Oscar Lewis Loudenslager

*This space is reserved
for the set certificate*

Yours very Truly,

James D. Richardson

A COMPILATION

OF THE

MESSAGES AND PAPERS

OF THE

PRESIDENTS

Prepared Under the Direction of the Joint Committee
on Printing, of the House and Senate,
Pursuant to an Act of the Fifty-Second Congress
of the United States

(With Additions and Encyclopedic Index
by Private Enterprise)

VOLUME I

PUBLISHED BY

BUREAU OF NATIONAL LITERATURE

1913

Copyright, 1897,

BY

JAMES D. RICHARDSON

Resolution Authorizing the Compilation

JOINT COMMITTEE ON PRINTING,
UNITED STATES SENATE,
Washington, D. C., August 20, 1894.

Hon. JAMES D. RICHARDSON,
House of Representatives.

SIR: I am directed by Senator GORMAN, the Chairman of the Joint Committee on Printing, to transmit to you the accompanying resolution, adopted by the Joint Committee this day and entered upon its journal.

Very respectfully,

F. M. COX,
Clerk Joint Committee on Printing.

Whereas Congress has passed the following resolution, to wit:

Resolved by the House of Representatives, the Senate concurring, That there be printed and bound in cloth six thousand copies of the complete compilation of all the annual, special, and veto messages, proclamations, and inaugural addresses of the Presidents of the United States from 1789 to 1894, inclusive, two thousand copies for the use of the Senate and four thousand copies for the use of the House. The work shall be performed under the direction of the Joint Committee on Printing:

Therefore, resolved by the Joint Committee on Printing, That Hon. JAMES D. RICHARDSON be, and he is hereby, authorized and requested to take charge of the work contemplated in said resolution, and prepare, compile, and edit same. He is given full power and discretion to do this work for and on behalf of this Committee.

III

Prefatory Note

In compliance with the authorization of the Joint Committee on Printing, I have undertaken this compilation.

The messages of the several Presidents of the United States—annual, veto, and special—are among the most interesting, instructive, and valuable contributions to the public literature of our Republic. They discuss from the loftiest standpoint nearly all the great questions of national policy and many subjects of minor interest which have engaged the attention of the people from the beginning of our history, and so constitute important and often vital links in their progressive development. The proclamations, also, contain matter and sentiment no less elevating, interesting, and important. They inspire to the highest and most exalted degree the patriotic fervor and love of country in the hearts of the people.

It is believed that legislators and other public men, students of our national history, and many others will hail with satisfaction the compilation and publication of these messages and proclamations in such compact form as will render them easily accessible and of ready reference. The work can not fail to be exceedingly convenient and useful to all who have occasion to consult these documents. The Government has never heretofore authorized a like publication.

In executing the commission with which I have been charged I have sought to bring together in the several volumes of the series all Presidential proclamations, addresses, messages, and communications to Congress excepting those nominating persons to office and those which simply transmit treaties, and reports of heads of Departments which contain no recommendation from the Executive. The utmost effort has been made to render the compilation accurate and exhaustive.

Although not required by the terms of the resolution authorizing the compilation, it has been deemed wise and wholly consistent with its purpose to incorporate in the first volume authentic copies of the Declaration of Independence, the Articles of Confederation, and the Constitution of the United States, together with steel engravings of the Capitol, the Executive Mansion, and of the historical painting the "Signing of the Declaration of Independence." Steel portraits of the Presidents will be inserted each in its appropriate place.

The compilation has not been brought even to its present stage without much labor and close application, and the end is far from view; but if it shall prove satisfactory to Congress and the country, I will feel compensated for my time and effort.

JAMES D. RICHARDSON.

NOTE.

The pages of "The Messages and Papers of the Presidents" have been renumbered from page one to the end, and the division into volumes has been altered. This plan is required by the addition of new matter and the desirability of keeping the volumes as nearly uniform in size as possible.

ILLUSTRATIONS IN VOLUME ONE

Declaration of Independence

July 4, 1776

Declaration of Independence

"SIGNING THE DECLARATION OF INDEPENDENCE," by Col. John Trumbull, is the most famous of the historical paintings in the rotunda of the Capitol. It is the first painted of four ordered by Congress and was executed between 1817 and 1824. It is valued at $100,000. Jefferson and Franklin furnished the artist with the details as to the positions of the various figures, etc.

Declaration of Independence

In CONGRESS, July 4, 1776.

The unanimous Declaration of the thirteen united States of America,

When in the Course of human events, it becomes necessary for one people to dissolve the political bands which have connected them with another, and to assume among the powers of the earth, the separate and equal station to which the Laws of Nature and of Nature's God entitle them, a decent respect to the opinions of mankind requires that they should declare the causes which impel them to the separation.—We hold these truths to be self-evident, that all men are created equal, that they are endowed by their Creator with certain unalienable Rights, that among these are Life, Liberty and the pursuit of Happiness.—That to secure these rights, Governments are instituted among Men, deriving their just powers from the consent of the governed,—That whenever any Form of Government becomes destructive of these ends, it is the Right of the People to alter or to abolish it, and to institute new Government, laying its foundation on such principles and organizing its powers in such form, as to them shall seem most likely to effect their Safety and Happiness. Prudence, indeed, will dictate that Governments long established should not be changed for light and transient causes; and accordingly all experience hath shewn, that mankind are more disposed to suffer, while evils are sufferable, than to right themselves by abolishing the forms to which they are accustomed. But when a long train of abuses and usurpations, pursuing invariably the same Object evinces a design to reduce them under absolute Despotism, it is their right, it is their duty, to throw off such Government, and to provide new Guards for their future security.—Such has been the patient sufferance of these Colonies; and such is now the necessity which constrains them to alter their former Systems of Government. The history of the present King of Great Britain is a history of repeated injuries and usurpations, all having in direct object the establishment of an absolute Tyranny over

NOTE.—The words "Declaration of Independence" do not appear on the original.

these States.   To prove this, let Facts be submitted to a candid world.—
He has refused his Assent to Laws, the most wholesome and necessary
for the public good.—He has forbidden his Governors to pass Laws of
immediate and pressing importance, unless suspended in their operation
till his Assent should be obtained; and when so suspended, he has
utterly neglected to attend to them.—He has refused to pass other Laws
for the accommodation of large districts of people, unless those people
would relinquish the right of Representation in the Legislature, a right
inestimable to them and formidable to tyrants only.—He has called
together legislative bodies at places unusual, uncomfortable, and distant
from the depository of their public Records, for the sole purpose of
fatiguing them into compliance with his measures.—He has dissolved
Represtative Houses repeatedly, for opposing with manly firmness his
invasions on the rights of the people.—He has refused for a long time,
after such dissolutions, to cause others to be elected; whereby the Legislative powers, incapable of Annihilation, have returned to the People at
large for their exercise; the State remaining in the mean time exposed
to all the dangers of invasion from without, and convulsions within.—
He has endeavoured to prevent the population of these States; for that
purpose obstructing the Laws for Naturalization of Foreigners; refusing to pass others to encourage their migrations hither, and raising
the conditions of new Appropriations of Lands.—He has obstructed
the Administration of Justice, by refusing his Assent to Laws for establishing Judiciary powers.—He has made Judges dependent on his Will
alone, for the tenure of their offices, and the amount and payment of
their salaries.—He has erected a multitude of New Offices, and sent
hither swarms of Officers to harrass our people, and eat out their substance.—He has kept among us, in times of peace, Standing Armies
without the Consent of our legislatures.—He has affected to render the
Military independent of and superior to the Civil power.—He has combined with others to subject us to a jurisdiction foreign to our constitution, and unacknowledged by our laws; giving his Assent to their
Acts of pretended Legislation:—For quartering large bodies of armed
troops among us:—For protecting them, by a mock Trial, from punishment for any Murders which they should commit on the Inhabitants of
these States:—For cutting off our Trade with all parts of the world:—
For imposing Taxes on us without our Consent:—For depriving us in
many cases, of the benefits of Trial by Jury:—For transporting us beyond
Seas to be tried for pretended offences:—For abolishing the free System

of English Laws in a neighbouring Province, establishing therein an Arbitrary government, and enlarging its Boundaries so as to render it at once an example and fit instrument for introducing the same absolute rule into these Colonies:—For taking away our Charters, abolishing our most valuable Laws, and altering fundamentally the Forms of our Governments:—For suspending our own Legislatures, and declaring themselves invested with power to legislate for us in all cases whatsoever.— He has abdicated Government here, by declaring us out of his Protection and waging War against us.—He has plundered our seas, ravaged our Coasts, burnt our towns, and destroyed the Lives of our people.—He is at this time transporting large Armies of foreign Mercenaries to compleat the works of death, desolation and tyranny, already begun with circumstances of Cruelty & perfidy scarcely paralleled in the most barbarous ages, and totally unworthy the Head of a civilized nation.—He has constrained our fellow Citizens taken Captive on the high Seas to bear Arms against their Country, to become the executioners of their friends and Brethren, or to fall themselves by their Hands.—He has excited domestic insurrections amongst us, and has endeavoured to bring on the inhabitants of our frontiers, the merciless Indian Savages, whose known rule of warfare, is an undistinguished destruction of all ages, sexes and conditions.   In every stage of these Oppressions We have Petitioned for Redress in the most humble terms: Our repeated Petitions have been answered only by repeated injury.   A Prince, whose character is thus marked by every act which may define a Tyrant, is unfit to be the ruler of a free people.   Nor have We been wanting in attentions to our Brittish brethren.   We have warned them from time to time of attempts by their legislature to extend an unwarrantable jurisdiction over us.   We have reminded them of the circumstances of our emigration and settlement here.   We have appealed to their native justice and magnanimity, and we have conjured them by the ties of our common kindred to disavow these usurpations, which, would inevitably interrupt our connections and correspondence They too have been deaf to the voice of justice and of consanguinity.   We must, therefore, acquiesce in the necessity, which denounces our Separation, and hold them, as we hold the rest of mankind, Enemies in War, in Peace Friends.—

We, therefore, the Representatives of the **united States of America,** in General Congress, Assembled, appealing to the Supreme Judge of the world for the rectitude of our intentions, do, in the Name, and by Authority of the good People of these Colonies, solemnly publish and declare, That these United Colonies are, and of Right ought to be 𝕱𝖗𝖊𝖊 𝖆𝖓𝖉 𝕴𝖓𝖉𝖊𝖕𝖊𝖓𝖉𝖊𝖓𝖙 𝕾𝖙𝖆𝖙𝖊𝖘; that they are Absolved from all Allegiance to the British Crown, and that all political connection between them and the State of Great Britain, is and ought to be totally dissolved; and that as Free and Independent States, they have full Power to levy War, conclude Peace, contract Alliances, establish Commerce, and to do all other Acts and Things which Independent States may of right do.—And for the support of this Declaration, with a firm reliance on the protection of divine Providence, we mutually pledge to each other our Lives, our Fortunes and our sacred Honor.

JOHN HANCOCK

Josiah Bartlett	Geo. Taylor
Wᴹ Whipple	James Wilson
Samˡ Adams	Geo. Ross
John Adams	Cæsar Rodney
Robᵀ Treat Paine	Geo Read
Elbridge Gerry	Tho M:Kean
Step. Hopkins	Samuel Chase
William Ellery	Wᴹ Paca
Roger Sherman	Thoˢ Stone
Samᴱᴸ Huntington	Charles Carroll of Carrollton
Wᴹ Williams	George Wythe
Oliver Wolcott	Richard Henry Lee.
Matthew Thornton	Th Jefferson
Wᴹ Floyd	Benjᴬ Harrison
Phil. Livingston	Thoˢ Nelson jr.
Franˢ Lewis	Francis Lightfoot Lee
Lewis Morris	Carter Braxton
Richᴰ Stockton	Wᴹ Hooper
Jnᴼ Witherspoon	Joseph Hewes,
Fraˢ Hopkinson	John Penn
John Hart	Edward Rutledge.
Abra Clark	Thoˢ Heyward Junʳ
Robᵀ Morris	Thomas Lynch Junʳ
Benjamin Rush	Arthur Middleton
Benjᴬ Franklin	Button Gwinnett
John Morton	Lyman Hall
Geo Clymer	Geo Walton.
Jaˢ Smith.	

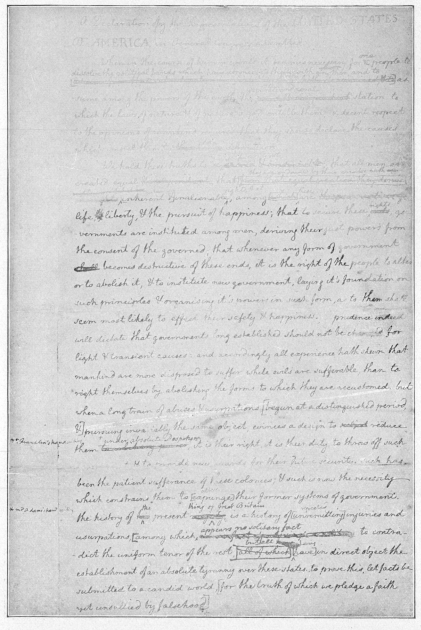

FACSIMILE OF PARTS OF JEFFERSON'S ORIGINAL DRAFT OF
THE DECLARATION OF INDEPENDENCE.

for taking away our charters, & altering fundamentally the forms of our governments

for suspending our own legislatures & declaring themselves invested with power to

legislate for us in all cases whatsoever.

he has abdicated government here, withdrawing his governors, & declaring us out

of his allegiance & protection.

he has plundered our seas, ravaged our coasts, burnt our towns & destroyed the

lives of our people.

he is at this time transporting large armies of foreign mercenaries to compleat

the works of death, desolation & tyranny, already begun with circumstances

of cruelty & perfidy, unworthy the head of a civilized nation:

he has endeavored to bring on the inhabitants of our frontiers the merciless Indian

savages, whose known rule of warfare is an undistinguished destruction of

all ages, sexes, & conditions [of existence:]

he has incited treasonable insurrections of our fellow-citizens, with the

allurements of forfeiture & confiscation of our property.

he has waged cruel war against human nature itself, violating it's most sa-

-cred rights of life & liberty in the persons of a distant people who never of-

-fended him, captivating & carrying them into slavery in another hemis-

-sphere, or to incur miserable death in their transportation thither. this

piratical warfare, the opprobrium of infidel powers, is the warfare of the

Christian king of Great Britain. determined to keep open a market

where MEN should be bought & sold. he has prostituted his negative

for suppressing every legislative attempt to prohibit or to restrain this

execrable commerce: and that this assemblage of horrors might want no fact

of distinguished die, he is now exciting those very people to rise in arms

among us, and to purchase that liberty of which he has deprived them,

by murdering the people upon whom he also obtruded them: thus paying

off former crimes committed against the liberties of one people, with crimes

which he urges them to commit against the lives of another.]

in every stage of these oppressions we have petitioned for redress in the most humble

terms; our repeated petitions have been answered only by repeated injuries. a prince

whose character is thus marked by every act which may define a tyrant, is unfit

to be the ruler of a people who mean to be free. future ages will scarce believe

that the hardiness of one man, adventured within the short compass of twelve years

only, to lay a foundation so broad & undisguised for tyranny over a people fostered & fixed in principles

he has refused his assent to laws the most wholesome and necessary for the public good:

he has forbidden his governors to pass laws of immediate & pressing importance,
unless suspended in their operation till his assent should be obtained;
and when so suspended, he has utterly neglected utterly to attend to them.

he has refused to pass other laws for the accomodation of large districts of people
unless those people would relinquish the right of representation in the legislature, a right
inestimable to them, & formidable to tyrants only:

he has called together legislative bodies at places unusual, uncomfortable & distant from
the depository of their public records for the sole purpose of fatiguing them into compliance
with his measures:

he has refused for a long time after such dissolutions to cause others to be elected,
whereby the legislative powers, incapable of annihilation, have returned to
the people at large for their exercise, the state remaining in the mean time
exposed to all the dangers of invasion from without & convulsions within:

he has endeavored to prevent the population of these states; for that purpose
obstructing the laws for naturalization of foreigners; refusing to pass others
to encourage their migrations hither; & raising the conditions of new appropriations of lands:

he has suffered the administration of justice totally to cease in some of these
states refusing his assent to laws for establishing judiciary powers:

he has made our judges dependant on his will alone, for the tenure of their offices
& payment & amount of their salaries:

he has erected a multitude of new offices by a self-assumed power, & sent hither
their swarms of officers to harrass our people & eat out their substance:

he has kept among us in times of peace standing armies & ships of war without the consent of our legislatures

he has affected to render the military independent of & superior to the civil power

Nor have we been wanting in attentions to our British brethren. we have
warned them from time to time of attempts by their legislature to extend a juris-
-diction over these our states. we have reminded them of the circumstances of
our emigration & settlement here, no one of which could warrant so strange a
pretension: that these were effected at the expence of our own blood & treasure,
unassisted by the wealth or the strength of Great Britain: that in constituting
indeed our several forms of government, we had adopted one common king, thereby
laying a foundation for perpetual league & amity with them: but that submission to their
parliament was no part of our constitution, nor ever in idea, if history may be
credited: and we appealed to their native justice & magnanimity, as well as to the ties
of our common kindred to disavow these usurpations which were likely to interrupt
our correspondence & connection & correspondence. they too have been deaf to the voice of justice &
of consanguinity. & when occasions have been given them by the regular course of
their laws, of removing from their councils the disturbers of our harmony, they
have by their free election re-established them in power. at this very time too they
are permitting their chief magistrate to send over not only soldiers of our common
blood, but Scotch & foreign mercenaries to invade & destroy us. these facts
have given the last stab to agonizing affection, and manly spirit bids us to re-
-nounce for ever these unfeeling brethren. we must endeavor to forget our former
love for them, and to hold them as we hold the rest of mankind, enemies in war,
in peace friends. we might have been a free & a great people together; but a communication of grandeur & of freedom it seems is below their dignity. be it so, since they
will have it. the road to happiness & to glory is open to us too; we will tread it
apart from them, and acquiesce in the necessity which pronounces our
everlasting Adieu! separation!

    We therefore the representatives of the United States of America in General Con-
-gress assembled, do in the name & by authority of the good people of these states,
reject and renounce all allegiance & subjection to the kings of Great Britain
& all others who may hereafter claim by, through, or under them; we utterly
dissolve & break off all political connection which may have heretofore sub-
-sisted between us & the people or parliament of Great Britain; and finally
we do assert and declare these colonies to be free and independent states,
and that as free & independent states they shall hereafter have full power to levy
war, conclude peace, contract alliances, establish commerce, & to do all other
acts & things which independent states may of right do. and for the
support of this declaration we mutually pledge to each other our lives, our
fortunes, & our sacred honour.

Articles of Confederation

Important

❖

*Be sure and examine
the eleventh volume
of this set first. It
is the key to the mine
of information con-
tained in the balance
of the set*

Important

⊞

Be sure and examine the eleventh volume of this set first. It is the key to the mine of information contained in the balance of the set

Articles of Confederation

To all to whom these Presents shall come, we the undersigned Delegates of the States affixed to our Names send greeting. Whereas the Delegates of the United States of America in Congress assembled did on the fifteenth day of November in the Year of our Lord One Thousand Seven Hundred and Seventy seven, and in the Second Year of the Independence of America agree to certain articles of Confederation and perpetual Union between the States of Newhampshire, Massachusetts-bay, Rhodeisland and Providence Plantations, Connecticut, New York, New Jersey, Pennsylvania, Delaware, Maryland, Virginia, North-Carolina, South-Carolina and Georgia in the Words following, viz. "Articles of Confederation and perpetual Union between the states of Newhampshire, Massachusetts-bay, Rhodeisland and Providence Plantations, Connecticut, New-York, New-Jersey, Pennsylvania, Delaware, Maryland, Virginia, North-Carolina, South-Carolina and Georgia.

Article I. The Stile of this confederacy shall be "The United States of America."

Article II. Each state retains its sovereignty, freedom and independence, and every Power, Jurisdiction and right, which is not by this confederation expressly delegated to the United States, in Congress assembled.

Article III. The said states hereby severally enter into a firm league of friendship with each other, for their common defence, the security of their Liberties, and their mutual and general welfare, binding themselves to assist each other, against all force offered to, or attacks made upon them, or any of them, on account of religion, sovereignty, trade, or any other pretence whatsoever.

NOTE.—The original is indorsed: Act of Confederation of The United States of America.

Article IV. The better to secure and perpetuate mutual friendship and intercourse among the people of the different states in this union, the free inhabitants of each of these states, paupers, vagabonds and fugitives from Justice excepted, shall be entitled to all privileges and immunities of free citizens in the several states; and the people of each state shall have free ingress and regress to and from any other state, and shall enjoy therein all the privileges of trade and commerce, subject to the same duties, impositions and restrictions as the inhabitants thereof respectively, provided that such restriction shall not extend so far as to prevent the removal of property imported into any state, to any other state of which the Owner is an inhabitant; provided also that no imposition, duties or restriction shall be laid by any state, on the property of the united states, or either of them.

If any Person guilty of, or charged with treason, felony, or other high misdemeanor in any state, shall flee from Justice, and be found in any of the united states, he shall upon demand of the Governor or executive power, of the state from which he fled, be delivered up and removed to the state having jurisdiction of his offence.

Full faith and credit shall be given in each of these states to the records, acts and judicial proceedings of the courts and magistrates of every other state.

Article V. For the more convenient management of the general interests of the united states, delegates shall be annually appointed in such manner as the legislature of each state shall direct, to meet in Congress on the first Monday in November, in every year, with a power reserved to each state, to recal its delegates, or any of them, at any time within the year, and to send others in their stead, for the remainder of the Year.

No state shall be represented in Congress by less than two, nor by more than seven Members; and no person shall be capable of being a delegate for more than three years in any term of six years; nor shall any person, being a delegate, be capable of holding any office under the united states, for which he, or another for his benefit receives any salary, fees or emolument of any kind.

Each state shall maintain its own delegates in a meeting of the states, and while they act as members of the committee of the states.

In determining questions in the united states, in Congress assembled, each state shall have one vote.

Freedom of speech and debate in Congress shall not be impeached or questioned in any Court, or place out of Congress, and the members of congress shall be protected in their persons from arrests and imprisonments, during the time of their going to and from, and attendance on congress, except for treason, felony, or breach of the peace.

Article VI. No state without the Consent of the united states in congress assembled, shall send any embassy to, or receive any embassy from, or enter into any conferrence, agreement, alliance or treaty with any King prince or state; nor shall any person holding any office of profit or trust under the united states, or any of them, accept of any present, emolument, office or title of any kind whatever from any king, prince or foreign state; nor shall the united states in congress assembled, or any of them, grant any title of nobility.

No two or more states shall enter into any treaty, confederation or alliance whatever between them, without the consent of the united states in congress assembled, specifying accurately the purposes for which the same is to be entered into, and how long it shall continue.

No state shall lay any imposts or duties, which may interfere with any stipulations in treaties, entered into by the united states in congress assembled, with any king, prince or state, in pursuance of any treaties already proposed by congress, to the courts of France and Spain.

No vessels of war shall be kept up in time of peace by any state, except such number only, as shall be deemed necessary by the united states in congress assembled, for the defence of such state, or its trade; nor shall any body of forces be kept up by any state, in time of peace, except such number only, as in the judgment of the united states, in congress assembled, shall be deemed requisite to garrison the forts necessary for the defence of such state; but every state shall always keep up a well regulated and disciplined militia, sufficiently armed and accoutred, and shall provide and constantly have ready for use, in public stores, a due number of field pieces and tents, and a proper quantity of arms, ammunition and camp equipage.

No state shall engage in any war without the consent of the united states in congress assembled, unless such state be actually invaded by enemies, or shall have received certain advice of a resolution being formed by some nation of Indians to invade such state, and the danger is so imminent as not to admit of a delay, till the united states in congress assembled can be consulted: nor shall any state grant commissions to any ships or vessels of war, nor letters of marque or reprisal, except it be after a declaration of war by the united states in congress assembled, and then only against the kingdom or state and the subjects thereof, against which war has been so declared, and under such regula-/tions as shall be established by the united states in congress assembled, unless such state be infested by pirates, in which case vessels of war may be fitted out for that occasion, and kept so long as the danger shall continue, or until the united states in congress assembled shall determine otherwise.

Article VII. When land-forces are raised by any state for the common defence, all officers of or under the rank of colonel, shall be appointed by the legislature of each state respectively by whom such forces shall be raised, or in such manner as such state shall direct, and all vacancies shall be filled up by the state which first made the appointment.

Article VIII. All charges of war, and all other expences that shall be incurred for the common defence or general welfare, and allowed by the united states in congress assembled, shall be defrayed out of a common treasury, which shall be supplied by the several states, in proportion to the value of all land within each state, granted to or surveyed for any Person, as such land and the buildings and improvements thereon shall be estimated according to such mode as the united states in congress assembled, shall from time to time direct and appoint. The taxes for paying that proportion shall be laid and levied by the authority and direction of the legislatures of the several states within the time agreed upon by the united states in congress assembled.

Article IX. The united states in congress assembled, shall have the sole and exclusive right and power of determining on peace and war, except in the cases mentioned in the sixth article—of sending and receiving ambassadors—entering into treaties and alliances, provided that no treaty of commerce shall be made whereby the legislative power of the respective states shall be restrained from imposing such imposts and duties on foreigners, as their own people are subjected to, or from prohibiting the exportation or importation of any species of goods or commodities whatsoever—of establishing rules for deciding in all cases, what captures on land or water shall be legal, and in what manner prizes taken by land or naval forces in the service of the united states shall be divided or appropriated.—of granting letters of marque and reprisal in times of peace—appointing courts for the trial of piracies and felonies committed on the high seas and establishing courts for receiving and determining finally appeals in all cases of captures, provided that no member of congress shall be appointed a judge of any of the said courts.

The united states in congress assembled shall also be the last resort on appeal in all disputes and differences now subsisting or that hereafter may arise between two or more states concerning boundary, jurisdiction or any other cause whatever; which authority shall always be exercised in the manner following. Whenever the legislative or executive authority or lawful agent of any state in controversy with another shall present a petition to congress. stating the matter in question and praying for a hearing, notice thereof shall be given by order of congress to the legislative or executive authority of the other state in controversy, and a day assigned for the appearance of the parties by their lawful agents, who shall then be directed to appoint by joint consent, commissioners or judges to constitute a court for hearing and determining the matter in question: but if they cannot agree, congress shall name three persons out of each of the united states, and from the list of such persons each party shall alternately strike out one, the petitioners beginning, until the number shall be reduced to thirteen; and from that number not less than seven, nor more than nine names as congress shall direct, shall in the presence of congress be drawn out by lot, and the persons whose names shall be so drawn or any five of them, shall be commissioners or judges, to hear and finally determine the controversy, so always as a major part of the judges who shall hear the cause shall agree in the determination: and if either party shall neglect to attend at the day appointed, without shewing reasons, which congress shall judge sufficient, or being present shall refuse to strike, the congress shall proceed to nominate three persons out of each state, and the secretary of congress shall strike in behalf of such party absent or refusing; and the judgment and sentence of the court to be appointed, in the manner before prescribed, shall be final and conclusive; and if any of the parties shall refuse to submit to the authority of such court, or to appear or defend their claim or cause, the court shall nevertheless proceed to pronounce sentence, or judgment, which shall in like manner be final and decisive, the judgment or sentence and other proceedings being in either case transmitted to congress, and lodged among the acts of congress for the security of the parties concerned: provided that every commissioner, before he sits in judgment, shall take an oath to be administred by one of the judges of the supreme or superior court of the state, where the cause shall be tried, "well and truly to hear and determine the matter in question, according to the best of his judgment, without favour, affection or hope of reward:" provided also that no state shall be deprived of territory for the benefit of the united states.

All controversies concerning the private right of soil claimed under different grants of two or more states, whose jurisdictions as they may respect such lands, and the states which passed such grants are adjusted, the said grants or either of them being at the same time claimed to have originated antecedent to such settlement of jurisdiction, shall on the petition of either party to the congress of the united states, be finally determined as near as may be in the same manner as is before prescribed for deciding disputes respecting territorial jurisdiction between different states.

The united states in congress assembled shall also have the sole and exclusive right and power of regulating the alloy and value of coin struck by their own authority, or by that of the respective states—fixing the standard of weights and measures throughout the united states.—regulating the trade and managing all affairs with the Indians, not members of any of the states, provided that the legislative right of any state within its own limits be not infringed or violated—establishing and regulating post-offices from one state to another, throughout all the united states, and exacting such postage on the papers passing thro' the same as may be requisite to defray the expences of the said office—appointing all officers of the land forces, in the service of the united states, excepting regimental officers.—appointing all the officers of the naval forces, and commissioning all officers whatever in the service of the united states—making rules for the government and regulation of the said land and naval forces, and directing their operations.

The united states in congress assembled shall have authority to appoint a committee, to sit in the recess of congress, to be denominated "A Committee of the States," and to consist of one delegate from each state; and to appoint such other committees and civil officers as may be necessary for managing the general affairs of the united states under their direction—to appoint one of their number to preside, provided that no person be allowed to serve in the office of president more than one year in any term of three years; to ascertain the necessary sums of Money to be raised for the service of the united states, and to appropriate and apply the same for defraying the public expences—to borrow money, or emit bills on the credit of the united states, transmitting every half year to the respective states an account of the sums of money so borrowed or emitted,—to build and equip a navy—to agree upon the number of land forces, and to make requisitions from each state for its quota, in proportion to the number of white inhabitants in such state; which requisition shall be binding, and thereupon the legislature of each state shall appoint the regimental officers, raise the men and cloath, arm and equip them in a soldier like manner, at the expence of the united states, and the officers and men so cloathed, armed and equipped shall march to the place appointed, and within the time agreed on by the united states in congress assembled: But if the united states in congress assembled shall, on consideration of circumstances judge proper that any state should not raise men, or should raise a smaller number than its quota, and that any other state should raise a greater number of men than the quota thereof, such extra number shall be raised, officered, cloathed, armed and equipped in the same manner as the quota of such state, unless the legislature of such state shall judge that such extra number cannot be safely spared out of the same, in which case they shall raise officer, cloath, arm and equip as many of such extra number as they judge can be safely spared. And the officers and men so cloathed, armed and equipped, shall march to the place appointed, and within the time agreed on by the united states in congress assembled.

The united states in congress assembled shall never engage in a war, nor grant letters of marque and reprisal in time of peace, nor enter into any treaties or alliances, nor coin money, nor regulate the value thereof, nor ascertain the sums and expences necessary for the defence and welfare of the united states, or any of them, nor emit bills, nor borrow money on the credit of the united states, nor appropriate money, nor agree upon the number of vessels of war, to be built or purchased, or the number of land or sea forces to be raised, nor appoint a commander in chief of the army or navy, unless nine states assent to the same: nor shall a question on any other point, except for adjourning from day to day be determined, unless by the votes of a majority of the united states in congress assembled.

The congress of the united states shall have power to adjourn to any time within the year, and to any place within the united states, so that no period of adjournment be for a longer duration than the space of six Months, and shall publish the Journal of their proceedings monthly, except such parts thereof relating to treaties, alliances or military operations, as in their judgment require secrecy; and the yeas and nays of the delegates of each state on any question shall be entered on the Journal, when it is desired by any delegate; and the delegates of a state, or any of them, at his or their request shall be furnished with a transcript of the said Journal, except such parts as are above excepted, to lay before the legislatures of the several states.

Article X. The committee of the states, or any nine of them, shall be authorised to execute, in the recess of congress, such of the powers of congress as the united states in congress assembled, by the consent of nine states, shall from time to time think expedient to vest them with; provided that no power be delegated to the said committee, for the exercise of which, by the articles of confederation, the voice of nine states in the congress of the united states assembled is requisite.

Article XI. Canada acceding to this confederation, and joining in the measures of the united states, shall be admitted into, and entitled to all the advantages of this union: but no other colony shall be admitted into the same, unless such admission be agreed to by nine states.

Article XII. All bills of credit emitted, monies borrowed and debts contracted by, or under the authority of congress, before the assembling of the united states, in pursuance of the present confederation, shall be deemed and considered as a charge against the united states, for payment and satisfaction whereof the said united states, and the public faith are hereby solemnly pledged.

Article XIII. Every state shall abide by the determinations of the united states in congress assembled, on all questions which by this confederation are submitted to them. And the Articles of this confederation shall be inviolably observed by every state, and the union shall be perpetual; nor shall any alteration at any time hereafter be made in any of them; unless such alteration be agreed to in a congress of the united states, and be afterwards confirmed by the legislatures of every state.

And Whereas it hath pleased the Great Governor of the World to incline the hearts of the legislatures we respectively represent in congress, to approve of, and to authorize us to ratify the said articles of confederation and perpetual union. Know Ye that we the under-signed delegates, by virtue of the power and authority to us given for that purpose, do by these presents, in the name and in behalf of our respective constituents, fully and entirely ratify and confirm each and every of the said articles of confederation and perpetual union, and all and singular the matters and things therein contained: And we do further solemnly plight and engage the faith of our respective constituents, that they shall abide by the determinations of the united states in congress assembled, on all questions, which by the said confederation are submitted to them. And that the articles thereof shall be inviolably observed by the states we repectively represent, and that the union shall be perpetual. In Witness whereof we have hereunto set our hands in Congress. Done at Philadelphia in the state of Pennsylvania the ninth Day of July in the Year of our Lord one Thousand seven Hundred and Seventy-eight, and in the third year of the independence of America.

JOSIAH BARTLETT
JOHN WENTWORTH Junr
　　　　August 8th 1778

On the part & behalf of the State of New Hampshire

JOHN HANCOCK
SAMUEL ADAMS
ELBRIDGE GERRY
FRANCIS DANA
JAMES LOVELL
SAMUEL HOLTEN

On the part and behalf of The State of Massachusetts Bay

WILLIAM ELLERY
HENRY MARCHANT
JOHN COLLINS

On the part and behalf of the State of Rhode-Island and Providence Plantations

ROGER SHERMAN
SAMUEL HUNTINGTON
OLIVER WOLCOTT
TITUS HOSMER
ANDREW ADAMS

on the part and behalf of the State of Connecticut

JA^S DUANE
FRA^S LEWIS
W^M DUER.
GOUV MORRIS

On the Part and Behalf of the State of New York

JNO WITHERSPOON
NATH^L SCUDDER

On the Part and in Behalf of the State of New Jersey. Novr 26, 1778.—

ROB^T MORRIS
DANIEL ROBERDEAU
JON^A BAYARD SMITH.
WILLIAM CLINGAN
JOSEPH REED 22^d July 1778

On the part and behalf of the State of Pennsylvania

THO M:KEAN Feby 12 1779
JOHN DICKINSON May 5th 1779   } On the part & behalf of the State of
NICHOLAS VAN DYKE,   Delaware

JOHN HANSON March 1 1781   } on the part and behalf of the State
DANIEL CARROLL   do   of Maryland

RICHARD HENRY LEE
JOHN BANISTER
THOMAS ADAMS   } On the Part and Behalf of the State
JNO HARVIE   of Virginia
FRANCIS LIGHTFOOT LEE

JOHN PENN July 21st 1778   } On the part and Behalf of the State
CORNS HARNETT   of No Carolina
JNO WILLIAMS

HENRY LAURENS.
WILLIAM HENRY DRAYTON
JNO MATHEWS   } On the part & behalf of the State of
RICHD HUTSON.   South-Carolina
THOS HEYWARD Junr

JNO WALTON 24th July 1778   } On the part & behalf of the State of
EDWD TELFAIR.   Georgia
EDWD LANGWORTHY.

CONSTITUTIONAL CONVENTION, PHILADELPHIA, MAY, 1787

CONSTITUTIONAL CONVENTION, PHILADELPHIA

May, 1787

"The United States of America never wore a more majestic aspect than in the convention. . . . The purpose of the assembly was sufficient to invest it with solemnity. To meet in the design of strengthening instead of enfeebling authority, of forming a government which should enable the nation to fulfil instead of eluding its obligations alike to the citizen and the stranger—to meet with these intentions was to do what the world had never witnessed. . . . Thus was completed the most extraordinary transaction of which merely human history bears record. A nation enfeebled, dismembered and dispirited, broken by the losses of war, by the dissensions of peace, incapacitated for its duties to its own citizens or to foreign powers, suddenly bestirred itself and prepared to create a government. It chose its representatives. . . . They came together, at first only to disagree, to threaten and to fail. But against the spells of individual selfishness and sectional passion, the inspiration of the national cause proved potent. The representatives of the nation consented to the measures on which the common honor and the common safety depended. . . . The work thus achieved was not merely for the nation that achieved it. In the midst of their doubts and their dangers a few generous spirits, if no more, gathered fresh courage by looking beyond the limits of their country. Let Washington speak for them: "I conceive," says he, "under an energetic general government, such regulations might be made, and such measures taken, as would render this country the asylum of pacific and industrious characters from all parts of Europe—a kind of asylum for mankind."

JOHN FISKE, "The Critical Period of American History."

See the article "Constitution" in the index (volume eleven), and also the list of celebrated cases, which are discussed in the index, under the heading, "Constitution, Supreme Court Decisions On."

The Constitution

The Constitution

𝕸𝖊 𝖙𝖍𝖊 𝕻𝖊𝖔𝖕𝖑𝖊 of the United States, in Order to form a more perfect Union, establish Justice, insure domestic Tranquility, provide for the common defence, promote the general Welfare, and secure the Blessings of Liberty to ourselves and our Posterity, do ordain and establish this Constitution for the United States of America.

Article. I.

Section. 1. All legislative Powers herein granted shall be vested in a Congress of the United States, which shall consist of a Senate and House of Representatives.

Section. 2. The House of Representatives shall be composed of Members chosen every second Year by the People of the several States, and the Electors in each State shall have the Qualifications requisite for Electors of the most numerous Branch of the State Legislature.

No Person shall be a Representative who shall not have attained to the Age of twenty five Years, and been seven Years a Citizen of the United States, and who shall not, when elected, be an Inhabitant of that State in which he shall be chosen.

Representatives and direct Taxes shall be apportioned among the several States which may be included within this Union, according to their respective Numbers, which shall be determined by adding to the whole Number of free Persons, including those bound to Service for a Term of Years, and excluding Indians not taxed, three fifths of all other Persons. The actual Enumeration shall be made within three Years after the first Meeting of the Congress of the United States, and within every subsequent Term of ten Years, in such Manner as they shall by

NOTE.—The words "The Constitution" do not appear on the original.

Law direct. The Number of Representatives shall not exceed one for every thirty Thousand, but each State shall have at Least one Representative; and until such enumeration shall be made, the State of New Hampshire shall be entitled to chuse three, Massachusetts eight, Rhode-Island and Providence Plantations one, Connecticut five, New-York six, New Jersey four, Pennsylvania eight, Delaware one, Maryland six, Virginia ten, North Carolina five, South Carolina five, and Georgia three.

When vacancies happen in the Representation from any State, the Executive Authority thereof shall issue Writs of Election to fill such Vacancies.

The House of Representatives shall chuse their Speaker and other Officers; and shall have the sole Power of Impeachment.

Section. 3. The Senate of the United States shall be composed of two Senators from each State, chosen by the Legislature thereof, for six Years; and each Senator shall have one Vote.

Immediately after they shall be assembled in Consequence of the first Election, they shall be divided as equally as may be into three Classes. The Seats of the Senators of the first Class shall be vacated at the Expiration of the second Year, of the second Class at the Expiration of the fourth Year, and of the third Class at the Expiration of the sixth Year, so that one third may be chosen every second Year; and if Vacancies happen by Resignation, or otherwise, during the Recess of the Legislature of any State, the Executive thereof may make temporary Appointments until the next Meeting of the Legislature, which shall then fill such Vacancies.

No Person shall be a Senator who shall not have attained to the Age of thirty Years, and been nine Years a Citizen of the United States, and who shall not, when elected, be an Inhabitant of that State for which he shall be chosen.

The Vice President of the United States shall be President of the Senate, but shall have no Vote, unless they be equally divided.

The Senate shall chuse their other Officers, and also a President pro tempore, in the Absence of the Vice President, or when he shall exercise the Office of President of the United States.

The Senate shall have the sole Power to try all Impeachments. When sitting for that Purpose, they shall be on Oath or Affirmation. When the President of the United States is tried, the Chief Justice shall preside: And no Person shall be convicted without the Concurrence of two thirds of the Members present.

Judgment in Cases of Impeachment shall not extend further than to removal from Office, and disqualification to hold and enjoy any Office of honor, Trust or Profit under the United States: but the Party convicted shall nevertheless be liable and subject to Indictment, Trial, Judgment and Punishment, according to Law.

Section. 4. The Times, Places and Manner of holding Elections for Senators and Representatives, shall be prescribed in each State by the Legislature thereof; but the Congress may at any time by Law make or alter such Regulations, except as to the Places of chusing Senators.

The Congress shall assemble at least once in every Year, and such Meeting shall be on the first Monday in December, unless they shall by Law appoint a different Day.

Section. 5. Each House shall be the Judge of the Elections, Returns and Qualifications of its own Members, and a Majority of each shall constitute a Quorum to do Business; but a smaller Number may adjourn from day to day, and may be authorized to compel the Attendance of absent Members, in such Manner, and under such Penalties as each House may provide.

Each House may determine the Rules of its Proceedings, punish its Members for disorderly Behaviour, and, with the Concurrence of two thirds, expel a Member.

Each House shall keep a Journal of its Proceedings, and from time to time publish the same, excepting such Parts as may in their Judgment require Secrecy; and the Yeas and Nays of the Members of either House on any question shall, at the Desire of one fifth of those Present, be entered on the Journal.

Neither House, during the Session of Congress, shall, without the Consent of the other, adjourn for more than three days, nor to any other Place than that in which the two Houses shall be sitting.

Section. 6. The Senators and Representatives shall receive a Compensation for their Services, to be ascertained by Law, and paid out of the Treasury of the United States. They shall in all Cases, except Treason, Felony and Breach of the Peace, be privileged from Arrest during their Attendance at the Session of their respective Houses, and in going to and returning from the same; and for any Speech or Debate in either House, they shall not be questioned in any other Place.

No Senator or Representative shall, during the Time for which he was elected, be appointed to any civil Office under the Authority of the United States which shall have been created, or the Emoluments whereof shall have been encreased during such time; and no Person holding any Office under the United States, shall be a Member of either House during his Continuance in Office.

Section. 7. All Bills for raising Revenue shall originate in the House of Representatives; but the Senate may propose or concur with Amendments as on other Bills.

Every Bill which shall have passed the House of Representatives and the Senate, shall, before it become a Law, be presented to the President of the United States; If he approve he shall sign it, but if not he shall return it, with his Objections to that House in which it shall have originated, who shall enter the Objections at large on their Journal, and proceed to reconsider it. If after such Reconsideration two thirds of that House shall agree to pass the Bill, it shall be sent, together with the Objections, to the other House, by which it shall likewise be reconsidered, and if approved by two thirds of that House, it shall become a Law. But in all such Cases the Votes of both Houses shall be determined by yeas and Nays, and the Names of the Persons voting for and against the Bill shall be entered on the Journal of each House respectively. If any Bill shall not be returned by the President within ten Days (Sundays excepted) after it shall have been presented to him, the Same shall be a Law, in like Manner as if he had signed it, unless the Congress by their Adjournment prevent its Return, in which Case it shall not be a Law.

Every Order, Resolution, or Vote to which the Concurrence of the Senate and House of Representatives may be necessary (except on a question of Adjournment) shall be presented to the President of the United States; and before the Same shall take Effect, shall be approved by him, or being disapproved by him, shall be repassed by two thirds of the Senate and House of Representatives, according to the Rules and Limitations prescribed in the Case of a Bill.

Section. 8. The Congress shall have Power To lay and collect Taxes, Duties, Imposts and Excises, to pay the Debts and provide for the common Defence and general Welfare of the United States; but all Duties, Imposts and Excises shall be uniform throughout the United States;

To borrow Money on the credit of the United States;

To regulate Commerce with foreign Nations, and among the several States, and with the Indian Tribes;

To establish an uniform Rule of Naturalization, and uniform Laws on the subject of Bankruptcies throughout the United States;

To coin Money, regulate the Value thereof, and of foreign Coin, and fix the Standard of Weights and Measures;

To provide for the Punishment of counterfeiting the Securities and current Coin of the United States;

To establish Post Offices and post Roads;

To promote the Progress of Science and useful Arts, by securing for limited Times to Authors and Inventors the exclusive Right to their respective Writings and Discoveries;

To constitute Tribunals inferior to the supreme Court;

To define and punish Piracies and Felonies committed on the high Seas, and Offences against the Law of Nations;

To declare War, grant Letters of Marque and Reprisal, and make Rules concerning Captures on Land and Water;

To raise and support Armies, but no Appropriation of Money to that Use shall be for a longer Term than two Years;

To provide and maintain a Navy;

To make Rules for the Government and Regulation of the land and naval Forces;

To provide for calling forth the Militia to execute the Laws of the Union, suppress Insurrections and repel Invasions;

To provide for organizing, arming, and disciplining, the Militia, and for governing such Part of them as may be employed in the Service of the United States, reserving to the States respectively, the Appointment of the Officers, and the Authority of training the Militia according to the discipline prescribed by Congress;

To exercise exclusive Legislation in all Cases whatsoever, over such District (not exceeding ten Miles square) as may, by Cession of particular States, and the Acceptance of Congress, become the Seat of the Government of the United States, and to exercise like Authority over all Places purchased by the Consent of the Legislature of the State in which the Same shall be, for the Erection of Forts, Magazines, Arsenals, dock-Yards, and other needful Buildings;—And

To make all Laws which shall be necessary and proper for carrying into Execution the foregoing Powers, and all other Powers vested by this Constitution in the Government of the United States, or in any Department or Officer thereof.

Section. 9. The Migration or Importation of such Persons as any of the States now existing shall think proper to admit, shall not be prohibited by the Congress prior to the Year one thousand eight hundred and eight, but a Tax or duty may be imposed on such Importation, not exceeding ten dollars for each Person.

The Privilege of the Writ of Habeas Corpus shall not be suspended, unless when in Cases of Rebellion or Invasion the public Safety may require it.

No Bill of Attainder or ex post facto Law shall be passed.

No Capitation, or other direct, Tax shall be laid, unless in Proportion to the Census or Enumeration herein before directed to be taken.

No Tax or Duty shall be laid on Articles exported from any State.

No Preference shall be given by any Regulation of Commerce or Revenue to the Ports of one State over those of another: nor shall Vessels bound to, or from, one State, be obliged to enter, clear, or pay Duties in another.

No Money shall be drawn from the Treasury, but in Consequence of Appropriations made by Law; and a regular Statement and Account of the Receipts and Expenditures of all public Money shall be published from time to time.

No Title of Nobility shall be granted by the United States: And no Person holding any Office of Profit or Trust under them, shall, without the Consent of the Congress, accept of any present, Emolument, Office, or Title, of any kind whatever, from any King, Prince, or foreign State.
Section. 10. No State shall enter into any Treaty, Alliance, or Confederation; grant Letters of Marque and Reprisal; coin Money; emit Bills of Credit; make any Thing but gold and silver Coin a Tender in Payment of Debts; pass any Bill of Attainder, ex post facto Law, or Law impairing the Obligation of Contracts, or grant any Title of Nobility.

No State shall, without the Consent of ˄the Congress, lay any Imposts or Duties on Imports or Exports, except what may be absolutely necessary for executing it's inspection Laws: and the net Produce of all Duties and Imposts, laid by any State on Imports or Exports, shall be for the Use of the Treasury of the United States; and all such Laws shall be subject to the Revision and Controul of ˄the Congress.

No State shall, without the Consent of Congress, lay any Duty of Tonnage, keep Troops, or Ships of War in time of Peace, enter into any Agreement or Compact with another State, or with a foreign Power, or engage in War, unless actually invaded, or in such imminent Danger as will not admit of delay.

Article. II.

Section. 1. The executive Power shall be vested in a President of the United States of America. He shall hold his Office during the Term of four Years, and, together with the Vice President, chosen for the same Term, be elected, as follows

Each State shall appoint, in such Manner as the Legislature thereof may direct, a Number of Electors, equal to the whole Number of Senators and Representatives to which the State may be entitled in the Congress: but no Senator or Representative, or Person holding an Office of Trust or Profit under the United States, shall be appointed an Elector.

The Electors shall meet in their respective States, and vote by Ballot for two Persons, of whom one at least shall not be an Inhabitant of the same State with themselves. And they shall make a List of all the Persons voted for, and of the Number of Votes for each; which List they shall sign and certify, and transmit sealed to the Seat of the Government of the United States, directed to the President of the Senate. The President of the Senate shall, in the Presence of the Senate and House of Representatives, open all the Certificates, and the Votes shall then be counted. The Person having the greatest Number of Votes shall be the President, if such Number be a Majority of the whole Number of Electors appointed ; and if there be more than one who have such Majority, and have an equal Number of Votes, then the House of Representatives shall immediately chuse by Ballot one of them for President ; and if no Person have a Majority, then from the five highest on the List the said House shall in like Manner chuse the President. But in chusing the President, the Votes shall be taken by States, the Representation from each State having one Vote ; A quorum for this Purpose shall consist of a Member or Members from two thirds of the States, and a Majority of all the States shall be necessary to a Choice. In every Case, after the Choice of the President, the Person having the greatest Number of Votes of the Electors shall be the Vice President. But if there should remain two or more who have equal Votes, the Senate shall chuse from them by Ballot the Vice President.

The Congress may determine the Time of chusing the Electors, and the Day on which they shall give their Votes ; which Day shall be the same throughout the United States.

No Person except a natural born Citizen, or a Citizen of the United States, at the time of the Adoption of this Constitution, shall be eligible to the Office of President; neither shall any Person be eligible to that Office who shall not have attained to the Age of thirty five Years, and been fourteen Years a Resident within the United States.

In Case of the Removal of the President from Office, or of his Death, Resignation, or Inability to discharge the Powers and Duties of the said Office, the Same shall devolve on the Vice President, and the Congress may by Law provide for the Case of Removal, Death, Resignation or Inability, both of the President and Vice President, declaring what Officer shall then act as President, and such Officer shall act accordingly, until the Disability be removed, or a President shall be elected.

The President shall, at stated Times, receive for his Services, a Compensation, which shall neither be encreased nor diminished during the Period for which he shall have been elected, and he shall not receive within that Period any other Emolument from the United States, or any of them.

Before he enter on the Execution of his Office, he shall take the following Oath or Affirmation:—"I do solemnly swear (or affirm) that I will faithfully execute the Office of President of the United States, and will to the best of my Ability, preserve, protect and defend the Constitution of the United States."

Section. 2. The President shall be Commander in Chief of the Army and Navy of the United States, and of the Militia of the several States, when called into the actual Service of the United States; he may require the Opinion, in writing, of the principal Officer in each of the executive Departments, upon any Subject relating to the Duties of their respective Offices, and he shall have Power to grant Reprieves and Pardons for Offences against the United States, except in Cases of Impeachment.

He shall have Power, by and with the Advice and Consent of the Senate, to make Treaties, provided two thirds of the Senators present concur; and he shall nominate, and by and with the Advice and Consent of the Senate, shall appoint Ambassadors, other public Ministers and Consuls, Judges of the supreme Court, and all other Officers of the United States, whose Appointments are not herein otherwise provided for, and which shall be established by Law: but the Congress may by Law vest the Appointment of such inferior Officers, as they think proper, in the President alone, in the Courts of Law, or in the Heads of Departments.

The President shall have Power to fill up all Vacancies that may happen during the Recess of the Senate, by granting Commissions which shall expire at the End of their next Session.

Section. 3. He shall from time to time give to the Congress Information of the State of the Union, and recommend to their Consideration such Measures as he shall judge necessary and expedient; he may, on extraordinary Occasions, convene both Houses, or either of them, and in Case of Disagreement between them, with Respect to the Time of Adjournment, he may adjourn them to such Time as he shall think proper; he shall receive Ambassadors and other public Ministers; he shall take Care that the Laws be faithfully executed, and shall Commission all the Officers of the United States.

Section. 4. The President, Vice President and all civil Officers of the United States, shall be removed from Office on Impeachment for, and Conviction of, Treason, Bribery, or other high Crimes and Misdemeanors.

Article III.

Section. 1. The judicial Power of the United States, shall be vested in one supreme Court, and in such inferior Courts as the Congress may from time to time ordain and establish. The Judges, both of the supreme and inferior Courts, shall hold their Offices during good Behaviour, and shall, at stated Times, receive for their Services, a Compensation, which shall not be diminished during their Continuance in Office.

Section. 2. The judicial Power shall extend to all Cases, in Law and Equity, arising under this Constitution, the Laws of the United States, and Treaties made, or which shall be made, under their Authority;—to all Cases affecting Ambassadors, other public Ministers and Consuls;—to all Cases of admiralty and maritime Jurisdiction;—to Controversies to which the United States shall be a Party;—to Controversies between two or more States;—between a State and Citizens of another State;—between Citizens of different States,—between Citizens of the same State claiming Lands under Grants of different States, and between a State, or the Citizens thereof, and foreign States, Citizens or Subjects.

In all Cases affecting Ambassadors, other public Ministers and Consuls, and those in which a State shall be Party, the supreme Court shall have original Jurisdiction. In all the other Cases before mentioned, the supreme Court shall have appellate Jurisdiction, both as to Law and

Fact, with such Exceptions, and under such Regulations as the Congress shall make.

The Trial of all Crimes, except in Cases of Impeachment, shall be by Jury; and such Trial shall be held in the State where the said Crimes shall have been committed; but when not committed within any State, the Trial shall be at such Place or Places as the Congress may by Law have directed.

Section. 3. Treason against the United States, shall consist only in levying War against them, or in adhering to their Enemies, giving them Aid and Comfort. No Person shall be convicted of Treason unless on the Testimony of two Witnesses to the same overt Act, or on Confession in open Court.

The Congress shall have Power to declare the Punishment of Treason, but no Attainder of Treason shall work Corruption of Blood, or Forfeiture except during the Life of the Person attainted.

Article. IV.

Section. 1. Full Faith and Credit shall be given in each State to the public Acts, Records, and judicial Proceedings of every other State. And the Congress may by general Laws prescribe the Manner in which such Acts, Records and Proceedings shall be proved, and the Effect thereof.

Section. 2. The Citizens of each State shall be entitled to all Privileges and Immunities of Citizens in the several States.

A Person charged in any State with Treason, Felony, or other Crime, who shall flee from Justice, and be found in another State, shall on Demand of the executive Authority of the State from which he fled, be delivered up, to be removed to the State having Jurisdiction of the Crime.

No Person held to Service or Labour in one State, under the Laws thereof, escaping into another, shall, in Consequence of any Law or Regulation therein, be discharged from such Service or Labour, but shall be delivered up on Claim of the Party to whom such Service or Labour may be due.

Section. 3. New States may be admitted by the Congress into this Union; but no new State shall be formed or erected within the Jurisdiction of any other State; nor any State be formed by the Junction of two or more States, or Parts of States, without the Consent of the Legislatures of the States concerned as well as of the Congress.

The Congress shall have Power to dispose of and make all needful Rules and Regulations respecting the Territory or other Property belonging to the United States; and nothing in this Constitution shall be so construed as to Prejudice any Claims of the United States, or of any particular State.

Section. 4. The United States shall guarantee to every State in this Union a Republican Form of Government, and shall protect each of them against Invasion; and on Application of the Legislature, or of the Executive (when the Legislature cannot be convened) against domestic Violence.

Article. V.

The Congress, whenever two thirds of both Houses shall deem it necessary, shall propose Amendments to this Constitution, or, on the Application of the Legislatures of two thirds of the several States, shall call a Convention for proposing Amendments, which, in either Case, shall be valid to all Intents and Purposes, as Part of this Constitution, when ratified by the Legislatures of three fourths of the several States, or by Conventions in three fourths thereof, as the one or the other Mode of Ratification may be proposed by the Congress; Provided that no Amendment which may be made prior to the Year One thousand eight hundred and eight shall in any Manner affect the first and fourth Clauses in the Ninth Section of the first Article; and that no State, without its Consent, shall be deprived of it's equal Suffrage in the Senate.

Article. VI.

All Debts contracted and Engagements entered into, before the Adoption of this Constitution, shall be as valid against the United States under this Constitution, as under the Confederation.

This Constitution, and the Laws of the United States which shall be made in Pursuance thereof; and all Treaties made, or which shall be made, under the Authority of the United States, shall be the supreme Law of the Land; and the Judges in every State shall be bound thereby, any Thing in the Constitution or Laws of any State to the Contrary notwithstanding.

The Senators and Representatives before mentioned, and the Members of the several State Legislatures, and all executive and judicial Officers, both of the United States and of the several States, shall be bound by

Oath or Affirmation, to support this Constitution; but no religious Test shall ever be required as a Qualification to any Office or public Trust under the United States.

Article. VII.

The Ratification of the Conventions of nine States, shall be sufficient for the Establishment of this Constitution between the States so ratifying the Same.

The Word, "the," being interlined between the seventh and eighth Lines of the first Page, The Word "Thirty" being partly written on an Erazure in the fifteenth Line of the first Page, The Words "is tried" being interlined between the thirty second and thirty third Lines of the first Page and the Word "the" being interlined between the forty third and forty fourth Lines of the second Page.

Attest WILLIAM JACKSON Secretary

done in Convention by the Unanimous Consent of the States present the Seventeenth Day of September in the Year of our Lord one thousand seven hundred and Eighty seven and of the Independance of the United States of America the Twelfth In witness whereof We have hereunto subscribed our Names,

G? WASHINGTON—Presid^t

and deputy from Virginia

New Hampshire { JOHN LANGDON
NICHOLAS GILMAN }

Massachusetts { NATHANIEL GORHAM
RUFUS KING

Connecticut { W^M SAM^L JOHNSON
ROGER SHERMAN

New York . . . ALEXANDER HAMILTON

New Jersey { WIL: LIVINGSTON
DAVID BREARLEY.
W^M PATERSON.
JONA: DAYTON

Pensylvania { B FRANKLIN
THOMAS MIFFLIN
ROB^T MORRIS
GEO. CLYMER
THO^S FITZSIMONS
JARED INGERSOLL
JAMES WILSON
GOUV MORRIS

Delaware
{ GEO: READ
GUNNING BEDFORD jun
JOHN DICKINSON
RICHARD BASSETT
JACO: BROOM

Maryland
{ JAMES M^C^HENRY
DAN OF S^T THO^S JENIFER
DAN^L CARROLL

Virginia
{ JOHN BLAIR—
JAMES MADISON Jr.

North Carolina
{ W^M BLOUNT
RICH^D DOBBS SPAIGHT.
HU WILLIAMSON

South Carolina
{ J. RUTLEDGE
CHARLES COTESWORTH PINCKNEY
CHARLES PINCKNEY
PIERCE BUTLER.

Georgia
{ WILLIAM FEW
ABR BALDWIN

In Convention Monday September 17th 1787.

Present

The States of

New Hampshire, Massachusetts, Connecticut, Mr Hamilton from New York, New Jersey, Pennsylvania, Delaware, Maryland, Virginia, North Carolina, South Carolina and Georgia.

Resolved,

That the preceeding Constitution be laid before the United States in Congress assembled, and that it is the Opinion of this Convention, that it should afterwards be submitted to a Convention of Delegates, chosen in each State by the People thereof, under the Recommendation of its Legislature, for their Assent and Ratification; and that each Convention assenting to, and ratifying the Same, should give Notice thereof to the United States in Congress assembled.

Resolved, That it is the Opinion of this Convention, that as soon as the Conventions of nine States shall have ratified this Constitution, the United States in Congress assembled should fix a Day on which Electors should be appointed by the States which shall have ratified the same, and a Day on which the Electors should assemble to vote for the President, and the Time and Place for commencing Proceedings under this Constitution. That after such Publication the Electors should be appointed, and the Senators and Representatives elected: That the Electors should meet on the Day fixed for the Election of the President, and should transmit their Votes certified, signed, sealed and directed, as the Constitution requires, to the Secretary of the United States in Congress assembled, that the Senators and Representatives should convene at the Time and Place assigned; that the Senators should appoint a President of the Senate, for the sole Purpose of receiving, opening and counting the Votes for President; and, that after he shall be chosen, the Congress, together with the President, should, without Delay, proceed to execute this Constitution.

By the Unanimous Order of the Convention

                                        GO WASHINGTON Presidt

W. JACKSON Secretary.

Articles in addition to, and Amendment of the Constitution of the United States of America, proposed by Congress, and ratified by the Legislatures of the several States, pursuant to the fifth Article of the original Constitution.

[Article I.]

Congress shall make no law respecting an establishment of religion, or prohibiting the free exercise thereof; or abridging the freedom of speech, or of the press; or the right of the people peaceably to assemble, and to petition the Government for a redress of grievances.

[Article II.]

A well regulated Militia, being necessary to the security of a free State, the right of the people to keep and bear Arms, shall not be infringed.

[Article III.]

No Soldier shall, in time of peace be quartered in any house, without the consent of the Owner, nor in time of war, but in a manner to be prescribed by law.

[Article IV.]

The right of the people to be secure in their persons, houses, papers, and effects, against unreasonable searches and seizures, shall not be violated, and no Warrants shall issue, but upon probable cause, supported by Oath or affirmation, and particularly describing the place to be searched, and the persons or things to be seized.

[Article V.]

No person shall be held to answer for a capital, or otherwise infamous crime, unless on a presentment or indictment of a Grand Jury, except in cases arising in the land or naval forces, or in the Militia, when in actual service in time of War or public danger; nor shall any person be subject for the same offence to be twice put in jeopardy of life or limb; nor shall be compelled in any criminal case to be a witness against himself, nor be deprived of life, liberty, or property, without due process of law; nor shall private property be taken for public use, without just compensation.

[Article VI.]

In all criminal prosecutions, the accused shall enjoy the right to a speedy and public trial, by an impartial jury of the State and district wherein the crime shall have been committed, which district shall have been previously ascertained by law, and to be informed of the nature and cause of the accusation; to be confronted with the witnesses against him; to have compulsory process for obtaining witnesses in his favor, and to have the Assistance of Counsel for his defence.

[Article VII.]

In Suits at common law, where the value in controversy shall exceed twenty dollars, the right of trial by jury shall be preserved, and no fact tried by a jury, shall be otherwise re-examined in any Court of the United States, than according to the rules of the common law.

[Article VIII.]

Excessive bail shall not be required, nor excessive fines imposed, nor cruel and unusual punishments inflicted.

[Article IX.]

The enumeration in the Constitution, of certain rights, shall not be construed to deny or disparage others retained by the people.

[Article X.]

The powers not delegated to the United States by the Constitution, nor prohibited by it to the States, are reserved to the States respectively, or to the people.

[Article XI.]

The Judicial power of the United States shall not be construed to extend to any suit in law or equity, commenced or prosecuted against one of the United States by Citizens of another State, or by Citizens or Subjects of any Foreign State.

[Article XII.]

The Electors shall meet in their respective states, and vote by ballot for President and Vice-President, one of whom, at least, shall not be an inhabitant of the same state with themselves; they shall name in their ballots the person voted for as President, and in distinct ballots the person voted for as Vice-President, and they shall make distinct lists of all persons voted for as President, and of all persons voted for as Vice-President, and of the number of votes for each, which lists they shall sign and certify, and transmit sealed to the seat of the government of the United States, directed to the President of the Senate;—The President of the Senate shall, in the presence of the Senate and House of Representatives, open all the certificates and the votes shall then be counted;—The person having the greatest number of votes for President, shall be the President, if such number be a majority of the whole number of Electors appointed; and if no person have such majority, then from the persons having the highest numbers not exceeding three on the list of those

voted for as President, the House of Representatives shall choose immediately, by ballot, the President. But in choosing the President, the
votes shall be taken by states, the representation from each state having
one vote; a quorum for this purpose shall consist of a member or members from two-thirds of the states, and a majority of all the states shall
be necessary to a choice. And if the House of Representatives shall not
choose a President whenever the right of choice shall devolve upon
them, before the fourth day of March next following, then the Vice-
President shall act as President, as in the case of the death or other
constitutional disability of the President.—The person having the greatest number of votes as Vice-President, shall be the Vice-President, if
such number be a majority of the whole number of Electors appointed,
and if no person have a majority, then from the two highest numbers on
the list, the Senate shall choose the Vice-President; a quorum for the
purpose shall consist of two-thirds of the whole number of Senators, and
a majority of the whole number shall be necessary to a choice. But
no person constitutionally ineligible to the office of President shall be
eligible to that of Vice-President of the United States.

Article XIII.

Section 1. Neither slavery nor involuntary servitude, except as a punishment for crime whereof the party shall have been duly convicted,
shall exist within the United States, or any place subject to their jurisdiction.
Section. 2. Congress shall have power to enforce this article by appropriate legislation.

Article XIV.

Section 1. All persons born or naturalized in the United States, and
subject to the jurisdiction thereof, are citizens of the United States and
of the State wherein they reside. No State shall make or enforce any
law which shall abridge the privileges or immunities of citizens of the
United States; nor shall any State deprive any person of life, liberty, or
property, without due process of law; nor deny to any person within its
jurisdiction the equal protection of the laws.
Section 2. Representatives shall be apportioned among the several
States according to their respective numbers, counting the whole number
of persons in each State, excluding Indians not taxed. But when the

right to vote at any election for the choice of electors for President and
Vice President of the United States, Representatives in Congress, the
Executive and Judicial officers of a State, or the members of the Legislature thereof, is denied to any of the male inhabitants of such State,
being twenty-one years of age, and citizens of the United States, or in
any way abridged, except for participation in rebellion, or other crime,
the basis of representation therein shall be reduced in the proportion
which the number of such male citizens shall bear to the whole number
of male citizens twenty-one years of age in such State.

Section 3. No person shall be a Senator or Representative in Congress, or elector of President and Vice President, or hold any office, civil
or military, under the United States, or under any State, who, having
previously taken an oath, as a member of Congress, or as an officer of
the United States, or as a member of any State legislature, or as an executive or judicial officer of any State, to support the Constitution of the
United States, shall have engaged in insurrection or rebellion against
the same, or given aid or comfort to the enemies thereof. But Congress
may by a vote of two-thirds of each House, remove such disability.

Section 4. The validity of the public debt of the United States, authorized by law, including debts incurred for payment of pensions and
bounties for services in suppressing insurrection or rebellion, shall not
be questioned. But neither the United States nor any State shall assume
or pay any debt or obligation incurred in aid of insurrection or rebellion
against the United States, or any claim for the loss or emancipation of
any slave; but all such debts, obligations and claims shall be held illegal
and void.

Section 5. The Congress shall have power to enforce, by appropriate
legislation, the provisions of this article.

Article XV.

Section 1. The right of citizens of the United States to vote shall not
be denied or abridged by the United States or by any State on account
of race, color, or previous condition of servitude—

Section 2. The Congress shall have power to enforce this article by
appropriate legislation—

George Washington

April 30, 1789, to March 4, 1797

SEE VOLUME XI.

Volume eleven is not only an index to the other volumes, not only a key that unlocks the treasures of the entire publication, but it is in itself an alphabetically arranged brief history or story of the great controlling events constituting the History of the United States.

Under its proper alphabetical classification the story is told of every great subject referred to by any of the Presidents in their official Messages, and at the end of each story the official utterances of the Presidents themselves are cited upon the subject, so that you may readily turn to the page in the body of the work itself for this original information.

Next to the possession of knowledge is the ability to turn at will to where knowledge is to be found.

HOME, ON THE POTOMAC, OF THE PARENTS OF

GEORGE WASHINGTON

With official portrait engraved from copy of original in steel

George Washington

GEORGE WASHINGTON was born at Bridges Creek, on the Potomac River, in Westmoreland County, Va., on the 22d day of February (or 11th, old style), 1732. Augustine Washington, his father, was a son of Lawrence Washington, whose father, John Washington, came to Virginia from England in 1657, and settled at Bridges Creek. Augustine Washington died in 1743, leaving several children, George being the eldest by his second wife, Mary Ball. At the early age of 19 years he was appointed adjutant-general of one of the districts of Virginia, with the rank of major. In November, 1753, he was sent by Lieutenant-Governor Dinwiddie, of Virginia, to visit the French army in the Ohio Valley on important business. War followed, and in 1754 he was promoted to the rank of lieutenant-colonel, and engaged in the war. In 1755 he acted as aid-de-camp to General Braddock. Soon after this he was appointed by the legislature commander in chief of all the forces of the Colony, and for three years devoted himself to recruiting and organizing troops for her defense. In 1758 he commanded a successful expedition to Fort Du Quesne. He then left the Army, and was married to Mrs. Martha Custis, a widow lady of Virginia. For sixteen years he resided at Mount Vernon, occasionally acting as a magistrate or as a member of the legislature. He was a delegate to the Williamsburg convention, August, 1773, which resolved that taxation and representation were inseparable. In 1774 he was sent to the Continental Congress as a delegate from Virginia. The following year he was unanimously chosen commander in chief, and assumed the command of the Continental Army July 2, 1775. He commanded the armies throughout the War for Independence. At the close he resigned his commission, December 23, 1783, and retired to private life. He was a delegate to, and president of, the National Convention which met in Philadelphia, Pa., in May, 1787, and adopted a new Constitution, that greatly increased the power of the Federal Government. He was unanimously elected the first President of the United States, and was inaugurated on the 30th of April, 1789, in New York City, and at the end of his first term was unanimously reelected. He retired March 4, 1797, having declined a third term. In September, 1796, he issued his Farewell Address to the people. July 3, 1798, he was again appointed to the command of the armies of the United States, with the rank of lieutenant-general. He was a Freemason, and served as master of his lodge. He died at Mount Vernon, Va., after a short illness, December 14, 1799, and was buried there.

PROCEEDINGS INITIATORY TO THE FIRST PRESIDENTIAL INAUGURATION.

[From the Washington Papers (Executive Proceedings, vol. 17), Department of State.]

Charles Thomson, esq., Secretary of the late Congress, being appointed by the Senate of the United States to carry to General Washington the official information of his unanimous election to the office of President of the United States of America, arrived at Mount Vernon on the 14th day of April, A. D. 1789, when he communicated to General Washington the purport of his mission in the following words:

SIR: The President of the Senate chosen for the special purpose, having opened and counted the votes of the electors in presence of the Senate and House of Representatives, I was honored with the commands of the Senate to wait upon Your Excellency with the information of your being elected to the office of President of the United States of America. This commission was intrusted to me on account of my having been long in the confidence of the late Congress, and charged with the duties of one of the principal civil departments of Government.

I have now, sir, to inform you that the proofs you have given of your patriotism, and of your readiness to sacrifice domestic ease and private enjoyments to preserve the happiness of your country, did not permit the two Houses to harbor a doubt of your undertaking this great and important office, to which you are called, not only by the unanimous vote of the electors, but by the voice of America.

I have it, therefore, in command to accompany you to New York, where the Senate and House of Representatives are convened for the dispatch of public business.

To which General Washington replied:

SIR: I have been accustomed to pay so much respect to the opinion of my fellow-citizens that the knowledge of their having given their unanimous suffrages in my favor scarcely leaves me the alternative for an option. I can not, I believe, give a greater evidence of my sensibility of the honor which they have done me than by accepting the appointment.

I am so much affected by this fresh proof of my country's esteem and confidence that silence can best explain my gratitude. While I realize the arduous nature of the task which is imposed upon me, and feel my own inability to perform it, I wish, however, that there may not be reason for regretting the choice, for, indeed, all I can promise is only to accomplish that which can be done by an honest zeal.

Upon considering how long time some of the gentlemen of both Houses of Congress have been at New York, how anxiously desirous they must be to proceed to business, and how deeply the public mind appears to be impressed with the necessity of doing it speedily, I can not find myself at liberty to delay my journey. I shall therefore be in readiness to set out the day after to-morrow, and shall be happy in the pleasure of your company, for you will permit me to say that it is a peculiar gratification to have received the communication from you.

OFFICIAL INFORMATION OF THE ELECTION OF THE PRESIDENT OF THE UNITED STATES, APRIL 6, 1789.

Be it known that the Senate and House of Representatives of the United States of America, being convened in the city and State of New York, this 6th day of April, A. D. 1789, the underwritten, appointed President of the Senate for the sole purpose of receiving, opening, and counting the votes of the electors, did, in the presence of the said Senate and House of Representatives, open all the certificates and count all the votes of the electors for a President and Vice-President, by which it appears that His Excellency George Washington, esq., was unanimously elected, agreeably to the Constitution, to the office of President of the said United States of America.

In testimony whereof I have hereunto set my hand and seal.

JOHN LANGDON.

MOUNT VERNON, *April 14, 1789.*

To the Honorable JOHN LANGDON,
   President pro tempore of the Senate of the United States.

SIR: I had the honor to receive your official communication, by the hand of Mr. Secretary Thomson, about 1 o'clock this day. Having concluded to obey the important and flattering call of my country, and having been impressed with an idea of the expediency of my being with Congress at as early a period as possible, I propose to commence my journey on Thursday morning, which will be the day after to-morrow.

I have the honor to be, with sentiments of esteem, sir, your most obedient servant,

G? WASHINGTON.

RESOLVE OF THE SENATE OF THE UNITED STATES RESPECTING MR. OSGOOD'S PREPARING HIS HOUSE FOR THE RECEPTION OF THE PRESIDENT OF THE UNITED STATES.

UNITED STATES OF AMERICA,
   In Senate, April 15, 1789.

The committee to whom it was referred to consider of and report to the House respecting the ceremonial of receiving the President, and to whom also was referred a letter from the chairman of a committee of the

Senate to the Speaker, communicating an instruction from that House to a committee thereof to report if any and what arrangements are necessary for the reception of the Vice-President, have agreed to the following report:

That Mr. Osgood, the proprietor of the house lately occupied by the President of Congress, be requested to put the same and the furniture thereof in proper condition for the residence and use of the President of the United States, and otherwise, at the expense of the United States, to provide for his temporary accommodation.

That it will be more eligible, in the first instance, that a committee of three members from the Senate and five members from the House of Representatives, to be appointed by the two Houses respectively, attend to receive the President at such place as he shall embark from New Jersey for this city, and conduct him without form to the house lately occupied by the President of Congress, and at such time thereafter as the President shall signify it will be most convenient for him, he be formally received by both Houses.

Read and accepted.

IN SENATE, *April 16, 1789.*

The Senate proceeded by ballot to the choice of a committee, agreeably to the report of the committee of both Houses agreed to the 15th instant, when the Honorable Mr. Langdon, the Honorable Mr. Carroll, and the Honorable Mr. Johnson were chosen.

A true copy from the Journals of the Senate.

Attest:

SAM. A. OTIS, *Secretary.*

RESOLVE OF THE HOUSE OF REPRESENTATIVES OF THE UNITED STATES RESPECTING MR. OSGOOD'S PREPARING HIS HOUSE FOR THE RECEPTION OF THE PRESIDENT OF THE UNITED STATES.

IN THE HOUSE OF REPRESENTATIVES
OF THE UNITED STATES,
Wednesday, April 15, 1789.

Mr. Benson reported from the committee to whom it was referred to consider of and report to the House respecting the ceremonial of receiving the President, and to whom was also referred a letter from the chairman of a committee of the Senate to the Speaker, communicating an instruction from that House to a committee thereof to report if any and what arrangements are necessary for the reception of the Vice-President, that the committee had, according to order, considered of the same, and had agreed to a report thereupon, which he delivered in at the Clerk's table, and where the same was thrice read, and the question put thereupon agreed to by the House as followeth :

That Mr. Osgood, the proprietor of the house lately occupied by the President of Congress, be requested to put the same and the furniture therein in proper order for the residence and use of the President of the United States, and otherwise, at the expense of the United States, to provide for his temporary accommodation.

That it will be most eligible, in the first instance, that a committee of three members from the Senate and five members from the House of Representatives, to be appointed by the Houses respectively, attend to receive the President at such place as he shall embark from New Jersey for this city, and conduct him without form to the house lately occupied by the President of Congress, and that at such time thereafter as the President shall signify it will be most convenient for him, he be formally received by both Houses.

Extract from the Journal.

JOHN BECKLEY, *Clerk.*

RESOLVE OF THE HOUSE OF REPRESENTATIVES RESPECTING A COMMITTEE TO MEET THE PRESIDENT OF THE UNITED STATES.

IN THE HOUSE OF REPRESENTATIVES
OF THE UNITED STATES,
Wednesday, April 15, 1789.

Resolved, That it will be most eligible, in the first instance, that a committee of three members from the Senate and five members from the House of Representatives, to be appointed by the Houses respectively, attend to receive the President at such place as he shall embark from New Jersey for this city, and conduct him without form to the house lately occupied by the President of Congress, and that at such time thereafter as the President shall signify, he be formally received by both Houses.

THURSDAY, *April 16, 1789.*

The committee elected on the part of this House, Mr. Boudinot, Mr. Bland, Mr. Tucker, Mr. Benson, and Mr. Lawrance.

Extract from the Journal.

JOHN BECKLEY, *Clerk.*

REQUEST OF THE COMMITTEE APPOINTED BY CONGRESS TO KNOW WHEN THEY SHOULD MEET THE PRESIDENT.

The committee appointed in consequence of the resolutions of both Houses of Congress, and which accompany this note, most respectfully communicate their appointment to the President of the United States, with a request that he will please to have it signified to them when they shall attend, with a barge which has been prepared for that purpose, to receive him at Elizabeth Town, or at such other place as he shall choose to embark from New Jersey for this city.

NEW YORK, *April 17, 1789.*

> JOHN LANGDON.
> CHARLES CARROLL, of Carrollton.
> WM. SAMUEL JOHNSON.
> ELIAS BOUDINOT.
> THEODORICK BLAND.
> THOS. TUDR. TUCKER.
> EGBT. BENSON.
> JOHN LAWRANCE.

TO THE COMMITTEE OF CONGRESS RESPECTING THE TIME OF THE PRESIDENT MEETING THEM AT ELIZABETH TOWN.

PHILADELPHIA, *April 20, 1789.*

GENTLEMEN: Upon my arrival in this city I received your note, with the resolutions of the two Houses which accompanied it, and in answer thereto beg leave to inform you that, knowing how anxious both Houses must be to proceed to business, I shall continue my journey dispatch as possible. To-morrow evening I purpose to be at Trenton, the night following at Brunswick, and hope to have the pleasure of meeting you at Elizabeth Town point on Thursday at 12 o'clock.

GO WASHINGTON.

LETTER FROM THE HONORABLE ELIAS BOUDINOT.

NEW YORK, *April 21, 1789.*

His Excellency GEORGE WASHINGTON, Esq.

SIR: The committee have just received Your Excellency's letter of the 20th, and will be at Elizabeth Town on Thursday morning.

I must beg Your Excellency will alight at my house, where the committee will attend, and where it will give me (in a particular manner) the utmost pleasure to receive you.

I have the honor to be, with the most profound respect, sir, your most obedient and very humble servant,

ELIAS BOUDINOT.

LETTER FROM THE HONORABLE ELIAS BOUDINOT, APRIL 23, 1789.

ELIZABETH TOWN, *Wednesday Evening.*

His Excellency GEORGE WASHINGTON, Esq.

SIR: I have the honor of informing Your Excellency that the committees of both Houses arrived here this afternoon, and will be ready to receive Your Excellency at my house as soon as you can arrive here to-morrow morning.

If you, sir, will honor us with your company at breakfast, it will give us great pleasure. We shall wait Your Excellency's arrival in hopes of that gratification. You can have a room to dress in, if you should think it necessary, as convenient as you can have it in town.

I have the honor to be Your Excellency's most obedient humble servant,

ELIAS BOUDINOT

REPORT OF THE COMMITTEE OF CONGRESS RESPECTING THE TIME OF THE INAUGURATION OF THE PRESIDENT.

IN THE HOUSE OF REPRESENTATIVES
OF THE UNITED STATES,
Saturday, April 25, 1789.

Mr. Benson, from the committee appointed to consider of the time, place, and manner in which, and of the person by whom, the oath prescribed by the Constitution shall be administered to the President of the United States, and to confer with a committee of the Senate, appointed for the purpose, reported as followeth:

That the President hath been pleased to signify to them that any time or place which both Houses may think proper to appoint and any manner which shall appear most eligible to them will be convenient and acceptable to him.

That requisite preparations can not probably be made before Thursday next; that the President be on that day formally received in the Senate Chamber; that the Representatives' Chamber being capable of receiving the greater number of persons, that therefore the President do take the oath in that place and in the presence of both Houses; that after the formal reception of the President in the Senate Chamber he be attended by both Houses to the Representatives' Chamber, and that the oath be administered by the chancellor of this State.

The committee further report it as their opinion that it will be proper that a committee of both Houses be appointed to take order for further conducting the ceremonial.

The said report was twice read, and on the question put thereupon was agreed to by the House.

Ordered, That Mr. Benson, Mr. Ames, and Mr. Carroll be a committee on the part of this House pursuant to the said report.

Extract from the Journal.

JOHN BECKLEY, *Clerk.*

REPORT OF THE COMMITTEE OF CONGRESS TO THE SENATE RESPECTING THE TIME OF THE INAUGURATION OF THE PRESIDENT.

UNITED STATES OF AMERICA,
In Senate, April 25, 1789.

The committee appointed to consider of the time, place, and manner in which and of the person by whom the oath prescribed by the Constitution shall be administered to the President of the United States, and to confer with a committee of the House appointed for that purpose, report:

That the President hath been pleased to signify to them that any time or place which both Houses may think proper to appoint and any manner which shall appear most eligible to them will be convenient and acceptable to him; that requisite preparations can not probably be made before Thursday next; that the President be on that day formally received in the Senate Chamber by both Houses; that the Representatives' Chamber being capable of receiving the greater number of persons, that therefore the President do take the oath in that place in presence of both Houses; that after the formal reception of the President in the Senate Chamber he be attended by both Houses to the Representatives' Chamber, and that the oath be administered by the chancellor of this State.

The committee further report it as their opinion that it will be proper that a committee of both Houses be appointed to take order for conducting the ceremonial.

Read and accepted.

And Mr. Lee, Mr. Izard, and Mr. Dalton, on the part of the Senate, together with the committee that may be appointed on the part of the House, are empowered to take order for conducting the business.

A true copy from the Journals of Senate.

IN SENATE, *April 27, 1789.*

The committees appointed to take order for conducting the ceremonial of the formal reception, etc., of the President report that it appears to them more eligible that the oath should be administered to the President in the outer gallery adjoining the Senate Chamber than in the Representatives' Chamber, and therefore submit to the respective Houses the propriety of authorizing their committees to take order as to the place where the oath shall be administered to the President, the resolutions of Saturday assigning the Representatives' Chamber as the place notwithstanding.

Read and accepted.

A true copy from the Journals of the Senate.

SAM. A. OTIS, *Secretary.*

ORDER FOR CONDUCTING THE CEREMONIAL FOR THE INAUGURATION OF THE PRESIDENT.

The committees of both Houses of Congress appointed to take order for conducting the ceremonial for the formal reception, etc., of the President of the United States on Thursday next have agreed to the following order thereon, viz :

That General Webb, Colonel Smith, Lieutenant-Colonel Fish, Major Franks, Major L'Enfant, Major Bleeker, and Mr. John R. Livingston be requested to serve as assistants on the occasion.

That a chair be placed in the Senate Chamber for the President.

That a chair be placed in the Senate Chamber for the Vice-President, to the right of the President's chair, and that the Senators take their seats on that side of the Chamber on which the Vice-President's chair shall be placed. That a chair be placed in the Senate Chamber for the Speaker of the House of Representatives, to the left of the President's chair, and that the Representatives take their seats on that side of the Chamber on which the Speaker's chair shall be placed.

That seats be provided in the Senate Chamber sufficient to accommodate the late President of Congress, the governor of the Western Territory, the five persons being the heads of the great Departments, the minister plenipotentiary of France, the encargado de negocios of Spain, the chaplains of Congress, the persons in the suite of the President, and also to accommodate the following public officers of the State, viz: The governor, lieutenant-governor, the chancellor, the chief justice of the supreme court and other judges thereof, and the mayor of the city.

That one of the assistants wait on these gentlemen and inform them that seats are provided for their accommodation, and also to signify to them that no precedence of seats is intended, and that no salutation is expected from them on their entrance into or their departure from the Senate Chamber.

That the members of both Houses assemble in their respective chambers precisely at 12 o'clock, and that the Representatives, preceded by their Speaker and attended by their Clerk and other officers, proceed to the Senate Chamber, there to be received by the Vice-President and Senators rising.

That the committees attend the President from his residence to the Senate Chamber, and that he be there received by the Vice-President, the Senators and Representatives rising, and by the Vice-President conducted to his chair.

That after the President shall be seated in his chair and the Vice-President, Senators, and Representatives shall be again seated, the Vice-President shall announce to the President that the members of both Houses will attend him to be present at his taking the oath of office required by the Constitution.

To the end that the oath of office may be administered to the President in the most public manner and that the greatest number of the people of the United States, and without distinction, may be witnesses to the solemnity, that therefore the oath be administered in the outer gallery adjoining to the Senate Chamber.

That when the President shall proceed to the gallery to take the oath he be attended by the Vice-President, and be followed by the chancellor of the State, and pass through the middle door; that the Senators pass through the door on the right, and the Representatives pass through the door on the left, and such of the persons who may have been admitted into the Senate Chamber and may be desirous to go into the gallery are then also to pass through the door on the right.

That when the President shall have taken the oath and returned into the Senate Chamber, attended by the Vice-President, and shall be seated in his chair, that Senators and Representatives also return into the Senate Chamber, and that the Vice-President and they resume their respective seats.

That when the President retire from the Senate Chamber he be conducted by the Vice-President to the door, the members of both Houses rising, and that he be there received by the committees and attended to his residence.

That immediately as the President shall retire the Representatives do also return from the Senate Chamber to their own.

That it be intrusted to the assistants to take proper precautions for keeping the avenues to the hall open, and for that purpose they wait on his excellency the governor of this State, and in the name of the committees request his aid by an order or recommendation to the civil officers or militia of the city to attend and serve on the occasion as he shall judge most proper.

RESOLVE OF THE HOUSE OF REPRESENTATIVES UPON THE REPORT OF THE COMMITTEE RESPECTING THE INAUGURATION OF THE PRESIDENT.

IN THE HOUSE OF REPRESENTATIVES
OF THE UNITED STATES,
Monday, April 27, 1789.

Mr. Benson, from the committee of both Houses appointed to take order for conducting the ceremonial of the formal reception of the President of the United States, reported as followeth:

That it appears to the committee more eligible that the oath should be administered to the President in the outer gallery adjoining the Senate Chamber than in the Representatives' Chamber, and therefore submits to the respective Houses the propriety of authorizing their committees to take order as to the place where the oath shall be administered to the

INAUGURATION OF WASHINGTON

INAUGURATION MORNING, 1789

President, the resolutions of Saturday assigning the Representatives' Chamber as the place notwithstanding.

The said report being twice read,

Resolved, That this House doth concur in the said report and authorize the committee to take order for the change of place thereby proposed.

Extract from the Journal.

JOHN BECKLEY, *Clerk.*

FIRST INAUGURAL ADDRESS.

IN THE CITY OF NEW YORK.

APRIL 30, 1789.

Fellow-Citizens of the Senate and of the House of Representatives:

Among the vicissitudes incident to life no event could have filled me with greater anxieties than that of which the notification was transmitted by your order, and received on the 14th day of the present month. On the one hand, I was summoned by my country, whose voice I can never hear but with veneration and love, from a retreat which I had chosen with the fondest predilection, and, in my flattering hopes, with an immutable decision, as the asylum of my declining years— a retreat which was rendered every day more necessary as well as more dear to me by the addition of habit to inclination, and of frequent interruptions in my health to the gradual waste committed on it by time. On the other hand, the magnitude and difficulty of the trust to which the voice of my country called me, being sufficient to awaken in the wisest and most experienced of her citizens a distrustful scrutiny into his qualifications, could not but overwhelm with despondence one who (inheriting inferior endowments from nature and unpracticed in the duties of civil administration) ought to be peculiarly conscious of his own deficiencies. In this conflict of emotions all I dare aver is that it has been my faithful study to collect my duty from a just appreciation of every circumstance by which it might be affected. All I dare hope is that if, in executing this task, I have been too much swayed by a grateful remembrance of former instances, or by an affectionate sensibility to this transcendent proof of the confidence of my fellow-citizens, and have thence too little consulted my incapacity as well as disinclination for the weighty and untried cares before me, my error will be palliated by the motives which mislead me, and its consequences be judged by my country with some share of the partiality in which they originated.

Such being the impressions under which I have, in obedience to the public summons, repaired to the present station, it would be peculiarly improper to omit in this first official act my fervent supplications to that Almighty Being who rules over the universe, who presides in the councils of nations, and whose providential aids can supply every human defect, that His benediction may consecrate to the liberties and happiness of the people of the United States a Government instituted by themselves for these essential purposes, and may enable every instrument employed in its administration to execute with success the functions allotted to his charge. In tendering this homage to the Great Author of every public and private good, I assure myself that it expresses your sentiments not less than my own, nor those of my fellow-citizens at large less than either. No people can be bound to acknowledge and adore the Invisible Hand which conducts the affairs of men more than those of the United States. Every step by which they have advanced to the character of an independent nation seems to have been distinguished by some token of providential agency; and in the important revolution just accomplished in the system of their united government the tranquil deliberations and voluntary consent of so many distinct communities from which the event has resulted can not be compared with the means by which most governments have been established without some return of pious gratitude, along with an humble anticipation of the future blessings which the past seem to presage. These reflections, arising out of the present crisis, have forced themselves too strongly on my mind to be suppressed. You will join with me, I trust, in thinking that there are none under the influence of which the proceedings of a new and free government can more auspiciously commence.

By the article establishing the executive department it is made the duty of the President "to recommend to your consideration such measures as he shall judge necessary and expedient." The circumstances under which I now meet you will acquit me from entering into that subject further than to refer to the great constitutional charter under which you are assembled, and which, in defining your powers, designates the objects to which your attention is to be given. It will be more consistent with those circumstances, and far more congenial with the feelings which actuate me, to substitute, in place of a recommendation of particular measures, the tribute that is due to the talents, the rectitude, and the patriotism which adorn the characters selected to devise and adopt them. In these honorable qualifications I behold the surest pledges that as on one side no local prejudices or attachments, no separate views nor party animosities, will misdirect the comprehensive and equal eye which ought to watch over this great assemblage of communities and interests, so, on another, that the foundation of our national policy will be laid in the pure and immutable principles of private morality, and the preeminence of free government be exemplified by all the attributes which can win the affections of its citizens and command the respect of the world. I dwell on this prospect with every satisfaction which an ardent love for my country can inspire, since there is no truth more thoroughly established than that there exists in the economy and course of nature an indissoluble union between virtue and happiness; between duty and advantage; between the genuine maxims of an honest and magnanimous policy and the solid rewards of public prosperity and felicity; since we ought to be no less persuaded that the propitious smiles of Heaven can never be expected on a nation that disregards the eternal rules of order and right which Heaven itself has ordained; and since the preservation of the sacred fire of liberty and the destiny of the republican model of government are justly considered, perhaps, as *deeply*, as *finally*, staked on the experiment intrusted to the hands of the American people.

Besides the ordinary objects submitted to your care, it will remain with your judgment to decide how far an exercise of the occasional power delegated by the fifth article of the Constitution is rendered expedient at the present juncture by the nature of objections which have been urged against the system, or by the degree of inquietude which has given birth to them. Instead of undertaking particular recommendations on this subject, in which I could be guided by no lights derived from official opportunities, I shall again give way to my entire confidence in your discernment and pursuit of the public good; for I assure myself that whilst you carefully avoid every alteration which might endanger the benefits of an united and effective government, or which ought to await the future lessons of experience, a reverence for the characteristic rights of freemen and a regard for the public harmony will sufficiently influence your deliberations on the question how far the former can be impregnably fortified or the latter be safely and advantageously promoted.

To the foregoing observations I have one to add, which will be most properly addressed to the House of Representatives. It concerns myself, and will therefore be as brief as possible. When I was first honored with a call into the service of my country, then on the eve of an arduous struggle for its liberties, the light in which I contemplated my duty required that I should renounce every pecuniary compensation. From this resolution I have in no instance departed; and being still under the impressions which produced it, I must decline as inapplicable to myself any share in the personal emoluments which may be indispensably included in a permanent provision for the executive department, and must accordingly pray that the pecuniary estimates for the station in which I am placed may during my continuance in it be limited to such actual expenditures as the public good may be thought to require.

Having thus imparted to you my sentiments as they have been awakened by the occasion which brings us together, I shall take my present leave; but not without resorting once more to the benign Parent of the Human Race in humble supplication that, since He has been pleased to favor the American people with opportunities for deliberating in perfect tranquillity, and dispositions for deciding with unparalleled unanimity on a form of government for the security of their union and the advancement of their happiness, so His divine blessing may be equally *conspicuous* in the enlarged views, the temperate consultations, and the wise measures on which the success of this Government must depend.

ADDRESS OF THE SENATE TO GEORGE WASHINGTON, PRESIDENT OF THE UNITED STATES.

SIR: We, the Senate of the United States, return you our sincere thanks for your excellent speech delivered to both Houses of Congress, congratulate you on the complete organization of the Federal Government, and felicitate ourselves and our fellow-citizens on your elevation to the office of President, an office highly important by the powers constitutionally annexed to it and extremely honorable from the manner in which the appointment is made. The unanimous suffrage of the elective body in your favor is peculiarly expressive of the gratitude, confidence, and affection of the citizens of America, and is the highest testimonial at once of your merit and their esteem. We are sensible, sir, that nothing but the voice of your fellow-citizens could have called you from a retreat chosen with the fondest predilection, endeared by habit, and consecrated to the repose of declining years. We rejoice, and with us all America, that in obedience to the call of our common country you have returned once more to public life. In you all parties confide; in you all interests unite; and we have no doubt that your past services, great as they have been, will be equaled by your future exertions, and that your prudence and sagacity as a statesman will tend to avert the dangers to which we were exposed, to give stability to the present Government and dignity and splendor to that country which your skill and valor as a soldier so eminently contributed to raise to independence and empire.

When we contemplate the coincidence of circumstances and wonderful combination of causes which gradually prepared the people of this country for independence; when we contemplate the rise, progress, and termination of the late war, which gave them a name among the nations of the earth, we are with you unavoidably led to acknowledge and adore the Great Arbiter of the Universe, by whom empires rise and fall. A review of the many signal instances of divine interposition in favor of this country claims our most pious gratitude; and permit us, sir, to observe that among the great events which have led to the formation and establishment of a Federal Government we esteem your acceptance of the office of President as one of the most propitious and important.

In the execution of the trust reposed in us we shall endeavor to pursue that enlarged and liberal policy to which your speech so happily directs. We are conscious that the prosperity of each State is inseparably connected with the welfare of all, and that in promoting the latter we shall effectually advance the former. In full persuasion of this truth, it shall be our invariable aim to divest ourselves of local prejudices and attachments, and to view the great assemblage of communities and interests committed to our charge with an equal eye. We feel, sir, the force and acknowledge the justness of the observation that the foundation of our national policy should be laid in private morality. If individuals be not influenced by moral principles, it is in vain to look for public virtue. It is therefore the duty of legislators to enforce, both by precept and example, the utility as well as the necessity of a strict adherence to the rules of distributive justice. We beg you to be assured that the Senate will at all times cheerfully cooperate in every measure which may strengthen the Union, conduce to the happiness or secure and perpetuate the liberties of this great confederated Republic.

We commend you, sir, to the protection of Almighty God, earnestly beseeching Him long to preserve a life so valuable and dear to the people of the United States, and that your Administration may be prosperous to the nation and glorious to yourself.

MAY 7, 1789.

REPLY OF THE PRESIDENT.

GENTLEMEN: I thank you for your address, in which the most affectionate sentiments are expressed in the most obliging terms. The coincidence of circumstances which led to this auspicious crisis, the confidence reposed in me by my fellow-citizens, and the assistance I may expect from counsels which will be dictated by an enlarged and liberal policy seem to presage a more prosperous issue to my Administration than a diffidence of my abilities had taught me to anticipate. I now feel myself inexpressibly happy in a belief that Heaven, which has done so much for our infant nation, will not withdraw its providential influence before our political felicity shall have been completed, and in a conviction that the Senate will at all times cooperate in every measure which may tend to promote the welfare of this confederated Republic. Thus supported by a firm trust in the Great Arbiter of the Universe, aided by the collected wisdom of the Union, and imploring the divine benediction on our joint exertions in the service of our country, I readily engage with you in the arduous but pleasing task of attempting to make a nation happy.

G⁹ WASHINGTON.

MAY 18, 1789.

ADDRESS OF THE HOUSE OF REPRESENTATIVES TO GEORGE
WASHINGTON, PRESIDENT OF THE UNITED STATES.

SIR: The Representatives of the people of the United States present
their congratulations on the event by which your fellow-citizens have
attested the preeminence of your merit.   You have long held the first
place in their esteem.   You have often received tokens of their affection.
You now possess the only proof that remained of their gratitude for your
services, of their reverence for your wisdom, and of their confidence in
your virtues.   You enjoy the highest, because the truest, honor of being
the first Magistrate by the unanimous choice of the freest people on the
face of the earth.

We well know the anxieties with which you must have obeyed a summons from the repose reserved for your declining years into public scenes,
of which you had taken your leave forever.   But the obedience was due
to the occasion.   It is already applauded by the universal joy which wel-
comes you to your station.   And we can not doubt that it will be rewarded
with all the satisfaction with which an ardent love for your fellow-citizens
must review successful efforts to promote their happiness.

This anticipation is not justified merely by the past experience of your
signal services.   It is particularly suggested by the pious impressions
under which you commence your Administration and the enlightened
maxims by which you mean to conduct it.   We feel with you the strongest obligations to adore the Invisible Hand which has led the American
people through so many difficulties, to cherish a conscious responsibility
for the destiny of republican liberty, and to seek the only sure means of
preserving and recommending the precious deposit in a system of legislation founded on the principles of an honest policy and directed by the
spirit of a diffusive patriotism.

The question arising out of the fifth article of the Constitution will
receive all the attention demanded by its importance, and will, we trust,
be decided under the influence of all the considerations to which you
allude.

In forming the pecuniary provisions for the executive department
we shall not lose sight of a wish resulting from motives which give it a
peculiar claim to our regard.   Your resolution, in a moment critical to the
liberties of your country, to renounce all personal emolument, was among
the many presages of your patriotic services which have been amply fulfilled; and your scrupulous adherence now to the law then imposed on
yourself can not fail to demonstrate the purity, whilst it increases the
luster, of a character which has so many titles to admiration.

Such are the sentiments which we have thought fit to address to you.
They flow from our own hearts, and we verily believe that among the
millions we represent there is not a virtuous citizen whose heart will
disown them.

All that remains is that we join in our fervent supplications for the blessings of Heaven on our country, and that we add our own for the choicest of these blessings on the most beloved of her citizens.

MAY 5, 1789.

REPLY OF THE PRESIDENT.

GENTLEMEN: Your very affectionate address produces emotions which I know not how to express. I feel that my past endeavors in the service of my country are far overpaid by its goodness, and I fear much that my future ones may not fulfill your kind anticipation. All that I can promise is that they will be invariably directed by an honest and an ardent zeal. Of this resource my heart assures me. For all beyond I rely on the wisdom and patriotism of those with whom I am to cooperate and a continuance of the blessings of Heaven on our beloved country.

G? WASHINGTON.

MAY 8, 1789.

SPECIAL MESSAGES.

NEW YORK, *May 25, 1789.*

Gentlemen of the Senate:

In pursuance of the order of the late Congress, treaties between the United States and several nations of Indians have been negotiated and signed. These treaties, with sundry papers respecting them, I now lay before you, for your consideration and advice, by the hands of General Knox, under whose official superintendence the business was transacted, and who will be ready to communicate to you any information on such points as may appear to require it.

G? WASHINGTON.

NEW YORK, *June 11, 1789.*

Gentlemen of the Senate:

A convention between His Most Christian Majesty and the United States, for the purposes of determining and fixing the functions and prerogatives of their respective consuls, vice-consuls, agents, and commissaries, was signed by their respective plenipotentiaries on the 29th of July, 1784.

It appearing to the late Congress that certain alterations in that convention ought to be made, they instructed their minister at the Court of France to endeavor to obtain them.

It has accordingly been altered in several respects, and as amended was signed by the plenipotentiaries of the contracting powers on the 14th of November, 1788.

The sixteenth article provides that it shall be in force during the term of twelve years, to be counted from the day of the exchange *of ratifications, which shall be given in proper form*, and exchanged on both sides within the space of one year, or sooner if possible.

I now lay before you the original by the hands of Mr. Jay for your consideration and advice. The papers relative to this negotiation are in his custody, and he has my orders to communicate to you whatever official papers and information on the subject he may possess and you may require.

G? WASHINGTON.

NEW YORK, *June 15, 1789.*

Gentlemen of the Senate:

Mr. Jefferson, the present minister of the United States at the Court of France, having applied for permission to return home for a few months, and it appearing to me proper to comply with his request, it becomes necessary that some person be appointed *to take charge* of our affairs at that Court during his absence.

For this purpose I nominate William Short, esq., and request your advice on the propriety of appointing him.

There are in the Office for Foreign Affairs papers which will acquaint you with his character, and which Mr. Jay has my directions to lay before you at such time as you may think proper to assign.

G? WASHINGTON.

NEW YORK, *August 6, 1789.*

Gentlemen of the Senate:

My nomination of Benjamin Fishbourn for the place of naval officer of the port of Savannah not having met with your concurrence, I now nominate Lachlan McIntosh for that office.

Whatever may have been the reasons which induced your dissent, I am persuaded they were such as you deemed sufficient. Permit me to submit to your consideration whether on occasions where the propriety of nominations appear questionable to you it would not be expedient to communicate that circumstance to me, and thereby avail yourselves of the information which led me to make them, and which I would with pleasure lay before you. Probably my reasons for nominating Mr. Fishbourn may tend to show that such a mode of proceeding in such cases might be useful. I will therefore detail them.

First. While Colonel Fishbourn was an officer in actual service and chiefly under my own eye, his conduct appeared to me irreproachable;

nor did I ever hear anything injurious to his reputation as an officer or a gentleman. At the storm of Stony Point his behavior was represented to have been active and brave, and he was charged by his general to bring the account of that success to the headquarters of the Army.

Secondly. Since his residence in Georgia he has been repeatedly elected to the assembly as a representative of the county of Chatham, in which the port of Savannah is situated, and sometimes of the counties of Glynn and Camden; he has been chosen a member of the executive council of the State and has lately been president of the same; he has been elected by the officers of the militia in the county of Chatham lieutenant-colonel of the militia in that district, and on a very recent occasion, to wit, in the month of May last, he has been appointed by the council (on the suspension of the late collector) to an office in the port of Savannah nearly similar to that for which I nominated him, which office he actually holds at this time. To these reasons for nominating Mr. Fishbourn I might add that I received private letters of recommendation and oral testimonials in his favor from some of the most respectable characters in that State; but as they were secondary considerations with me, I do not think it necessary to communicate them to you.

It appeared, therefore, to me that Mr. Fishbourn must have enjoyed the *confidence* of the militia officers in order to have been elected to a military rank; the *confidence* of the freemen to have been elected to the assembly; the *confidence* of the assembly to have been selected for the council, and the *confidence* of the council to have been appointed collector of the port of Savannah.

G^o WASHINGTON.

NEW YORK, *August 7, 1789.*

Gentlemen of the Senate:

The business which has hitherto been under the consideration of Congress has been of so much importance that I was unwilling to draw their attention from it to any other subject; but the disputes which exist between some of the United States and several powerful tribes of Indians within the limits of the Union, and the hostilities which have in several instances been committed on the frontiers, seem to require the immediate interposition of the General Government.

I have therefore directed the several statements and papers which have been submitted to me on this subject by General Knox to be laid before you for your information.

While the measures of Government ought to be calculated to protect its citizens from all injury and violence, a due regard should be extended to those Indian tribes whose happiness in the course of events so materially depends on the national justice and humanity of the United States.

If it should be the judgment of Congress that it would be most expedient to terminate all differences in the Southern district, and to lay the foundation for future confidence by an amicable treaty with the Indian tribes in that quarter, I think proper to suggest the consideration of the expediency of instituting a temporary commission for that purpose, to consist of three persons, whose authority should expire with the occasion. How far such a measure, unassisted by posts, would be competent to the establishment and preservation of peace and tranquillity on the frontiers is also a matter which merits your serious consideration.

Along with this object I am induced to suggest another, with the national importance and necessity of which I am deeply impressed; I mean some uniform and effective system for the militia of the United States. It is unnecessary to offer arguments in recommendation of a measure on which the honor, safety, and well-being of our country so evidently and so essentially depend; but it may not be amiss to observe that I am particularly anxious it should receive as early attention as circumstances will admit, because it is now in our power to avail ourselves of the military knowledge disseminated throughout the several States by means of the many well-instructed officers and soldiers of the late Army, a resource which is daily diminishing by death and other causes. To suffer this peculiar advantage to pass away unimproved would be to neglect an opportunity which will never again occur, unless, unfortunately, we should again be involved in a long and arduous war.

G<u>O</u> WASHINGTON

NEW YORK, *August 10, 1789.*

Gentlemen of the Senate:

I have directed a statement of the troops in the service of the United States to be laid before you for your information.

These troops were raised by virtue of the resolves of Congress of the 20th October, 1786, and the 3d of October, 1787, in order to protect the frontiers from the depredations of the hostile Indians, to prevent all intrusions on the public lands, and to facilitate the surveying and selling of the same for the purpose of reducing the public debt.

As these important objects continue to require the aid of the troops, it is necessary that the establishment thereof should in all respects be conformed by law to the Constitution of the United States.

G<u>O</u> WASHINGTON.

NEW YORK, *August 20, 1789.*

Gentlemen of the Senate:

In consequence of an act providing for the expenses which may attend negotiations or treaties with the Indian tribes and the appointment of commissioners for managing the same, I nominate Benjamin Lincoln as one of three commissioners whom I shall propose to be employed to negotiate a treaty with the Southern Indians. My reason for nominating nim at this early moment is that it will not be possible for the public to avail itself of his services on this occasion unless his appointment can be forwarded to him by the mail which will leave this place to-morrow morning.

GO WASHINGTON.

NEW YORK, *August 21, 1789.*

Gentlemen of the Senate:

The President of the United States will meet the Senate in the Senate Chamber at half past 11 o'clock to-morrow, to advise with them on the terms of the treaty to be negotiated with the Southern Indians.

GO WASHINGTON.

SEPTEMBER 16, 1789.

Gentlemen of the Senate:

The governor of the Western territory has made a statement to me of the reciprocal hostilities of the Wabash Indians and the people inhabiting the frontiers bordering on the river Ohio, which I herewith lay before Congress.

The United States in Congress assembled, by their acts of the 21st day of July, 1787, and of the 12th August, 1788, made a provisional arrangement for calling forth the militia of Virginia and Pennsylvania in the proportions therein specified.

As the circumstances which occasioned the said arrangement continue nearly the same, I think proper to suggest to your consideration the expediency of making some temporary provision for calling forth the militia of the United States for the purposes stated in the Constitution, which would embrace the cases apprehended by the governor of the Western territory.

GO WASHINGTON.

SEPTEMBER 17, 1789.

Gentlemen of the Senate:

It doubtless is important that all treaties and compacts formed by the United States with other nations, whether civilized or not, should be made with caution and executed with fidelity.

It is said to be the general understanding and practice of nations, as a check on the mistakes and indiscretions of ministers or commissioners, not to consider any treaty negotiated and signed by such officers as final and conclusive until ratified by the sovereign or government from whom they derive their powers. This practice has been adopted by the United States respecting their treaties with European nations, and I am inclined to think it would be advisable to observe it in the conduct of our treaties with the Indians; for though such treaties, being on their part made by their chiefs or rulers, need not be ratified by them, yet, being formed on our part by the agency of subordinate officers, it seems to be both prudent and reasonable that their acts should not be binding on the nation until approved and ratified by the Government. It strikes me that this point should be well considered and settled, so that our national proceedings in this respect may become uniform and be directed by fixed and stable principles.

The treaties with certain Indian nations, which were laid before you with my message of the 25th May last, suggested two questions to my mind, viz: First, whether those treaties were to be considered as perfected and consequently as obligatory without being ratified. If not, then secondly, whether both or either, and which, of them ought to be ratified. On these questions I request your opinion and advice.

You have, indeed, advised me "*to execute and enjoin an observance of*" the treaty with the Wyandottes, etc. You, gentlemen, doubtless intended to be clear and explicit, and yet, without further explanation, I fear I may misunderstand your meaning, for if by my *executing* that treaty you mean that I should make it (in a more particular and immediate manner than it now is) the act of Government, then it follows that I am to ratify it. If you mean by my *executing it* that I am to see that it be carried into effect and operation, then I am led to conclude either that you consider it as being perfect and obligatory in its present state, and therefore to be executed and observed, or that you consider it as to derive its completion and obligation from the silent approbation and ratification which my proclamation may be construed to imply. Although I am inclined to think that the latter is your intention, yet it certainly is best that all doubts respecting it be removed.

Permit me to observe that it will be proper for me to be informed of your sentiments relative to the treaty with the Six Nations previous to the departure of the governor of the Western territory, and therefore I recommend it to your early consideration.

G⁰ WASHINGTON.

UNITED STATES, *September 29, 1789.*

Gentlemen of the Senate:

His Most Christian Majesty, by a letter dated the 7th of June last, addressed to the President and members of the General Congress of the United States of North America, announces the much lamented death of his son, the Dauphin. The generous conduct of the French monarch and nation toward this country renders every event that may affect his or their prosperity interesting to us, and I shall take care to assure him of the sensibility with which the United States participate in the affliction which a loss so much to be regretted must have occasioned both to him and to them.

G⁰ WASHINGTON.

UNITED STATES, *September 29, 1789.*

Gentlemen of the Senate:

Agreeably to the act of Congress for adapting the establishment of the troops in public service to the Constitution of the United States, I nominate the persons specified in the inclosed list to be the commissioned officers thereof.

This nomination differs from the existing arrangement only in the following cases, to wit: Lieutenant Erkuries Beatty, promoted to a vacant captaincy in the infantry; Ensign Edward Spear, promoted to a vacant lieutenancy of artillery; Jacob Melcher, who has been serving as a volunteer, to be an ensign, vice Benjamin Lawrence, who was appointed nearly three years past and has never been mustered or joined the troops.

It is to be observed that the order in which the captains and subalterns are named is not to affect their relative rank, which has been hitherto but imperfectly settled owing to the perplexity of promotions in the State quotas conformably to the late Confederation.

G? WASHINGTON.

UNITED STATES, *September 29, 1789.*

Gentlemen of the Senate:

Having been yesterday informed by a joint committee of both Houses of Congress that they had agreed to a recess to commence this day and to continue until the first Monday of January next, I take the earliest opportunity of acquainting you that, considering how long and laborious this session has been and the reasons which I presume have produced this resolution, it does not appear to me expedient to recommend any measures to their consideration at present, or now to call your attention, gentlemen, to any of those matters in my department which require your advice and consent and yet remain to be dispatched.

G? WASHINGTON.

UNITED STATES, *September 29, 1789.*

Gentlemen of the House of Representatives:

Having been yesterday informed by a joint committee of both Houses of Congress that they had agreed to a recess to commence this day and to continue until the first Monday of January next, I take the earliest opportunity of acquainting you that, considering how long and laborious this session has been and the reasons which I presume have produced this resolution, it does not appear to me expedient to recommend any measures to their consideration at present.

G? WASHINGTON.

PROCLAMATION.

A NATIONAL THANKSGIVING.

[From Sparks's Washington, Vol. XII, p. 119.]

Whereas it is the duty of all nations to acknowledge the providence of Almighty God, to obey His will, to be grateful for His benefits, and humbly to implore His protection and favor; and

Whereas both Houses of Congress have, by their joint committee, requested me "to recommend to the people of the United States a day of public thanksgiving and prayer, to be observed by acknowledging with grateful hearts the many and signal favors of Almighty God, especially by affording them an opportunity peaceably to establish a form of government for their safety and happiness:"

Now, therefore, I do recommend and assign Thursday, the 26th day of November next, to be devoted by the people of these States to the service of that great and glorious Being who is the beneficent author of all the good that was, that is, or that will be; that we may then all unite in rendering unto Him our sincere and humble thanks for His kind care and protection of the people of this country previous to their becoming a nation; for the signal and manifold mercies and the favorable interpositions of His providence in the course and conclusion of the late war; for the great degree of tranquillity, union, and plenty which we have since enjoyed; for the peaceable and rational manner in which we have been enabled to establish constitutions of government for our safety and happiness, and particularly the national one now lately instituted; for the civil and religious liberty with which we are blessed, and the means we have of acquiring and diffusing useful knowledge; and, in general, for all the great and various favors which He has been pleased to confer upon us.

And also that we may then unite in most humbly offering our prayers and supplications to the great Lord and Ruler of Nations, and beseech Him to pardon our national and other trangressions; to enable us all, whether in public or private stations, to perform our several and relative duties properly and punctually; to render our National Government a blessing to all the people by constantly being a Government of wise, just, and constitutional laws, discreetly and faithfully executed and obeyed; to protect and guide all sovereigns and nations (especially such as have shown kindness to us), and to bless them with good governments, peace, and concord; to promote the knowledge and practice of true religion and virtue, and the increase of science among them and us; and, generally, to grant unto all mankind such a degree of temporal prosperity as He alone knows to be best.

Given under my hand, at the city of New York, the 3d day of October, A. D. 1789.

GO WASHINGTON.

KNOX   RANDOLPH   WASHINGTON

        JEFFERSON   HAMILTON

THE FIRST CABINET

THE FIRST CABINET

Knox and Randolph obeyed orders; Jefferson and Hamilton alone counseled. Judging by his later greatness, one would presume that Jefferson dominated in the first cabinet. Not so; there was a stronger, clearer, more energetic character there, in the person of Hamilton. The financial policy of the country, the funding of the State debts, the machinery of the executive departments, the suppression of the Whiskey Rebellion,—in a word, all those positive and far-reaching measures that make the first Administration so great in our annals,—were achieved by Washington and Hamilton. Jefferson's constitutional scruples were uncontrollable; in his eyes the Federal Government had no powers but those specifically conferred by the States; even the founding of a military academy was unconstitutional; but Hamilton, the man of action, chose to consider that the Federal Government had, either by express declaration or implication, been given sufficient power to be respectable in the eyes of men.

These two gathered about themselves partisans, Hamilton's being called Federalists and Jefferson's Republicans. Washington espoused neither party, but relied chiefly on Hamilton for counsel, merely using Jefferson's facile pen when he desired to put a handsome dress on his thoughts.

Hamilton's genius glows in the words of the Farewell Address, he having elaborated and revised Washington's first draft of that immortal utterance. See the articles entitled "Assumption of State Debts," "Federalist Party," "Whiskey Insurrection," and "Republican Party," in the encyclopedic index (volume eleven).

FIRST ANNUAL ADDRESS.

UNITED STATES, *January 8, 1790.*

Fellow-Citizens of the Senate and House of Representatives:

I embrace with great satisfaction the opportunity which now presents itself of congratulating you on the present favorable prospects of our public affairs. The recent accession of the important State of North Carolina to the Constitution of the United States (of which official information has been received), the rising credit and respectability of our country, the general and increasing good will toward the Government of the Union, and the concord, peace, and plenty with which we are blessed are circumstances auspicious in an eminent degree to our national prosperity.

In resuming your consultations for the general good you can not but derive encouragement from the reflection that the measures of the last session have been as satisfactory to your constituents as the novelty and difficulty of the work allowed you to hope. Still further to realize their expectations and to secure the blessings which a gracious Providence has placed within our reach will in the course of the present important session call for the cool and deliberate exertion of your patriotism, firmness, and wisdom.

Among the many interesting objects which will engage your attention that of providing for the common defense will merit particular regard. To be prepared for war is one of the most effectual means of preserving peace.

A free people ought not only to be armed, but disciplined; to which end a uniform and well-digested plan is requisite; and their safety and interest require that they should promote such manufactories as tend to render them independent of others for essential, particularly military, supplies.

The proper establishment of the troops which may be deemed indispensable will be entitled to mature consideration. In the arrangements which may be made respecting it it will be of importance to conciliate the comfortable support of the officers and soldiers with a due regard to economy.

There was reason to hope that the pacific measures adopted with regard to certain hostile tribes of Indians would have relieved the inhabitants of our Southern and Western frontiers from their depredations, but you will perceive from the information contained in the papers which I shall direct to be laid before you (comprehending a communication from the Commonwealth of Virginia) that we ought to be prepared to afford protection to those parts of the Union, and, if necessary, to punish aggressors.

The interests of the United States require that our intercourse with other nations should be facilitated by such provisions as will enable me to fulfill my duty in that respect in the manner which circumstances may render most conducive to the public good, and to this end that the compensations to be made to the persons who may be employed should, according to the nature of their appointments, be defined by law, and a competent fund designated for defraying the expenses incident to the conduct of our foreign affairs.

Various considerations also render it expedient that the terms on which foreigners may be admitted to the rights of citizens should be speedily ascertained by a uniform rule of naturalization.

Uniformity in the currency, weights, and measures of the United States is an object of great importance, and will, I am persuaded, be duly attended to.

The advancement of agriculture, commerce, and manufactures by all proper means will not, I trust, need recommendation; but I can not forbear intimating to you the expediency of giving effectual encouragement as well to the introduction of new and useful inventions from abroad as to the exertions of skill and genius in producing them at home, and of facilitating the intercourse between the distant parts of our country by a due attention to the post-office and post-roads.

Nor am I less persuaded that you will agree with me in opinion that there is nothing which can better deserve your patronage than the promotion of science and literature. Knowledge is in every country the surest basis of public happiness. In one in which the measures of government receive their impressions so immediately from the sense of the community as in ours it is proportionably essential. To the security of a free constitution it contributes in various ways—by convincing those who are intrusted with the public administration that every valuable end of government is best answered by the enlightened confidence of the people, and by teaching the people themselves to know and to value their own rights; to discern and provide against invasions of them; to distinguish between oppression and the necessary exercise of lawful authority; between burthens proceeding from a disregard to their convenience and those resulting from the inevitable exigencies of society; to discriminate the spirit of liberty from that of licentiousness—cherishing the first, avoiding the last—and uniting a speedy but temperate vigilance against encroachments, with an inviolable respect to the laws.

Whether this desirable object will be best promoted by affording aids to seminaries of learning already established, by the institution of a national university, or by any other expedients will be well worthy of a place in the deliberations of the Legislature.

Gentlemen of the House of Representatives:

I saw with peculiar pleasure at the close of the last session the resolution entered into by you expressive of your opinion that an adequate provision for the support of the public credit is a matter of high importance to the national honor and prosperity. In this sentiment I entirely concur; and to a perfect confidence in your best endeavors to devise such a provision as will be truly consistent with the end I add an equal reliance on the cheerful cooperation of the other branch of the Legislature. It would be superfluous to specify inducements to a measure in which the character and permanent interests of the United States are so obviously and so deeply concerned, and which has received so explicit a sanction from your declaration.

Gentlemen of the Senate and House of Representatives:

I have directed the proper officers to lay before you, respectively, such papers and estimates as regard the affairs particularly recommended to your consideration, and necessary to convey to you that information of the state of the Union which it is my duty to afford.

The welfare of our country is the great object to which our cares and efforts ought to be directed, and I shall derive great satisfaction from a cooperation with you in the pleasing though arduous task of insuring to our fellow-citizens the blessings which they have a right to expect from a free, efficient, and equal government.

G? WASHINGTON.

ADDRESS OF THE SENATE TO GEORGE WASHINGTON, PRESIDENT OF THE UNITED STATES.

The PRESIDENT OF THE UNITED STATES.

SIR: We, the Senate of the United States, return you our thanks for your speech delivered to both Houses of Congress. The accession of the State of North Carolina to the Constitution of the United States gives us much pleasure, and we offer you our congratulations on that event, which at the same time adds strength to our Union and affords a proof that the more the Constitution has been considered the more the goodness of it has appeared. The information which we have received, that the measures of the last session have been as satisfactory to our constituents as we had reason to expect from the difficulty of the work in which we were engaged, will afford us much consolation and encouragement in resuming our deliberations in the present session for the public good, and every exertion on our part shall be made to realize and secure to our country those blessings which a gracious Providence has placed within her reach. We are persuaded that one of the most effectual means of preserving peace is to be prepared for war, and our attention shall be directed to the objects of common defense and to the adoption of such plans as shall appear the most likely to prevent our dependence on other countries ror essential supplies. In the arrangements to be made respecting the establishment of such troops as may be deemed indispensable we shall with pleasure provide for the comfortable support of the officers and soldiers, with a due regard to economy. We regret that the pacific measures adopted by Government with regard to certain hostile tribes of Indians have not been attended with the beneficial effects toward the inhabitants of our Southern and Western frontiers which we had reason to hope; and we shall cheerfully cooperate in providing the most effectual means for their protection, and, if necessary, for the punishment of aggressors. The uniformity of the currency and of weights and measures, the introduction of new and useful inventions from abroad and the exertions of skill and genius in producing them at home, the facilitating the communication between the distant parts of our country by means of the post-office and post-roads, a provision for the support of the Department of Foreign Affairs, and a uniform rule of naturalization, by which foreigners may be admitted to the rights of citizens, are objects which shall receive such early attention as their respective importance requires. Literature and science are essential to the preservation of a free constitution; the measures of Government should therefore be calculated to strengthen the confidence that is due to that important truth. Agriculture, commerce, and manufactures, forming the basis of the wealth and strength of our confederated Republic, must be the frequent subject of our deliberation, and shall be advanced by all proper means in our power. Public credit being an object of great importance, we shall cheerfully cooperate in all proper measures for its support. Proper attention shall be given to such papers and estimates as you may be pleased to lay before us. Our cares and efforts shall be directed to the welfare of our country, and we have the most perfect dependence upon your cooperating with us on all occasions in such measures as will insure to our fellow-citizens the blessings which they have a right to expect from a free, efficient, and equal government.

JANUARY 11, 1790.

REPLY OF THE PRESIDENT.

GENTLEMEN: I thank you for your address, and for the assurances which it contains of attention to the several matters suggested by me to your consideration.

Relying on the continuance of your exertions for the public good, I anticipate for our country the salutary effects of upright and prudent counsels.

G° WASHINGTON.

JANUARY 14, 1790.

ADDRESS OF THE HOUSE OF REPRESENTATIVES TO GEORGE
WASHINGTON, PRESIDENT OF THE UNITED STATES.

SIR: The Representatives of the people of the United States have
taken into consideration your speech to both Houses of Congress at the
opening of the present session.

We reciprocate your congratulations on the accession of the State of
North Carolina, an event which, while it is a testimony of the increasing
good will toward the Government of the Union, can not fail to give
additional dignity and strength to the American Republic, already rising
in the estimation of the world in national character and respectability.

The information that our measures of the last session have not proved
dissatisfactory to our constituents affords us much encouragement at
this juncture, when we are resuming the arduous task of legislating for
so extensive an empire.

Nothing can be more gratifying to the Representatives of a free people
than the reflection that their labors are rewarded by the approbation of
their fellow-citizens. Under this impression we shall make every exertion to realize their expectations, and to secure to them those blessings
which Providence has placed within their reach. Still prompted by the
same desire to promote their interests which then actuated us, we shall
in the present session diligently and anxiously pursue those measures
which shall appear to us conducive to that end.

We concur with you in the sentiment that agriculture, commerce, and
manufactures are entitled to legislative protection, and that the promotion of science and literature will contribute to the security of a free
Government; in the progress of our deliberations we shall not lose sight
of objects so worthy of our regard.

The various and weighty matters which you have judged necessary to
recommend to our attention appear to us essential to the tranquillity and
welfare of the Union, and claim our early and most serious consideration.
We shall proceed without delay to bestow on them that calm discussion
which their importance requires.

We regret that the pacific arrangements pursued with regard to certain
hostile tribes of Indians have not been attended with that success which
we had reason to expect from them. We shall not hesitate to concur in
such further measures as may best obviate any ill effects which might be
apprehended from the failure of those negotiations.

Your approbation of the vote of this House at the last session respecting the provision for the public creditors is very acceptable to us. The
proper mode of carrying that resolution into effect, being a subject in
which the future character and happiness of these States are deeply
involved, will be among the first to deserve our attention.

The prosperity of the United States is the primary object of all our
deliberations, and we cherish the reflection that every measure which we

may adopt for its advancement will not only receive your cheerful concurrence, but will at the same time derive from your cooperation additional efficacy, in insuring to our fellow-citizens the blessings of a free, efficient, and equal government.

JANUARY 12, 1790.

REPLY OF THE PRESIDENT.

GENTLEMEN: I receive with pleasure the assurances you give me that you will diligently and anxiously pursue such measures as shall appear to you conducive to the interest of your constituents, and that an early and serious consideration will be given to the various and weighty matters recommended by me to your attention.

I have full confidence that your deliberations will continue to be directed by an enlightened and virtuous zeal for the happiness of our country.

Gᵒ WASHINGTON.

JANUARY 14, 1790.

SPECIAL MESSAGES.

UNITED STATES, *January 11, 1790.*

Gentlemen of the Senate:

Having advised with you upon the terms of a treaty to be offered to the Creek Nation of Indians, I think it proper you should be informed of the result of that business previous to its coming before you in your legislative capacity. I have therefore directed the Secretary for the Department of War to lay before you my instructions to the commissioners and their report in consequence thereof.

The apparently critical state of the Southern frontier will render it expedient for me to communicate to both Houses of Congress, with other papers, the whole of the transactions relative to the Creeks, in order that they may be enabled to form a judgment of the measures which the case may require.

GᵒWASHINGTON.

UNITED STATES, *January 11, 1790.*

Gentlemen of the House of Representatives:

I have directed Mr. Lear, my private secretary, to lay before you a copy of the adoption and ratification of the Constitution of the United States by the State of North Carolina, together with a copy of a letter from His Excellency Samuel Johnston, president of the convention of said State, to the President of the United States.

The originals of the papers which are herewith transmitted to you will be lodged in the office of the Secretary of State.

G⁹ WASHINGTON.

UNITED STATES, *January 12, 1790.*

Gentlemen of the Senate and House of Representatives:

I lay before you a statement of the Southwestern frontiers and of the Indian Department, which have been submitted to me by the Secretary for the Department of War.

I conceive that an unreserved but confidential communication of all the papers relative to the recent negotiations with some of the Southern tribes of Indians is indispensably requisite for the information of Congress. I am persuaded that they will effectually prevent either transcripts or publications of all such circumstances as might be injurious to the public interests.

G⁹ WASHINGTON.

UNITED STATES, *January 21, 1790.*

Gentlemen of the Senate and House of Representatives:

The Secretary for the Department of War has submitted to me certain principles to serve as a plan for the general arrangement of the militia of the United States.

Conceiving the subject to be of the highest importance to the welfare of our country and liable to be placed in various points of view, I have directed him to lay the plan before Congress for their information, in order that they may make such use thereof as they may judge proper.

G⁹ WASHINGTON.

UNITED STATES, *January 25, 1790.*

Gentlemen of the Senate and House of Representatives:

I have received from His Excellency John E. Howard, governor of the State of Maryland, an act of the legislature of Maryland to ratify certain articles in addition to and amendment of the Constitution of the United States of America, proposed by Congress to the legislatures of the several States, and have directed my secretary to lay a copy of the same before you, together with the copy of a letter, accompanying the above act, from his excellency the governor of Maryland to the President of the United States.

The originals will be deposited in the office of the Secretary of State.

G⁹ WASHINGTON.

UNITED STATES, *January 28, 1790.*

Gentlemen of the Senate and House of Representatives:

I have directed my secretary to lay before you the copy of an act of the legislature of Rhode Island and Providence Plantations entitled "An act for calling a convention to take into consideration the Constitution proposed for the United States, passed on the 17th day of September, A. D. 1787, by the General Convention held at Philadelphia," together with the copy of a letter, accompanying said act, from His Excellency John Collins, governor of the State of Rhode Island and Providence Plantations, to the President of the United States.

The originals of the foregoing act and letter will be deposited in the office of the Secretary of State.

G9 WASHINGTON.

UNITED STATES, *February 1, 1790.*

Gentlemen of the Senate and House of Representatives:

I have received from His Excellency Alexander Martin, governor of the State of North Carolina, an act of the general assembly of that State entitled "An act for the purpose of ceding to the United States of America certain western lands therein described," and have directed my secretary to lay a copy of the same before you, together with a copy of a letter, accompanying said act, from His Excellency Governor Martin to the President of the United States.

The originals of the foregoing act and letter will be deposited in the office of the Secretary of State.

G9 WASHINGTON.

UNITED STATES, *February 9, 1790.*

Gentlemen of the Senate:

You will perceive from the papers herewith delivered, and which are enumerated in the annexed list, that a difference subsists between Great Britain and the United States relative to the boundary line between our eastern and their territories. A plan for deciding this difference was laid before the late Congress, and whether that or some other plan of a like kind would not now be eligible is submitted to your consideration.

In my opinion, it is desirable that all questions between this and other nations be speedily and amicably settled, and in this instance I think it advisable to postpone any negotiations on the subject until I shall be informed of the result of your deliberations and receive your advice as to the propositions most proper to be offered on the part of the United States.

As I am taking measures for learning the intentions of Great Britain respecting the further detention of our posts, etc., I am the more solicitous that the business now submitted to you may be prepared for negotiation as soon as the other important affairs which engage your attention will permit.

G⁇ WASHINGTON.

UNITED STATES, *February 15, 1790.*

Gentlemen of the Senate and House of Representatives:

I have directed my secretary to lay before you the copy of a vote of the legislature of the State of New Hampshire, to accept the articles proposed in addition to and amendment of the Constitution of the United States of America, except the second article. At the same time will be delivered to you the copy of a letter from his excellency the president of the State of New Hampshire to the President of the United States.

The originals of the above-mentioned vote and letter will be lodged in the office of the Secretary of State.

G⁇ WASHINGTON.

UNITED STATES, *February 18, 1790.*

Gentlemen of the Senate:

By the mail of last evening I received a letter from His Excellency John Hancock, governor of the Commonwealth of Massachusetts, inclosing a resolve of the senate and house of representatives of that Commonwealth and sundry documents relative to the eastern boundary of the United States.

I have directed a copy of the letter and resolve to be laid before you. The documents which accompanied them being but copies of some of the papers which were delivered to you with my communication of the 9th of this month, I have thought it unnecessary to lay them before you at this time. They will be deposited in the office of the Secretary of State, together with the originals of the above-mentioned letters and resolve.

G⁇ WASHINGTON.

UNITED STATES, *March 8, 1790.*

Gentlemen of the Senate and House of Representatives:

I have received from His Excellency Joshua Clayton, president of the State of Delaware, the articles proposed by Congress to the legislatures of the several States as amendments to the Constitution of the United States, which articles were transmitted to him for the consideration of the legislature of Delaware, and are now returned with the following resolutions annexed to them, viz:

The general assembly of Delaware having taken into their consideration the above amendments, proposed by Congress to the respective legislatures of the several States,

Resolved, That the first article be postponed;

Resolved, That the general assembly do agree to the second, third, fourth, fifth, sixth, seventh, eighth, ninth, tenth, eleventh, and twelfth articles, and we do hereby assent to, ratify, and confirm the same as part of the Constitution of the United States.

In testimony whereof we have caused the great seal of the State to be hereunto affixed this 28th day of January, A. D. 1790, and in the fourteenth year of the independence of the Delaware State.

Signed by order of council.

GEORGE MITCHELL, *Speaker*.

Signed by order of the house of assembly.

JEHU DAVIS, *Speaker*.

I have directed a copy of the letter which accompanied the said articles, from His Excellency Joshua Clayton to the President of the United States, to be laid before you.

The before-mentioned articles and the original of the letter will be lodged in the office of the Secretary of State.

G⁰ WASHINGTON.

UNITED STATES, *March 16, 1790*.

Gentlemen of the Senate and House of Representatives:

I have directed my secretary to lay before you the copy of an act and the form of ratification of certain articles of amendment to the Constitution of the United States by the legislature of the State of Pennsylvania, together with the copy of a letter which accompanied the said act, from the speaker of the house of assembly of Pennsylvania to the President of the United States.

The originals of the above will be lodged in the office of the Secretary of State.

G⁰ WASHINGTON.

UNITED STATES, *April 1, 1790*.

Gentlemen of the Senate and House of Representatives:

I have directed my private secretary to lay before you a copy of the adoption by the legislature of South Carolina of the articles proposed by Congress to the legislatures of the several States as amendments to the Constitution of the United States, together with the copy of a letter from the governor of the State of South Carolina to the President of the United States, which have lately come to my hands.

The originals of the foregoing will be lodged in the office of the Secretary of State.

G⁰ WASHINGTON.

By the President of the United States of America:

A Proclamation

When we review the calamities which afflict so many other Nations the present condition of the United States affords much matter of consolation and satisfaction. Our exemption hitherto from foreign war, an increasing prospect of the continuance of that exemption, the great degree of internal tranquillity we have enjoyed, the recent confirmation of that tranquility by the suppression of an insurrection which so wantonly threatened it, the happy course of our public affairs in general, the unexampled prosperity of all classes of our Citizens — are circumstances which peculiarly mark our situation with indications of the Divine Beneficence towards us. In such a state of things it is, in an especial manner, our duty as a people, with devout reverence and affectionate gratitude, to acknowledge our many and great obligations to Almighty God and to implore him to continue and confirm the blessings we experience.

Deeply penetrated with this sentiment I George Washington President of the United States do recommend to all Religious societies and Denominations and to all persons whomsoever within the united States to set apart and observe thursday the nineteenth day of February next as a day of public thanksgiving and prayer; and on that day to meet together and render their sincere and hearty thanks to the great ruler of Nations for the manifold and signal mercies, which distinguish our lot as a Nation; particularly for the possession of Constitutions of Government which unite and by their union establish liberty with order, for the preservation of our peace foreign and domestic for the seasonable controul which has been given to a spirit of disorder in the suppression of the late insurrection, and generally for the prosperous course of our affairs public and private; and at the same time humbly

and

WASHINGTON'S THANKSGIVING PROCLAMATION.

and fervently to beseech the kind author of these blessings graciously to prolong them to us — to imprint on our hearts a deep and solemn sense of our obligations to him for them — to teach us rightly to estimate their immense value — to preserve us from the arrogance of prosperity and from hazarding the advantages we enjoy by delusive pursuits — to dispose us to merit the continuance ___ of his favors, by not abusing them, by our gratitude for them, and by a correspondent conduct as citizens and as men — to render this Country more and more a safe and propitious asylum for the unfortunate of other Countries — to extend — among us true and useful knowledge — to diffuse and establish habits of sobriety, order, morality, and piety and finally to impart all the blessings we possess, or ask for ourselves, to the whole family of mankind.

In Testimony whereof I have caused the Seal of the united States of America to be affixed to these presents and signed the same with my hand. Done at the City of Philadelphia the First day of January one thousand seven hundred and ninety five, and of the Independence of the United States of America the nineteenth.

G Washington

By the President
Edm Randolph

UNITED STATES, *April 5, 1790.*

Gentlemen of the Senate and House of Representatives:

I have directed my private secretary to lay before you copies of three acts of the legislature of the State of New York, which have been transmitted to me by the governor thereof, viz:

"An act declaring it to be the duty of the sheriffs of the several counties within this State to receive and safe keep such prisoners as shall be committed under the authority of the United States."

"An act for vesting in the United States of America the light-house and the lands thereunto belonging at Sandy Hook."

"An act ratifying certain articles in addition to and amendment of the Constitution of the United States of America, proposed by Congress."

A copy of a letter accompanying said acts, from the governor of the State of New York to the President of the United States, will at the same time be laid before you, and the originals be deposited in the office of the Secretary of State.

G? WASHINGTON.

UNITED STATES, *May 31, 1790.*

Gentlemen of the Senate:

Mr. de Poiery served in the American Army for several of the last years of the late war as secretary to Major-General the Marquis de Lafayette, and might probably at that time have obtained the commission of captain from Congress upon application to that body. At present he is an officer in the French national guards, and solicits a brevet commission from the United States of America. I am authorized to add, that while the compliance will involve no expense on our part, it will be particularly grateful to that friend of America, the Marquis de Lafayette. I therefore nominate M. de Poiery to be a captain by brevet.

G? WASHINGTON.

UNITED STATES, *June 1, 1790.*

Gentlemen of the Senate and House of Representatives:

Having received official information of the accession of the State of Rhode Island and Providence Plantations to the Constitution of the United States, I take the earliest opportunity of communicating the same to you, with my congratulations on this happy event, which unites under the General Government all the States which were originally confederated, and have directed my secretary to lay before you a copy of the letter from the president of the convention of the State of Rhode Island to the President of the United States.

GO WASHINGTON.

UNITED STATES, *June 11, 1790.*

Gentlemen of the Senate and House of Representatives:

I have directed my secretary to lay before you a copy of the ratification of the amendments to the Constitution of the United States by the State of North Carolina, together with an extract from a letter, accompanying said ratification, from the governor of the State of North Carolina to the President of the United States.

G? WASHINGTON.

UNITED STATES, *June 16, 1790.*

Gentlemen of the Senate and House of Representatives:

The ratification of the Constitution of the United States of America by the State of Rhode Island and Providence Plantations was received by me last night, together with a letter to the President of the United States from the president of the convention. I have directed my secretary to lay before you a copy of each.

G? WASHINGTON.

UNITED STATES, *June 30, 1790.*

Gentlemen of the Senate and House of Representatives:

An act of the legislature of the State of Rhode Island and Providence Plantations, for ratifying certain articles as amendments to the Constitution of the United States, was yesterday put into my hands, and I have directed my secretary to lay a copy of the same before you.

G? WASHINGTON.

UNITED STATES, *August 4, 1790.*

Gentlemen of the Senate:

In consequence of the general principles agreed to by the Senate in August, 1789, the adjustment of the terms of a treaty is far advanced between the United States and the chiefs of the Creek Indians, now in this city, in behalf of themselves and the whole Creek Nation.

In preparing the articles of this treaty the present arrangements of the trade with the Creeks have caused much embarrassment. It seems to be well ascertained that the said trade is almost exclusively in the hands of a company of British merchants, who by agreement make their importations of goods from England into the Spanish ports.

As the trade of the Indians is a main mean of their political management, it is therefore obvious that the United States can not possess any security for the performance of treaties with the Creeks while their trade is liable to be interrupted or withheld at the caprice of two foreign powers.

Hence it becomes an object of real importance to form new channels for the commerce of the Creeks through the United States. But this operation will require time, as the present arrangements can not be suddenly broken without the greatest violation of faith and morals.

It therefore appears to be important to form a secret article of a treaty similar to the one which accompanies this message.

If the Senate should require any further explanation, the Secretary of War will attend them for that purpose.

G⁰ WASHINGTON.

The President of the United States states the following question for the consideration and advice of the Senate: If it should be found essential to a treaty for the firm establishment of peace with the Creek Nation of Indians that an article to the following effect should be inserted therein, will such an article be proper? viz:

SECRET ARTICLE.

The commerce necessary for the Creek Nation shall be carried on through the ports and by the citizens of the United States if substantial and effectual arrangements shall be made for that purpose by the United States on or before the 1st day of August, 1792. In the meantime the said commerce may be carried on through its present channels and according to its present regulations.

And whereas the trade of the said Creek Nation is now carried on wholly or principally through the territories of Spain, and obstructions thereto may happen by war or prohibitions of the Spanish Government, it is therefore agreed between the said parties that in the event of any such obstructions happening it shall be lawful for such persons as ——— ——— shall designate to introduce into and transport through the territories of the United States to the country of the said Creek Nation any quantity of goods, wares, and merchandise not exceeding in value in any one year $60,000, and that free from any duties or impositions whatsoever, but subject to such regulations for guarding against abuse as the United States shall judge necessary, which privilege shall continue as long as such obstruction shall continue.

G⁰ WASHINGTON.

UNITED STATES, *August 6, 1790.*

Gentlemen of the Senate:

Considering the circumstances which prevented the late commissioners from concluding a peace with the Creek Nation of Indians, it appeared to me most prudent that all subsequent measures for disposing them to a treaty should in the first instance be informal.

I informed you on the 4th instant that the adjustment of the terms of a treaty with their chiefs, now here, was far advanced. Such further progress has since been made that I think measures may at present be taken for conducting and concluding that business in form. It therefore becomes necessary that a proper person be appointed and authorized to treat with these chiefs and to conclude a treaty with them. For this purpose I nominate to you Henry Knox.

G⁰ WASHINGTON.

UNITED STATES, *August 6, 1790.*

Gentlemen of the Senate and House of Representatives:

I have directed my secretary to lay before you a copy of an exemplified copy of a law to ratify on the part of the State of New Jersey certain amendments to the Constitution of the United States, together with a copy of a letter, which accompanied said ratification, from Hon. Elisha Lawrence, esq., vice-president of the State of New Jersey, to the President of the United States,

G⁰ WASHINGTON.

UNITED STATES, *August 7, 1790.*

Gentlemen of the Senate:

I lay before you a treaty between the United States and the chiefs of the Creek Nation, now in this city, in behalf of themselves and the whole Creek Nation, subject to the ratification of the President of the United States with the advice and consent of the Senate.

While I flatter myself that this treaty will be productive of present peace and prosperity to our Southern frontier, it is to be expected that it will also in its consequences be the means of firmly attaching the Creeks and the neighboring tribes to the interests of the United States.

At the same time it is to be hoped that it will afford solid grounds of satisfaction to the State of Georgia, as it contains a regular, full, and definitive relinquishment on the part of the Creek Nation of the Oconee land in the utmost extent in which it has been claimed by that State, and thus extinguishes the principal cause of those hostilities from which it has more than once experienced such severe calamities.

But although the most valuable of the disputed land is included, yet there is a certain claim of Georgia, arising out of the treaty made by that State at Galphinston in November, 1785, of land to the eastward of a new temporary line from the forks of the Oconee and Oakmulgee in a southwest direction to the St. Marys River, which tract of land the Creeks in this city absolutely refuse to yield.

This land is reported to be generally barren, sunken, and unfit for cultivation, except in some instances on the margin of the rivers, on which by improvement rice might be cultivated, its chief value depending on the timber fit for the building of ships, with which it is represented as abounding.

While it is thus circumstanced on the one hand, it is stated by the Creeks on the other to be of the highest importance to them as constituting some of their most valuable winter hunting ground.

I have directed the commissioner to whom the charge of adjusting this treaty has been committed to lay before you such papers and documents and to communicate to you such information relatively to it as you may require.

G? WASHINGTON.

UNITED STATES, *August 11, 1790.*

Gentlemen of the Senate:

Although the treaty with the Creeks may be regarded as the main foundation of the future peace and prosperity of the Southwestern frontier of the United States, yet in order fully to effect so desirable an object the treaties which have been entered into with the other tribes in that quarter must be faithfully performed on our parts.

During the last year I laid before the Senate a particular statement of the case of the Cherokees. By a reference to that paper it will appear that the United States formed a treaty with the Cherokees in November, 1785; that the said Cherokees thereby placed themselves under the protection of the United States and had a boundary assigned them; that the white people settled on the frontiers had openly violated the said boundary by intruding on the Indian lands; that the United States in Congress assembled did, on the 1st day of September, 1788, issue their proclamation forbidding all such unwarrantable intrusions, and enjoined all those who had settled upon the hunting grounds of the Cherokees to depart with their families and effects without loss of time, as they would answer their disobedience to the injunctions and prohibitions expressed at their peril.

But information has been received that notwithstanding the said treaty and proclamation upward of 500 families have settled on the Cherokee lands exclusively of those settled between the fork of French Broad and Holstein rivers, mentioned in the said treaty.

As the obstructions to a proper conduct on this matter have been removed since it was mentioned to the Senate on the 22d of August, 1789, by the accession of North Carolina to the present Union and the cessions of the land in question, I shall conceive myself bound to exert the powers intrusted to me by the Constitution in order to carry into faithful execution the treaty of Hopewell, unless it shall be thought proper to attempt to arrange a new boundary with the Cherokees, embracing the settlements, and compensating the Cherokees for the cessions they shall make on the occasion. On this point, therefore, I state the following questions and request the advice of the Senate thereon:

First. Is it the judgment of the Senate that overtures shall be made to the Cherokees to arrange a new boundary so as to embrace the settlements made by the white people since the treaty of Hopewell, in November, 1785?

Second. If so, shall compensation to the amount of ———— dollars annually, or of ———— dollars in gross, be made to the Cherokees for the land they shall relinquish, holding the occupiers of the land accountable to the United States for its value?

Third. Shall the United States stipulate solemnly to guarantee the new boundary which may be arranged?

G⁰ WASHINGTON.

PROCLAMATIONS.

[From the Gazette of the United States (New York), September 15, 1790, in the Library of Congress.]

BY THE PRESIDENT OF THE UNITED STATES OF AMERICA.

A PROCLAMATION.

Whereas a treaty of peace and friendship between the United States and the Creek Nation was made and concluded on the 7th day of the present month of August; and

Whereas I have, by and with the advice and consent of the Senate, in due form ratified the said treaty:

Now, therefore, to the end that the same may be observed and performed with good faith on the part of the United States, I have ordered the said treaty to be herewith published; and I do hereby enjoin and require all officers of the United States, civil and military, and all other citizens and inhabitants thereof, faithfully to observe and fulfill the same.

Given under my hand and the seal of the United States, in the city of New York, the 14th day of August, A. D. 1790, and in the [SEAL.] fifteenth year of the Sovereignty and Independence of the United States.

G⁰ WASHINGTON.

By the President:
  TH: JEFFERSON.

[From Miscellaneous Letters, Department of State, vol. 3.]

BY THE PRESIDENT OF THE UNITED STATES OF AMERICA.

A PROCLAMATION.

Whereas it hath at this time become peculiarly necessary to warn the citizens of the United States against a violation of the treaties made at Hopewell, on the Keowee, on the 28th day of November, 1785, and on the 3d and 10th days of January, 1786, between the United States and the Cherokee, Choctaw, and Chickasaw nations of Indians, and to enforce an act entitled "An act to regulate trade and intercourse with the Indian tribes," copies of which treaties and act are hereunto annexed, I have therefore thought fit to require, and I do by these presents require, all officers of the United States, as well civil as military, and all other citizens and inhabitants thereof, to govern themselves according to the treaties and act aforesaid, as they will answer the contrary at their peril.

Given under my hand and the seal of the United States, in the city of New York, the 26th day of August, A. D. 1790, and in the [SEAL.] fifteenth year of the Sovereignty and Independence of the United States.

GO WASHINGTON.

By the President:
TH: JEFFERSON.

SECOND ANNUAL ADDRESS.

UNITED STATES, *December 8, 1790.*

Fellow-Citizens of the Senate and House of Representatives:

In meeting you again I feel much satisfaction in being able to repeat my congratulations on the favorable prospects which continue to distinguish our public affairs. The abundant fruits of another year have blessed our country with plenty and with the means of a flourishing commerce. The progress of public credit is witnessed by a considerable rise of American stock abroad as well as at home, and the revenues allotted for this and other national purposes have been productive beyond the calculations by which they were regulated. This latter circumstance is the more pleasing, as it is not only a proof of the fertility of our resources, but as it assures us of a further increase of the national respectability and credit, and, let me add, as it bears an honorable testimony to the patriotism and integrity of the mercantile and marine part of our citizens. The punctuality of the former in discharging their engagements has been exemplary.

In conformity to the powers vested in me by acts of the last session, a loan of 3,000,000 florins, toward which some provisional measures had previously taken place, has been completed in Holland. As well the celerity with which it has been filled as the nature of the terms (considering the more than ordinary demand for borrowing created by the situation of Europe) give a reasonable hope that the further execution of those powers may proceed with advantage and success. The Secretary of the Treasury has my directions to communicate such further particulars as may be requisite for more precise information.

Since your last sessions I have received communications by which it appears that the district of Kentucky, at present a part of Virginia, has concurred in certain propositions contained in a law of that State, in consequence of which the district is to become a distinct member of the Union, in case the requisite sanction of Congress be added. For this sanction application is now made. I shall cause the papers on this very important transaction to be laid before you. The liberality and harmony with which it has been conducted will be found to do great honor to both the parties, and the sentiments of warm attachment to the Union and its present Government expressed by our fellow-citizens of Kentucky can not fail to add an affectionate concern for their particular welfare to the great national impressions under which you will decide on the case submitted to you.

It has been heretofore known to Congress that frequent incursions have been made on our frontier settlements by certain banditti of Indians from the northwest side of the Ohio. These, with some of the tribes dwelling on and near the Wabash, have of late been particularly active in their depredations, and being emboldened by the impunity of their crimes and aided by such parts of the neighboring tribes as could be seduced to join in their hostilities or afford them a retreat for their prisoners and plunder, they have, instead of listening to the humane invitations and overtures made on the part of the United States, renewed their violences with fresh alacrity and greater effect. The lives of a number of valuable citizens have thus been sacrificed, and some of them under circumstances peculiarly shocking, whilst others have been carried into a deplorable captivity.

These aggravated provocations rendered it essential to the safety of the Western settlements that the aggressors should be made sensible that the Government of the Union is not less capable of punishing their crimes than it is disposed to respect their rights and reward their attachments. As this object could not be effected by defensive measures, it became necessary to put in force the act which empowers the President to call out the militia for the protection of the frontiers, and I have accordingly authorized an expedition in which the regular troops in that quarter are combined with such drafts of militia as were deemed sufficient. The event of the measure is yet unknown to me. The Secretary of War is directed to lay before you a statement of the information on which it is founded, as well as an estimate of the expense with which it will be attended.

The disturbed situation of Europe, and particularly the critical posture of the great maritime powers, whilst it ought to make us the more thankful for the general peace and security enjoyed by the United States, reminds us at the same time of the circumspection with which it becomes us to preserve these blessings. It requires also that we should not overlook the tendency of a war, and even of preparations for a war, among the nations most concerned in active commerce with this country to abridge the means, and thereby at least enhance the price, of transporting its valuable productions to their proper markets. I recommend it to your serious reflections how far and in what mode it may be expedient to guard against embarrassments from these contingencies by such encouragements to our own navigation as will render our commerce and agriculture less dependent on foreign bottoms, which may fail us in the very moments most interesting to both of these great objects. Our fisheries and the transportation of our own produce offer us abundant means for guarding ourselves against this evil.

Your attention seems to be not less due to that particular branch of our trade which belongs to the Mediterranean. So many circumstances unite in rendering the present state of it distressful to us that you will not think any deliberations misemployed which may lead to its relief and protection.

The laws you have already passed for the establishment of a judiciary system have opened the doors of justice to all descriptions of persons. You will consider in your wisdom whether improvements in that system may yet be made, and particularly whether an uniform process of execution on sentences issuing from the Federal courts be not desirable through all the States.

The patronage of our commerce, of our merchants and seamen, has called for the appointment of consuls in foreign countries. It seems expedient to regulate by law the exercise of that jurisdiction and those functions which are permitted them, either by express convention or by a friendly indulgence, in the places of their residence. The consular convention, too, with His Most Christian Majesty has stipulated in certain cases the aid of the national authority to his consuls established here. Some legislative provision is requisite to carry these stipulations into full effect.

The establishment of the militia, of a mint, of standards of weights and measures, of the post-office and post-roads are subjects which I presume you will resume of course, and which are abundantly urged by their own importance.

Gentlemen of the House of Representatives:

The sufficiency of the revenues you have established for the objects to which they are appropriated leaves no doubt that the residuary provisions will be commensurate to the other objects for which the public faith stands now pledged. Allow me, moreover, to hope that it will be a favorite policy with you, not merely to secure a payment of the interest of the debt funded, but as far and as fast as the growing resources of the country will permit to exonerate it of the principal itself. The appropriation you have made of the Western land explains your dispositions on this subject, and I am persuaded that the sooner that valuable fund can be made to contribute, along with other means, to the actual reduction of the public debt the more salutary will the measure be to every public interest, as well as the more satisfactory to our constituents.

Gentlemen of the Senate and House of Representatives:

In pursuing the various and weighty business of the present session I indulge the fullest persuasion that your consultations will be equally marked with wisdom and animated by the love of your country. In whatever belongs to my duty you shall have all the cooperation which an undiminished zeal for its welfare can inspire. It will be happy for us both, and our best reward, if, by a successful administration of our respective trusts, we can make the established Government more and more instrumental in promoting the good of our fellow-citizens, and more and more the object of their attachment and confidence.

G⁰ WASHINGTON.

ADDRESS OF THE SENATE TO GEORGE WASHINGTON, PRESIDENT OF THE UNITED STATES.

The PRESIDENT OF THE UNITED STATES OF AMERICA:

We receive, sir, with particular satisfaction the communications contained in your speech, which confirm to us the progressive state of the public credit and afford at the same time a new proof of the solidity of the foundation on which it rests; and we cheerfully join in the acknowledgment which is due to the probity and patriotism of the mercantile and marine part of our fellow-citizens, whose enlightened attachment to the principles of good government is not less conspicuous in this than it has been in other important respects.

In confidence that every constitutional preliminary has been observed, we assure you of our disposition to concur in giving the requisite sanction to the admission of Kentucky as a distinct member of the Union; in doing which we shall anticipate the happy effects to be expected from the sentiments of attachment toward the Union and its present Government which have been expressed by the patriotic inhabitants of that district.

While we regret that the continuance and increase of the hostilities and depredations which have distressed our Northwestern frontiers should have rendered offensive measures necessary, we feel an entire confidence in the sufficiency of the motives which have produced them and in the wisdom of the dispositions which have been concerted in pursuance of the powers vested in you, and whatever may have been the event, we shall cheerfully concur in the provisions which the expedition that has been undertaken may require on the part of the Legislature, and in any other which the future peace and safety of our frontier settlements may call for.

The critical posture of the European powers will engage a due portion of our attention, and we shall be ready to adopt any measures which a prudent circumspection may suggest for the preservation of the blessings of peace. The navigation and the fisheries of the United States are objects too interesting not to inspire a disposition to promote them by all the means which shall appear to us consistent with their natural progress and permanent prosperity.

Impressed with the importance of a free intercourse with the Mediterranean, we shall not think any deliberations misemployed which may conduce to the adoption of proper measures for removing the impediments that obstruct it.

The improvement of the judiciary system and the other important objects to which you have pointed our attention will not fail to engage the consideration they respectively merit.

In the course of our deliberations upon every subject we shall rely upon that cooperation which an undiminished zeal and incessant anxiety for the public welfare on your part so thoroughly insure; and as it is our anxious desire so it shall be our constant endeavor to render the established Government more and more instrumental in promoting the good of our fellow-citizens, and more and more the object of their attachment and confidence.

DECEMBER 10, 1790.

REPLY OF THE PRESIDENT.

GENTLEMEN: These assurances of favorable attention to the subjects I have recommended and of entire confidence in my views make the impression on me which I ought to feel. I thank you for them both, and shall continue to rely much for the success of all our measures for the public good on the aid they will receive from the wisdom and integrity of your councils.

G⁰ WASHINGTON.

DECEMBER 13, 1790.

ADDRESS OF THE HOUSE OF REPRESENTATIVES TO GEORGE WASHINGTON, PRESIDENT OF THE UNITED STATES.

SIR: The Representatives of the people of the United States have taken into consideration your address to the two Houses at the opening of the present session of Congress.

We share in the satisfaction inspired by the prospects which continue to be so auspicious to our public affairs. The blessings resulting from the smiles of Heaven on our agriculture, the rise of public credit, with the further advantages promised by it, and the fertility of resources which are found so little burdensome to the community, fully authorize our mutual congratulations on the present occasion. Nor can we learn without an additional gratification that the energy of the laws for providing adequate revenues have been so honorably seconded by those classes of citizens whose patriotism and probity were more immediately concerned.

The success of the loan opened in Holland, under the disadvantages of the present moment, is the more important, as it not only denotes the confidence already placed in the United States, but as the effect of a judicious application of that aid will still further illustrate the solidity of the foundation on which the public credit rests.

The preparatory steps taken by the State of Virginia, in concert with the district of Kentucky, toward the erection of the latter into a distinct member of the Union exhibit a liberality mutually honorable to the parties.   We shall bestow on this important subject the favorable consideration which it merits, and, with the national policy which ought to govern our decision, shall not fail to mingle the affectionate sentiments which are awakened by those expressed on behalf of our fellow-citizens of Kentucky.

Whilst we regret the necessity which has produced offensive hostilities against some of the Indian tribes northwest of the Ohio, we sympathize too much with our Western brethren not to behold with approbation the watchfulness and vigor which have been exerted by the executive authority for their protection, and which we trust will make the aggressors sensible that it is their interest to merit by a peaceable behavior the friendship and humanity which the United States are always ready to extend to them.

The encouragement of our own navigation has at all times appeared to us highly important.   The point of view under which you have recommended it to us is strongly enforced by the actual state of things in Europe.   It will be incumbent on us to consider in what mode our commerce and agriculture can be best relieved from an injurious dependence on the navigation of other nations, which the frequency of their wars renders a too precarious resource for conveying the productions of our country to market.

The present state of our trade to the Mediterranean seems not less to demand, and will accordingly receive, the attention which you have recommended.

Having already concurred in establishing a judiciary system which opens the doors of justice to all, without distinction of persons, it will be our disposition to incorporate every improvement which experience may suggest.   And we shall consider in particular how far the uniformity which in other cases is found convenient in the administration of the General Government through all the States may be introduced into the forms and rules of executing sentences issuing from the Federal courts.

The proper regulation of the jurisdiction and functions which may be exercised by consuls of the United States in foreign countries, with the provisions stipulated to those of His Most Christian Majesty established here, are subjects of too much consequence to the public interest and honor not to partake of our deliberations.

We shall renew our attention to the establishment of the militia and the other subjects unfinished at the last session, and shall proceed in them with all the dispatch which the magnitude of all and the difficulty of some of them will allow.

Nothing has given us more satisfaction than to find that the revenues heretofore established have proved adequate to the purposes to which they were allotted. In extending the provision to the residuary objects it will be equally our care to secure sufficiency and punctuality in the payments due from the Treasury of the United States. We shall also never lose sight of the policy of diminishing the public debt as fast as the increase of the public resources will permit, and are particularly sensible of the many considerations which press a resort to the auxiliary resource furnished by the public lands.

In pursuing every branch of the weighty business of the present session it will be our constant study to direct our deliberations to the public welfare. Whatever our success may be, we can at least answer for the fervent love of our country, which ought to animate our endeavors. In your cooperation we are sure of a resource which fortifies our hopes that the fruits of the established Government will justify the confidence which has been placed in it, and recommend it more and more to the affection and attachment of our fellow-citizens.

DECEMBER 11, 1790.

REPLY OF THE PRESIDENT.

GENTLEMEN: The sentiments expressed in your address are entitled to my particular acknowledgment.

Having no object but the good of our country, this testimony of approbation and confidence from its immediate Representatives must be among my best rewards, as the support of your enlightened patriotism has been among my greatest encouragements. Being persuaded that you will continue to be actuated by the same auspicious principle, I look forward to the happiest consequences from your deliberations during the present session.

G⁰ WASHINGTON.

DECEMBER 13, 1790.

SPECIAL MESSAGES.

UNITED STATES, *December 23, 1790.*

Gentlemen of the Senate and House of Representatives:

It appearing by the report of the secretary of the government northwest of the Ohio that there are certain cases respecting grants of land within that territory which require the interference of the Legislature of the United States, I have directed a copy of said report and the papers therein referred to to be laid before you, together with a copy of the report of the Secretary of State upon the same subject.

G⁰ WASHINGTON.

UNITED STATES, *December 30, 1790.*

Gentlemen of the Senate and House of Representatives:

I lay before you a report of the Secretary of State on the subject of the citizens of the United States in captivity at Algiers, that you may provide on their behalf what to you shall seem most expedient.

G⁰ WASHINGTON.

UNITED STATES, *January 3, 1791.*

Gentlemen of the Senate and House of Representatives:

I lay before you a copy of an exemplified copy of an act passed by the legislature of the State of New Jersey for vesting in the United States of America the jurisdiction of a lot of land at Sandy Hook, in the county of Monmouth, and a copy of a letter which accompanied said act, from the governor of the State of New Jersey to the President of the United States.

G⁰ WASHINGTON.

UNITED STATES, *January 17, 1791.*

Gentlemen of the Senate and House of Representatives:

I lay before you an official statement of the appropriation of $10,000, granted to defray the contingent expenses of Government by an act of the 26th March, 1790.

A copy of two resolutions of the legislature of Virginia, and a petition of sundry officers and assignees of officers and soldiers of the Virginia line on continental establishment, on the subject of bounty lands allotted to them on the northwest side of the Ohio; and

A copy of an act of the legislature of Maryland to empower the wardens of the port of Baltimore to levy and collect the duty therein mentioned.

G⁰ WASHINGTON.

UNITED STATES, *January 17, 1791.*

Gentlemen of the Senate:

I lay before you a letter from His Most Christian Majesty, addressed to the President and Members of Congress of the United States of America.

G⁰ WASHINGTON.

To our very dear friends and allies, the President and Members of the General Congress of the United States of North America.

VERY DEAR GREAT FRIENDS AND ALLIES: We have received the letter by which you inform us of the new mark of confidence that you have shown to Mr. Jefferson, and which puts a period to his appointment of minister plenipotentiary at our Court.

The manner in which he conducted during his residence with us has merited our esteem and entire approbation, and it is with pleasure that we now give him this testimony of it.

It is with the most sincere pleasure that we embrace this opportunity of renewing these assurances of regard and friendship which we feel for the United States in general and for each of them in particular. Under their influence we pray God that He will keep you, very dear friends and allies, under His holy and beneficent protection.

Done at Paris this 11th September, 1790.

Your good friend and ally,

LOUIS.

MONTMORIN. [SEAL.]

The UNITED STATES OF NORTH AMERICA.

UNITED STATES, *January 19, 1791.*

Gentlemen of the Senate:

I lay before you a representation of the chargé d'affaires of France, made by order of his Court, on the acts of Congress of the 20th of July, 1789 and 1790, imposing an extra tonnage on foreign vessels, not excepting those of that country, together with the report of the Secretary of State thereon, and I recommend the same to your consideration, that I may be enabled to give to it such answer as may best comport with the justice and the interests of the United States.

GO WASHINGTON.

DOCUMENTS.

JANUARY 18, 1791.

The Secretary of State having received from the chargé d'affaires of France a note on the tonnage payable by French vessels in the ports of the United States, has had the same under his consideration, and thereupon makes the following report to the President of the United States:

The chargé d'affaires of France, by a note of the 13th of December, represents, by order of his Court, that they consider so much of the acts of Congress of July 20, 1789 and 1790, as imposes an extraordinary tonnage on foreign vessels without excepting those of France, to be in contravention of the fifth article of the treaty of amity and commerce between the two nations; that this would have authorized on their part a proportional modification in the favors granted to the American navigation, but that his Sovereign had thought it more conformable to his principles of friendship and attachment to the United States to order him to make representations thereon, and to ask in favor of French vessels a modification of the acts which impose an extraordinary tonnage on foreign vessels.

The Secretary of State, in giving in this paper to the President of the United States, thinks it his duty to accompany it with the following observations:

The third and fourth articles of the treaty of amity and commerce between France and the United States subject the vessels of each nation to pay in the ports of the other only such duties as are paid by the most favored nation, and give them reciprocally all the privileges and exemptions in navigation and commerce which are given by either to the most favored nations. Had the contracting parties stopped here, they would have been free to raise or lower their tonnage as they should find it expedient, only taking care to keep the other on the footing of the most favored nation. The question, then, is whether the fifth article cited in the note is anything more than an application of the principle comprised in the third and fourth to a particular object, or whether it is an additional stipulation of something not so comprised.

I. That it is merely an application of a principle comprised in the preceding articles is declared by the express words of the article, to wit: "*Dans l'exemption ci-dessus est nommément compris,*" etc., "*in the above exemption is particularly comprised,* the imposition of 100 sols per ton established in France on foreign vessels." Here, then, is at once an express declaration that the exemption from the duty of 100 sols is *comprised* in the third and fourth articles; that is to say, it was one of the exemptions enjoyed by the most favored nations, and as such extended to us by those articles. If the exemption spoken of in this first member of the fifth article was *comprised* in the third and fourth articles, as is expressly declared, then the reservation by France out of that exemption (which makes the second member of the same article) *was also comprised;* that is to say, if *the whole* was comprised, *the part* was comprised. And if this reservation of France in the second member was comprised in the third and fourth articles, then the counter reservation by the United States (which constitutes the third and last member of the same article) was also comprised, because it is but a corresponding portion of a similar whole on our part, which had been comprised by the same terms with theirs.

In short, the whole article relates to a particular duty of 100 sols, laid by some antecedent law of France on the vessels of foreign nations, relinquished as to the most favored, and consequently to us. It is not a new and additional stipulation, then, but a declared application of the stipulations comprised in the preceding articles to a particular case by way of greater caution.

The doctrine laid down generally in the third and fourth articles, and exemplified specially in the fifth, amounts to this: "The vessels of the most favored nations coming from foreign ports are exempted from the duty of 100 sols; therefore you are exempted from it by the third and fourth articles. The vessels of the most favored nations coming coastwise pay that duty; therefore you are to pay it by the third and fourth articles. We shall not think it unfriendly in you to lay a like duty on coasters, because it will be no more than we have done ourselves. You are free also to lay that or any other duty on vessels coming from foreign ports, provided they apply to all other nations, even the most favored. We are free to do the same under the same restriction. Our exempting you from a duty which the most favored nations do not pay does not exempt you from one which they do pay."

In this view, it is evident that the fifth article neither enlarges nor abridges the stipulations of the third and fourth. The effect of the treaty would have been precisely the same had it been omitted altogether; consequently it may be truly said that the reservation by the United States in this article is completely useless. And it may be added with equal truth that the equivalent reservation by France is completely useless, as well as her previous abandonment of the same duty, and, in short, the whole article. Each party, then, remains free to raise or lower its tonnage, provided the change operates on all nations, even the most favored.

Without undertaking to affirm, we may obviously conjecture that this article has been inserted on the part of the United States from an overcaution to guard, *nommément, by name,* against a particular aggrievance, which they thought they could never be too well secured against; and that has happened which generally happens—doubts have been produced by the too great number of words used to prevent doubt.

II. The Court of France, however, understands this article as intended to introduce something to which the preceding articles had not reached, and not merely as an application of them to a particular case. Their opinion seems to be founded on the general rule in the construction of instruments, to leave no words merely useless for which any rational meaning can be found. They say that the reservation by the United States of a right to lay a duty equivalent to that of the 100 sols, reserved by France, would have been completely useless if they were left free by the preceding articles to lay a tonnage to any extent whatever; consequently, that the reservation of a part proves a relinquishment of the residue.

If some meaning, and such a one, is to be given to the last member of the article, some meaning, and a similar one, must be given to the corresponding member. If the reservation by the United States of a right to lay an equivalent duty implies a relinquishment of their right to lay any other, the reservation by France of a right to continue the specified duty to which it is an equivalent must imply a relinquishment of the right on her part to lay or continue any other. Equivalent reservations by both must imply equivalent restrictions on both. The exact reciprocity stipulated in the preceding articles, and which pervades every part of the treaty, insures a counter right to each party for every right ceded to the other.

Let it be further considered that the duty called *tonnage* in the United States is in lieu of the duties for anchorage, for the support of buoys, beacons, and light-houses, to guide the mariner into harbor and along the coast, which are provided and supported at the expense of the United States, and for fees to measurers, weighers, gaugers, etc., who are paid by the United States, for which articles, among many others (light-house money excepted), duties are paid by us in the ports of France under their specific names. That Government has hitherto thought these duties consistent with the treaty, and consequently the same duties under a general instead of specific names, with us, must be equally consistent with it. It is not the name, but the thing, which is essential. If we have renounced the right to lay any port duties, they must be understood to have equally renounced that of either laying new or continuing the old. If we ought to refund the port duties received from their vessels since the date of the act of Congress, they should refund the port duties they have received from our vessels since the date of the treaty, for nothing short of this is the reciprocity of the treaty.

If this construction be adopted, then each party has forever renounced the right of laying any duties on the vessels of the other coming from any foreign port, or more than 100 sols on those coming coastwise. Could this relinquishment be confined to the two contracting parties alone, the United States would be the gainers, for it is well known that a much greater number of American than of French vessels are employed in the commerce between the two countries; but the exemption once conceded by the one nation to the other becomes immediately the property of all others who are on the footing of the most favored nations. It is true that those others would be obliged to yield the same compensation, that is to say, to receive our vessels duty free. Whether we should gain or lose in the exchange of the measure with them is not easy to say.

Another consequence of this construction will be that the vessels of the most favored nations paying no duties will be on a better footing than those of natives which pay a moderate duty; consequently either the duty on these also must be given up or they will be supplanted by foreign vessels in our own ports.

The resource, then, of duty on vessels for the purposes either of revenue or regulation will be forever lost to both. It is hardly conceivable that either party looking forward to all these consequences would see their interest in them.

III. But if France persists in claiming this exemption, what is to be done? The claim, indeed, is couched in mild and friendly terms; but the idea leaks out that a refusal would authorize them to modify proportionally the favors granted by the same article to our navigation. Perhaps they may do what we should feel much more severely, they may turn their eyes to the favors granted us by their arrets of December 29, 1787, and December 7, 1788, which hang on their will alone, unconnected with the treaty. Those arrets, among other advantages, admit our whale oils to the exclusion of that of all other foreigners. And this monopoly procures a vent for seven-twelfths of the produce of that fishery, which experience has taught us could find no other market. Near two-thirds of the produce of our cod fisheries, too, have lately found a free vent in the colonies of France. This, indeed, has been an irregularity growing out of the anarchy reigning in those colonies. Yet the demands of the colonists, even of the Government party among them (if an auxiliary disposition can be excited by some marks of friendship and distinction on our part), may perhaps produce a constitutional concession to them to procure their provisions at the cheapest market; that is to say, at ours.

Considering the value of the interests we have at stake and considering the smallness of difference between foreign and native tonnage on French vessels alone, it might perhaps be thought advisable to make the sacrifice asked, and especially if it can be so done as to give no title to other the most favored nations to claim it. If the act should put French vessels on the footing of those of natives, and declare it to be in consideration of the favors granted us by the arrets of December 29, 1787, and December 7, 1788 (and perhaps this would satisfy them), no nation could then demand the same favor without offering an equivalent compensation. It might strengthen, too, the tenure by which those arrets are held, which must be precarious so long as they are gratuitous.

It is desirable in many instances to exchange mutual advantages by legislative acts rather than by treaty, because the former, though understood to be in consideration of each other, and therefore greatly respected, yet when they become too inconvenient can be dropped at the will of either party; whereas stipulations by treaty are forever irrevocable but by joint consent, let a change of circumstances render them ever so burdensome.

On the whole, if it be the opinion that the first construction is to be insisted on as ours, in opposition to the second urged by the Court of France, and that no relaxation is to be admitted, an answer shall be given to that Court defending that construction, and explaining in as friendly terms as possible the difficulties opposed to the exemption they claim.

2. If it be the opinion that it is advantageous for us to close with France in her interpretation of a reciprocal and perpetual exemption from tonnage, a repeal of so much of the tonnage law will be the answer.

3. If it be thought better to waive rigorous and nice discussions of right and to make the modification an act of friendship and of compensation for favors received, the passage of such a bill will then be the answer.

TH: JEFFERSON.

[Translation.]

L. G. Otto to the Secretary of State.

PHILADELPHIA, *December 13, 1790.*

SIR: During the long stay you made in France you had opportunities of being satisfied of the favorable dispositions of His Majesty to render permanent the ties that united the two nations and to give stability to the treaties of alliance and of commerce which form the basis of this union. These treaties were so well maintained by the Congress formed under the ancient Confederation that they thought it their duty to interpose their authority whenever any laws made by individual States appeared to infringe their stipulations, and particularly in 1785, when the States of New Hampshire and of Massachusetts had imposed an extraordinary tonnage on foreign vessels without exempting those of the French nation. The reflections that I have the honor to address to you in the subjoined note being founded on the same principles, I flatter myself that they will merit on the part of the Government of the United States the most serious attention.

I am, with respect, etc.,

L. G. OTTO.

L. G. Otto to the Secretary of State.

PHILADELPHIA, *December 13, 1790.*

NOTE.—The underwritten, chargé d'affaires of France, has received the express order of his Court to represent to the United States that the act passed by Congress the 20th July, 1789, and renewed the 20th July of the present year, which imposes an extraordinary tonnage on foreign vessels without excepting French vessels, is directly contrary to the spirit and to the object of the treaty of commerce which unites the two nations, and of which His Majesty has not only scrupulously observed the tenor, but of which he has extended the advantages by many regulations very favorable to the commerce and navigation of the United States.

By the fifth article of this treaty the citizens of these States are declared exempt from the tonnage duty imposed in France on foreign vessels, and they are not subject to that duty but in the coasting business. Congress has reserved the privilege of establishing *a duty equivalent to this last,* a stipulation founded on the state in which matters were in America at the time of the signature of the treaty. There did not exist at that epoch any duty on tonnage in the United States.

It is evident that it was the nonexistence of this duty and the motive of a perfect reciprocity stipulated in the preamble of the treaty that had determined the King to grant the exemption contained in the article fifth; and a proof that Congress had no intention to contravene this reciprocity is that *it only reserves a privilege of establishing on the coasting business a duty equivalent to that which is levied in France.* This reservation would have been completely useless if by the words of the treaty Congress thought themselves at liberty to lay *any* tonnage they should think proper on French vessels.

The undersigned has the honor to observe that this contravention of the fifth article of the treaty of commerce might have authorized His Majesty to modify proportionately the favors granted by the same article to the American navigation; but the King, always faithful to the principles of friendship and attachment to the United States, and desirous of strengthening more and more the ties which subsist so happily between the French nation and these States, thinks it more conformable to these views to order the undersigned to make representations on this subject, and to ask in favor of French vessels a modification of the act which imposes an extraordinary tonnage on foreign vessels. His Majesty does not doubt but that the United States will acknowledge the justice of this claim, and will be disposed to restore things to the footing on which they were at the signature of the treaty of the 6th February, 1778.

L. G. OTTO.

L. G. Otto to the Secretary of State.

NEW YORK, *January 8, 1791.*

His Excellency M. JEFFERSON,
    Secretary of State.

SIR: I have the honor herewith to send you a letter from the King to Congress, and one which M. de Montmorin has written to yourself. You will find therein the sincere sentiments with which you have inspired our Government, and the regret of the minister in not having a more near relation of correspondence with you. In these every person who has had the advantage of knowing you in France participates.

At the same time, it gives me pain, sir, to be obliged to announce to you that the complaints of our merchants on the subject of the tonnage duty increase, and that they have excited not only the attention of the King but that of several departments of the Kingdom. I have received new orders to request of the United States a decision on this matter and to solicit in favor of the aggrieved merchants the restitution of the duties which have already been paid. I earnestly beg of you, sir, not to lose sight of an object which, as I have already had the honor to tell you verbally, is of the greatest importance for cementing the future commercial connections between the two nations.

In more particularly examining this question you will perhaps find that motives of convenience are as powerful as those of justice to engage the United States to give to His Majesty the satisfaction which he requires. At least twice as many American vessels enter the ports of France as do those of France the ports of America. The exemption of the tonnage of duty, then, is evidently less advantageous for the French than for the navigators of the United States. Be this as it may, I can assure you, sir, that the delay of a decision in this respect by augmenting the just complaints of the French merchants will only augment the difficulties.

I therefore beg of you to enable me before the sailing of the packet, which will take place toward the last of this month, to give to my Court a satisfactory answer.

I have the honor to be, etc.,

L. G. OTTO.

UNITED STATES, *January 24, 1791.*

Gentlemen of the Senate and House of Representatives:

I lay before you a statement relative to the frontiers of the United States, which has been submitted to me by the Secretary for the Department of War.

I rely upon your wisdom to make such arrangements as may be essential for the preservation of good order and the effectual protection of the frontiers.

G⁰ WASHINGTON.

UNITED STATES, *January 24, 1791.*

Gentlemen of the Senate and House of Representatives:

In execution of the powers with which Congress were pleased to invest me by their act entitled "An act for establishing the temporary and permanent seat of Government of the United States," and on mature consideration of the advantages and disadvantages of the several positions within the limits prescribed by the said act, I have by a proclamation bearing date this day (a copy of which is herewith transmitted) directed commissioners, appointed in pursuance of the act, to survey and limit a part of the territory of 10 miles square on both sides of the river Potomac, so as to comprehend Georgetown, in Maryland, and extend to the Eastern Branch.

I have not by this first act given to the said territory the whole extent of which it is susceptible in the direction of the river, because I thought it important that Congress should have an opportunity of considering whether by an amendatory law they would authorize the location of the residue at the lower end of the present, so as to comprehend the Eastern Branch itself and some of the country on its lower side, in the State of Maryland, and the town of Alexandria, in Virginia. If, however, they are of opinion that the Federal territory should be bounded by the water edge of the Eastern Branch, the location of the residue will be to be made at the upper end of what is now directed.

I have thought best to await a survey of the territory before it is decided on what particular spot on the northeastern side of the river the public buildings shall be erected.

GQ WASHINGTON.

UNITED STATES, *January 26, 1791.*

Gentlemen of the Senate and House of Representatives:

I lay before you the copy of a letter from the President of the National Assembly of France to the President of the United States, and of a decree of that Assembly, which was transmitted with the above-mentioned letter.

GQ WASHINGTON.

UNITED STATES, *January 27, 1791.*

Gentlemen of the Senate and House of Representatives:

In order that you may be fully informed of the situation of the frontiers and the prospect of hostility in that quarter, I lay before you the intelligence of some recent depredations, received since my message to you upon this subject of the 24th instant.

GQ WASHINGTON.

UNITED STATES, *February 9, 1791.*

Gentlemen of the Senate and House of Representatives:

I have received from the governor of Vermont authentic documents, expressing the consent of the legislatures of New York and of the Territory of Vermont that the said Territory shall be admitted to be a distinct member of our Union; and a memorial of Nathaniel Chipman and Lewis R. Morris, commissioners from the said Territory, praying the consent of Congress to that admission, by the name and style of the State of Vermont, copies of which I now lay before Congress, with whom the Constitution has vested the object of these proceedings.

GQ WASHINGTON.

UNITED STATES, *February 14, 1791.*

Gentlemen of the Senate and House of Representatives:

Soon after I was called to the administration of the Government I found it important to come to an understanding with the Court of London on several points interesting to the United States, and particularly to know whether they were disposed to enter into arrangements by mutual consent which might fix the commerce between the two nations on principles of reciprocal advantage. For this purpose I authorized informal conferences with their ministers, and from these I do not infer any disposition on their part to enter into any arrangements merely commercial. I have thought it proper to give you this information, as it might at some time have influence on matters under your consideration.

G⁰ WASHINGTON.

UNITED STATES, *February 14, 1791.*

Gentlemen of the Senate:

Conceiving that in the possible event of a refusal of justice on the part of Great Britain we should stand less committed should it be made to a private rather than to a public person, I employed Mr. Gouverneur Morris, who was on the spot, and without giving him any definite character, to enter informally into the conferences before mentioned. For your more particular information I lay before you the instructions I gave him and those parts of his communications wherein the British ministers appear either in conversation or by letter. These are two letters from the Duke of Leeds to Mr. Morris, and three letters of Mr. Morris giving an account of two conferences with the Duke of Leeds and one with him and Mr. Pitt. The sum of these is that they declare without scruple they do not mean to fulfill what remains of the treaty of peace to be fulfilled on their part (by which we are to understand the delivery of the posts and payment for property carried off) till performance on our part, and compensation where the delay has rendered the performance now impracticable; that on the subject of a treaty of commerce they avoided direct answers, so as to satisfy Mr. Morris they did not mean to enter into one unless it could be extended to a treaty of alliance offensive and defensive, or unless in the event of a rupture with Spain.

As to the sending a minister here, they made excuses at the first conference, seemed disposed to it in the second, and in the last express an intention of so doing.

Their views being thus sufficiently ascertained, I have directed Mr. Morris to discontinue his communications with them.

G⁰ WASHINGTON.

UNITED STATES, *February 18, 1791.*

Gentlemen of the Senate:

The aspect of affairs in Europe during the last summer, and especially between Spain and England, gave reason to expect a favorable occasion for pressing to accommodation the unsettled matters between them and us. Mr. Carmichael, our chargé d'affaires at Madrid, having been long absent from his country, great changes having taken place in our circumstances and sentiments during that interval, it was thought expedient to send some person, in a private character, fully acquainted with the present state of things here, to be the bearer of written and confidential instructions to him, and at the same time to possess him in full and frequent conversations of all those details of facts and topics of argument which could not be conveyed in writing, but which would be necessary to enable him to meet the reasonings of that Court with advantage. Colonel David Humphreys was therefore sent for these purposes.

An additional motive for this confidential mission arose in the same quarter. The Court of Lisbon had on several occasions made the most amicable advances for cultivating friendship and intercourse with the United States. The exchange of a diplomatic character had been informally, but repeatedly, suggested on their part. It was our interest to meet this nation in its friendly dispositions and to concur in the exchange proposed. But my wish was at the same time that the character to be exchanged should be of the lowest and most economical grade. To this it was known that certain rules of long standing at that Court would produce obstacles. Colonel Humphreys was charged with dispatches to the prime minister of Portugal and with instructions to endeavor to arrange this to our views. It happened, however, that previous to his arrival at Lisbon the Queen had appointed a minister *resident* to the United States. This embarrassment seems to have rendered the difficulty completely insurmountable. The minister of that Court in his conferences with Colonel Humphreys, professing every wish to accommodate, yet expresses his regrets that circumstances do not permit them to concur in the grade of chargé d'affaires, a grade of little privilege or respectability by the rules of their Court and held in so low estimation with them that no proper character would accept it to go abroad. In a letter to the Secretary of State he expresses the same sentiments, and announces the appointment on their part of a minister *resident* to the United States, and the pleasure with which the Queen will receive one from us at her Court. A copy of his letter, and also of Colonel Humphreys's giving the details of this transaction, will be delivered to you.

On consideration of all circumstances I have determined to accede to the desire of the Court of Lisbon in the article of grade. I am aware that the consequences will not end here, and that this is not the only instance in which a like change may be pressed. But should it be necessary to yield elsewhere also, I shall think it a less evil than to disgust a government so friendly and so interesting to us as that of Portugal.

I do not mean that the change of grade shall render the mission more expensive.

I have therefore nominated David Humphreys minister resident from the United States to Her Most Faithful Majesty the Queen of Portugal.

G⁰ WASHINGTON.

UNITED STATES, *February 22, 1791.*
Gentlemen of the Senate:

I will proceed to take measures for the ransom of our citizens in captivity at Algiers, in conformity with your resolution of advice of the 1st instant, so soon as the moneys necessary shall be appropriated by the Legislature and shall be in readiness.

The recognition of our treaty with the new Emperor of Morocco requires also previous appropriation and provision. The importance of this last to the liberty and property of our citizens induces me to urge it on your earliest attention.

G⁰ WASHINGTON.

UNITED STATES, *February 23, 1791.*
Gentlemen of the Senate:

Information having been received from Thomas Auldjo, who was appointed vice-consul of the United States at Cowes, in Great Britain, that his commission has not been recognized by that Government because it is a port at which no foreign consul has yet been received, and that it has been intimated to him that his appointment to the port of Poole and parts nearer to that than to the residence of any other consul of the United States would be recognized and his residence at Cowes not noticed, I have therefore thought it expedient to nominate Thomas Auldjo to be vice-consul for the United States at the port of Poole, in Great Britain, and such parts within the allegiance of His Britannic Majesty as shall be nearer thereto than to the residence of any other consul or vice-consul of the United States within the same allegiance.

I also nominate James Yard, of Pennsylvania, to be consul for the United States in the island of Santa Cruz and such other parts within the allegiance of His Danish Majesty as shall be nearer thereto than to the residence of any other consul or vice-consul of the United States within the same allegiance.

G⁰ WASHINGTON.

UNITED STATES, *March 4, 1791.*
Gentlemen of the Senate:

The act for the admission of the State of Vermont into this Union having fixed on this as the day of its admission, it was thought that this would also be the first day on which any officer of the Union might legally perform any act of authority relating to that State. I therefore required your attendance to receive nominations of the several officers necessary to put the Federal Government into motion in that State.*

For this purpose I nominate Nathaniel Chipman to be judge of the district of Vermont; Stephen Jacobs to be attorney for the United States in the district of Vermont; Lewis R. Morris to be marshal of the district of Vermont, and Stephen Keyes to be collector of the port of Allburgh, in the State of Vermont.

G<u>o</u> WASHINGTON

UNITED STATES, *March 4, 1791.*

Gentlemen of the Senate:

Pursuant to the powers vested in me by the act entitled "An act repealing after the last day of June next the duties heretofore laid upon distilled spirits imported from abroad and laying others in their stead, and also upon spirits distilled within the United States, and for appropriating the same," I have thought fit to divide the United States into the following districts, namely:

The district of New Hampshire, to consist of the State of New Hampshire; the district of Massachusetts, to consist of the State of Massachusetts; the district of Rhode Island and Providence Plantations, to consist of the State of Rhode Island and Providence Plantations; the district of Connecticut, to consist of the State of Connecticut; the district of Vermont, to consist of the State of Vermont; the district of New York, to consist of the State of New York; the district of New Jersey, to consist of the State of New Jersey; the district of Pennsylvania, to consist of the State of Pennsylvania; the district of Delaware, to consist of the State of Delaware; the district of Maryland, to consist of the State of Maryland; the district of Virginia, to consist of the State of Virginia; the district of North Carolina, to consist of the State of North Carolina; the district of South Carolina, to consist of the State of South Carolina; and the district of Georgia, to consist of the State of Georgia.

And I hereby nominate as supervisors of the said districts, respectively, the following persons, viz:

For the district of New Hampshire, Joshua Wentworth; for the district of Massachusetts, Nathaniel Gorham; for the district of Rhode Island and Providence Plantations, John S. Dexter; for the district of Connecticut, John Chester; for the district of Vermont, Noah Smith; for the district of New York, William S. Smith; for the district of New Jersey, Aaron Dunham; for the district of Pennsylvania, George Clymer; for the district of Delaware, Henry Latimer; for the district of Maryland, George Gale; for the district of Virginia, Edward Carrington; for the district of North Carolina, William Polk; for the district of South Carolina, Daniel Stevens; for the district of Georgia, John Mathews.

G<u>o</u> WASHINGTON.

*For proclamation convening Senate in extraordinary session see p. 571

PROCLAMATIONS.

[From a broadside in the archives of the Department of State.]

By the President of the United States of America.

A PROCLAMATION.

Whereas the general assembly of the State of Maryland, by an act passed on the 23d day of December, A. D. 1788, intituled "An act to cede to Congress a district of 10 miles square in this State for the seat of the Government of the United States," did enact that the Representatives of the said State in the House of Representatives of the Congress of the United States, appointed to assemble at New York on the first Wednesday of March then next ensuing, should be, and they were thereby, authorized and required on the behalf of the said State to cede to the Congress of the United States any district in the said State not exceeding 10 miles square which the Congress might fix upon and accept for the seat of Government of the United States;

And the general assembly of the Commonwealth of Virginia, by an act passed on the 3d day of December, 1789, and intituled "An act for the cession of 10 miles square, or any lesser quantity, of territory within this State to the United States in Congress assembled, for the permanent seat of the General Government," did enact that a tract of country not exceeding 10 miles square, or any lesser quantity, to be located within the limits of the said State, and in any part thereof, as Congress might by law direct, should be, and the same was thereby, forever ceded and relinquished to the Congress and Government of the United States, in full and absolute right and exclusive jurisdiction, as well of soil as of persons residing or to reside thereon, pursuant to the tenor and effect of the eighth section of the first article of the Constitution of Government of the United States;

And the Congress of the United States, by their act passed the 16th day of July, 1790, and intituled "An act for establishing the temporary and permanent seat of the Government of the United States," authorized the President of the United States to appoint three commissioners to survey under his direction and by proper metes and bounds to limit a district of territory, not exceeding 10 miles square, on the river Potomac, at some place between the mouths of the Eastern Branch and Connogocheque, which district, so to be located and limited, was accepted by the said act of Congress as the district for the permanent seat of the Government of the United States:

Now, therefore, in pursuance of the powers to me confided, and after duly examining and weighing the advantages and disadvantages of the several situations within the limits aforesaid, I do hereby declare and make known that the location of one part of the said district of 10 miles square shall be found by running four lines of experiment in the following manner, that is to say: Running from the court-house of Alexandria, in Virginia, due southwest half a mile, and thence a due southeast course till it shall strike Hunting Creek, to fix the beginning of the said four lines of experiment.

Then beginning the first of the said four lines of experiment at the point on Hunting Creek where the said southeast course shall have struck the same, and running the said first line due northwest 10 miles; thence the second line into Maryland due northeast 10 miles; thence the third line due southeast 10 miles, and thence the fourth line due southwest 10 miles to the beginning on Hunting Creek.

And the said four lines of experiment being so run, I do hereby declare and make known that all that part within the said four lines of experiment which shall be within the State of Maryland and above the Eastern Branch, and all that part within the same four lines of experiment which shall be within the Commonwealth of Virginia and above a line to be run from the point of land forming the upper cape of the mouth of the Eastern Branch due southwest, and no more, is now fixed upon and directed to be surveyed, defined, limited, and located for a part of the said district accepted by the said act of Congress for the permanent seat of the Government of the United States (hereby expressly reserving the direction of the survey and location of the remaining part of the said district to be made hereafter contiguous to such part or parts of the present location as is or shall be agreeable to law).

And I do accordingly direct the said commissioners, appointed agreeably to the tenor of the said act, to proceed forthwith to run the said lines of experiment, and the same being run, to survey and by proper metes and bounds to define and limit the part within the same which is hereinbefore directed for immediate location and acceptance, and thereof to make due report to me under their hands and seals.

In testimony whereof I have caused the seal of the United States to be affixed to these presents and signed the same with my hand.

[SEAL.] Done at the city of Philadelphia, the 24th day of January, A. D. 1791, and of the Independence of the United States the fifteenth.

GO WASHINGTON.

By the President:

TH: JEFFERSON.

[From a broadside in the archives of the Department of State.]

BY THE PRESIDENT OF THE UNITED STATES OF AMERICA.
A PROCLAMATION.

Whereas it hath been represented to me that James O'Fallon is levying an armed force in that part of the State of Virginia which is called Kentucky, disturbs the public peace, and sets at defiance the treaties of the United States with the Indian tribes, the act of Congress intituled

"An act to regulate trade and intercourse with the Indian tribes," and my proclamations of the 14th and 26th days of August last founded thereon; and it is my earnest desire that those who have incautiously associated themselves with the said James O'Fallon may be warned of their danger, I have therefore thought fit to publish this proclamation, hereby declaring that all persons violating the treaties and act aforesaid shall be prosecuted with the utmost rigor of the law.

And I do, moreover, require all officers of the United States whom it may concern to use their best exertions to bring to justice any persons offending in the premises.

In testimony whereof I have caused the seal of the United States to be affixed to these presents and signed the same with my hand.

[SEAL.]   Done at the city of Philadelphia, the 19th day of March, A. D. 1791, and of the Independence of the United States the fifteenth.   GO WASHINGTON.

By the President:

TH: JEFFERSON.

[From the Washington Papers (Executive Proceedings), vol. 20, p. 191.]

BY THE PRESIDENT OF THE UNITED STATES OF AMERICA.

A PROCLAMATION.

Whereas by a proclamation bearing date the 24th day of January of this present year, and in pursuance of certain acts of the States of Maryland and Virginia and of the Congress of the United States, therein mentioned, certain lines of experiment were directed to be run in the neighborhood of Georgetown, in Maryland, for the purpose of determining the location of a part of the territory of 10 miles square for the permanent seat of the Government of the United States, and a certain part was directed to be located within the said lines of experiment on both sides of the Potomac and above the limit of the Eastern Branch prescribed by the said act of Congress;

And Congress by an amendatory act passed on the 3d day of the present month of March have given further authority to the President of the United States "to make any part of the territory below the said limit and above the mouth of Hunting Creek a part of the said district, so as to include a convenient part of the Eastern Branch and of the lands lying on the lower side thereof, and also the town of Alexandria":

Now, therefore, for the purpose of amending and completing the location of the whole of the said territory of 10 miles square in conformity with the said amendatory act of Congress, I do hereby declare and make known that the whole of the said territory shall be located and included within the four lines following, that is to say:

Beginning at Jones's Point, being the upper cape of Hunting Creek, in Virginia, and at an angle in the outset of 45 degrees west of the north, and running in a direct line 10 miles for the first line; then beginning again at the same Jones's Point and running another direct line at a right angle with the first across the Potomac 10 miles for the second line; then from the termination of the said first and second lines running two other direct lines of 10 miles each, the one crossing the Eastern Branch aforesaid and the other the Potomac, and meeting each other in a point.

And I do accordingly direct the commissioners named under the authority of the said first-mentioned act of Congress to proceed forthwith to have the said four lines run, and by proper metes and bounds defined and limited, and thereof to make due report under their hands and seals; and the territory so to be located, defined, and limited shall be the whole territory accepted by the said acts of Congress as the district for the permanent seat of the Government of the United States.

In testimony whereof I have caused the seal of the United States to be affixed to these presents and signed the same with my hand.

[SEAL.] Done at Georgetown aforesaid, the 30th day of March, A. D. 1791, and of the Independence of the United States the fifteenth.

GO WASHINGTON.

THIRD ANNUAL ADDRESS.

UNITED STATES, *October 25, 1791.*

Fellow-Citizens of the Senate and of the House of Representatives:

I meet you upon the present occasion with the feelings which are naturally inspired by a strong impression of the prosperous situation of our common country, and by a persuasion equally strong that the labors of the session which has just commenced will, under the guidance of a spirit no less prudent than patriotic, issue in measures conducive to the stability and increase of national prosperity.

Numerous as are the providential blessings which demand our grateful acknowledgments, the abundance with which another year has again rewarded the industry of the husbandman is too important to escape recollection.

Your own observations in your respective situations will have satisfied you of the progressive state of agriculture, manufactures, commerce, and navigation. In tracing their causes you will have remarked with particular pleasure the happy effects of that revival of confidence, public as well as private, to which the Constitution and laws of the United States have so eminently contributed; and you will have observed with no less interest new and decisive proofs of the increasing reputation and credit of the nation. But you nevertheless can not fail to derive satisfaction from the confirmation of these circumstances which will be disclosed in the several official communications that will be made to you in the course of your deliberations.

The rapid subscriptions to the Bank of the United States, which completed the sum allowed to be subscribed in a single day, is among the striking and pleasing evidences which present themselves, not only of confidence in the Government, but of resource in the community.

In the interval of your recess due attention has been paid to the execution of the different objects which were specially provided for by the laws and resolutions of the last session.

Among the most important of these is the defense and security of the Western frontiers. To accomplish it on the most humane principles was a primary wish.

Accordingly, at the same time that treaties have been provisionally concluded and other proper means used to attach the wavering and to confirm in their friendship the well-disposed tribes of Indians, effectual measures have been adopted to make those of a hostile description sensible that a pacification was desired upon terms of moderation and justice.

Those measures having proved unsuccessful, it became necessary to convince the refractory of the power of the United States to punish their depredations. Offensive operations have therefore been directed, to be conducted, however, as consistently as possible with the dictates of humanity. Some of these have been crowned with full success and others are yet depending. The expeditions which have been completed were carried on under the authority and at the expense of the United States by the militia of Kentucky, whose enterprise, intrepidity, and good conduct are entitled to peculiar commendation.

Overtures of peace are still continued to the deluded tribes, and considerable numbers of individuals belonging to them have lately renounced all further opposition, removed from their former situations, and placed themselves under the immediate protection of the United States.

It is sincerely to be desired that all need of coercion in future may cease and that an intimate intercourse may succeed, calculated to advance the happiness of the Indians and to attach them firmly to the United States.

In order to this it seems necessary—

That they should experience the benefits of an impartial dispensation of justice.

That the mode of alienating their lands, the main source of discontent and war, should be so defined and regulated as to obviate imposition and as far as may be practicable controversy concerning the reality and extent of the alienations which are made.

That commerce with them should be promoted under regulations tending to secure an equitable deportment toward them, and that such rational experiments should be made for imparting to them the blessings of civilization as may from time to time suit their condition.

That the Executive of the United States should be enabled to employ the means to which the Indians have been long accustomed for uniting their immediate interests with the preservation of peace.

And that efficacious provision should be made for inflicting adequate penalties upon all those who, by violating their rights, shall infringe the treaties and endanger the peace of the Union.

A system corresponding with the mild principles of religion and philanthropy toward an unenlightened race of men, whose happiness materially depends on the conduct of the United States, would be as honorable to the national character as conformable to the dictates of sound policy.

The powers specially vested in me by the act laying certain duties on distilled spirits, which respect the subdivisions of the districts into surveys, the appointment of officers, and the assignment of compensations, have likewise been carried into effect. In a matter in which both materials and experience were wanting to guide the calculation it will be readily conceived that there must have been difficulty in such an adjustment of the rates of compensation as would conciliate a reasonable competency with a proper regard to the limits prescribed by the law. It is hoped that the circumspection which has been used will be found in the result to have secured the last of the two objects; but it is probable that with a view to the first in some instances a revision of the provision will be found advisable.

The impressions with which this law has been received by the community have been upon the whole such as were to be expected among enlightened and well-disposed citizens from the propriety and necessity of the measure. The novelty, however, of the tax in a considerable part of the United States and a misconception of some of its provisions have given occasion in particular places to some degree of discontent; but it is satisfactory to know that this disposition yields to proper explanations and more just apprehensions of the true nature of the law, and I entertain a full confidence that it will in all give way to motives which arise out of a just sense of duty and a virtuous regard to the public welfare.

If there are any circumstances in the law which consistently with its main design may be so varied as to remove any well-intentioned objections that may happen to exist, it will consist with a wise moderation to make the proper variations. It is desirable on all occasions to unite with a steady and firm adherence to constitutional and necessary acts of Government the fullest evidence of a disposition as far as may be practicable to consult the wishes of every part of the community and to lay the foundations of the public administration in the affections of the people.

Pursuant to the authority contained in the several acts on that subject, a district of 10 miles square for the permanent seat of the Government of the United States has been fixed and announced by proclamation, which district will comprehend lands on both sides of the river Potomac and the towns of Alexandria and Georgetown. A city has also been laid out agreeably to a plan which will be placed before Congress, and as there is a prospect, favored by the rate of sales which have already taken place, of ample funds for carrying on the necessary public buildings, there is every expectation of their due progress.

The completion of the census of the inhabitants, for which provision was made by law, has been duly notified (excepting one instance in which the return has been informal, and another in which it has been omitted or miscarried), and the returns of the officers who were charged with this duty, which will be laid before you, will give you the pleasing assurance that the present population of the United States borders on 4,000,000 persons.

It is proper also to inform you that a further loan of 2,500,000 florins has been completed in Holland, the terms of which are similar to those of the one last announced, except as to a small reduction of charges. Another, on like terms, for 6,000,000 florins, had been set on foot under circumstances that assured an immediate completion.

Gentlemen of the Senate:

Two treaties which have been provisionally concluded with the Cherokees and Six Nations of Indians will be laid before you for your consideration and ratification.

Gentlemen of the House of Representatives:

In entering upon the discharge of your legislative trust you must anticipate with pleasure that many of the difficulties necessarily incident to the first arrangements of a new government for an extensive country have been happily surmounted by the zealous and judicious exertions of your predecessors in cooperation with the other branch of the Legislature. The important objects which remain to be accomplished will, I am persuaded, be conducted upon principles equally comprehensive and equally well calculated for the advancement of the general weal.

The time limited for receiving subscriptions to the loans proposed by the act making provision for the debt of the United States having expired, statements from the proper department will as soon as possible apprise you of the exact result. Enough, however, is known already to afford an assurance that the views of that act have been substantially fulfilled. The subscription in the domestic debt of the United States has embraced by far the greatest proportion of that debt, affording at the same time proof of the general satisfaction of the public creditors

THE CAPITOL was begun September 1, 1793, and finished in 1867. Estimated cost $13,000,000. Cornerstone was ... The building is 751 x 350 feet. It is 288 feet high. Construction was ... Beneath the dome ... a tomb is prepared, ... where body ... for Washington, ... It is now ... where all senators empty ... called Washington's Tomb.

THE CAPITOL was begun September 1, 1793, and finished in 1863. Estimated cost $15,000,000. It is 751 x 350 feet. The dome is 288 feet high. Corner-stone was laid by Washington, for whose body the builders prepared a tomb beneath the dome called "undercroft," which still remains empty.

Capitol

with the system which has been proposed to their acceptance and of the spirit of accommodation to the convenience of the Government with which they are actuated. The subscriptions in the debts of the respective States as far as the provisions of the law have permitted may be said to be yet more general. The part of the debt of the United States which remains unsubscribed will naturally engage your further deliberations.

It is particularly pleasing to me to be able to announce to you that the revenues which have been established promise to be adequate to their objects, and may be permitted, if no unforeseen exigency occurs, to supersede for the present the necessity of any new burthens upon our constituents.

An object which will claim your early attention is a provision for the current service of the ensuing year, together with such ascertained demands upon the Treasury as require to be immediately discharged, and such casualties as may have arisen in the execution of the public business, for which no specific appropriation may have yet been made; of all which a proper estimate will be laid before you.

Gentlemen of the Senate and of the House of Representatives:

I shall content myself with a general reference to former communications for several objects upon which the urgency of other affairs has hitherto postponed any definitive resolution. Their importance will recall them to your attention, and I trust that the progress already made in the most arduous arrangements of the Government will afford you leisure to resume them with advantage.

There are, however, some of them of which I can not forbear a more particular mention. These are the militia, the post-office and post-roads, the mint, weights and measures, a provision for the sale of the vacant lands of the United States.

The first is certainly an object of primary importance whether viewed in reference to the national security to the satisfaction of the community or to the preservation of order. In connection with this the establishment of competent magazines and arsenals and the fortification of such places as are peculiarly important and vulnerable naturally present themselves to consideration. The safety of the United States under divine protection ought to rest on the basis of systematic and solid arrangements, exposed as little as possible to the hazards of fortuitous circumstances.

The importance of the post-office and post-roads on a plan sufficiently liberal and comprehensive, as they respect the expedition, safety, and facility of communication, is increased by their instrumentality in diffusing a knowledge of the laws and proceedings of the Government, which, while it contributes to the security of the people, serves also to guard them against the effects of misrepresentation and misconception. The establishment of additional cross posts, especially to some of the important points in the Western and Northern parts of the Union, can not fail to be of material utility.

The disorders in the existing currency, and especially the scarcity of small change, a scarcity so peculiarly distressing to the poorer classes, strongly recommend the carrying into immediate effect the resolution already entered into concerning the establishment of a mint. Measures have been taken pursuant to that resolution for procuring some of the most necessary artists, together with the requisite apparatus.

An uniformity in the weights and measures of the country is among the important objects submitted to you by the Constitution, and if it can be derived from a standard at once invariable and universal, must be no less honorable to the public councils than conducive to the public convenience.

A provision for the sale of the vacant lands of the United States is particularly urged, among other reasons, by the important considerations that they are pledged as a fund for reimbursing the public debt; that if timely and judiciously applied they may save the necessity of burthening our citizens with new taxes for the extinguishment of the principal; and that being free to discharge the principal but in a limited proportion, no opportunity ought to be lost for availing the public of its right.

G⁰ WASHINGTON.

ADDRESS OF THE SENATE TO GEORGE WASHINGTON, PRESIDENT OF THE UNITED STATES.

The PRESIDENT OF THE UNITED STATES.

SIR: The Senate of the United States have received with the highest satisfaction the assurances of public prosperity contained in your speech to both Houses. The multiplied blessings of Providence have not escaped our notice or failed to excite our gratitude.

The benefits which flow from the restoration of public and private confidence are conspicuous and important, and the pleasure with which we contemplate them is heightened by your assurance of those further communications which shall confirm their existence and indicate their source.

While we rejoice in the success of those military operations which have been directed against the hostile Indians, we lament with you the necessity that has produced them, and we participate the hope that the present prospect of a general peace on terms of moderation and justice may be wrought into complete and permanent effect, and that the measures of Government may equally embrace the security of our frontiers and the general interests of humanity, our solicitude to obtain which will insure our zealous attention to an object so warmly espoused by the principles of benevolence and so highly interesting to the honor and welfare of the nation.

The several subjects which you have particularly recommended and those which remain of former sessions will engage our early consideration. We are encouraged to prosecute them with alacrity and steadiness by the belief that they will interest no passion but that for the general welfare, by the assurance of concert, and by a view of those arduous and important arrangements which have been already accomplished.

We observe, sir, the constancy and activity of your zeal for the public good. The example will animate our efforts to promote the happiness of our country.

OCTOBER 28, 1791.

REPLY OF THE PRESIDENT.

GENTLEMEN: This manifestation of your zeal for the honor and the happiness of our country derives its full value from the share which your deliberations have already had in promoting both.

I thank you for the favorable sentiments with which you view the part I have borne in the arduous trust committed to the Government of the United States, and desire you to be assured that all my zeal will continue to second those further efforts for the public good which are insured by the spirit in which you are entering on the present session.

G9 WASHINGTON.

OCTOBER 31, 1791.

ADDRESS OF THE HOUSE OF REPRESENTATIVES TO GEORGE WASHINGTON, PRESIDENT OF THE UNITED STATES.

SIR: In receiving your address at the opening of the present session the House of Representatives have taken an ample share in the feelings inspired by the actual prosperity and flattering prospects of our country, and whilst with becoming gratitude to Heaven we ascribe this happiness to the true source from which it flows, we behold with an animating pleasure the degree in which the Constitution and laws of the United States have been instrumental in dispensing it.

It yields us particular satisfaction to learn the success with which the different important measures of the Government have proceeded, as well those specially provided for at the last session as those of preceding date. The safety of our Western frontier, in which the lives and repose of so many of our fellow-citizens are involved, being peculiarly interesting, your communications on that subject are proportionally grateful to us. The gallantry and good conduct of the militia, whose services were called for, is an honorable confirmation of the efficacy of that precious resource of a free state, and we anxiously wish that the consequences of their successful enterprises and of the other proceedings to which you have referred may leave the United States free to pursue the most benevolent policy toward the unhappy and deluded race of people in our neighborhood.

The amount of the population of the United States, determined by the returns of the census, is a source of the most pleasing reflections whether it be viewed in relation to our national safety and respectability or as a proof of that felicity in the situation of our country which favors so unexampled a rapidity in its growth. Nor ought any to be insensible to the additional motive suggested by this important fact to perpetuate the free Government established, with a wise administration of it, to a portion of the earth which promises such an increase of the number which is to enjoy those blessings within the limits of the United States.

We shall proceed with all the respect due to your patriotic recommendations and with a deep sense of the trust committed to us by our fellow-citizens to take into consideration the various and important matters falling within the present session; and in discussing and deciding each we shall feel every disposition whilst we are pursuing the public welfare, which must be the supreme object with all our constituents, to accommodate as far as possible the means of attaining it to the sentiments and wishes of every part of them.

OCTOBER 27, 1791.

REPLY OF THE PRESIDENT.

GENTLEMEN: The pleasure I derive from an assurance of your attention to the objects I have recommended to you is doubled by your concurrence in the testimony I have borne to the prosperous condition of our public affairs.

Relying on the sanctions of your enlightened judgment and on your patriotic aid, I shall be the more encouraged in all my endeavors for the public weal, and particularly in those which may be required on my part for executing the salutary measures I anticipate from your present deliberations.

G? WASHINGTON.

OCTOBER 28, 1791.

SPECIAL MESSAGES.

UNITED STATES, *October 26, 1791.*

Gentlemen of the Senate and of the House of Representatives:

I lay before you copies of the following acts, which have been transmitted to me during the recess of Congress, viz:

An act passed by the legislature of New Hampshire for ceding to the United States the fort and light-house belonging to the said State.

An act of the legislature of Pennsylvania ratifying on behalf of said

State the first article of amendment to the Constitution of the United States as proposed by Congress; and

An act of the legislature of North Carolina granting the use of the jails within that State to the United States.

GQ WASHINGTON.

UNITED STATES, *October 26, 1791.*

Gentlemen of the Senate:

I have directed the Secretary of War to lay before you for your consideration all the papers relative to the late negotiations with the Cherokee Indians, and the treaty concluded with that tribe on the 2d day of July last by the superintendent of the southern district, and I request your advice whether I shall ratify the same.

I also lay before you the instructions to Colonel Pickering and his conferences with the Six Nations of Indians. These conferences were for the purpose of conciliation, and at a critical period, to withdraw those Indians to a greater distance from the theater of war, in order to prevent their being involved therein.

It might not have been necessary to have requested your opinion on this business had not the commissioner, with good intentions, but incautiously, made certain ratifications of lands unauthorized by his instructions and unsupported by the Constitution.

It therefore became necessary to disavow the transaction explicitly in a letter written by my orders to the governor of New York on the 17th of August last.

The speeches to the Cornplanter and other Seneca chiefs, the instructions to Colonel Proctor, and his report, and other messages and directions are laid before you for your information and as evidences that all proper lenient measures preceded the exercise of coercion.

The letters to the chief of the Creeks are also laid before you, to evince that the requisite steps have been taken to produce a full compliance with the treaty made with that nation on the 7th of August, 1790.

GQ WASHINGTON.

UNITED STATES, *October 27, 1791.*

Gentlemen of the Senate and of the House of Representatives:

I lay before you a copy of a letter and of sundry documents which I have received from the governor of Pennsylvania, respecting certain persons who are said to have fled from justice out of the State of Pennsylvania into that of Virginia, together with a report of the Attorney-General of the United States upon the same subject.

I have received from the governor of North Carolina a copy of an act of the general assembly of that State, authorizing him to convey to the United States the right and jurisdiction of the said State over 1 acre of land in Occacock Island and 10 acres on the Cape Island, within the said State, for the purpose of erecting light-houses thereon, together with the deed of the governor in pursuance thereof and the original conveyances made to the State by the individual proprietors, which original conveyances contain conditions that the light-house on Occacock shall be built before the 1st day of January, 1801, and that on the Cape Island before the 8th day of October, 1800. And I have caused these several papers to be deposited in the office of the Secretary of State.

A statement of the returns of the enumeration of the inhabitants of the United States which have been received will at this time be laid before you.

GQ WASHINGTON.

UNITED STATES, *October 27, 1791.*

Gentlemen of the Senate and of the House of Representatives:

I have directed the Secretary of War to lay before you, for your information, the reports of Brigadier-General Scott and Lieutenant-Colonel Commandant Wilkinson, the officers who commanded the two expeditions against the Wabash Indians in the months of June and August last, together with the instructions by virtue of which the said expeditions were undertaken. When the operations now depending shall be terminated, the reports relative thereto shall also be laid before you.

GQ WASHINGTON.

UNITED STATES, *October 31, 1791.*

Gentlemen of the Senate and of the House of Representatives:

I send you herewith the arrangement which has been made by me, pursuant to the act entitled "An act repealing after the last day of June next the duties heretofore laid upon distilled spirits imported from abroad and laying others in their stead, and also upon spirits distilled within the United States, and for appropriating the same," in respect to the subdivision of the several districts created by the said act into surveys of inspection, the appointment of officers for the same, and the assignment of compensations.

GQ WASHINGTON.

UNITED STATES, *November 1, 1791.*

Gentlemen of the Senate and of the House of Representatives:

I received yesterday from the judge of the district of South Carolina a letter, inclosing the presentments of the grand jury to him, and stating the causes which have prevented the return of the census from that district, copies of which are now laid before you.

GQ WASHINGTON.

UNITED STATES, *November 10, 1791.*

Gentlemen of the Senate and of the House of Representatives:

The resolution passed at the last session of Congress, requesting the President of the United States to cause an estimate to be laid before Congress at their next session of the quantity and situation of the lands not claimed by the Indians nor granted to nor claimed by any of the citizens of the United States within the territory ceded to the United States by the State of North Carolina and within the territory of the United States northwest of the river Ohio, has been referred to the Secretary of State, a copy of whose report on that subject I now lay before you, together with the copy of a letter accompanying it.

GQ WASHINGTON.

UNITED STATES, *November 11, 1791.*

Gentlemen of the Senate and of the House of Representatives:

I have received from the governor of Virginia a resolution of the general assembly of that Commonwealth, ratifying the first article of the amendments proposed by Congress to the Constitution of the United States, a copy of which and of the letter accompanying it I now lay before you.

Sundry papers relating to the purchase by Judge Symmes of the lands on the Great Miami having been communicated to me, I have thought it proper to lay the same before you for your information on that subject.

GQ WASHINGTON.

UNITED STATES, *December 12, 1791.*

Gentlemen of the Senate and of the House of Representatives:

It is with great concern that I communicate to you the information received from Major-General St. Clair of the misfortune which has befallen the troops under his command.

Although the national loss is considerable according to the scale of the event, yet it may be repaired without great difficulty, excepting as to the brave men who have fallen on the occasion, and who are a subject of public as well as private regret.

A further communication will shortly be made of all such matters as shall be necessary to enable the Legislature to judge of the future measures which it may be proper to pursue.

GQ WASHINGTON.

UNITED STATES, *December 13, 1791.*

Gentlemen of the Senate and of the House of Representatives:

I place before you the plan of a city that has been laid out within the district of 10 miles square, which was fixed upon for the permanent seat of the Government of the United States.

GQ WASHINGTON.

UNITED STATES, *December 20, 1791.*

Gentlemen of the Senate and of the House of Representatives:

I lay before you the copy of a letter which I have received from the governor of the Commonwealth of Pennsylvania, and of sundry documents which accompanied it, relative to a contract for the purchase of a certain tract of land bounding on Lake Erie, together with a copy of a report of the Secretary of State on the same subject.

G⁰ WASHINGTON.

UNITED STATES, *December 30, 1791.*

Gentlemen of the Senate and of the House of Representatives:

I lay before you a copy of the ratification by the Commonwealth of Virginia of the articles of amendment proposed by Congress to the Constitution of the United States, and a copy of a letter which accompanied said ratification from the governor of Virginia.

G⁰ WASHINGTON.

UNITED STATES, *January 11, 1792.*

Gentlemen of the Senate:

I lay before you the following report, which has been made to me by the Secretary of State:

DECEMBER 22, 1791.

The Secretary of State reports to the President of the United States that one of the commissioners of Spain, in the name of both, has lately communicated to him verbally, by order of his Court, that His Catholic Majesty, apprised of our solicitude to have some arrangements made respecting our free navigation of the river Mississippi and the use of a port thereon, is ready to enter into treaty thereon at Madrid.

The Secretary of State is of opinion that this overture should be attended to without delay, and that the proposal of treating at Madrid, though not what might have been desired, should yet be accepted, and a commission plenipotentiary made out for the purpose.

That Mr. Carmichael, the present chargé d'affaires of the United States at Madrid, from the local acquaintance which he must have acquired with persons and circumstances, would be an useful and proper member of the commission, but that it would be useful also to join with him some person more particularly acquainted with the circumstances of the navigation to be treated of.

That the fund appropriated by the act providing the means of intercourse between the United States and foreign nations will insufficiently furnish the ordinary and regular demands on it, and is consequently inadequate to the mission of an additional commissioner express from hence.

That therefore it will be advisable on this account, as well as for the sake of dispatch, to constitute some one of the ministers of the United States in Europe, jointly with Mr. Carmichael, commissioners plenipotentiary for the special purpose of negotiating and concluding with any person or persons duly authorized by His Catholic Majesty a convention or treaty for the free navigation of the river Mississippi by the citizens of the United States under such accommodations with respect to a port and other circumstances as may render the said navigation practicable, useful, and free from dispute, saving to the President and Senate their respective rights as to the ratification of the same, and that the said negotiation be at Madrid, or such other place in Spain as shall be desired by His Catholic Majesty.

TH: JEFFERSON.

In consequence of the communication from the Court of Spain, as stated in the preceding report, I nominate William Carmichael, present chargé d'affaires of the United States at Madrid, and William Short, present chargé d'affaires of the United States at Paris, to be commissioners plenipotentiary for negotiating and concluding with any person or persons who shall be duly authorized by His Catholic Majesty a convention or treaty concerning the navigation of the river Mississippi by the citizens of the United States, saving to the President and Senate their respective rights as to the ratification of the same.

G♀ WASHINGTON.

UNITED STATES, *January 11, 1792.*

Gentlemen of the Senate and of the House of Representatives:

I lay before you, in confidence, two reports, made to me by the Secretary for the Department of War, relatively to the present state of affairs on the Western frontiers of the United States.

In these reports the causes of the present war with the Indians, the measures taken by the Executive to terminate it amicably, and the military preparations for the late campaign are stated and explained, and also a plan suggested of such further measures on the occasion as appear just and expedient.

I am persuaded, gentlemen, that you will take this important subject into your immediate and serious consideration, and that the result of your deliberations will be the adoption of such wise and efficient measures as will reflect honor on our national councils and promote the welfare of our country.

G♀ WASHINGTON.

UNITED STATES, *January 18, 1792.*

Gentlemen of the Senate and of the House of Representatives:

I lay before you a copy of an exemplified copy of an act of the legislature of Vermont, ratifying on behalf of that State the articles of amendment proposed by Congress to the Constitution of the United States together with a copy of a letter which accompanied said ratification.

G♀ WASHINGTON.

UNITED STATES, *January 18, 1792.*

Gentlemen of the Senate:

I lay before you the communications of a deputation from the Cherokee Nation of Indians now in this city, and I request your advice whether

an additional article shall be made to the Cherokee treaty to the following effect, to wit:

That the sum to be paid annually by the United States to the Cherokee Nation of Indians in consideration of the relinquishment of lands as
stated in the treaty made with them on the 2d day of July, 1791, shall
be $1,500 instead of $1,000 mentioned in the said treaty.

G⁰ WASHINGTON.

UNITED STATES, *January 23, 1792.*

Gentlemen of the Senate and of the House of Representatives:

Having received from the governor of Virginia a letter, inclosing a
resolution of the general assembly of that State and a report of a committee of the House of Delegates respecting certain lands located by the
officers and soldiers of the Virginia line under the laws of that State, and
since ceded to the Chickasaw Indians, I lay copies of the same before you,
together with a report of the Secretary of State on this subject.

G⁰ WASHINGTON.

UNITED STATES, *February 8, 1792.*

Gentlemen of the Senate and of the House of Representatives:

An article of expense having occurred in the Department of Foreign
Affairs for which no provision has been made by law, I lay before you a
letter from the Secretary of State explaining the same, in order that you
may do thereon what you shall find to be right.

G⁰ WASHINGTON.

UNITED STATES, *March 3, 1792.*

Gentlemen of the Senate and of the House of Representatives:

I lay before you a copy of a return of the number of inhabitants in the
district of South Carolina as made to me by the marshal thereof, and a
copy of a letter which accompanied said return.

G⁰ WASHINGTON.

UNITED STATES, *March 5, 1792.*

Gentlemen of the Senate and of the House of Representatives:

Knowing the friendly interest you take in whatever may promote the
happiness and prosperity of the French nation, it is with pleasure that I
lay before you the translation of a letter which I have received from His
Most Christian Majesty, announcing to the United States of America
his acceptance of the constitution presented to him by his nation.

G⁰ WASHINGTON.

Very Dear Great Friends and Allies:

We make it our duty to inform you that we have accepted the constitution which has been presented to us in the name of the nation, and according to which France will be henceforth governed.

We do not doubt that you take an interest in an event so important to our Kingdom and to us, and it is with real pleasure we take this occasion to renew to you assurances of the sincere friendship we bear you. Whereupon we pray God to have you, very dear great friends and allies, in His just and holy keeping.

Written at Paris the 19th of September, 1791.

Your good friend and ally,

LOUIS.

MONTMORIN.

The UNITED STATES OF NORTH AMERICA.

UNITED STATES, *March 6, 1792.*

Gentlemen of the Senate:

I lay before you the following report, which has been submitted to me by the Secretary of State:

JANUARY 10, 1792.

The Secretary of State having received information that the merchants and merchandise of the United States are subject in Copenhagen and other ports of Denmark to considerable extra duties, from which they might probably be relieved by the presence of a consul there—

Reports to the President of the United States that it would be expedient to name a consul to be resident in the port of Copenhagen; that he has not been able to find that there is any citizen of the United States residing there; that there is a certain Hans Rudolph Saaby, a Danish subject and merchant of that place, of good character, of wealth and distinction, and well qualified and disposed to act there for the United States, who would probably accept the commission of consul; but that that of vice-consul, hitherto given by the President to foreigners in ports where there was no proper American citizen, would probably not be accepted because in this, as in some other ports of Europe, usage has established it as a subordinate grade.

And that he is therefore of the opinion that the said Hans Rudolph Saaby should be nominated consul of the United States of America for the port of Copenhagen and such other places within the allegiance of His Danish Majesty as shall be nearer to the said port than to the residence of any other consul or vice-consul of the United States within the same allegiance.

TH: JEFFERSON.

With a view to relieve the merchants and merchandise of the United States from the extra duties to which they are or may be subjected in the ports of Denmark, I have thought it for the interest of the United States that a consul be appointed to reside at Copenhagen. I therefore nominate Hans Rudolph Saaby, a Danish subject and merchant of Copenhagen, to be consul for the United States of America at the port of Copenhagen and for such other places within the allegiance of His Danish Majesty as shall be nearer to the said port than to the residence of any other consul or vice-consul of the United States within the same allegiance.

GO WASHINGTON.

UNITED STATES, *March 7, 1792.*

Gentlemen of the Senate:

I submit to your consideration the report of the Secretary of State, which accompanies this, stating the reasons for extending the negotiation proposed at Madrid to the subject of commerce, and explaining, under the form of instructions to the commissioners lately appointed to that Court, the principles on which commercial arrangements with Spain might, if desired on her part, be acceded to on ours ; and I have to request your decision whether you will advise and consent to the extension of the powers of the commissioners as proposed, and to the ratification of a treaty which shall conform to those instructions should they enter into such a one with that Court.

G<u>o</u> WASHINGTON.

MARCH 7, 1792.

The Secretary of State having understood from communications with the commissioners of His Catholic Majesty, subsequent to that which he reported to the President on the 22d of December last, that though they considered the navigation of the Mississippi as the principal object of negotiation between the two countries, yet it was expected by their Court that the conferences would extend to all the matters which were under negotiation on the former occasion with Mr. Gardoqui, and particularly to some arrangements of commerce, is of opinion that to renew the conferences on this subject also, since they desire it, will be but friendly and respectful, and can lead to nothing without our own consent, and that to refuse it might obstruct the settlement of the questions of navigation and boundary; and therefore reports to the President of the United States the following observations and instructions to the commissioners of the United States appointed to negotiate with the Court of Spain a treaty or convention relative to the navigation of the Mississippi, which observations and instructions he is of opinion should be laid before the Senate of the United States, and their decision be desired whether they will advise and consent that a treaty be entered into by the commissioners of the United States with Spain conformably thereto.

After stating to our commissioners the foundation of our rights to navigate the Mississippi and to hold our southern boundary at the thirty-first degree of latitude, and that each of these is to be a sine qua non, it is proposed to add as follows:

On the former conferences on the navigation of the Mississippi, Spain chose to blend with it the subject of commerce, and accordingly specific propositions thereon passed between the negotiators. Her object then was to obtain our renunciation of the navigation and to hold out commercial arrangements perhaps as a lure to us. Perhaps, however, she might then, and may now, really set a value on commercial arrangements with us, and may receive them as a consideration for accommodating us in the navigation, or may wish for them to have the appearance of receiving a consideration. Commercial arrangements, if acceptable in themselves, will not be the less so if coupled with those relating to navigation and boundary. We have only to take care that they be acceptable in themselves.

There are two principles which may be proposed as the basis of a commercial treaty: First, that of exchanging the privileges of native citizens, or, second, those of the most favored nation.

First. With the nations holding important possessions in America we are ready to exchange the rights of native citizens, provided they be extended through the whole possessions of both parties; but the propositions of Spain made on the former occasion (a copy of which accompanies this) were that we should give their merchants, vessels, and productions the privileges of native merchants, vessels, and productions through the whole of our possessions, and they give the same to ours only in Spain and the Canaries. This is inadmissible, because unequal; and as we believe that Spain is not ripe for an equal exchange on this basis, we avoid proposing it.

Second. Though treaties which merely exchange the rights of the most favored nations are not without all inconvenience, yet they have their conveniences also. It is an important one that they leave each party free to make what internal regulations they please, and to give what preferences they find expedient to native merchants, vessels, and productions; and as we already have treaties on this basis with France, Holland, Sweden, and Prussia, the two former of which are perpetual, it will be but small additional embarrassment to extend it to Spain. On the contrary, we are sensible it is right to place that nation on the most favored footing, whether we have a treaty with them or not, and it can do us no harm to secure by treaty a reciprocation of the right.

Of the four treaties before mentioned, either the French or the Prussian might be taken as a model; but it would be useless to propose the Prussian, because we have already supposed that Spain would never consent to those articles which give to each party access to all the dominions of the other; and without this equivalent we would not agree to tie our own hands so materially in war as would be done by the twenty-third article, which renounces the right of fitting out privateers or of capturing merchant vessels. The French treaty, therefore, is proposed as the model. In this, however, the following changes are to be made:

We should be admitted to all the dominions of Spain to which any other foreign nation is or may be admitted.

Article 5, being an exemption from a particular duty in France, will of course be omitted as inapplicable to Spain.

Article 8 to be omitted as unnecessary with Morocco, and inefficacious and little honorable with any of the Barbary powers; but it may furnish occasion to sound Spain on the project of a convention of the powers at war with the Barbary States to keep up by rotation a constant cruise of a given force on their coasts till they shall be compelled to renounce forever and against all nations their predatory practices. Perhaps the infidelities of the Algerines to their treaty of peace with Spain, though the latter does not choose to break openly, may induce her to subsidize *us* to cruise against them with a given force.

Articles 9 and 10, concerning fisheries, to be omitted as inapplicable.

Article 11. The first paragraph of this article respecting the droit d'aubaine to be omitted, that law being supposed peculiar to France.

Article 17, giving asylum in the ports of either to the armed vessels of the other with the prizes taken from the enemies of that other, must be qualified as it is in the nineteenth article of the Prussian treaty, as the stipulation in the latter part of the article that "no shelter or refuge shall be given in the ports of the one to such as shall have made prize on the subjects of the other of the parties" would forbid us, in case of a war between France and Spain, to give shelter in our ports to prizes made by the latter on the former, while the first part of the article would oblige us to shelter those made by the former on the latter—a very dangerous covenant, and which ought never to be repeated in any other instance.

Article 29. Consuls should be received at all the ports at which the vessels of either party may be received.

Article 30, concerning free ports in Europe and America, free ports in the Spanish possessions in America, and particularly at The Havannah, are more to be desired than expected. It can therefore only be recommended to the best endeavors of the commissioners to obtain them. It will be something to obtain for our vessels, flour, etc., admission to those ports during their pleasure. In like manner, if they could be prevailed on to reestablish our right of cutting logwood in the Bay of Campeachy on the footing on which it stood before the treaty of 1763, it would be desirable and not endanger to us any contest with the English, who by the revolution treaty are restrained to the southeastern parts of Yucatan.

Article 31. The *act* of ratification on our part may require a twelvemonth from the date of the treaty, as the Senate meets regularly but once a year; and to return it to Madrid for *exchange* may require four months more.

The treaty must not exceed —— years' duration, except the clauses relating to boundary and the navigation of the Mississippi, which must be perpetual and final. Indeed, these two subjects had better be in a separate instrument.

There might have been mentioned a third species of arrangement—that of making special agreements on every special subject of commerce, and of settling a tariff of duty to be paid on each side on every particular article; but this would require in our commissioners a very minute knowledge of our commerce, as it is impossible to foresee every proposition of this kind which might be brought into discussion and to prepare them for it by information and instruction from hence. Our commerce, too, is as yet rather in a course of experiment, and the channels in which it will ultimately flow are not sufficiently known to enable us to provide for it by special agreement; nor have the exigencies of our new Government as yet so far developed themselves as that we can know to what degree we may or must have recourse to commerce for the purposes of revenue. No common consideration, therefore, ought to induce us as yet to arrangements of this kind. Perhaps nothing should do it with any nation short of the privileges of natives in all their possessions, foreign and domestic.

It were to be wished, indeed, that some positively favorable stipulations respecting our grain, flour, and fish could be obtained, even on our giving reciprocal advantages to some of the commodities of Spain, say her wines and brandies; but,

First. If we quit the ground of the most *favored nation* as to certain articles for our convenience, Spain may insist on doing the same for other articles for her convenience, and thus our commissioners will get themselves on the ground of *a treaty of detail*, for which they will not be prepared.

Second. If we grant favor to the wines and brandies of Spain, then Portugal and France will demand the same; and in order to create an equivalent Portugal may lay a duty on our fish and grain, and France a prohibition on our whale oils, the removal of which will be proposed as an equivalent.

Thus much, however, as to grain and flour may be attempted. There has not long since been a considerable duty laid on them in Spain. This was while a treaty on the subject of commerce was pending between us and Spain, as that Court considers the matter. It is not generally thought right to change the state of things pending a treaty concerning them. On this consideration and on the motive of cultivating our friendship, perhaps the commissioners may induce them to restore this commodity to the footing on which it was on opening the conferences with Mr. Gardoqui, on the 26th day of July, 1785. If Spain says, "Do the same by your tonnage on our vessels," the answer may be that "Our foreign tonnage affects Spain very little and other nations very much; whereas the duty on flour in Spain affects us very much and other nations very little; consequently there would be no equality in reciprocal relinquishment, as there had been none in the reciprocal innovation; and Spain, by insisting on this, would in fact only be aiding the interests of her rival nations, to whom we should be forced to extend the same indulgence." At the time of opening the conferences, too, we had as yet not erected any system, our Government itself being not yet erected. Innovation then was unavoidable on our part, if it be innovation to establish a system. We did it on fair and general ground, on ground favorable to Spain; but they had a system, and therefore innovation was avoidable on their part.

TH: JEFFERSON.

ARTICLES PROPOSED BY DON DIEGO GARDOQUI TO BE INSERTED IN THE TREATY
WITH THE UNITED STATES.

First. That all commercial regulations affecting each other shall be founded in perfect reciprocity. Spanish merchants shall enjoy all the commercial privileges of native merchants in the United States, and American merchants shall enjoy all the commercial privileges of native merchants in the Kingdom of Spain and in the Canaries and other islands belonging to and adjacent thereto. The same privileges shall extend to their respective vessels and merchandise consisting of the manufactures and products of their respective countries.

Second. Each party may establish consuls in the countries of the other (excepting such provinces in Spain into which none have heretofore been admitted, viz, Bilboa and Guipusca), with such powers and privileges as shall be ascertained by a particular convention.

Third. That the bona fide manufactures and productions of the United States (tobacco only excepted, which shall continue under its present regulation) may be imported in American or Spanish vessels into any parts of His Majesty's European dominions and islands aforesaid in like manner as if they were the productions of Spain, and, on the other hand, that the bona fide manufactures and productions of His Majesty's dominions may be imported into the United States in Spanish or American vessels in like manner as if they were the manufactures and productions of the said States. And further, that all such duties and imposts as may mutually be thought necessary to lay on them by either party shall be ascertained and regulated on principles of exact reciprocity by a tariff, to be formed by a convention for that purpose, to be negotiated and made within *one* year after the exchange of the ratification of this treaty; and in the meantime that no other duties or imposts shall be exacted from each other's merchants and ships than such as may be payable by natives in like cases.

Fourth. That inasmuch as the United States, from not having mines of gold and silver, may often want supplies of specie for a circulating medium, His Catholic Majesty, as a proof of his good will, agrees to order the masts and timber which may from time to time be wanted for his royal navy to be purchased and paid for in specie in the United States, provided the said masts and timber shall be of equal quality and when brought to Spain shall not cost more than the like may there be had for from other countries.

Fifth. It is agreed that the articles commonly inserted in other treaties of commerce for mutual and reciprocal convenience shall be inserted in this, and that this treaty and every article and stipulation therein shall continue in full force for —— years, to be computed from the day of the date hereof.

UNITED STATES, *March 9, 1792.*

Gentlemen of the Senate and of the House of Representatives:

I now lay before you a general account rendered by the bankers of the United States at Amsterdam of the payments they had made between the 1st of July, 1790 and 1791, from the fund deposited in their hands for the purposes of the act providing the means of intercourse between the United States and foreign nations, and of the balance remaining in their hands, together with a letter from the Secretary of State on the subject.

GO WASHINGTON.

UNITED STATES, *March 20, 1792.*

Gentlemen of the Senate and of the House of Representatives:

The several acts which have been passed relatively to the military establishment of the United States and the protection of the frontiers do not appear to have made provision for more than one brigadier-general. It is incumbent upon me to observe that, with a view merely to the organization of the troops designated by those acts, a greater number of officers of that grade would, in my opinion, be conducive to the good of the public service. But an increase of the number becomes still more desirable in reference to a different organization which is contemplated, pursuant to the authority vested in me for that purpose, and which, besides other advantages expected from it, is recommended by considerations of economy. I therefore request that you will be pleased to take this subject into your early consideration and to adopt such measures thereon as you shall judge proper.

GO WASHINGTON.

UNITED STATES, *March 23, 1792.*

Gentlemen of the Senate:

At the conferences which Colonel Pickering had with the Five Nations at the Painted Post the last year ideas were then held out of introducing among them some of the primary principles of civilization, in consequence of which, as well as more firmly to attach them to the interests of the United States, they have been invited to the seat of the General Government.

As the representation now here is respectable for its character and influence, it is of some importance that the chiefs should be well satisfied of the entire good faith and liberality of the United States.

In managing the affairs of the Indian tribes generally it appears proper to teach them to expect annual presents, conditioned on the evidence of their attachment to the interests of the United States. The situation of the Five Nations and the present crisis of affairs would seem to render the extension of this measure to them highly judicious. I therefore request the advice of the Senate whether an article shall be stipulated with the Five Nations to the following purport, to wit:

The United States, in order to promote the happiness of the Five Nations of Indians, will cause to be expended annually the amount of $1,500 in purchasing for them clothing, domestic animals, and implements of husbandry, and for encouraging useful artificers to reside in their villages,

GO WASHINGTON.

APRIL 13, 1792.

Gentlemen of the Senate and of the House of Representatives:

I have thought it proper to lay before you a communication of the 11th instant from the minister plenipotentiary of Great Britain to the Secretary of State, relative to the commerce of the two countries, together with their explanatory correspondence and the Secretary of State's letter to me on the subject.

G⁰ WASHINGTON.

UNITED STATES, *April 16, 1792.*

Gentlemen of the Senate and of the House of Representatives:

I lay before you a copy of a letter from the judges of the circuit court of the United States held for the New York district, and of their opinion and agreement respecting the "Act to provide for the settlement of the claims of widows and orphans barred by the limitations heretofore established, and to regulate the claims to invalid pensions."

G⁰ WASHINGTON.

UNITED STATES, *April 21, 1792.*

Gentlemen of the Senate and of the House of Representatives:

I lay before you the copy of a letter which I have received from the judges of the circuit court of the United States held for the Pennsylvania district relatively to the "Act to provide for the settlement of the claims of widows and orphans barred by the limitations heretofore established, and to regulate the claims to invalid pensions."

G⁰ WASHINGTON.

UNITED STATES, *May 8, 1792.*

Gentlemen of the Senate:

If the President of the United States should conclude a convention or treaty with the Government of Algiers for the ransom of the thirteen Americans in captivity there for a sum not exceeding $40,000, all expenses included, will the Senate approve the same? Or is there any, and what, greater or lesser sum which they would fix on as the limit beyond which they would not approve the ransom?

If the President of the United States should conclude a treaty with the Government of Algiers for the establishment of peace with them, at an expense not exceeding $25,000, paid at the signature, and a like sum to be paid annually afterwards during the continuance of the treaty, would the Senate approve the same? Or are there any greater or lesser sums which they would fix on as the limits beyond which they would not approve of such treaty?

G⁰ WASHINGTON.

VETO MESSAGE.

UNITED STATES, *April 5, 1792.*

Gentlemen of the House of Representatives:

I have maturely considered the act passed by the two Houses entitled "An act for an apportionment of Representatives among the several States according to the first enumeration," and I return it to your House, wherein it originated, with the following objections:

First. The Constitution has prescribed that Representatives shall be apportioned among the several States according to their respective numbers, and there is no one proportion or divisor which, applied to the respective numbers of the States, will yield the number and allotment of Representatives proposed by the bill.

Second. The Constitution has also provided that the number of Representatives shall not exceed 1 for every 30,000, which restriction is by the context and by fair and obvious construction to be applied to the separate and respective numbers of the States; and the bill has allotted to eight of the States more than 1 for every 30,000.

G? WASHINGTON.

[From Sparks's Washington, Vol. X, p. 532.]

PROCLAMATION.

Whereas certain violent and unwarrantable proceedings have lately taken place tending to obstruct the operation of the laws of the United States for raising a revenue upon spirits distilled within the same, enacted pursuant to express authority delegated in the Constitution of the United States, which proceedings are subversive of good order, contrary to the duty that every citizen owes to his country and to the laws, and of a nature dangerous to the very being of a government; and

Whereas such proceedings are the more unwarrantable by reason of the moderation which has been heretofore shown on the part of the Government and of the disposition which has been manifested by the Legislature (who alone have authority to suspend the operation of laws) to obviate causes of objection and to render the laws as acceptable as possible; and

Whereas it is the particular duty of the Executive "to take care that the laws be faithfully executed," and not only that duty but the permanent interests and happiness of the people require that every legal and necessary step should be pursued as well to prevent such violent and unwarrantable proceedings as to bring to justice the infractors of the laws and secure obedience thereto:

Now, therefore, I, George Washington, President of the United States, do by these presents most earnestly admonish and exhort all persons whom it may concern to refrain and desist from all unlawful combinations and proceedings whatsoever having for object or tending to obstruct the operation of the laws aforesaid, inasmuch as all lawful ways and means will be strictly put in execution for bringing to justice the infractors thereof and securing obedience thereto.

And I do moreover charge and require all courts, magistrates, and officers whom it may concern, according to the duties of their several offices, to exert the powers in them respectively vested by law for the purposes aforesaid, hereby also enjoining and requiring all persons whomsoever, as they tender the welfare of their country, the just and due authority of Government, and the preservation of the public peace, to be aiding and assisting therein according to law.

In testimony whereof I have caused the seal of the United States to be affixed to these presents, and signed the same with my hand.

[SEAL.]　　Done this 15th of September, A. D. 1792, and of the Independence of the United States the seventeenth.

G<u>o</u> WASHINGTON.

FOURTH ANNUAL ADDRESS.

UNITED STATES, *November 6, 1792.*

Fellow-Citizens of the Senate and of the House of Representatives:

It is some abatement of the satisfaction with which I meet you on the present occasion that, in felicitating you on a continuance of the national prosperity generally, I am not able to add to it information that the Indian hostilities which have for some time past distressed our Northwestern frontier have terminated.

You will, I am persuaded, learn with no less concern than I communicate it that reiterated endeavors toward effecting a pacification have hitherto issued only in new and outrageous proofs of persevering hostility on the part of the tribes with whom we are in contest. An earnest desire to procure tranquillity to the frontier, to stop the further effusion of blood, to arrest the progress of expense, to forward the prevalent wish of the nation for peace has led to strenuous efforts through various channels to accomplish these desirable purposes; in making which efforts I consulted less my own anticipations of the event, or the scruples which some considerations were calculated to inspire, than the wish to find the object attainable, or if not attainable, to ascertain unequivocally that such is the case.

A detail of the measures which have been pursued and of their consequences, which will be laid before you, while it will confirm to you the want of success thus far, will, I trust, evince that means as proper and as efficacious as could have been devised have been employed. The issue of some of them, indeed, is still depending, but a favorable one, though not to be despaired of, is not promised by anything that has yet happened.

In the course of the attempts which have been made some valuable citizens have fallen victims to their zeal for the public service. A sanction commonly respected even among savages has been found in this instance insufficient to protect from massacre the emissaries of peace. It will, I presume, be duly considered whether the occasion does not call for an exercise of liberality toward the families of the deceased.

It must add to your concern to be informed that, besides the continuation of hostile appearances among the tribes north of the Ohio, some threatening symptoms have of late been revived among some of those south of it.

A part of the Cherokees, known by the name of Chickamaugas, inhabiting five villages on the Tennessee River, have long been in the practice of committing depredations on the neighboring settlements.

It was hoped that the treaty of Holston, made with the Cherokee Nation in July, 1791, would have prevented a repetition of such depredations; but the event has not answered this hope. The Chickamaugas, aided by some banditti of another tribe in their vicinity, have recently perpetrated wanton and unprovoked hostilities upon the citizens of the United States in that quarter. The information which has been received on this subject will be laid before you. Hitherto defensive precautions only have been strictly enjoined and observed.

It is not understood that any breach of treaty or aggression whatsoever on the part of the United States or their citizens is even alleged as a pretext for the spirit of hostility in this quarter.

I have reason to believe that every practicable exertion has been made (pursuant to the provision by law for that purpose) to be prepared for the alternative of a prosecution of the war in the event of a failure of pacific overtures. A large proportion of the troops authorized to be raised have been recruited, though the number is still incomplete, and pains have been taken to discipline and put them in condition for the particular kind of service to be performed. A delay of operations (besides being dictated by the measures which were pursuing toward a pacific termination of the war) has been in itself deemed preferable to immature efforts. A statement from the proper department with regard to the number of troops raised, and some other points which have been suggested, will afford more precise information as a guide to the legislative consultations, and among other things will enable Congress to judge whether some additional stimulus to the recruiting service may not be advisable.

In looking forward to the future expense of the operations which may be found inevitable I derive consolation from the information I receive that the product of the revenues for the present year is likely to supersede the necessity of additional burthens on the community for the service of the ensuing year. This, however, will be better ascertained in the course of the session, and it is proper to add that the information alluded to proceeds upon the supposition of no material extension of the spirit of hostility.

I can not dismiss the subject of Indian affairs without again recommending to your consideration the expediency of more adequate provision for giving energy to the laws throughout our interior frontier and for restraining the commission of outrages upon the Indians, without which all pacific plans must prove nugatory. To enable, by competent rewards, the employment of qualified and trusty persons to reside among them as agents would also contribute to the preservation of peace and good neighborhood. If in addition to these expedients an eligible plan could be devised for promoting civilization among the friendly tribes and for carrying on trade with them upon a scale equal to their wants and under regulations calculated to protect them from imposition and extortion, its influence in cementing their interest with ours could not but be considerable.

The prosperous state of our revenue has been intimated. This would be still more the case were it not for the impediments which in some places continue to embarrass the collection of the duties on spirits distilled within the United States. These impediments have lessened and are lessening in local extent, and, as applied to the community at large, the contentment with the law appears to be progressive.

But symptoms of increased opposition having lately manifested themselves in certain quarters, I judged a special interposition on my part proper and advisable, and under this impression have issued a proclamation warning against all unlawful combinations and proceedings having for their object or tending to obstruct the operation of the law in question, and announcing that all lawful ways and means would be strictly put in execution for bringing to justice the infractors thereof and securing obedience thereto.

Measures have also been taken for the prosecution of offenders, and Congress may be assured that nothing within constitutional and legal limits which may depend upon me shall be wanting to assert and maintain the just authority of the laws. In fulfilling this trust I shall count entirely upon the full cooperation of the other departments of the Government and upon the zealous support of all good citizens.

I can not forbear to bring again into the view of the Legislature the subject of a revision of the judiciary system. A representation from the judges of the Supreme Court, which will be laid before you, points out some of the inconveniences that are experienced. In the course of the execution of the laws considerations arise out of the structure of that system which in some cases tend to relax their efficacy. As connected with this subject, provisions to facilitate the taking of bail upon processes out of the courts of the United States and a supplementary definition of offenses against the Constitution and laws of the Union and of the punishment for such offenses will, it is presumed, be found worthy of particular attention.

Observations on the value of peace with other nations are unnecessary. It would be wise, however, by timely provisions to guard against those acts of our own citizens which might tend to disturb it, and to put ourselves in a condition to give that satisfaction to foreign nations which we may sometimes have occasion to require from them. I particularly recommend to your consideration the means of preventing those aggressions by our citizens on the territory of other nations, and other infractions of the law of nations, which, furnishing just subject of complaint, might endanger our peace with them; and, in general, the maintenance of a friendly intercourse with foreign powers will be presented to your attention by the expiration of the law for that purpose, which takes place, if not renewed, at the close of the present session.

In execution of the authority given by the Legislature measures have been taken for engaging some artists from abroad to aid in the establishment of our mint. Others have been employed at home. Provision has been made of the requisite buildings, and these are now putting into proper condition for the purposes of the establishment. There has also been a small beginning in the coinage of half dimes, the want of small coins in circulation calling the first attention to them.

The regulation of foreign coins in correspondency with the principles of our national coinage, as being essential to their due operation and to order in our money concerns, will, I doubt not, be resumed and completed.

It is represented that some provisions in the law which establishes the post-office operate, in experiment, against the transmission of newspapers to distant parts of the country. Should this, upon due inquiry, be found to be the fact, a full conviction of the importance of facilitating the circulation of political intelligence and information will, I doubt not, lead to the application of a remedy.

The adoption of a constitution for the State of Kentucky has been notified to me. The Legislature will share with me in the satisfaction which arises from an event interesting to the happiness of the part of the nation to which it relates and conducive to the general order.

It is proper likewise to inform you that since my last communication on the subject, and in further execution of the acts severally making provision for the public debt and for the reduction thereof, three new loans have been effected, each for 3,000,000 florins—one at Antwerp, at the annual interest of 4½ per cent, with an allowance of 4 per cent in lieu of all charges, and the other two at Amsterdam, at the annual interest of 4 per cent, with an allowance of 5½ per cent in one case and of 5 per cent in the other in lieu of all charges. The rates of these loans and the circumstances under which they have been made are confirmations of the high state of our credit abroad.

Among the objects to which these funds have been directed to be applied, the payment of the debts due to certain foreign officers, according to the provision made during the last session, has been embraced.

Gentlemen of the House of Representatives:

I entertain a strong hope that the state of the national finances is now sufficiently matured to enable you to enter upon a systematic and effectual arrangement for the regular redemption and discharge of the public debt, according to the right which has been reserved to the Government. No measure can be more desirable, whether viewed with an eye to its intrinsic importance or to the general sentiment and wish of the nation.

Provision is likewise requisite for the reimbursement of the loan which has been made of the Bank of the United States, pursuant to the eleventh section of the act by which it is incorporated. In fulfilling the public stipulations in this particular it is expected a valuable saving will be made.

Appropriations for the current service of the ensuing year and for such extraordinaries as may require provision will demand, and I doubt not will engage, your early attention.

Gentlemen of the Senate and of the House of Representatives:

I content myself with recalling your attention generally to such objects, not particularized in my present, as have been suggested in my former communications to you.

Various temporary laws will expire during the present session. Among these, that which regulates trade and intercourse with the Indian tribes will merit particular notice.

The results of your common deliberations hitherto will, I trust, be productive of solid and durable advantages to our constituents, such as, by conciliating more and more their ultimate suffrage, will tend to strengthen and confirm their attachment to that Constitution of Government upon which, under Divine Providence, materially depend their union, their safety, and their happiness.

Still further to promote and secure these inestimable ends there is nothing which can have a more powerful tendency than the careful cultivation of harmony, combined with a due regard to stability, in the public councils.

G⁰ WASHINGTON.

ADDRESS OF THE SENATE TO GEORGE WASHINGTON, PRESIDENT
OF THE UNITED STATES.

The PRESIDENT OF THE UNITED STATES:

Accept, sir, our grateful acknowledgments for your address at the opening of the present session. We participate with you in the satisfaction arising from the continuance of the general prosperity of the nation, but it is not without the most sincere concern that we are informed that the reiterated efforts which have been made to establish peace with the hostile Indians have hitherto failed to accomplish that desired object. Hoping that the measures still depending may prove more successful than those which have preceded them, we shall nevertheless concur in every necessary preparation for the alternative, and should the Indians on either side of the Ohio persist in their hostilities, fidelity to the Union, as well as affection for our fellow-citizens on the frontiers, will insure our decided cooperation in every measure which shall be deemed requisite for their protection and safety.

At the same time that we avow the obligation of the Government to afford its protection to every part of the Union, we can not refrain from expressing our regret that even a small portion of our fellow-citizens in any quarter of it should have combined to oppose the operation of the law for the collection of duties on spirits distilled within the United States, a law repeatedly sanctioned by the authority of the nation, and at this juncture materially connected with the safety and protection of those who oppose it. Should the means already adopted fail in securing obedience to this law, such further measures as may be thought necessary to carry the same into complete operation can not fail to receive the approbation of the Legislature and the support of every patriotic citizen.

It yields us particular pleasure to learn that the productiveness of the revenue of the present year will probably supersede the necessity of any additional tax for the service of the next.

The organization of the government of the State of Kentucky being an event peculiarly interesting to a part of our fellow-citizens and conducive to the general order, affords us particular satisfaction.

We are happy to learn that the high state of our credit abroad has been evinced by the terms on which the new loans have been negotiated.

In the course of the session we shall proceed to take into consideration the several objects which you have been pleased to recommend to our attention, and keeping in view the importance of union and stability in the public councils, we shall labor to render our decisions conducive to the safety and happiness of our country.

We repeat with pleasure our assurances of confidence in your Administration and our ardent wish that your unabated zeal for the public good may be rewarded by the durable prosperity of the nation, and every ingredient of personal happiness.

JOHN LANGDON,

NOVEMBER 9, 1792.   *President pro tempore.*

REPLY OF THE PRESIDENT.

I derive much pleasure, gentlemen, from your very satisfactory address. The renewed assurances of your confidence in my Administration and the expression of your wish for my personal happiness claim and receive my particular acknowledgments. In my future endeavor for the public welfare, to which my duty may call me, I shall not cease to count upon the firm, enlightened, and patriotic support of the Senate.

GO WASHINGTON.

NOVEMBER 9, 1792.

ADDRESS OF THE HOUSE OF REPRESENTATIVES TO GEORGE WASHINGTON, PRESIDENT OF THE UNITED STATES.

SIR: The House of Representatives, who always feel a satisfaction in meeting you, are much concerned that the occasion for mutual felicitation afforded by the circumstances favorable to the national prosperity should be abated by a continuance of the hostile spirit of many of the Indian tribes, and particularly that the reiterated efforts for effecting a general pacification with them should have issued in new proofs of their persevering enmity and the barbarous sacrifice of citizens who, as the messengers of peace, were distinguishing themselves by their zeal for the public service. In our deliberations on this important department of our affairs we shall be disposed to pursue every measure that may be dictated by the sincerest desire, on one hand, of cultivating peace and manifesting by every practicable regulation our benevolent regard for the welfare of those misguided people, and by the duty we feel, on the other, to provide effectually for the safety and protection of our fellow-citizens.

While with regret we learn that symptoms of opposition to the law imposing duties on spirits distilled within the United States have manifested themselves, we reflect with consolation that they are confined to a small portion of our fellow-citizens. It is not more essential to the preservation of true liberty that a government should be always ready to listen to the representations of its constituents and to accommodate its measures to the sentiments and wishes of every part of them, as far as will consist with the good of the whole, than it is that the just authority of the laws should be steadfastly maintained. Under this impression every department of the Government and all good citizens must approve the measures you have taken and the purpose you have formed to execute this part of your trust with firmness and energy; and be assured, sir, of every constitutional aid and cooperation which may become requisite on our part. And we hope that, while the progress of contentment under the law in question is as obvious as it is rational, no particular part of the community may be permitted to withdraw from the general burthens of the country by a conduct as irreconcilable to national justice as it is inconsistent with public decency.

The productive state of the public revenue and the confirmation of the credit of the United States abroad, evinced by the loans at Antwerp and Amsterdam, are communications the more gratifying as they enforce the obligation to enter on systematic and effectual arrangements for discharging the public debt as fast as the conditions of it will permit, and we take pleasure in the opportunity to assure you of our entire concurrence in the opinion that no measure can be more desirable, whether viewed with an eye to the urgent wish of the community or the intrinsic importance of promoting so happy a change in our situation.

The adoption of a constitution for the State of Kentucky is an event on which we join in all the satisfaction you have expressed. It may be considered as particularly interesting since, besides the immediate benefits resulting from it, it is another auspicious demonstration of the facility and success with which an enlightened people is capable of providing, by free and deliberate plans of government, for their own safety and happiness.

The operation of the law establishing the post-office, as it relates to the transmission of newspapers, will merit our particular inquiry and attention, the circulation of political intelligence through these vehicles being justly reckoned among the surest means of preventing the degeneracy of a free government, as well as of recommending every salutary public measure to the confidence and cooperation of all virtuous citizens.

The several other matters which you have communicated and recommended will in their order receive the attention due to them, and our discussions will in all cases, we trust, be guided by a proper respect for harmony and stability in the public councils and a desire to conciliate more and more the attachment of our constituents to the Constitution, by measures accommodated to the true ends for which it was established.

NOVEMBER 10, 1792.

REPLY OF THE PRESIDENT.

GENTLEMEN: It gives me pleasure to express to you the satisfaction which your address affords me. I feel, as I ought, the approbation you manifest of the measures I have taken and the purpose I have formed to maintain, pursuant to the trust reposed in me by the Constitution, the respect which is due to the laws, and the assurance which you at the same time give me of every constitutional aid and cooperation that may become requisite on your part.

This is a new proof of that enlightened solicitude for the establishment and confirmation of public order which, embracing a zealous regard for the principles of true liberty, has guided the deliberations of the House of Representatives, a perseverance in which can alone secure, under the livine blessing, the real and permanent felicity of our common country.

G⁰ WASHINGTON.

NOVEMBER 12, 1792.

SPECIAL MESSAGES.

UNITED STATES, *November 7, 1792.*
Gentlemen of the Senate and of the House of Representatives:

In pursuance of the law, I now lay before you a statement of the administration of the funds appropriated to certain foreign purposes, together with a letter from the Secretary of State explaining the same.

I also lay before you a copy of a letter and representation from the Chief Justice and associate judges of the Supreme Court of the United States, stating the difficulties and inconveniences which attend the discharge of their duties according to the present judiciary system.

A copy of a letter from the judges attending the circuit court of the United States for the North Carolina district in June last, containing their observations on an act, passed during the last session of Congress, entitled "An act to provide for the settlement of the claims of widows and orphans barred by the limitations heretofore established, and to regulate the claims to invalid pensions;" and

A copy of the constitution formed for the State of Kentucky.

GQ WASHINGTON.

UNITED STATES, *November 9, 1792.*
Gentlemen of the Senate and of the House of Representatives:

I now lay before you a letter from the Secretary of State, covering the copy of one from the governor of Virginia, with the several papers therein referred to, on the subject of the boundary between that State and the territory of the United States south of the Ohio. It will remain with the Legislature to take such measures as it shall think best for settling the said boundary with that State, and at the same time, if it thinks proper, for extending the settlement to the State of Kentucky, between which and the same territory the boundary is as yet undetermined.

GQ WASHINGTON.

UNITED STATES, *November 22, 1792.*
Gentlemen of the Senate and of the House of Representatives:

I send you herewith the abstract of a supplementary arrangement which has been made by me, pursuant to the acts of the 3d day of March, 1791, and the 8th day of May, 1792, for raising a revenue upon foreign and domestic distilled spirits, in respect to the subdivisions and officers which have appeared to me necessary and to the allowances for their respective services to the supervisors, inspectors, and other officers of inspection, together with the estimates of the amount of compensations and charges.

GQ WASHINGTON.

UNITED STATES, *December 6, 1792.*

Gentlemen of the Senate and of the House of Representatives:

The several measures which have been pursued to induce the hostile Indian tribes north of the Ohio to enter into a conference or treaty with the United States at which all causes of difference might be fully understood and justly and amicably arranged have already been submitted to both Houses of Congress.

The papers herewith sent will inform you of the result.

G⁰ WASHINGTON.

UNITED STATES, *December 7, 1792.*

Gentlemen of the Senate and of the House of Representatives:

I lay before you two letters, with their inclosures, from the governor of the Southwestern territory, and an extract of a letter to him from the Department of War.

These and a letter of the 9th of October last, which has been already communicated to you, from the same Department to the governor, will shew in what manner the first section of the act of the last session which provides for calling out the militia for the repelling of Indian invasions has been executed. It remains to be considered by Congress whether in the present situation of the United States it be advisable or not to pursue any further or other measures than those which have been already adopted. The nature of the subject does of itself call for your immediate attention to it, and I must add that upon the result of your deliberations the future conduct of the Executive will on this occasion materially depend.

G⁰ WASHINGTON.

UNITED STATES, *January 23, 1793.*

Gentlemen of the Senate and of the House of Representatives:

Since my last communication to you on the subject of the revenue on distilled spirits it has been found necessary, on experience, to revise and amend the arrangements relative thereto in regard to certain surveys and the officers thereof in the district of North Carolina, which I have done accordingly in the manner following:

First. The several counties of the said district originally and heretofore contained within the first, second, and third surveys have been allotted into and are now contained in two surveys, one of which (to be hereafter denominated the first) comprehends the town of Wilmington and the counties of Onslow, New Hanover, Brunswick, Robertson, Sampson, Craven, Jones, Lenox, Glascow, Johnston, and Wayne, and the other of which (to be hereafter denominated the second) comprehends the counties of Kurrituck, Camden, Pasquotank, Perquimans, Chowan, Gates, Hartford, Tyrrel, Bertie, Carteret, Hyde, Beaufort, and Pitt.

Secondly. The several counties of the said district originally and here-tofore contained within the fifth survey of the district aforesaid has been allotted into and is contained in two surveys, one of which (to be here-after denominated the third) comprehends the counties of Mecklenburg, Rowan, Iredell, Montgomery, Guilford, Rockingham, Stokes, and Surrey, and the other of which (to be hereafter denominated the fifth) compre-hends the counties of Lincoln, Rutherford, Burke, Buncombe, and Wilkes.

Thirdly. The duties of the inspector of the revenue in and for the third survey as constituted above is to be performed for the present by the supervisor.

Fourthly. The compensations of the inspector of the revenue for the first survey as above constituted are to be a salary of $250 per annum and commissions and other emoluments similar to those heretofore allowed to the inspector of the late first survey as it was originally constituted.

Fifthly. The compensations of the inspector of the revenue for the second survey as above constituted are to be a salary of $100 per annum and the commissions and other emoluments heretofore allowed to the inspector of the late third survey as it was originally constituted.

Sixthly. The compensations of the inspector of the revenue for the fifth survey as above constituted are to be a salary of $120 per annum and the commissions and other emoluments similar to those heretofore allowed to the inspector of the late fifth survey as it was originally constituted.

G? WASHINGTON.

UNITED STATES, *January 25, 1793.*

Gentlemen of the Senate and of the House of Representatives:

I lay before you an official statement of the expenditure to the year 1792 from the sum of $10,000, granted to defray the contingent expenses of Government by an act passed on the 26th of March, 1790.

Also an abstract of a supplementary arrangement made in the district of North Carolina in regard to certain surveys to facilitate the execu-tion of the law laying a duty on distilled spirits.

G? WASHINGTON.

UNITED STATES, *February 13, 1793.*

Gentlemen of the Senate:

I lay before you for your consideration and advice a treaty of peace and friendship made and concluded on the 27th day of September, 1792, by Brigadier-General Rufus Putnam, in behalf of the United States, with the Wabash and Illinois tribes of Indians, and also the proceedings attending the said treaty, the explanation of the fourth article thereof, and a map explanatory of the reservation to the French inhabitants and the general claim of the said Indians.

In connection with this subject I also lay before the Senate the copy of a paper which has been delivered by a man by the name of John Baptiste Mayeé, who has accompanied the Wabash Indians at present in this city.

It will appear by the certificate of Brigadier-General Putnam that the Wabash Indians disclaimed the validity of the said paper, excepting a certain tract upon the Wabash, as mentioned in the proceedings.

The instructions to Brigadier-General Putnam of the 22d of May, together with a letter to him of the 7th of August, 1792, were laid before the Senate on the 7th of November, 1792.

After the Senate shall have considered this treaty, I request that they would give me their advice whether the same shall be ratified and confirmed; and if to be ratified and confirmed, whether it would not be proper, in order to prevent any misconception hereafter of the fourth article, to guard in the ratification the exclusive preemption of the United States to the lands of the said Indians.

GỌ WASHINGTON.

UNITED STATES, *February 18, 1793.*

Gentlemen of the Senate and of the House of Representatives:

I now lay before you a report and plat of the territory of the United States on the Potomac as given in by the commissioners of that territory, together with a letter from the Secretary of State which accompanied them. These papers, being original, are to be again deposited with the records of the Department of State after having answered the purpose of your information.

GỌ WASHINGTON.

UNITED STATES, *February 19, 1793.*

Gentlemen of the House of Representatives:

It has been agreed on the part of the United States that a treaty or conference shall be held at the ensuing season with the hostile Indians northwest of the Ohio, in order to remove, if possible, all causes of difference and to establish a solid peace with them.

As the estimates heretofore presented to the House for the current year did not contemplate this object, it will be proper that an express provision be made by law as well for the general expenses of the treaty as to establish the compensation to be allowed the commissioners who shall be appointed for the purpose.

I shall therefore direct the Secretary of War to lay before you an estimate of the expenses which may probably attend this measure.

GỌ WASHINGTON.

UNITED STATES, *February 27, 1793.*

Gentlemen of the Senate and of the House of Representatives:

I lay before you a copy of an exemplification of an act of the legislature of New York ceding to the United States the jurisdiction of certain lands on Montauk Point for the purpose mentioned in said act, and the copy of a letter from the governor of New York to the Secretary of State, which accompanied said exemplification.

GO WASHINGTON.

UNITED STATES, *February 28, 1793.*

Gentlemen of the Senate:

I was led by a consideration of the qualifications of William Patterson, of New Jersey, to nominate him an associate justice of the Supreme Court of the United States. It has since occurred that he was a member of the Senate when the law creating that office was passed, and that the time for which he was elected is not yet expired. I think it my duty, therefore, to declare that I deem the nomination to have been null by the Constitution.

GO WASHINGTON.

PROCLAMATIONS.

[From Freneau's National Gazette of December 15, 1792.]

BY THE PRESIDENT OF THE UNITED STATES.

Whereas I have received authentic information that certain lawless and wicked persons of the western frontier in the State of Georgia did lately invade, burn, and destroy a town belonging to the Cherokee Nation, although in amity with the United States, and put to death several Indians of that nation; and

Whereas such outrageous conduct not only violates the rights of humanity, but also endangers the public peace, and it highly becomes the honor and good faith of the United States to pursue all legal means for the punishment of those atrocious offenders:

I have therefore thought fit to issue this my proclamation, hereby exhorting all the citizens of the United States and requiring all the officers thereof, according to their respective stations, to use their utmost endeavors to apprehend and bring those offenders to justice. And I do moreover offer a reward of $500 for each and every of the above-named persons who shall be so apprehended and brought to justice and shall be proved to have assumed or exercised any command or authority among the perpetrators of the crimes aforesaid at the time of committing the same.

In testimony whereof I have caused the seal of the United States to be affixed to these presents, and signed the same with my hand.

[SEAL.]   Done at the city of Philadelphia, the 12th day of December, A. D. 1792, and of the Independence of the United States the seventeenth.   GO WASHINGTON.

By the President:
    TH: JEFFERSON.

[From Annals of Congress, Second Congress, 666.]

MARCH 1, 1793.

The President of the United States to the President of the Senate:

Certain matters touching the public good requiring that the Senate shall be convened on Monday, the 4th instant, I have desired their attendance, as I do yours, by these presents, at the Senate Chamber, in Philadelphia, on that day, then and there to receive and deliberate on such communications as shall be made to you on my part.

GO WASHINGTON.

SECOND INAUGURAL ADDRESS.

IN THE CITY OF PHILADELPHIA, PA.

FELLOW-CITIZENS: I am again called upon by the voice of my country to execute the functions of its Chief Magistrate. When the occasion proper for it shall arrive, I shall endeavor to express the high sense I entertain of this distinguished honor, and of the confidence which has been reposed in me by the people of united America.

Previous to the execution of any official act of the President the Constitution requires an oath of office. This oath I am now about to take, and in your presence: That if it shall be found during my administration of the Government I have in any instance violated willingly or knowingly the injunctions thereof, I may (besides incurring constitutional punishment) be subject to the upbraidings of all who are now witnesses of the present solemn ceremony.

MARCH 4, 1793.

FIFTH ANNUAL ADDRESS.

PHILADELPHIA, *December 3, 1793.*

Fellow-Citizens of the Senate and of the House of Representatives:

Since the commencement of the term for which I have been again called into office no fit occasion has arisen for expressing to my fellow-citizens at large the deep and respectful sense which I feel of the renewed testimony of public approbation. While on the one hand it awakened my gratitude for all those instances of affectionate partiality with which I have been honored by my country, on the other it could not prevent an earnest wish for that retirement from which no private consideration should ever have torn me. But influenced by the belief that my conduct would be estimated according to its real motives, and that the people, and the authorities derived from them, would support exertions having nothing personal for their object, I have obeyed the suffrage which commanded me to resume the Executive power; and I humbly implore that Being on whose will the fate of nations depends to crown with success our mutual endeavors for the general happiness.

As soon as the war in Europe had embraced those powers with whom the United States have the most extensive relations there was reason to apprehend that our intercourse with them might be interrupted and our disposition for peace drawn into question by the suspicions too often entertained by belligerent nations. It seemed, therefore, to be my duty to admonish our citizens of the consequences of a contraband trade and of hostile acts to any of the parties, and to obtain by a declaration of the existing legal state of things an easier admission of our right to the immunities belonging to our situation. Under these impressions the proclamation which will be laid before you was issued.

In this posture of affairs, both new and delicate, I resolved to adopt general rules which should conform to the treaties and assert the privileges of the United States. These were reduced into a system, which will be communicated to you. Although I have not thought myself at liberty to forbid the sale of the prizes permitted by our treaty of commerce with France to be brought into our ports, I have not refused to cause them to be restored when they were taken within the protection of our territory, or by vessels commissioned or equipped in a warlike form within the limits of the United States.

It rests with the wisdom of Congress to correct, improve, or enforce this plan of procedure; and it will probably be found expedient to extend the legal code and the jurisdiction of the courts of the United States to many cases which, though dependent on principles already recognized, demand some further provisions.

Where individuals shall, within the United States, array themselves in hostility against any of the powers at war, or enter upon military expeditions or enterprises within the jurisdiction of the United States, or usurp and exercise judicial authority within the United States, or where the penalties on violations of the law of nations may have been indistinctly marked, or are inadequate—these offenses can not receive too early and close an attention, and require prompt and decisive remedies.

Whatsoever those remedies may be, they will be well administered by the judiciary, who possess a long-established course of investigation, effectual process, and officers in the habit of executing it.

In like manner, as several of the courts have doubted, under particular circumstances, their power to liberate the vessels of a nation at peace, and even of a citizen of the United States, although seized under a false color of being hostile property, and have denied their power to liberate certain captures within the protection of our territory, it would seem proper to regulate their jurisdiction in these points. But if the Executive is to be the resort in either of the two last-mentioned cases, it is hoped that he will be authorized by law to have facts ascertained by the courts when for his own information he shall request it.

I can not recommend to your notice measures for the fulfillment of our duties to the rest of the world without again pressing upon you the necessity of placing ourselves in a condition of complete defense and of exacting from them the fulfillment of their duties toward us. The United States ought not to indulge a persuasion that, contrary to the order of human events, they will forever keep at a distance those painful appeals to arms with which the history of every other nation abounds. There is a rank due to the United States among nations which will be withheld, if not absolutely lost, by the reputation of weakness. If we desire to avoid insult, we must be able to repel it; if we desire to secure peace, one of the most powerful instruments of our rising prosperity, it must be known that we are at all times ready for war. The documents which will be presented to you will shew the amount and kinds of arms and military stores now in our magazines and arsenals; and yet an addition even to these supplies can not with prudence be neglected, as it would leave nothing to the uncertainty of procuring of warlike apparatus in the moment of public danger.

Nor can such arrangements, with such objects, be exposed to the censure or jealousy of the warmest friends of republican government. They are incapable of abuse in the hands of the militia, who ought to possess a pride in being the depository of the force of the Republic, and may be trained to a degree of energy equal to every military exigency of the United States. But it is an inquiry which can not be too solemnly pursued, whether the act "more effectually to provide for the national defense by establishing an uniform militia throughout the United States" has organized them so as to produce their full effect; whether your own experience in the several States has not detected some imperfections in the scheme, and whether a material feature in an improvement of it ought not to be to afford an opportunity for the study of those branches of the military art which can scarcely ever be attained by practice alone.

The connection of the United States with Europe has become extremely interesting. The occurrences which relate to it and have passed under the knowledge of the Executive will be exhibited to Congress in a subsequent communication.

When we contemplate the war on our frontiers, it may be truly affirmed that every reasonable effort has been made to adjust the causes of dissension with the Indians north of the Ohio. The instructions given to the commissioners evince a moderation and equity proceeding from a sincere love of peace, and a liberality having no restriction but the essential interests and dignity of the United States. The attempt, however, of an amicable negotiation having been frustrated, the troops have marched to act offensively. Although the proposed treaty did not arrest the progress of military preparation, it is doubtful how far the advance of the season, before good faith justified active movements, may retard them during the remainder of the year. From the papers and intelligence which relate to this important subject you will determine whether the deficiency in the number of troops granted by law shall be compensated by succors of militia, or additional encouragements shall be proposed to recruits.

An anxiety has been also demonstrated by the Executive for peace with the Creeks and the Cherokees. The former have been relieved with corn and with clothing, and offensive measures against them prohibited during the recess of Congress. To satisfy the complaints of the latter, prosecutions have been instituted for the violences committed upon them. But the papers which will be delivered to you disclose the critical footing on which we stand in regard to both those tribes, and it is with Congress to pronounce what shall be done.

After they shall have provided for the present emergency, it will merit their most serious labors to render tranquillity with the savages permanent by creating ties of interest. Next to a rigorous execution of justice on the violators of peace, the establishment of commerce with the Indian nations in behalf of the United States is most likely to conciliate their attachment. But it ought to be conducted without fraud, without extortion, with constant and plentiful supplies, with a ready market for the commodities of the Indians and a stated price for what they give in payment and receive in exchange. Individuals will not pursue such a traffic unless they be allured by the hope of profit; but it will be enough for the United States to be reimbursed only. Should this recommendation accord with the opinion of Congress, they will recollect that it can not be accomplished by any means yet in the hands of the Executive.

Gentlemen of the House of Representatives:

The commissioners charged with the settlement of accounts between the United States and individual States concluded their important functions within the time limited by law, and the balances struck in their report, which will be laid before Congress, have been placed on the books of the Treasury.

On the 1st day of June last an installment of 1,000,000 florins became payable on the loans of the United States in Holland. This was adjusted by a prolongation of the period of reimbursement in nature of a new loan at an interest of 5 per cent for the term of ten years, and the expenses of this operation were a commission of 3 per cent.

The first installment of the loan of $2,000,000 from the Bank of the United States has been paid, as was directed by law. For the second it is necessary that provision should be made.

No pecuniary consideration is more urgent than the regular redemption and discharge of the public debt. On none can delay be more injurious or an economy of time more valuable.

The productiveness of the public revenues hitherto has continued to equal the anticipations which were formed of it, but it is not expected to prove commensurate with all the objects which have been suggested. Some auxiliary provisions will therefore, it is presumed, be requisite, and it is hoped that these may be made consistently with a due regard to the convenience of our citizens, who can not but be sensible of the true wisdom of encountering a small present addition to their contributions to obviate a future accumulation of burthens.

But here I can not forbear to recommend a repeal of the tax on the transportation of public prints. There is no resource so firm for the Government of the United States as the affections of the people, guided by an enlightened policy ; and to this primary good nothing can conduce more than a faithful representation of public proceedings, diffused without restraint throughout the United States.

An estimate of the appropriations necessary for the current service of the ensuing year and a statement of a purchase of arms and military stores made during the recess will be presented to Congress.

Gentlemen of the Senate and of the House of Representatives:

The several subjects to which I have now referred open a wide range to your deliberations and involve some of the choicest interests of our common country. Permit me to bring to your remembrance the magnitude of your task. Without an unprejudiced coolness the welfare of the Government may be hazarded ; without harmony as far as consists with freedom of sentiment its dignity may be lost. But as the legislative proceedings of the United States will never, I trust, be reproached for the want of temper or of candor, so shall not the public happiness languish from the want of my strenuous and warmest cooperation.

G? WASHINGTON.

ADDRESS OF THE SENATE TO GEORGE WASHINGTON, PRESIDENT
OF THE UNITED STATES.

The PRESIDENT OF THE UNITED STATES:

Accept, sir, the thanks of the Senate for your speech delivered to both Houses of Congress at the opening of the session. Your reelection to the Chief Magistracy of the United States gives us sincere pleasure. We consider it as an event every way propitious to the happiness of our country, and your compliance with the call as a fresh instance of the patriotism which has so repeatedly led you to sacrifice private inclination to the public good. In the unanimity which a second time marks this important national act we trace with particular satisfaction, besides the distinguished tribute paid to the virtues and abilities which it recognizes, another proof of that just discernment and constancy of sentiments and views which have hitherto characterized the citizens of the United States.

As the European powers with whom the United States have the most extensive relations were involved in war, in which we had taken no part, it seemed necessary that the disposition of the nation for peace should be promulgated to the world, as well for the purpose of admonishing our citizens of the consequences of a contraband trade and of acts hostile to any of the belligerent parties as to obtain by a declaration of the existing legal state of things an easier admission of our right to the immunities of our situation. We therefore contemplate with pleasure the proclamation by you issued, and give it our hearty approbation. We deem it a measure well timed and wise, manifesting a watchful solicitude for the welfare of the nation and calculated to promote it.

The several important matters presented to our consideration will, in the course of the session, engage all the attention to which they are respectively entitled, and as the public happiness will be the sole guide of our deliberations, we are perfectly assured of receiving your strenuous and most zealous cooperation.

JOHN ADAMS,
Vice-President of the United States and President of the Senate.
DECEMBER 9, 1793.

REPLY OF THE PRESIDENT.

GENTLEMEN: The pleasure expressed by the Senate on my reelection to the station which I fill commands my sincere and warmest acknowledgments. If this be an event which promises the smallest addition to the happiness of our country, as it is my duty so shall it be my study to realize the expectation.

The decided approbation which the proclamation now receives from your House, by completing the proofs that this measure is considered as manifesting a vigilant attention to the welfare of the United States, brings with it a peculiar gratification to my mind.

The other important subjects which have been communicated to you will, I am confident, receive a due discussion, and the result will, I trust, prove fortunate to the United States.

Gº WASHINGTON.

DECEMBER 10, 1793.

ADDRESS OF THE HOUSE OF REPRESENTATIVES TO GEORGE WASHINGTON, PRESIDENT OF THE UNITED STATES.

SIR: The Representatives of the people of the United States, in meeting you for the first time since you have been again called by an unanimous suffrage to your present station, find an occasion which they embrace with no less sincerity than promptitude for expressing to you their congratulations on so distinguished a testimony of public approbation, and their entire confidence in the purity and patriotism of the motives which have produced this obedience to the voice of your country. It is to virtues which have commanded long and universal reverence and services from which have flowed great and lasting benefits that the tribute of praise may be paid without the reproach of flattery, and it is from the same sources that the fairest anticipations may be derived in favor of the public happiness.

The United States having taken no part in the war which had embraced in Europe the powers with whom they have the most extensive relations, the maintenance of peace was justly to be regarded as one of the most important duties of the Magistrate charged with the faithful execution of the laws. We accordingly witness with approbation and pleasure the vigilance with which you have guarded against an interruption of that blessing by your proclamation admonishing our citizens of the consequences of illicit or hostile acts toward the belligerent parties, and promoting by a declaration of the existing legal state of things an easier admission of our right to the immunities belonging to our situation.

The connection of the United States with Europe has evidently become extremely interesting. The communications which remain to be exhibited to us will no doubt assist in giving us a fuller view of the subject and in guiding our deliberations to such results as may comport with the rights and true interests of our country.

We learn with deep regret that the measures, dictated by love of peace, for obtaining an amicable termination of the afflicting war on our frontiers have been frustrated, and that a resort to offensive measures should have again become necessary. As the latter, however, must be rendered more satisfactory in proportion to the solicitude for peace manifested by the former, it is to be hoped they will be pursued under the better auspices on that account, and be finally crowned with more happy success.

In relation to the particular tribes of Indians against whom offensive measures have been prohibited, as well as on all the other important subjects which you have presented to our view, we shall bestow the attention which they claim. We can not, however, refrain at this time from particularly expressing our concurrence in your anxiety for the regular discharge of the public debts as fast as circumstances and events will permit and in the policy of removing any impediments that may be found in the way of a faithful representation of public proceedings throughout the United States, being persuaded with you that on no subject more than the former can delay be more injurious or an economy of time more valuable, and that with respect to the latter no resource is so firm for the Government of the United States as the affections of the people, guided by an enlightened policy.

Throughout our deliberations we shall endeavor to cherish every sentiment which may contribute to render them conducive to the dignity as well as to the welfare of the United States; and we join with you in imploring that Being on whose will the fate of nations depends to crown with success our mutual endeavors.

DECEMBER 6, 1793.

REPLY OF THE PRESIDENT.

GENTLEMEN: I shall not affect to conceal the cordial satisfaction which I derive from the address of the House of Representatives. Whatsoever those services may be which you have sanctioned by your favor, it is a sufficient reward that they have been accepted as they were meant. For the fulfillment of your anticipations of the future I can give no other assurance than that the motives which you approve shall continue unchanged.

It is truly gratifying to me to learn that the proclamation has been considered as a seasonable guard against the interruption of the public peace. Nor can I doubt that the subjects which I have recommended to your attention as depending on legislative provisions will receive a discussion suited to their importance. With every reason, then, it may be expected that your deliberations, under the divine blessing, will be matured to the honor and happiness of the United States.

G⁰ WASHINGTON.

DECEMBER 7, 1793.

SPECIAL MESSAGES.

UNITED STATES, *December 5, 1793.*

Gentlemen of the Senate and of the House of Representatives:

As the present situation of the several nations of Europe, and especially of those with which the United States have important relations, can not but render the state of things between them and us matter of interesting inquiry to the Legislature, and may indeed give rise to deliberations to which they alone are competent, I have thought it my duty to communicate to them certain correspondences which have taken place.

The representative and executive bodies of France have manifested generally a friendly attachment to this country; have given advantages to our commerce and navigation, and have made overtures for placing these advantages on permanent ground. A decree, however, of the National Assembly subjecting vessels laden with provisions to be carried into their ports and making enemy goods lawful prize in the vessel of a friend, contrary to our treaty, though revoked at one time as to the United States, has been since extended to their vessels also, as has been recently stated to us. Representations on this subject will be immediately given in charge to our minister there, and the result shall be communicated to the Legislature.

It is with extreme concern I have to inform you that the proceedings of the person whom they have unfortunately appointed their minister plenipotentiary here have breathed nothing of the friendly spirit of the nation which sent him. Their tendency, on the contrary, has been to involve us in war abroad and discord and anarchy at home. So far as his acts or those of his agents have threatened our immediate commitment in the war, or flagrant insult to the authority of the laws, their effect has been counteracted by the ordinary cognizance of the laws and by an exertion of the powers confided to me. Where their danger was not imminent they have been borne with from sentiments of regard to his nation, from a sense of their friendship toward us, from a conviction that they would not suffer us to remain long exposed to the action of a person who has so little respected our mutual dispositions, and, I will add, from a reliance on the firmness of my fellow-citizens in their principles of peace and order. In the meantime I have respected and pursued the stipulations of our treaties according to what I judged their true sense, and have withheld no act of friendship which their affairs have called for from us, and which justice to others left us free to perform. I have gone farther. Rather than employ force for the restitution of certain vessels which I deemed the United States bound to restore, I thought it more advisable to satisfy the parties by avowing it to be my opinion that if restitution were not made it would be incumbent on the United States to make compensation. The papers now communicated will more particularly apprise you of these transactions.

The vexations and spoliation understood to have been committed on our vessels and commerce by the cruisers and officers of some of the belligerent powers appear to require attention. The proofs of these, however, not having been brought forward, the descriptions of citizens supposed to have suffered were notified that, on furnishing them to the Executive, due measures would be taken to obtain redress of the past and more effectual provisions against the future. Should such documents be furnished, proper representations will be made thereon, with a just reliance on a redress proportioned to the exigency of the case.

The British Government having undertaken, by orders to the commanders of their armed vessels, to restrain generally our commerce in **corn and other provisions to their own ports and those of their friends,** the instructions now communicated were immediately forwarded to our minister at that Court. In the meantime some discussions on the subject took place between him and them. These are also laid before you, and I may expect to learn the result of his special instructions in time to make it known to the Legislature during their present session.

Very early after the arrival of a British minister here mutual explanations on the inexecution of the treaty of peace were entered into with that minister. These are now laid before you for your information.

On the subjects of mutual interest between this country and Spain negotiations and conferences are now depending. The public good requiring that the present state of these should be made known to the Legislature *in confidence only*, they shall be the subject of a separate and subsequent communication.

G? WASHINGTON.

UNITED STATES, *December 16, 1793.*

Gentlemen of the Senate and of the House of Representatives:

The situation of affairs in Europe in the course of the year 1790 having rendered it possible that a moment might arrive favorable for the arrangement of our unsettled matters with Spain, it was thought proper to prepare our representative at that Court to avail us of it. A confidential person was therefore dispatched to be the bearer of instructions to him, and to supply, by verbal communications, any additional information of which he might find himself in need. The Government of France was at the same time applied to for its aid and influence in this negotiation. Events, however, took a turn which did not present the occasion hoped for.

About the close of the ensuing year I was informed through the representatives of Spain here that their Government would be willing to renew at Madrid the former conferences on these subjects. Though the transfer of scene was not what would have been desired, yet I did not think it important enough to reject the proposition, and therefore, with the advice and consent of the Senate, I appointed commissioners plenipotentiary for negotiating and concluding a treaty with that country on the several subjects of boundary, navigation, and commerce, and gave them the instructions now communicated. Before these negotiations, however, could be got into train the new troubles which had arisen in Europe had produced new combinations among the powers there, the effects of which are but too visible in the proceedings now laid before you.

In the meantime some other points of discussion had arisen with that country, to wit, the restitution of property escaping into the territories of each other, the mutual exchange of fugitives from justice, and, above all, the mutual interferences with the Indians lying between us. I had the best reason to believe that the hostilities threatened and exercised by the Southern Indians on our border were excited by the agents of that Government. Representations were thereon directed to be made by our commissioners to the Spanish Government, and a proposal to cultivate with good faith the peace of each other with those people. In the meantime corresponding suspicions were entertained, or pretended to be entertained, on their part of like hostile excitements by our agents to disturb their peace with the same nations. These were brought forward by the representatives of Spain here in a style which could not fail to produce attention. A claim of patronage and protection of those Indians was asserted; a mediation between them and us by that sovereign assumed; their boundaries with us made a subject of his interference, and at length, at the very moment when these savages were committing daily inroads upon our frontier, we were informed by them that "the continuation of the peace, good harmony, and perfect friendship of the two nations was very problematical for the future, unless the United States should take more convenient measures and of greater energy than those adopted for a long time past."

If their previous correspondence had worn the appearance of a desire to urge on a disagreement, this last declaration left no room to evade it, since it could not be conceived we would submit to the scalping knife and tomahawk of the savage without any resistance. I thought it time, therefore, to know if these were the views of their sovereign, and dispatched a special messenger with instructions to our commissioners, which are among the papers now communicated. Their last letter gives us reason to expect very shortly to know the result. I must add that the Spanish representatives here, perceiving that their last communication had made considerable impression, endeavored to abate this by some subsequent professions, which, being also among the communications to the Legislature, they will be able to form their own conclusions.

G? WASHINGTON.

UNITED STATES, *December 16, 1793.*

Gentlemen of the Senate and of the House of Representatives:

I lay before you a report of the Secretary of State on the measures which have been taken on behalf of the United States for the purpose of obtaining a recognition of our treaty with Morocco and for the ransom of our citizens and establishment of peace with Algiers.

While it is proper our citizens should know that subjects which so much concern their interest and their feelings have duly engaged the attention of their Legislature and Executive, it would still be improper that some particulars of this communication should be made known. The confidential conversation stated in one of the last letters sent herewith is one of these. Both justice and policy require that the source of that information should remain secret. So a knowledge of the sums meant to have been given for peace and ransom might have a disadvantageous influence on future proceedings for the same objects.

G? WASHINGTON.

UNITED STATES, *December 23, 1793.*

Gentlemen of the Senate and of the House of Representatives:

Since the communications which were made to you on the affairs of the United States with Spain and on the truce between Portugal and Algiers some other papers have been received, which, making a part of the same subjects, are now communicated for your information.

G? WASHINGTON.

UNITED STATES, *December 30, 1793.*

Gentlemen of the Senate and of the House of Representatives:

I lay before you, for your consideration, a letter from the Secretary of State, informing me of certain impediments which have arisen to the coinage of the precious metals at the Mint, as also a letter from the same officer relative to certain advances of money which have been made on public account. Should you think proper to sanction what has been done, or be of opinion that anything more shall be done in the same way, you will judge whether there are not circumstances which would render secrecy expedient.

G? WASHINGTON.

UNITED STATES, *January 7, 1794.*

Gentlemen of the Senate and of the House of Representatives:

Experience has shewn that it would be useful to have an officer particularly charged, under the direction of the Department of War, with the duties of receiving, safe-keeping, and distributing the public supplies in all cases in which the laws and the course of service do not devolve them upon other officers, and also with that of superintending in all cases the issues in detail of supplies, with power for that purpose to bring to account all persons intrusted to make such issues in relation thereto.

An establishment of this nature, by securing a regular and punctual accountability for the issues of public supplies, would be a great guard against abuse, would tend to insure their due application and to give public satisfaction on that point.

I therefore recommend to the consideration of Congress the expediency of an establishment of this nature, under such regulations as shall appear to them advisable.

G? WASHINGTON.

UNITED STATES, *January 20, 1794.*

Gentlemen of the Senate and of the House of Representatives:

Having already laid before you a letter of the 16th of August, 1793, from the Secretary of State to our minister at Paris, stating the conduct and urging the recall of the minister plenipotentiary of the Republic of France, I now communicate to you that his conduct has been unequivocally disapproved, and that the strongest assurances have been given that his recall should be expedited without delay.

G⁹ WASHINGTON.

UNITED STATES, *January 21, 1794.*

Gentlemen of the Senate and of the House of Representatives:

It is with satisfaction I announce to you that the alterations which have been made by law in the original plan for raising a duty on spirits distilled within the United States, and on stills, cooperating with better information, have had a considerable influence in obviating the difficulties which have embarrassed that branch of the public revenue. But the obstacles which have been experienced, though lessened, are not yet entirely surmounted, and it would seem that some further legislative provisions may usefully be superadded, which leads me to recall the attention of Congress to the subject. Among the matters which may demand regulation is the effect, in point of organization, produced by the separation of Kentucky from the State of Virginia, and the situation with regard to the law of the territories northwest and southwest of the Ohio.

The laws respecting light-house establishments require, as a condition of their permanent maintenance at the expense of the United States, a complete cession of soil and jurisdiction. The cessions of different States having been qualified with a reservation of the right of serving legal process within the ceded jurisdiction are understood to be inconclusive as annexing a qualification not consonant with the terms of the law. I present this circumstance to the view of Congress, that they may judge whether any alteration ought to be made.

As it appears to be conformable with the intention of the "ordinance for the government of the territory of the United States northwest of the river Ohio," although it is not expressly directed that the laws of that territory should be laid before Congress, I now transmit to you a copy of such as have been passed from July to December, 1792, inclusive, being the last which have been received by the Secretary of State.

G⁹ WASHINGTON.

UNITED STATES, *January 30, 1794.*

Gentlemen of the Senate and of the House of Representatives:

Communications have been made to Congress during the present session with the intention of affording a full view of the posture of affairs on the Southwestern frontiers. By the information which has lately been laid before Congress it appeared that the difficulties with the Creeks had been amicably and happily terminated; but it will be perceived with regret by the papers herewith transmitted that the tranquillity has, unfortunately, been of short duration, owing to the murder of several friendly Indians by some lawless white men.

The condition of things in that quarter requires the serious and immediate consideration of Congress, and the adoption of such wise and vigorous laws as will be competent to the preservation of the national character and of the peace made under the authority of the United States with the several Indian tribes. Experience demonstrates that the existing legal provisions are entirely inadequate to those great objects.

G° WASHINGTON.

UNITED STATES, *February 7, 1794.*

Gentlemen of the Senate and of the House of Representatives:

I transmit to you an act and three ordinances passed by the government of the territory of the United States south of the river Ohio on the 13th and 21st of March and the 7th of May, 1793, and also certain letters from the minister plenipotentiary of the French Republic to the Secretary of State, inclosing dispatches from the general and extraordinary commission of Guadaloupe.

G° WASHINGTON.

UNITED STATES, *February 19, 1794.*

Gentlemen of the Senate and of the House of Representatives:

I lay before you the copy of a letter which I have received from the Chief Justice and associate justices of the Supreme Court of the United States, and, at their desire, the representation mentioned in the said letter, pointing out certain defects in the judiciary system.

G° WASHINGTON.

UNITED STATES, *February 24, 1794.*

Gentlemen of the Senate and of the House of Representatives:

The extracts which I now lay before you, from a letter of our minister at London, are supplementary to some of my past communications, and will appear to be of a confidential nature.

I also transmit to you copies of a letter from the Secretary of State to the minister plenipotentiary of His Britannic Majesty, and of the answer thereto, upon the subject of the treaty between the United States and Great Britain, together with the copy of a letter from Messrs. Carmichael and Short, relative to our affairs with Spain, which letter is connected with a former confidential message.

G° WASHINGTON.

UNITED STATES, *February 26, 1794.*

Gentlemen of the Senate:

I have caused the correspondence which is the subject of your resolution of the 24th day of January last to be laid before me. After an
examination of it I directed copies and translations to be made, except
in those particulars which, in my judgment, for public considerations,
ought not to be communicated.

These copies and translations are now transmitted to the Senate; but
the nature of them manifests the propriety of their being received as
confidential.

G⁰ WASHINGTON.

UNITED STATES, *March 3, 1794.*

Gentlemen of the Senate and of the House of Representatives:

I transmit to you an extract from a letter of Mr. Short, relative to our
affairs with Spain, and copies of two letters from our minister at Lisbon,
with their inclosures, containing intelligence from Algiers. The whole
of these communications are made in confidence, except the passage in
Mr. Short's letter which respects the Spanish convoy.

G⁰ WASHINGTON.

UNITED STATES, *March 5, 1794.*

Gentlemen of the Senate and of the House of Representatives:

The Secretary of State having reported to me upon the several
complaints which have been lodged in his office against the vexations
and spoliations on our commerce since the commencement of the European war, I transmit to you a copy of his statement, together with the
documents upon which it is founded.

G⁰ WASHINGTON.

UNITED STATES, *March 18, 1794.*

Gentlemen of the Senate and of the House of Representatives:

The minister plenipotentiary of the French Republic having requested
an advance of money, I transmit to Congress certain documents relative
to that subject.

G⁰ WASHINGTON.

UNITED STATES, *March 28, 1794.*

Gentlemen of the Senate and of the House of Representatives:

In the execution of the resolution of Congress bearing date the 26th
of March, 1794, and imposing an embargo, I have requested the governors
of the several States to call forth the force of their militia, if it should be
necessary, for the detention of vessels. This power is conceived to be
incidental to an embargo.

It also deserves the attention of Congress how far the clearances from one district to another, under the law as it now stands, may give rise to evasions of the embargo. As one security the collectors have been instructed to refuse to receive the surrender of coasting licenses for the purpose of taking out registers, and to require bond from registered vessels bound from one district to another, for the delivery of the cargo within the United States.

It is not understood that the resolution applies to fishing vessels, although their occupations lie generally in parts beyond the United States. But without further restrictions there is an opportunity of their privileges being used as means of eluding the embargo.

All armed vessels possessing public commissions from any foreign power (letters of marque excepted) are considered as not liable to the embargo.

These circumstances are transmitted to Congress for their consideration.

G⁹ WASHINGTON.

UNITED STATES, *April 4, 1794.*

Gentlemen of the Senate and of the House of Representatives:

I lay before you three letters from our minister in London, advices concerning the Algerine mission from our minister at Lisbon and others, and a letter from the minister plenipotentiary of the French Republic to the Secretary of State, with his answer.

G⁹ WASHINGTON.

UNITED STATES, *April 15, 1794.*

Gentlemen of the Senate and of the House of Representatives:

I lay before you a letter from the minister plenipotentiary of His Britannic Majesty to the Secretary of State; a letter from the secretary of the territory south of the river Ohio, inclosing an ordinance and proclamation of the governor thereof; the translation of so much of a petition of the inhabitants of Post Vincennes, addressed to the President, as relates to Congress, and certain dispatches lately received from our commissioners at Madrid. These dispatches from Madrid being a part of the business which has been hitherto deemed confidential, they are forwarded under that view.

G⁹ WASHINGTON.

UNITED STATES, *April 16, 1794.*

Gentlemen of the Senate:

The communications which I have made to you during your present session from the dispatches of our minister in London contain a serious aspect of our affairs with Great Britain. But as peace ought to be pursued with unremitted zeal before the last resource, which has so often been the scourge of nations, and can not fail to check the advanced prosperity of the United States, is contemplated, I have thought proper to nominate, and do hereby nominate, John Jay as envoy extraordinary of the United States to His Britannic Majesty.

My confidence in our minister plenipotentiary in London continues undiminished. But a mission like this, while it corresponds with the solemnity of the occasion, will announce to the world a solicitude for a friendly adjustment of our complaints and a reluctance to hostility. Going immediately from the United States, such an envoy will carry with him a full knowledge of the existing temper and sensibility of our country, and will thus be taught to vindicate our rights with firmness and to cultivate peace with sincerity.

G? WASHINGTON.

UNITED STATES, *May 12, 1794.*

Gentlemen of the Senate and of the House of Representatives:

As the letter which I forwarded to Congress on the 15th day of April last, from the minister plenipotentiary of His Britannic Majesty to the Secretary of State, in answer to a memorial of our minister in London, related to a very interesting subject, I thought it proper not to delay its communication. But since that time the memorial itself has been received in a letter from our minister, and a reply has been made to that answer by the Secretary of State. Copies of them are therefore now transmitted.

I also send the copy of a letter from the governor of Rhode Island, inclosing an act of the legislature of that State empowering the United States to hold lands within the same for the purpose of erecting fortifications, and certain papers concerning patents for the donation lands to the ancient settlers of Vincennes upon the Wabash.

G? WASHINGTON.

UNITED STATES, *May 20, 1794.*

Gentlemen of the Senate and of the House of Representatives:

In the communications which I have made to Congress during the present session relative to foreign nations I have omitted no opportunity of testifying my anxiety to preserve the United States in peace. It is peculiarly, therefore, my duty at this time to lay before you the present state of certain hostile threats against the territories of Spain in our neighborhood.

The documents which accompany this message develop the measures which I have taken to suppress them, and the intelligence which has been lately received.

It will be seen from thence that the subject has not been neglected; that every power vested in the Executive on such occasions has been exerted, and that there was reason to believe that the enterprise pro-jected against the Spanish dominions was relinquished.

But it appears to have been revived upon principles which set public order at defiance and place the peace of the United States in the discretion of unauthorized individuals. The means already deposited in the different departments of Government are shewn by experience not to be adequate to these high exigencies, although such of them as are lodged in the hands of the Executive shall continue to be used with promptness, energy, and decision proportioned to the case. But I am impelled by the position of our public affairs to recommend that provision be made for a stronger and more vigorous opposition than can be given to such hostile movements under the laws as they now stand.

GƠ WASHINGTON.

UNITED STATES, *May 21, 1794.*

Gentlemen of the Senate and of the House of Representatives:

I lay before you in confidence sundry papers, by which you will perceive the state of affairs between us and the Six Nations, and the probable cause to which it is owing, and also certain information whereby it would appear that some encroachment was about to be made on our territory by an officer and party of British troops. Proceeding upon a supposition of the authenticity of this information, although of a private nature, I have caused the representation to be made to the British minister a copy of which accompanies this message.

It can not be necessary to comment upon the very serious nature of such an encroachment, nor to urge that this new state of things suggests the propriety of placing the United States in a posture of effectual preparation for an event which, notwithstanding the endeavors making to avert it, may by circumstances beyond our control be forced upon us.

GƠ WASHINGTON.

UNITED STATES, *May 26, 1794.*

Gentlemen of the Senate and of the House of Representatives:

The commissioners of His Catholic Majesty having communicated to the Secretary of State the form of a certificate without which the vessels of the United States can not be admitted into the ports of Spain, I think it proper to lay it before Congress.

GƠ WASHINGTON.

UNITED STATES, *May 27, 1794.*

Gentlemen of the Senate:

The Executive Provisory Council of the French Republic having requested me to recall Gouverneur Morris, our minister plenipotentiary in France, I have thought proper, in pursuance of that request, to recall him.   I therefore nominate James Monroe, of Virginia, as minister plenipotentiary of the United States to the said Republic.

I also nominate William Short, now minister resident for the United States with Their High Mightinesses the States-General of the United Netherlands, to be minister resident for the United States to His Catholic Majesty, in the room of William Carmichael, who is recalled.

G？ WASHINGTON.

UNITED STATES, *June 2, 1794.*

Gentlemen of the Senate and of the House of Representatives:

I send you certain communications, recently received from Georgia, which materially change the prospect of affairs in that quarter, and seem to render a war with the Creek Nations more probable than it has been at any antecedent period.   While the attention of Congress will be directed to the consideration of measures suited to the exigency, it can not escape their observation that this intelligence brings a fresh proof of the insufficiency of the existing provisions of the laws toward the effectual cultivation and preservation of peace with our Indian neighbors.

G？ WASHINGTON.

PROCLAMATIONS.

[From a broadside in the archives of the Department of State.]

BY THE PRESIDENT OF THE UNITED STATES OF AMERICA.

A PROCLAMATION.

Whereas it appears that a state of war exists between Austria, Prussia, Sardinia, Great Britain, and the United Netherlands of the one part and France on the other, and the duty and interest of the United States require that they should with sincerity and good faith adopt and pursue a conduct friendly and impartial toward the belligerent powers:

I have therefore thought fit by these presents to declare the disposition of the United States to observe the conduct aforesaid toward those powers respectively, and to exhort and warn the citizens of the United States carefully to avoid all acts and proceedings whatsoever which may in any manner tend to contravene such disposition.

And I do hereby also make known that whosoever of the citizens of the United States shall render himself liable to punishment or forfeiture under the law of nations by committing, aiding, or abetting hostilities against any of the said powers, or by carrying to any of them those articles which are deemed contraband by the modern usage of nations, will not receive the protection of the United States against such punishment or forfeiture; and further, that I have given instructions to those officers to whom it belongs to cause prosecutions to be instituted against all persons who shall, within the cognizance of the courts of the United States, violate the law of nations with respect to the powers at war, or any of them.

In testimony whereof I have caused the seal of the United States of America to be affixed to these presents, and signed the same with my hand.

[SEAL.]   Done at the city of Philadelphia, the 22d day of April, 1793, and of the Independence of the United States of America the seventeenth.

GO WASHINGTON.

By the President:

TH: JEFFERSON.

¶BY THE PRESIDENT OF THE UNITED STATES OF AMERICA.

A PROCLAMATION.

Whereas I have received information that certain persons, in violation of the laws, have presumed, under color of a foreign authority, to enlist citizens of the United States and others within the State of Kentucky, and have there assembled an armed force for the purpose of invading and plundering the territories of a nation at peace with the said United States; and

Whereas such unwarrantable measures, being contrary to the laws of nations and to the duties incumbent on every citizen of the United States, tend to disturb the tranquillity of the same, and to involve them in the calamities of war; and

Whereas it is the duty of the Executive to take care that such criminal proceedings should be suppressed, the offenders brought to justice, and all good citizens cautioned against measures likely to prove so pernicious to their country and themselves, should they be seduced into similar infractions of the laws:

I have therefore thought proper to issue this proclamation, hereby solemnly warning every person, not authorized by the laws, against enlisting any citizen or citizens of the United States, or levying troops, or assembling any persons within the United States for the purposes aforesaid, or proceeding in any manner to the execution thereof, as they will answer for the same at their peril; and I do also admonish and require all citizens to refrain from enlisting, enrolling, or assembling themselves for such unlawful purposes and from being in anywise concerned, aiding, or abetting therein, as they tender their own welfare, inasmuch as all lawful means will be strictly put in execution for securing obedience to the laws and for punishing such dangerous and daring violations thereof.

And I do moreover charge and require all courts, magistrates, and other officers whom it may concern, according to their respective duties, to exert the powers in them severally vested to prevent and suppress all such unlawful assemblages and proceedings, and to bring to condign punishment those who may have been guilty thereof, as they regard the due authority of Government and the peace and welfare of the United States.

In testimony whereof I have caused the seal of the United States of America to be affixed to these presents, and signed the same with my hand.

[SEAL.]   Done at the city of Philadelphia, the 24th day of March, 1794, and of the Independence of the United States of America the eighteenth.

G<u>o</u> WASHINGTON.

By the President:

EDM: RANDOLPH.

[From Annals of Congress, Fourth Congress, second session, 2796.]

BY THE PRESIDENT OF THE UNITED STATES OF AMERICA.

A PROCLAMATION.

Whereas combinations to defeat the execution of the laws laying duties upon spirits distilled within the United States and upon stills have from the time of the commencement of those laws existed in some of the western parts of Pennsylvania; and

Whereas the said combinations, proceeding in a manner subversive equally of the just authority of government and of the rights of individuals, have hitherto effected their dangerous and criminal purpose by the influence of certain irregular meetings whose proceedings have tended to encourage and uphold the spirit of opposition by misrepresentations of the laws calculated to render them odious; by endeavors to deter those who might be so disposed from accepting offices under them through fear of public resentment and of injury to person and property, and to compel those who had accepted such offices by actual violence to surrender or forbear the execution of them; by circulating vindictive menaces against all those who should otherwise, directly or indirectly, aid in the execution of the said laws, or who, yielding to the dictates of conscience and to a sense of obligation, should themselves comply therewith; by actually injuring and destroying the property of persons who were understood to have so complied; by inflicting cruel and humiliating punishments upon private citizens for no other cause than that of appearing to be the friends of the laws; by intercepting the public officers on the highways, abusing, assaulting, and otherwise ill treating them; by going to their houses in the night, gaining admittance by force, taking away their papers, and committing other outrages, employing for these unwarrantable purposes the agency of armed banditti disguised in such manner as for the most part to escape discovery; and

Whereas the endeavors of the Legislature to obviate objections to the said laws by lowering the duties and by other alterations conducive to the convenience of those whom they immediately affect (though they have given satisfaction in other quarters), and the endeavors of the executive officers to conciliate a compliance with the laws by explanations, by forbearance, and even by particular accommodations founded on the suggestion of local considerations, have been disappointed of their effect by the machinations of persons whose industry to excite resistance has increased with every appearance of a disposition among the people to relax in their opposition and to acquiesce in the laws, insomuch that many persons in the said western parts of Pennsylvania have at length been hardy enough to perpetrate acts which I am advised amount to treason, being overt acts of levying war against the United States, the said persons having on the 16th and 17th July last past proceeded in arms (on the second day amounting to several hundreds) to the house of John Neville, inspector of the revenue for the fourth survey of the district of Pennsylvania; having repeatedly attacked the said house with the persons therein, wounding some of them; having seized David Lenox, marshal of the district of Pennsylvania, who previous thereto had been fired upon while in the execution of his duty by a party of armed men, detaining him for some time prisoner, till for the preservation of his life and the obtaining of his liberty he found it necessary to enter into stipulations to forbear the execution of certain official duties touching processes issuing out of a court of the United States; and having finally obliged the said inspector of the said revenue and the said marshal from considerations of personal safety to fly from that part of the country, in order, by a circuitous route, to proceed to the seat of Government, avowing as the motives of these outrageous proceedings an intention to prevent by force of arms the execution of the said laws, to oblige the said inspector of the revenue to renounce his said office, to withstand by open violence the lawful authority of the Government of the United States, and to compel thereby an alteration in the measures of the Legislature and a repeal of the laws aforesaid; and

Whereas by a law of the United States entitled "An act to provide for calling forth the militia to execute the laws of the Union, suppress insurrections, and repel invasions," it is enacted "that whenever the laws of the United States shall be opposed or the execution thereof obstructed in any State by combinations too powerful to be suppressed by the ordinary course of judicial proceedings or by the powers vested in the marshals by that act, the same being notified by an associate justice or the district judge, it shall be lawful for the President of the United States to call forth the militia of such State to suppress such combinations and to cause the laws to be duly executed. And if the militia of a State where such combinations may happen shall refuse or be insufficient to suppress the same, it shall be lawful for the President, if the Legislature of the United States shall not be in session, to call forth and employ such numbers of the militia of any other State or States most convenient thereto as may be necessary; and the use of the militia so to be called forth may be continued, if necessary, until the expiration of thirty days after the commencement of the ensuing session: *Provided always,* That whenever it may be necessary in the judgment of the President to use the military force hereby directed to be called forth, the President shall forthwith, and previous thereto, by proclamation, command such insurgents to disperse and retire peaceably to their respective abodes within a limited time;" and

Whereas James Wilson, an associate justice, on the 4th instant, by writing under his hand, did from evidence which had been laid before him notify to me that "in the counties of Washington and Allegany, in Pennsylvania, laws of the United States are opposed and the execution thereof obstructed by combinations too powerful to be suppressed by the ordinary course of judicial proceedings or by the powers vested in the marshal of that district;" and

Whereas it is in my judgment necessary under the circumstances of the case to take measures for calling forth the militia in order to suppress the combinations aforesaid, and to cause the laws to be duly executed; and I have accordingly determined so to do, feeling the deepest regret for the occasion, but withal the most solemn conviction that the essential interests of the Union demand it, that the very existence of Government and the fundamental principles of social order are materially involved in the issue, and that the patriotism and firmness of all good citizens are seriously called upon, as occasions may require, to aid in the effectual suppression of so fatal a spirit:

Wherefore, and in pursuance of the proviso above recited, I, George Washington, President of the United States, do hereby command all persons being insurgents as aforesaid, and all others whom it may concern, on or before the 1st day of September next to disperse and retire peaceably to their respective abodes. And I do moreover warn all persons whomsoever against aiding, abetting, or comforting the perpetrators of the aforesaid treasonable acts, and do require all officers and other citizens, according to their respective duties and the laws of the land, to exert their utmost endeavors to prevent and suppress such dangerous proceedings.

In testimony whereof I have caused the seal of the United States of America to be affixed to these presents, and signed the same with my hand.

[SEAL.]   Done at the city of Philadelphia, the 7th day of August, 1794, and of the Independence of the United States of America the nineteenth.

By the President: G⁹ WASHINGTON.

EDM: RANDOLPH

[From Annals of Congress, Third Congress, 1413.]

BY THE PRESIDENT OF THE UNITED STATES OF AMERICA.

A PROCLAMATION.

Whereas from a hope that the combinations against the Constitution and laws of the United States in certain of the western counties of Pennsylvania would yield to time and reflection I thought it sufficient in the first instance rather to take measures for calling forth the militia than immediately to embody them, but the moment is now come when the overtures of forgiveness, with no other condition than a submission to law, have been only partially accepted; when every form of conciliation not inconsistent with the being of Government has been adopted without effect; when the well-disposed in those counties are unable by their influence and example to reclaim the wicked from their fury, and are compelled to associate in their own defense; when the proffered lenity has been perversely misinterpreted into an apprehension that the citizens will march with reluctance; when the opportunity of examining the serious consequences of a treasonable opposition has been employed in propagating principles of anarchy, endeavoring through emissaries to alienate the friends of order from its support, and inviting its enemies to perpetrate similar acts of insurrection; when it is manifest that violence would continue to be exercised upon every attempt to enforce the laws; when, therefore, Government is set at defiance, the contest being whether a small portion of the United States shall dictate to the whole Union, and, at the expense of those who desire peace, indulge a desperate ambition:

Now, therefore, I, George Washington, President of the United States, in obedience to that high and irresistible duty consigned to me by the Constitution "to take care that the laws be faithfully executed," deploring that the American name should be sullied by the outrages of citizens on their own Government, commiserating such as remain obstinate from delusion, but resolved, in perfect reliance on that gracious Providence which so signally displays its goodness towards this country, to reduce the refractory to a due subordination to the law, do hereby declare and make known that, with a satisfaction which can be equaled only by the merits of the militia summoned into service from the States of New Jersey, Pennsylvania, Maryland, and Virginia, I have received intelligence of their patriotic alacrity in obeying the call of the present, though painful, yet commanding necessity; that a force which, according to every reasonable expectation, is adequate to the exigency is already in motion to the scene of disaffection; that those who have confided or shall confide in the protection of Government shall meet full succor under the standard and from the arms of the United States; that those who, having offended against the laws, have since entitled themselves to indemnity will be treated with the most liberal good faith if they shall not have forfeited their claim by any subsequent conduct, and that instructions are given accordingly.

And I do moreover exhort all individuals, officers, and bodies of men to contemplate with abhorrence the measures leading directly or indirectly to those crimes which produce this resort to military coercion; to check in their respective spheres the efforts of misguided or designing men to substitute their misrepresentation in the place of truth and their discontents in the place of stable government, and to call to mind that, as the people of the United States have been permitted, under the Divine favor, in perfect freedom, after solemn deliberation, and in an enlightened age, to elect their own government, so will their gratitude for this inestimable blessing be best distinguished by firm exertions to maintain the Constitution and the laws.

And, lastly, I again warn all persons whomsoever and wheresoever not to abet, aid, or comfort the insurgents aforesaid, as they will answer the contrary at their peril; and I do also require all officers and other citizens, according to their several duties, as far as may be in their power, to bring under the cognizance of the laws all offenders in the premises.

In testimony whereof I have caused the seal of the United States of America to be affixed to these presents, and signed the same with my hand.

[SEAL.]   Done at the city of Philadelphia, the 25th day of September, 1794, and of the Independence of the United States of America the nineteenth.

G⁹ WASHINGTON.

By the President:
EDM: RANDOLPH.

SIXTH ANNUAL ADDRESS.

UNITED STATES, *November 19, 1794.*

Fellow-Citizens of the Senate and of the House of Representatives:

When we call to mind the gracious indulgence of Heaven by which the American people became a nation; when we survey the general prosperity of our country, and look forward to the riches, power, and happiness to which it seems destined, with the deepest regret do I announce to you that during your recess some of the citizens of the United States have been found capable of an insurrection. It is due, however, to the character of our Government and to its stability, which can not be shaken by the enemies of order, freely to unfold the course of this event.

During the session of the year 1790 it was expedient to exercise the legislative power granted by the Constitution of the United States "to

MOB OF WHISKEY INSURRECTIONISTS MALTREATING EXCISE OFFICER

Pittsburg in 1790

THE WHISKEY REBELLION, 1791-4

The story of the first rebellion against the Federal Government is told in the article entitled "Whiskey Insurrection," in the index (volume eleven), and if the reader so desires he may read the history of that occurrence, as written by the pen of George Washington, on the pages cited beneath the above-mentioned article.

The crushing of this revolt was a crisis in our national life. If any section or class could, with impunity, defy the will of the majority as expressed in the Acts of Congress, the new Government would disintegrate as did the Confederation. For three years Washington temporized with the Pennsylvanians, because he feared that a call upon the militia to uphold the Government would be repudiated, and that the Constitution, thus shown to have no hold upon the people's affections, would perish in mockery and derision. But when the new Government had established its credit by Hamilton's financial plans, the number of colonists who imbibed their principles and fashions from Europe decreased, in proportion as the number of Americans who were proud of the Republic increased. Then came Washington's call for volunteers, the ready answer of the militia and the suppression of the rebellion.

lay and collect excises." In a majority of the States scarcely an objection was heard to this mode of taxation. In some, indeed, alarms were at first conccived, until they were banished by reason and patriotism. In the four western counties of Pennsylvania a prejudice, fostered and imbittered by the artifice of men who labored for an ascendency over the will of others by the guidance of their passions, produced symptoms of riot and violence. It is well known that Congress did not hesitate to examine the complaints which were presented, and to relieve them as far as justice dictated or general convenience would permit. But the impression which this moderation made on the discontented did not correspond with what it deserved. The arts of delusion were no longer confined to the efforts of designing individuals. The very forbearance to press prosecutions was misinterpreted into a fear of urging the execution of the laws, and associations of men began to denounce threats against the officers employed. From a belief that by a more formal concert their operation might be defeated, certain self-created societies assumed the tone of condemnation. Hence, while the greater part of Pennsylvania itself were conforming themselves to the acts of excise, a few counties were resolved to frustrate them. It was now perceived that every expectation from the tenderness which had been hitherto pursued was unavailing, and that further delay could only create an opinion of impotency or irresolution in the Government. Legal process was therefore delivered to the marshal against the rioters and delinquent distillers.

No sooner was he understood to be engaged in this duty than the vengeance of armed men was aimed at *his* person and the person and property of the inspector of the revenue. They fired upon the marshal, arrested him, and detained him for some time as a prisoner. He was obliged, by the jeopardy of his life, to renounce the service of other process on the west side of the Allegheny Mountain, and a deputation was afterwards sent to him to demand a surrender of that which he *had* served. A numerous body repeatedly attacked the house of the inspector, seized his papers of office, and finally destroyed by fire his buildings and whatsoever they contained. Both of these officers, from a just regard to their safety, fled to the seat of Government, it being avowed that the motives to such outrages were to compel the resignation of the inspector, to withstand by force of arms the authority of the United States, and thereby to extort a repeal of the laws of excise and an alteration in the conduct of Government.

Upon the testimony of these facts an associate justice of the Supreme Court of the United States notified to me that "in the counties of Washington and Allegheny, in Pennsylvania, laws of the United States were opposed, and the execution thereof obstructed, by combinations too powerful to be suppressed by the ordinary course of judicial proceedings or by the powers vested in the marshal of that district." On this call, momentous in the extreme, I sought and weighed what might best subdue the crisis. On the one hand the judiciary was pronounced to be stripped of its capacity to enforce the laws; crimes which reached the very existence of social order were perpetrated without control; the friends of Government were insulted, abused, and overawed into silence or an apparent acquiescence; and to yield to the treasonable fury of so small a portion of the United States would be to violate the fundamental principle of our Constitution, which enjoins that the will of the majority shall prevail. On the other, to array citizen against citizen, to publish the dishonor of such excesses, to encounter the expense and other embarrassments of so distant an expedition, were steps too delicate, too closely interwoven with many affecting considerations, to be lightly adopted. I postponed, therefore, the summoning the militia immediately into the field, but I required them to be held in readiness, that if my anxious endeavors to reclaim the deluded and to convince the malignant of their danger should be fruitless, military force might be prepared to act before the season should be too far advanced.

My proclamation of the 7th of August last was accordingly issued, and accompanied by the appointment of commissioners, who were charged to repair to the scene of insurrection. They were authorized to confer with any bodies of men or individuals. They were instructed to be candid and explicit in stating the sensations which had been excited in the Executive, and his earnest wish to avoid a resort to coercion; to represent, however, that, without submission, coercion *must* be the resort; but to invite them, at the same time, to return to the demeanor of faithful citizens, by such accommodations as lay within the sphere of Executive power. Pardon, too, was tendered to them by the Government of the United States and that of Pennsylvania, upon no other condition than a satisfactory assurance of obedience to the laws.

Although the report of the commissioners marks their firmness and abilities, and must unite all virtuous men, by shewing that the means of conciliation have been exhausted, all of those who had committed or abetted the tumults did not subscribe the mild form which was proposed as the atonement, and the indications of a peaceable temper were neither sufficiently general nor conclusive to recommend or warrant the further suspension of the march of the militia.

Thus the painful alternative could not be discarded. I ordered the militia to march, after once more admonishing the insurgents in my proclamation of the 25th of September last

It was a task too difficult to ascertain with precision the lowest degree of force competent to the quelling of the insurrection. From a respect, indeed, to economy and the ease of my fellow-citizens belonging to the militia, it would have gratified me to accomplish such an estimate. My very reluctance to ascribe too much importance to the opposition, had its extent been accurately seen, would have been a decided inducement to the smallest efficient numbers. In this uncertainty, therefore, I put into motion 15,000 men, as being an army which, according to all human calculation, would be prompt and adequate in every view, and might, perhaps, by rendering resistance desperate, prevent the effusion of blood. Quotas had been assigned to the States of New Jersey, Pennsylvania, Maryland, and Virginia, the governor of Pennsylvania having declared on this occasion an opinion which justified a requisition to the other States.

As commander in chief of the militia when called into the actual service of the United States, I have visited the places of general rendezvous to obtain more exact information and to direct a plan for ulterior movements. Had there been room for a persuasion that the laws were secure from obstruction; that the civil magistrate was able to bring to justice such of the most culpable as have not embraced the proffered terms of amnesty, and may be deemed fit objects of example; that the friends to peace and good government were not in need of that aid and countenance which they ought always to receive, and, I trust, ever will receive, against the vicious and turbulent, I should have caught with avidity the opportunity of restoring the militia to their families and homes. But succeeding intelligence has tended to manifest the necessity of what has been done, it being now confessed by those who were not inclined to exaggerate the ill conduct of the insurgents that their malevolence was not pointed merely to a particular law, but that a spirit inimical to all order has actuated many of the offenders. If the state of things had afforded reason for the continuance of my presence with the army, it would not have been withholden. But every appearance assuring such an issue as will redound to the reputation and strength of the United States, I have judged it most proper to resume my duties at the seat of Government, leaving the chief command with the governor of Virginia.

Still, however, as it is probable that in a commotion like the present, whatsoever may be the pretense, the purposes of mischief and revenge may not be laid aside, the stationing of a small force for a certain period in the four western counties of Pennsylvania will be indispensable, whether we contemplate the situation of those who are connected with the execution of the laws or of others who may have exposed themselves by an honorable attachment to them. Thirty days from the commencement of this session being the legal limitation of the employment of the militia, Congress can not be too early occupied with this subject.

Among the discussions which may arise from this aspect of our affairs, and from the documents which will be submitted to Congress, it will not escape their observation that not only the inspector of the revenue, but other officers of the United States in Pennsylvania have, from their fidelity in the discharge of their functions, sustained material injuries to their property. The obligation and policy of indemnifying them are strong and obvious. It may also merit attention whether policy will not enlarge this provision to the retribution of other citizens who, though not under the ties of office, may have suffered damage by their generous exertions for upholding the Constitution and the laws. The amount, even if all the injured were included, would not be great, and on future emergencies the Government would be amply repaid by the influence of an example that he who incurs a loss in its defense shall find a recompense in its liberality.

While there is cause to lament that occurrences of this nature should have disgraced the name or interrupted the tranquillity of any part of our community, or should have diverted to a new application any portion of the public resources, there are not wanting real and substantial consolations for the misfortune. It has demonstrated that our prosperity rests on solid foundations, by furnishing an additional proof that my fellow-citizens understand the true principles of government and liberty; that they feel their inseparable union; that notwithstanding all the devices which have been used to sway them from their interest and duty, they are now as ready to maintain the authority of the laws against licentious invasions as they were to defend their rights against usurpation. It has been a spectacle displaying to the highest advantage the value of republican government to behold the most and the least wealthy of our citizens standing in the same ranks as private soldiers, preeminently distinguished by being the army of the Constitution—undeterred by a march of 300 miles over rugged mountains, by the approach of an inclement season, or by any other discouragement. Nor ought I to omit to acknowledge the efficacious and patriotic cooperation which I have experienced from the chief magistrates of the States to which my requisitions have been addressed.

To every description of citizens, indeed, let praise be given. But let them persevere in their affectionate vigilance over that precious depository of American happiness, the Constitution of the United States. Let them cherish it, too, for the sake of those who, from every clime, are daily seeking a dwelling in our land. And when in the calm moments of reflection they shall have retraced the origin and progress of the insurrection, let them determine whether it has not been fomented by combinations of men who, careless of consequences and disregarding the unerring truth that those who rouse can not always appease a civil convulsion, have disseminated, from an ignorance or perversion of facts, suspicions, jealousies, and accusations of the whole Government.

Having thus fulfilled the engagement which I took when I entered into office, "to the best of my ability to preserve, protect, and defend the Constitution of the United States," on you, gentlemen, and the people by whom you are deputed, I rely for support.

In the arrangements to which the possibility of a similar contingency will naturally draw your attention it ought not to be forgotten that the militia laws have exhibited such striking defects as could not have been supplied but by the zeal of our citizens. Besides the extraordinary expense and waste. which are not the least of the defects, every appeal to those laws is attended with a doubt on its success.

The devising and establishing of a well-regulated militia would be a genuine source of legislative honor and a perfect title to public gratitude. I therefore entertain a hope that the present session will not pass without carrying to its full energy the power of organizing, arming, and disciplining the militia, and thus providing, in the language of the Constitution, for calling them forth to execute the laws of the Union, suppress insurrections, and repel invasions.

As auxiliary to the state of our defense, to which Congress can never too frequently recur, they will not omit to inquire whether the fortifications which have been already licensed by law be commensurate with our exigencies.

The intelligence from the army under the command of General Wayne is a happy presage to our military operations against the hostile Indians north of the Ohio. From the advices which have been forwarded, the advance which he has made must have damped the ardor of the savages and weakened their obstinacy in waging war against the United States. And yet, even at this late hour, when our power to punish them can not be questioned, we shall not be unwilling to cement a lasting peace upon terms of candor, equity, and good neighborhood.

Toward none of the Indian tribes have overtures of friendship been spared. The Creeks in particular are covered from encroachment by the interposition of the General Government and that of Georgia. From a desire also to remove the discontents of the Six Nations, a settlement meditated at Presque Isle, on Lake Erie, has been suspended, and an agent is now endeavoring to rectify any misconception into which they may have fallen. But I can not refrain from again pressing upon your deliberations the plan which I recommended at the last session for the improvement of harmony with all the Indians within our limits by the fixing and conducting of trading houses upon the principles then expressed.

Gentlemen of the House of Representatives:

The time which has elapsed since the commencement of our fiscal measures has developed our pecuniary resources so as to open the way for a definite plan for the redemption of the public debt. It is believed that the result is such as to encourage Congress to consummate this work without delay. Nothing can more promote the permanent welfare of the nation and nothing would be more grateful to our constituents. Indeed, whatsoever is unfinished of our system of public credit can not be benefited by procrastination; and as far as may be practicable we ought to place that credit on grounds which can not be disturbed, and to prevent that progressive accumulation of debt which must ultimately endanger all governments.

An estimate of the necessary appropriations, including the expenditures into which we have been driven by the insurrection, will be submitted to Congress.

Gentlemen of the Senate and of the House of Representatives.

The Mint of the United States has entered upon the coinage of the precious metals, and considerable sums of defective coins and bullion have been lodged with the Director by individuals. There is a pleasing prospect that the institution will at no remote day realize the expectation which was originally formed of its utility.

In subsequent communications certain circumstances of our intercourse with foreign nations will be transmitted to Congress. However, it may not be unseasonable to announce that my policy in our foreign transactions has been to cultivate peace with all the world; to observe treaties with pure and absolute faith; to check every deviation from the line of impartiality; to explain what may have been misapprehended and correct what may have been injurious to any nation, and having thus acquired the right, to lose no time in acquiring the ability to insist upon justice being done to ourselves.

Let us unite, therefore, in imploring the Supreme Ruler of Nations to spread his holy protection over these United States; to turn the machinations of the wicked to the confirming of our Constitution; to enable us at all times to root out internal sedition and put invasion to flight; to perpetuate to our country that prosperity which His goodness has already conferred, and to verify the anticipations of this Government being a safeguard to human rights.

GO WASHINGTON.

ADDRESS OF THE SENATE TO GEORGE WASHINGTON, PRESIDENT OF THE UNITED STATES.

SIR: We receive with pleasure your speech to the two Houses of Congress. In it we perceive renewed proofs of that vigilant and paternal concern for the prosperity, honor, and happiness of our country which has uniformly distinguished your past Administration.

Our anxiety arising from the licentious and open resistance to the laws in the western counties of Pennsylvania has been increased by the proceedings of certain self-created societies relative to the laws and administration of the Government; proceedings, in our apprehension, founded in political error, calculated, if not intended, to disorganize our Government, and which, by inspiring delusive hopes of support, have been influential in misleading our fellow-citizens in the scene of insurrection.

In a situation so delicate and important the lenient and persuasive measures which you adopted merit and receive our affectionate approbation. These failing to procure their proper effect, and coercion having become inevitable, we have derived the highest satisfaction from the enlightened patriotism and animating zeal with which the citizens of New Jersey, Pennsylvania, Maryland, and Virginia have rallied around the standard of Government in opposition to anarchy and insurrection.

Our warm and cordial acknowledgments are due to you, sir, for the wisdom and decision with which you arrayed the militia to execute the public will, and to them for the disinterestedness and alacrity with which they obeyed your summons.

The example is precious to the theory of our Government, and confers the brightest honor upon the patriots who have given it.

We shall readily concur in such further provisions for the security of internal peace and a due obedience to the laws as the occasion manifestly requires.

The effectual organization of the militia and a prudent attention to the fortifications of our ports and harbors are subjects of great national importance, and, together with the other measures you have been pleased to recommend, will receive our deliberate consideration.

The success of the troops under the command of General Wayne can not fail to produce essential advantages. The pleasure with which we acknowledge the merits of that gallant general and army is enhanced by the hope that their victories will lay the foundation of a just and durable peace with the Indian tribes.

At a period so momentous in the affairs of nations the temperate, just, and firm policy that you have pursued in respect to foreign powers has been eminently calculated to promote the great and essential interest of our country, and has created the fairest title to the public gratitude and thanks.

JOHN ADAMS,

Vice-President of the United States and President of the Senate.

NOVEMBER 21, 1794.

REPLY OF THE PRESIDENT.

GENTLEMEN: Among the occasions which have been afforded for expressing my sense of the zealous and steadfast cooperation of the Senate in the maintenance of Government, none has yet occurred more forcibly demanding my unqualified acknowledgments than the present.

Next to the consciousness of upright intentions, it is the highest pleasure to be approved by the enlightened representatives of a free nation. With the satisfaction, therefore, which arises from an unalterable attachment to public order do I learn that the Senate discountenance those proceedings which would arrogate the direction of our affairs without any degree of authority derived from the people.

It has been more than once the lot of our Government to be thrown into new and delicate situations, and of these the insurrection has not been the least important. Having been compelled at length to lay aside my repugnance to resort to arms, I derive much happiness from being confirmed by your judgment in the necessity of decisive measures, and from the support of my fellow-citizens of the militia, who were the patriotic instruments of that necessity.

With such demonstrations of affection for our Constitution; with an adequate organization of the militia; with the establishment of necessary fortifications; with a continuance of those judicious and spirited exertions which have brought victory to our Western army; with a due attention to public credit, and an unsullied honor toward all nations, we may meet, under every assurance of success, our enemies from within and from without.

G⁰ WASHINGTON.

NOVEMBER 22, 1794.

ADDRESS OF THE HOUSE OF REPRESENTATIVES TO GEORGE WASHINGTON, PRESIDENT OF THE UNITED STATES.

SIR: The House of Representatives, calling to mind the blessings enjoyed by the people of the United States, and especially the happiness of living under constitutions and laws which rest on their authority alone, could not learn with other emotions than those you have expressed that any part of our fellow-citizens should have shewn themselves capable of an insurrection. And we learn with the greatest concern that any misrepresentations whatever of the Government and its proceedings, either by individuals or combinations of men, should have been made and so far credited as to foment the flagrant outrage which has been committed on the laws. We feel with you the deepest regret at so painful an occurrence in the annals of our country. As men regardful of the tender interests of humanity, we look with grief at scenes which might have stained our land with civil blood; as lovers of public order, we lament that it has suffered so flagrant a violation; as zealous friends of republican government, we deplore every occasion which in the hands of its enemies may be turned into a calumny against it.

This aspect of the crisis, however, is happily not the only one which it presents. There is another, which yields all the consolations which you have drawn from it. It has demonstrated to the candid world, as well as to the American people themselves, that the great body of them everywhere are equally attached to the luminous and vital principle of our Constitution, which enjoins that the will of the majority shall prevail; that they understand the indissoluble union between true liberty and regular government; that they feel their duties no less than they are watchful over their rights; that they will be as ready at all times to crush licentiousness as they have been to defeat usurpation. In a word, that they are cap⸺ of carrying into execution that noble plan of self-government which they have chosen as the guaranty of their own happiness and the asylum for that of all, from every clime, who may wish to unite their destiny with ours.

These are the just inferences flowing from the promptitude with which the summons to the standard of the laws has been obeyed, and from the sentiments which have been witnessed in every description of citizens in every quarter of the Union. The spectacle, therefore, when viewed in its true light, may well be affirmed to display in equal luster the virtues of the American character and the value of republican government. All must particularly acknowledge and applaud the patriotism of that portion of citizens who have freely sacrificed everything less dear than the love of their country to the meritorious task of defending its happiness.

In the part which you have yourself borne through this delicate and distressing period we trace the additional proofs it has afforded of your solicitude for the public good. Your laudable and successful endeavors to render lenity in executing the laws conducive to their real energy, and to convert tumult into order without the effusion of blood, form a particular title to the confidence and praise of your constituents. In all that may be found necessary on our part to complete this benevolent purpose, and to secure the ministers and friends of the laws against the remains of danger, our due cooperation will be afforded.

The other subjects which you have recommended or communicated, and of which several are peculiarly interesting, will all receive the attention which they demand. We are deeply impressed with the importance of an effectual organization of the militia. We rejoice at the intelligence of the advance and success of the army under the command of General Wayne, whether we regard it as a proof of the perseverance, prowess, and superiority of our troops, or as a happy presage to our military operations against the hostile Indians, and as a probable prelude to the establishment of a lasting peace upon terms of candor, equity, and good neighborhood. We receive it with the greater pleasure as it increases the probability of sooner restoring a part of the public resources to the desirable object of reducing the public debt.

We shall on this, as on all occasions, be disposed to adopt any measures which may advance the safety and prosperity of our country. In nothing can we more cordially unite with you than in imploring the Supreme Ruler of Nations to multiply his blessings on these United States; to guard our free and happy Constitution against every machination and danger, and to make it the best source of public happiness, by verifying its character of being the best safeguard of human rights.

NOVEMBER 28, 1794.

REPLY OF THE PRESIDENT.

GENTLEMEN: I anticipated with confidence the concurrence of the House of Representatives in the regret produced by the insurrection. Every effort ought to be used to discountenance what has contributed to foment it, and thus discourage a repetition of like attempts; for notwith-standing the consolations which may be drawn from the issue of this event, it is far better that the artful approaches to such a situation of things should be checked by the vigilant and duly admonished patri-otism of our fellow-citizens than that the evil should increase until it becomes necessary to crush it by the strength of their arm.

I am happy that the part which I have myself borne on this occasion receives the approbation of your House. For the discharge of a consti-tutional duty it is a sufficient reward to me to be assured that you will unite in consummating what remains to be done.

I feel also great satisfaction in learning that the other subjects which I have communicated or recommended will meet with due attention; that you are deeply impressed with the importance of an effectual organ-ization of the militia, and that the advance and success of the army under the command of General Wayne is regarded by you, no less than myself, as a proof of the perseverance, prowess, and superiority of our troops.

G^o WASHINGTON.

NOVEMBER 29, 1794.

SPECIAL MESSAGES.

UNITED STATES, *November 21, 1794.*

Gentlemen of the Senate and of the House of Representatives:

I lay before Congress copies of a letter from the governor of the State of New York and of the exemplification of an act of the legislature thereof ratifying the amendment of the Constitution of the United States proposed by the Senate and House of Representatives at their last session, respecting the judicial power.

G^o WASHINGTON.

UNITED STATES, *November 21, 1794.*

Gentlemen of the Senate:

In the negotiation between the United States and His Catholic Majesty I have received satisfactory proofs of attention and ability exerted in behalf of the United States to bring it to a happy and speedy issue. But it is probable that by complying with an intimation made to the Secretary of State by the commissioners of His Catholic Majesty much further delay in concluding it may be prevented. Notwithstanding, therefore, I retain full confidence in our minister resident at Madrid, who is charged with powers as commissioner plenipotentiary, I nominate Thomas Pinckney to be envoy extraordinary of the United States to

His Catholic Majesty, for the purpose of negotiating of and concerning the navigation of the river Mississippi, and such other matters relative to the confines of their territories, and the intercourse to be had thereon, as the mutual interests and general harmony of neighboring and friendly nations require should be precisely adjusted and regulated, and of and concerning the general commerce between the United States and the kingdoms and dominions of his said Catholic Majesty.

It is believed that by his temporary absence from London in the discharge of these new functions no injury will arise to the United States.

I also nominate :

John Miller Russell, of Massachusetts, to be consul of the United States of America for the port of St. Petersburg, in Russia, and for such other places as shall be nearer to the said port than to the residence of any other consul or vice-consul of the United States within the same allegiance ;

Joseph Pitcairn, of New York, to be vice-consul of the United States of America at Paris, vice Alexander Duvernet, superseded ; and

Nathaniel Brush, of Vermont, to be supervisor for the United States in the district of Vermont, vice Noah Smith, who has resigned.

Gº WASHINGTON.

UNITED STATES, *November 25, 1794.*

Gentlemen of the Senate and of the House of Representatives:

I lay before you a statement of the troops in the service of the United States, which has been submitted to me by the Secretary of War. It will rest with Congress to consider and determine whether further inducements shall be held out for entering into the military service of the United States in order to complete the establishment authorized by law.

Gº WASHINGTON.

UNITED STATES, *December 17, 1794.*

Gentlemen of the Senate and of the House of Representatives:

I lay before Congress copies of the journal of the proceedings of the executive department of the government of the United States south of the river Ohio to the 1st of September, 1794.

Gº WASHINGTON.

UNITED STATES, *December 30, 1794.*

Gentlemen of the Senate and of the House of Representatives:

I lay before you a report, made to me by the Secretary of War, respecting the frontiers of the United States. The disorders and the great expenses which incessantly arise upon the frontiers are of a nature and magnitude to excite the most serious considerations.

I feel a confidence that Congress will devise such constitutional and efficient measures as shall be equal to the great objects of preserving our treaties with the Indian tribes and of affording an adequate protection to our frontiers.

G⁰ WASHINGTON

UNITED STATES, *January 2, 1795.*

Gentlemen of the Senate:

A spirit of discontent, from several causes, arose in the early part of the present year among the Six Nations of Indians, and particularly on the ground of a projected settlement by Pennsylvania, at Presque Isle, upon Lake Erie. The papers upon this point have already been laid before Congress. It was deemed proper on my part to endeavor to tranquillize the Indians by pacific measures. Accordingly a time and place was appointed at which a free conference should be had upon all the causes of discontent, and an agent was appointed with the instructions of which No. 1, herewith transmitted, is a copy.

A numerous assembly of Indians was held in Canandaigua, in the State of New York the proceedings whereof accompany this message, marked No. 2.

The two treaties, the one with the Six Nations and the other with the Oneida, Tuscorora, and Stockbridge Indians dwelling in the country of the Oneidas, which have resulted from the mission of the agent, are herewith laid before the Senate for their consideration and advice.

The original engagement of the United States to the Oneidas is also sent herewith.

G⁰ WASHINGTON.

UNITED STATES, *January 8, 1795.*

Gentlemen of the Senate and of the House of Representatives:

I lay before Congress copies of acts passed by the legislatures of the States of Vermont, Massachusetts, and New York, ratifying the amendment proposed by the Senate and House of Representatives at their last session to the Constitution of the United States respecting the judicial power thereof.

The minister of the French Republic having communicated to the Secretary of State certain proceedings of the committee of public safety respecting weights and measures, I lay these also before Congress.

The letter from the governor of the Western territory, copies of which are now transmitted, refers to a defect in the judicial system of that territory deserving the attention of Congress.

The necessary absence of the judge of the district of Pennsylvania upon business connected with the late insurrection is stated by him in a letter of which I forward copies to have produced certain interruptions in the judicial proceedings of that district which can not be removed without the interposition of Congress.

GO WASHINGTON.

UNITED STATES, *February 4, 1795.*

Gentlemen of the Senate and of the House of Representatives:

I lay before Congress, for their consideration, a letter from the Secretary of State upon the subject of a loan which is extremely interesting and urgent.

GO WASHINGTON.

UNITED STATES, *February 17, 1795.*

Gentlemen of the Senate and of the House of Representatives:

I transmit to Congress copies of a letter from the governor of the State of New Hampshire and of an act of the legislature thereof "ratifying the article proposed in amendment to the Constitution of the United States respecting the judicial power."

I also lay before Congress copies of a letter from the governor of the State of North Carolina and of an act of the legislature thereof ceding to the United States certain lands upon the conditions therein mentioned.

GO WASHINGTON.

UNITED STATES, *February 17, 1795.*

Gentlemen of the Senate and of the House of Representatives:

I have received copies of two acts of the legislature of Georgia, one passed on the 28th day of December and the other on the 7th day of January last, for appropriating and selling the Indian lands within the territorial limits claimed by that State. These copies, though not officially certified, have been transmitted to me in such a manner as to leave no room to doubt their authenticity. These acts embrace an object of such magnitude, and in their consequences may so deeply affect the peace and welfare of the United States, that I have thought it necessary now to lay them before Congress.

In *confidence*, I also forward copies of several documents and papers received from the governor of the Southwestern territory. By these it seems that hostilities with the Cherokees have ceased, and that there is a pleasing prospect of a permanent peace with that nation; but from all the communications of the governor it appears that the Creeks, in small parties, continue their depredations, and it is uncertain to what they may finally lead.

The several papers now communicated deserve the immediate attention of Congress, who will consider how far the subjects of them may require their cooperation.

GO WASHINGTON.

UNITED STATES, *February 25, 1795.*

Gentlemen of the Senate and of the House of Representatives:

I communicate to Congress copies of a letter from the governor of the State of Georgia and of an act of the legislature thereof "to ratify the resolution of Congress explanatory of the judicial power of the United States."

G⁰ WASHINGTON.

UNITED STATES, *February 28, 1795.*

Gentlemen of the Senate and of the House of Representatives:

In my first communication to Congress during their present session I gave them reason to expect that "certain circumstances of our intercourse with foreign nations" would be transmitted to them. There was at that time every assurance for believing that some of the most important of our foreign affairs would have been concluded and others considerably matured before they should rise. But notwithstanding I have waited until this moment, it has so happened that, either from causes unknown to me or from events which could not be controlled, I am yet unable to execute my original intention. That I may, however, fulfill the expectation given as far as the actual situation of things will in my judgment permit, I now, *in confidence*, lay before Congress the following general statement:

Our minister near the French Republic has urged compensation for the injuries which our commerce has sustained from captures by French cruisers, from the nonfulfillment of the contracts of the agents of that Republic with our citizens, and from the embargo at Bordeaux. He has also pressed an allowance for the money voted by Congress for relieving the inhabitants of St. Domingo. It affords me the highest pleasure to inform Congress that perfect harmony reigns between the two Republics, and that those claims are in a train of being discussed with candor and of being amicably adjusted.

So much of our relation to Great Britain may depend upon the result of our late negotiations in London that until that result shall arrive I can not undertake to make any communication upon this subject.

After the negotiation with Spain had been long depending unusual and unexpected embarrassments were raised to interrupt its progress. But the commissioner of His Catholic Majesty near the United States having declared to the Secretary of State that if a particular accommodation should be made in the *conducting* of the business no further delay would ensue, I thought proper, under all circumstances, to send to His Catholic Majesty an envoy extraordinary specially charged to bring to a conclusion the discussions which have been formerly announced to Congress.

The friendship of Her Most Faithful Majesty has been often manifested in checking the passage of the Algerine corsairs into the Atlantic Ocean. She has also furnished occasional convoys to the vessels of the United States, even when bound to other ports than her own. We may therefore promise ourselves that, as in the ordinary course of things few causes can exist for dissatisfaction between the United States and Portugal, so the temper with which accidental difficulties will be met on each side will speedily remove them.

Between the Executive of the United States and the Government of the United Netherlands but little intercourse has taken place during the last year. It may be acceptable to Congress to learn that our credit in Holland is represented as standing upon the most respectable footing.

Upon the death of the late Emperor of Morocco an agent was dispatched to renew with his successor the treaty which the United States had made with *him*. The agent, unfortunately, died after he had reached Europe in the prosecution of his mission. But until lately it was impossible to determine with any degree of probability who of the competitors for that Empire would be ultimately fixed in the supreme power. Although the measures which have been since adopted for the renewal of the treaty have been obstructed by the disturbed situation of Amsterdam, there are good grounds for presuming as yet upon the pacific disposition of the Emperor, in fact, toward the United States, and that the past miscarriage will be shortly remedied.

Congress are already acquainted with the failure of the loan attempted in Holland for the relief of our unhappy fellow-citizens in Algiers. This subject, than which none deserves a more affectionate zeal, has constantly commanded my best exertions. I am happy, therefore, in being able to say that from the last authentic accounts the Dey was disposed to treat for a peace and ransom, and that both would in all probability have been accomplished had we not been disappointed in the means. Nothing which depends upon the Executive shall be left undone for carrying into immediate effect the supplementary act of Congress.

G⁰ WASHINGTON.

UNITED STATES, *March 2, 1795.*

Gentlemen of the Senate and of the House of Representatives:

It appears from the information which I have lately received that it may be probably necessary to the more successful conduct of our affairs on the coast of Barbary that one consul should reside in Morocco, another in Algiers, and a third in Tunis or Tripoli. As no appointment for these offices will be accepted without some emolument annexed, I submit to the consideration of Congress whether it may not be advisable to authorize a stipend to be allowed to two consuls for that coast in addition to the one already existing.

G⁰ WASHINGTON.

UNITED STATES, *March 2, 1795.*

Gentlemen of the Senate and of the House of Representatives:

I transmit to you copies of a letter from the governor of the State of Delaware and of an act inclosed "declaring the assent of that State to an amendment therein mentioned to the Constitution of the United States.'

G? WASHINGTON.

UNITED STATES, *June 8, 1795.**

Gentlemen of the Senate:

In pursuance of my nomination of John Jay as envoy extraordinary to His Britannic Majesty on the 16th day of April, 1794, and of the advice and consent of the Senate thereto on the 19th, a negotiation was opened in London. On the 7th of March, 1795, the treaty resulting therefrom was delivered to the Secretary of State. I now transmit to the Senate that treaty and other documents connected with it. They will, therefore, in their wisdom decide whether they will advise and consent that the said treaty be made between the United States and His Britannic Majesty.

G? WASHINGTON.

UNITED STATES, *June 25, 1795.*

Gentlemen of the Senate:

It has been represented by our minister plenipotentiary near the French Republic that such of our commercial relations with France as may require the support of the United States in *detail* can not be well executed without a consul-general. Of this I am satisfied when I consider the extent of the mercantile claims now depending before the French Government, the necessity of bringing into the hands of one agent the various applications to the several committees of administration residing at Paris, the attention which must be paid to the conduct of consuls and vice-consuls, and the nature of the services which are the peculiar objects of a minister's care, and leave no leisure for his intervention in business to which consular functions are competent. I therefore nominate Fulwar Skipwith to be consul-general of the United States in France.

G? WASHINGTON.

UNITED STATES, *June 25, 1795.*

Gentlemen of the Senate:

Just at the close of the last session of Congress I received from one of the Senators and one of the Representatives of the State of Georgia an application for a treaty to be held with the tribes or nations of Indians claiming the right of soil to certain lands lying beyond the present temporary boundary line of that State, and which were described in an act of the legislature of Georgia passed on the 28th of December last.

*For proclamation convening Senate in extraordinary session see p. 171

which has already been laid before the Senate. This application and the subsequent correspondence with the governor of Georgia are herewith transmitted. The subject being very important, I thought proper to postpone a decision upon that application. The views I have since taken of the matter, with the information received of a more pacific disposition on the part of the Creeks, have induced me now to accede to the request, but with this explicit declaration, that neither my assent nor the treaty which may be made shall be considered as affecting any question which may arise upon the supplementary act passed by the legislature of the State of Georgia on the 7th of January last, upon which inquiries have been instituted in pursuance of a resolution of the Senate and House of Representatives, and that any cession or relinquishment of the Indian claims shall be made in the general terms of the treaty of New York, which are contemplated as the form proper to be generally used on such occasions, and on the condition that one-half of the expense of the supplies of provisions for the Indians assembled at the treaty be borne by the State of Georgia.

Having concluded to hold the treaty requested by that State, I was willing to embrace the opportunity it would present of inquiring into the causes of the dissatisfaction of the Creeks which has been manifested since the treaty of New York by their numerous and distressing depredations on our Southwestern frontiers. Their depredations on the Cumberland have been so frequent and so peculiarly destructive as to lead me to think they must originate in some claim to the lands upon that river. But whatever may have been the cause, it is important to trace it to its source; for, independent of the destruction of lives and property, it occasions a very serious annual expense to the United States. The commissioners for holding the proposed treaty will, therefore, be instructed to inquire into the causes of the hostilities to which I have referred, and to enter into such reasonable stipulations as will remove them and give permanent peace to those parts of the United States.

I now nominate Benjamin Hawkins, of North Carolina; George Clymer, of Pennsylvania, and Andrew Pickens, of South Carolina, to be commissioners to hold a treaty with the Creek Nation of Indians, for the purposes hereinbefore expressed.

G⁹ WASHINGTON.

PROCLAMATIONS.

BY THE PRESIDENT OF THE UNITED STATES OF AMERICA.

A PROCLAMATION.

When we review the calamities which afflict so many other nations, the present condition of the United States affords much matter of consolation and satisfaction. Our exemption hitherto from foreign war, an increasing prospect of the continuance of that exemption, the great degree of internal tranquillity we have enjoyed, the recent confirmation of that tranquillity by the suppression of an insurrection which so wantonly threatened it, the happy course of our public affairs in general, the unexampled prosperity of all classes of our citizens, are circumstances which peculiarly mark our situation with indications of the Divine beneficence toward us. In such a state of things it is in an especial manner our duty as a people, with devout reverence and affectionate gratitude, to acknowledge our many and great obligations to Almighty God and to implore Him to continue and confirm the blessings we experience.

Deeply penetrated with this sentiment, I, George Washington, President of the United States, do recommend to all religious societies and denominations, and to all persons whomsoever, within the United States to set apart and observe Thursday, the 19th day of February next, as a day of public thanksgiving and prayer, and on that day to meet together and render their sincere and hearty thanks to the Great Ruler of Nations for the manifold and signal mercies which distinguish our lot as a nation, particularly for the possession of constitutions of government which unite and by their union establish liberty with order; for the preservation of our peace, foreign and domestic; for the seasonable control which has been given to a spirit of disorder in the suppression of the late insurrection, and generally, for the prosperous course of our affairs, public and private; and at the same time humbly and fervently to beseech the kind Author of these blessings graciously to prolong them to us; to imprint on our hearts a deep and solemn sense of our obligations to Him for them; to teach us rightly to estimate their immense value; to preserve us from the arrogance of prosperity, and from hazarding the advantages we enjoy by delusive pursuits; to dispose us to merit the continuance of His favors by not abusing them; by our gratitude for them, and by a correspondent conduct as citizens and men; to render this country more and more a safe and propitious asylum for the unfortunate of other countries; to extend among us true and useful knowledge; to diffuse and establish habits of sobriety, order, morality, and piety, and finally, to impart all the blessings we possess, or ask for ourselves, to the whole family of mankind.

In testimony whereof I have caused the seal of the United States of America to be affixed to these presents, and signed the same with my hand.

[SEAL.]   Done at the city of Philadelphia, the 1st day of January 1795, and of the Independence of the United States of America the nineteenth.

G⁰ WASHINGTON.

By the President:
    EDM: RANDOLPH.

[From Sparks's Washington, Vol. XII, p. 134.]

PROCLAMATION.

Whereas the commissioners appointed by the President of the United States to confer with the citizens in the western counties of Pennsylvania during the late insurrection which prevailed therein, by their act and agreement bearing date the 2d day of September last, in pursuance of the powers in them vested, did promise and engage that, if assurances of submission to the laws of the United States should be bona fide given by the citizens resident in the fourth survey of Pennsylvania, in the manner and within the time in the said act and agreement specified, a general pardon should be granted on the 10th day of July then next ensuing of all treasons and other indictable offenses against the United States committed within the said survey before the 22d day of August last, excluding therefrom, nevertheless, every person who should refuse or neglect to subscribe such assurance and engagement in manner aforesaid, or who should after such subscription violate the same, or willfully obstruct or attempt to obstruct the execution of the acts for raising a revenue on distilled spirits and stills, or be aiding or abetting therein; and

Whereas I have since thought proper to extend the said pardon to all persons guilty of the said treasons, misprisions of treasons, or otherwise concerned in the late insurrection within the survey aforesaid who have not since been indicted or convicted thereof, or of any other offense against the United States:

Therefore be it known that I, George Washington, President of the said United States, have granted, and by these presents do grant, a full, free, and entire pardon to all persons (excepting as is hereinafter excepted) of all treasons, misprisions of treason, and other indictable offenses against the United States committed within the fourth survey of Pennsylvania before the said 22d day of August last past, excepting and excluding therefrom, nevertheless, every person who refused or neglected to give and subscribe the said assurances in the manner aforesaid (or having subscribed hath violated the same) and now standeth indicted or convicted of any treason, misprision of treason, or other offense against the said United States, hereby remitting and releasing unto all persons, except as before excepted, all penalties incurred, or supposed to be incurred, for or on account of the premises.

In testimony whereof I have hereunto set my hand and caused the seal of the United States to be affixed, this 10th day of July, [SEAL.] A. D. 1795, and the twentieth year of the Independence of the said United States.

G⁰ WASHINGTON.

SEVENTH ANNUAL ADDRESS.

UNITED STATES, *December 8, 1795.*

Fellow-Citizens of the Senate and of the House of Representatives:

I trust I do not deceive myself when I indulge the persuasion that I have never met you at any period when more than at the present the situation of our public affairs has afforded just cause for mutual congratulation, and for inviting you to join with me in profound gratitude to the Author of all Good for the numerous and extraordinary blessings we enjoy.

The termination of the long, expensive, and distressing war in which we have been engaged with certain Indians northwest of the Ohio is placed in the option of the United States by a treaty which the commander of our army has concluded provisionally with the hostile tribes in that region.

In the adjustment of the terms the satisfaction of the Indians was deemed an object worthy no less of the policy than of the liberality of the United States as the necessary basis of durable tranquillity. The object, it is believed, has been fully attained. The articles agreed upon will immediately be laid before the Senate for their consideration.

The Creek and Cherokee Indians, who alone of the Southern tribes had annoyed our frontiers, have lately confirmed their preexisting treaties with us, and were giving evidence of a sincere disposition to carry them into effect by the surrender of the prisoners and property they had taken. But we have to lament that the fair prospect in this quarter has been once more clouded by wanton murders, which some citizens of Georgia are represented to have recently perpetrated on hunting parties of the Creeks, which have again subjected that frontier to disquietude and danger, which will be productive of further expense, and may occasion more effusion of blood. Measures are pursuing to prevent or mitigate the usual consequences of such outrages, and with the hope of their succeeding at least to avert general hostility.

A letter from the Emperor of Morocco announces to me his recognition of our treaty made with his father, the late Emperor, and consequently the continuance of peace with that power. With peculiar satisfaction I add that information has been received from an agent deputed on our part to Algiers importing that the terms of the treaty with the Dey and Regency of that country had been adjusted in such a manner as to authorize the expectation of a speedy peace and the restoration of our unfortunate fellow-citizens from a grievous captivity.

The latest advices from our envoy at the Court of Madrid give, moreover, the pleasing information that he had received assurances of a speedy and satisfactory conclusion of his negotiation. While the event depending upon unadjusted particulars can not be regarded as ascertained, it is agreeable to cherish the expectation of an issue which, securing amicably very essential interests of the United States, will at the same time lay the foundation of lasting harmony with a power whose friendship we have uniformly and sincerely desired to cultivate.

Though not before officially disclosed to the House of Representatives, you, gentlemen, are all apprised that a treaty of amity, commerce, and navigation has been negotiated with Great Britain, and that the Senate have advised and consented to its ratification upon a condition which excepts part of one article. Agreeably thereto, and to the best judgment I was able to form of the public interest after full and mature deliberation, I have added my sanction. The result on the part of His Britannic Majesty is unknown. When received, the subject will without delay be placed before Congress.

This interesting summary of our affairs with regard to the foreign powers between whom and the United States controversies have subsisted, and with regard also to those of our Indian neighbors with whom we have been in a state of enmity or misunderstanding, opens a wide field for consoling and gratifying reflections. If by prudence and moderation on every side the extinguishment of all the causes of external discord which have heretofore menaced our tranquillity, on terms compatible with our national rights and honor, shall be the happy result, how firm and how precious a foundation will have been laid for accelerating, maturing, and establishing the prosperity of our country.

Contemplating the internal situation as well as the external relations of the United States, we discover equal cause for contentment and satisfaction. While many of the nations of Europe, with their American dependencies, have been involved in a contest unusually bloody, exhausting, and calamitous, in which the evils of foreign war have been aggravated by domestic convulsion and insurrection; in which many of the arts most useful to society have been exposed to discouragement and decay; in which scarcity of subsistence has imbittered other sufferings; while even the anticipations of a return of the blessings of peace and repose are alloyed by the sense of heavy and accumulating burthens, which press upon all the departments of industry and threaten to clog the future springs of government, our favored country, happy in a striking contrast, has enjoyed general tranquillity—a tranquillity the more satisfactory because maintained at the expense of no duty. Faithful to ourselves, we have violated no obligation to others. Our agriculture, commerce, and manufactures prosper beyond former example, the molestations of our trade (to prevent a continuance of which, however, very pointed remonstrances have been made) being overbalanced by the aggregate benefits which it derives from a neutral position. Our population advances with a celerity which, exceeding the most sanguine calculations. proportionally augments our strength and resources, and guarantees our future security. Every part of the Union displays indications of rapid and various improvement; and with burthens so light as scarcely to be perceived, with resources fully adequate to our present exigencies, with governments founded on the genuine principles of rational liberty, and with mild and wholesome laws, is it too much to say that our country exhibits a spectacle of national happiness never surpassed, if ever before equaled?

Placed in a situation every way so auspicious, motives of commanding force impel us, with sincere acknowledgment to Heaven and pure love to our country, to unite our efforts to preserve, prolong, and improve our immense advantages. To cooperate with you in this desirable work is a fervent and favorite wish of my heart.

It is a valuable ingredient in the general estimate of our welfare that the part of our country which was lately the scene of disorder and insurrection now enjoys the blessings of quiet and order. The misled have abandoned their errors, and pay the respect to our Constitution and laws which is due from good citizens to the public authorities of the society. These circumstances have induced me to pardon generally the offenders here referred to, and to extend forgiveness to those who had been adjudged to capital punishment. For though I shall always think it a sacred duty to exercise with firmness and energy the constitutional powers with which I am vested, yet it appears to me no less consistent with the public good than it is with my personal feelings to mingle in the operations of Government every degree of moderation and tenderness which the national justice, dignity, and safety may permit.

GENTLEMEN: Among the objects which will claim your attention in the course of the session, a review of our military establishment is not the least important. It is called for by the events which have changed, and may be expected still further to change, the relative situation of our frontiers. In this review you will doubtless allow due weight to the considerations that the questions between us and certain foreign powers are not yet finally adjusted, that the war in Europe is not yet terminated, and that our Western posts, when recovered, will demand provision for garrisoning and securing them. A statement of our present military force will be laid before you by the Department of War.

With the review of our Army establishment is naturally connected that of the militia. It will merit inquiry what imperfections 'n the existing plan further experience may have unfolded. The subject is of so much moment in my estimation as to excite a constant solicitude that the consideration of it may be renewed until the greatest attainable perfection shall be accomplished. Time is wearing away some advantages for forwarding the object, while none better deserves the persevering attention of the public councils.

While we indulge the satisfaction which the actual condition of our

Western borders so well authorizes, it is necessary that we should not lose sight of an important truth which continually receives new confirmations, namely, that the provisions heretofore made with a view to the protection of the Indians from the violences of the lawless part of our frontier inhabitants are insufficient. It is demonstrated that these violences can now be perpetrated with impunity, and it can need no argument to prove that unless the murdering of Indians can be restrained by bringing the murderers to condign punishment, all the exertions of the Government to prevent destructive retaliations by the Indians will prove fruitless and all our present agreeable prospects illusory. The frequent destruction of innocent women and children, who are chiefly the victims of retaliation, must continue to shock humanity, and an enormous expense to drain the Treasury of the Union.

To enforce upon the Indians the observance of justice it is indispensable that there shall be competent means of rendering justice to them. If these means can be devised by the wisdom of Congress, and especially if there can be added an adequate provision for supplying the necessities of the Indians on reasonable terms (a measure the mention of which I the more readily repeat, as in all the conferences with them they urge it with solicitude), I should not hesitate to entertain a strong hope of rendering our tranquillity permanent. I add with pleasure that the probability even of their civilization is not diminished by the experiments which have been thus far made under the auspices of Government. The accomplishment of this work, if practicable, will reflect undecaying luster on our national character and administer the most grateful consolations that virtuous minds can know.

Gentlemen of the House of Representatives:

The state of our revenue, with the sums which have been borrowed and reimbursed pursuant to different acts of Congress, will be submitted from the proper Department, together with an estimate of the appropriations necessary to be made for the service of the ensuing year.

Whether measures may not be advisable to reenforce the provision for the redemption of the public debt will naturally engage your examination. Congress have demonstrated their sense to be, and it were superfluous to repeat mine, that whatsoever will tend to accelerate the honorable extinction of our public debt accords as much with the true interest of our country as with the general sense of our constituents.

Gentlemen of the Senate and of the House of Representatives:

The statements which will be laid before you relative to the Mint will shew the situation of that institution and the necessity of some further legislative provisions for carrying the business of it more completely into effect, and for checking abuses which appear to be arising in particular quarters.

The progress in providing materials for the frigates and in building them, the state of the fortifications of our harbors, the measures which have been pursued for obtaining proper sites for arsenals and for replenishing our magazines with military stores, and the steps which have been taken toward the execution of the law for opening a trade with the Indians will likewise be presented for the information of Congress.

Temperate discussion of the important subjects which may arise in the course of the session and mutual forbearance where there is a difference of opinion are too obvious and necessary for the peace, happiness, and welfare of our country to need any recommendation of mine.

G⁰ WASHINGTON.

ADDRESS OF THE SENATE TO GEORGE WASHINGTON, PRESIDENT OF THE UNITED STATES.

SIR: It is with peculiar satisfaction that we are informed by your speech to the two Houses of Congress that the long and expensive war in which we have been engaged with the Indians northwest of the Ohio is in a situation to be finally terminated; and though we view with concern the danger of an interruption of the peace so recently confirmed with the Creeks, we indulge the hope that the measures that you have adopted to prevent the same, if followed by those legislative provisions that justice and humanity equally demand, will succeed in laying the foundation of a lasting peace with the Indian tribes on the Southern as well as on the Western frontiers.

The confirmation of our treaty with Morocco, and the adjustment of a treaty of peace with Algiers, in consequence of which our captive fellow-citizens shall be delivered from slavery, are events that will prove no less interesting to the public humanity than they will be important in extending and securing the navigation and commerce of our country.

As a just and equitable conclusion of our depending negotiations with Spain will essentially advance the interest of both nations, and thereby cherish and confirm the good understanding and friendship which we have at all times desired to maintain, it will afford us real pleasure to receive an early confirmation of our expectations on this subject.

The interesting prospect of our affairs with regard to the foreign powers between whom and the United States controversies have subsisted is not more satisfactory than the review of our internal situation. If from the former we derive an expectation of the extinguishment of all the causes of external discord that have heretofore endangered our tranquillity, and on terms consistent with our national honor and safety, in the latter we discover those numerous and widespread tokens of prosperity which in so peculiar a manner distinguish our happy country.

Circumstances thus every way auspicious demand our gratitude and sincere acknowledgments to Almighty God, and require that we should unite our efforts in imitation of your enlightened, firm, and persevering example to establish and preserve the peace, freedom, and prosperity of our country.

The objects which you have recommended to the notice of the Legislature will in the course of the session receive our careful attention, and with a true zeal for the public welfare we shall cheerfully cooperate in every measure that shall appear to us best calculated to promote the same.

JOHN ADAMS,
Vice-President of the United States and President of the Senate.

DECEMBER 11, 1795.

REPLY OF THE PRESIDENT.

GENTLEMEN: With real pleasure I receive your address, recognizing the prosperous situation of our public affairs, and giving assurances of your careful attention to the objects demanding legislative consideration, and that with a true zeal for the public welfare you will cheerfully cooperate in every measure which shall appear to you best calculated to promote the same.

But I derive peculiar satisfaction from your concurrence with me in the expressions of gratitude to Almighty God, which a review of the auspicious circumstances that distinguish our happy country have excited, and I trust the sincerity of our acknowledgments will be evinced by a union of efforts to establish and preserve its peace, freedom, and prosperity.

G⁰ WASHINGTON.

DECEMBER 12, 1795.

ADDRESS OF THE HOUSE OF REPRESENTATIVES TO GEORGE WASHINGTON, PRESIDENT OF THE UNITED STATES.

The PRESIDENT OF THE UNITED STATES.

SIR: As the Representatives of the people of the United States, we can not but participate in the strongest sensibility to every blessing which they enjoy, and cheerfully join with you in profound gratitude to the Author of all Good for the numerous and extraordinary blessings which He has conferred on our favored country.

A final and formal termination of the distressing war which has ravaged our Northwestern frontier will be an event which must afford a satisfaction proportionate to the anxiety with which it has long been sought, and in the adjustment of the terms we perceive the true policy of making them satisfactory to the Indians as well as to the United States as the best basis of a durable tranquillity. The disposition of such of the Southern tribes as had also heretofore annoyed our frontier is another prospect in our situation so important to the interest and happiness of the United States that it is much to be lamented that any clouds should be thrown over it, more especially by excesses on the part of our own citizens.

While our population is advancing with a celerity which exceeds the most sanguine calculations; while every part of the United States displays indications of rapid and various improvement; while we are in the enjoyment of protection and security by mild and wholesome laws, administered by governments founded on the genuine principles of rational liberty, a secure foundation will be laid for accelerating, maturing, and establishing the prosperity of our country if, by treaty and amicable negotiation, all those causes of external discord which heretofore menaced our tranquillity shall be extinguished on terms compatible with our national rights and honor and with our Constitution and great commercial interests.

Among the various circumstances in our internal situation none can be viewed with more satisfaction and exultation than that the late scene of disorder and insurrection has been completely restored to the enjoyment of order and repose.   Such a triumph of reason and of law is worthy of the free Government under which it happened, and was justly to be hoped from the enlightened and patriotic spirit which pervades and actuates the people of the United States.

In contemplating that spectacle of national happiness which our country exhibits, and of which you, sir, have been pleased to make an interesting summary, permit us to acknowledge and declare the very great share which your zealous and faithful services have contributed to it, and to express the affectionate attachment which we feel for your character.

The several interesting subjects which you recommend to our consideration will receive every degree of attention which is due to them; and whilst we feel the obligation of temperance and mutual indulgence in all our discussions, we trust and pray that the result to the happiness and welfare of our country may correspond with the pure affection we bear to it.

DECEMBER 16, 1795.

REPLY OF THE PRESIDENT.

GENTLEMEN: Coming as you do from all parts of the United States, I receive great satisfaction from the concurrence of your testimony in the justness of the interesting summary of our national happiness which, as the result of my inquiries, I presented to your view.   The sentiments we have mutually expressed of profound gratitude to the source of those numerous blessings, the Author of all Good, are pledges of our obligations to unite our sincere and zealous endeavors, as the instruments of Divine Providence, to preserve and perpetuate them.

Accept, gentlemen, my thanks for your declaration that to my agency you ascribe the enjoyment of a great share of these benefits.   So far as my services contribute to the happiness of my country, the acknowledgment thereof by my fellow-citizens and their affectionate attachment will ever prove an abundant reward.

G? WASHINGTON.

DECEMBER 17, 1795.

SPECIAL MESSAGES.

UNITED STATES, *December 9, 1795.*

Gentlemen of the Senate:

I lay before you, for your consideration, a treaty of peace which has been negotiated by General Wayne, on behalf of the United States, with all the late hostile tribes of Indians northwest of the river Ohio, together with the instructions which were given to General Wayne and the proceedings at the place of treaty.

G? WASHINGTON.

UNITED STATES, *December 21, 1795.*

Gentlemen of the Senate:

Herewith I transmit, for your information and consideration, the original letter from the Emperor of Morocco, recognizing the treaty of peace and friendship between the United States and his father, the late Emperor, accompanied with a translation thereof, and various documents relating to the negotiation by which the recognition was effected.

G? WASHINGTON.

UNITED STATES, *January 4, 1796.*

Gentlemen of the Senate and of the House of Representatives:

A letter from the minister plenipotentiary of the French Republic, received on the 22d of the last month, covered an address, dated the 21st of October, 1794, from the committee of public safety to the Representatives of the United States in Congress, and also informed me that he was instructed by the committee to present to the United States the colors of France. I thereupon proposed to receive them last Friday, the first day of the new year, a day of general joy and congratulation. On that day the minister of the French Republic delivered the colors, with an address, to which I returned an answer. By the latter Congress will see that I have informed the minister that the colors will be deposited with the archives of the United States. But it seemed to me proper previously to exhibit to the two Houses of Congress these evidences of the continued friendship of the French Republic, together with the sentiments expressed by me on the occasion in behalf of the United States. They are herewith communicated.

G⁰ WASHINGTON.

UNITED STATES, *January 8, 1796.*

Gentlemen of the Senate and of the House of Representatives:

I transmit to you a memorial of the commissioners appointed by virtue of an act entitled "An act for establishing the temporary and permanent seat of the Government of the United States," on the subject of the public buildings under their direction.

Since locating a district for the permanent seat of the Government of the United States, as heretofore announced to both Houses of Congress, I have accepted the grants of money and of land stated in the memorial of the commissioners. I have directed the buildings therein mentioned to be commenced on plans which I deemed consistent with the liberality of the grants and proper for the purposes intended.

I have not been inattentive to this important business intrusted by the Legislature to my care. I have viewed the resources placed in my hands, and observed the manner in which they have been applied. The progress is pretty fully detailed in the memorial from the commissioners, and one of them attends to give further information if required. In a case new and arduous, like the present, difficulties might naturally be expected. Some have occurred, but they are in a great degree surmounted, and I have no doubt, if the remaining resources are properly cherished, so as to prevent the loss of property by hasty and numerous sales, that all the buildings required for the accommodation of the Government of the United States may be completed in season without aid from the Federal Treasury. The subject is therefore recommended to the consideration of Congress, and the result will determine the measures which I shall cause to be pursued with respect to the property remaining unsold.

G⁰ WASHINGTON.

UNITED STATES, *January 29, 1796.*

Gentlemen of the Senate and of the House of Representatives:

I send herewith for the information of Congress:

First. An act of the legislature of the State of Rhode Island, ratifying an amendment to the Constitution of the United States to prevent suits in certain cases against a State.

Second. An act of the State of North Carolina making the like ratification.

Third. An act of the State of North Carolina, assenting to the purchase by the United States of a sufficient quantity of land on Shell Castle

Island for the purpose of erecting a beacon thereon, and ceding the jurisdiction thereof to the United States.

Fourth. A copy from the journal of proceedings of the governor in his executive department of the territory of the United States northwest of the river Ohio from July 1 to December 31, 1794.

Fifth. A copy from the records of the executive proceedings of the same governor from January 1 to June 30, 1795; and

Sixth and seventh. A copy of the journal of the proceedings of the governor in his executive department of the territory of the United States south of the river Ohio from September 1, 1794, to September 1, 1795.

Eighth. The acts of the first and second sessions of the general assembly of the same territory.

GO WASHINGTON.

UNITED STATES, *January 29, 1796.*

Gentlemen of the Senate and of the House of Representatives:

In pursuance of the authority vested in the President of the United States by an act of Congress passed the 3d of March last, to reduce the weights of the copper coin of the United States whenever he should think it for the benefit of the United States, provided that the reduction should not exceed 2 pennyweights in each cent, and in the like proportion in a half cent, I have caused the same to be reduced since the 27th of last December, to wit, 1 pennyweight and 16 grains in each cent, and in the like proportion in a half cent; and I have given notice thereof by proclamation.

By the letter of the judges of the circuit court of the United States, held at Boston in June last, and the inclosed application of the under-keeper of the jail at that place, of which copies are herewith transmitted, Congress will perceive the necessity of making a suitable provision for the maintenance of prisoners committed to the jails of the several States under the authority of the United States.

GO WASHINGTON.

UNITED STATES, *February 2, 1796.*

Gentlemen of the Senate and of the House of Representatives:

I transmit herewith the copy of a letter, dated the 19th of December last, from Governor Blount to the Secretary of War, stating the avowed and daring designs of certain persons to take possession of the lands belonging to the Cherokees, and which the United States have by treaty solemnly guaranteed to that nation. The injustice of such intrusions and the mischievous consequences which must necessarily result therefrom demand that effectual provision be made to prevent them.

GO WASHINGTON.

UNITED STATES, *February 15, 1796.*

Gentlemen of the Senate:

Herewith I transmit, for your consideration and advice, a treaty of peace and amity, concluded on the 5th day of last September by Joseph Donaldson, jr., on the part of the United States, with the Dey of Algiers, for himself, his Divan, and his subjects.

The instructions and other necessary papers relative to this negotiation are also sent herewith, for the information of the Senate.

GO WASHINGTON.

UNITED STATES, *February 26, 1796.*

Gentlemen of the Senate:

I send herewith the treaty concluded on the 27th of October last between the United States and Spain by their respective plenipotentiaries.

The communications to the Senate referred to in my message of the 16th of December, 1793, contain the instructions to the commissioners of the United States, Messrs. Carmichael and Short, and various details relative to the negotiations with Spain. Herewith I transmit copies of the documents authorizing Mr. Pinckney, the envoy extraordinary from the United States to the Court of Spain, to conclude the negotiation agreeably to the original instructions above mentioned, and to adjust the claims of the United States for the spoliations committed by the armed vessels of His Catholic Majesty on the commerce of our citizens.

The numerous papers exhibiting the progress of the negotiation under the conduct of Mr. Pinckney, being in the French and Spanish languages, will be communicated to the Senate as soon as the translations which appear necessary shall be completed.

GO WASHINGTON.

UNITED STATES, *March 1, 1796.*

Gentlemen of the Senate and of the House of Representatives:

The treaty of amity, commerce, and navigation concluded between the United States of America and His Britannic Majesty having been duly ratified, and the ratifications having been exchanged at London on the 28th day of October, 1795, I have directed the same to be promulgated, and herewith transmit a copy thereof for the information of Congress.

GO WASHINGTON.

UNITED STATES, *March 8, 1796.*

Gentlemen of the Senate and of the House of Representatives:

I send herewith, for the information of Congress, the treaty concluded between the United States and the Dey and Regency of Algiers.

GO WASHINGTON.

UNITED STATES, *March 15, 1796.*

Gentlemen of the Senate and of the House of Representatives:

By the ninth section of the act entitled "An act to provide a naval armament" it is enacted "that if a peace shall take place between the United States and the Regency of Algiers, that no further proceedings be had under this act."

The peace which is here contemplated having taken place, it is incumbent upon the Executive to suspend all orders respecting the building of the frigates, procuring materials for them, or preparing materials already obtained, which may be done without intrenching upon contracts or agreements made and entered into before this event.

But inasmuch as the loss which the public would incur might be considerable from dissipation of workmen, from certain works or operations being suddenly dropped or left unfinished, and from the derangement in the whole system consequent upon an immediate suspension of all proceedings under it, I have therefore thought advisable, before taking such a step, to submit the subject to the Senate and House of Representatives, that such measures may be adopted in the premises as may best comport with the public interest.

G? WASHINGTON.

UNITED STATES, *March 25, 1796.*

Gentlemen of the Senate and of the House of Representatives:

I send herewith, for your information, the translation of a letter from the minister plenipotentiary of the French Republic to the Secretary of State, announcing the peace made by the Republic with the Kings of Prussia and Spain, the Grand Duke of Tuscany, and the Landgrave of Hesse Cassel, and that the republican constitution decreed by the National Convention had been accepted by the people of France and was in operation. I also send you a copy of the answer given by my direction to this communication from the French minister. My sentiments therein expressed I am persuaded will harmonize with yours and with those of all my fellow-citizens.

G? WASHINGTON.

UNITED STATES, *March 29, 1796.*

Gentlemen of the House of Representatives:

I send herewith a copy of the treaty of friendship, limits, and navigation, concluded on the 27th of October last, between the United States and His Catholic Majesty. This treaty has been ratified by me agreeably to the Constitution, and the ratification has been dispatched for Spain, where it will doubtless be immediately ratified by His Catholic Majesty.

This early communication of the treaty with Spain has become necessary because it is stipulated in the third article that commissioners for running the boundary line between the territory of the United States and the Spanish colonies of East and West Florida shall meet at the Natchez before the expiration of six months from the ratification; and as that period will undoubtedly arrive before the next meeting of Congress, the House will see the necessity of making provision in their present session for the object here mentioned. It will also be necessary to provide for the expense to be incurred in executing the twenty-first article of the treaty, to enable our fellow-citizens to obtain with as little delay as possible compensation for the losses they have sustained by the capture of their vessels and cargoes by the subjects of His Catholic Majesty during the late war between France and Spain.

Estimates of the moneys necessary to be provided for the purposes of this and several other treaties with foreign nations and the Indian tribes will be laid before you by the proper Department.

G^O WASHINGTON.

UNITED STATES, *March 30, 1796.*

To the House of Representatives of the United States:

With the utmost attention I have considered your resolution of the 24th instant, requesting me to lay before your House a copy of the instructions to the minister of the United States who negotiated the treaty with the King of Great Britain, together with the correspondence and other documents relative to that treaty, excepting such of the said papers as any existing negotiation may render improper to be disclosed.

In deliberating upon this subject it was impossible for me to lose sight of the principle which some have avowed in its discussion, or to avoid extending my views to the consequences which must flow from the admission of that principle.

I trust that no part of my conduct has ever indicated a disposition to withhold any information which the Constitution has enjoined upon the President as a duty to give, or which could be required of him by either House of Congress as a right; and with truth I affirm that it has been, as it will continue to be while I have the honor to preside in the Government, my constant endeavor to harmonize with the other branches thereof so far as the trust delegated to me by the people of the United States and my sense of the obligation it imposes to "preserve, protect, and defend the Constitution" will permit.

The nature of foreign negotiations requires caution, and their success must often depend on secrecy; and even when brought to a conclusion a full disclosure of all the measures, demands, or eventual concessions which may have been proposed or contemplated would be extremely impolitic; for this might have a pernicious influence on future negotiations, or produce immediate inconveniences, perhaps danger and mischief, in relation to other powers. The necessity of such caution and secrecy was one cogent reason for vesting the power of making treaties in the President, with the advice and consent of the Senate, the principle on which that body was formed confining it to a small number of members. To admit, then, a right in the House of Representatives to demand and to have as a matter of course all the papers respecting a negotiation with a foreign power would be to establish a dangerous precedent.

It does not occur that the inspection of the papers asked for can be relative to any purpose under the cognizance of the House of Representatives, except that of an impeachment, which the resolution has not expressed. I repeat that I have no disposition to withhold any information which the duty of my station will permit or the public good shall require to be disclosed; and, in fact, all the papers affecting the negotiation with Great Britain were laid before the Senate when the treaty itself was communicated for their consideration and advice.

The course which the debate has taken on the resolution of the House leads to some observations on the mode of making treaties under the Constitution of the United States.

Having been a member of the General Convention, and knowing the principles on which the Constitution was formed, I have ever entertained but one opinion on this subject; and from the first establishment of the Government to this moment my conduct has exemplified that opinion— that the power of making treaties is exclusively vested in the President, by and with the advice and consent of the Senate, provided two-thirds of the Senators present concur; and that every treaty so made and promulgated thenceforward became the law of the land. It is thus that the treaty-making power has been understood by foreign nations, and in all the treaties made with them *we* have declared and *they* have believed that, when ratified by the President, with the advice and consent of the Senate, they became obligatory. In this construction of the Constitution every House of Representatives has heretofore acquiesced, and until the present time not a doubt or suspicion has appeared, to my knowledge, that this construction was not the true one. Nay, they have more than acquiesced; for till now, without controverting the obligation of such treaties, they have made all the requisite provisions for carrying them into effect.

There is also reason to believe that this construction agrees with the opinions entertained by the State conventions when they were deliberating on the Constitution, especially by those who objected to it because there was not required in *commercial treaties* the consent of two-third, of the whole number of the members of the Senate instead of two-thirds of the Senators present, and because in treaties respecting territorial and certain other rights and claims the concurrence of three-fourths of the whole number of the members of both Houses, respectively, was not made necessary.

It is a fact declared by the General Convention and universally understood that the Constitution of the United States was the result of a spirit of amity and mutual concession; and it is well known that under this influence the smaller States were admitted to an equal representation in the Senate with the larger States, and that this branch of the Government was invested with great powers, for on the equal participation of those powers the sovereignty and political safety of the smaller States were deemed essentially to depend.

If other proofs than these and the plain letter of the Constitution itself be necessary to ascertain the point under consideration, they may be found in the journals of the General Convention, which I have deposited in the office of the Department of State. In those journals it will appear that a proposition was made "that no treaty should be binding on the United States which was not ratified by a law," and that the proposition was explicitly rejected.

As, therefore, it is perfectly clear to my understanding that the assent of the House of Representatives is not necessary to the validity of a treaty; as the treaty with Great Britain exhibits in itself all the objects requiring legislative provision, and on these the papers called for can throw no light, and as it is essential to the due administration of the Government that the boundaries fixed by the Constitution between the different departments should be preserved, a just regard to the Constitution and to the duty of my office, under all the circumstances of this case, forbids a compliance with your request.

G<u>o</u> WASHINGTON.

UNITED STATES, *March 31, 1796.*

Gentlemen of the Senate:

The treaty of amity, commerce, and navigation between the United States and Great Britain requiring that commissioners should be appointed to fix certain boundaries between the territories of the contracting parties, and to ascertain the losses and damages represented to have been sustained by their respective citizens and subjects, as set forth in the fifth, sixth, and seventh articles of the treaty, in order to carry those articles into execution I nominate as commissioners on the part of the United States:

For the purpose mentioned in the fifth article, Henry Knox, of Massachusetts;

For the purpose mentioned in the sixth article, Thomas Fitzsimons, of Pennsylvania, and James Innes, of Virginia; and

For the purposes mentioned in the seventh article, Christopher Gore, of Massachusetts, and William Pinckney, of Maryland.

G<u>o</u> WASHINGTON.

UNITED STATES, *April 8, 1796.*

Gentlemen of the Senate and of the House of Representatives:

By an act of Congress passed on the 26th of May, 1790, it was declared that the inhabitants of the territory of the United States south of the river Ohio should enjoy all the privileges, benefits, and advantages set forth in the ordinance of Congress for the government of the territory of the United States northwest of the river Ohio, and that the government of the said territory south of the Ohio should be similar to that which was then exercised in the territory northwest of the Ohio, except so far as was otherwise provided in the conditions expressed in an act of Congress passed the 2d of April, 1790, entitled "An act to accept a cession of the claims of the State of North Carolina to a certain district of western territory."

Among the privileges, benefits, and advantages thus secured to the inhabitants of the territory south of the river Ohio appear to be the right of forming a permanent constitution and State government, and of admission as a State, by its Delegates, into the Congress of the United States, on an equal footing with the original States in all respects whatever, when it should have therein 60,000 free inhabitants; provided the constitution and government so to be formed should be republican, and in conformity to the principles contained in the articles of the said ordinance.

As proofs of the several requisites to entitle the territory south of the river Ohio to be admitted as a State into the Union, Governor Blount has transmitted a return of the enumeration of its inhabitants and a printed copy of the constitution and form of government on which they have agreed, which, with his letters accompanying the same, are herewith laid before Congress.

GO WASHINGTON.

UNITED STATES, *April 28, 1796.*

Gentlemen of the Senate and of the House of Representatives:

Herewith I lay before you a letter from the Attorney-General of the United States, relative to compensation to the attorneys of the United States in the several districts, which is recommended to your consideration.

GO WASHINGTON.

UNITED STATES, *May 2, 1796.*

Gentlemen of the Senate:

Some time last year Jeremiah Wadsworth was authorized to hold a treaty with the Cohnawaga Indians, styling themselves the Seven Nations of Canada, to enable the State of New York to extinguish, by purchase, a claim which the said Indians had set up to a parcel of land lying within that State. The negotiation having issued without effecting its object, and the State of New York having requested a renewal of the negotiation, and the Indians having come forward with an application on the same subject, I now nominate Jeremiah Wadsworth to be a commissioner to hold a treaty with the Cohnawaga Indians, styling themselves the Seven Nations of Canada, for the purpose of enabling the State of New York to extinguish the aforesaid claim.

G? WASHINGTON.

UNITED STATES, *May 5, 1796.*

Gentlemen of the Senate:

I lay before you, for your consideration and advice, an explanatory article proposed to be added to the treaty of amity, commerce, and navigation between the United States and Great Britain, together with a copy of the full power to the Secretary of State to negotiate the same.

G? WASHINGTON.

UNITED STATES, *May 25, 1796.*

Gentlemen of the Senate and of the House of Representatives:

The measures now in operation for taking possession of the posts of Detroit and Michilimackinac render it proper that provision should be made for extending to these places and any others alike circumstanced the civil authority of the Northwestern Territory. To do this will require an expense to defray which the ordinary salaries of the governor and secretary of that Territory appear to be incompetent.

The forming of a new county, or new counties, and the appointment of the various officers, which the just exercise of government must require, will oblige the governor and secretary to visit those places, and to spend considerable time in making the arrangements necessary for introducing and establishing the Government of the United States. Congress will consider what provision will in this case be proper.

G? WASHINGTON.

UNITED STATES, *May 28, 1796.*

Gentlemen of the Senate and of the House of Representatives:

The extraordinary expenses to be incurred in the present year in supporting our foreign intercourse I find will require a provision beyond the ordinary appropriation and the additional $20,000 already granted.

I have directed an estimate to be made, which is sent herewith, and will exhibit the deficiency for which an appropriation appears to be necessary.

G? WASHINGTON.

EIGHTH ANNUAL ADDRESS.

UNITED STATES, *December 7, 1796.*

Fellow-Citizens of the Senate and of the House of Representatives:

In recurring to the internal situation of our country since I had last the pleasure to address you, I find ample reason for a renewed expression of that gratitude to the Ruler of the Universe which a continued series of prosperity has so often and so justly called forth.

The acts of the last session which required special arrangements have been as far as circumstances would admit carried into operation.

Measures calculated to insure a continuance of the friendship of the Indians and to preserve peace along the extent of our interior frontier have been digested and adopted. In the framing of these care has been taken to guard on the one hand our advanced settlements from the predatory incursions of those unruly individuals who can not be restrained by their tribes, and on the other hand to protect the rights secured to the Indians by treaty—to draw them nearer to the civilized state and inspire them with correct conceptions of the power as well as justice of the Government.

The meeting of the deputies from the Creek Nation at Colerain, in the State of Georgia, which had for a principal object the purchase of a parcel of their land by that State, broke up without its being accomplished, the nation having previous to their departure instructed them against making any sale. The occasion, however, has been improved to confirm by a new treaty with the Creeks their preexisting engagements with the United States, and to obtain their consent to the establishment of trading houses and military posts within their boundary, by means of which their friendship and the general peace may be more effectually secured.

The period during the late session at which the appropriation was passed for carrying into effect the treaty of amity, commerce, and navigation between the United States and His Britannic Majesty necessarily procrastinated the reception of the posts stipulated to be delivered beyond the date assigned for that event. As soon, however, as the Governor-General of Canada could be addressed with propriety on the subject, arrangements were cordially and promptly concluded for their evacuation, and the United States took possession of the principal of them, comprehending Oswego, Niagara, Detroit, Michilimackinac, and Fort Miami, where such repairs and additions have been ordered to be made as appeared indispensable.

The commissioners appointed on the part of the United States and of Great Britain to determine which is the river St. Croix mentioned in the treaty of peace of 1783, agreed in the choice of Egbert Benson, esq., of New York, for the third commissioner. The whole met at St. Andrews, in Passamaquoddy Bay, in the beginning of October, and directed surveys to be made of the rivers in dispute; but deeming it impracticable to have these surveys completed before the next year, they adjourned to meet at Boston in August, 1797, for the final decision of the question.

Other commissioners appointed on the part of the United States, agreeably to the seventh article of the treaty with Great Britain, relative to captures and condemnation of vessels and other property, met the commissioners of His Britannic Majesty in London in August last, when John Trumbull, esq., was chosen by lot for the fifth commissioner. In October following the board were to proceed to business. As yet there has been no communication of commissioners on the part of Great Britain to unite with those who have been appointed on the part of the United States for carrying into effect the sixth article of the treaty.

The treaty with Spain required that the commissioners for running the boundary line between the territory of the United States and His Catholic Majesty's provinces of East and West Florida should meet at the Natchez before the expiration of six months after the exchange of the ratifications, which was effected at Aranjuez on the 25th day of April; and the troops of His Catholic Majesty occupying any posts within the limits of the United States were within the same period to be withdrawn. The commissioner of the United States therefore commenced his journey for the Natchez in September, and troops were ordered to occupy the posts from which the Spanish garrisons should be withdrawn. Information has been recently received of the appointment of a commissioner on the part of His Catholic Majesty for running the boundary line, but none of any appointment for the adjustment of the claims of our citizens whose vessels were captured by the armed vessels of Spain.

In pursuance of the act of Congress passed in the last session for the protection and relief of American seamen, agents were appointed, one to reside in Great Britain and the other in the West Indies. The effects of the agency in the West Indies are not yet fully ascertained, but those which have been communicated afford grounds to believe the measure will be beneficial. The agent destined to reside in Great Britain declining to accept the appointment, the business has consequently devolved on the minister of the United States in London, and will command his attention until a new agent shall be appointed.

After many delays and disappointments arising out of the European war, the final arrangements for fulfilling the engagements made to the Dey and Regency of Algiers will in all present appearance be crowned with success, but under great, though inevitable, disadvantages in the pecuniary transactions occasioned by that war, which will render further provision necessary. The actual liberation of all our citizens who were prisoners in Algiers, while it gratifies every feeling heart, is itself an earnest of a satisfactory termination of the whole negotiation. Measures are in operation for effecting treaties with the Regencies of Tunis and Tripoli.

To an active external commerce the protection of a naval force is indispensable. This is manifest with regard to wars in which a State is itself a party. But besides this, it is in our own experience that the most sincere neutrality is not a sufficient guard against the depredations of nations at war. To secure respect to a neutral flag requires a naval force organized and ready to vindicate it from insult or aggression. This may even prevent the necessity of going to war by discouraging belligerent powers from committing such violations of the rights of the neutral party as may, first or last, leave no other option. From the best information I have been able to obtain it would seem as if our trade to the Mediterranean without a protecting force will always be insecure and our citizens exposed to the calamities from which numbers of them have but just been relieved.

These considerations invite the United States to look to the means, and to set about the gradual creation of a navy. The increasing progress of their navigation promises them at no distant period the requisite supply of seamen, and their means in other respects favor the undertaking. It is an encouragement, likewise, that their particular situation will give weight and influence to a moderate naval force in their hands. Will it not, then, be advisable to begin without delay to provide and lay up the materials for the building and equipping of ships of war, and to proceed in the work by degrees, in proportion as our resources shall render it practicable without inconvenience, so that a future war of Europe may not find our commerce in the same unprotected state in which it was found by the present?

Congress have repeatedly, and not without success, directed their attention to the encouragement of manufactures. The object is of too much consequence not to insure a continuance of their efforts in every way which shall appear eligible. As a general rule, manufactures on public account are inexpedient; but where the state of things in a country leaves little hope that certain branches of manufacture will for a great length of time obtain, when these are of a nature essential to the furnishing and equipping of the public force in time of war, are not establishments for procuring them on public account to the extent of the ordinary demand for the public service recommended by strong considerations of national policy as an exception to the general rule? Ought our country to remain in such cases dependent on foreign supply, precarious because liable to be interrupted? If the necessary article should in this mode cost more in time of peace, will not the security and independence thence arising form an ample compensation? Establishments of this sort, commensurate only with the calls of the public service in time of peace, will in time of war easily be extended in proportion to the exigencies of the Government, and may even perhaps be made to yield a surplus for the supply of our citizens at large, so as to mitigate the privations from the interruption of their trade. If adopted, the plan ought to exclude all those branches which are already, or likely soon to be, established in the country, in order that there may be no danger of interference with pursuits of individual industry.

It will not be doubted that with reference either to individual or national welfare agriculture is of primary importance. In proportion as nations advance in population and other circumstances of maturity this truth becomes more apparent, and renders the cultivation of the soil more and more an object of public patronage. Institutions for promoting it grow up, supported by the public purse; and to what object can it be dedicated with greater propriety? Among the means which have been employed to this end none have been attended with greater success than the establishment of boards (composed of proper characters) charged with collecting and diffusing information, and enabled by premiums and small pecuniary aids to encourage and assist a spirit of discovery and improvement. This species of establishment contributes doubly to the increase of improvement by stimulating to enterprise and experiment, and by drawing to a common center the results everywhere of individual skill and observation, and spreading them thence over the whole nation. Experience accordingly has shewn that they are very cheap instruments of immense national benefits.

I have heretofore proposed to the consideration of Congress the expediency of establishing a national university and also a military academy. The desirableness of both these institutions has so constantly increased with every new view I have taken of the subject that I can not omit the opportunity of once for all recalling your attention to them.

The assembly to which I address myself is too enlightened not to be fully sensible how much a flourishing state of the arts and sciences contributes to national prosperity and reputation.

True it is that our country, much to its honor, contains many seminaries of learning highly respectable and useful; but the funds upon which they rest are too narrow to command the ablest professors in the different departments of liberal knowledge for the institution contemplated, though they would be excellent auxiliaries.

Amongst the motives to such an institution, the assimilation of the principles, opinions, and manners of our countrymen by the common education of a portion of our youth from every quarter well deserves attention. The more homogeneous our citizens can be made in these particulars the greater will be our prospect of permanent union; and a primary object of such a national institution should be the education of our youth in the science of *government*. In a republic what species of knowledge can be equally important and what duty more pressing on its legislature than to patronize a plan for communicating it to those who are to be the future guardians of the liberties of the country?

The institution of a military academy is also recommended by cogent reasons. However pacific the general policy of a nation may be, it ought never to be without an adequate stock of military knowledge for emergencies. The first would impair the energy of its character, and both would hazard its safety or expose it to greater evils when war could not be avoided ; besides that, war might often not depend upon its own choice. In proportion as the observance of pacific maxims might exempt a nation from the necessity of practicing the rules of the military art ought to be its care in preserving and transmitting, by proper establishments, the knowledge of that art. Whatever argument may be drawn from particular examples superficially viewed, a thorough examination of the subject will evince that the art of war is at once comprehensive and complicated, that it demands much previous study, and that the possession of it in its most improved and perfect state is always of great moment to the security of a nation. This, therefore, ought to be a serious care of every government, and for this purpose an academy where a regular course of instruction is given is an obvious expedient which different nations have successfully employed.

The compensations to the officers of the United States in various instances, and in none more than in respect to the most important stations, appear to call for legislative revision. The consequences of a defective provision are of serious import to the Government. If private wealth is to supply the defect of public retribution, it will greatly contract the sphere within which the selection of character for office is to be made, and will proportionally diminish the probability of a choice of men able as well as upright. Besides that, it would be repugnant to the vital principles of our Government virtually to exclude from public trusts talents and virtue unless accompanied by wealth.

While in our external relations some serious inconveniences and embarrassments have been overcome and others lessened, it is with much pain and deep regret I mention that circumstances of a very unwelcome nature have lately occurred. Our trade has suffered and is suffering extensive injuries in the West Indies from the cruisers and agents of the French Republic, and communications have been received from its minister here which indicate the danger of a further disturbance of our commerce by its authority, and which are in other respects far from agreeable.

It has been my constant, sincere, and earnest wish, in conformity with that of our nation, to maintain cordial harmony and a perfectly friendly understanding with that Republic. This wish remains unabated, and I shall persevere in the endeavor to fulfill it to the utmost extent of what shall be consistent with a just and indispensable regard to the rights and honor of our country; nor will I easily cease to cherish the expectation that a spirit of justice, candor, and friendship on the part of the Republic will eventually insure success.

In pursuing this course, however, I can not forget what is due to the character of our Government and nation, or to a full and entire confidence in the good sense, patriotism, self-respect, and fortitude of my countrymen.

I reserve for a special message a more particular communication on this interesting subject.

Gentlemen of the House of Representatives:

I have directed an estimate of the appropriations necessary for the service of the ensuing year to be submitted from the proper Department, with a view of the public receipts and expenditures to the latest period to which an account can be prepared.

It is with satisfaction I am able to inform you that the revenues of the United States continue in a state of progressive improvement.

A reenforcement of the existing provisions for discharging our public debt was mentioned in my address at the opening of the last session. Some preliminary steps were taken toward it, the maturing of which will no doubt engage your zealous attention during the present. I will only add that it will afford me a heartfelt satisfaction to concur in such further measures as will ascertain to our country the prospect of a speedy extinguishment of the debt. Posterity may have cause to regret if from any motive intervals of tranquillity are left unimproved for accelerating this valuable end.

Gentlemen of the Senate and of the House of Representatives:

My solicitude to see the militia of the United States placed on an efficient establishment has been so often and so ardently expressed that I shall but barely recall the subject to your view on the present occasion, at the same time that I shall submit to your inquiry whether our harbors are yet sufficiently secured.

The situation in which I now stand for the last time, in the midst of the representatives of the people of the United States, naturally recalls the period when the administration of the present form of government commenced, and I can not omit the occasion to congratulate you and my country on the success of the experiment, nor to repeat my fervent supplications to the Supreme Ruler of the Universe and Sovereign Arbiter of Nations that His providential care may still be extended to the United States, that the virtue and happiness of the people may be preserved, and that the Government which they have instituted for the protection of their liberties may be perpetual.

G° WASHINGTON.

ADDRESS OF THE SENATE TO GEORGE WASHINGTON, PRESIDENT OF THE UNITED STATES.

We thank you, sir, for your faithful and detailed exposure of the existing situation of our country, and we sincerely join in sentiments of gratitude to an overruling Providence for the distinguished share of public prosperity and private happiness which the people of the United States so peculiarly enjoy.

We are fully sensible of the advantages that have resulted from the adoption of measures (which you have successfully carried into effect) to preserve peace, cultivate friendship, and promote civilization amongst the Indian tribes on the Western frontiers. Feelings of humanity and the most solid political interests equally encourage the continuance of this system.

We observe with pleasure that the delivery of the military posts lately occupied by the British forces within the territory of the United States was made with cordiality and promptitude as soon as circumstances would admit, and that the other provisions of our treaties with Great Britain and Spain that were objects of eventual arrangement are about being carried into effect with entire harmony and good faith.

The unfortunate but unavoidable difficulties that opposed a timely compliance with the terms of the Algerine treaty are much to be lamented, as they may occasion a temporary suspension of the advantages to be derived from a solid peace with that power and a perfect security from its predatory warfare. At the same time, the lively impressions that affected the public mind on the redemption of our captive fellow-citizens afford the most laudable incentive to our exertions to remove the remaining obstacles.

We perfectly coincide with you in opinion that the importance of our commerce demands a naval force for its protection against foreign insult and depredation, and our solicitude to attain that object will be always proportionate to its magnitude.

The necessity of accelerating the establishment of certain useful manufactures by the intervention of legislative aid and protection and the encouragement due to agriculture by the creation of boards (composed of intelligent individuals) to patronize this primary pursuit of society are subjects which will readily engage our most serious attention.

A national university may be converted to the most useful purposes. The science of legislation being so essentially dependent on the endowments of the mind, the public interests must receive effectual aid from the general diffusion of knowledge, and the United States will assume a more dignified station among the nations of the earth by the successful cultivation of the higher branches of literature.

A military academy may be likewise rendered equally important. To aid and direct the physical force of the nation by cherishing a military spirit, enforcing a proper sense of discipline, and inculcating a scientific system of tactics is consonant to the soundest maxims of public policy. Connected with and supported by such an establishment a well-regulated militia, constituting the natural defense of the country, would prove the most effectual as well as economical preservative of peace.

We can not but consider with serious apprehensions the inadequate compensations of the public officers, especially of those in the more important stations.   It is not only a violation of the spirit of a public contract, but is an evil so extensive in its operation and so destructive in its consequences that we trust it will receive the most pointed legislative attention.

We sincerely lament that, whilst the conduct of the United States has been uniformly impressed with the character of equity, moderation, and love of peace in the maintenance of all their foreign relationships, our trade should be so harassed by the cruisers and agents of the Republic of France throughout the extensive departments of the West Indies.

Whilst we are confident that no cause of complaint exists that could authorize an interruption of our tranquillity or disengage that Republic from the bonds of amity, cemented by the faith of treaties, we can not but express our deepest regrets that official communications have been made to you indicating a more serious disturbance of our commerce. Although we cherish the expectation that a sense of justice and a consideration of our mutual interests will moderate their councils, we are not unmindful of the situation in which events may place us, nor unprepared to adopt that system of conduct which, compatible with the dignity of a respectable nation, necessity may compel us to pursue.

We cordially acquiesce in the reflection that the United States, under the operation of the Federal Government, have experienced a most rapid aggrandizement and prosperity as well political as commercial.

Whilst contemplating the causes that produce this auspicious result, we must acknowledge the excellence of the constitutional system and the wisdom of the legislative provisions; but we should be deficient in gratitude and justice did we not attribute a great portion of these advantages to the virtue, firmness, and talents of your Administration, which have been conspicuously displayed in the most trying time and on the most critical occasions.   It is therefore with the sincerest regret that we now receive an official notification of your intentions to retire from the public employments of your country.

When we review the various scenes of your public life, so long and so successfully devoted to the most arduous services, civil and military, as well during the struggles of the American Revolution as the convulsive periods of a recent date, we can not look forward to your retirement without our warmest affections and most anxious regards accompanying you, and without mingling with our fellow-citizens at large in the sincerest wishes for your personal happiness that sensibility and attachment can express.

The most effectual consolation that can offer for the loss we are about to sustain arises from the animating reflection that the influence of your example will extend to your successors, and the United States thus continue to enjoy an able, upright, and energetic administration.

JOHN ADAMS,
Vice-President of the United States and President of the Senate.
DECEMBER 10, 1796.

REPLY OF THE PRESIDENT.

GENTLEMEN: It affords me great satisfaction to find in your address a concurrence in sentiment with me on the various topics which I presented for your information and deliberation, and that the latter will receive from you an attention proportioned to their respective importance.

For the notice you take of my public services, civil and military, and your kind wishes for my personal happiness, I beg you to accept my cordial thanks. Those services, and greater had I possessed ability to render them, were due to the unanimous calls of my country, and its approbation is my abundant reward.

When contemplating the period of my retirement, I saw virtuous and enlightened men among whom I relied on the discernment and patriotism of my fellow-citizens to make the proper choice of a successor—men who would require no influential example to insure to the United States "an able, upright, and energetic administration." To such men I shall cheerfully yield the palm of genius and talents to serve our common country; but at the same time I hope I may be indulged in expressing the consoling reflection (which consciousness suggests), and to bear it with me to my grave, that none can serve it with purer intentions than I have done or with a more disinterested zeal.

GQ WASHINGTON.

DECEMBER 12, 1796.

ADDRESS OF THE HOUSE OF REPRESENTATIVES TO GEORGE WASHINGTON, PRESIDENT OF THE UNITED STATES.

SIR: The House of Representatives have attended to your communication respecting the state of our country with all the sensibility that the contemplation of the subject and a sense of duty can inspire.

We are gratified by the information that measures calculated to insure a continuance of the friendship of the Indians and to maintain the tranquillity of the Western frontier have been adopted, and we indulge the hope that these, by impressing the Indian tribes with more correct conceptions of the justice as well as power of the United States, will be attended with success.

While we notice with satisfaction the steps that you have taken in pursuance of the late treaties with several foreign nations, the liberation of our citizens who were prisoners at Algiers is a subject of peculiar felicitation. We shall cheerfully cooperate in any further measures that shall appear on consideration to be requisite.

We have ever concurred with you in the most sincere and uniform disposition to preserve our neutral relations inviolate, and it is of course with anxiety and deep regret we hear that any interruption of our harmony with the French Republic has occurred, for we feel with you and with our constituents the cordial and unabated wish to maintain a perfectly friendly understanding with that nation.   Your endeavors to fulfill that wish, and by all honorable means to preserve peace, and to restore that harmony and affection which have heretofore so happily subsisted between the French Republic and the United States, can not fail, therefore, to interest our attention.   And while we participate in the full reliance you have expressed on the patriotism, self-respect, and fortitude of our countrymen, we cherish the pleasing hope that a mutual spirit of justice and moderation will insure the success of your perseverance.

The various subjects of your communication will respectively meet with the attention that is due to their importance.

When we advert to the internal situation of the United States, we deem it equally natural and becoming to compare the present period with that immediately antecedent to the operation of the Government, and to contrast it with the calamities in which the state of war still involves several of the European nations, as the reflections deduced from both tend to justify as well as to excite a warmer admiration of our free Constitution, and to exalt our minds to a more fervent and grateful sense of piety toward Almighty God for the beneficence of His providence, by which its administration has been hitherto so remarkably distinguished.

And while we entertain a grateful conviction that your wise, firm, and patriotic Administration has been signally conducive to the success of the present form of government, we can not forbear to express the deep sensations of regret with which we contemplate your intended retirement from office.

As no other suitable occasion may occur, we can not suffer the present to pass without attempting to disclose some of the emotions which it can not fail to awaken.

The gratitude and admiration of your countrymen are still drawn to the recollection of those resplendent virtues and talents which were so eminently instrumental to the achievement of the Revolution, and of which that glorious event will ever be the memorial.   Your obedience to the voice of duty and your country when you quitted reluctantly a second time the retreat you had chosen and first accepted the Presidency afforded a new proof of the devotedness of your zeal in its service and an earnest of the patriotism and success which have characterized your Administration.   As the grateful confidence of the citizens in the virtues of their Chief Magistrate has essentially contributed to that success, we persuade ourselves that the millions whom we represent participate with us in the anxious solicitude of the present occasion.

Yet we can not be unmindful that your moderation and magnanimity, twice displayed by retiring from your exalted stations, afford examples no less rare and instructive to mankind than valuable to a republic.

Although we are sensible that this event of itself completes the luster of a character already conspicuously unrivaled by the coincidence of virtue, talents, success, and public estimation, yet we conceive we owe it to you, sir, and still more emphatically to ourselves and to our nation (of the language of whose hearts we presume to think ourselves at this moment the faithful interpreters), to express the sentiments with which it is contemplated.

The spectacle of a free and enlightened nation offering, by its Representatives, the tribute of unfeigned approbation to its first citizen, however novel and interesting it may be, derives all its luster (a luster which accident or enthusiasm could not bestow, and which adulation would tarnish) from the transcendent merit of which it is the voluntary testimony.

May you long enjoy that liberty which is so dear to you, and to which your name will ever be so dear. May your own virtues and a nation's prayers obtain the happiest sunshine for the decline of your days and the choicest of future blessings. For our country's sake, for the sake of republican liberty, it is our earnest wish that your example may be the guide of your successors, and thus, after being the ornament and safeguard of the present age, become the patrimony of our descendants.

DECEMBER 15, 1796.

REPLY OF THE PRESIDENT.

GENTLEMEN: To a citizen whose views were unambitious, who preferred the shade and tranquillity of private life to the splendor and solicitude of elevated stations, and whom the voice of duty and his country could alone have drawn from his chosen retreat, no reward for his public services can be so grateful as public approbation, accompanied by a consciousness that to render those services useful to that country has been his single aim; and when this approbation is expressed by the Representatives of a free and enlightened nation, the reward will admit of no addition. Receive, gentlemen, my sincere and affectionate thanks for this signal testimony that my services have been acceptable and useful to my country. The strong confidence of my fellow-citizens, while it animated all my actions, insured their zealous cooperation, which rendered those services successful. The virtue and wisdom of my successors, joined with the patriotism and intelligence of the citizens who compose the other branches of Government, I firmly trust will lead them to the adoption of measures which, by the beneficence of Providence, will give stability to our system of government, add to its success, and secure to ourselves and to posterity that liberty which is to all of us so dear.

While I acknowledge with pleasure the sincere and uniform disposition of the House of Representatives to preserve our neutral relations inviolate, and with them deeply regret any degree of interruption of our good understanding with the French Republic, I beg you, gentlemen, to rest assured that my endeavors will be earnest and unceasing by all honorable means to preserve peace and to restore that harmony and affection which have heretofore so happily subsisted between our two nations; and with you I cherish the pleasing hope that a mutual spirit of justice and moderation will crown those endeavors with success.

I shall cheerfully concur in the beneficial measures which your deliberations shall mature on the various subjects demanding your attention; and while directing your labors to advance the real interests of our country, you receive its blessings. With perfect sincerity my individual wishes will be offered for your present and future felicity.

G⁰ WASHINGTON.

DECEMBER 16. 1796.

SPECIAL MESSAGES.

UNITED STATES, *January 4, 1797.*

Gentlemen of the Senate:

I lay before you for your consideration a treaty which has been negotiated and concluded on the 29th day of June last by Benjamin Hawkins, Andrew Pickens, and George Clymer, commissioners on behalf of the United States, with the Creek Indians, together with the instructions which were given to the said commissioners and the proceedings at the place of treaty.

I submit also the proceedings and result of a treaty, held at the city of New York, on behalf of the State of New York, with certain nations or tribes of Indians denominating themselves the Seven Nations of Canada.

G⁰ WASHINGTON.

UNITED STATES, *January 9, 1797.*

Gentlemen of the Senate and of the House of Representatives:

Herewith I lay before you in confidence reports from the Departments of State and the Treasury, by which you will see the present situation of our affairs with the Dey and Regency of Algiers.

G⁰ WASHINGTON.

UNITED STATES, *January 19, 1797.*

Gentlemen of the Senate and of the House of Representatives:

At the opening of the present session of Congress I mentioned that some circumstances of an unwelcome nature had lately occurred in relation to France; that our trade had suffered, and was suffering, extensive injuries in the West Indies from the cruisers and agents of the French Republic, and that communications had been received from its minister here which indicated danger of a further disturbance of our commerce by its authority, and that were in other respects far from agreeable, but that I reserved for a special message a more particular communication on this interesting subject. This communication I now make.

The complaints of the French minister embraced most of the transactions of our Government in relation to France from an early period of the present war, which, therefore, it was necessary carefully to review. A collection has been formed of letters and papers relating to those transactions, which I now lay before you, with a letter to Mr. Pinckney, our minister at Paris, containing an examination of the notes of the French minister and such information as I thought might be useful to Mr. Pinckney in any further representations he might find necessary to be made to the French Government. The immediate object of his mission was to make to that Government such explanations of the principles and conduct of our own as, by manifesting our good faith, might remove all jealousy and discontent and maintain that harmony and good understanding with the French Republic which it has been my constant solicitude to preserve. A government which required only a knowledge of the *truth* to justify its measures could not but be anxious to have this fully and frankly displayed.

G? WASHINGTON.

UNITED STATES, *March 2, 1797.*

Gentlemen of the Senate:

Application having been made to me to permit a treaty to be held with the Seneca Nation of Indians to effect the purchase of a parcel of their land under a preemption right derived from the State of Massachusetts and situated within the State of New York, and it appearing to me reasonable that such opportunity should be afforded, provided the negotiation shall be conducted at the expense of the applicant, and at the desire and with the consent of the Indians, always considering these as prerequisites, I now nominate Isaac Smith to be a commissioner to hold a treaty with the Seneca Nation for the aforesaid purpose.

G? WASHINGTON.

VETO MESSAGE.

UNITED STATES, *February 28, 1797.*

Gentlemen of the House of Representatives:

Having maturely considered the bill to alter and amend an act entitled "An act to ascertain and fix the military establishment of the United States," which was presented to me on the 22d day of this month, I now return it to the House of Representatives, in which it originated, with my objections:

First. If the bill passes into a law, the two companies of light dragoons will be from that moment *legally* out of service, though they will afterwards continue *actually* in service; and for their services during this interval, namely, from the time of *legal* to the time of *actual* discharge, it will not be lawful to pay them, unless some future provision be made by law. Though they may be discharged at the pleasure of Congress, in justice they ought to receive their pay, not only to the time of passing the law, but at least to the time of their actual discharge.

Secondly. It will be inconvenient and injurious to the public to dismiss the light dragoons as soon as notice of the law can be conveyed to them, one of the companies having been lately destined to a necessary and important service.

Thirdly. The companies of light dragoons consist of 126 noncommissioned officers and privates, who are bound to serve as dismounted dragoons when ordered so to do. They have received in bounties about $2,000. One of them is completely equipped, and above half of the noncommissioned officers and privates have yet to serve more than one-third of the time of their enlistment; and besides, there will in the course of the year be a considerable deficiency in the complement of infantry intended to be continued. Under these circumstances, to discharge the dragoons does not seem to comport with economy.

Fourthly. It is generally agreed that some cavalry, either militia or regular, will be necessary; and according to the best information I have been able to obtain, it is my opinion that the latter will be less expensive and more useful than the former in preserving peace between the frontier settlers and the Indians, and therefore a part of the military establishment should consist of cavalry.

G° WASHINGTON.

PROCLAMATION.

[From Senate Journal, vol. 2, p. 397.]

MARCH 1, 1797.

To the Vice-President and Senators of the United States, respectively.

SIR: It appearing to me proper that the Senate of the United State should be convened on Saturday, the 4th of March instant, you are desired to attend in the Chamber of the Senate on that day, at 10 o'clock in the forenoon, to receive any communications which the President of the United States may then lay before you touching their interests.

G° WASHINGTON

FAREWELL ADDRESS.

UNITED STATES, *September 17, 1796.*

Friends and Fellow-Citizens:

The period for a new election of a citizen to administer the Executive Government of the United States being not far distant, and the time actually arrived when your thoughts must be employed in designating the person who is to be clothed with that important trust, it appears to me proper, especially as it may conduce to a more distinct expression of the public voice, that I should now apprise you of the resolution I have formed to decline being considered among the number of those out of whom a choice is to be made.

I beg you at the same time to do me the justice to be assured that this resolution has not been taken without a strict regard to all the considerations appertaining to the relation which binds a dutiful citizen to his country; and that in withdrawing the tender of service, which silence in my situation might imply, I am influenced by no diminution of zeal for your future interest, no deficiency of grateful respect for your past kindness, but am supported by a full conviction that the step is compatible with both.

The acceptance of and continuance hitherto in the office to which your suffrages have twice called me have been a uniform sacrifice of inclination to the opinion of duty and to a deference for what appeared to be your desire. I constantly hoped that it would have been much earlier in my power, consistently with motives which I was not at liberty to disregard, to return to that retirement from which I had been reluctantly drawn. The strength of my inclination to do this previous to the last election had even led to the preparation of an address to declare it to you; but mature reflection on the then perplexed and critical posture of our affairs with foreign nations and the unanimous advice of persons entitled to my confidence impelled me to abandon the idea. I rejoice that the state of your concerns, external as well as internal, no longer renders the pursuit of inclination incompatible with the sentiment of duty or propriety, and am persuaded, whatever partiality may be retained for my services, that in the present circumstances of our country you will not disapprove my determination to retire.

The impressions with which I first undertook the arduous trust were explained on the proper occasion. In the discharge of this trust I will only say that I have, with good intentions, contributed toward the organization and administration of the Government the best exertions of which a very fallible judgment was capable. Not unconscious in the outset of the inferiority of my qualifications, experience in my own eyes, perhaps still more in the eyes of others, has strengthened the motives to diffidence of myself; and every day the increasing weight of years admonishes me more and more that the shade of retirement is as necessary to me as it will be welcome. Satisfied that if any circumstances have given peculiar value to my services they were temporary, I have the consolation to believe that, while choice and prudence invite me to quit the political scene, patriotism does not forbid it.

In looking forward to the moment which is intended to terminate the career of my political life my feelings do not permit me to suspend the deep acknowledgment of that debt of gratitude which I owe to my beloved country for the many honors it has conferred upon me; still more for the steadfast confidence with which it has supported me, and for the opportunities I have thence enjoyed of manifesting my inviolable attachment by services faithful and persevering, though in usefulness unequal to my zeal. If benefits have resulted to our country from these services, let it always be remembered to your praise and as an instructive example in our annals that under circumstances in which the passions, agitated in every direction, were liable to mislead; amidst appearances sometimes dubious; vicissitudes of fortune often discouraging; in situations in which not unfrequently want of success has countenanced the spirit of criticism, the constancy of your support was the essential prop of the efforts and a guaranty of the plans by which they were effected. Profoundly penetrated with this idea, I shall carry it with me to my grave as a strong incitement to unceasing vows that Heaven may continue to you the choicest tokens of its beneficence; that your union and brotherly affection may be perpetual; that the free Constitution which is the work of your hands may be sacredly maintained; that its administration in every department may be stamped with wisdom and virtue; that, in fine, the happiness of the people of these States, under the auspices of liberty, may be made complete by so careful a preservation and so prudent a use of this blessing as will acquire to them the glory of recommending it to the applause, the affection, and adoption of every nation which is yet a stranger to it.

Here, perhaps, I ought to stop. But a solicitude for your welfare which can not end but with my life, and the apprehension of danger natural to that solicitude, urge me on an occasion like the present to offer to your solemn contemplation and to recommend to your frequent review some sentiments which are the result of much reflection, of no inconsiderable observation, and which appear to me all important to the permanency of your felicity as a people. These will be offered to you with the more freedom as you can only see in them the disinterested warnings of a parting friend, who can possibly have no personal motive to bias his counsel. Nor can I forget as an encouragement to it your indulgent reception of my sentiments on a former and not dissimilar occasion.

Interwoven as is the love of liberty with every ligament of your hearts, no recommendation of mine is necessary to fortify or confirm the attachment.

The unity of government which constitutes you one people is also now dear to you. It is justly so, for it is a main pillar in the edifice of your real independence, the support of your tranquillity at home, your peace abroad, of your safety, of your prosperity, of that very liberty which you so highly prize. But as it is easy to foresee that from different causes and from different quarters much pains will be taken, many artifices employed, to weaken in your minds the conviction of this truth, as this is the point in your political fortress against which the batteries of internal and external enemies will be most constantly and actively (though often covertly and insidiously) directed, it is of infinite moment that you should properly estimate the immense value of your national union to your collective and individual happiness; that you should cherish a cordial, habitual, and immovable attachment to it; accustoming yourselves to think and speak of it as of the palladium of your political safety and prosperity; watching for its preservation with jealous anxiety; discountenancing whatever may suggest even a suspicion that it can in any event be abandoned, and indignantly frowning upon the first dawning of every attempt to alienate any portion of our country from the rest or to enfeeble the sacred ties which now link together the various parts.

For this you have every inducement of sympathy and interest. Citizens by birth or choice of a common country, that country has a right to concentrate your affections. The name of American, which belongs to you in your national capacity, must always exalt the just pride of patriotism more than any appellation derived from local discriminations. With slight shades of difference, you have the same religion, manners, habits, and political principles. You have in a common cause fought and triumphed together. The independence and liberty you possess are the work of joint councils and joint efforts, of common dangers, sufferings, and successes.

But these considerations, however powerfully they address themselves to your sensibility, are greatly outweighed by those which apply more immediately to your interest. Here every portion of our country finds the most commanding motives for carefully guarding and preserving the union of the whole.

The *North*, in an unrestrained intercourse with the *South*, protected by the equal laws of a common government, finds in the productions of the latter great additional resources of maritime and commercial enterprise and precious materials of manufacturing industry. The *South*, in the same intercourse, benefiting by the same agency of the *North*, sees its agriculture grow and its commerce expand. Turning partly into its own channels the seamen of the *North*, it finds its particular navigation invigorated; and while it contributes in different ways to nourish and increase the general mass of the national navigation, it looks forward to the protection of a maritime strength to which itself is unequally adapted. The *East*, in a like intercourse with the *West*, already finds, and in the progressive improvement of interior communications by land and water will more and more find, a valuable vent for the commodities which it brings from abroad or manufactures at home. The *West* derives from the *East* supplies requisite to its growth and comfort, and what is perhaps of still greater consequence, it must of necessity owe the *secure* enjoyment of indispensable *outlets* for its own productions to the weight, influence, and the future maritime strength of the Atlantic side of the Union, directed by an indissoluble community of interest as *one nation*. Any other tenure by which the *West* can hold this essential advantage, whether derived from its own separate strength or from an apostate and unnatural connection with any foreign power, must be intrinsically precarious.

While, then, every part of our country thus feels an immediate and particular interest in union, all the parts combined can not fail to find in the united mass of means and efforts greater strength, greater resource, proportionably greater security from external danger, a less frequent interruption of their peace by foreign nations, and what is of inestimable value, they must derive from union an exemption from those broils and wars between themselves which so frequently afflict neighboring countries not tied together by the same governments, which their own rivalships alone would be sufficient to produce, but which opposite foreign alliances, attachments, and intrigues would stimulate and imbitter. Hence, likewise, they will avoid the necessity of those overgrown military establishments which, under any form of government, are inauspicious to liberty, and which are to be regarded as particularly hostile to republican liberty. In this sense it is that your union ought to be considered as a main prop of your liberty, and that the love of the one ought to endear to you the preservation of the other.

These considerations speak a persuasive language to every reflecting and virtuous mind, and exhibit the continuance of the union as a primary object of patriotic desire. Is there a doubt whether a common government can embrace so large a sphere? Let experience solve it. To listen to mere speculation in such a case were criminal. We are authorized to hope that a proper organization of the whole, with the auxiliary agency of governments for the respective subdivisions, will afford a happy issue to the experiment. It is well worth a fair and full experiment. With such powerful and obvious motives to union affecting all parts of our country, while experience shall not have demonstrated its impracticability, there will always be reason to distrust the patriotism of those who in any quarter may endeavor to weaken its bands.

In contemplating the causes which may disturb our union it occurs as matter of serious concern that any ground should have been furnished for characterizing parties by *geographical* discriminations—*Northern* and *Southern*, *Atlantic* and *Western*—whence designing men may endeavor to excite a belief that there is a real difference of local interests and views.

One of the expedients of party to acquire influence within particular districts is to misrepresent the opinions and aims of other districts. You can not shield yourselves too much against the jealousies and heartburnings which spring from these misrepresentations; they tend to render alien to each other those who ought to be bound together by fraternal affection. The inhabitants of our Western country have lately had a useful lesson on this head. They have seen in the negotiation by the Executive and in the unanimous ratification by the Senate of the treaty with Spain, and in the universal satisfaction at that event throughout the United States, a decisive proof how unfounded were the suspicions propagated among them of a policy in the General Government and in the Atlantic States unfriendly to their interests in regard to the Mississippi. They have been witnesses to the formation of two treaties—that with Great Britain and that with Spain—which secure to them everything they could desire in respect to our foreign relations toward confirming their prosperity. Will it not be their wisdom to rely for the preservation of these advantages on the union by which they were procured? Will they not henceforth be deaf to those advisers, if such there are, who would sever them from their brethren and connect them with aliens?

To the efficacy and permanency of your union a government for the whole is indispensable. No alliances, however strict, between the parts can be an adequate substitute. They must inevitably experience the infractions and interruptions which all alliances in all times have experienced. Sensible of this momentous truth, you have improved upon your first essay by the adoption of a Constitution of Government better calculated than your former for an intimate union and for the efficacious management of your common concerns. This Government, the offspring of our own choice, uninfluenced and unawed, adopted upon full investigation and mature deliberation, completely free in its principles, in the distribution of its powers, uniting security with energy, and containing within itself a provision for its own amendment, has a just claim to your confidence and your support. Respect for its authority, compliance with its laws, acquiescence in its measures, are duties enjoined by the fundamental maxims of true liberty. The basis of our political systems is the right of the people to make and to alter their constitutions of government. But the constitution which at any time exists till changed by an explicit and authentic act of the whole people is sacredly obligatory upon all. The very idea of the power and the right of the people to establish government presupposes the duty of every individual to obey the established government.

All obstructions to the execution of the laws, all combinations and associations, under whatever plausible character, with the real design to direct, control, counteract, or awe the regular deliberation and action of the constituted authorities, are destructive of this fundamental principle and of fatal tendency. They serve to organize faction; to give it an artificial and extraordinary force; to put in the place of the delegated will of the nation the will of a party, often a small but artful and enterprising minority of the community, and, according to the alternate triumphs of different parties, to make the public administration the mirror of the ill-concerted and incongruous projects of faction rather than the organ of consistent and wholesome plans, digested by common counsels and modified by mutual interests.

However combinations or associations of the above description may now and then answer popular ends, they are likely in the course of time and things to become potent engines by which cunning, ambitious, and unprincipled men will be enabled to subvert the power of the people, and to usurp for themselves the reins of government, destroying afterwards the very engines which have lifted them to unjust dominion.

Toward the preservation of your Government and the permanency of your present happy state, it is requisite not only that you steadily discountenance irregular oppositions to its acknowledged authority, but also that you resist with care the spirit of innovation upon its principles, however specious the pretexts. One method of assault may be to effect in the forms of the Constitution alterations which will impair the energy of the system, and thus to undermine what can not be directly overthrown. In all the changes to which you may be invited remember that time and habit are at least as necessary to fix the true character of governments as of other human institutions; that experience is the surest standard by which to test the real tendency of the existing constitution of a country; that facility in changes upon the credit of mere hypothesis and opinion exposes to perpetual change, from the endless variety of hypothesis and opinion; and remember especially that for the efficient management of your common interests in a country so extensive as ours a government of as much vigor as is consistent with the perfect security of liberty is indispensable. Liberty itself will find in such a government, with powers properly distributed and adjusted, its surest guardian. It is, indeed, little else than a name where the government is too feeble to withstand the enterprises of faction, to confine each member of the society within the limits prescribed by the laws, and to maintain all in the secure and tranquil enjoyment of the rights of person and property.

I have already intimated to you the danger of parties in the State, with particular reference to the founding of them on geographical discriminations. Let me now take a more comprehensive view, and warn you in the most solemn manner against the baneful effects of the spirit of party generally.

This spirit, unfortunately, is inseparable from our nature, having its root in the strongest passions of the human mind. It exists under different shapes in all governments, more or less stifled, controlled, or repressed; but in those of the popular form it is seen in its greatest rankness and is truly their worst enemy.

The alternate domination of one faction over another, sharpened by the spirit of revenge natural to party dissension, which in different ages and countries has perpetrated the most horrid enormities, is itself a frightful despotism. But this leads at length to a more formal and permanent despotism. The disorders and miseries which result gradually incline the minds of men to seek security and repose in the absolute power of an individual, and sooner or later the chief of some prevailing faction, more able or more fortunate than his competitors, turns this disposition to the purposes of his own elevation on the ruins of public liberty.

Without looking forward to an extremity of this kind (which nevertheless ought not to be entirely out of sight), the common and continual mischiefs of the spirit of party are sufficient to make it the interest and duty of a wise people to discourage and restrain it.

It serves always to distract the public councils and enfeeble the public administration. It agitates the community with ill-founded jealousies and false alarms; kindles the animosity of one part against another; foments occasionally riot and insurrection. It opens the door to foreign influence and corruption, which find a facilitated access to the government itself through the channels of party passion. Thus the policy and the will of one country are subjected to the policy and will of another.

There is an opinion that parties in free countries are useful checks upon the administration of the government, and serve to keep alive the spirit of liberty. This within certain limits is probably true; and in governments of a monarchical cast patriotism may look with indulgence, if not with favor, upon the spirit of party. But in those of the popular character, in governments purely elective, it is a spirit not to be encouraged. From their natural tendency it is certain there will always be enough of that spirit for every salutary purpose; and there being constant danger of excess, the effort ought to be by force of public opinion to mitigate and assuage it. A fire not to be quenched, it demands a uniform vigilance to prevent its bursting into a flame, lest, instead of warming, it should consume.

It is important, likewise, that the habits of thinking in a free country should inspire caution in those intrusted with its administration to confine themselves within their respective constitutional spheres, avoiding in the exercise of the powers of one department to encroach upon another. The spirit of encroachment tends to consolidate the powers of all the departments in one, and thus to create, whatever the form of government, a real despotism. A just estimate of that love of power and proneness to abuse it which predominates in the human heart is sufficient to satisfy us of the truth of this position. The necessity of reciprocal checks in the exercise of political power, by dividing and distributing it into different depositories, and constituting each the guardian of the public weal against invasions by the others, has been evinced by experiments ancient and modern, some of them in our country and under our own eyes. To preserve them must be as necessary as to institute them. If in the opinion of the people the distribution or modification of the constitutional powers be in any particular wrong, let it be corrected by an amendment in the way which the Constitution designates. But let there be no change by usurpation; for though this in one instance may be the instrument of good, it is the customary weapon by which free governments are destroyed. The precedent must always greatly overbalance in permanent evil any partial or transient benefit which the use can at any time yield.

Of all the dispositions and habits which lead to political prosperity, religion and morality are indispensable supports. In vain would that man claim the tribute of patriotism who should labor to subvert these great pillars of human happiness—these firmest props of the duties of men and citizens. The mere politician, equally with the pious man, ought to respect and to cherish them. A volume could not trace all their connections with private and public felicity. Let it simply be asked, Where is the security for property, for reputation, for life, if the sense of religious obligation *desert* the oaths which are the instruments of investigation in courts of justice? And let us with caution indulge the supposition that morality can be maintained without religion. Whatever may be conceded to the influence of refined education on minds of peculiar structure, reason and experience both forbid us to expect that national morality can prevail in exclusion of religious principle.

It is substantially true that virtue or morality is a necessary spring of popular government. The rule indeed extends with more or less force to every species of free government. Who that is a sincere friend to it can look with indifference upon attempts to shake the foundation of the fabric? Promote, then, as an object of primary importance, institutions for the general diffusion of knowledge. In proportion as the structure of a government gives force to public opinion, it is essential that public opinion should be enlightened.

As a very important source of strength and security, cherish public credit. One method of preserving it is to use it as sparingly as possible, avoiding occasions of expense by cultivating peace, but remembering also that timely disbursements to prepare for danger frequently prevent much greater disbursements to repel it; avoiding likewise the accumulation of debt, not only by shunning occasions of expense, but by vigorous exertions in time of peace to discharge the debts which unavoidable wars have occasioned, not ungenerously throwing upon posterity the burthen which we ourselves ought to bear. The execution of these maxims belongs to your representatives; but it is necessary that public opinion should cooperate. To facilitate to them the performance of their duty it is essential that you should practically bear in mind that toward the payment of debts there must be revenue; that to have revenue there must be taxes; that no taxes can be devised which are not more or less inconvenient and unpleasant; that the intrinsic embarrassment inseparable frcm the selection of the proper objects (which is always a choice of difficulties), ought to be a decisive motive for a candid construction of the conduct of the Government in making it, and for a spirit of acquiescence in the measures for obtaining revenue which the public exigencies may at any time dictate.

Observe good faith and justice toward all nations. Cultivate peace and harmony with all. Religion and morality enjoin this conduct. And can it be that good policy does not equally enjoin it? It will be worthy of a free, enlightened, and at no distant period a great nation to give to mankind the magnanimous and too novel example of a people always guided by an exalted justice and benevolence. Who can doubt that in the course of time and things the fruits of such a plan would richly repay any temporary advantages which might be lost by a steady adherence to it? Can it be that Providence has not connected the permanent felicity of a nation with its virtue? The experiment, at least, is recommended by every sentiment which ennobles human nature. Alas! is it rendered impossible by its vices?

In the execution of such a plan nothing is more essential than that permanent, inveterate antipathies against particular nations and passionate attachments for others should be excluded, and that in place of them just and amicable feelings toward all should be cultivated. The nation which indulges toward another an habitual hatred or an habitual fondness is in some degree a slave. It is a slave to its animosity or to its affection, either of which is sufficient to lead it astray from its duty and its interest. Antipathy in one nation against another disposes each more readily to offer insult and injury, to lay hold of slight causes of umbrage, and to be haughty and intractable when accidental or trifling occasions of dispute occur.

Hence frequent collisions, obstinate, envenomed, and bloody contests. The nation prompted by ill will and resentment sometimes impels to war the government contrary to the best calculations of policy. The government sometimes participates in the national propensity, and adopts through passion what reason would reject. At other times it makes the animosity of the nation subservient to projects of hostility, instigated by pride, ambition, and other sinister and pernicious motives. The peace often, sometimes perhaps the liberty, of nations has been the victim.

So, likewise, a passionate attachment of one nation for another produces a variety of evils. Sympathy for the favorite nation, facilitating the illusion of an imaginary common interest in cases where no real common interest exists, and infusing into one the enmities of the other, betrays the former into a participation in the quarrels and wars of the latter without adequate inducement or justification. It leads also to concessions to the favorite nation of privileges denied to others, which is apt doubly to injure the nation making the concessions by unnecessarily parting with what ought to have been retained, and by exciting jealousy, ill will, and a disposition to retaliate in the parties from whom equal privileges are withheld; and it gives to ambitious, corrupted, or deluded citizens (who devote themselves to the favorite nation) facility to betray or sacrifice the interests of their own country without odium, sometimes even with popularity, gilding with the appearances of a virtuous sense of obligation, a commendable deference for public opinion, or a laudable zeal for public good the base or foolish compliances of ambition, corruption, or infatuation.

As avenues to foreign influence in innumerable ways, such attachments are particularly alarming to the truly enlightened and independent patriot. How many opportunities do they afford to tamper with domestic factions, to practice the arts of seduction, to mislead public opinion, to influence or awe the public councils! Such an attachment of a small or weak toward a great and powerful nation dooms the former to be the satellite of the latter. Against the insidious wiles of foreign influence (I conjure you to believe me, fellow-citizens) the jealousy of a free people ought to be *constantly* awake, since history and experience prove that foreign influence is one of the most baneful foes of republican government. But that jealousy, to be useful, must be impartial, else it becomes the instrument of the very influence to be avoided, instead of a defense against it. Excessive partiality for one foreign nation and excessive dislike of another cause those whom they actuate to see danger only on one side, and serve to veil and even second the arts of influence on the other. Real patriots who may resist the intrigues of the favorite are liable to become suspected and odious, while its tools and dupes usurp the applause and confidence of the people to surrender their interests.

The great rule of conduct for us in regard to foreign nations is, in extending our commercial relations to have with them as little *political* connection as possible. So far as we have already formed engagements let them be fulfilled with perfect good faith. Here let us stop.

Europe has a set of primary interests which to us have none or a very remote relation. Hence she must be engaged in frequent controversies, the causes of which are essentially foreign to our concerns. Hence, therefore, it must be unwise in us to implicate ourselves by artificial ties in the ordinary vicissitudes of her politics or the ordinary combinations and collisions of her friendships or enmities.

Our detached and distant situation invites and enables us to pursue a different course. If we remain one people, under an efficient government, the period is not far off when we may defy material injury from external annoyance; when we may take such an attitude as will cause the neutrality we may at any time resolve upon to be scrupulously respected; when belligerent nations, under the impossibility of making acquisitions upon us, will not lightly hazard the giving us provocation; when we may choose peace or war, as our interest, guided by justice, shall counsel.

Why forego the advantages of so peculiar a situation? Why quit our own to stand upon foreign ground? Why, by interweaving our destiny with that of any part of Europe, entangle our peace and prosperity in the toils of European ambition, rivalship, interest, humor, or caprice?

It is our true policy to steer clear of permanent alliances with any portion of the foreign world, so far, I mean, as we are now at liberty to do it; for let me not be understood as capable of patronizing infidelity to existing engagements. I hold the maxim no less applicable to public than to private affairs that honesty is always the best policy. I repeat, therefore, let those engagements be observed in their genuine sense. But in my opinion it is unnecessary and would be unwise to extend them.

Taking care always to keep ourselves by suitable establishments on a respectable defensive posture, we may safely trust to temporary alliances for extraordinary emergencies.

Harmony, liberal intercourse with all nations are recommended by policy, humanity, and interest. But even our commercial policy should hold an equal and impartial hand, neither seeking nor granting exclusive favors or preferences; consulting the natural course of things; diffusing and diversifying by gentle means the streams of commerce, but forcing nothing; establishing with powers so disposed, in order to give trade a stable course, to define the rights of our merchants, and to enable the Government to support them, conventional rules of intercourse, the best that present circumstances and mutual opinion will permit, but temporary and liable to be from time to time abandoned or varied as experience and circumstances shall dictate; constantly keeping in view that it is folly in one nation to look for disinterested favors from another; that it must pay with a portion of its independence for whatever it may accept under that character; that by such acceptance it may place itself in the condition of having given equivalents for nominal favors, and yet of being reproached with ingratitude for not giving more. There can be no greater error than to expect or calculate upon real favors from nation to nation. It is an illusion which experience must cure, which a just pride ought to discard.

In offering to you, my countrymen, these counsels of an old and affectionate friend I dare not hope they will make the strong and lasting impression I could wish—that they will control the usual current of the passions or prevent our nation from running the course which has hitherto marked the destiny of nations. But if I may even flatter myself that they may be productive of some partial benefit, some occasional good—that they may now and then recur to moderate the fury of party spirit, to warn against the mischiefs of foreign intrigue, to guard against the impostures of pretended patriotism—this hope will be a full recompense for the solicitude for your welfare by which they have been dictated.

How far in the discharge of my official duties I have been guided by the principles which have been delineated the public records and other evidences of my conduct must witness to you and to the world. To myself, the assurance of my own conscience is that I have at least believed myself to be guided by them.

In relation to the still subsisting war in Europe my proclamation of the 22d of April, 1793, is the index to my plan. Sanctioned by your approving voice and by that of your representatives in both Houses of Congress, the spirit of that measure has continually governed me, uninfluenced by any attempts to deter or divert me from it.

After deliberate examination, with the aid of the best lights I could obtain, I was well satisfied that our country, under all the circumstances of the case, had a right to take, and was bound in duty and interest to take, a neutral position. Having taken it, I determined as far as should depend upon me to maintain it with moderation, perseverance, and firmness.

The considerations which respect the right to hold this conduct it is not necessary on this occasion to detail. I will only observe that, according to my understanding of the matter, that right, so far from being denied by any of the belligerent powers, has been virtually admitted by all.

The duty of holding a neutral conduct may be inferred, without anything more, from the obligation which justice and humanity impose on every nation, in cases in which it is free to act, to maintain inviolate the relations of peace and amity toward other nations.

The inducements of interest for observing that conduct will best be referred to your own reflections and experience. With me a predominant motive has been to endeavor to gain time to our country to settle and mature its yet recent institutions, and to progress without interruption to that degree of strength and consistency which is necessary to give it, humanly speaking, the command of its own fortunes.

Though in reviewing the incidents of my Administration I am unconscious of intentional error, I am nevertheless too sensible of my defects not to think it probable that I may have committed many errors. Whatever they may be, I fervently beseech the Almighty to avert or mitigate the evils to which they may tend. I shall also carry with me the hope that my country will never cease to view them with indulgence, and that, after forty-five years of my life dedicated to its service with an upright zeal, the faults of incompetent abilities will be consigned to oblivion, as myself must soon be to the mansions of rest.

Relying on its kindness in this as in other things, and actuated by that fervent love toward it which is so natural to a man who views in it the native soil of himself and his progenitors for several generations, I anticipate with pleasing expectation that retreat in which I promise myself to realize without alloy the sweet enjoyment of partaking in the midst of my fellow-citizens the benign influence of good laws under a free government—the ever-favorite object of my heart, and the happy reward, as I trust, of our mutual cares, labors, and dangers.

G⁰ WASHINGTON.

John Adams

March 4, 1797, to March 4, 1801

SEE VOLUME XI.

Volume eleven is not only an index to the other volumes, not only a key that unlocks the treasures of the entire publication, but it is in itself an alphabetically arranged brief history or story of the great controlling events constituting the History of the United States.

Under its proper alphabetical classification the story is told of every great subject referred to by any of the Presidents in their official Messages, and at the end of each story the official utterances of the Presidents themselves are cited upon the subject, so that you may readily turn to the page in the body of the work itself for this original information.

Next to the possession of knowledge is the ability to turn at will to where knowledge is to be found.

HOME AT QUINCY, MASSACHUSETTS, OF
JOHN ADAMS
With official portrait engraved from copy of original in steel

John Adams

John Adams

JOHN ADAMS was born on October 19 (old style), 1735, near Boston, Mass., in the portion of the town of Braintree which has since been incorporated as Quincy. He was fourth in descent from Henry Adams, who fled from persecution in Devonshire, England, and settled in Massachusetts about 1630. Another of his ancestors was John Adams, a founder of the Plymouth Colony in 1620. Entered Harvard College in 1751, and graduated therefrom four years later. Studied the law and taught school at Worcester; was admitted to the bar of Suffolk County in 1758. In 1768 removed to Boston, where he won distinction at the bar. In 1764 married Abigail Smith, whose father was Rev. William Smith and whose grandfather was Colonel Quincy. In 1770 was chosen a representative from Boston in the legislature of Massachusetts. In 1774 was a member of the Continental Congress, and in 1776 was the adviser and great supporter of the Declaration of Independence. The same year was a deputy to treat with Lord Howe for the pacification of the Colonies. He declined the offer of chief justice of Massachusetts. In December, 1777, was appointed a commissioner to France, and returned home in the summer of 1779. He was then chosen a member of the Massachusetts convention for framing a State constitution. On September 29, 1779, was appointed by Congress minister plenipotentiary to negotiate a peace treaty with Great Britain. In 1781 was a commissioner to conclude treaties of peace with European powers. In 1783 negotiated with others a commercial treaty with Great Britain. Was one of the commissioners to sign the provisional treaty of peace with that nation November 30, 1782, and the definite treaty September 3, 1783. In 1784 remained in Holland, and in 1785 was by Congress appointed minister of the United States at the Court of Great Britain. He returned to his home in June, 1788. Was chosen Vice-President on the ticket with Washington, and on the assembling of the Senate took his seat as President of that body, at New York in April, 1789. Was reelected Vice-President in 1792. On the retirement of Washington in 1796 he was elected President, and was inaugurated March 4, 1797. He retired March 4, 1801, to his home at Quincy, Mass. In 1816 was chosen to head the list of Presidential electors of his party in the State. Was a member of the State convention to revise the constitution of Massachusetts; was unanimously elected president of that convention, but declined it on account of his age. His wife died in 1818. On July 4, 1826, he died, and was buried at Quincy.

INAUGURAL ADDRESS.

IN THE CITY OF PHILADELPHIA, PA

When it was first perceived, in early times, that no middle course for America remained between unlimited submission to a foreign legislature and a total independence of its claims, men of reflection were less apprehensive of danger from the formidable power of fleets and armies they must determine to resist than from those contests and dissensions which would certainly arise concerning the forms of government to be instituted over the whole and over the parts of this extensive country. Relying, however, on the purity of their intentions, the justice of their cause, and the integrity and intelligence of the people, under an overruling Providence which had so signally protected this country from the first, the representatives of this nation, then consisting of little more than half its present number, not only broke to pieces the chains which were forging and the rod of iron that was lifted up, but frankly cut asunder the ties which had bound them, and launched into an ocean of uncertainty.

The zeal and ardor of the people during the Revolutionary war, supplying the place of government, commanded a degree of order sufficient at least for the temporary preservation of society. The Confederation which was early felt to be necessary was prepared from the models of the Batavian and Helvetic confederacies, the only examples which remain with any detail and precision in history, and certainly the only ones which the people at large had ever considered. But reflecting on the striking difference in so many particulars between this country and those where a courier may go from the seat of government to the frontier in a single day, it was then certainly foreseen by some who assisted in Congress at the formation of it that it could not be durable.

Negligence of its regulations, inattention to its recommendations, if not disobedience to its authority, not only in individuals but in States, soon appeared with their melancholy consequences—universal languor, jealousies and rivalries of States, decline of navigation and commerce, discouragement of necessary manufactures, universal fall in the value of lands and their produce, contempt of public and private faith, loss of consideration and credit with foreign nations, and at length in discontents, animosities, combinations, partial conventions, and insurrection, threatening some great national calamity.

In this dangerous crisis the people of America were not abandoned by their usual good sense, presence of mind, resolution, or integrity. Measures were pursued to concert a plan to form a more perfect union, establish justice, insure domestic tranquillity, provide for the common defense, promote the general welfare, and secure the blessings of liberty. The public disquisitions, discussions, and deliberations issued in the present happy Constitution of Government.

Employed in the service of my country abroad during the whole course of these transactions, I first saw the Constitution of the United States in a foreign country. Irritated by no literary altercation, animated by no public debate, heated by no party animosity, I read it with great sat isfaction, as the result of good heads prompted by good hearts, as an experiment better adapted to the genius, character, situation, and rela tions of this nation and country than any which had ever been proposed or suggested. In its general principles and great outlines it was con formable to such a system of government as I had ever most esteemed, and in some States, my own native State in particular, had contributed to establish. Claiming a right of suffrage, in common with my fellow-citizens, in the adoption or rejection of a constitution which was to rule me and my posterity, as well as them and theirs, I did not hesitate to express my approbation of it on all occasions, in public and in private. It was not then, nor has been since, any objection to it in my mind that the Executive and Senate were not more permanent. Nor have I ever entertained a thought of promoting any alteration in it but such as the people themselves, in the course of their experience, should see and feel to be necessary or expedient, and by their representatives in Congress and the State legislatures, according to the Constitution itself, adopt and ordain.

Returning to the bosom of my country after a painful separation from it for ten years, I had the honor to be elected to a station under the new order of things, and I have repeatedly laid myself under the most serious obligations to support the Constitution. The operation of it has equaled the most sanguine expectations of its friends, and from an habitual atten tion to it, satisfaction in its administration, and delight in its effects upon the peace, order, prosperity, and happiness of the nation I have acquired an habitual attachment to it and veneration for it.

What other form of government, indeed, can so well deserve our esteem and love?

There may be little solidity in an ancient idea that congregations of men into cities and nations are the most pleasing objects in the sight of superior intelligences, but this is very certain, that to a benevolent human mind there can be no spectacle presented by any nation more pleasing, more noble, majestic, or august, than an assembly like that which has so often been seen in this and the other Chamber of Congress, of a Gov ernment in which the Executive authority, as well as that of all the branches of the Legislature, are exercised by citizens selected at regular periods by their neighbors to make and execute laws for the general good. Can anything essential, anything more than mere ornament and deco ration, be added to this by robes and diamonds? Can authority be more amiable and respectable when it descends from accidents or institutions established in remote antiquity than when it springs fresh from the hearts and judgments of an honest and enlightened people? For it is the people only that are represented. It is their power and majesty that is reflected, and only for their good, in every legitimate government, under whatever form it may appear. The existence of such a government as ours for any length of time is a full proof of a general dissemination of knowledge and virtue throughout the whole body of the people. And what object or consideration more pleasing than this can be presented to the human mind? If national pride is ever justifiable or excusable it is when it springs, not from power or riches, grandeur or glory, but from conviction of national innocence, information, and benevolence.

In the midst of these pleasing ideas we should be unfaithful to ourselves if we should ever lose sight of the danger to our liberties if anything partial or extraneous should infect the purity of our free, fair, virtuous, and independent elections. If an election is to be determined by a majority of a single vote, and that can be procured by a party through artifice or corruption, the Government may be the choice of a party for its own ends, not of the nation for the national good. If that solitary suffrage can be obtained by foreign nations by flattery or menaces, by fraud or violence, by terror, intrigue, or venality, the Government may not be the choice of the American people, but of foreign nations. It may be foreign nations who govern us, and not we, the people, who govern ourselves; and candid men will acknowledge that in such cases choice would have little advantage to boast of over lot or chance.

Such is the amiable and interesting system of government (and such are some of the abuses to which it may be exposed) which the people of America have exhibited to the admiration and anxiety of the wise and virtuous of all nations for eight years under the administration of a citizen who, by a long course of great actions, regulated by prudence, justice, temperance, and fortitude, conducting a people inspired with the same virtues and animated with the same ardent patriotism and love of liberty to independence and peace, to increasing wealth and unexampled prosperity, has merited the gratitude of his fellow-citizens, commanded the highest praises of foreign nations, and secured immortal glory with posterity.

In that retirement which is his voluntary choice may he long live to enjoy the delicious recollection of his services, the gratitude of mankind, the happy fruits of them to himself and the world, which are daily increasing, and that splendid prospect of the future fortunes of this country which is opening from year to year. His name may be still a rampart, and the knowledge that he lives a bulwark, against all open or secret enemies of his country's peace. This example has been recommended to the imitation of his successors by both Houses of Congress and by the voice of the legislatures and the people throughout the nation.

On this subject it might become me be er to be silent or to speak with diffidence; but as something may be expected, the occasion, I hope, will be admitted as an apology if I venture to say that if a preference, upon principle, of a free republican government, formed upon long and serious reflection, after a diligent and impartial inquiry after truth; if an attachment to the Constitution of the United States, and a conscientious determination to support it until it shall be altered by the judgments and wishes of the people, expressed in the mode prescribed in it; if a respectful attention to the constitutions of the individual States and a constant caution and delicacy toward the State governments; if an equal and impartial regard to the rights, interest, honor, and happiness of all the States in the Union, without preference or regard to a northern or southern, an eastern or western, position, their various political opinions on unessential points or their personal attachments; if a love of virtuous men of all parties and denominations; if a love of science and letters and a wish to patronize every rational effort to encourage schools, colleges, universities, academies, and every institution for propagating knowledge, virtue, and religion among all classes of the people, not only for their benign influence on the happiness of life in all its stages and classes, and of society in all its forms, but as the only means of preserving our Constitution from its natural enemies, the spirit of sophistry, the spirit of party, the spirit of intrigue, the profligacy of corruption, and the pestilence of foreign influence, which is the angel of destruction to elective governments; if a love of equal laws, of justice, and humanity in the interior administration; if an inclination to improve agriculture, commerce, and manufactures for necessity, convenience, and defense; if a spirit of equity and humanity toward the aboriginal nations of America, and a disposition to meliorate their condition by inclining them to be more friendly to us, and our citizens to be more friendly to them; if an inflexible determination to maintain peace and inviolable faith with all nations, and that system of neutrality and impartiality among the belligerent powers of Europe which has been adopted by this Government and so solemnly sanctioned by both Houses of Congress and applauded by the legislatures of the States and the public opinion, until it shall be otherwise ordained by Congress; if a personal esteem for the French nation, formed in a residence of seven years chiefly among them, and a sincere desire to preserve the friendship which has been so much for the honor and interest of both nations; if, while the conscious honor and integrity of the people of America and the internal sentiment of their own power and energies must be preserved, an earnest endeavor to investigate every just cause and remove every colorable pretense of complaint; if an intention to pursue by amicable negotiation a reparation for the injuries that have been committed on the commerce of our fellow-citizens by whatever nation, and if success can not be obtained, to lay the facts before the Legislature, that they may consider what further measures the honor and interest of the Government and its constituents demand; if a resolution to do justice as far as may depend upon me, at all times and to all nations, and maintain peace, friendship, and benevolence with all the world; if an unshaken confidence in the honor, spirit, and resources of the American people, on which I have so often hazarded my all and never been deceived; if elevated ideas of the high destinies of this country and of my own duties toward it, founded on a knowledge of the moral principles and intellectual improvements of the people deeply engraven on my mind in early life, and not obscured but exalted by experience and age; and, with humble reverence, I feel it to be my duty to add, if a veneration for the religion of a people who profess and call themselves Christians, and a fixed resolution to consider a decent respect for Christianity among the best recommendations for the public service, can enable me in any degree to comply with your wishes, it shall be my strenuous endeavor that this sagacious injunction of the two Houses shall not be without effect.

With this great example before me, with the sense and spirit, the faith and honor, the duty and interest, of the same American people pledged to support the Constitution of the United States, I entertain no doubt of its continuance in all its energy, and my mind is prepared without hesitation to lay myself under the most solemn obligations to support it to the utmost of my power.

And may that Being who is supreme over all, the Patron of Order, the Fountain of Justice, and the Protector in all ages of the world of virtuous liberty, continue His blessing upon this nation and its Government and give it all possible success and duration consistent with the ends of His providence.

MARCH 4, 1797.

PROCLAMATION.

[From Annals of Congress, Fifth Congress, Vol. I, 49.]

BY THE PRESIDENT OF THE UNITED STATES OF AMERICA.

A PROCLAMATION.

Whereas the Constitution of the United States of America provides that the President may, on extraordinary occasions, convene both Houses of Congress; and

Whereas an extraordinary occasion exists for convening Congress, and divers weighty matters claim their consideration:

I have therefore thought it necessary to convene, and I do by these presents convene, the Congress of the United States of America at the city of Philadelphia, in the Commonwealth of Pennsylvania, on Monday, the 15th day of May next, hereby requiring the Senators and Representatives in the Congress of the United States of America, and every of them, that, laying aside all other matters and cares, they then and there meet and assemble in Congress in order to consult and determine on such measures as in their wisdom shall be deemed meet for the safety and welfare of the said United States.

In testimony whereof I have caused the seal of the United States of America to be affixed to these presents, and signed the same with my hand.

[SEAL.]   Done at the city of Philadelphia, the 25th day of March, A. D. 1797, and of the Independence of the United States of America the twenty-first.

JOHN ADAMS.

By the President:
  TIMOTHY PICKERING,
    Secretary of State.

SPECIAL SESSION MESSAGE.

UNITED STATES, *May 16, 1797.*

Gentlemen of the Senate and Gentlemen of the House of Representatives:

The personal inconveniences to the members of the Senate and of the House of Representatives in leaving their families and private affairs at this season of the year are so obvious that I the more regret the extraordinary occasion which has rendered the convention of Congress indispensable.

It would have afforded me the highest satisfaction to have been able to congratulate you on a restoration of peace to the nations of Europe whose animosities have endangered our tranquillity; but we have still abundant cause of gratitude to the Supreme Dispenser of National Blessings for general health and promising seasons, for domestic and social happiness, for the rapid progress and ample acquisitions of industry through extensive territories, for civil, political, and religious liberty. While other states are desolated with foreign war or convulsed with intestine divisions, the United States present the pleasing prospect of a nation governed by mild and equal laws, generally satisfied with the possession of their rights, neither envying the advantages nor fearing the power of other nations, solicitous only for the maintenance of order and justice and the preservation of liberty, increasing daily in their attachment to a system of government in proportion to their experience of its utility, yielding a ready and general obedience to laws flowing from the reason and resting on the only solid foundation—the affections of the people

It is with extreme regret that I shall be obliged to turn your thoughts to other circumstances, which admonish us that some of these felicities may not be lasting. But if the tide of our prosperity is full and a reflux commencing, a vigilant circumspection becomes us, that we may meet our reverses with fortitude and extricate ourselves from their consequences with all the skill we possess and all the efforts in our power.

In giving to Congress information of the state of the Union and recommending to their consideration such measures as appear to me to be necessary or expedient, according to my constitutional duty, the causes and the objects of the present extraordinary session will be explained.

After the President of the United States received information that the French Government had expressed serious discontents at some proceedings of the Government of these States said to affect the interests of France, he thought it expedient to send to that country a new minister, fully instructed to enter on such amicable discussions and to give such candid explanations as might happily remove the discontents and suspicions of the French Government and vindicate the conduct of the United States. For this purpose he selected from among his fellow-citizens a character whose integrity, talents, experience, and services had placed him in the rank of the most esteemed and respected in the nation. The direct object of his mission was expressed in his letter of credence to the French Republic, being "to maintain that good understanding which from the commencement of the alliance had subsisted between the two nations, and to efface unfavorable impressions, banish suspicions, and restore that cordiality which was at once the evidence and pledge of a friendly union." And his instructions were to the same effect, "faithfully to represent the disposition of the Government and people of the United States (their disposition being one), to remove jealousies and obviate complaints by shewing that they were groundless, to restore that mutual confidence which had been so unfortunately and injuriously impaired, and to explain the relative interests of both countries and the real sentiments of his own."

A minister thus specially commissioned it was expected would have proved the instrument of restoring mutual confidence between the two Republics. The first step of the French Government corresponded with that expectation. A few days before his arrival at Paris the French minister of foreign relations informed the American minister then resident at Paris of the formalities to be observed by himself in taking leave, and by his successor preparatory to his reception. These formalities they observed, and on the 9th of December presented officially to the minister of foreign relations, the one a copy of his letters of recall, the other a copy of his letters of credence.

These were laid before the Executive Directory. Two days afterwards the minister of foreign relations informed the recalled American minister that the Executive Directory had determined not to receive another minister plenipotentiary from the United States until after the redress of grievances demanded of the American Government, and which the French Republic had a right to expect from it. The American minister immediately endeavored to ascertain whether by refusing to receive him it was intended that he should retire from the territories of the French Republic, and verbal answers were given that such was the intention of the Directory. For his own justification he desired a written answer, but obtained none until toward the last of January, when, receiving notice in writing to quit the territories of the Republic, he proceeded to Amsterdam, where he proposed to wait for instruction from this Government. During his residence at Paris cards of hospitality were refused him, and he was threatened with being subjected to the jurisdiction of the minister of police; but with becoming firmness he insisted on the protection of the law of nations due to him as the known minister of a foreign power. You will derive further information from his dispatches, which will be laid before you.

As it is often necessary that nations should treat for the mutual advantage of their affairs, and especially to accommodate and terminate differences, and as they can treat only by ministers, the right of embassy is well known and established by the law and usage of nations. The refusal on the part of France to receive our minister is, then, the denial of a right; but the refusal to receive him until we have acceded to their demands without discussion and without investigation is to treat us neither as allies nor as friends, nor as a sovereign state.

With this conduct of the French Government it will be proper to take into view the public audience given to the late minister of the United States on his taking leave of the Executive Directory. The speech of the President discloses sentiments more alarming than the refusal of a minister, because more dangerous to our independence and union, and at the same time studiously marked with indignities toward the Government of the United States. It evinces a disposition to separate the people of the United States from the Government, to persuade them that they have different affections, principles, and interests from those of their fellow-citizens whom they themselves have chosen to manage their common concerns, and thus to produce divisions fatal to our peace. Such attempts ought to be repelled with a decision which shall convince France and the world that we are not a degraded people, humiliated under a colonial spirit of fear and sense of inferiority, fitted to be the miserable instruments of foreign influence, and regardless of national honor, character, and interest.

I should have been happy to have thrown a veil over these transactions if it had been possible to conceal them; but they have passed on the great theater of the world, in the face of all Europe and America, and with such circumstances of publicity and solemnity that they can not be disguised and will not soon be forgotten. They have inflicted a wound in the American breast. It is my sincere desire, however, that it may be healed.

It is my sincere desire, and in this I presume I concur with you and with our constituents, to preserve peace and friendship with all nations; and believing that neither the honor nor the interest of the United States absolutely forbid the repetition of advances for securing these desirable objects with France, I shall institute a fresh attempt at negotiation, and shall not fail to promote and accelerate an accommodation on terms compatible with the rights, duties, interests, and honor of the nation. If we have committed errors, and these can be demonstrated, we shall be willing to correct them; if we have done injuries, we shall be willing on conviction to redress them; and equal measures of justice we have a right to expect from France and every other nation.

The diplomatic intercourse between the United States and France being at present suspended, the Government has no means of obtaining official information from that country. Nevertheless, there is reason to believe that the Executive Directory passed a decree on the 2d of March last contravening in part the treaty of amity and commerce of 1778, injurious to our lawful commerce and endangering the lives of our citizens. A copy of this decree will be laid before you.

While we are endeavoring to adjust all our differences with France by amicable negotiation, the progress of the war in Europe, the depredations on our commerce, the personal injuries to our citizens, and the general complexion of affairs render it my indispensable duty to recommend to your consideration effectual measures of defense.

The commerce of the United States has become an interesting object of attention, whether we consider it in relation to the wealth and finances or the strength and resources of the nation. With a seacoast of near 2,000 miles in extent, opening a wide field for fisheries, navigation, and commerce, a great portion of our citizens naturally apply their industry and enterprise to these objects. Any serious and permanent injury to commerce would not fail to produce the most embarrassing disorders. To prevent it from being undermined and destroyed it is essential that it receive an adequate protection.

The naval establishment must occur to every man who considers the injuries committed on our commerce, the insults offered to our citizens, and the description of vessels by which these abuses have been practiced. As the sufferings of our mercantile and seafaring citizens can not be ascribed to the omission of duties demandable, considering the neutral situation of our country, they are to be attributed to the hope of impunity arising from a supposed inability on our part to afford protection. To resist the consequences of such impressions on the minds of foreign nations and to guard against the degradation and servility which they must finally stamp on the American character is an important duty of Government.

A naval power, next to the militia, is the natural defense of the United States. The experience of the last war would be sufficient to shew that a moderate naval force, such as would be easily within the present abilities of the Union, would have been sufficient to have baffled many formidable transportations of troops from one State to another, which were then practiced. Our seacoasts, from their great extent, are more easily annoyed and more easily defended by a naval force than any other. With all the materials our country abounds; in skill our naval architects and navigators are equal to any, and commanders and seamen will not be wanting.

But although the establishment of a permanent system of naval defense appears to be requisite, I am sensible it can not be formed so speedily and extensively as the present crisis demands. Hitherto I have thought proper to prevent the sailing of armed vessels except on voyages to the East Indies, where general usage and the danger from pirates appeared to render the permission proper. Yet the restriction has originated solely from a wish to prevent collisions with the powers at war, contravening the act of Congress of June, 1794, and not from any doubt entertained by me of the policy and propriety of permitting our vessels to employ means of defense while engaged in a lawful foreign commerce. It remains for Congress to prescribe such regulations as will enable our seafaring citizens to defend themselves against violations of the law of nations, and at the same time restrain them from committing acts of hostility against the powers at war. In addition to this voluntary provision for defense by individual citizens, it appears to me necessary to equip the frigates, and provide other vessels of inferior force, to take under convoy such merchant vessels as shall remain unarmed.

The greater part of the cruisers whose depredations have been most injurious have been built and some of them partially equipped in the United States. Although an effectual remedy may be attended with difficulty, yet I have thought it my duty to present the subject generally to your consideration. If a mode can be devised by the wisdom of Congress to prevent the resources of the United States from being converted into the means of annoying our trade, a great evil will be prevented. With the same view, I think it proper to mention that some of our citizens resident abroad have fitted out privateers, and others have voluntarily taken the command, or entered on board of them, and committed spoliations on the commerce of the United States. Such unnatural and iniquitous practices can be restrained only by severe punishments.

But besides a protection of our commerce on the seas, I think it highly necessary to protect it at home, where it is collected in our most important ports. The distance of the United States from Europe and the well-known promptitude, ardor, and courage of the people in defense of their country happily diminish the probability of invasion. Nevertheless, to guard against sudden and predatory incursions the situation of some of our principal seaports demands your consideration. And as our country is vulnerable in other interests besides those of its commerce, you will seriously deliberate whether the means of general defense ought not to be increased by an addition to the regular artillery and cavalry, and by arrangements for forming a provisional army.

With the same view, and as a measure which, even in a time of universal peace, ought not to be neglected, I recommend to your consideration a revision of the laws for organizing, arming, and disciplining the militia, to render that natural and safe defense of the country efficacious.

Although it is very true that we ought not to involve ourselves in the political system of Europe, but to keep ourselves always distinct and separate from it if we can, yet to effect this separation, early, punctual, and continual information of the current chain of events and of the political projects in contemplation is no less necessary than if we were directly concerned in them. It is necessary, in order to the discovery of the efforts made to draw us into the vortex, in season to make preparations against them. However we may consider ourselves, the maritime and commercial powers of the world will consider the United States of America as forming a weight in that balance of power in Europe which never can be forgotten or neglected. It would not only be against our interest, but it would be doing wrong to one-half of Europe, at least, if we should voluntarily throw ourselves into either scale. It is a natural policy for a nation that studies to be neutral to consult with other nations engaged in the same studies and pursuits. At the same time that measures might be pursued with this view, our treaties with Prussia and Sweden, one of which is expired and the other near expiring, might be renewed.

Gentlemen of the House of Representatives:

It is particularly your province to consider the state of the public finances, and to adopt such measures respecting them as exigencies shall be found to require. The preservation of public credit, the regular extinguishment of the public debt, and a provision of funds to defray any extraordinary expenses will of course call for your serious attention. Although the imposition of new burthens can not be in itself agreeable, yet there is no ground to doubt that the American people will expect from you such measures as their actual engagements, their present security, and future interests demand.

Gentlemen of the Senate and Gentlemen of the House of Representatives:

The present situation of our country imposes an obligation on all the departments of Government to adopt an explicit and decided conduct. In my situation an exposition of the principles by which my Administration will be governed ought not to be omitted.

It is impossible to conceal from ourselves or the world what has been before observed, that endeavors have been employed to foster and establish a division between the Government and people of the United States. To investigate the causes which have encouraged this attempt is not necessary; but to repel, by decided and united councils, insinuations so derogatory to the honor and aggressions so dangerous to the Constitution, union, and even independence of the nation is an indispensable duty.

It must not be permitted to be doubted whether the people of the United States will support the Government established by their voluntary consent and appointed by their free choice, or whether, by surrendering themselves to the direction of foreign and domestic factions, in opposition to their own Government, they will forfeit the honorable station they have hitherto maintained.

For myself, having never been indifferent to what concerned the interests of my country, devoted the best part of my life to obtain and support its independence, and constantly witnessed the patriotism, fidelity, and perseverance of my fellow-citizens on the most trying occasions, it is not for me to hesitate or abandon a cause in which my heart has been so long engaged.

Convinced that the conduct of the Government has been just and impartial to foreign nations, that those internal regulations which have been established by law for the preservation of peace are in their nature proper, and that they have been fairly executed, nothing will ever be done by me to impair the national engagements, to innovate upon principles which have been so deliberately and uprightly established, or to surrender in any manner the rights of the Government. To enable me to maintain this declaration I rely, under God, with entire confidence on the firm and enlightened support of the National Legislature and upon the virtue and patriotism of my fellow-citizens.

JOHN ADAMS.

ADDRESS OF THE SENATE TO JOHN ADAMS, PRESIDENT OF THE UNITED STATES.

SIR: The Senate of the United States request you to accept their acknowledgments for the comprehensive and interesting detail you have given in your speech to both Houses of Congress on the existing state of the Union.

While we regret the necessity of the present meeting of the Legislature, we wish to express our entire approbation of your conduct in convening it on this momentous occasion.

The superintendence of our national faith, honor, and dignity being in a great measure constitutionally deposited with the Executive, we observe with singular satisfaction the vigilance, firmness, and promptitude exhibited by you in this critical state of our public affairs, and from thence derive an evidence and pledge of the rectitude and integrity of your Administration. And we are sensible it is an object of primary importance that each branch of the Government should adopt a language and system of conduct which shall be cool, just, and dispassionate, but firm, explicit, and decided.

We are equally desirous with you to preserve peace and friendship with all nations, and are happy to be informed that neither the honor nor interests of the United States forbid advances for securing those desirable objects by amicable negotiation with the French Republic. This method of adjusting national differences is not only the most mild, but the most rational and humane, and with governments disposed to be just can seldom fail of success when fairly, candidly, and sincerely used. If we have committed errors and can be made sensible of them, we agree with you in opinion that we ought to correct them, and compensate the injuries which may have been consequent thereon; and we trust the French Republic will be actuated by the same just and benevolent principles of national policy.

We do therefore most sincerely approve of your determination to promote and accelerate an accommodation of our existing differences with that Republic by negotiation, on terms compatible with the rights, duties, interests, and honor of our nation. And you may rest assured of our most cordial cooperation so far as it may become necessary in this pursuit.

Peace and harmony with all nations is our sincere wish; but such being the lot of humanity that nations will not always reciprocate peaceable dispositions, it is our firm belief that effectual measures of defense will tend to inspire that national self-respect and confidence at *home* which is the unfailing source of respectability *abroad*, to check aggression and prevent war.

While we are endeavoring to adjust our differences with the French Republic by amicable negotiation, the progress of the war in Europe, the depredations on our commerce, the personal injuries to our citizens, and the general complexion of affairs prove to us your vigilant care in recommending to our attention effectual measures of defense.

Those which you recommend, whether they relate to external defense by permitting our citizens to arm for the purpose of repelling aggressions on their commercial rights, and by providing sea convoys, or to internal defense by increasing the establishments of artillery and cavalry, by forming a provisional army, by revising the militia laws, and fortifying more completely our ports and harbors, will meet our consideration under the influence of the same just regard for the security, interest, and honor of our country which dictated your recommendation.

Practices so unnatural and iniquitous as those you state, of our own citizens converting their property and personal exertions into the means of annoying our trade and injuring their fellow-citizens, deserve legal severity commensurate with their turpitude.

Although the Senate believe that the prosperity and happiness of our country does not depend on general and extensive political connections with European nations, yet we can never lose sight of the propriety as well as necessity of enabling the Executive, by sufficient and liberal supplies, to maintain and even extend our foreign intercourse as exigencies may require, reposing full confidence in the Executive, in whom the Constitution has placed the powers of negotiation.

We learn with sincere concern that attempts are in operation to alienate the affections of our fellow-citizens from their Government. Attempts so wicked, wherever they exist, can not fail to excite our utmost abhorrence. A government chosen by the people for their own safety and happiness, and calculated to secure both, can not lose their affections so long as its administration pursues the principles upon which it was erected; and your resolution to observe a conduct just and impartial to all nations, a sacred regard to our national engagements, and not to impair the rights of our Government, contains principles which can not fail to secure to your Administration the support of the National Legislature to render abortive every attempt to excite dangerous jealousies among us, and to convince the world that our Government and your administration of it can not be separated from the affectionate support of every good citizen. And the Senate can not suffer the present occasion to pass without thus publicly and solemnly expressing their attachment to the Constitution and Government of their country; and as they hold themselves responsible to their constituents, their consciences, and their God, it is their determination by all their exertions to repel every attempt to alienate the affections of the people from the Government, so highly injurious to the honor, safety, and independence of the United States.

We are happy, since our sentiments on the subject are in perfect unison with yours, in this public manner to declare that we believe the conduct of the Government has been just and impartial to foreign nations, and that those internal regulations which have been established for the preservation of peace are in their nature proper and have been fairly executed.

And we are equally happy in possessing an entire confidence in your abilities and exertions in your station to maintain untarnished the honor, preserve the peace, and support the independence of our country, to acquire and establish which, in connection with your fellow-citizens, has been the virtuous effort of a principal part of your life.

To aid you in these arduous and honorable exertions, as it is our duty so it shall be our faithful endeavor ; and we flatter ourselves, sir, that the proceedings of the present session of Congress will manifest to the world that although the United States love peace, they will be independent; that they are sincere in their declarations to be just to the French and all other nations, and expect the same in return.

If a sense of justice, a love of moderation and peace, shall influence their councils, which we sincerely hope we shall have just grounds to expect, peace and amity between the United States and all nations will be preserved.

But if we are so unfortunate as to experience injuries from any foreign power, and the ordinary methods by which differences are amicably adjusted between nations shall be rejected, the determination "not to surrender in any manner the rights of the Government," being so inseparably connected with the dignity, interest, and independence of our country, shall by us be steadily and inviolably supported.

TH: JEFFERSON,
Vice-President of the United States and President of the Senate.
MAY 23, 1797.

REPLY OF THE PRESIDENT.

Mr. Vice-President and Gentlemen of the Senate:

It would be an affectation in me to dissemble the pleasure I feel on receiving this kind address.

My long experience of the wisdom, fortitude, and patriotism of the Senate of the United States enhances in my estimation the value of those obliging expressions of your approbation of my conduct, which are a generous reward for the past and an affecting encouragement to constancy and perseverance in future.

Our sentiments appear to be so entirely in unison that I can not but believe them to be the rational result of the understandings and the natural feelings of the hearts of Americans in general on contemplating the present state of the nation.

While such principles and affections prevail they will form an indissoluble bond of union and a sure pledge that our country has no essential injury to apprehend from any portentous appearances abroad. In a humble reliance on Divine Providence we may rest assured that while we reiterate with sincerity our endeavors to accommodate all our differences with France, the independence of our country can not be diminished, its dignity degraded, or its glory tarnished by any nation or combination of nations, whether friends or enemies.

JOHN ADAMS.

MAY 24, 1797.

ADDRESS OF THE HOUSE OF REPRESENTATIVES TO JOHN ADAMS, PRESIDENT OF THE UNITED STATES.

SIR: The interesting details of those events which have rendered the convention of Congress at this time indispensable (communicated in your speech to both Houses) has excited in us the strongest emotions. Whilst we regret the occasion, we can not omit to testify our approbation of the measure, and pledge ourselves that no considerations of private inconvenience shall prevent on our part a faithful discharge of the duties to which we are called.

We have constantly hoped that the nations of Europe, whilst desolated by foreign wars or convulsed by intestine divisions, would have left the United States to enjoy that peace and tranquillity to which the impartial conduct of our Government has entitled us, and it is now with extreme regret we find the measures of the French Republic tending to endanger a situation so desirable and interesting to our country.

Upon this occasion we feel it our duty to express in the most explicit manner the sensations which the present crisis has excited, and to assure you of our zealous cooperation in those measures which may appear necessary for our security or peace.

Although it is the earnest wish of our hearts that peace may be maintained with the French Republic and with all the world, yet we never will surrender those rights which belong to us as a nation; and whilst we view with satisfaction the wisdom, dignity, and moderation which have marked the measures of the Supreme Executive of our country in his attempt to remove by candid explanations the complaints and jealousies of France, we feel the full force of that indignity which has been offered our country in the rejection of its minister. No attempts to wound our rights as a sovereign State will escape the notice of our constituents. They will be felt with indignation and repelled with that decision which shall convince the world that we are not a degraded people; that we can never submit to the demands of a foreign power without examination and without discussion.

Knowing as we do the confidence reposed by the people of the United States in their Government, we can not hesitate in expressing our indignation at any sentiments tending to derogate from that confidence. Such sentiments, wherever entertained, serve to evince an imperfect knowledge of the opinions of our constituents. An attempt to separate the people of the United States from their Government is an attempt to separate them from themselves; and although foreigners who know not the genius of our country may have conceived the project, and foreign emissaries may attempt the execution, yet the united efforts of our fellow-citizens will convince the world of its impracticability.

Sensibly as we feel the wound which has been inflicted by the transactions disclosed in your communications, yet we think with you that neither the honor nor the interest of the United States forbid the repetition of advances for preserving peace; we therefore receive with the utmost satisfaction your information that a fresh attempt at negotiation will be instituted, and we cherish the hope that a mutual spirit of conciliation, and a disposition on the part of France to compensate for any injuries which may have been committed upon our neutral rights, and on the part of the United States to place France on grounds similar to those of other countries in their relation and connection with us (if any inequalities shall be found to exist), will produce an accommodation compatible with the engagements, rights, duties, and honor of the United States.

Fully, however, impressed with the uncertainty of the result, we shall prepare to meet with fortitude any unfavorable events which may occur, and to extricate ourselves from their consequences with all the skill we possess and all the efforts in our power. Believing with you that the conduct of the Government has been just and impartial to foreign nations, that the laws for the preservation of peace have been proper, and that they have been fairly executed, the Representatives of the people do not hesitate to declare that they will give their most cordial support to the execution of principles so deliberately and uprightly established.

The many interesting subjects which you have recommended to our consideration, and which are so strongly enforced by this momentous occasion, will receive every attention which their importance demands, and we trust that, by the decided and explicit conduct which will govern our deliberations, every insinuation will be repelled which is derogatory to the honor and independence of our country.

Permit us in offering this address to express our satisfaction at your promotion to the first office in the Government and our entire confidence that the preeminent talents and patriotism which have placed you in this distinguished situation will enable you to discharge its various duties with satisfaction to yourself and advantage to our common country.

JUNE 2, 1797.

REPLY OF THE PRESIDENT.

Mr. Speaker and Gentlemen of the House of Representatives:

I receive with great satisfaction your candid approbation of the convention of Congress, and thank you for your assurances that the interesting subjects recommended to your consideration shall receive the attention which their importance demands, and that your cooperation may be expected in those measures which may appear necessary for our security or peace.

The declarations of the Representatives of this nation of their satisfaction at my promotion to the first office in this Government and of their confidence in my sincere endeavors to discharge the various duties of it with advantage to our common country have excited my most grateful sensibility.

I pray you, gentlemen, to believe and to communicate such assurance to our constituents that no event which I can foresee to be attainable by any exertions in the discharge of my duties can afford me so much cordial satisfaction as to conduct a negotiation with the French Republic to a removal of prejudices, a correction of errors, a dissipation of umbrages, an accommodation of all differences, and a restoration of harmony and affection to the mutual satisfaction of both nations. And whenever the legitimate organs of intercourse shall be restored and the real sentiments of the two Governments can be candidly communicated to each other, although strongly impressed with the necessity of collecting ourselves into a manly posture of defense, I nevertheless entertain an encouraging confidence that a mutual spirit of conciliation, a disposition to compensate injuries and accommodate each other in all our relations and connections, will produce an agreement to a treaty consistent with the engagements, rights, duties, and honor of both nations.

JOHN ADAMS.

JUNE 3, 1797.

SPECIAL MESSAGES.

UNITED STATES, *May 26, 1797.*

Gentlemen of the Senate:

I lay before you, for your consideration and advice, a treaty of perpetual peace and friendship between the United States of America and the Bey and subjects of Tripoli, of Barbary, concluded at Tripoli on the 4th day of November, 1796.

JOHN ADAMS.

UNITED STATES, *May 31, 1797.*

Gentlemen of the Senate:

I nominate General Charles Cotesworth Pinckney, of South Carolina, Francis Dana, chief justice of the State of Massachusetts, and General John Marshall, of Virginia, to be jointly and severally envoys extraordinary and ministers plenipotentiary to the French Republic.

After mature deliberation on the critical situation of our relations with France, which have long engaged my most serious attention, I have determined on these nominations of persons to negotiate with the French Republic to dissipate umbrages, to remove prejudices, to rectify errors, and adjust all differences by a treaty between the two powers.

It is in the present critical and singular circumstances of great importance to engage the confidence of the great portions of the Union in the characters employed and the measures which may be adopted. I have therefore thought it expedient to nominate persons of talents and integrity, long known and intrusted in the three great divisions of the Union, and at the same time, to provide against the cases of death, absence, indisposition, or other impediment. to invest any one or more of them with full powers.

JOHN ADAMS.

UNITED STATES, *June 12, 1797.*

Gentlemen of the Senate and Gentlemen of the House of Representatives:

I have received information from the commissioner appointed on the part of the United States, pursuant to the third article of our treaty with Spain, that the running and marking of the boundary line between the colonies of East and West Florida and the territory of the United States have been delayed by the officers of His Catholic Majesty, and that they have declared their intention to maintain his jurisdiction, and to suspend the withdrawing his troops from the military posts they occupy within the territory of the United States until the two Governments shall, by negotiation, have settled the meaning of the second article respecting the withdrawing of the troops, garrisons, or settlements of either party in the territory of the other—that is, whether, when the Spanish garrisons withdraw, they are to leave the works standing or to demolish them—and until, by an additional article to the treaty, the real property of the inhabitants shall be secured, and, likewise, until the Spanish officers are sure the Indians will be pacific. The two first questions, if to be determined by negotiation, might be made subjects of discussion for years, and as no limitation of time can be prescribed to the other, a certainty in the opinion of the Spanish officers that the Indians will be pacific, it will be impossible to suffer it to remain an obstacle to the fulfillment of the treaty on the part of Spain.

To remove the first difficulty, I have determined to leave it to the discretion of the officers of His Catholic Majesty when they withdraw his troops from the forts within the territory of the United States, either to leave the works standing or to demolish them; and to remove the second I shall cause an assurance to be published and to be particularly communicated to the minister of His Catholic Majesty and to the governor of Louisiana that the settlers or occupants of the lands in question shall not be disturbed in their possessions by the troops of the United States, but, on the contrary, that they shall be protected in all their lawful claims; and to prevent or remove every doubt on this point it merits the consideration of Congress whether it will not be expedient immediately to pass a law giving positive assurances to those inhabitants who, by fair and regular grants or by occupancy, have obtained legal titles or equitable claims to lands in that country prior to the final ratification of the treaty between the United States and Spain on the 25th of April, 1796.

This country is rendered peculiarly valuable by its inhabitants, who are represented to amount to nearly 4,000, generally well affected and much attached to the United States, and zealous for the establishment of a government under their authority.

I therefore recommend to your consideration the expediency of erecting a government in the district of the Natchez similar to that established for the territory northwest of the river Ohio, but with certain modifications relative to titles or claims of land, whether of individuals or companies, or to claims of jurisdiction of any individual State.

JOHN ADAMS.

UNITED STATES, *June 22, 1797.*

Gentlemen of the House of Representatives:

Immediately after I had received your resolution of the 10th of June, requesting a report respecting the depredations committed on the commerce of the United States since the 1st of October, 1796, specifying the name of the vessel taken, where bound to or from, species of lading, the value (when it can be ascertained) of the vessel and cargo taken, and by what power captured, particularizing those which have been actually condemned, together with the proper documents to ascertain the same, I directed a collection to be made of all such information as should be found in the possession of the Government; in consequence of which the Secretary of State has made the report and the collection of documents which accompany this message, and are now laid before the House of Representatives in compliance with their desire.

JOHN ADAMS.

UNITED STATES, *June 23, 1797.*

Gentlemen of the Senate and of the House of Representatives:

The Dey of Algiers has manifested a predilection for American-built vessels, and in consequence has desired that two vessels might be constructed and equipped as cruisers according to the choice and taste of Captain O'Brien. The cost of two such vessels built with live oak and cedar, and coppered, with guns and all other equipments complete, is estimated at $45,000. The expense of navigating them to Algiers may perhaps be compensated by the freight of the stores with which they may be loaded on account of our stipulations by treaty with the Dey.

A compliance with the Dey's request appears to me to be of serious importance. He will repay the whole expense of building and equipping the two vessels, and as he has advanced the price of our peace with Tripoli, and become pledged for that of Tunis, the United States seem to be under peculiar obligations to provide this accommodation, and I trust that Congress will authorize the advance of money necessary for that purpose.

It also appears to be of importance to place at Algiers a person as consul in whose integrity and ability much confidence may be placed, to whom a considerable latitude of discretion should be allowed, for the interest of the United States in relation to their commerce. That country is so remote as to render it impracticable for the consul to ask and receive instructions in sudden emergencies. He may sometimes find it necessary to make instant engagements for money or its equivalent, to prevent greater expenses or more serious evils. We can hardly hope to escape occasions of discontent proceeding from the Regency or arising from the misconduct or even the misfortunes of our commercial vessels navigating in the Mediterranean Sea, and unless the causes of discontent are speedily removed the resentment of the Regency may be exerted with precipitation on our defenseless citizens and their property, and thus occasion a tenfold expense to the United States. For these reasons it appears to me to be expedient to vest the consul at Algiers with a degree of discretionary power which can be requisite in no other situation; and to encourage a person deserving the public confidence to accept so expensive and responsible a situation, it appears indispensable to allow him a handsome salary. I should confer on such a consul a superintending power over the consulates for the States of Tunis and Tripoli, especially in respect to pecuniary engagements, which should not be made without his approbation.

While the present salary of $2,000 a year appears adequate to the consulates of Tunis and Tripoli, twice that sum probably will be requisite for Algiers.

JOHN ADAMS.

UNITED STATES, *July 3, 1797.*

Gentlemen of the Senate and Gentlemen of the House of Representatives:

The whole of the intelligence which has for some time past been received from abroad, the correspondences between this Government and the ministers of the belligerent powers residing here, and the advices from the officers of the United States, civil and military, upon the frontiers all conspire to shew in a very strong light the critical situation of our country. That Congress might be enabled to form a more perfect judgment of it and of the measures necessary to be taken, I have directed the proper officers to prepare such collections of extracts from the public correspondences as might afford the clearest information. The reports made to me from the Secretary of State and the Secretary of War, with a collection of documents from each of them, are now communicated to both Houses of Congress. I have desired that the message, reports, and documents may be considered as confidential merely that the members of both Houses of Congress may be apprised of their contents before they should be made public. As soon as the two Houses shall have heard them, I shall submit to their discretion the publication of the whole, or any such parts of them as they shall judge necessary or expedient for the public good.

JOHN ADAMS.

PROCLAMATION.

By John Adams, the President of the United States of America.

A PROCLAMATION.

Whereas an act of the Congress of the United States was passed on the 9th day of February, 1793, entitled "An act regulating foreign coins, and for other purposes," in which it was enacted "that foreign gold and silver coins shall pass current as money within the United States and be a legal tender for the payment of all debts and demands" at the several and respective rates therein stated; and that "at the expiration of three years next ensuing the time when the coinage of gold and silver agreeably to the act intituled "An act establishing a mint and regulating the coins of the United States" shall commence at the Mint of the United States (which time shall be announced by the proclamation of the President of the United States), all foreign gold coins and all foreign silver coins, except Spanish milled dollars and parts of such dollars, shall cease to be a legal tender as aforesaid:

Now, therefore, I, the said John Adams, President of the United States, hereby proclaim, announce, and give notice to all whom it may concern that, agreeably to the act last above mentioned, the coinage of silver at the Mint of the United States commenced on the 15th day of October, 1794, and the coinage of gold on the 31st day of July, 1795; and that consequently, in conformity to the act first above mentioned, all foreign silver coins, except Spanish milled dollars and parts of such dollars, will cease to pass current as money within the United States and to be a legal tender for the payment of any debts or demands after the 15th day of October next, and all foreign gold coins will cease to pass current as money within the United States and to be a legal tender as aforesaid for the payment of any debts or demands after the 31st day of July, which will be A. D. 1798.

In testimony whereof I have caused the seal of the United States to be affixed to these presents, and signed the same with my hand.

[SEAL.]   Done at Philadelphia, the 22d day of July, A. D. 1797, and of the Independence of the United States the twenty-second.

JOHN ADAMS.

By the President:

TIMOTHY PICKERING,
Secretary of State.

FIRST ANNUAL ADDRESS.

UNITED STATES, *November 22, 1797.*

Gentlemen of the Senate and Gentlemen of the House of Representatives:

I was for some time apprehensive that it would be necessary, on account of the contagious sickness which afflicted the city of Philadelphia, to convene the National Legislature at some other place. This measure it was desirable to avoid, because it would occasion much public inconvenience and a considerable public expense and add to the calamities of the inhabitants of this city, whose sufferings must have excited the sympathy of all their fellow-citizens. Therefore, after taking measures to ascertain the state and decline of the sickness, I postponed my determination, having hopes, now happily realized, that, without hazard to the lives or health of the members, Congress might assemble at this place, where it was next by law to meet. I submit, however, to your consideration whether a power to postpone the meeting of Congress, without passing the time fixed by the Constitution upon such occasions, would not be a useful amendment to the law of 1794.

Although I can not yet congratulate you on the reestablishment of peace in Europe and the restoration of security to the persons and properties of our citizens from injustice and violence at sea, we have, nevertheless, abundant cause of gratitude to the source of benevolence and influence for interior tranquillity and personal security, for propitious seasons, prosperous agriculture, productive fisheries, and general improvements, and, above all, for a rational spirit of civil and religious liberty and a calm but steady determination to support our sovereignty, as well as our moral and our religious principles, against all open and secret attacks.

Our envoys extraordinary to the French Republic embarked—one in July, the other early in August—to join their colleague in Holland. I have received intelligence of the arrival of both of them in Holland, from whence they all proceeded on their journeys to Paris within a few days of the 19th of September. Whatever may be the result of this mission, I trust that nothing will have been omitted on my part to conduct the negotiation to a successful conclusion, on such equitable terms as may be compatible with the safety, honor, and interest of the United States. Nothing, in the meantime, will contribute so much to the preservation of peace and the attainment of justice as a manifestation of that energy and unanimity of which on many former occasions the people of the United States have given such memorable proofs, and the exertion of those resources for national defense which a beneficent Providence has kindly placed within their power.

It may be confidently asserted that nothing has occurred since the adjournment of Congress which renders inexpedient those precautionary measures recommended by me to the consideration of the two Houses at the opening of your late extraordinary session. If that system was then prudent, it is more so now, as increasing depredations strengthen the reasons for its adoption.

Indeed, whatever may be the issue of the negotiation with France, and whether the war in Europe is or is not to continue, I hold it most certain that permanent tranquillity and order will not soon be obtained. The state of society has so long been disturbed, the sense of moral and religious obligations so much weakened, public faith and national honor have been so impaired, respect to treaties has been so diminished, and the law of nations has lost so much of its force, while pride, ambition, avarice, and violence have been so long unrestrained, there remains no reasonable ground on which to raise an expectation that a commerce without protection or defense will not be plundered.

The commerce of the United States is essential, if not to their existence, at least to their comfort, their growth, prosperity, and happiness. The genius, character, and habits of the people are highly commercial. Their cities have been formed and exist upon commerce. Our agriculture, fisheries, arts, and manufactures are connected with and depend upon it. In short, commerce has made this country what it is, and it can not be destroyed or neglected without involving the people in poverty and distress. Great numbers are directly and solely supported by navigation. The faith of society is pledged for the preservation of the rights of commercial and seafaring no less than of the other citizens. Under this view of our affairs, I should hold myself guilty of a neglect of duty if I forbore to recommend that we should make every exertion to protect our commerce and to place our country in a suitable posture of defense as the only sure means of preserving both.

I have entertained an expectation that it would have been in my power at the opening of this session to have communicated to you the agreeable information of the due execution of our treaty with His Catholic Majesty respecting the withdrawing of his troops from our territory and the demarcation of the line of limits, but by the latest authentic intelligence Spanish garrisons were still continued within our country, and the running of the boundary line had not been commenced. These circumstances are the more to be regretted as they can not fail to affect the Indians in a manner injurious to the United States. Still, however, indulging the hope that the answers which have been given will remove the objections offered by the Spanish officers to the immediate execution of the treaty, I have judged it proper that we should continue in readiness to receive the posts and to run the line of limits. Further information on this subject will be communicated in the course of the session.

In connection with this unpleasant state of things on our western frontier it is proper for me to mention the attempts of foreign agents to alienate the affections of the Indian nations and to excite them to actual hostilities against the United States. Great activity has been exerted by those persons who have insinuated themselves among the Indian tribes residing within the territory of the United States to influence them to transfer their affections and force to a foreign nation, to form them into a confederacy, and prepare them for war against the United States. Although measures have been taken to counteract these infractions of our rights, to prevent Indian hostilities, and to preserve entire their attachment to the United States, it is my duty to observe that to give a better effect to these measures and to obviate the consequences of a repetition of such practices a law providing adequate punishment for such offenses may be necessary.

The commissioners appointed under the fifth article of the treaty of amity, commerce, and navigation between the United States and Great Britain to ascertain the river which was truly intended under the name of the river St. Croix mentioned in the treaty of peace, met at Passamaquoddy Bay in October, 1796, and viewed the mouths of the rivers in question and the adjacent shores and islands, and, being of opinion that actual surveys of both rivers to their sources were necessary, gave to the agents of the two nations instructions for that purpose, and adjourned to meet at Boston in August. They met, but the surveys requiring more time than had been supposed, and not being then completed, the commissioners again adjourned, to meet at Providence, in the State of Rhode Island, in June next, when we may expect a final examination and decision.

The commissioners appointed in pursuance of the sixth article of the treaty met at Philadelphia in May last to examine the claims of British subjects for debts contracted before the peace and still remaining due to them from citizens or inhabitants of the United States. Various causes have hitherto prevented any determinations, but the business is now resumed, and doubtless will be prosecuted without interruption.

Several decisions on the claims of citizens of the United States for losses and damages sustained by reason of irregular and illegal captures or condemnations of their vessels or other property have been made by the commissioners in London comformably to the seventh article of the treaty. The sums awarded by the commissioners have been paid by the British Government. A considerable number of other claims, where costs and damages, and not captured property, were the only objects in question, have been decided by arbitration, and the sums awarded to the citizens of the United States have also been paid.

The commissioners appointed agreeably to the twenty-first article of our treaty with Spain met at Philadelphia in the summer past to examine and decide on the claims of our citizens for losses they have sustained in consequence of their vessels and cargoes having been taken by the subjects of His Catholic Majesty during the late war between

Spain and France. Their sittings have been interrupted, but are now resumed.

The United States being obligated to make compensation for the losses and damages sustained by British subjects, upon the award of the commissioners acting under the sixth article of the treaty with Great Britain, and for the losses and damages sustained by British subjects by reason of the capture of their vessels and merchandise taken within the limits and jurisdiction of the United States and brought into their ports, or taken by vessels originally armed in ports of the United States, upon the awards of the commissioners acting under the seventh article of the same treaty, it is necessary that provision be made for fulfilling these obligations.

The numerous captures of American vessels by the cruisers of the French Republic and of some by those of Spain have occasioned considerable expenses in making and supporting the claims of our citizens before their tribunals. The sums required for this purpose have in divers instances been disbursed by the consuls of the United States. By means of the same captures great numbers of our seamen have been thrown ashore in foreign countries, destitute of all means of subsistence, and the sick in particular have been exposed to grievous sufferings. The consuls have in these cases also advanced moneys for their relief. For these advances they reasonably expect reimbursements from the United States.

The consular act relative to seamen requires revision and amendment. The provisions for their support in foreign countries and for their return are found to be inadequate and ineffectual. Another provision seems necessary to be added to the consular act. Some foreign vessels have been discovered sailing under the flag of the United States and with forged papers. It seldom happens that the consuls can detect this deception, because they have no authority to demand an inspection of the registers and sea letters.

Gentlemen of the House of Representatives:

It is my duty to recommend to your serious consideration those objects which by the Constitution are placed particularly within your sphere—the national debts and taxes.

Since the decay of the feudal system, by which the public defense was provided for chiefly at the expense of individuals, the system of loans has been introduced, and as no nation can raise within the year by taxes sufficient sums for its defense and military operations in time of war, the sums loaned and debts contracted have necessarily become the subjects of what have been called funding systems. The consequences arising from the continual accumulation of public debts in other countries ought to admonish us to be careful to prevent their growth in our own. The national defense must be provided for as well as the support of

Government; but both should be accomplished as much as possible by immediate taxes, and as little as possible by loans.

The estimates for the service of the ensuing year will by my direction be laid before you.

Gentlemen of the Senate and Gentlemen of the House of Representatives:

We are met together at a most interesting period. The situations of the principal powers of Europe are singular and portentous. Connected with some by treaties and with all by commerce, no important event there can be indifferent to us. Such circumstances call with peculiar importunity not less for a disposition to unite in all those measures on which the honor, safety, and prosperity of our country depend than for all the exertions of wisdom and firmness.

In all such measures you may rely on my zealous and hearty concurrence.

JOHN ADAMS.

ADDRESS OF THE SENATE TO JOHN ADAMS, PRESIDENT OF THE UNITED STATES.

The PRESIDENT OF THE UNITED STATES.

SIR: The communications you thought proper to make in your speech to both Houses of Congress on the opening of their present session afford additional proofs of the attention, integrity, and firmness which have always marked your official character.

We can not but approve of the measures you had taken to ascertain the state and decline of the contagious sickness which has so lately afflicted the city of Philadelphia, and the pleasing circumstance that Congress is now assembled at that place without hazard to the health of its members evinces the propriety of your having postponed a determination to convene the National Legislature at another place. We shall take into consideration the law of 1794 on this subject, and will readily concur in any amendment which may be deemed expedient.

It would have given us much pleasure to have received your congratulations on the reestablishment of peace in Europe and the restoration of security to the persons and property of our citizens from injustice and violence at sea; but though these events, so desirable to our country and the world, have not taken place, yet we have abundant cause of gratitude to the Great Disposer of Human Events for interior tranquillity and personal security, for propitious seasons, prosperous agriculture, productive fisheries, and general improvement, and, above all, for a rational spirit of civil and religious liberty and a calm but steady determination to support our sovereignty against all open and secret attacks.

We learn with satisfaction that our envoys extraordinary to the French

Republic had safely arrived in Europe and were proceeding to the scene of negotiation, and whatever may be the result of the mission, we are perfectly satisfied that nothing on your part has been omitted which could in any way conduce to a successful conclusion of the negotiation upon terms compatible with the safety, honor, and interest of the United States; and we are fully convinced that in the meantime a manifestation of that unanimity and energy of which the people of the United States have given such memorable proofs and a proper exertion of those resources of national defense which we possess will essentially contribute to the preservation of peace and the attainment of justice.

We think, sir, with you that the commerce of the United States is essential to the growth, comfort, and prosperity of our country, and that the faith of society is pledged for the preservation of the rights of commercial and seafaring no less than of other citizens. And even if our negotiation with France should terminate favorably and the war in Europe cease, yet the state of society which unhappily prevails in so great a portion of the world and the experience of past times under better circumstances unite in warning us that a commerce so extensive and which holds out so many temptations to lawless plunderers can never be safe without protection; and we hold ourselves obliged by every tie of duty which binds us to our constituents to promote and concur in such measures of marine defense as may convince our merchants and seamen that their rights are not sacrificed nor their injuries forgotten.

We regret that, notwithstanding the clear and explicit terms of the treaty between the United States and His Catholic Majesty, the Spanish garrisons are not yet withdrawn from our territory nor the running of the boundary line commenced. The United States have been faithful in the performance of their obligations to Spain, and had reason to expect a compliance equally prompt on the part of that power. We still, however, indulge the hope that the convincing answers which have been given to the objections stated by the Spanish officers to the immediate execution of the treaty will have their proper effect, and that this treaty, so mutually beneficial to the contracting parties, will be finally observed with good faith. We therefore entirely approve of your determination to continue in readiness to receive the posts and to run the line of partition between our territory and that of the King of Spain.

Attempts to alienate the affections of the Indians, to form them into a confederacy, and to excite them to actual hostility against the United States, whether made by foreign agents or by others, are so injurious to our interests at large and so inhuman with respect to our citizens inhabiting the adjacent territory as to deserve the most exemplary punishment, and we will cheerfully afford our aid in framing a law which may prescribe a punishment adequate to the commission of crimes so heinous.

The several objects you have pointed out to the attention of the Legislature, whether they regard our internal or external relations, shall receive from us that consideration which they merit, and we will readily concur in all such measures as may be necessary either to enable us to fulfill our engagements at home or to cause ourselves to be respected abroad; and at this portentous period, when the powers of Europe with whom we are connected by treaty or commerce are in so critical a situation, and when the conduct of some of those powers toward the United States is so hostile and menacing, the several branches of the Government are, in our opinion, called upon with peculiar importunity to unite, and by union not only to devise and carry into effect those measures on which the safety and prosperity of our country depend, but also to undeceive those nations who, regarding us as a weak and divided people, have pursued systems of aggression inconsistent with a state of peace between independent nations.   And, sir, we beg leave to assure you that we derive a singular consolation from the reflection that at such a time the executive part of our Government has been committed to your hands, for in your integrity, talents, and firmness we place the most entire confidence.

JACOB READ,
President of the Senate pro tempore.

NOVEMBER 27, 1797.

REPLY OF THE PRESIDENT.

UNITED STATES, *November 28, 1797.*

Gentlemen of the Senate:

I thank you for this address.

When, after the most laborious investigation and serious reflection, without partial considerations or personal motives, measures have been adopted or recommended, I can receive no higher testimony of their rectitude than the approbation of an assembly so independent, patriotic, and enlightened as the Senate of the United States.

Nothing has afforded me more entire satisfaction than the coincidence of your judgment with mine in the opinion of the essential importance of our commerce and the absolute necessity of a maritime defense.   What is it that has drawn to Europe the superfluous riches of the three other quarters of the globe but a marine?   What is it that has drained the wealth of Europe itself into the coffers of two or three of its principal commercial powers but a marine?

The world has furnished no example of a flourishing commerce without a maritime protection, and a moderate knowledge of man and his history will convince anyone that no such prodigy ever can arise.   A mercantile marine and a military marine must grow up together; one can not long exist without the other.

JOHN ADAMS.

ADDRESS OF THE HOUSE OF REPRESENTATIVES TO JOHN ADAMS, PRESIDENT OF THE UNITED STATES.

SIR: While our sympathy is excited by the recent sufferings of the citizens of Philadelphia, we participate in the satisfaction which you are pleased to express that the duration of the late calamity was so limited as to render unnecessary the expense and inconvenience that would have been incident to the convention of Congress in another place; and we shall readily attend to every useful amendment of the law which contemplates the event of contagious sickness at the seat of Government.

In lamenting the increase of the injuries offered to the persons and property of our citizens at sea we gratefully acknowledge the continuance of interior tranquillity and the attendant blessings of which you remind us as alleviations of these fatal effects of injustice and violence.

Whatever may be the result of the mission to the French Republic, your early and uniform attachment to the interest of our country, your important services in the struggle for its independence, and your unceasing exertions for its welfare afford no room to doubt of the sincerity of your efforts to conduct the negotiation to a successful conclusion on such terms as may be compatible with the safety, honor, and interest of the United States. We have also a firm reliance upon the energy and unanimity of the people of these States in the assertion of their rights, and on their determination to exert upon all proper occasions their ample resources in providing for the national defense.

The importance of commerce and its beneficial influence upon agriculture, arts, and manufactures have been verified in the growth and prosperity of our country. It is essentially connected with the other great interests of the community; they must flourish and decline together; and while the extension of our navigation and trade naturally excites the jealousy and tempts the avarice of other nations, we are firmly persuaded that the numerous and deserving class of citizens engaged in these pursuits and dependent on them for their subsistence has a strong and indisputable claim to our support and protection.

The delay of the Spanish officers to fulfill the treaty existing with His Catholic Majesty is a source of deep regret. We learn, however, with satisfaction that you still indulge hopes of removing the objections which have been made to its execution, and that you have continued in readiness to receive the posts. Disposed to perform with fidelity our national engagements, nothing shall be wanting on our part to obtain the same justice from others which we exercise toward them.

Our abhorrence can not be too strongly expressed of the intrigues of foreign agents to alienate the affections of the Indians and to rouse them to acts of hostility against the United States. No means in our power should be omitted of providing for the suppression of such cruel practices and for the adequate punishment of their atrocious authors.

Upon the other interesting subjects noticed in your address we shall bestow the requisite attention. To preserve inviolable the public faith by providing for the due execution of our treaties, to indemnify those who may have just claims to retribution upon the United States for expenses incurred in defending the property and relieving the necessities of our unfortunate fellow-citizens, to guard against evasions of the laws intended to secure advantages to the navigation of our own vessels, and especially to prevent by all possible means an unnecessary accumulation of the public debt, are duties which we shall endeavor to keep in view and discharge with assiduity.

We regard with great anxiety the singular and portentous situation of the principal powers of Europe. It were devoutly to be wished that the United States, remote from this seat of war and discord, unambitious of conquests, respecting the rights of other nations, and desirous merely to avail themselves of their natural resources, might be permitted to behold the scenes which desolate that quarter of the globe with only those sympathetic emotions which are natural to the lovers of peace and friends of the human race. But we are led by events to associate with these feelings a sense of the dangers which menace our security and peace. We rely upon your assurances of a zealous and hearty concurrence in such measures as may be necessary to avert these dangers, and nothing on our part shall be wanting to repel them which the honor, safety, and prosperity of our country may require.

NOVEMBER 28, 1797.

REPLY OF THE PRESIDENT.

UNITED STATES, *November 29, 1797.*

Gentlemen of the House of Representatives:

I receive this address from the House of Representatives of the United States with peculiar pleasure.

Your approbation of the meeting of Congress in this city and of those other measures of the Executive authority of Government communicated in my address to both Houses at the opening of the session afford me great satisfaction, as the strongest desire of my heart is to give satisfaction to the people and their Representatives by a faithful discharge of my duty.

The confidence you express in the sincerity of my endeavors and in the unanimity of the people does me much honor and gives me great joy.

I rejoice in that harmony which appears in the sentiments of all the branches of the Government on the importance of our commerce and our obligations to defend it, as well as in all the other subjects recommended to your consideration, and sincerely congratulate you and our fellow-citizens at large on this appearance, so auspicious to the honor, interest, and happiness of the nation.

SPECIAL MESSAGES.

UNITED STATES, *December 6, 1797.*

Gentlemen of the Senate:

Isaac Smith, esq., who was appointed, with the advice and consent of the Senate, to hold a treaty with the Seneca Nation of Indians, to superintend the purchase of a parcel of their land under a right of preemption derived from the State of Massachusetts, and situated within the State of New York, having declined that service, Jeremiah Wadsworth, esq., was appointed during your recess to hold a treaty, which has terminated in a deed of bargain and sale, herewith submitted to your consideration.

It being represented to me that the immediate investment in bank stock of the moneys which are to be the consideration of this deed might be attended with considerable loss to the Indians by raising the market price of that article, it is suggested whether it would not be expedient that the ratification should be made conclusive and binding on the parties only after the President shall be satisfied that the investment of the moneys has been made conformably to the intention of the treaty.

JOHN ADAMS.

UNITED STATES, *December 13, 1797.*

Gentlemen of the Senate and Gentlemen of the House of Representatives:

I lay before you the copy of a letter from the judges of the Supreme Court of the United States, representing the inconvenience arising from altering the time of holding the circuit court for the State of Delaware from April to June, and desiring that the existing law may be altered by restoring the spring session of the circuit court in Delaware to the 27th of April.

JOHN ADAMS.

UNITED STATES, *December 30, 1797.*

Gentlemen of the Senate and Gentlemen of the House of Representatives:

In compliance with the desire of the two Houses of Congress, expressed in their resolution of the 2d of March, 1797, that some speedy and effectual means might be adopted of obtaining information from the States of Connecticut, New Jersey, Pennsylvania, Maryland, Virginia, Kentucky, Tennessee, and South Carolina whether they have ratified the amendment proposed by Congress to the Constitution concerning the suability of States, and if they have, to obtain proper evidences, measures have been taken and information and evidences obtained the particulars of which will appear in the report from the Secretary of State made by my direction on the 28th day of this month, and now presented to the two Houses for their consideration.

JOHN ADAMS.

UNITED STATES, *January 5, 1798.*

Gentlemen of the Senate and Gentlemen of the House of Representatives:

The Secretary for the Department of War on the 30th day of December last made a representation to me of the situation of affairs in his office, which I now transmit to the Senate and House of Representatives. and recommend to their consideration and decision.

JOHN ADAMS.

UNITED STATES, *January 8, 1798.*

Gentlemen of the Senate:

The situation of affairs between some of the citizens of the United States and the Cherokee Indians has evinced the propriety of holding a treaty with that nation to extinguish by purchase their right to certain parcels of land and to adjust and settle other points relative to the safety and conveniency of our citizens. With this view I nominate Fisher Ames, of Dedham, in the State of Massachusetts; Bushrod Washington, of Richmond, in the State of Virginia, and Alfred Moore, of North Carolina, to be commissioners of the United States with full powers to hold conferences and conclude a treaty with the Cherokee Nation of Indians for the purposes before mentioned.

JOHN ADAMS.

UNITED STATES, *January 8, 1798.*

Gentlemen of the Senate and Gentlemen of the House of Representatives:

I have now an opportunity of transmitting to Congress a report of the Secretary of State, with a copy of an act of the legislature of the State of Kentucky consenting to the ratification of the amendment of the Constitution of the United States proposed by Congress in their resolution of the 2d day of December, 1793, relative to the suability of States. This amendment, having been adopted by three-fourths of the several States, may now be declared to be a part of the Constitution of the United States.

JOHN ADAMS.

UNITED STATES, *January 17, 1798.*

Gentlemen of the Senate and Gentlemen of the House of Representatives:

The situation of affairs between the United States and the Cherokee Indians having evinced the expediency of a treaty with that nation for the promotion of justice to them, as well as of the interests and convenience of our citizens, I have nominated and, by and with the advice and consent of the Senate, appointed commissioners to hold conferences and conclude a treaty as early as the season of the year and the convenience of the parties will admit.

As we know very well by experience such negotiations can not be carried on without considerable expenses, I recommend to your consideration the propriety of making an appropriation at this time for defraying such as may be necessary for holding and concluding a treaty.

That you may form your judgments with greater facility, I shall direct the proper officer to lay before you an estimate of such articles and expenses as may be thought indispensable.

JOHN ADAMS.

UNITED STATES, *January 18, 1798.*

Gentlemen of the Senate and Gentlemen of the House of Representatives:

A representation has been made to me by the judge of the Pennsylvania district of the United States of certain inconveniences and disagreeable circumstances which have occurred in the execution of the law passed on the 28th day of May, 1796, entitled "An act for the relief of persons imprisoned for debt," as well as of certain doubts which have been raised concerning its construction. This representation, together with a report of the Attorney-General on the same subject, I now transmit to Congress for their consideration, that if any amendments or explanations of that law should be thought advisable they may be adopted.

JOHN ADAMS.

UNITED STATES, *January 23, 1798.*

Gentlemen of the Senate and Gentlemen of the House of Representatives:

At the commencement of this session of Congress I proposed in the course of it to communicate to both Houses further information concerning the situation of our affairs in the territories of the United States situated on the Mississippi River and in its neighborhood; our intercourse with the Indian nations; our relations with the Spanish Government, and the conduct of their officers and agents. This information will be found in a report of the Secretary of State and the documents attending it, which I now present to the Senate and House of Representatives.

JOHN ADAMS.

UNITED STATES, *February 2, 1798.*

Gentlemen of the Senate and Gentlemen of the House of Representatives:

I have received from our minister in London two acts of the Parliament of Great Britain, one passed on the 4th of July, 1797, entitled "An act for carrying into execution the treaty of amity, commerce, and navigation concluded between His Majesty and the United States of America," the other passed on the 19th day of July, 1797, entitled "An act for regulating the trade to be carried on with the British possessions in India by the ships of nations in amity with His Majesty.'' These acts have such connections with the commercial and political interests of the United States that it is proper they should be communicated to Congress. I have accordingly transmitted copies of them with this message.

JOHN ADAMS.

UNITED STATES, *February 5, 1798.*

Gentlemen of the Senate and Gentlemen of the House of Representatives:

I have received a letter from His Excellency Charles Pinckney, esq., governor of the State of South Carolina, dated the 22d of October, 1797, inclosing a number of depositions of witnesses to several captures and outrages committed within and near the limits of the United States by a French privateer belonging to Cape François, or Monte Christo, called the *Vertitude* or *Fortitude*, and commanded by a person of the name of Jordan or Jourdain, and particularly upon an English merchant ship named the *Oracabissa*, which he first plundered and then burned, with the rest of her cargo, of great value, within the territory of the United States, in the harbor of Charleston, on the 17th day of October last, copies of which letter and depositions, and also of several other depositions relative to the same subject, received from the collector of Charleston, are herewith communicated.

Whenever the channels of diplomatical communication between the United States and France shall be opened, I shall demand satisfaction for the insult and reparation for the injury.

I have transmitted these papers to Congress not so much for the purpose of communicating an account of so daring a violation of the territory of the United States as to shew the propriety and necessity of enabling the Executive authority of Government to take measures for protecting the citizens of the United States and such foreigners as have a right to enjoy their peace and the protection of their laws within their limits in that as well as some other harbors which are equally exposed.

JOHN ADAMS.

UNITED STATES, *February 12, 1798.*

Gentlemen of the Senate and Gentlemen of the House of Representatives:

In obedience to the law, I now present to both Houses of Congress my annual account of expenditures from the contingent fund during the year 1797, by which it appears that on the 1st day of January last there remained in the Treasury a balance of $15,494.24 subject to future dispositions of Government.

JOHN ADAMS.

UNITED STATES, *February 18, 1798.*

Gentlemen of the House of Representatives:

In the report of the Secretary of State and the documents herewith transmitted will be found such information as is in our possession of the losses recovered by the citizens of the United States under the treaty made with Great Britain, which are now presented to the House of Representatives in compliance with their request in their resolution of the 1st of this month.

JOHN ADAMS.

UNITED STATES, *February 20, 1798.*

Gentlemen of the Senate and Gentlemen of the House of Representatives:

In obedience to the law of the United States of the 3d of March, 1797, entitled "An act authorizing an expenditure and making an appropriation for the prosecution of the claims of certain citizens of the United States for property captured by the belligerent powers," I submit to Congress the account exhibited to me by the Secretary of State with his report of the 17th of this month.

JOHN ADAMS.

UNITED STATES, *February 21, 1798.*

Gentlemen of the Senate:

Having received the original treaty concluded between the United States and the Government of Tunis, I lay it before the Senate of the United States whether they advise and consent to its ratification.

JOHN ADAMS.

UNITED STATES, *February 23, 1798.*

Gentlemen of the Senate and Gentlemen of the House of Representatives:

The inclosed memorial from the commissioners appointed under an act of the United States entitled "An act for establishing the temporary and permanent seat of the Government of the United States," representing the situation and circumstances of the city of Washington, I take this opportunity to present to both Houses of the Legislature and recommend to their consideration. Alexander White, esq., one of those commissioners, is now in this city, and will be able to give to Congress, or any of their committees, any explanation or further information which the subject may require.

JOHN ADAMS.

UNITED STATES, *March 5, 1798.*

Gentlemen of the Senate and Gentlemen of the House of Representatives:

The first dispatches from our envoys extraordinary since their arrival at Paris were received at the Secretary of State's office at a late hour last evening.   They are all in a character which will require some days to be deciphered, except the last, which is dated the 8th of January, 1798. The contents of this letter are of so much importance to be immediately made known to Congress and to the public, especially to the mercantile part of our fellow-citizens, that I have thought it my duty to communicate them to both Houses without loss of time.

JOHN ADAMS.

UNITED STATES, *March 12, 1798.*

Gentlemen of the Senate:

Insinuations having been repeatedly made in the name of the Court of Sweden of an inclination to renew the connection between the United States and that power, I sent, in the recess of the Senate, to our minister at Berlin a full power to negotiate that business, with such alterations as might be agreeable to both parties; but as that commission, if not renewed with the advice and consent of the Senate, will expire with the present session of Congress, I now nominate John Quincy Adams to be a commissioner with full powers to negotiate a treaty of amity and commerce with His Majesty the King of Sweden.

JOHN ADAMS.

UNITED STATES, *March 19, 1798.*

Gentlemen of the Senate and Gentlemen of the House of Representatives:

The dispatches from the envoys extraordinary of the United States to the French Republic, which were mentioned in my message to both Houses of Congress of the 5th instant, have been examined and maturely considered.

While I feel a satisfaction in informing you that their exertions for the adjustment of the differences between the two nations have been sincere and unremitted, it is incumbent on me to declare that I perceive no ground of expectation that the objects of their mission can be accomplished on terms compatible with the safety, the honor, or the essential interests of the nation.

This result can not with justice be attributed to any want of moderation on the part of this Government, or to any indisposition to forego secondary interests for the preservation of peace.   Knowing it to be my duty, and believing it to be your wish, as well as that of the great body of the people, to avoid by all reasonable concessions any participation in the contentions of Europe, the powers vested in our envoys were commensurate with a liberal and pacific policy and that high confidence which might justly be reposed in the abilities, patriotism, and integrity of the characters to whom the negotiation was committed.   After a careful review of the whole subject, with the aid of all the information I have received, I can discern nothing which could have insured or contributed to success that has been omitted on my part, and nothing further which can be attempted consistently with maxims for which our country has contended at every hazard, and which constitute the basis of our national sovereignty.

Under these circumstances I can not forbear to reiterate the recommendations which have been formerly made, and to exhort you to adopt with promptitude, decision, and unanimity such measures as the ample resources of the country afford for the protection of our seafaring and commercial citizens, for the defense of any exposed portions of our territory, for replenishing our arsenals, establishing foundries and military manufactures, and to provide such efficient revenue as will be necessary to defray extraordinary expenses and supply the deficiencies which may be occasioned by depredations on our commerce.

The present state of things is so essentially different from that in which instructions were given to the collectors to restrain vessels of the United States from sailing in an armed condition that the principle on which those orders were issued has ceased to exist. I therefore deem it proper to inform Congress that I no longer conceive myself justifiable in continuing them, unless in particular cases where there may be reasonable ground of suspicion that such vessels are intended to be employed contrary to law.

In all your proceedings it will be important to manifest a zeal, vigor, and concert in defense of the national rights proportioned to the danger with which they are threatened.

JOHN ADAMS.

UNITED STATES, *April 3, 1798.*

Gentlemen of the Senate and Gentlemen of the House of Representatives:

In compliance with the request of the House of Representatives expressed in their resolution of the 2d of this month, I transmit to both Houses those instructions to and dispatches from the envoys extraordinary of the United States to the French Republic which were mentioned in my message of the 19th of March last, omitting only some names and a few expressions descriptive of the persons.

I request that they may be considered in confidence until the members of Congress are fully possessed of their contents and shall have had opportunity to deliberate on the consequences of their publication, after which time I submit them to your wisdom.

JOHN ADAMS.

UNITED STATES, *April 12, 1798.*

Gentlemen of the Senate:

A treaty with the Mohawk Nation of Indians has by accident lain long neglected. It was executed under the authority of the Honorable Isaac Smith, a commissioner of the United States. I now submit it to the Senate for their consideration.

JOHN ADAMS.

UNITED STATES, *May 3, 1798.*

Gentlemen of the Senate:

His Excellency John Jay, esq., governor of New York, has informed me that the Oneida tribe of Indians have proposed to sell a part of their land to the said State, and that the legislature at their late session authorized the purchase, and to accomplish this object the governor has desired that a commissioner may be appointed to hold a treaty with the Oneida tribe of Indians, at which the agents of the State of New York may agree with them on the terms of the purchase. I therefore nominate Joseph Hopkinson, esq., of Pennsylvania, to be the commissioner to hold a treaty with the said Oneida tribe of Indians for the purpose above mentioned.

JOHN ADAMS.

UNITED STATES, *June 21, 1798.*

Gentlemen of the Senate and Gentlemen of the House of Representatives:

While I congratulate you on the arrival of General Marshall, one of our late envoys extraordinary to the French Republic, at a place of safety, where he is justly held in honor, I think it my duty to communicate to you a letter received by him from Mr. Gerry, the only one of the three who has not received his congé. This letter, together with another from the minister of foreign relations to him of the 3d of April, and his answer of the 4th, will shew the situation in which he remains—his intentions and prospects.

I presume that before this time he has received fresh instructions (a copy of which accompanies this message) to consent to no loans, and therefore the negotiation may be considered at an end.

I will never send another minister to France without assurances that he will be received, respected, and honored as the representative of a great, free, powerful, and independent nation.

JOHN ADAMS.

UNITED STATES, *June 27, 1798.*

Gentlemen of the Senate and Gentlemen of the House of Representatives:

I have received a letter from His Excellency Thomas Mifflin, governor of Pennsylvania, inclosing some documents which I judge it my duty to lay before Congress without loss of time.

As my opinion coincides entirely with that of his excellency the governor, I recommend the subject to the consideration of both Houses of Congress, whose authority alone appears to me adequate to the occasion.

JOHN ADAMS.

By John Adams

The President of the United States of America

A Proclamation

Whereas an act of the Congress of the United States, was passed on the ninth day of February 1793 intitled "An Act regulating foreign coins and for other purposes," in which it was enacted "that foreign gold and silver coins shall pass current as money within the United States "and be a legal tender for the payment of all debts and demands" at the several and respective rates therein stated and that "at the expiration of three years, next ensuing the time when the Coinage of gold and silver agreeably to the act intituled "An Act establishing a Mint and regulating the Coins of the United States" shall commence at the Mint of the United States, which time shall be announced by the Proclamation of the President of the United States, all foreign gold coins and all foreign silver coins, except spanish milled dollars and parts of such dollars, shall cease to be a legal tender as aforesaid." Now therefore I the said John Adams President of the United States hereby proclaim announce and give notice to all whom it may concern, that agreeably to the Act last above mentioned the Coinage of silver at the Mint of the United States commenced on the fifteenth day of October one thousand seven hundred and ninety four and the Coinage of Gold on the thirty first day of July one thousand seven hundred and ninety five and that consequently in conformity to the Act first above mentioned, all foreign silver coins, except spanish Milled dollars and parts of such dollars, will cease to pass current as money within the United States and to be a legal tender for the payment of any debts or demands, after the fifteenth day of October next, and all foreign gold coins will cease to pass current as money within the United States and to be a legal tender as aforesaid for the payment of any debts or demands after the thirty first day of July, which will be in the year of our Lord one thousand seven hundred and ninety eight. In Testimony whereof I have caused the Seal of the United States to be affixed to these presents, and signed the same with my hand. Done at Philadelphia the twenty second day of June in the year of our Lord one thousand seven hundred and ninety seven and of the Independence of the United States the twenty second.

John Adams

By the President
Timothy Pickering, Secretary of State

COINAGE PROCLAMATION BY PRESIDENT JOHN ADAMS.

UNITED STATES, *July 2, 1798.*

Gentlemen of the Senate:

I nominate George Washington, of Mount Vernon, to be Lieutenant-General and Commander in Chief of all the armies raised or to be raised in the United States.

JOHN ADAMS.

UNITED STATES, *July 13, 1798.*

Gentlemen of the Senate:

A resolution of both Houses of Congress authorizing an adjournment on Monday, the 16th of this month, has been laid before me. Sensible of the severity of the service in so long a session, it is with great reluctance that I find myself obliged to offer any consideration which may operate against the inclinations of the members; but certain measures of Executive authority which will require the consideration of the Senate, and which can not be matured, in all probability, before Monday or Tuesday, oblige me to request of the Senate that they would continue their session until Wednesday or Thursday.

JOHN ADAMS.

UNITED STATES, *July 17, 1798.*

Gentlemen of the Senate:

Believing that the letter received this morning from General Washington will give high satisfaction to the Senate, I transmit them a copy of it, and congratulate them and the public on this great event—the General's acceptance of his appointment as Lieutenant-General and Commander in Chief of the Army.

JOHN ADAMS.

MOUNT VERNON, *July 13, 1798.*

JOHN ADAMS,
    President of the United States.

DEAR SIR: I had the honor, on the evening of the 11th instant, to receive from the hands of the Secretary of War your favor of the 7th, announcing that you had, with the advice and consent of the Senate, appointed me "Lieutenant-General and Commander in Chief of all the armies raised or to be raised for the service of the United States."

I can not express how greatly affected I am at this new proof of public confidence and the highly flattering manner in which you have been pleased to make the communication. At the same time I must not conceal from you my earnest wish that the choice had fallen upon a man less declined in years and better qualified to encounter the usual vicissitudes of war.

You know, sir, what calculation I had made relative to the probable course of events on my retiring from office, and the determination I had consoled myself with of closing the remnant of my days in my present peaceful abode. You will therefore be at no loss to conceive and appreciate the sensations I must have experienced to bring my mind to any conclusion that would pledge me, at so late a period of life, to leave scenes I sincerely love to enter upon the boundless field of public action, incessant trouble, and high responsibility.

It was not possible for me to remain ignorant of or indifferent to recent transactions. The conduct of the Directory of France toward our country, their insidious hostility to its Government, their various practices to withdraw the affections of the people from it, the evident tendency of their acts and those of their agents to countenance and invigorate opposition, their disregard of solemn treaties and the laws of nations, their war upon our defenseless commerce, their treatment of our ministers of peace, and their demands amounting to tribute could not fail to excite in me corresponding sentiments with those my countrymen have so generally expressed in their affectionate addresses to you. Believe me, sir, no one can more cordially approve of the wise and prudent measures of your Administration. They ought to inspire universal confidence, and will no doubt, combined with the state of things, call from Congress such laws and means as will enable you to meet the full force and extent of the crisis.

Satisfied, therefore, that you have sincerely wished and endeavored to avert war, and exhausted to the last drop the cup of reconciliation, we can with pure hearts appeal to Heaven for the justice of our cause, and may confidently trust the final result to that kind Providence who has heretofore and so often signally favored the people of these United States.

Thinking in this manner, and feeling how incumbent it is upon every person, of every description, to contribute at all times to his country's welfare, and especially in a moment like the present, when everything we hold dear and sacred is so seriously threatened, I have finally determined to accept the commission of Commander in Chief of the armies of the United States, with the reserve only that I shall not be called into the field until the Army is in a situation to require my presence or it becomes indispensable by the urgency of circumstances.

In making this reservation I beg it to be understood that I do not mean to withhold any assistance to arrange and organize the Army which you may think I can afford. I take the liberty also to mention that I must decline having my acceptance considered as drawing after it any immediate charge upon the public, or that I can receive any emoluments annexed to the appointment before entering into a situation to incur expense.

The Secretary of War being anxious to return to the seat of Government, I have detained him no longer than was necessary to a full communication upon the several points he had in charge.

With very great respect and consideration, I have the honor to be, dear sir, your most obedient and humble servant,

G? WASHINGTON.

PROCLAMATIONS.

BY THE PRESIDENT OF THE UNITED STATES OF AMERICA.

A PROCLAMATION.

As the safety and prosperity of nations ultimately and essentially depend on the protection and the blessing of Almighty God, and the national acknowledgment of this truth is not only an indispensable duty which the people owe to Him, but a duty whose natural influence is favorable to the promotion of that morality and piety without which social happiness can not exist nor the blessings of a free government be enjoyed; and as this duty, at all times incumbent, is so especially in sea-sons of difficulty or of danger, when existing or threatening calamities, the just judgments of God against prevalent iniquity, are a loud call to repentance and reformation; and as the United States of America are at present placed in a hazardous and afflictive situation by the unfriendly disposition, conduct, and demands of a foreign power, evinced by repeated refusals to receive our messengers of reconciliation and peace, by depre-dations on our commerce, and the infliction of injuries on very many of our fellow-citizens while engaged in their lawful business on the seas—under these considerations it has appeared to me that the duty of implor-ing the mercy and benediction of Heaven on our country demands at this time a special attention from its inhabitants.

I have therefore thought fit to recommend, and I do hereby recom-mend, that Wednesday, the 9th day of May next, be observed throughout the United States as a day of solemn humiliation, fasting, and prayer; that the citizens of these States, abstaining on that day from their cus-tomary worldly occupations, offer their devout addresses to the Father of Mercies agreeably to those forms or methods which they have severally adopted as the most suitable and becoming; that all religious congrega-tions do, with the deepest humility, acknowledge before God the manifold sins and transgressions with which we are justly chargeable as individ-uals and as a nation, beseeching Him at the same time, of His infinite grace, through the Redeemer of the World, freely to remit all our offenses, and to incline us by His Holy Spirit to that sincere repentance and reformation which may afford us reason to hope for his inestimable favor and heavenly benediction; that it be made the subject of particular and earnest supplication that our country may be protected from all the dangers which threaten it; that our civil and religious privileges may be preserved inviolate and perpetuated to the latest generations; that our public councils and magistrates may be especially enlightened and directed at this critical period; that the American people may be united in those bonds of amity and mutual confidence and inspired with that vigor and fortitude by which they have in times past been so highly distinguished and by which they have obtained such invaluable advan-tages; that the health of the inhabitants of our land may be preserved, and their agriculture, commerce, fisheries, arts, and manufactures be blessed and prospered; that the principles of genuine piety and sound morality may influence the minds and govern the lives of every descrip-tion of our citizens, and that the blessings of peace, freedom, and pure religion may be speedily extended to all the nations of the earth.

And finally, I recommend that on the said day the duties of humili-ation and prayer be accompanied by fervent thanksgiving to the Bestower of Every Good Gift, not only for His having hitherto protected and pre-served the people of these United States in the independent enjoyment of their religious and civil freedom, but also for having prospered them in a wonderful progress of population, and for conferring on them many and great favors conducive to the happiness and prosperity of a nation.

Given under my hand and the seal of the United States of America, at Philadelphia, this 23d day of March, A. D. 1798, and of the Independence of the said States the twenty-second.

[SEAL.]

JOHN ADAMS.

By the President:
    TIMOTHY PICKERING,
        Secretary of State.

[From C. F. Adams's Works of John Adams, Vol. IX, p. 170.]

PROCLAMATION.

JULY 13, 1798.

The citizen Joseph Philippe Letombe having heretofore produced to the President of the United States his commission as consul-general of the French Republic within the United States of America, and another commission as consul of the French Republic at Philadelphia; and, in like manner, the citizen Rosier having produced his commission as vice-consul of the French Republic at New York; and the citizen Arcambal having produced his commission as vice-consul of the French Republic at Newport; and citizen Theodore Charles Mozard having produced his commission as consul of the French Republic within the States of New Hampshire, Massachusetts, and Rhode Island; and the President of the United States having thereupon granted an exequatur to each of the French citizens above named, recognizing them in their respective consular offices above mentioned, and declaring them respectively free to exercise and enjoy such functions, powers, and privileges as are allowed to a consul-general, consuls, and vice-consuls of the French Republic by their treaties, conventions, and laws in that case made and provided; and the Congress of the United States, by their act passed the 7th day of July, 1798, having declared "that the United States are of right freed and exonerated from the stipulations of the treaties and of the consular convention heretofore concluded between the United States and France, and that the same shall not henceforth be regarded as legally obligatory on the Government or citizens of the United States," and by a former act, passed the 13th day of May, 1798, the Congress of the United States having "suspended the commercial intercourse between the United States and France and the dependencies thereof," which commercial intercourse was the direct and chief object of the consular establishment; and

Whereas actual hostilities have long been practiced on the commerce of the United States by the cruisers of the French Republic under the orders of its Government, which orders that Government refuses to revoke or relax; and hence it has become improper any longer to allow the consul-general, consuls, and vice-consuls of the French Republic above named, or any of its consular persons or agents heretofore admitted in these United States, any longer to exercise their consular functions:

These are therefore to declare that I do no longer recognize the said citizen Letombe as consul-general or consul, nor the said citizens Rosier and Arcambal as vice-consuls, nor the said citizen Mozard as consul of the French Republic in any part of these United States, nor permit them or any other consular persons or agents of the French Republic heretofore admitted in the United States to exercise their functions as such; and I do hereby wholly revoke the exequaturs heretofore given to them respectively, and do declare them absolutely null and void from this day forward.

In testimony whereof, etc.

JOHN ADAMS.

SECOND ANNUAL ADDRESS.

UNITED STATES, *December 8, 1798.*

Gentlemen of the Senate and Gentlemen of the House of Representatives:

While with reverence and resignation we contemplate the dispensations of Divine Providence in the alarming and destructive pestilence with which several of our cities and towns have been visited, there is cause for gratitude and mutual congratulations that the malady has disappeared and that we are again permitted to assemble in safety at the seat of Government for the discharge of our important duties. But when we reflect that this fatal disorder has within a few years made repeated ravages in some of our principal seaports, and with increased malignancy, and when we consider the magnitude of the evils arising from the interruption of public and private business, whereby the national interests are deeply affected, I think it my duty to invite the Legislature of the Union to examine the expediency of establishing suitable regulations in aid of the health laws of the respective States; for these being formed on the idea that contagious sickness may be communicated through the channels of commerce, there seems to be a necessity that Congress, who alone can regulate trade, should frame a system which, while it may tend to preserve the general health, may be compatible with the interests of commerce and the safety of the revenue.

While we think on this calamity and sympathize with the immediate sufferers, we have abundant reason to present to the Supreme Being our annual oblations of gratitude for a liberal participation in the ordinary blessings of His providence. To the usual subjects of gratitude I can not omit to add one of the first importance to our well-being and safety; I mean that spirit which has arisen in our country against the menaces and aggression of a foreign nation. A manly sense of national honor, dignity, and independence has appeared which, if encouraged and invigorated by every branch of the Government, will enable us to view undismayed the enterprises of any foreign power and become the sure foundation of national prosperity and glory.

The course of the transactions in relation to the United States and France which have come to my knowledge during your recess will be made the subject of a future communication. That communication will confirm the ultimate failure of the measures which have been taken by the Government of the United States toward an amicable adjustment of differences with that power. You will at the same time perceive that the French Government appears solicitous to impress the opinion that it is averse to a rupture with this country, and that it has in a qualified manner declared itself willing to receive a minister from the United States for the purpose of restoring a good understanding. It is unfortunate for professions of this kind that they should be expressed in terms which may countenance the inadmissible pretension of a right to prescribe the qualifications which a minister from the United States should possess, and that while France is asserting the existence of a disposition on her part to conciliate with sincerity the differences which have arisen, the sincerity of a like disposition on the part of the United States, of which so many demonstrative proofs have been given, should even be indirectly questioned. It is also worthy of observation that the decree of the Directory alleged to be intended to restrain the depredations of French cruisers on our commerce has not given, and can not give, any relief. It enjoins them to conform to all the laws of France relative to cruising and prizes, while these laws are themselves the sources of the depredations of which we have so long, so justly, and so fruitlessly complained.

The law of France enacted in January last, which subjects to capture and condemnation neutral vessels and their cargoes if any portion of the latter are of British fabric or produce, although the entire property belong to neutrals, instead of being rescinded has lately received a confirmation by the failure of a proposition for its repeal. While this law, which is an unequivocal act of war on the commerce of the nations it attacks, continues in force those nations can see in the French Government only a power regardless of their essential rights, of their independence and sovereignty; and if they possess the means they can reconcile nothing with their interest and honor but a firm resistance.

Hitherto, therefore, nothing is discoverable in the conduct of France which ought to change or relax our measures of defense. On the contrary, to extend and invigorate them is our true policy. We have no reason to regret that these measures have been thus far adopted and pursued, and in proportion as we enlarge our view of the portentous and incalculable situation of Europe we shall discover new and cogent motives for the full development of our energies and resources.

But in demonstrating by our conduct that we do not fear war in the necessary protection of our rights and honor we shall give no room to infer that we abandon the desire of peace. An efficient preparation for war can alone insure peace. It is peace that we have uniformly and perseveringly cultivated, and harmony between us and France may be restored at her option. But to send another minister without more determinate assurances that he would be received would be an act of humiliation to which the United States ought not to submit. It must therefore be left with France (if she is indeed desirous of accommodation) to take the requisite steps. The United States will steadily observe the maxims by which they have hitherto been governed. They will respect the sacred rights of embassy; and with a sincere disposition on the part of France to desist from hostility, to make reparation for the injuries heretofore inflicted on our commerce, and to do justice in future, there will be no obstacle to the restoration of a friendly intercourse. In making to you this declaration I give a pledge to France and the world that the Executive authority of this country still adheres to the humane and pacific policy which has invariably governed its proceedings, in conformity with the wishes of the other branches of the Government and of the people of the United States. But considering the late manifestations of her policy toward foreign nations, I deem it a duty deliberately and solemnly to declare my opinion that whether we negotiate with her or not, vigorous preparations for war will be alike indispensable. These alone will give to us an equal treaty and insure its observance.

Among the measures of preparation which appear expedient, I take the liberty to recall your attention to the naval establishment. The beneficial effects of the small naval armament provided under the acts of the last session are known and acknowledged. Perhaps no country ever experienced more sudden and remarkable advantages from any measure of policy than we have derived from the arming for our maritime protection and defense. We ought without loss of time to lay the foundation for an increase of our Navy to a size sufficient to guard our coast and protect our trade. Such a naval force as it is doubtless in the power of the United States to create and maintain would also afford to them the best means of general defense by facilitating the safe transportation of troops and stores to every part of our extensive coast. To accomplish this important object, a prudent foresight requires that systematical measures be adopted for procuring at all times the requisite timber and other supplies. In what manner this shall be done I leave to your consideration.

I will now advert, gentlemen, to some matters of less moment, but proper to be communicated to the National Legislature.

After the Spanish garrisons had evacuated the posts they occupied at the Natchez and Walnut Hills the commissioner of the United States commenced his observations to ascertain the point near the Mississippi which terminated the northernmost part of the thirty-first degree of north latitude. From thence he proceeded to run the boundary line between the United States and Spain. He was afterwards joined by the Spanish commissioner, when the work of the former was confirmed, and they proceeded together to the demarcation of the line. Recent information renders it probable that the Southern Indians, either instigated to oppose the demarcation or jealous of the consequences of suffering white people to run a line over lands to which the Indian title had not been extinguished, have ere this time stopped the progress of the commissioners; and considering the mischiefs which may result from continuing the demarcation in opposition to the will of the Indian tribes, the great expense attending it, and that the boundaries which the commissioners have actually established probably extend at least as far as the Indian title has been extinguished, it will perhaps become expedient and necessary to suspend further proceedings by recalling our commissioner.

The commissioners appointed in pursuance of the fifth article of the treaty of amity, commerce, and navigation between the United States and His Britannic Majesty to determine what river was truly intended under the name of the river St. Croix mentioned in the treaty of peace, and forming a part of the boundary therein described, have finally decided that question. On the 25th of October they made their declaration that a river called Scoodiac, which falls into Passamaquoddy Bay at its northwestern quarter, was the true St. Croix intended in the treaty of peace, as far as its great fork, where one of its streams comes from the westward and the other from the northward, and that the latter stream is the continuation of the St. Croix to its source. This decision, it is understood, will preclude all contention among individual claimants, as it seems that the Scoodiac and its northern branch bound the grants of land which have been made by the respective adjoining Governments. A subordinate question, however, it has been suggested, still remains to be determined. Between the mouth of the St. Croix as now settled and what is usually called the Bay of Fundy lie a number of valuable islands. The commissioners have not continued the boundary line through any channel of these islands, and unless the bay of Passamaquoddy be a part of the Bay of Fundy this further adjustment of boundary will be necessary. But it is apprehended that this will not be a matter of any difficulty.

Such progress has been made in the examination and decision of cases of captures and condemnations of American vessels which were the subject of the seventh article of the treaty of amity, commerce, and navigation between the United States and Great Britain that it is supposed the commissioners will be able to bring their business to a conclusion in August of the ensuing year.

The commissioners acting under the twenty-fifth article of the treaty between the United States and Spain have adjusted most of the claims of our citizens for losses sustained in consequence of their vessels and cargoes having been taken by the subjects of His Catholic Majesty during the late war between France and Spain.

Various circumstances have concurred to delay the execution of the law for augmenting the military establishment, among these the desire of obtaining the fullest information to direct the best selection of officers. As this object will now be speedily accomplished, it is expected that the raising and organizing of the troops will proceed without obstacle and with effect.

Gentlemen of the House of Representatives:

I have directed an estimate of the appropriations which will be necessary for the service of the ensuing year to be laid before you, accompanied with a view of the public receipts and expenditures to a recent period. It will afford you satisfaction to infer the great extent and solidity of the public resources from the prosperous state of the finances, notwithstanding the unexampled embarrassments which have attended commerce. When you reflect on the conspicuous examples of patriotism and liberality which have been exhibited by our mercantile fellow-citizens, and how great a proportion of the public resources depends on their enterprise, you will naturally consider whether their convenience can not be promoted and reconciled with the security of the revenue by a revision of the system by which the collection is at present regulated.

During your recess measures have been steadily pursued for effecting the valuations and returns directed by the act of the last session, preliminary to the assessment and collection of a direct tax. No other delays or obstacles have been experienced except such as were expected to arise from the great extent of our country and the magnitude and novelty of the operation, and enough has been accomplished to assure a fulfillment of the views of the Legislature.

Gentlemen of the Senate and Gentlemen of the House of Representatives:

I can not close this address without once more adverting to our political situation and inculcating the essential importance of uniting in the maintenance of our dearest interests; and I trust that by the temper and wisdom of your proceedings and by a harmony of measures we shall secure to our country that weight and respect to which it is so justly entitled.   JOHN ADAMS.

ADDRESS OF THE SENATE TO JOHN ADAMS, PRESIDENT OF THE UNITED STATES.

The President of the United States.

Sir: The Senate of the United States join you in thanks to Almighty God for the removal of the late afflicting dispensations of His providence and for the patriotic spirit and general prosperity of our country. Sympathy for the sufferings of our fellow-citizens from disease and the important interests of the Union demand of the National Legislature a ready cooperation with the State governments in the use of such means as seem best calculated to prevent the return of this fatal calamity.

Although we have sincerely wished that an adjustment of our differences with the Republic of France might be effected on safe and honorable terms, yet the information you have given us of the ultimate failure of the negotiation has not surprised us. In the general conduct of that Republic we have seen a design of universal influence incompatible with the self-government and destructive of the independence of other States. In its conduct toward these United States we have seen a plan of hostility pursued with unremitted constancy, equally disregarding the obligations of treaties and the rights of individuals. We have seen two embassies, formed for the purpose of mutual explanations and clothed with the most extensive and liberal powers, dismissed without recognition and even without a hearing. The Government of France has not only refused to repeal but has recently enjoined the observance of its former edict respecting merchandise of British fabric or produce the property of neutrals, by which the interruption of our lawful commerce and the spoliation of the property of our citizens have again received a public sanction. These facts indicate no change of system or disposition; they speak a more intelligible language than professions of solicitude to avoid a rupture, however ardently made. But if, after the repeated proofs we have given of a sincere desire for peace, these professions should be accompanied by insinuations implicating the integrity with which it has been pursued; if, neglecting and passing by the constitutional and authorized agents of the Government, they are made through the medium of individuals without public character or authority, and, above all, if they carry with them a claim to prescribe the political qualifications of the minister of the United States to be employed in the negotiation, they are not entitled to attention or consideration, but ought to be regarded as designed to separate the people from their Government and to bring about by intrigue that which open force could not effect.

We are of opinion with you, sir, that there has nothing yet been discovered in the conduct of France which can justify a relaxation of the means of defense adopted during the last session of Congress, the happy result of which is so strongly and generally marked. If the force by sea and land which the existing laws authorize should be judged inadequate to the public defense, we will perform the indispensable duty of bringing forward such other acts as will effectually call forth the resources and force of our country.

A steady adherence to this wise and manly policy, a proper direction of the noble spirit of patriotism which has arisen in our country, and which ought to be cherished and invigorated by every branch of the Government, will secure our liberty and independence against all open and secret attacks.

We enter on the business of the present session with an anxious solicitude for the public good, and shall bestow that consideration on the several objects pointed out in your communication which they respectively merit.

Your long and important services, your talents and firmness, so often displayed in the most trying times and most critical situations, afford a sure pledge of a zealous cooperation in every measure necessary to secure us justice and respect.

JOHN LAURANCE,
President of the Senate pro tempore.

DECEMBER 11, 1798.

REPLY OF THE PRESIDENT.

DECEMBER 12, 1798.

To the Senate of the United States.

GENTLEMEN: I thank you for this address, so conformable to the spirit of our Constitution and the established character of the Senate of the United States for wisdom, honor, and virtue.

I have seen no real evidence of any change of system or disposition in the French Republic toward the United States. Although the officious interference of individuals without public character or authority is not entitled to any credit, yet it deserves to be considered whether that temerity and impertinence of individuals affecting to interfere in public affairs between France and the United States, whether by their secret correspondence or otherwise, and intended to impose upon the people and separate them from their Government, ought not to be inquired into and corrected.

I thank you, gentlemen, for your assurances that you will bestow that consideration on the several objects pointed out in my communication which they respectively merit.

If I have participated in that understanding, sincerity, and constancy which have been displayed by my fellow-citizens and countrymen in the most trying times and critical situations, and fulfilled my duties to them, I am happy. The testimony of the Senate of the United States in my favor is an high and honorable reward, which receives, as it merits, my grateful acknowledgments. My zealous cooperation in measures necessary to secure us justice and consideration may be always depended on.

JOHN ADAMS.

ADDRESS OF THE HOUSE OF REPRESENTATIVES TO JOHN ADAMS, PRESIDENT OF THE UNITED STATES.

JOHN ADAMS,
President of the United States.

SIR: The House of Representatives unite with you in deploring the effects of the desolating malady by which the seat of Government and other parts of our country have recently been visited. In calling our attention to the fatality of its repeated ravages and inviting us to consider the expediency of exercising our constitutional powers in aid of the health laws of the respective States, your recommendation is sanctioned by the dictates of humanity and liberal policy. On this interesting subject we feel the necessity of adopting every wise expedient for preventing a calamity so distressing to individual sufferers and so prejudicial to our national commerce.

That our finances are in a prosperous state notwithstanding the commercial derangements resulting from this calamity and from external embarrassments is a satisfactory manifestation of the great extent and solidity of the public resources. Connected with this situation of our fiscal concerns, the assurance that the legal provisions for obtaining revenue by direct taxation will fulfill the views of the Legislature is peculiarly acceptable.

Desirous as we are that all causes of hostility may be removed by the amicable adjustment of national differences, we learn with satisfaction that in pursuance of our treaties with Spain and with Great Britain advances have been made for definitively settling the controversies relative to the southern and northeastern limits of the United States. With similar sentiments have we received your information that the proceedings under commissions authorized by the same treaties afford to a respectable portion of our citizens the prospect of a final decision on their claims for maritime injuries committed by subjects of those powers.

It would be the theme of mutual felicitation were we assured of experiencing similar moderation and justice from the French Republic, between which and the United States differences have unhappily arisen; but this is denied us by the ultimate failure of the measures which have been taken by this Government toward an amicable adjustment of those differences and by the various inadmissible pretensions on the part of that nation.

The continuing in force the decree of January last, to which you have more particularly pointed our attention, ought of itself to be considered as demonstrative of the real intentions of the French Government. That decree proclaims a predatory warfare against the unquestionable rights of neutral commerce which with our means of defense our interest and our honor command us to repel. It therefore now becomes the United States to be as determined in resistance as they have been patient in suffering and condescending in negotiation.

While those who direct the affairs of France persist in the enforcement of decrees so hostile to our essential rights, their conduct forbids us to confide in any of their professions of amity.

As, therefore, the conduct of France hitherto exhibits nothing which ought to change or relax our measures of defense, the policy of extending and invigorating those measures demands our sedulous attention. The sudden and remarkable advantages which this country has experienced from a small naval armament sufficiently prove the utility of its establishment. As it respects the guarding of our coast, the protection of our trade, and the facility of safely transporting the means of territorial defense to every part of our maritime frontier, an adequate naval force must be considered as an important object of national policy. Nor do we hesitate to adopt the opinion that, whether negotiations with France are resumed or not, vigorous preparations for war will be alike indispensable.

In this conjuncture of affairs, while with you we recognize our abundant cause of gratitude to the Supreme Disposer of Events for the ordinary blessings of Providence, we regard as of high national importance the manifestation in our country of a magnanimous spirit of resistance to foreign domination. This spirit merits to be cherished and invigorated by every branch of Government as the estimable pledge of national prosperity and glory.

Disdaining a reliance on foreign protection, wanting no foreign guaranty of our liberties, resolving to maintain our national independence against every attempt to despoil us of this inestimable treasure, we confide under Providence in the patriotism and energies of the people of these United States for defeating the hostile enterprises of any foreign power.

To adopt with prudent foresight such systematical measures as may be expedient for calling forth those energies wherever the national exigencies may require, whether on the ocean or on our own territory, and to reconcile with the proper security of revenue the convenience of mercantile enterprise, on which so great a proportion of the public resources depends, are objects of moment which shall be duly regarded in the course of our deliberations.

Fully as we accord with you in the opinion that the United States ought not to submit to the humiliation of sending another minister to France without previous assurances sufficiently determinate that he will be duly accredited, we have heard with cordial approbation the declaration of your purpose steadily to observe those maxims of humane and pacific policy by which the United States have hitherto been governed. While it is left with France to take the requisite steps for accommodation, it is worthy the Chief Magistrate of a free people to make known to the world that justice on the part of France will annihilate every obstacle to the restoration of a friendly intercourse, and that the Executive authority of this country will respect the sacred rights of embassy. At the same time, the wisdom and decision which have characterized your past Administration assure us that no illusory professions will seduce you into any abandonment of the rights which belong to the United States as a free and independent nation.

DECEMBER 13, 1798.

REPLY OF THE PRESIDENT.

DECEMBER 14, 1798.

To the House of Representatives of the United States of America.

GENTLEMEN: My sincere acknowledgments are due to the House of Representatives of the United States for this excellent address so consonant to the character of representatives of a great and free people. The judgment and feelings of a nation, I believe, were never more truly expressed by their representatives than those of our constituents by your decided declaration that with our means of defense our interest and honor command us to repel a predatory warfare against the unquestionable rights of neutral commerce; that it becomes the United States to be as determined in resistance as they have been patient in suffering and condescending in negotiation; that while those who direct the affairs of France persist in the enforcement of decrees so hostile to our essential rights their conduct forbids us to confide in any of their professions of amity; that an adequate naval force must be considered as an important object of national policy, and that, whether negotiations with France are resumed or not, vigorous preparations for war will be alike indispensable.

The generous disdain you so coolly and deliberately express of a reliance on foreign protection, wanting no foreign guaranty of our liberties, resolving to maintain our national independence against every attempt to despoil us of this inestimable treasure, will meet the full approbation of every sound understanding and exulting applauses from the heart of every faithful American.

I thank you, gentlemen, for your candid approbation of my sentiments on the subject of negotiation and for the declaration of your opinion that the policy of extending and invigorating our measures of defense and the adoption with prudent foresight of such systematical measures as may be expedient for calling forth the energies of our country wherever the national exigencies may require, whether on the ocean or on our own territory, will demand your sedulous attention.

At the same time, I take the liberty to assure you it shall be my vigilant endeavor that no illusory professions shall seduce me into any abandonment of the rights which belong to the United States as a free and independent nation.

JOHN ADAMS.

SPECIAL MESSAGES.

JANUARY 8, 1799.

Gentlemen of the House of Representatives:

In compliance with your desire expressed in your resolution of the 2d of this month, I lay before you an extract of a letter from George C. Moreton, acting consul of the United States at The Havannah, dated the

13th of November, 1798, to the Secretary of State, with a copy of a letter from him to L. Tresevant and William Timmons, esquires, with their answer.

Although your request extends no further than such information as has been received, yet it may be a satisfaction to you to know that as soon as this intelligence was communicated to me circular orders were given by my direction to all the commanders of our vessels of war, a copy of which is also herewith transmitted. I also directed this intelligence and these orders to be communicated to His Britannic Majesty's envoy extraordinary and minister plenipotentiary to the United States and to our minister plenipotentiary to the Court of Great Britain, with instructions to him to make the proper representation to that Government upon this subject.

It is but justice to say that this is the first instance of misbehavior of any of the British officers toward our vessels of war that has come to my knowledge. According to all the representations that I have seen, the flag of the United States and their officers and men have been treated by the civil and military authority of the British nation in Nova Scotia, the West India islands, and on the ocean with uniform civility, politeness, and friendship. I have no doubt that this first instance of misconduct will be readily corrected.

JOHN ADAMS.

JANUARY 15, 1799.

Gentlemen of the Senate:

I transmit to you the treaty between the United States and the Cherokee Indians, signed near Tellico on the 2d day of October, 1798, for your consideration. I have directed the Secretary of War to lay before you the journal of the commissioners and a copy of their instructions.

JOHN ADAMS.

JANUARY 18, 1799.

Gentlemen of the Senate and Gentlemen of the House of Representatives:

The communication relative to our affairs with France alluded to in my address to both Houses at the opening of the session is contained in the sheets which accompany this. A report of the Secretary of State, containing some observations on them, will be sent to Congress on Monday.

JOHN ADAMS.

JANUARY 28, 1799.

Gentlemen of the Senate and Gentlemen of the House of Representatives:

An edict of the Executive Directory of the French Republic of the 29th of October, 1798, inclosed in a letter from our minister plenipotentiary in London of the 16th of November, is of so much importance that it can not be too soon communicated to you and the public.

JOHN ADAMS.

FEBRUARY 6, 1799.

Gentlemen of the Senate:

In consequence of intimations from the Court of Russia to our minister plenipotentiary at the Court of Great Britain of the desire of that power to have a treaty of amity and commerce with the United States, and that the negotiation might be conducted in London, I nominate Rufus King, our minister plenipotentiary at the Court of Great Britain, to be a minister plenipotentiary for the special purpose of negotiating with any minister of equal rank and powers a treaty of amity and commerce between the United States and the Emperor of all the Russias.

JOHN ADAMS.

UNITED STATES, *February 15, 1799.*

Gentlemen of the House of Representatives:

In pursuance of the request in your resolve of yesterday, I lay before you such information as I have received touching a suspension of the arrêt of the French Republic, communicated to your House by my message of the 28th of January last. But if the execution of that arrêt be suspended, or even if it were repealed, it should be remembered that the arrêt of the Executive Directory of the 2d of March, 1797, remains in force, the third article of which subjects, explicitly and exclusively, American seamen to be treated as pirates if found on board ships of the enemies of France.

JOHN ADAMS.

FEBRUARY 18, 1799.

Gentlemen of the Senate:

I transmit to you a document which seems to be intended to be a compliance with a condition mentioned at the conclusion of my message to Congress of the 21st of June last.

Always disposed and ready to embrace every plausible appearance of probability of preserving or restoring tranquillity, I nominate William Vans Murray, our minister resident at The Hague, to be minister plenipotentiary of the United States to the French Republic.

If the Senate shall advise and consent to his appointment, effectual care shall be taken in his instructions that he shall not go to France without direct and unequivocal assurances from the French Government, signified by their minister of foreign relations, that he shall be received in character, shall enjoy the privileges attached to his character by the law of nations, and that a minister of equal rank, title, and powers shall be appointed to treat with him, to discuss and conclude all controversies between the two Republics by a new treaty.

JOHN ADAMS.

[Translation.]

PARIS, *the 7th Vendémiaire of the 7th Year
of the French Republic, One and Indivisible.*

The Minister of Exterior Relations to Citizen Pichon, Secretary of Legation of the French Republic near the Batavian Republic:

I have received successively, Citizen, your letters of the 22d and 27th Fructidor [8th and 13th September]. They afford me more and more reason to be pleased with the measure you have adopted, to detail to me your conversations with Mr. Murray. These conversations, at first merely friendly, have acquired consistency by the sanction I have given to them by my letter of the 11th Fructidor. I do not regret that you have trusted to Mr. Murray's honor a copy of my letter. It was intended for you only, and contains nothing but what is conformable to the intentions of Government. I am thoroughly convinced that should explanations take place with confidence between the two Cabinets, irritation would cease, a crowd of misunderstandings would disappear, and the ties of friendship would be the more strongly united as each party would discover the hand which sought to disunite them. But I will not conceal from you that your letters of the 2d and 3d Vendémiaire, just received, surprised me much. What Mr. Murray is still dubious of has been very explicitly declared, even before the President's message to Congress of the 3d Messidor [21st June] last was known in France. I had written it to Mr. Gerry, namely, on the 24th Messidor and 4th Thermidor; I did repeat it to him before he sat out. A whole paragraph of my letter to you of the 11th Fructidor, of which Mr. Murray has a copy, is devoted to develop still more the fixed determination of the French Government. According to these bases, you were right to assert that whatever plenipotentiary the Government of the United States might send to France to put an end to the existing differences between the two countries would be undoubtedly received with the respect due to the representative of a free, independent, and powerful nation.

I can not persuade myself, Citizen, that the American Government need any further declarations from us to induce them, in order to renew the negotiations, to adopt such measures as would be suggested to them by their desire to bring the differences to a peaceable end. If misunderstandings on both sides have prevented former explanations from reaching that end, it is presumable that, those misunderstandings being done away, nothing henceforth will bring obstacles to the reciprocal dispositions. The President's instructions to his envoys at Paris, which I have only known by the copy given you by Mr. Murray, and received by me the 21st Messidor [9th July], announce, if they contain the whole of the American Government's intentions, dispositions which could only have added to those which the Directory has always entertained; and, notwithstanding the posterior acts of that Government, notwithstanding the irritating and almost hostile measures they have adopted, the Directory has manifested its perseverance in the sentiments which are deposited both in my correspondence with Mr. Gerry and in my letter to you of the 11th Fructidor, and which I have hereinbefore repeated in the most explicit manner. Carry, therefore, Citizen, to Mr. Murray those positive expressions in order to convince him of our sincerity, and prevail upon him to transmit them to his Government.

I presume, Citizen, that this letter will find you at The Hague; if not, I ask it may be sent back to you at Paris.

Salute and fraternity,

CH: MAU: TALLEYRAND.

FEBRUARY 25, 1799.

Gentlemen of the Senate:

The proposition of a fresh negotiation with France in consequence of advances made by the French Government has excited so general an attention and so much conversation as to have given occasion to many manifestations of the public opinion, from which it appears to me that a new modification of the embassy will give more general satisfaction to the Legislature and to the nation, and perhaps better answer the purposes we have in view.

It is upon this supposition and with this expectation that I now nominate Oliver Ellsworth, esq., Chief Justice of the United States; Patrick Henry, esq., late governor of Virginia, and William Vans Murray, esq., our minister resident at The Hague, to be envoys extraordinary and ministers plenipotentiary to the French Republic, with full powers to discuss and settle by a treaty all controversies between the United States and France.

It is not intended that the two former of these gentlemen shall embark for Europe until they shall have received from the Executive Directory assurances, signified by their secretary of foreign relations, that they shall be received in character, that they shall enjoy all the prerogatives attached to that character by the law of nations, and that a minister or ministers of equal powers shall be appointed and commissioned to treat with them.

JOHN ADAMS.

MARCH 2, 1799.

Gentlemen of the Senate and Gentlemen of the House of Representatives:

Judging it of importance to the public that the Legislature should be informed of the gradual progress of their maritime resources, I transmit to Congress a statement of the vessels, with their tonnage, warlike force, and complement of men, to which commissions as private armed vessels have been issued since the 9th day of July last.

JOHN ADAMS.

PROCLAMATIONS.

[From C. F. Adams's Works of John Adams, Vol. IX, p. 172.]

PROCLAMATION.

MARCH 6, 1799.

As no truth is more clearly taught in the Volume of Inspiration, nor any more fully demonstrated by the experience of all ages, than that a deep sense and a due acknowledgment of the governing providence of a Supreme Being and of the accountableness of men to Him as the searcher of hearts and righteous distributer of rewards and punishments are conducive equally to the happiness and rectitude of individuals and to the well-being of communities; as it is also most reasonable in itself that men who are made capable of social acts and relations, who owe their improvements to the social state, and who derive their enjoyments from it, should, as a society, make their acknowledgments of dependence and obligation to Him who hath endowed them with these capacities and elevated them in the scale of existence by these distinctions; as it is likewise a plain dictate of duty and a strong sentiment of nature that in circumstances of great urgency and seasons of imminent danger earnest and particular supplications should be made to Him who is able to defend or to destroy; as, moreover, the most precious interests of the people of the United States are still held in jeopardy by the hostile designs and insidious acts of a foreign nation, as well as by the dissemination among them of those principles, subversive of the foundations of all religious, moral, and social obligations, that have produced incalculable mischief and misery in other countries; and as, in fine, the observance of special seasons for public religious solemnities is happily calculated to avert the evils which we ought to deprecate and to excite to the performance of the duties which we ought to discharge by calling and fixing the attention of the people at large to the momentous truths already recited, by affording opportunity to teach and inculcate them by animating devotion and giving to it the character of a national act:

For these reasons I have thought proper to recommend, and I do hereby recommend accordingly, that Thursday, the 25th day of April next, be observed throughout the United States of America as a day of solemn humiliation, fasting, and prayer; that the citizens on that day abstain as far as may be from their secular occupations, devote the time to the sacred duties of religion in public and in private; that they call to mind our numerous offenses against the Most High God, confess them before Him with the sincerest penitence, implore His pardoning mercy, through the Great Mediator and Redeemer, for our past transgressions, and that through the grace of His Holy Spirit we may be disposed and enabled to yield a more suitable obedience to His righteous requisitions in time to come; that He would interpose to arrest the progress of that impiety and licentiousness in principle and practice so offensive to Himself and so ruinous to mankind; that He would make us deeply sensible that "righteousness exalteth a nation, but sin is a reproach to any people;" that He would turn us from our transgressions and turn His displeasure from us; that He would withhold us from unreasonable discontent, from disunion, faction, sedition, and insurrection; that He would preserve our country from the desolating sword; that He would save our cities and towns from a repetition of those awful pestilential visitations under which they have lately suffered so severely, and that the health of our inhabitants generally may be precious in His sight; that He would favor us with fruitful seasons and so bless the labors of the husbandman as that there may be food in abundance for man and beast; that He would prosper our commerce, manufactures, and fisheries, and give success to the people in all their lawful industry and enterprise; that He would smile on our colleges, academies, schools, and seminaries of learning, and make them nurseries of sound science, morals, and religion; that He would bless all magistrates, from the highest to the lowest, give them the true spirit of their station, make them a terror to evil doers and a praise to them that do well; that He would preside over the councils of the nation at this critical period, enlighten them to a just discernment of the public interest, and save them from mistake, division, and discord; that He would make succeed our preparations for defense and bless our armaments by land and by sea; that He would put an end to the effusion of human blood and the accumulation of human misery among the contending nations of the earth by disposing them to justice, to equity, to benevolence, and to peace; and that he would extend the blessings of knowledge, of true liberty, and of pure and undefiled religion throughout the world.

And I do also recommend that with these acts of humiliation, penitence, and prayer fervent thanksgiving to the Author of All Good be united for the countless favors which He is still continuing to the people of the United States, and which render their condition as a nation eminently happy when compared with the lot of others.

Given, etc.

JOHN ADAMS.

By the President of the United States of America.

A PROCLAMATION.

Whereas combinations to defeat the execution of the laws for the valuation of lands and dwelling houses within the United States have existed in the counties of Northampton, Montgomery, and Bucks, in the State of Pennsylvania, and have proceeded in a manner subversive of the just authority of the Government, by misrepresentations, to render the laws odious, by deterring the public officers of the United States to forbear the execution of their functions, and by openly threatening their lives; and

Whereas the endeavors of the well-affected citizens, as well as of the executive officers, to conciliate a compliance with those laws have failed of success, and certain persons in the county of Northampton aforesaid have been hardy enough to perpetrate certain acts which I am advised amount to treason, being overt acts of levying war against the United States, the said persons, exceeding one hundred in number and armed and arrayed in a warlike manner, having, on the 7th day of this present month of March, proceeded to the house of Abraham Lovering, in the town of Bethlehem, and there compelled William Nichols, marshal of the United States in and for the district of Pennsylvania, to desist from the execution of certain legal process in his hands to be executed, and having compelled him to discharge and set at liberty certain persons whom he had arrested by virtue of criminal process duly issued for offenses against the United States, and having impeded and prevented the commissioner and the assessors, appointed in conformity with the laws aforesaid, in the county of Northampton aforesaid, by threats and personal injury, from executing the said laws, avowing as the motives of these illegal and treasonable proceedings an intention to prevent by force of arms the execution of the said laws and to withstand by open violence the lawful authority of the Government of the United States; and

Whereas by the Constitution and laws of the United States I am authorized, whenever the laws of the United States shall be opposed or the execution thereof obstructed in any State by combinations too powerful to be suppressed by the ordinary course of judicial proceedings or by the powers vested in the marshals, to call forth military force to suppress such combinations and to cause the laws to be duly executed; and

Whereas it is in my judgment necessary to call forth military force in order to suppress the combinations aforesaid and to cause the laws aforesaid to be duly executed, and I have accordingly determined so to do, under the solemn conviction that the essential interests of the United States demand it:

Wherefore I, John Adams, President of the United States, do hereby command all persons being insurgents as aforesaid, and all others whom it may concern, on or before Monday next, being the 18th day of this present month, to disperse and retire peaceably to their respective abodes; and I do moreover warn all persons whomsoever against aiding, abetting, or comforting the perpetrators of the aforesaid treasonable acts; and I do require all officers and others, good and faithful citizens, according to their respective duties and the laws of the land, to exert their utmost endeavors to prevent and suppress such dangerous and unlawful proceedings.

In testimony whereof I have caused the seal of the United States of America to be affixed to these presents, and signed the same with my hand.

[SEAL.]   Done at the city of Philadelphia, the 12th day of March, A. D. 1799, and of the Independence of the said United States of America the twenty-third.

JOHN ADAMS.

By the President:
    TIMOTHY PICKERING,
      Secretary of State.

[From a broadside in the archives of the Department of State.]

By the President of the United States of America.

A PROCLAMATION.

Whereas by an act of the Congress of the United States passed the 9th day of February last, entitled "An act further to suspend the commercial intercourse between the United States and France and the dependencies thereof," it is provided that at any time after the passing of this act it shall be lawful for the President of the United States, if he shall deem it expedient and consistent with the interests of the United States, by his order to remit and discontinue for the time being the restraints and prohibitions by the said act imposed, either with respect to the French Republic or to any island, port, or place belonging to the said Republic with which a commercial intercourse may safely be renewed, and also to revoke such order whenever, in his opinion, the interest of the United States shall require; and he is authorized to make proclamation thereof accordingly; and

Whereas the arrangements which have been made at St. Domingo for the safety of the commerce of the United States and for the admission of American vessels into certain ports of that island do, in my opinion, render it expedient and for the interest of the United States to renew a commercial intercourse with such ports:

Therefore I, John Adams, President of the United States, by virtue of the powers vested in me by the above-recited act, do hereby remit and discontinue the restraints and prohibitions therein contained within the limits and under the regulations here following, to wit:

1. It shall be lawful for vessels which have departed or may depart from the United States to enter the ports of Cape François and Port Republicain, formerly called Port-au-Prince, in the said island of St. Domingo, on and after the 1st day of August next.

2. No vessel shall be cleared for any other port in St. Domingo than Cape François and Port Republicain.

3. It shall be lawful for vessels which shall enter the said ports of Cape François and Port Republicain after the 31st day of July next to depart from thence to any other port in said island between Monte Christi on the north and Petit Goave on the west; provided it be done with the consent of the Government of St. Domingo and pursuant to certificates or passports expressing such consent, signed by the consul-general of the United States or consul residing at the port of departure.

4. All vessels sailing in contravention of these regulations will be out of the protection of the United States and be, moreover, liable to capture, seizure, and confiscation

Given under my hand and the seal of the United States, at Philadelphia,
the 26th day of June, A. D. 1799, and of the Independence of
[SEAL.] the said States the twenty-third.

JOHN ADAMS.

By the President:
TIMOTHY PICKERING,
Secretary of State.

THIRD ANNUAL ADDRESS.

UNITED STATES, *December 3, 1799.*

Gentlemen of the Senate and Gentlemen of the House of Representatives:

It is with peculiar satisfaction that I meet the Sixth Congress of the
United States of America. Coming from all parts of the Union at this
critical and interesting period, the members must be fully possessed of
the sentiments and wishes of our constituents.

The flattering prospects of abundance from the labors of the people by
land and by sea; the prosperity of our extended commerce, notwithstanding interruptions occasioned by the belligerent state of a great part of the
world; the return of health, industry, and trade to those cities which
have lately been afflicted with disease, and the various and inestimable
advantages, civil and religious, which, secured under our happy frame
of government, are continued to us unimpaired, demand of the whole
American people sincere thanks to a benevolent Deity for the merciful
dispensations of His providence.

But while these numerous blessings are recollected, it is a painful duty
to advert to the ungrateful return which has been made for them by some
of the people in certain counties of Pennsylvania, where, seduced by the
arts and misrepresentations of designing men, they have openly resisted
the law directing the valuation of houses and lands. Such defiance was
given to the civil authority as rendered hopeless all further attempts
by judicial process to enforce the execution of the law, and it became
necessary to direct a military force to be employed, consisting of some
companies of regular troops, volunteers, and militia, by whose zeal and
activity, in cooperation with the judicial power, order and submission
were restored and many of the offenders arrested. Of these, some have
been convicted of misdemeanors, and others, charged with various crimes,
remain to be tried.

To give due effect to the civil administration of Government and to
insure a just execution of the laws, a revision and amendment of the
judiciary system is indispensably necessary. In this extensive country it
can not but happen that numerous questions respecting the interpretation

of the laws and the rights and duties of officers and citizens must arise. On the one hand, the laws should be executed; on the other, individuals should be guarded from oppression. Neither of these objects is sufficiently assured under the present organization of the judicial department. I therefore earnestly recommend the subject to your serious consideration.

Persevering in the pacific and humane policy which had been invariably professed and sincerely pursued by the Executive authority of the United States, when indications were made on the part of the French Republic of a disposition to accommodate the existing differences between the two countries, I felt it to be my duty to prepare for meeting their advances by a nomination of ministers upon certain conditions which the honor of our country dictated, and which its moderation had given it a right to prescribe. The assurances which were required of the French Government previous to the departure of our envoys have been given through their minister of foreign relations, and I have directed them to proceed on their mission to Paris. They have full power to conclude a treaty, subject to the constitutional advice and consent of the Senate. The characters of these gentlemen are sure pledges to their country that nothing incompatible with its honor or interest, nothing inconsistent with our obligations of good faith or friendship to any other nation, will be stipulated.

It appearing probable from the information I received that our commercial intercourse with some ports in the island of St. Domingo might safely be renewed, I took such steps as seemed to me expedient to ascertain that point. The result being satisfactory, I then, in conformity with the act of Congress on the subject, directed the restraints and prohibitions of that intercourse to be discontinued on terms which were made known by proclamation. Since the renewal of this intercourse our citizens trading to those ports, with their property, have been duly respected, and privateering from those ports has ceased.

In examining the claims of British subjects by the commissioners at Philadelphia, acting under the sixth article of the treaty of amity, commerce, and navigation with Great Britain, a difference of opinion on points deemed essential in the interpretation of that article has arisen between the commissioners appointed by the United States and the other members of that board, from which the former have thought it their duty to withdraw. It is sincerely to be regretted that the execution of an article produced by a mutual spirit of amity and justice should have been thus unavoidably interrupted. It is, however, confidently expected that the same spirit of amity and the same sense of justice in which it originated will lead to satisfactory explanations. In consequence of the obstacles to the progress of the commission in Philadelphia, His Britannic Majesty has directed the commissioners appointed by him under the seventh article of the treaty relating to the British captures of American vessels to withdraw from the board sitting in London, but with the express declaration of his determination to fulfill with punctuality and good faith the engagements which His Majesty has contracted by his treaty with the United States, and that they will be instructed to resume their functions whenever the obstacles which impede the progress of the commission at Philadelphia shall be removed. It being in like manner my sincere determination, so far as the same depends on me, that with equal punctuality and good faith the engagements contracted by the United States in their treaties with His Britannic Majesty shall be fulfilled, I shall immediately instruct our minister at London to endeavor to obtain the explanations necessary to a just performance of those engagements on the part of the United States. With such dispositions on both sides, I can not entertain a doubt that all difficulties will soon be removed and that the two boards will then proceed and bring the business committed to them respectively to a satisfactory conclusion.

The act of Congress relative to the seat of the Government of the United States requiring that on the first Monday of December next it should be transferred from Philadelphia to the District chosen for its permanent seat, it is proper for me to inform you that the commissioners appointed to provide suitable buildings for the accommodation of Congress and of the President and of the public offices of the Government have made a report of the state of the buildings designed for those purposes in the city of Washington, from which they conclude that the removal of the seat of Government to that place at the time required will be practicable and the accommodation satisfactory. Their report will be laid before you.

Gentlemen of the House of Representatives:

I shall direct the estimates of the appropriations necessary for the service of the ensuing year, together with an account of the revenue and expenditure, to be laid before you. During a period in which a great portion of the civilized world has been involved in a war unusually calamitous and destructive, it was not to be expected that the United States could be exempted from extraordinary burthens. Although the period is not arrived when the measures adopted to secure our country against foreign attacks can be renounced, yet it is alike necessary for the honor of the Government and the satisfaction of the community that an exact economy should be maintained. I invite you, gentlemen, to investigate the different branches of the public expenditure. The examination will lead to beneficial retrenchments or produce a conviction of the wisdom of the measures to which the expenditure relates.

Gentlemen of the Senate and Gentlemen of the House of Representatives:

At a period like the present, when momentous changes are occurring and every hour is preparing new and great events in the political world, when a spirit of war is prevalent in almost every nation with whose affairs the interests of the United States have any connection, unsafe and precarious would be our situation were we to neglect the means of maintaining our just rights. The result of the mission to France is uncertain; but however it may terminate, a steady perseverance in a system of national defense commensurate with our resources and the situation of our country is an obvious dictate of wisdom; for, remotely as we are placed from the belligerent nations, and desirous as we are, by doing justice to all, to avoid offense to any, nothing short of the power of repelling aggressions will secure to our country a rational prospect of escaping the calamities of war or national degradation. As to myself, it is my anxious desire so to execute the trust reposed in me as to render the people of the United States prosperous and happy. I rely with entire confidence on your cooperation in objects equally your care, and that our mutual labors will serve to increase and confirm union among our fellow-citizens and an unshaken attachment to our Government.

JOHN ADAMS.

ADDRESS OF THE SENATE TO JOHN ADAMS, PRESIDENT OF THE UNITED STATES.

The PRESIDENT OF THE UNITED STATES:

Accept, sir, the respectful acknowledgments of the Senate of the United States for your speech delivered to both Houses of Congress at the opening of the present session.

While we devoutly join you in offering our thanks to Almighty God for the return of health to our cities and for the general prosperity of the country, we can not refrain from lamenting that the arts and calumnies of factious, designing men have excited open rebellion a second time in Pennsylvania, and thereby compelled the employment of a military force to aid the civil authority in the execution of the laws. We rejoice that your vigilance, energy, and well-timed exertions have crushed so daring an opposition and prevented the spreading of such treasonable combinations. The promptitude and zeal displayed by the troops called to suppress this insurrection deserve our highest commendation and praise, and afford a pleasing proof of the spirit and alacrity with which our fellow-citizens are ready to maintain the authority of our excellent Government.

Knowing as we do that the United States are sincerely anxious for a fair and liberal execution of the treaty of amity, commerce, and navigation entered into with Great Britain, we learn with regret that the progress of adjustment has been interrupted by a difference of opinion among the commissioners. We hope, however, that the justice, the moderation, and the obvious interests of both parties will lead to satisfactory explanations, and that the business will then go forward to an amicable close of all differences and demands between the two countries. We are fully persuaded that the Legislature of the United States will cheerfully enable you to realize your assurances of performing on our part all engagements under our treaties with punctuality and the most scrupulous good faith.

When we reflect upon the uncertainty of the result of the late mission to France and upon the uncommon nature, extent, and aspect of the war now raging in Europe, which affects materially our relations with the powers at war, and which has changed the condition of their colonies in our neighborhood, we are of opinion with you that it would be neither wise nor safe to relax our measures of defense or to lessen any of our preparations to repel aggression.

Our inquiries and attention shall be carefully directed to the various other important subjects which you have recommended to our consideration, and from our experience of your past Administration we anticipate with the highest confidence your strenuous cooperation in all measures which have a tendency to promote and extend our national interests and happiness.

SAMUEL LIVERMORE,
President of the Senate pro tempore.

DECEMBER 9, 1799.

REPLY OF THE PRESIDENT.

UNITED STATES, *December 10, 1799.*

Gentlemen of the Senate:

I thank you for this address. I wish you all possible success and satisfaction in your deliberations on the means which have a tendency to promote and extend our national interests and happiness, and I assure you that in all your measures directed to those great objects you may at all times rely with the highest confidence on my cordial cooperation.

The praise of the Senate, so judiciously conferred on the promptitude and zeal of the troops called to suppress the insurrection, as it falls from so high authority, must make a deep impression, both as a terror to the disobedient and an encouragement of such as do well.

JOHN ADAMS.

ADDRESS OF THE HOUSE OF REPRESENTATIVES TO JOHN ADAMS, PRESIDENT OF THE UNITED STATES.

The PRESIDENT OF THE UNITED STATES

SIR: While the House of Representatives contemplate the flattering prospects of abundance from the labors of the people by land and by sea, the prosperity of our extended commerce notwithstanding the interruptions occasioned by the belligerent state of a great part of the world, the return of health, industry, and trade to those cities which have lately been afflicted with disease, and the various and inestimable advantages, civil and religious, which, secured under our happy frame of Government, are continued to us unimpaired, we can not fail to offer up to a benevolent Deity our sincere thanks for these the merciful dispensations of His protecting providence.

That any portion of the people of America should permit themselves, amid such numerous blessings, to be seduced by the arts and misrepresentations of designing men into an open resistance of a law of the United States can not be heard without deep and serious regret.   Under a Constitution where the public burthens can only be imposed by the people themselves for their own benefit and to promote their own objects, a hope might well have been indulged that the general interest would have been too well understood and the general welfare too highly prized to have produced in any of our citizens a disposition to hazard so much felicity by the criminal effort of a part to oppose with lawless violence the will of the whole.   While we lament that depravity which could produce a defiance of the civil authority and render indispensable the aid of the military force of the nation, real consolation is to be derived from the promptness and fidelity with which that aid was afforded.   That zealous and active cooperation with the judicial power of the volunteers and militia called into service, which has restored order and submission to the laws, is a pleasing evidence of the attachment of our fellow-citizens to their own free Government, and of the truly patriotic alacrity with which they will support it.

To give due effect to the civil administration of Government and to insure a just execution of the laws are objects of such real magnitude as to secure a proper attention to your recommendation of a revision and amendment of the judiciary system.

Highly approving as we do the pacific and humane policy which has been invariably professed and sincerely pursued by the Executive authority of the United States, a policy which our best interests enjoined, and of which honor has permitted the observance, we consider as the most unequivocal proof of your inflexible perseverance in the same well-chosen system your preparation to meet the first indications on the part of the French Republic of a disposition to accommodate the existing differences between the two countries by a nomination of ministers, on certain conditions which the honor of our country unquestionably dictated, and which its moderation had certainly given it a right to prescribe.   When the assurances thus required of the French Government, previous to the departure of our envoys, had been given through their minister of foreign relations, the direction that they should proceed on their mission was on your part a completion of the measure, and manifests the sincerity with which it was commenced.   We offer up our fervent prayers to the Supreme Ruler of the Universe for the success of their embassy, and that it may be productive of peace and happiness to our common country. The uniform tenor of your conduct through a life useful to your fellow-citizens and honorable to yourself gives a sure pledge of the sincerity with which the avowed objects of the negotiation will be pursued on your part, and we earnestly pray that similar dispositions may be displayed on the part of France. The differences which unfortunately subsist between the two nations can not fail in that event to be happily terminated. To produce this end, to all so desirable, firmness, moderation, and union at home constitute, we are persuaded, the surest means. The character of the gentlemen you have deputed, and still more the character of the Government which deputes them, are safe pledges to their country that nothing incompatible with its honor or interest, nothing inconsistent with our obligations of good faith or friendship to any other nation, will be stipulated.

We learn with pleasure that our citizens, with their property, trading to those ports of St. Domingo with which commercial intercourse has been renewed have been duly respected, and that privateering from those ports has ceased.

With you we sincerely regret that the execution of the sixth article of the treaty of amity, commerce, and navigation with Great Britain, an article produced by a mutual spirit of amity and justice, should have been unavoidably interrupted. We doubt not that the same spirit of amity and the same sense of justice in which it originated will lead to satisfactory explanations, and we hear with approbation that our minister at London will be immediately instructed to obtain them. While the engagements which America has contracted by her treaty with Great Britain ought to be fulfilled with that scrupulous punctuality and good faith to which our Government has ever so tenaciously adhered, yet no motive exists to induce, and every principle forbids us to adopt, a construction which might extend them beyond the instrument by which they are created. We cherish the hope that the Government of Great Britain will disclaim such extension, and by cordially uniting with that of the United States for the removal of all difficulties will soon enable the boards appointed under the sixth and seventh articles of our treaty with that nation to proceed and bring the business committed to them respectively to a satisfactory conclusion.

The buildings for the accommodation of Congress and of the President and for the public offices of the Government at its permanent seat being in such a state as to admit of a removal to that District by the time prescribed by the act of Congress, no obstacle, it is presumed, will exist to a compliance with the law.

With you, sir, we deem the present period critical and momentous. The important changes which are occurring, the new and great events which are every hour preparing in the political world, the spirit of war which is prevalent in almost every nation with whose affairs the interests of the United States have any connection, demonstrate how unsafe and precarious would be our situation should we neglect the means of maintaining our just rights. Respecting, as we have ever done, the rights of others, America estimates too correctly the value of her own and has received evidence too complete that they are only to be preserved by her own vigilance ever to permit herself to be seduced by a love of ease or by other considerations into that deadly disregard of the means of self-defense which could only result from a carelessness as criminal as it would be fatal concerning the future destinies of our growing Republic. The result of the mission to France is indeed, sir, uncertain. It depends not on America alone. The most pacific temper will not always insure peace. We should therefore exhibit a system of conduct as indiscreet as it would be new in the history of the world if we considered the negotiation happily terminated because we have attempted to commence it, and peace restored because we wish its restoration. But, sir, however this mission may terminate, a steady perseverance in a system of national defense commensurate with our resources and the situation of our country is an obvious dictate of duty. Experience, the parent of wisdom and the great instructor of nations, has established the truth of your position, that, remotely as we are placed from the belligerent nations and desirous as we are, by doing justice to all, to avoid offense to any, yet nothing short of the power of repelling aggressions will secure to our country a rational prospect of escaping the calamities of war or national degradation.

In the progress of the session we shall take into our serious consideration the various and important matters recommended to our attention.

A life devoted to the service of your country, talents and integrity which have so justly acquired and so long retained the confidence and affection of your fellow-citizens, attest the sincerity of your declaration that it is your anxious desire so to execute the trust reposed in you as to render the people of the United States prosperous and happy.

DECEMBER 9, 1799.

REPLY OF THE PRESIDENT.

UNITED STATES, *December 10, 1799.*

Gentlemen of the House of Representatives:

This very respectful address from the Representatives of the people of the United States, at their first assembly after a fresh election, under the strong impression of the public opinion and national sense, at this interesting and singular crisis of our public affairs, has excited my sensibility and receives my sincere and grateful acknowledgments.

As long as we can maintain with harmony and affection the honor of our country consistently with its peace, externally and internally, while that is attainable, or in war when that becomes necessary, assert its real independence and sovereignty, and support the constitutional energies and dignity of its Government, we may be perfectly sure, under the smiles of Divine Providence, that we shall effectually promote and extend our national interest and happiness.

The applause of the Senate and House of Representatives, so justly bestowed upon the volunteers and militia for their zealous and active cooperation with the judicial power, which has restored order and submission to the laws, as it comes with peculiar weight and propriety from the Legislature, can not fail to have an extensive and permanent effect for the support of Government upon all those ingenuous minds who receive delight from the approving and animating voice of their country.

JOHN ADAMS.

SPECIAL MESSAGES.

UNITED STATES, *December 5, 1799.*

Gentlemen of the Senate and Gentlemen of the House of Representatives:

I transmit to Congress certain documents which have relation to the communications made on Tuesday, on the subjects of the insurrection in Pennsylvania, the renewal of commerce with St. Domingo, and the mission to the French Republic.

JOHN ADAMS.

UNITED STATES, *December 6, 1799.*

Gentlemen of the Senate:

I lay before you, for your consideration, a treaty of amity and commerce between the United States and the King of Prussia, signed by their ministers on the 11th of July last.

JOHN ADAMS.

UNITED STATES, *December 19, 1799.*

Gentlemen of the Senate and Gentlemen of the House of Representatives:

The letter herewith transmitted will inform you that it has pleased Divine Providence to remove from this life our excellent fellow-citizen, George Washington, by the purity of his character and a long series of services to his country rendered illustrious through the world. It remains for an affectionate and grateful people, in whose hearts he can never die, to pay suitable honors to his memory.

JOHN ADAMS.

MOUNT VERNON, *December 15, 1799.*

The PRESIDENT OF THE UNITED STATES.

SIR: It is with inexpressible grief that I have to announce to you the death of the great and good General Washington. He died last evening between 10 and 11 o'clock, after a short illness of about twenty hours. His disorder was an inflammatory sore throat, which proceeded from a cold of which he made but little complaint on Friday. On Saturday morning about 3 o'clock he became ill. Dr. Craik attended him in the morning, and Dr. Dick, of Alexandria, and Dr. Brown, of Port Tobacco, were soon after called in. Every medical assistance was offered, but without the desired effect. His last scene corresponded with the whole tenor of his life; not a groan nor a complaint escaped him in extreme distress. With perfect resignation and in full possession of his reason, he closed his well-spent life.

I have the honor to be, with the highest respect, sir, your most obedient and very humble servant,

TOBIAS LEAR.

The Senate, having resolved to wait on the President of the United States "to condole with him on the distressing event of the death of General George Washington," proceeded to the house of the President, when the President of the Senate, in their name, presented the address which had previously been agreed to, as follows:

The PRESIDENT OF THE UNITED STATES:

The Senate of the United States respectfully take leave, sir, to express to you their deep regret for the loss their country sustains in the death of General George Washington.

This event, so distressing to all our fellow-citizens, must be peculiarly heavy to you, who have long been associated with him in deeds of patriotism. Permit us, sir, to mingle our tears with yours. On this occasion it is manly to weep. To lose such a man at such a crisis is no common calamity to the world. Our country mourns her father. The Almighty Disposer of Human Events has taken from us our greatest benefactor and ornament. It becomes us to submit with reverence to Him who maketh darkness His pavilion.

With patriotic pride we review the life of our Washington and compare him with those of other countries who have been preeminent in fame. Ancient and modern names are diminished before him. Greatness and guilt have too often been allied, but his fame is whiter than it is brilliant. The destroyers of nations stood abashed at the majesty of his virtue. It reproved the intemperance of their ambition and darkened the splendor of victory. The scene is closed, and we are no longer anxious lest misfortune should sully his glory. He has traveled on to the end of his journey and carried with him an increasing weight of honor. He has deposited it safely, where misfortune can not tarnish it, where malice can not blast it. Favored of Heaven, he departed without exhibiting the weakness of humanity. Magnanimous in death, the darkness of the grave could not obscure his brightness.

Such was the man whom we deplore. Thanks to God, his glory is consummated. Washington yet lives on earth in his spotless example; his spirit is in Heaven.

Let his countrymen consecrate the memory of the heroic general, the patriotic statesman, and the virtuous sage. Let them teach their children never to forget that the fruit of his labors and his example are their inheritance.

SAMUEL LIVERMORE,
President of the Senate pro tempore.

DECEMBER 23, 1799.

To which the President replied as follows:

UNITED STATES, *December 23, 1799.*

Gentlemen of the Senate:

I receive with the most respectful and affectionate sentiments in this impressive address the obliging expressions of your regard for the loss our country has sustained in the death of her most esteemed, beloved, and admired citizen.

In the multitude of my thoughts and recollections on this melancholy event you will permit me only to say that I have seen him in the days of adversity, in some of the scenes of his deepest distress and most trying perplexities; I have also attended him in his highest elevation and most prosperous felicity, with uniform admiration of his wisdom, moderation, and constancy.

Among all our original associates in that memorable league of the continent in 1774, which first expressed the sovereign will of a free nation in America, he was the only one remaining in the General Government. Although with a constitution more enfeebled than his at an age when he thought it necessary to prepare for retirement, I feel myself alone bereaved of my last brother; yet I derive a strong consolation from the unanimous disposition which appears in all ages and classes to mingle their sorrows with mine on this common calamity to the world.

The life of our Washington can not suffer by comparison with those of other countries who have been most celebrated and exalted by fame. The attributes and decorations of royalty could have only served to eclipse the majesty of those virtues which made him, from being a modest citizen, a more resplendent luminary.

Misfortune, had he lived, could hereafter have sullied his glory only with those superficial minds who, believing that characters and actions are marked by success alone, rarely deserve to enjoy it. Malice could never blast his honor, and envy made him a singular exception to her universal rule. For himself, he had lived enough to life and to glory. For his fellow-citizens, if their prayers could have been answered, he would have been immortal. For me, his departure is at a most unfortunate moment. Trusting, however, in the wise and righteous dominion of Providence over the passions of men and the results of their councils and actions, as well as over their lives, nothing remains for me but humble resignation.

His example is now complete, and it will teach wisdom and virtue to magistrates, citizens, and men, not only in the present age, but in future generations as long as our history shall be read. If a Trajan found a Pliny, a Marcus Aurelius can never want biographers, eulogists, or historians.

JOHN ADAMS.

The House of Representatives having resolved unanimously to wait on the President of the United States "in condolence of this national calamity," the Speaker, attended by the House, withdrew to the house of the President, when the Speaker addressed the President as follows:

SIR: The House of Representatives, penetrated with a sense of the irreparable loss sustained by the nation in the death of that great and good man, the illustrious and beloved Washington, wait on you, sir, to express their condolence on this melancholy and distressing event.

To which the President replied as follows:

UNITED STATES *December 19, 1799.*

Gentlemen of the House of Representatives:

I receive with great respect and affection the condolence of the House of Representatives on the melancholy and affecting event in the death of the most illustrious and beloved personage which this country ever produced. I sympathize with you, with the nation, and with good men through the world in this irreparable loss sustained by us all.

JOHN ADAMS.

UNITED STATES, *December 31, 1799.*

Gentlemen of the Senate:

I nominate Timothy Pickering, Secretary of State; Oliver Wolcott, Secretary of the Treasury, and Samuel Sitgreaves, esq., of Pennsylvania, to be commissioners to adjust and determine, with commissioners appointed under the legislative authority of the State of Georgia, all interfering claims of the United States and that State to territories situate west of the river Chatahouchee, north of the thirty-first degree of north latitude, and south of the cession made to the United States by South Carolina; and also to receive any proposals for the relinquishment or cession of the whole or any part of the other territory claimed by the State of Georgia, and out of the ordinary jurisdiction thereof, according to the law of the United States of the 7th of April, 1798.

JOHN ADAMS.

UNITED STATES, *January 8, 180-*

Gentlemen of the Senate and Gentlemen of the House of Representatives:

In compliance with the request in one of the resolutions of Congress of the 21st of December last, I transmitted a copy of these resolutions, by my secretary, Mr. Shaw, to Mrs. Washington, assuring her of the profound respect Congress will ever bear to her person and character, of their condolence in the late afflicting dispensation of Providence, and entreating her assent to the interment of the remains of General George Washington in the manner expressed in the first resolution. As the sentiments of that virtuous lady, not less beloved by this nation than she is at present greatly afflicted, can never be so well expressed as in her own words, I transmit to Congress her original letter.

It would be an attempt of too much delicacy to make any comments upon it, but there can be no doubt that the nation at large, as well as all the branches of the Government, will be highly gratified by any arrangement which may diminish the sacrifice she makes of her individual feelings.

JOHN ADAMS.

MOUNT VERNON, *December 31, 1799.*
The PRESIDENT OF THE UNITED STATES.

SIR: While I feel with keenest anguish the late dispensation of Divine Providence, I can not be insensible to the mournful tributes of respect and veneration which are paid to the memory of my dear deceased husband; and as his best services and most anxious wishes were always devoted to the welfare and happiness of his country, to know that they were truly appreciated and gratefully remembered affords no inconsiderable consolation.

Taught by the great example which I have so long had before me never to oppose my private wishes to the public will, I must consent to the request made by Congress, which you have had the goodness to transmit to me; and in doing this I need not, I can not, say what a sacrifice of individual feeling I make to a sense of public duty.

With grateful acknowledgments and unfeigned thanks for the personal respect and evidences of condolence expressed by Congress and yourself, I remain, very respectfully, sir, your most obedient, humble servant,

MARTHA WASHINGTON.

UNITED STATES, *January 13, 1800.*
Gentlemen of the Senate and Gentlemen of the House of Representatives:

A report made to me on the 5th of this month by the Secretary of War contains various matters in which the honor and safety of the nation are deeply interested. I transmit it, therefore, to Congress and recommend it to their serious consideration.

JOHN ADAMS.

UNITED STATES, *January 14, 1800.*
Gentlemen of the House of Representatives:

As the inclosed letter from a member of your House received by me in the night of Saturday, the 11th instant, relates to the privileges of the House, which, in my opinion, ought to be inquired into in the House itself, if anywhere, I have thought proper to submit the whole letter and its tendencies to your consideration without any other comments on its matter or style; but as no gross impropriety of conduct on the part of persons holding commissions in the Army or Navy of the United States ought to pass without due animadversion, I have directed the Secretary of War and the Secretary of the Navy to investigate the conduct complained of and to report to me without delay such a statement of facts as will enable me to decide on the course which duty and justice shall appear to prescribe.

JOHN ADAMS.

UNITED STATES, *January 23, 1800.*
Gentlemen of the Senate and Gentlemen of the House of Representatives:

I transmit to Congress for the information of the members a report of the Secretary of State of the 9th instant, a letter from Matthew Clarkson, esq., to him of the 2d, and a list of the claims adjusted by the commissioners under the twenty-first article of our treaty with Spain.

JOHN ADAMS.

UNITED STATES, *February 14, 1800.*
Gentlemen of the House of Representatives:

I transmit herewith a copy of the laws enacted by the governor and judges of the Mississippi Territory, for the inspection of Congress. There being but this one copy, I must request the House, when they have made the requisite examination, to send it to the Senate.

JOHN ADAMS.

PROCLAMATIONS.

[From C. F. Adams's Works of John Adams, Vol. IX, p. 177.]

PROCLAMATION.

MAY 9, 1800.

Whereas by an act of Congress of the United States passed the 27th day of February last, entitled "An act further to suspend the commercial intercourse between the United States and France and the dependencies thereof," it is enacted that at any time after the passing of the said act it shall be lawful for the President of the United States, by his order, to remit and discontinue for the time being, whenever he shall deem it expedient and for the interest of the United States, all or any of the restraints and prohibitions imposed by the said act in respect to the territories of the French Republic, or to any island, port, or place belonging to the said Republic with which, in his opinion, a commercial intercourse may be safely renewed, and to make proclamation thereof accordingly; and it is also thereby further enacted that the whole of the island of Hispaniola shall, for the purposes of the said act, be considered as a dependence of the French Republic; and

Whereas the circumstances of certain ports and places of the said island not comprised in the proclamation of the 26th day of June, 1799, are such that I deem it expedient and for the interest of the United States to remit and discontinue the restraints and prohibitions imposed by the said act in respect to those ports and places in order that a commercial intercourse with the same may be renewed:

Therefore I, John Adams, President of the United States, by virtue of the powers vested in me as aforesaid, do hereby remit and discontinue the restraints and prohibitions imposed by the act aforesaid in respect to all the ports and places in the said island of Hispaniola from Monte Christi on the north, round by the eastern end thereof as far as the port of Jacmel on the south, inclusively. And it shall henceforth be lawful for vessels of the United States to enter and trade at any of the said ports and places, provided it be done with the consent of the Government of St. Domingo. And for this purpose it is hereby required that such vessels first enter the port of Cape François or Port Republicain, in the said island, and there obtain the passports of the said Government, which shall also be signed by the consul-general or consul of the United States residing at Cape François or Port Republicain, permitting such vessel to go thence to the other ports and places of the said island hereinbefore mentioned and described. Of all which the collectors of the customs and all other officers and citizens of the United States are to take due notice and govern themselves.

In testimony, etc.

JOHN ADAMS.

[From Annals of Congress, Seventh Congress, second session, 1552.]

PROCLAMATION.

BY JOHN ADAMS, PRESIDENT OF THE UNITED STATES OF AMERICA.

Whereas the late wicked and treasonable insurrection against the just authority of the United States of sundry persons in the counties of Northampton, Montgomery, and Bucks, in the State of Pennsylvania, in the year 1799, having been speedily suppressed without any of the calamities usually attending rebellion; whereupon peace, order, and submission to the laws of the United States were restored in the aforesaid counties, and the ignorant, misguided, and misinformed in the counties have returned to a proper sense of their duty, whereby it is become unnecessary for the public good that any future prosecutions should be commenced or carried on against any person or persons by reason of their being concerned in the said insurrection:

Wherefore be it known that I, John Adams, President of the United States of America, have granted, and by these presents do grant, a full, free, and absolute pardon to all and every person or persons concerned in the said insurrection, excepting as hereinafter excepted, of all treasons, misprisions of treason, felonies, misdemeanors, and other crimes by them respectively done or committed against the United States in either of the said counties before the 12th day of March, in the year 1799, excepting and excluding therefrom every person who now standeth indicted or convicted of any treason, misprision of treason, or other offense against the United States, whereby remedying and releasing unto all persons, except as before excepted, all pains and penalties incurred, or supposed to be incurred, for or on account of the premises.

Given under my hand and the seal of the United States of America, at the city of Philadelphia, this 21st day of May, A. D. 1800, [SEAL.] and of the Independence of the said States the twenty-fourth.

JOHN ADAMS.

By JOHN ADAMS, PRESIDENT OF THE UNITED STATES OF AMERICA.

A PROCLAMATION.

Whereas by an act of the Congress of the United States passed on the 27th day of February last, entitled "An act further to suspend the commercial intercourse between the United States and France and the dependencies thereof," it is enacted "that at any time after the passing of the said act it shall be lawful for the President of the United States, by his order, to remit and discontinue for the time being, whenever he shall deem it expedient and for the interest of the United States, all or any of the restraints and prohibitions imposed by the said act in respect to the territories of the French Republic, or to any island, port, or place belonging to the said Republic with which, in his opinion, a commercial intercourse may be safely renewed, and to make proclamation thereof accordingly;" and it is also thereby further enacted that the whole of the island of Hispaniola shall, for the purposes of the said act, be considered as a dependence of the French Republic; and

Whereas the circumstances of the said island are such that, in my opinion, a commercial intercourse may safely be renewed with every part thereof, under the limitations and restrictions hereinafter mentioned:

Therefore I, John Adams, President of the United States, by virtue of the powers vested in me as aforesaid, do hereby remit and discontinue the restraints and prohibitions imposed by the act aforesaid in respect to every part of the said island, so that it shall be lawful for vessels of the United States to trade at any of the ports and places thereof, provided it be done with the consent of the Government of St. Domingo; and for this purpose it is hereby required that such vessels first clear for and enter the port of Cape Français or Port Republicain, in the said island, and there obtain the passports of the said Government, which shall also be signed by the consul-general of the United States, or their consul residing at Cape Français, or their consul residing at Port Republicain, permitting such vessels to go thence to the other ports and places of the said island. Of all which the collectors of the customs and all other officers and citizens of the United States are to take due notice and govern themselves accordingly.

Given under my hand and the seal of the United States of America, at the city of Washington, this 6th day of September, A. D. [SEAL.] 1800, and of the Independence of the said States the twenty-fifth.

JOHN ADAMS.

By the President:
J. MARSHALL,
Secretary of State.

FOURTH ANNUAL ADDRESS.

UNITED STATES, *November 22, 1800.*

Gentlemen of the Senate and Gentlemen of the House of Representatives:

Immediately after the adjournment of Congress at their last session in Philadelphia I gave directions, in compliance with the laws, for the removal of the public offices, records, and property. These directions have been executed, and the public officers have since resided and conducted the ordinary business of the Government in this place.

I congratulate the people of the United States on the assembling of Congress at the permanent seat of their Government, and I congratulate you, gentlemen, on the prospect of a residence not to be changed. Although there is cause to apprehend that accommodations are not now so complete as might be wished, yet there is great reason to believe that this inconvenience will cease with the present session.

It would be unbecoming the representatives of this nation to assemble for the first time in this solemn temple without looking up to the Supreme Ruler of the Universe and imploring His blessing.

May this territory be the residence of virtue and happiness! In this city may that piety and virtue, that wisdom and magnanimity, that constancy and self-government, which adorned the great character whose name it bears be forever held in veneration! Here and throughout our country may simple manners, pure morals, and true religion flourish forever!

It is with you, gentlemen, to consider whether the local powers over the District of Columbia vested by the Constitution in the Congress of the United States shall be immediately exercised. If in your opinion this important trust ought now to be executed, you can not fail while performing it to take into view the future probable situation of the territory for the happiness of which you are about to provide. You will consider it as the capital of a great nation advancing with unexampled rapidity in arts, in commerce, in wealth, and in population, and possessing within itself those energies and resources which, if not thrown away or lamentably misdirected, will secure to it a long course of prosperity and self-government.

In compliance with a law of the last session of Congress, the officers and soldiers of the temporary army have been discharged. It affords real pleasure to recollect the honorable testimony they gave of the patriotic motives which brought them into the service of their country, by the readiness and regularity with which they returned to the station of private citizens.

It is in every point of view of such primary importance to carry the laws into prompt and faithful execution, and to render that part of the administration of justice which the Constitution and laws devolve on the Federal courts as convenient to the people as may consist with their present circumstances, that I can not omit once more to recommend to your serious consideration the judiciary system of the United States. No subject is more interesting than this to the public happiness, and to none can those improvements which may have been suggested by experience be more beneficially applied.

A treaty of amity and commerce with the King of Prussia has been concluded and ratified. The ratifications have been exchanged, and I have directed the treaty to be promulgated by proclamation.

The difficulties which suspended the execution of the sixth article of our treaty of amity, commerce, and navigation with Great Britain have not yet been removed. The negotiation on this subject is still depending. As it must be for the interest and honor of both nations to adjust this difference with good faith, I indulge confidently the expectation that the sincere endeavors of the Government of the United States to bring it to an amicable termination will not be disappointed.

The envoys extraordinary and ministers plenipotentiary from the United States to France were received by the First Consul with the respect due to their character, and three persons with equal powers were appointed to treat with them. Although at the date of the last official intelligence the negotiation had not terminated, yet it is to be hoped that our efforts to effect an accommodation will at length meet with a success proportioned to the sincerity with which they have been so often repeated.

While our best endeavors for the preservation of harmony with all nations will continue to be used, the experience of the world and our own experience admonish us of the insecurity of trusting too confidently to their success. We can not, without committing a dangerous imprudence, abandon those measures of self-protection which are adapted to our situation and to which, notwithstanding our pacific policy, the violence and injustice of others may again compel us to resort   While our vast extent of seacoast, the commercial and agricultural habits of our people, the great capital they will continue to trust on the ocean, suggest the system of defense which will be most beneficial to ourselves, our distance from Europe and our resources for maritime strength will enable us to employ it with effect.   Seasonable and systematic arrangements, so far as our resources will justify, for a navy adapted to defensive war, and which may in case of necessity be quickly brought into use, seem to be as much recommended by a wise and true economy as by a just regard for our future tranquillity, for the safety of our shores, and for the protection of our property committed to the ocean.

The present Navy of the United States, called suddenly into existence by a great national exigency, has raised us in our own esteem, and by the protection afforded to our commerce has effected to the extent of our expectations the objects for which it was created.

In connection with a navy ought to be contemplated the fortification of some of our principal seaports and harbors.   A variety of considerations, which will readily suggest themselves, urge an attention to this measure of precaution.   To give security to our principal ports considerable sums have already been expended, but the works remain incomplete. It is for Congress to determine whether additional appropriations shall be made in order to render competent to the intended purposes the fortifications which have been commenced.

The manufacture of arms within the United States still invites the attention of the National Legislature.   At a considerable expense to the public this manufacture has been brought to such a state of maturity as, with continued encouragement, will supersede the necessity of future importations from foreign countries.

Gentlemen of the House of Representatives:

I shall direct the estimates of the appropriations necessary for the ensuing year, together with an account of the public revenue and expenditure to a late period, to be laid before you.   I observe with much satisfaction that the product of the revenue during the present year has been more considerable than during any former equal period.   This result affords conclusive evidence of the great resources of this country and of the wisdom and efficiency of the measures which have been adopted by Congress for the protection of commerce and preservation of public credit.

Gentlemen of the Senate and Gentlemen of the House of Representatives:

As one of the grand community of nations, our attention is irresistibly drawn to the important scenes which surround us.   If they have exhibited an uncommon portion of calamity, it is the province of humanity to deplore and of wisdom to avoid the causes which may have produced it. If, turning our eyes homeward, we find reason to rejoice at the prospect which presents itself; if we perceive the interior of our country prosperous, free, and happy; if all enjoy in safety, under the protection of laws emanating only from the general will, the fruits of their own labor, we ought to fortify and cling to those institutions which have been the source of such real felicity and resist with unabating perseverance the progress of those dangerous innovations which may diminish their influence.

To your patriotism, gentlemen, has been confided the honorable duty of guarding the public interests; and while the past is to your country a sure pledge that it will be faithfully discharged, permit me to assure you that your labors to promote the general happiness will receive from me the most zealous cooperation.

JOHN ADAMS.

ADDRESS OF THE SENATE TO JOHN ADAMS, PRESIDENT OF THE UNITED STATES.

The PRESIDENT OF THE UNITED STATES.

SIR: Impressed with the important truth that the hearts of rulers and people are in the hand of the Almighty, the Senate of the United States most cordially join in your invocations for appropriate blessings upon the Government and people of this Union.

We meet you, sir, and the other branch of the National Legislature in the city which is honored by the name of our late hero and sage, the illustrious Washington, with sensations and emotions which exceed our power of description.

While we congratulate ourselves on the convention of the Legislature at the permanent seat of Government, and ardently hope that permanence and stability may be communicated as well to the Government itself as to its seat, our minds are irresistibly led to deplore the death of him who bore so honorable and efficient a part in the establishment of both. Great indeed would have been our gratification if his sum of earthly happiness had been completed by seeing the Government thus peaceably convened at this place; but we derive consolation from a belief that the moment in which we were destined to experience the loss we deplore was fixed by that Being whose counsels can not err, and from a hope that since in this seat of Government, which bears his name, his earthly remains will be deposited, the members of Congress, and all who inhabit the city, with these memorials before them, will retain his virtues in lively recollection, and make his patriotism, morals, and piety models for imitation. And permit us to add, sir, that it is not among the least of our consolations that you, who have been his companion and friend from the dawning of our national existence, and trained in the same school of exertion to effect our independence, are still preserved by a gracious Providence in health and activity to exercise the functions of Chief Magistrate.

The question whether the local powers over the District of Columbia, vested by the Constitution in the Congress of the United States, shall be immediately exercised is of great importance, and in deliberating upon it we shall naturally be led to weigh the attending circumstances and every probable consequence of the measures which may be proposed.

The several subjects for legislative consideration contained in your speech to both Houses of Congress shall receive from the Senate all the attention which they can give, when contemplating those objects, both in respect to their national importance and the additional weight that is given them by your recommendation.

We deprecate with you, sir, all spirit of innovation from whatever quarter it may arise, which may impair the sacred bond that connects the different parts of this Empire, and we trust that, under the protection of Divine Providence the wisdom and virtue of the citizens of the United States will deliver our national compact unimpaired to a grateful posterity.

From past experience it is impossible for the Senate of the United States to doubt of your zealous cooperation with the Legislature in every effort to promote the general happiness and tranquillity of the Union.

Accept, sir, our warmest wishes for your health and happiness.

JOHN E. HOWARD,
President of the Senate pro tempore.

NOVEMBER 25, 1800.

REPLY OF THE PRESIDENT.

CITY OF WASHINGTON, *November 26, 1800.*

Mr. President and Gentlemen of the Senate:

For this excellent address, so respectful to the memory of my illustrious predecessor, which I receive from the Senate of the United States at this time and in this place with peculiar satisfaction, I pray you to accept of my unfeigned acknowledgments. With you I ardently hope that permanence and stability will be communicated as well to the Government itself as to its beautiful and commodious seat. With you I deplore the death of that hero and sage who bore so honorable and efficient a part in the establishment of both. Great indeed would have been my gratification if his sum of earthly happiness had been completed by seeing the Government thus peaceably convened at this place, himself at its head; but while we submit to the decisions of Heaven, whose councils are inscrutable to us, we can not but hope that the members of Congress, the officers of Government, and all who inhabit the city or the country will retain his virtues in lively recollection and make his patriotism, morals, and piety models for imitation.

I thank you, gentlemen, for your assurance that the several subjects for legislative consideration recommended in my communication to both Houses shall receive from the Senate a deliberate and candid attention.

With you, gentlemen, I sincerely deprecate all spirit of innovation which may weaken the sacred bond that connects the different parts of this nation and Government, and with you I trust that under the protection of Divine Providence the wisdom and virtue of our citizens will deliver our national compact unimpaired to a free, prosperous, happy, and grateful posterity. To this end it is my fervent prayer that in this city the foundations of wisdom may be always opened and the streams of eloquence forever flow. Here may the youth of this extensive country forever look up without disappointment, not only to the monuments and memorials of the dead, but to the examples of the living, in the members of Congress and officers of Government, for finished models of all those virtues, graces, talents, and accomplishments which constitute the dignity of human nature and lay the only foundation for the prosperity or duration of empires.

JOHN ADAMS.

ADDRESS OF THE HOUSE OF REPRESENTATIVES TO JOHN ADAMS, PRESIDENT OF THE UNITED STATES.

JOHN ADAMS,
President of the United States.

SIR: The House of Representatives have received with great respect the communication which you have been pleased to make to the two Houses of Congress at the commencement of the present session.

The final establishment of the seat of National Government, which has now taken place, within the District of Columbia is an event of no small importance in the political transactions of our country, and we cordially unite our wishes with yours that this Territory may be the residence of happiness and virtue.

Nor can we on this occasion omit to express a hope that the spirit which animated the great founder of this city may descend to future generations, and that the wisdom, magnanimity, and steadiness which marked the events of his public life may be imitated in all succeeding ages.

A consideration of those powers which have been vested in Congress over the District of Columbia will not escape our attention, nor shall we forget that in exercising these powers a regard must be had to those events which will necessarily attend the capital of America.

The cheerfulness and regularity with which the officers and soldiers of the temporary army have returned to the condition of private citizens is a testimony clear and conclusive of the purity of those motives which induced them to engage in the public service, and will remain a proof on all future occasions that an army of soldiers drawn from the citizens of our country deserve our confidence and respect.

No subject can be more important than that of the judiciary, which you have again recommended to our consideration, and it shall receive our early and deliberate attention.

The Constitution of the United States having confided the management of our foreign negotiations to the control of the Executive power, we cheerfully submit to its decisions on this important subject; and in respect to the negotiations now pending with France, we sincerely hope that the final result may prove as fortunate to our country as the most ardent mind can wish.

So long as a predatory war is carried on against our commerce we should sacrifice the interests and disappoint the expectations of our constituents should we for a moment relax that system of maritime defense which has resulted in such beneficial effects. At this period it is confidently believed that few persons can be found within the United States who do not admit that a navy, well organized, must constitute the natural and efficient defense of this country against all foreign hostility.

The progress which has been made in the manufacture of arms leaves no doubt that the public patronage has already placed this country beyond all necessary dependence on foreign markets for an article so indispensable for defense, and gives us assurances that, under the encouragement which Government will continue to extend to this important object, we shall soon rival foreign countries not only in the number but in the quality of arms completed from our own manufactories.

Few events could have been more pleasing to our constituents than that great and rapid increase of revenue which has arisen from permanent taxes. Whilst this event explains the great and increasing resources of our country, it carries along with it a proof which can not be resisted that those measures of maritime defense which were calculated to meet our enemy upon the ocean, and which have produced such extensive protection to our commerce, were founded in wisdom and policy. The mind must, in our opinion, be insensible to the plainest truths which can not discern the elevated ground on which this policy has placed our country. That national spirit which alone could vindicate our common rights has been roused, and those latent energies which had not been fully known were unfolded and brought into view, and our fellow-citizens were prepared to meet every event which national honor or national security could render necessary. Nor have its effects been much less important in other respects.

Whilst many of the nations of the earth have been impoverished and depopulated by internal commotions and national contests, our internal peace has not been materially impaired; our commerce has extended, under the protection of our infant Navy, to every part of the globe; wealth has flowed without intermission into our seaports, and the labors of the husbandman have been rewarded by a ready market for the productions of the soil.

Be assured, sir, that the various and important subjects recommended to our consideration shall receive our early and deliberate attention; and, confident of your cooperation in every measure which may be calculated to promote the general interest, we shall endeavor on our part to testify by our industry and dispatch the zeal and sincerity with which we regard the public good

NOVEMBER 26, 1800.

REPLY OF THE PRESIDENT.

WASHINGTON, *November 27, 1800.*

Mr. Speaker and Gentlemen of the House of Representatives:

Compelled by the habits of a long life, as well as by all the principles of society and government which I could ever understand and believe, to consider the great body of the people as the source of all legitimate authority no less than of all efficient power, it is impossible for me to receive this address from the immediate Representatives of the American people at this time and in this place without emotions which it would be improper to express if any language could convey them.

May the spirit which animated the great founder of this city descend to future generations, and may the wisdom, magnanimity, and steadiness which marked the events of his public life be imitated in all succeeding ages.

I thank you, gentlemen, for your assurance that the judiciary system shall receive your deliberate attention.

With you, gentlemen, I sincerely hope that the final result of the negotiations now pending with France may prove as fortunate to our country as they have been commenced with sincerity and prosecuted with deliberation and caution. With you I cordially agree that so long as a predatory war is carried on against our commerce we should sacrifice the interests and disappoint the expectations of our constituents should we for a moment relax that system of maritime defense which has resulted in such beneficial effects. With you I confidently believe that few persons can be found within the United States who do not admit that a navy, well organized, must constitute the natural and efficient defense of this country against all foreign hostility.

Those who recollect the distress and danger to this country in former periods from the want of arms must exult in the assurance from their Representatives that we shall soon rival foreign countries not only in the number but in the quality of arms completed from our own manufactories.

With you, gentlemen, I fully agree that the great increase of revenue is a proof that the measures of maritime defense were founded in wisdom. This policy has raised us in the esteem of foreign nations. That national spirit and those latent energies which had not been and are not yet fully known to any were not entirely forgotten by those who had lived long enough to see in former times their operation and some of their effects. Our fellow-citizens were undoubtedly prepared to meet every event which national honor or national security could render necessary. These, it is to be hoped, are secured at the cheapest and easiest rate; if not, they will be secured at more expense.

I thank you, gentlemen, for your assurance that the various subjects recommended to your consideration shall receive your deliberate attention. No further evidence is wanting to convince me of the zeal and sincerity with which the House of Representatives regard the public good.

I pray you, gentlemen, to accept of my best wishes for your health and happiness.

JOHN ADAMS.

SPECIAL MESSAGES.

UNITED STATES, *December 15, 1800.*

Gentlemen of the Senate:

I transmit to the Senate, for their consideration and decision, a convention, both in English and French, between the United States of America and the French Republic, signed at Paris on the 30th day of September last by the respective plenipotentiaries of the two powers. I also transmit to the Senate three manuscript volumes containing the journal of our envoys.

JOHN ADAMS.

UNITED STATES, *January 1, 1801.*

Gentlemen of the Senate and Gentlemen of the House of Representatives:

I transmit to both Houses of Congress, for their information and consideration, copies of laws enacted by the governor and judges of the Mississippi Territory from the 30th of June until the 31st of December, A. D. 1799.

JOHN ADAMS.

UNITED STATES, *January 17, 1801.*

Gentlemen of the Senate and Gentlemen of the House of Representatives:

I have received from Elias Boudinot, esq., Director of the Mint of the United States, a report of the 2d of January, representing the state of it, together with an abstract of the coins struck at the Mint from the 1st of January to the 31st of December, 1800; an abstract of the expenditures of the Mint from the 1st of January to the 31st of December, inclusive; a statement of gain on copper coined at the Mint from the 1st of January to the 31st of December, 1800, and a certificate from Joseph Richardson, assayer of the Mint, ascertaining the value of Spanish milled doubloons in proportion to the gold coins of the United States to be no more than 84 cents and $\frac{424}{500}$ parts of a cent for 1 pennyweight, or 28 grains and $\frac{24256}{84848}$ parts of a grain to one dollar. These papers I transmit to Congress for their consideration.

JOHN ADAMS.

UNITED STATES, *January 21, 1801.*

Gentlemen of the Senate:

In compliance with your request, signified in your resolution of the 20th day of this month, I transmit you a report made to me by the Secretary of State on the same day, a letter of our late envoys to him of the 4th of October last, an extract of a letter from our minister plenipotentiary in London to him of the 22d of November last, and an extract of another letter from the minister to the Secretary of the 31st of October last.

The reasoning in the letter of our late envoys to France is so fully supported by the writers on the law of nations, particularly by Vattel, as well as by his great masters, Grotius and Puffendorf, that nothing is left to be desired to settle the point that if there be a collision between two treaties made with two different powers the more ancient has the advantage, for no engagement contrary to it can be entered into in the treaty afterwards made; and if this last be found in any case incompatible with the more ancient one its execution is considered as impossible, because the person promising had not the power of acting contrary to his antecedent engagement. Although our right is very clear to negotiate treaties according to our own ideas of right and justice, honor and good faith, yet it must always be a satisfaction to know that the judgment of other nations with whom we have connection coincides with ours, and that we have no reason to apprehend that any disagreeable questions and discussions are likely to arise. The letters from Mr. King will therefore be read by the Senate with particular satisfaction.

The inconveniences to public officers and the mischiefs to the public arising from the publication of the dispatches of ministers abroad are so numerous and so obvious that I request of the Senate that these papers, especially the letters from Mr. King, be considered in close confidence.

JOHN ADAMS.

UNITED STATES, *January 30, 1801.*

Gentlemen of the Senate and Gentlemen of the House of Representatives:

I transmit to Congress for their consideration a letter from William Thornton, Alexander White, and William Cranch, esquires, commissioners of the city of Washington, with a representation of the affairs of the city made by them to the President of the United States, dated 28th of January, 1801, accompanied with a series of documents marked from A to H, inclusively,

JOHN ADAMS.

UNITED STATES, *February 16, 1801.*

Gentlemen of the Senate and Gentlemen of the House of Representatives:

I wish to know the pleasure of Congress and request their direction concerning the disposition of the property of the United States now in my possession; whether I shall deliver it into the hands of the heads of Departments, or of the commissioners of the city of Washington, or of a committee of Congress, or to any other persons Congress may appoint, to be delivered into the hands of my successor, or whether I shall present it myself to the President of the United States on the 4th of March next. Any of these modes will be agreeable to me.

JOHN ADAMS.

UNITED STATES, *February 20, 1801.*

Gentlemen of the Senate and Gentlemen of the House of Representatives:

I transmit to Congress a report received this morning from Elias Boudinot, esq., Director of the Mint, dated February 13, 1801, which will require the attention and decision of Congress before the close of the session.

JOHN ADAMS.

UNITED STATES, *March 2, 1801.*

Gentlemen of the Senate:

I have considered the advice and consent of the Senate to the ratification of the convention with France under certain conditions. Although it would have been more conformable to my own judgment and inclination to have agreed to that instrument unconditionally, yet as in this point I found I had the misfortune to differ in opinion from so high a constitutional authority as the Senate, I judged it more consistent with the honor and interest of the United States to ratify it under the conditions prescribed than not at all. I accordingly nominated Mr. Bayard minister plenipotentiary to the French Republic, that he might proceed without delay to Paris to negotiate the exchange of ratifications; but as that gentleman has declined his appointment, for reasons equally applicable to every other person suitable for the service, I shall take no further measures relative to this business, and leave the convention, with all the documents, in the Office of State, that my successor may proceed with them according to his wisdom.

JOHN ADAMS.

PROCLAMATION.

JANUARY 30, 1801.

To the Senators of the United States, respectively.

SIR: It appearing to me proper and necessary for the public service that the Senate of the United States should be convened on Wednesday, the 4th of March next, you are desired to attend in the Chamber of the Senate on that day, at 10 o'clock in the forenoon, to receive and act upon any communications which the President of the United States may then lay before you touching their interests, and to do and consider all other things which may be proper and necessary for the public service for the Senate to do and consider.

JOHN ADAMS,
President of the United States.

Thomas Jefferson

March 4, 1801, to March 4, 1809

SEE VOLUME XI.

Volume eleven is not only an index to the other volumes, not only a key that unlocks the treasures of the entire publication, but it is in itself an alphabetically arranged brief history or story of the great controlling events constituting the History of the United States.

Under its proper alphabetical classification the story is told of every great subject referred to by any of the Presidents in their official Messages, and at the end of each story the official utterances of the Presidents themselves are cited upon the subject, so that you may readily turn to the page in the body of the work itself for this original information.

Next to the possession of knowledge is the ability to turn at will to where knowledge is to be found.

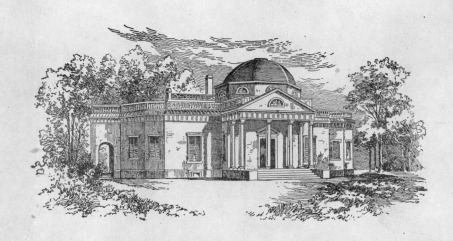

MONTICELLO, VIRGINIA, HOME OF

THOMAS JEFFERSON

With official portrait engraved from copy of original in steel

Thomas Jefferson

THOMAS JEFFERSON was born at Shadwell, Albemarle County, Va., on April 2 (old style), 1743. He was the oldest son of Peter Jefferson, who died in 1757. After attending private schools, he entered William and Mary College in 1760. In 1767 began the practice of the law. In 1769 was chosen to represent his county in the Virginia house of burgesses, a station he continued to fill up to the period of the Revolution. He married Mrs. Martha Skelton in 1772, she being a daughter of John Wayles, an eminent lawyer of Virginia. On March 12, 1773, was chosen a member of the first committee of correspondence established by the Colonial legislature. Was elected a delegate to the Continental Congress in 1775; was placed on the Committee of Five to prepare the Declaration of Independence, and at the request of that committee he drafted the Declaration, which, with slight amendments, was adopted July 4, 1776. Resigned his seat in Congress and occupied one in the Virginia legislature in October, 1776. Was elected governor of Virginia by the legislature on June 1, 1779, to succeed Patrick Henry. Retired to private life at the end of his term as governor, but was the same year elected again to the legislature. Was appointed commissioner with others to negotiate treaties with France in 1776, but declined. In 1782 he was appointed by Congress minister plenipotentiary to act with others in Europe in negotiating a treaty of peace with Great Britain. Was again elected a Delegate to Congress in 1783, and as a member of that body he advocated and had adopted the dollar as the unit and the present system of coins and decimals. In May, 1784, was appointed minister plenipotentiary to Europe to assist John Adams and Benjamin Franklin in negotiating treaties of commerce. In March, 1785, was appointed by Congress minister at the French Court to succeed Dr. Franklin, and remained in France until September, 1789. On his arrival at Norfolk, November 23, 1789, received a letter from Washington offering him the appointment of Secretary of State in his Cabinet. Accepted and became the first Secretary of State under the Constitution. December 31, 1793, resigned his place in the Cabinet and retired to private life at his home. In 1796 was brought forward by his friends as a candidate for President, but Mr. Adams, receiving the highest number of votes, was elected President, and Jefferson became Vice-President for four years from March 4, 1797. In 1800 was again voted for by his party for President. He and Mr. Burr received an equal number of electoral votes, and under the Constitution the House of Representatives was called upon to elect. Mr. Jefferson was chosen on the thirty-sixth ballot. Was reelected in 1804, and retired finally from public life March 4, 1809. He died on the 4th day of July, 1826, and was buried at Monticello, Va.

NOTIFICATION OF ELECTION.

Mr. Pinckney, from the committee instructed on the 18th instant to wait on the President elect to notify him of his election, reported that the committee had, according to order, performed that service, and addressed the President elect in the following words, to wit:

The committee beg leave to express their wishes for the prosperity of your Administration and their sincere desire that it may promote your own happiness and the welfare of our country.

To which the President elect was pleased to make the following reply:

I receive, gentlemen, with profound thankfulness this testimony of confidence from the great representative council of our nation. It fills up the measure of that grateful satisfaction which had already been derived from the suffrages of my fellow-citizens themselves, designating me as one of those to whom they were willing to commit this charge, the most important of all others to them. In deciding between the candidates whom their equal vote presented to your choice, I am sensible that age has been respected rather than more active and useful qualifications.

I know the difficulties of the station to which I am called, and feel and acknowledge my incompetence to them. But whatsoever of understanding, whatsoever of diligence, whatsoever of justice or of affectionate concern for the happiness of man, it has pleased Providence to place within the compass of my faculties shall be called forth for the discharge of the duties confided to me, and for procuring to my fellow-citizens all the benefits which our Constitution has placed under the guardianship of the General Government.

Guided by the wisdom and patriotism of those to whom it belongs to express the legislative will of the nation, I will give to that will a faithful execution.

I pray you, gentlemen, to convey to the honorable body from which you are deputed the homage of my humble acknowledgments and the sentiments of zeal and fidelity by which I shall endeavor to merit these proofs of confidence from the nation and its Representatives; and accept yourselves my particular thanks for the obliging terms in which you have been pleased to communicate their will.

TH: JEFFERSON.

FEBRUARY 20, 1801.

LETTER FROM THE PRESIDENT ELECT.

The President laid before the Senate a letter from the President elect of the United States, which was read, as follows:

WASHINGTON, *March 2, 1801.*

The PRESIDENT PRO TEMPORE OF THE SENATE.

SIR: I beg leave through you to inform the honorable the Senate of the United States that I propose to take the oath which the Constitution prescribes to the President of the United States before he enters on the execution of his office on Wednesday, the 4th instant, at 12 o'clock, in the Senate Chamber.

I have the honor to be, with the greatest respect, sir, your most obedient and most humble servant,

TH: JEFFERSON.

(The same letter was sent to the House of Representatives.)

FIRST INAUGURAL ADDRESS.

AT WASHINGTON, D. C.

Friends and Fellow-Citizens.

Called upon to undertake the duties of the first executive office of our country, I avail myself of the presence of that portion of my fellow-citizens which is here assembled to express my grateful thanks for the favor with which they have been pleased to look toward me, to declare a sincere consciousness that the task is above my talents, and that I approach it with those anxious and awful presentiments which the greatness of the charge and the weakness of my powers so justly inspire. A rising nation, spread over a wide and fruitful land, traversing all the seas with the rich productions of their industry, engaged in commerce with nations who feel power and forget right, advancing rapidly to destinies beyond the reach of mortal eye—when I contemplate these transcendent objects, and see the honor, the happiness, and the hopes of this beloved country committed to the issue and the auspices of this day, I shrink from the contemplation, and humble myself before the magnitude of the undertaking. Utterly, indeed, should I despair did not the presence of many whom I here see remind me that in the other high authorities provided by our Constitution I shall find resources of wisdom, of virtue, and of zeal on which to rely under all difficulties. To you, then, gentlemen, who are charged with the sovereign functions of legislation, and to those associated with you, I look with encouragement for that guidance and support which may enable us to steer with safety the vessel in which we are all embarked amidst the conflicting elements of a troubled world.

During the contest of opinion through which we have passed the animation of discussions and of exertions has sometimes worn an aspect which might impose on strangers unused to think freely and to speak and to write what they think; but this being now decided by the voice of the nation, announced according to the rules of the Constitution, all will, of course, arrange themselves under the will of the law, and unite in common efforts for the common good. All, too, will bear in mind this sacred principle, that though the will of the majority is in all cases to prevail, that will to be rightful must be reasonable; that the minority possess their equal rights, which equal law must protect, and to violate would be oppression. Let us, then, fellow-citizens, unite with one heart and one mind. Let us restore to social intercourse that harmony and affection without which liberty and even life itself are but dreary things. And let us reflect that, having banished from our land that religious intolerance under which mankind so long bled and suffered, we have yet gained little if we countenance a political intolerance as despotic, as wicked, and capable of as bitter and bloody persecutions. During the throes and convulsions of the ancient world, during the agonizing spasms of infuriated man, seeking through blood and slaughter his long-lost liberty, it was not wonderful that the agitation of the billows should reach even this distant and peaceful shore; that this should be more felt and feared by some and less by others, and should divide opinions as to measures of safety. But every difference of opinion is not a difference of principle. We have called by different names brethren of the same principle. We are all Republicans, we are all Federalists. If there be any among us who would wish to dissolve this Union or to change its republican form, let them stand undisturbed as monuments of the safety with which error of opinion may be tolerated where reason is left free to combat it. I know, indeed, that some honest men fear that a republican government can not be strong, that this Government is not strong enough; but would the honest patriot, in the full tide of successful experiment, abandon a government which has so far kept us free and firm on the theoretic and visionary fear that this Government, the world's best hope, may by possibility want energy to preserve itself? I trust not. I believe this, on the contrary, the strongest Government on earth. I believe it the only one where every man, at the call of the law, would fly to the standard of the law, and would meet invasions of the public order as his own personal concern. Sometimes it is said that man can not be trusted with the government of himself. Can he, then, be trusted with the government of others? Or have we found angels in the forms of kings to govern him? Let history answer this question.

Let us, then, with courage and confidence pursue our own Federal and Republican principles, our attachment to union and representative government. Kindly separated by nature and a wide ocean from the exterminating havoc of one quarter of the globe; too high-minded to endure the degradations of the others; possessing a chosen country, with room enough for our descendants to the thousandth and thousandth generation; entertaining a due sense of our equal right to the use of our own faculties, to the acquisitions of our own industry, to honor and confidence from our fellow-citizens, resulting not from birth, but from our actions and their sense of them; enlightened by a benign religion, professed, indeed, and practiced in various forms, yet all of them inculcating honesty, truth, temperance, gratitude, and the love of man; acknowledging and adoring an overruling Providence, which by all its dispensations proves that it delights in the happiness of man here and his greater happiness hereafter—with all these blessings, what more is necessary to make us a happy and a prosperous people? Still one thing more, fellow-citizens—a wise and frugal Government, which shall restrain men from injuring one another, shall leave them otherwise free to regulate their own pursuits of industry and improvement, and shall not take from the mouth of labor the bread it has earned. This is the sum of good government, and this is necessary to close the circle of our felicities.

About to enter, fellow-citizens, on the exercise of duties which comprehend everything dear and valuable to you, it is proper you should understand what I deem the essential principles of our Government, and consequently those which ought to shape its Administration. I will compress them within the narrowest compass they will bear, stating the general principle, but not all its limitations. Equal and exact justice to all men, of whatever state or persuasion, religious or political; peace, commerce, and honest friendship with all nations, entangling alliances with none; the support of the State governments in all their rights, as the most competent administrations for our domestic concerns and the surest bulwarks against antirepublican tendencies; the preservation of the General Government in its whole constitutional vigor, as the sheet anchor of our peace at home and safety abroad; a jealous care of the right of election by the people—a mild and safe corrective of abuses which are lopped by the sword of revolution where peaceable remedies are unprovided; absolute acquiescence in the decisions of the majority, the vital principle of republics, from which is no appeal but to force, the vital principle and immediate parent of despotism; a well-disciplined militia, our best reliance in peace and for the first moments of war, till regulars may relieve them; the supremacy of the civil over the military authority; economy in the public expense, that labor may be lightly burthened; the honest payment of our debts and sacred preservation of the public faith; encouragement of agriculture, and of commerce as its handmaid; the diffusion of information and arraignment of all abuses at the bar of the public reason; freedom of religion; freedom of the press, and freedom of person under the protection of the habeas corpus, and trial by juries impartially selected. These principles form the bright constellation which has gone before us and guided our steps through an age of revolution and reformation. The wisdom of our sages and blood of our heroes have been devoted to their attainment. They should be the creed of our political faith, the text of civic instruction, the touchstone by which to try the services of those we trust; and should we wander from them in moments of error or of alarm, let us hasten to retrace our steps and to regain the road which alone leads to peace, liberty, and safety.

I repair, then, fellow-citizens, to the post you have assigned me. With experience enough in subordinate offices to have seen the difficulties of this the greatest of all, I have learnt to expect that it will rarely fall to the lot of imperfect man to retire from this station with the reputation and the favor which bring him into it. Without pretensions to that high confidence you reposed in our first and greatest revolutionary character, whose preeminent services had entitled him to the first place in his country's love and destined for him the fairest page in the volume of faithful history, I ask so much confidence only as may give firmness and effect to the legal administration of your affairs. I shall often go wrong through defect of judgment. When right, I shall often be thought wrong by those whose positions will not command a view of the whole ground. I ask your indulgence for my own errors, which will never be intentional, and your support against the errors of others, who may condemn what they would not if seen in all its parts. The approbation implied by your suffrage is a great consolation to me for the past, and my future solicitude will be to retain the good opinion of those who have bestowed it in advance, to conciliate that of others by doing them all the good in my power, and to be instrumental to the happiness and freedom of all.

Relying, then, on the patronage of your good will, I advance with obedience to the work, ready to retire from it whenever you become sensible how much better choice it is in your power to make. And may that Infinite Power which rules the destinies of the universe lead our councils to what is best, and give them a favorable issue for your peace and prosperity.

MARCH 4, 1801.

PROCLAMATION.

[From the National Intelligencer, March 13, 1801.]

BY THE PRESIDENT OF THE UNITED STATES.

Whereas by the first article of the terms and conditions declared by the President of the United States on the 17th day of October, 1791, for regulating the materials and manner of buildings and improvements on the lots in the city of Washington, it is provided "that the outer and party walls of all houses in the said city shall be built of brick or stone;" and by the third article of the same terms and conditions it is declared "that the wall of no house shall be higher than 40 feet to the roof in any part of the city, nor shall any be lower than 35 feet in any of the avenues;" and

Whereas the above-recited articles were found to impede the settlement in the city of mechanics and others whose circumstances did not admit of erecting houses authorized by the said regulations, for which cause the President of the United States, by a writing under his hand, bearing date the 25th day of June, 1796, suspended the operation of the said articles until the first Monday of December, 1800, and the beneficial effects arising from such suspension having been experienced, it is deemed proper to revive the same:

Wherefore I, Thomas Jefferson, President of the United States, do declare that the operation of the first and third articles above recited shall be, and the same is hereby, suspended until the 1st day of January, 1802, and that all the houses which shall be erected in the said city of Washington previous to the said 1st day of January, 1802, conformable in other respects to the regulations aforesaid, shall be considered as lawfully erected, except that no wooden house shall be erected within 24 feet of any brick or stone house.

Given under my hand this 11th day of March, 1801.

TH: JEFFERSON.

In communicating his first message to Congress, President Jefferson addressed the following letter to the presiding officer of each branch of the National Legislature:

DECEMBER 8, 1801.

The Honorable the PRESIDENT OF THE SENATE.

SIR: The circumstances under which we find ourselves at this place rendering inconvenient the mode heretofore practiced of making by personal address the first communications between the legislative and executive branches, I have adopted that by message, as used on all subsequent occasions through the session. In doing this I have had principal regard to the convenience of the Legislature, to the economy of their time, to their relief from the embarrassment of immediate answers on subjects not yet fully before them, and to the benefits thence resulting to the public affairs. Trusting that a procedure founded in these motives will meet their approbation, I beg leave through you, sir, to communicate the inclosed message, with the documents accompanying it, to the honorable the Senate, and pray you to accept for yourself and them the homage of my high respect and consideration.

TH: JEFFERSON.

FIRST ANNUAL MESSAGE.

DECEMBER 8, 1801.

Fellow-Citizens of the Senate and House of Representatives:

It is a circumstance of sincere gratification to me that on meeting the great council of our nation I am able to announce to them on grounds of reasonable certainty that the wars and troubles which have for so many years afflicted our sister nations have at length come to an end, and that the communications of peace and commerce are once more opening among them. Whilst we devoutly return thanks to the beneficent Being who has been pleased to breathe into them the spirit of conciliation and forgiveness, we are bound with peculiar gratitude to be thankful to Him that our own peace has been preserved through so perilous a season, and ourselves permitted quietly to cultivate the earth and to practice and improve those arts which tend to increase our comforts. The assurances, indeed, of friendly disposition received from all the powers with whom we have principal relations had inspired a confidence that our peace with them would not have been disturbed. But a cessation of irregularities which had affected the commerce of neutral nations and of the irritations and injuries produced by them can not but add to this confidence, and strengthens at the same time the hope that wrongs committed on unoffending friends under a pressure of circumstances will now be reviewed with candor, and will be considered as founding just claims of retribution for the past and new assurance for the future.

Among our Indian neighbors also a spirit of peace and friendship generally prevails, and I am happy to inform you that the continued efforts to introduce among them the implements and the practice of husbandry and of the household arts have not been without success; that they are becoming more and more sensible of the superiority of this dependence for clothing and subsistence over the precarious resources of hunting and fishing, and already we are able to announce that instead of that constant diminution of their numbers produced by their wars and their wants, some of them begin to experience an increase of population.

To this state of general peace with which we have been blessed, one only exception exists. Tripoli, the least considerable of the Barbary States, had come forward with demands unfounded either in right or in compact, and had permitted itself to denounce war on our failure to comply before a given day. The style of the demand admitted but one answer. I sent a small squadron of frigates into the Mediterranean, with assurances to that power of our sincere desire to remain in peace, but with orders to protect our commerce against the threatened attack. The measure was seasonable and salutary. The Bey had already declared war. His cruisers were out. Two had arrived at Gibraltar.

Our commerce in the Mediterranean was blockaded and that of the Atlantic in peril. The arrival of our squadron dispelled the danger. One of the Tripolitan cruisers having fallen in with and engaged the small schooner *Enterprise*, commanded by Lieutenant Sterret, which had gone as a tender to our larger vessels, was captured, after a heavy slaughter of her men, without the loss of a single one on our part. The bravery exhibited by our citizens on that element will, I trust, be a testimony to the world that it is not the want of that virtue which makes us seek their peace, but a conscientious desire to direct the energies of our nation to the multiplication of the human race, and not to its destruction. Unauthorized by the Constitution, without the sanction of Congress, to go beyond the line of defense, the vessel, being disabled from committing further hostilities, was liberated with its crew. The Legislature will doubtless consider whether, by authorizing measures of offense also, they will place our force on an equal footing with that of its adversaries. I communicate all material information on this subject, that in the exercise of this important function confided by the Constitution to the Legislature exclusively their judgment may form itself on a knowledge and consideration of every circumstance of weight.

I wish I could say that our situation with all the other Barbary States was entirely satisfactory. Discovering that some delays had taken place in the performance of certain articles stipulated by us, I thought it my duty, by immediate measures for fulfilling them, to vindicate to ourselves the right of considering the effect of departure from stipulation on their side. From the papers which will be laid before you you will be enabled to judge whether our treaties are regarded by them as fixing at all the measure of their demands or as guarding from the exercise of force our vessels within their power, and to consider how far it will be safe and expedient to leave our affairs with them in their present posture.

I lay before you the result of the census lately taken of our inhabitants, to a conformity with which we are now to reduce the ensuing ratio of representation and taxation. You will perceive that the increase of numbers during the last ten years, proceeding in geometrical ratio, promises a duplication in little more than twenty-two years. We contemplate this rapid growth and the prospect it holds up to us, not with a view to the injuries it may enable us to do others in some future day, but to the settlement of the extensive country still remaining vacant within our limits to the multiplication of men susceptible of happiness, educated in the love of order, habituated to self-government, and valuing its blessings above all price.

Other circumstances, combined with the increase of numbers, have produced an augmentation of revenue arising from consumption in a ratio far beyond that of population alone; and though the changes in foreign relations now taking place so desirably for the whole world may for a season affect this branch of revenue, yet weighing all probabilities of expense as well as of income, there is reasonable ground of confidence that we may now safely dispense with all the internal taxes, comprehending excise, stamps, auctions, licenses, carriages, and refined sugars, to which the postage on newspapers may be added to facilitate the progress of information, and that the remaining sources of revenue will be sufficient to provide for the support of Government, to pay the interest of the public debts, and to discharge the principals within shorter periods than the laws or the general expectation had contemplated. War, indeed, and untoward events may change this prospect of things and call for expenses which the imposts could not meet; but sound principles will not justify our taxing the industry of our fellow-citizens to accumulate treasure for wars to happen we know not when, and which might not, perhaps, happen but from the temptations offered by that treasure.

These views, however, of reducing our burthens are formed on the expectation that a sensible and at the same time a salutary reduction may take place in our habitual expenditures. For this purpose those of the civil Government, the Army, and Navy will need revisal.

When we consider that this Government is charged with the external and mutual relations only of these States; that the States themselves have principal care of our persons, our property, and our reputation, constituting the great field of human concerns, we may well doubt whether our organization is not too complicated, too expensive; whether offices and officers have not been multiplied unnecessarily and sometimes injuriously to the service they were meant to promote. I will cause to be laid before you an essay toward a statement of those who, under public employment of various kinds, draw money from the Treasury or from our citizens. Time has not permitted a perfect enumeration, the ramifications of office being too multiplied and remote to be completely traced in a first trial. Among those who are dependent on Executive discretion I have begun the reduction of what was deemed unnecessary. The expenses of diplomatic agency have been considerably diminished. The inspectors of internal revenue who were found to obstruct the accountability of the institution have been discontinued. Several agencies created by Executive authority, on salaries fixed by that also, have been suppressed, and should suggest the expediency of regulating that power by law, so as to subject its exercises to legislative inspection and sanction. Other reformations of the same kind will be pursued with that caution which is requisite in removing useless things, not to injure what is retained. But the great mass of public offices is established by law, and therefore by law alone can be abolished. Should the Legislature think it expedient to pass this roll in review and try all its parts by the test of public utility, they may be assured of every aid and light which Executive information can yield. Considering the general tendency to multiply offices and dependencies and to increase expense to the ultimate term of burthen which the citizen can bear, it behooves us to avail ourselves of every occasion which presents itself for taking off the surcharge, that it never may be seen here that after leaving to labor the smallest portion of its earnings on which it can subsist, Government shall itself consume the whole residue of what it was instituted to guard.

In our care, too, of the public contributions intrusted to our direction it would be prudent to multiply barriers against their dissipation by appropriating specific sums to every specific purpose susceptible of definition; by disallowing all applications of money varying from the appropriation in object or transcending it in amount; by reducing the undefined field of contingencies and thereby circumscribing discretionary powers over money, and by bringing back to a single department all accountabilities for money, where the examinations may be prompt, efficacious, and uniform.

An account of the receipts and expenditures of the last year, as prepared by the Secretary of the Treasury, will, as usual, be laid before you. The success which has attended the late sales of the public lands shews that with attention they may be made an important source of receipt. Among the payments those made in discharge of the principal and interest of the national debt will shew that the public faith has been exactly maintained. To these will be added an estimate of appropriations necessary for the ensuing year. This last will, of course, be affected by such modifications of the system of expense as you shall think proper to adopt.

A statement has been formed by the Secretary of War, on mature consideration, of all the posts and stations where garrisons will be expedient and of the number of men requisite for each garrison. The whole amount is considerably short of the present military establishment. For the surplus no particular use can be pointed out. For defense against invasion their number is as nothing, nor is it conceived needful or safe that a standing army should be kept up in time of peace for that purpose. Uncertain as we must ever be of the particular point in our circumference where an enemy may choose to invade us, the only force which can be ready at every point and competent to oppose them is the body of neighboring citizens as formed into a militia. On these, collected from the parts most convenient in numbers proportioned to the invading force, it is best to rely not only to meet the first attack, but if it threatens to be permanent to maintain the defense until regulars may be engaged to relieve them. These considerations render it important that we should at every session continue to amend the defects which from time to time shew themselves in the laws for regulating the militia until they are sufficiently perfect. Nor should we now or at any time separate until we can say we have done everything for the militia which we could do were an enemy at our door.

The provision of military stores on hand will be laid before you, that you may judge of the additions still requisite.

With respect to the extent to which our naval preparations should be carried some difference of opinion may be expected to appear, but just attention to the circumstances of every part of the Union will doubtless reconcile all. A small force will probably continue to be wanted for actual service in the Mediterranean. Whatever annual sum beyond that you may think proper to appropriate to naval preparations would perhaps be better employed in providing those articles which may be kept without waste or consumption, and be in readiness when any exigence calls them into use. Progress has been made, as will appear by papers now communicated, in providing materials for 74-gun ships as directed by law.

How far the authority given by the Legislature for procuring and establishing sites for naval purposes has been perfectly understood and pursued in the execution admits of some doubt. A statement of the expenses already incurred on that subject is now laid before you. I have in certain cases suspended or slackened these expenditures, that the Legislature might determine whether so many yards are necessary as have been contemplated. The works at this place are among those permitted to go on, and five of the seven frigates directed to be laid up have been brought and laid up here, where, besides the safety of their position, they are under the eye of the Executive Administration, as well as of its agents, and where yourselves also will be guided by your own view in the legislative provisions respecting them which may from time to time be necessary. They are preserved in such condition, as well the vessels as whatever belongs to them, as to be at all times ready for sea on a short warning. Two others are yet to be laid up so soon as they shall have received the repairs requisite to put them also into sound condition. As a superintending officer will be necessary at each yard, his duties and emoluments, hitherto fixed by the Executive, will be a more proper subject for legislation. A communication will also be made of our progress in the execution of the law respecting the vessels directed to be sold.

The fortifications of our harbors, more or less advanced, present considerations of great difficulty. While some of them are on a scale sufficiently proportioned to the advantages of their position, to the efficacy of their protection, and the importance of the points within it, others are so extensive, will cost so much in their first erection, so much in their maintenance, and require such a force to garrison them as to make it questionable what is best now to be done. A statement of those commenced or projected, of the expenses already incurred, and estimates of their future cost, as far as can be foreseen, shall be laid before you, that you may be enabled to judge whether any alteration is necessary in the laws respecting this subject.

Agriculture, manufactures, commerce, and navigation, the four pillars of our prosperity, are then most thriving when left most free to individual enterprise. Protection from casual embarrassments, however, may sometimes be seasonably interposed. If in the course of your observations or inquiries they should appear to need any aid within the limits of our constitutional powers, your sense of their importance is a sufficient assurance they will occupy your attention. We can not, indeed, but all feel an anxious solicitude for the difficulties under which our carrying trade will soon be placed. How far it can be relieved, otherwise than by time, is a subject of important consideration.

The judiciary system of the United States, and especially that portion of it recently erected, will of course present itself to the contemplation of Congress, and, that they may be able to judge of the proportion which the institution bears to the business it has to perform, I have caused to be procured from the several States and now lay before Congress an exact statement of all the causes decided since the first establishment of the courts, and of those which were depending when additional courts and judges were brought in to their aid.

And while on the judiciary organization it will be worthy your consideration whether the protection of the inestimable institution of juries has been extended to all the cases involving the security of our persons and property. Their impartial selection also being essential to their value, we ought further to consider whether that is sufficiently secured in those States where they are named by a marshal depending on Executive will or designated by the court or by officers dependent on them.

I can not omit recommending a revisal of the laws on the subject of naturalization. Considering the ordinary chances of human life, a denial of citizenship under a residence of fourteen years is a denial to a great proportion of those who ask it, and controls a policy pursued from their first settlement by many of these States, and still believed of consequence to their prosperity; and shall we refuse to the unhappy fugitives from distress that hospitality which the savages of the wilderness extended to our fathers arriving in this land? Shall oppressed humanity find no asylum on this globe? The Constitution indeed has wisely provided that for admission to certain offices of important trust a residence shall be required sufficient to develop character and design. But might not the general character and capabilities of a citizen be safely communicated to everyone manifesting a bona fide purpose of embarking his life and fortunes permanently with us, with restrictions, perhaps, to guard against the fraudulent usurpation of our flag, an abuse which brings so much embarrassment and loss on the genuine citizen and so much danger to the nation of being involved in war that no endeavor should be spared to detect and suppress it?

These, fellow-citizens, are the matters respecting the state of the nation which I have thought of importance to be submitted to your consideration at this time. Some others of less moment or not yet ready for communication will be the subject of separate messages. I am happy in this opportunity of committing the arduous affairs of our Government to the collected wisdom of the Union. Nothing shall be wanting on my part to inform as far as in my power the legislative judgment, nor to carry that judgment into faithful execution. The prudence and temperance of your discussions will promote within your own walls that conciliation which so much befriends rational conclusion, and by its example will encourage among our constituents that progress of opinion which is tending to unite them in object and in will. That all should be satisfied with any one order of things is not to be expected; but I indulge the pleasing persuasion that the great body of our citizens will cordially concur in honest and disinterested efforts which have for their object to preserve the General and State Governments in their constitutional form and equilibrium; to maintain peace abroad, and order and obedience to the laws at home; to establish principles and practices of administration favorable to the security of liberty and property, and to reduce expenses to what is necessary for the useful purposes of Government.

TH: JEFFERSON.

SPECIAL MESSAGES.

DECEMBER 11, 1801.

Gentlemen of the Senate:

Early in the last month I received the ratification by the First Consul of France of the convention between the United States and that nation. His ratification not being pure and simple in the ordinary form, I have thought it my duty, in order to avoid all misconception, to ask a second advice and consent of the Senate before I give it the last sanction by proclaiming it to be a law of the land.

TH: JEFFERSON.

DECEMBER 22, 1801.

Gentlemen of the Senate:

The States of Georgia and Tennessee being peculiarly interested in our carrying into execution the two acts passed by Congress on the 19th of February, 1799 (chapter 115), and 13th May, 1800 (chapter 62), commissioners were appointed early in summer and other measures taken for the purpose. The objects of these laws requiring meetings with the Cherokees, Chickasaws, Choctaws, and Creeks, the inclosed instructions were prepared for the proceedings with the three first nations. Our applications to the Cherokees failed altogether. Those to the Chickasaws produced the treaty now laid before you for your advice and consent, whereby we obtained permission to open a road of communication with the Mississippi Territory. The commissioners are probably at this time in conference with the Choctaws. Further information having been wanting when these instructions were formed to enable us to prepare those respecting the Creeks, the commissioners were directed to proceed with the others. We have now reason to believe the conferences with the Creeks can not take place till the spring.

The journals and letters of the commissioners relating to the subject of the treaty now inclosed accompany it.

TH: JEFFERSON.

DECEMBER 22, 1801.

Gentlemen of the Senate and of the House of Representatives:

I now inclose sundry documents supplementary to those communicated to you with my message at the commencement of the session. Two others of considerable importance—the one relating to our transactions with the Barbary Powers, the other presenting a view of the offices of the Government—shall be communicated as soon as they can be completed.

TH: JEFFERSON.

DECEMBER 23, 1801.

Gentlemen of the Senate and of the House of Representatives:

Another return of the census of the State of Maryland is just received from the marshal of that State, which he desires may be substituted as more correct than the one first returned by him and communicated by me to Congress. This new return, with his letter, is now laid before you.

TH: JEFFERSON.

JANUARY 11, 1802.

Gentlemen of the Senate and of the House of Representatives.

I now communicate to you a memorial of the commissioners of the city of Washington, together with a letter of later date, which, with their memorial of January 28, 1801, will possess the Legislature fully of the state of the public interests and of those of the city of Washington confided to them. The moneys now due, and soon to become due, to the State of Maryland on the loan guaranteed by the United States call for an early attention. The lots in the city which are chargeable with the payment of these moneys are deemed not only equal to the indemnification of the public, but to insure a considerable surplus to the city to be employed for its improvement, provided they are offered for sale only in sufficient numbers to meet the existing demand. But the act of 1796 requires that they shall be positively sold in such numbers as shall be necessary for the punctual payment of the loans. Nine thousand dollars of interest are lately become due, $3,000 quarter yearly will continue to become due, and $50,000, an additional loan, are reimbursable on the 1st day of November next. These sums would require sales so far beyond the actual demand of the market that it is apprehended that the whole property may be thereby sacrificed, the public security destroyed, and the residuary interest of the city entirely lost. Under these circumstances I have thought it my duty before I proceed to direct a rigorous execution of the law to submit the subject to the consideration of the Legislature. Whether the public interest will be better secured in the end and that of the city saved by offering sales commensurate only to the demand at market, and advancing from the Treasury in the first instance what these may prove deficient, to be replaced by subsequent sales, rests for the determination of the Legislature. If indulgence for the funds can be admitted, they will probably form a resource of great and permanent value ; and their embarrassments have been produced only by overstrained exertions to provide accommodations for the Government of the Union.

TH: JEFFERSON.

JANUARY 12, 1802.

Gentlemen of the Senate:

I now communicate to you a letter from the Secretary of State inclosing an estimate of the expenses which appear at present necessary for carrying into effect the convention between the United States of America and the French Republic, which has been prepared at the request of the House of Representatives.

TH: JEFFERSON.

JANUARY 27, 1802.

Gentlemen of the Senate and of the House of Representatives:

I lay before you the accounts of our Indian trading houses, as rendered up to the 1st day of January, 1801, with a report of the Secretary of War thereon, explaining the effects and the situation of that commerce and the reasons in favor of its further extension. But it is believed that the act authorizing this trade expired so long ago as the 3d of March, 1799. Its revival, therefore, as well as its extension, is submitted to the consideration of the Legislature.

The act regulating trade and intercourse with the Indian tribes will also expire on the 3d day of March next. While on the subject of its continuance it will be worthy the consideration of the Legislature whether the provisions of the law inflicting on Indians, in certain cases, the punishment of death by hanging might not permit its commutation into death by military execution, the form of the punishment in the former way being peculiarly repugnant to their ideas and increasing the obstacles to the surrender of the criminal.

These people are becoming very sensible of the baneful effects produced on their morals, their health, and existence by the abuse of ardent spirits, and some of them earnestly desire a prohibition of that article from being carried among them. The Legislature will consider whether the effectuating that desire would not be in the spirit of benevolence and liberality which they have hitherto practiced toward these our neighbors, and which has had so happy an effect toward conciliating their friendship. It has been found, too, in experience that the same abuse gives frequent rise to incidents tending much to commit our peace with the Indians.

It is now become necessary to run and mark the boundaries between them and us in various parts. The law last mentioned has authorized this to be done, but no existing appropriation meets the expense.

Certain papers explanatory of the grounds of this communication are herewith inclosed.

TH: JEFFERSON.

FEBRUARY 2, 1802.

Gentlemen of the Senate and of the House of Representatives:

I now lay before you—

1. A return of ordnance, arms, and military stores the property of the United States.

2. Returns of muskets and bayonets fabricated at the armories of the United States at Springfield and Harpers Ferry, and of the expenditures at those places; and

3. An estimate of expenditures which may be necessary for fortifications and barracks for the present year.

Besides the permanent magazines established at Springfield, West Point, and Harpers Ferry, it is thought one should be established in some point convenient for the States of North Carolina, South Carolina, and Georgia. Such a point will probably be found near the border of the Carolinas, and some small provision by the Legislature preparatory to the establishment will be necessary for the present year.

We find the United States in possession of certain iron mines and works in the county of Berkeley and State of Virginia, purchased, as is presumable, on the idea of establishing works for the fabrication of cannon and other military articles by the public. Whether this method of supplying what may be wanted will be most advisable or that of purchasing at market where competition brings everything to its proper level of price and quality is for the Legislature to decide, and if the latter alternative be preferred, it will rest for their further consideration in what way the subjects of this purchase may be best employed or disposed of. The Attorney-General's opinion on the subject of the title accompanies this.

There are in various parts of the United States small parcels of land which have been purchased at different times for cantonments and other military purposes. Several of them are in situations not likely to be accommodated to future purposes. The loss of the records prevents a detailed statement of these until they can be supplied by inquiry. In the meantime, one of them, containing 88 acres, in the county of Essex, in New Jersey, purchased in 1799 and sold the following year to Cornelius Vermule and Andrew Codmas, though its price has been received, can not be conveyed without authority from the Legislature.

I inclose herewith a letter from the Secretary of War on the subject of the islands in the lakes and rivers of our northern boundary, and of certain lands in the neighborhood of some of our military posts, on which it may be expedient for the Legislature to make some provisions.

TH: JEFFERSON.

FEBRUARY 16, 1802.

Gentlemen of the Senate and of the House of Representatives:

I now transmit a statement of the expenses incurred by the United States in their transactions with the Barbary Powers, and a roll of the persons having office or employment under the United States, as was proposed in my messages of December 7 and 22. Neither is as perfect as could have been wished, and the latter not so much so as further time and inquiry may enable us to make it.

The great volume of these communications and the delay it would produce to make out a second copy will, I trust, be deemed a sufficient reason for sending one of them to the one House, and the other to the other, with a request that they may be interchanged for mutual information rather than to subject both to further delay.

TH: JEFFERSON.

FEBRUARY 18, 1802.

Gentlemen of the Senate and of the House of Representatives:

In a message of the 2d instant I inclosed a letter from the Secretary of War on the subject of certain lands in the neighborhood of our military posts on which it might be expedient for the Legislature to make some provisions. A letter recently received from the governor of Indiana presents some further views of the extent to which such provision may be needed. I therefore now transmit it for the information of Congress.

TH: JEFFERSON.

FEBRUARY 24, 1802.

Gentlemen of the Senate and of the House of Representatives:

I communicate to both Houses of Congress a report of the Secretary of the Treasury on the subject of our marine hospitals, which appear to require legislative attention.

As connected with the same subject, I also inclose information respecting the situation of our seamen and boatmen frequenting the port of New Orleans and suffering there from sickness and the want of accommodation. There is good reason to believe their numbers greater than stated in these papers. When we consider how great a proportion of the territory of the United States must communicate with that port singly, and how rapidly that territory is increasing its population and productions, it may perhaps be thought reasonable to make hospital provisions there of a different order from those at foreign ports generally.

TH: JEFFERSON.

FEBRUARY 25, 1802.

Gentlemen of the Senate and of the House of Representatives:

No occasion having arisen since the last account rendered by my predecessor of making use of any part of the moneys heretofore granted to defray the contingent charges of the Government, I now transmit to Congress an official statement thereof to the 31st day of December last, when the whole unexpended balance, amounting to $20,911.80, was carried to the credit of the surplus fund, as provided for by law, and this account consequently becomes finally closed.

TH: JEFFERSON.

FEBRUARY 26, 1802.

Gentlemen of the Senate and of the House of Representatives:

Some statements have been lately received of the causes decided or depending in the courts of the Union in certain States, supplementary or corrective of those from which was formed the general statement accompanying my message at the opening of the session. I therefore communicate them to Congress, with a report of the Secretary of State noting their effect on the former statement and correcting certain errors in it which arose partly from inexactitude in some of the returns and partly in analyzing, adding, and transcribing them while hurried in preparing the other voluminous papers accompanying that message.

TH: JEFFERSON.

MARCH 1, 1802.

Gentlemen of the Senate and of the House of Representatives:

I transmit for the information of Congress letters recently received from our consuls at Gibraltar and Algiers, presenting the latest view of the state of our affairs with the Barbary Powers. The sums due to the Government of Algiers are now fully paid up, and of the gratuity which had been promised to that of Tunis, and was in a course of preparation, a small portion only remains still to be finished and delivered.

TH: JEFFERSON.

MARCH 9, 1802.

Gentlemen of the Senate:

The governor of New York has desired that, in addition to the negotiations with certain Indians already authorized under the superintendence of John Taylor, further negotiations should be held with the Oneidas and other members of the Confederacy of the Six Nations for the purchase of lands in and for the State of New York, which they are willing to sell, as explained in the letter from the Secretary of War herewith sent. I have therefore thought it better to name a commissioner to superintend the negotiations specified with the Six Nations generally, or with any of them.

I do accordingly nominate John Taylor, of New York, to be commissioner for the United States, to hold a convention or conventions between the State of New York and the Confederacy of the Six Nations of Indians, or any of the nations composing it.

This nomination, if advised and consented to by the Senate, will comprehend and supersede that of February 1 of the same John Taylor so far as it respected the Seneca Indians.

TH: JEFFERSON.

MARCH 10, 1802.

Gentlemen of the Senate:

I now submit for the ratification of the Senate a treaty entered into by the commissioners of the United States with the Choctaw Nation of Indians, and I transmit therewith so much of the instructions to the commissioners as related to the Choctaws, with the minutes of their proceedings and the letter accompanying them.

TH: JEFFERSON.

MARCH 29, 1802.

Gentlemen of the Senate and of the House of Representatives:

The Secretary of State, charged with the civil affairs of the several Territories of the United States, has received from the marshal of Columbia a statement of the condition, unavoidably distressing, of the persons committed to his custody on civil or criminal process and the urgency for some legislative provisions for their relief. There are other important cases wherein the laws of the adjoining States under which the Territory is placed, though adapted to the purposes of those States, are insufficient for those of the Territory from the dissimilar or defective organization of its authorities. The letter and statement of the marshal and the disquieting state of the Territory generally are now submitted to the wisdom and consideration of the Legislature.

TH: JEFFERSON.

MARCH 29, 1802.

Gentlemen of the Senate:

The commissioners who were appointed to carry into execution the sixth article of the treaty of amity, commerce, and navigation between the United States and His Britannic Majesty having differed in opinion as to the objects of that article and discontinued their proceedings, the Executive of the United States took early measures, by instructions to our minister at the British Court, to negotiate explanations of that article. This mode of resolving the difficulty, however, proved unacceptable to the British Government, which chose rather to avoid all further discussion and expense under that article by fixing at a given sum the amount for which the United States should be held responsible under it. Mr. King was consequently authorized to meet this proposition, and a settlement in this way has been effected by a convention entered into with the British Government, and now communicated for your advice and consent, together with the instructions and correspondence relating to it. The greater part of these papers being originals, the return of them is requested at the convenience of the Senate.

TH: JEFFERSON.

MARCH 30, 1802.

Gentlemen of the Senate and of the House of Representatives:

The Secretary of War has prepared an estimate of expenditures for the Army of the United States during the year 1802, conformably to the act fixing the military peace establishment, which estimate, with his letter accompanying and explaining it, I now transmit to both Houses of Congress.

TH: JEFFERSON.

MARCH 31, 1802.

Gentlemen of the House of Representatives:

According to the desire expressed in your resolution of the 23d instant, I now transmit a report of the Secretary of State, with the letters it refers to, shewing the proceedings which have taken place under the resolution of Congress of the 16th of April, 1800. The term prescribed for the execution of the resolution having elapsed before the person appointed had sat out on the service, I did not deem it justifiable to commence a course of expenditure after the expiration of the resolution authorizing it. The correspondence which has taken place, having regard to dates, will place this subject properly under the view of the House of Representatives.

TH: JEFFERSON.

APRIL 8, 1802.

Gentlemen of the Senate:

In order to satisfy as far as it is in my power the desire expressed in your resolution of the 6th instant, I now transmit you a letter from John Read, agent for the United States before the board of commissioners under the sixth article of the treaty with Great Britain, to the Attorney-General, bearing date the 25th of April, 1801, in which he gives a summary view of the proceedings of those commissioners and of the principles established or insisted on by a majority of them.

Supposing it might be practicable for us to settle by negotiation with Great Britain the principles which ought to govern the decisions under the treaty, I caused instructions to be given to Mr. Read to analyze the claims before the board of commissioners, to class them under the principles on which they respectively depended, and to state the sum depending on each principle or the amount of each description of debt. The object of this was that we might know what principles were most important for us to contend for and what others might be conceded without much injury. He performed this duty, and gave in such a statement during the last summer, but the chief clerk of the Secretary of State's office being absent on account of sickness, and the only person acquainted with the arrangement of the papers of the office, this particular document can not at this time be found. Having, however, been myself in possession of it a few days after its receipt, I then transcribed from it for my own use the recapitulation of the amount of each description of debt. A copy of this transcript I shall subjoin hereto, with assurances that it is substantially correct, and with the hope that it will give a view of the subject sufficiently precise to fulfill the wishes of the Senate. To save them the delay of waiting till a copy of the agent's letter could be made, I send the original, with the request that it may be returned at the convenience of the Senate.

TH: JEFFERSON.

APRIL 15, 1802.

Gentlemen of the House of Representatives:

I now transmit the papers desired in your resolution of the 6th instant. Those respecting the *Berceau* will sufficiently explain themselves. The officer charged with her repairs states in his letter, received August 27, 1801, that he had been led by circumstances, which he explains, to go considerably beyond his orders. In questions between nations, who have no common umpire but reason, something must often be yielded of mutual opinion to enable them to meet in a common point.

The allowance which had been proposed to the officers of that vessel being represented as too small for their daily necessities, and still more so as the means of paying before their departure debts contracted with our citizens for subsistence, it was requested on their behalf that the daily pay of each might be the measure of their allowance.

This being solicited and reimbursement assumed by the agent of their nation, I deemed that the indulgence would have a propitious effect in the moment of returning friendship. The sum of $870.83 was accordingly furnished them for the five months of past captivity and a proportional allowance authorized until their embarkation.

TH: JEFFERSON.

APRIL 20, 1802.

Gentlemen of the House of Representatives:

I transmit you a report from the Secretary of State, with the information desired by the House of Representatives, of the 8th of January, relative to certain spoliations and other proceedings therein referred to.

TH: JEFFERSON.

APRIL 26, 1802.

Gentlemen of the Senate and of the House of Representatives:

In pursuance of the act entitled "An act supplemental to the act entitled 'An act for an amicable settlement of limits with the State of Georgia, and authorizing the establishment of a government in the Mississippi Territory,'" James Madison, Secretary of State, Albert Gallatin, Secretary of the Treasury, and Levi Lincoln, Attorney-General of the United States, were appointed commissioners to settle by compromise with the commissioners appointed by the State of Georgia the claims and cession to which the said act has relation.

Articles of agreement and cession have accordingly been entered into and signed by the said commissioners of the United States and of Georgia, which, as they leave a right to Congress to act upon them legislatively at any time within six months after their date, I have thought it my duty immediately to communicate to the Legislature.

TH: JEFFERSON.

APRIL 27, 1802.

Gentlemen of the Senate and of the House of Representatives:

The commissioners who were appointed to carry into execution the sixth article of the treaty of amity, commerce, and navigation between the United States and Great Britain having differed in their construction of that article, and separated in consequence of that difference, the President of the United States took immediate measures for obtaining conventional explanations of that article for the government of the commissioners. Finding, however, great difficulties opposed to a settlement in that way, he authorized our minister at the Court of London to meet a proposition that the United States by the payment of a fixed sum should discharge themselves from their responsibility for such debts as can not be recovered from the individual debtors. A convention has accordingly been signed, fixing the sum to be paid at £600,000 in three equal and annual installments, which has been ratified by me with the advice and consent of the Senate.

I now transmit copies thereof to both Houses of Congress, trusting that in the free exercise of the authority which the Constitution has given them on the subject of public expenditures they will deem it for the public interest to appropriate the sums necessary for carrying this convention into execution.

TH: JEFFERSON.

SECOND ANNUAL MESSAGE.

DECEMBER 15, 1802.

To the Senate and House of Representatives of the United States:

When we assemble together, fellow-citizens, to consider the state of our beloved country, our just attentions are first drawn to those pleasing circumstances which mark the goodness of that Being from whose favor they flow and the large measure of thankfulness we owe for His bounty. Another year has come around, and finds us still blessed with peace and friendship abroad; law, order, and religion at home; good affection and harmony with our Indian neighbors; our burthens lightened, yet our income sufficient for the public wants, and the produce of the year great beyond example. These, fellow-citizens, are the circumstances under which we meet, and we remark with special satisfaction those which under the smiles of Providence result from the skill, industry, and order of our citizens, managing their own affairs in their own way and for their own use, unembarrassed by too much regulation, unoppressed by fiscal exactions.

On the restoration of peace in Europe that portion of the general carrying trade which had fallen to our share during the war was abridged by the returning competition of the belligerent powers. This was to be expected, and was just. But in addition we find in some parts of Europe monopolizing discriminations, which in the form of duties tend effectually to prohibit the carrying thither our own produce in our own vessels. From existing amities and a spirit of justice it is hoped that friendly discussion will produce a fair and adequate reciprocity. But should false calculations of interest defeat our hope, it rests with the Legislature to decide whether they will meet inequalities abroad with countervailing inequalities at home, or provide for the evil in any other way.

It is with satisfaction I lay before you an act of the British Parliament anticipating this subject so far as to authorize a mutual abolition of the duties and countervailing duties permitted under the treaty of 1794. It shows on their part a spirit of justice and friendly accommodation which it is our duty and our interest to cultivate with all nations. Whether this would produce a due equality in the navigation between the two countries is a subject for your consideration.

Another circumstance which claims attention as directly affecting the very source of our navigal is the defect or the evasion of the law providing for the return of sea en, and particularly of those belonging to vessels sold abroad. Numbers of them, discharged in foreign ports, have been thrown on the hands of our consuls, who, to rescue them from the dangers into which their distresses might plunge them and save them to their country, have found it necessary in some cases to return them at the public charge.

The cession of the Spanish Province of Louisiana to France, which took place in the course of the late war, will, if carried into effect, make a change in the aspect of our foreign relations which will doubtless have just weight in any deliberations of the Legislature connected with that subject.

There was reason not long since to apprehend that the warfare in which we were engaged with Tripoli might be taken up by some other of the Barbary Powers. A reenforcement, therefore, was immediately ordered to the vessels already there. Subsequent information, however, has removed these apprehensions for the present. To secure our commerce in that sea with the smallest force competent, we have supposed it best to watch strictly the harbor of Tripoli. Still, however, the shallowness of their coast and the want of smaller vessels on our part has permitted some cruisers to escape unobserved, and to one of these an American vessel unfortunately fell a prey. The captain, one American seaman, and two others of color remain prisoners with them unless exchanged under an agreement formerly made with the Bashaw, to whom, on the faith of that, some of his captive subjects had been restored.

The convention with the State of Georgia has been ratified by their legislature, and a repurchase from the Creeks has been consequently made of a part of the Talasscee country. In this purchase has been also comprehended a part of the lands within the fork of Oconee and Oakmulgee rivers. The particulars of the contract will be laid before Congress so soon as they shall be in a state for communication.

In order to remove every ground of difference possible with our Indian neighbors, I have proceeded in the work of settling with them and marking the boundaries between us. That with the Choctaw Nation is fixed in one part and will be through the whole within a short time. The country to which their title had been extinguished before the Revolution is sufficient to receive a very respectable population, which Congress will probably see the expediency of encouraging so soon as the limits shall be declared. We are to view this position as an outpost of the United States, surrounded by strong neighbors and distant from its support; and how far that monopoly which prevents population should here be guarded against and actual habitation made a condition of the continuance of title will be for your consideration. A prompt settlement, too, of all existing rights and claims within this territory presents itself as a preliminary operation.

In that part of the Indiana Territory wh .includes Vincennes the lines settled with the neighboring tribes fix the extinction of their title at a breadth of 24 leagues from east to west and about the same length parallel with and including the Wabash. They have also ceded a tract of 4 miles square, including the salt springs near the mouth of that river.

In the Department of Finance it is with pleasure I inform you that the receipts of external duties for the last twelve months have exceeded those of any former year, and that the ratio of increase has been also greater than usual. This has enabled us to answer all the regular exigencies of Government, to pay from the Treasury within one year upward of $8,000,000, principal and interest, of the public debt, exclusive of upward of one million paid by the sale of bank stock, and making in the whole a reduction of nearly five millions and a half of principal, and to have now in the Treasury $4,500,000, which are in a course of application to the further discharge of debt and current demands. Experience, too, so far, authorizes us to believe, if no extraordinary event supervenes, and the expenses which will be actually incurred shall not be greater than were contemplated by Congress at their last session, that we shall not be disappointed in the expectations then formed. But nevertheless, as the effect of peace on the amount of duties is not yet fully ascertained, it is the more necessary to practice every useful economy and to incur no expense which may be avoided without prejudice.

The collection of the internal taxes having been completed in some of the States, the officers employed in it are of course out of commission. In others they will be so shortly. But in a few, where the arrangements for the direct tax had been retarded, it will be some time before the system is closed. It has not yet been thought necessary to employ the agent authorized by an act of the last session for transacting business in Europe relative to debts and loans. Nor have we used the power confided by the same act of prolonging the foreign debt by reloans, and of redeeming instead thereof an equal sum of the domestic debt. Should, however, the difficulties of remittance on so large a scale render it necessary at any time, the power shall be executed and the money thus unemployed abroad shall, in conformity with that law, be faithfully applied here in an equivalent extinction of domestic debt. When effects so salutary result from the plans you have already sanctioned; when merely by avoiding false objects of expense we are able, without a direct tax, without internal taxes, and without borrowing to make large and effectual payments toward the discharge of our public debt and the emancipation of our posterity from that mortal canker, it is an encouragement, fellow-citizens, of the highest order to proceed as we have begun in substituting economy for taxation, and in pursuing what is useful for a nation placed as we are, rather than what is practiced by others under different circumstances. And whensoever we are destined to meet events which shall call forth all the energies of our countrymen, we have the firmest reliance on those energies and the comfort of leaving for calls like these the extraordinary resources of loans and internal taxes. In the meantime, by payments of the principal of our debt, we are liberating annually portions of the external taxes and forming from them a growing fund still further to lessen the necessity of recurring to extraordinary resources.

The usual account of receipts and expenditures for the last year, with an estimate of the expenses of the ensuing one, will be laid before you by the Secretary of the Treasury.

No change being deemed necessary in our military establishment, an estimate of its expenses for the ensuing year on its present footing, as also of the sums to be employed in fortifications and other objects within that department, has been prepared by the Secretary of War, and will make a part of the general estimates which will be presented you.

Considering that our regular troops are employed for local purposes, and that the militia is our general reliance for great and sudden emergencies, you will doubtless think this institution worthy of a review, and give it those improvements of which you find it susceptible.

Estimates for the Naval Department, prepared by the Secretary of the Navy, for another year will in like manner be communicated with the general estimates. A small force in the Mediterranean will still be necessary to restrain the Tripoline cruisers, and the uncertain tenure of peace with some other of the Barbary Powers may eventually require that force to be augmented. The necessity of procuring some smaller vessels for that service will raise the estimate, but the difference in their maintenance will soon make it a measure of economy.

Presuming it will be deemed expedient to expend annually a convenient sum toward providing the naval defense which our situation may require, I can not but recommend that the first appropriations for that purpose may go to the saving what we already possess. No cares, no attentions, can preserve vessels from rapid decay which lie in water and exposed to the sun. These decays require great and constant repairs, and will consume, if continued, a great portion of the moneys destined to naval purposes. To avoid this waste of our resources it is proposed to add to our navy-yard here a dock within which our present vessels may be laid up dry and under cover from the sun. Under these circumstances experience proves that works of wood will remain scarcely at all affected by time. The great abundance of running water which this situation possesses, at heights far above the level of the tide, if employed as is practiced for lock navigation, furnishes the means for raising and laying up our vessels on a dry and sheltered bed. And should the measure be found useful here, similar depositories for laying up as well as for building and repairing vessels may hereafter be undertaken at other navy-yards offering the same means. The plans and estimates of the work, prepared by a person of skill and experience, will be presented to you without delay, and from this it will be seen that scarcely more than has been the cost of one vessel is necessary to save the whole, and that the annual sum to be employed toward its completion may be adapted to the views of the Legislature as to naval expenditure.

To cultivate peace and maintain commerce and navigation in all their lawful enterprises; to foster our fisheries as nurseries of navigation and for the nurture of man, and protect the manufactures adapted to our circumstances; to preserve the faith of the nation by an exact discharge of its debts and contracts, expend the public money with the same care and economy we would practice with our own, and impose on our citizens no unnecessary burthens; to keep in all things within the pale of our constitutional powers, and cherish the federal union as the only rock of safety— these, fellow-citizens, are the landmarks by which we are to guide ourselves in all our proceedings. By continuing to make these the rule of our action we shall endear to our countrymen the true principles of their Constitution and promote an union of sentiment and of action equally auspicious to their happiness and safety. On my part, you may count on a cordial concurrence in every measure for the public good and on all the information I possess which may enable you to discharge to advantage the high functions with which you are invested by your country.

TH: JEFFERSON.

SPECIAL MESSAGES.

DECEMBER 22, 1802.

Gentlemen of the House of Representatives:

I now transmit a report from the Secretary of State with the information requested in your resolution of the 17th instant.

In making this communication I deem it proper to observe that I was led by the regard due to the rights and interests of the United States and to the just sensibility of the portion of our fellow-citizens more immediately affected by the irregular proceeding at New Orleans to lose not a moment in causing every step to be taken which the occasion claimed from me, being equally aware of the obligation to maintain in all cases the rights of the nation and to employ for that purpose those just and honorable means which belong to the character of the United States.

TH: JEFFERSON.

DECEMBER 23, 1802.

Gentlemen of the House of Representatives.

In pursuance of the resolution of the House of Representatives of the 3d of May last, desiring a statement of expenditures from January 1, 1797, by the Quartermaster-General and the navy agents, for the contingencies of the naval and military establishments and the navy contracts for timber and stores, I now transmit such statements from the offices of the Secretaries of the Treasury, War, and Navy, where alone these expenditures are entered.

TH: JEFFERSON.

DECEMBER 27, 1802.

Gentlemen of the Senate:

I lay before you a treaty, which has been agreed to by commissioners duly authorized on the part of the United States and the Creek Nation of Indians, for the extinguishment of the native title to lands in the Talassee County, and others between the forks of Oconee and Oakmulgee rivers, in Georgia, in pursuance of the convention with that State, together with the documents explanatory thereof; and it is submitted to your determination whether you will advise and consent to the ratification thereof.

TH: JEFFERSON.

DECEMBER 27, 1802.

Gentlemen of the Senate:

I lay before you a treaty, which has been concluded between the State of New York and the Oneida Indians, for the purchase of lands within that State.

One other, between the same State and the Seneca Indians, for the purchase of other lands within the same State.

One other, between certain individuals styled the Holland Company with the Senecas, for the exchange of certain lands in the same State.

And one other, between Oliver Phelps, a citizen of the United States, and the Senecas, for the exchange of lands in the same State; with sundry explanatory papers, all of them conducted under the superintendence of a commissioner on the part of the United States, who reports that they have been adjusted with the fair and free consent and understanding of the parties. It is therefore submitted to your determination whether you will advise and consent to their respective ratifications.

TH: JEFFERSON.

DECEMBER 27, 1802.

Gentlemen of the Senate and of the House of Representatives:

In my message of the 15th instant I mentioned that plans and estimates of a dry dock for the preservation of our ships of war, prepared by a person of skill and experience, should be laid before you without delay. These are now transmitted, the report and estimates by duplicates; but the plans being single only, I must request an intercommunication of them between the Houses and their return when they shall no longer be wanting for their consideration.

TH: JEFFERSON.

DECEMBER 30, 1802.

Gentlemen of the House of Representatives:

In addition to the information accompanying my message of the 22d instant, I now transmit the copy of a letter on the same subject, recently received.

TH: JEFFERSON.

WASHINGTON, *December 30, 1802.*

The SPEAKER OF THE HOUSE OF REPRESENTATIVES.

SIR: Although an informal communication to the public of the substance of the inclosed letter may be proper for quieting the public mind, yet I refer to the consideration of the House of Representatives whether the publication of it in form might not give dissatisfaction to the writer and tend to discourage the freedom and confidence of communications between the agents of the two Governments. Accept assurances of my high consideration and respect.

TH: JEFFERSON.

NATCHEZ, *November 25, 1802.*

The Honorable the SECRETARY OF STATE,
Washington.

SIR: I have the honor to inclose you an original copy of a communication (together with a translation thereof) which I this morning received from the governor-general of the Province of Louisiana in answer to my letters of the 28th ultimo.

I am, sir, with respect and esteem, your humble servant,

WILLIAM C. C. CLAIBORNE.

[Translation.]

NEW ORLEANS, *November 15, 1802.*

His Excellency WILLIAM C. C. CLAIBORNE.

MOST EXCELLENT SIR: I received a few days past your excellency's esteemed letter of the 28th ultimo, in which your excellency, referring to the twenty-second article of the treaty of friendship, navigation, and limits agreed upon between the King, my master, and the United States of America, has been pleased to inquire, after transcribing the literal text of said article (which you find so explicit as not to require any comment nor to admit of dubious construction), if His Majesty has been pleased to designate any other position on the banks of the Mississippi, and where that is, if his royal pleasure does not continue the permission stipulated by the said treaty which entitled the citizens of the United States to deposit their merchandise and effects in the port of New Orleans; and you request at the same time that, as the affair is so interesting to the commerce of the United States and to the welfare of its citizens, I may do you the favor to send you an answer as early as possible. I can now assure your excellency that His Catholic Majesty has not hitherto issued any order for suspending the deposit, and consequently has not designated any other position on the banks of the Mississippi for that purpose. But I must inform you, in answer to your inquiry, that the intendant of these provinces (who in the affairs of his own department is independent of the general Government), at the same time that, in conformity with the royal commands (the peace in Europe having been published since the 4th of May last), he suspended the commerce of neutrals, also thought proper to suspend the tacit prolongation which continued, and to put a stop to the infinite abuses which resulted from the deposit, contrary to the interest of the State and of the commerce of these colonies, in consequence of the experience he acquired of the frauds which have been committed and which it has been endeavored to excuse under the pretext of ignorance, as is manifested by the number of causes which now await the determination of His Majesty, as soon as they can be brought to his royal knowledge, besides many others which have been dropt because the individuals have absconded who introduced their properties into the deposit and did not extract them, thus defrauding the royal interests.

It might appear on the first view that particular cases like these ought not to operate against a general privilege granted by a solemn treaty, and it is an incontestable principle that the happiness of nations consists in a great measure in maintaining a good harmony and correspondence with their neighbors by respecting their rights, by supporting their own, without being deficient in what is required by humanity and civil intercourse; but it is also indubitable that for a treaty, although solemn, to be entirely valid it ought not to contain any defect; and if it be pernicious and of an injurious tendency, although it has been effectuated with good faith but without a knowledge of its bad consequence, it will be necessary to undo it, because treaties ought to be viewed like other acts of public will, in which more attention ought to be paid to the intention than to the words in which they are expressed; and thus it will not appear so repugnant that the term of three years fixed by the twenty-second article being completed without the King's having granted a prolongation, the intendancy should not, after putting a stop to the commerce of neutrals, take upon itself the responsibility of continuing that favor without the express mandate of the King, a circumstance equally indispensable for designating another place on the banks of the Mississippi.

From the foregoing I trust that you will infer that as it is the duty of the intendant, who conducts the business of his ministry with a perfect independence of the Government, to have informed the King of what he has done in fulfillment of what has been expressly stipulated, it is to be hoped that His Majesty will take the measures which are convenient to give effect to the deposit, either in this capital, if he should not find it prejudicial to the interests of Spain, or in the place on the banks of the Mississippi which it may be his royal pleasure to designate; as it ought to be confided that the justice and generosity of the King will not refuse to afford to the American citizens all the advantages they can desire, a measure which does not depend upon discretion, nor can an individual chief take it upon himself. Besides these principles on which the regulation of the intendant is founded, I ought at the same time to inform you that I myself opposed on my part, as far as I reasonably could, the measure of suspending the deposit, until the reasons adduced by the intendant brought it to my view; that as all events can not be prevented, and as with time and different circumstances various others occur which can not be foreseen, a just and rational interpretation is always necessary. Notwithstanding the foregoing, the result of my own reflections, I immediately consulted on the occasion with my captain-general, whose answer, which can not be long delayed, will dissipate every doubt that may be raised concerning the steps which are to be taken. By all means your excellency may live in the firm persuasion that as there has subsisted, and does subsist, the most perfect and constant good harmony between the King, my master, and the United States of America, I will spare no pains to preserve it by all the means in my power, being assured of a reciprocity of equal good offices in observing the treaty with good faith, ever keeping it in view that the felicity and glory of nations are deeply concerned in the advantages of a wise and prudently conducted commerce.

I have the honor to assure your excellency of the respect and high consideration which I profess for you; and I pray the Most High to preserve your life many years.

I kiss your excellency's hands.

Your most affectionate servant,

MANUEL DE SALCEDO.

JANUARY 5, 1803.

Gentlemen of the House of Representatives:

Agreeably to the request of the House of Representatives, I now transmit a statement of the militia of those States from which any returns have been made to the War Office. They are, as you will perceive, but a small proportion of the whole. I send you also the copy of a circular letter written some time since for the purpose of obtaining returns from all the States. Should any others in consequence of this be made during the session of Congress, they shall be immediately communicated.

TH: JEFFERSON.

JANUARY 7, 1803.

Gentlemen of the Senate:

I submit for your approbation and consent a convention entered into with the Choctaw Nation of Indians for ascertaining and marking the limits of the territory ceded to our nation while under its former government, and lying between the Tombigbee and Mobile rivers on the east and the Chickasawhay River on the west.

We are now engaged in ascertaining and marking in like manner the limits of the former cessions of the Choctaws from the river Yazoo to our southern boundary, which will be the subject of another convention, and we expect to obtain from the same nation a new cession of lands of considerable extent between the Tombigbee and Alabama rivers.

These several tracts of country will compose that portion of the Mississippi Territory which, so soon as certain individual claims are arranged, the United States will be free to sell and settle immediately.

TH: JEFFERSON

JANUARY 11, 1803.

Gentlemen of the Senate:

The cession of the Spanish Province of Louisiana to France, and perhaps of the Floridas, and the late suspension of our right of deposit at New Orleans are events of primary interest to the United States. On both occasions such measures were promptly taken as were thought most likely amicably to remove the present and to prevent future causes of inquietude. The objects of these measures were to obtain the territory on the left bank of the Mississippi and eastward of that, if practicable, on conditions to which the proper authorities of our country would agree, or at least to prevent any changes which might lessen the secure exercise of our rights. While my confidence in our minister plenipotentiary at Paris is entire and undiminished, I still think that these objects might be promoted by joining with him a person sent from hence directly, carrying with him the feelings and sentiments of the nation excited on the late occurrence, impressed by full communications of all the views we entertain on this interesting subject, and thus prepared to meet and to improve to an useful result the counter propositions of the other contracting party, whatsoever form their interests may give to them, and to secure to us the ultimate accomplishment of our object.

I therefore nominate Robert R. Livingston to be minister plenipotentiary and James Monroe to be minister extraordinary and plenipotentiary, with full powers to both jointly, or to either on the death of the other, to enter into a treaty or convention with the First Consul of France for the purpose of enlarging and more effectually securing our rights and interests in the river Mississippi and in the Territories eastward thereof.

But as the possession of these provinces is still in Spain, and the course of events may retard or prevent the cession to France being carried into effect, to secure our object it will be expedient to address equal powers to the Government of Spain also, to be used only in the event of its being necessary.

I therefore nominate Charles Pinckney to be minister plenipotentiary, and James Monroe, of Virginia, to be minister extraordinary and plenipotentiary, with full powers to both jointly, or to either on the death of the other, to enter into a treaty or convention with His Catholic Majesty for the purpose of enlarging and more effectually securing our rights and interests in the river Mississippi and in the Territories eastward thereof.

TH: JEFFERSON.

JANUARY 11, 1803.

Gentlemen of the Senate:

The spoliations and irregularities committed on our commerce during the late war by subjects of Spain or by others deemed within her responsibility having called for attention, instructions were accordingly given to our minister at Madrid to urge our right to just indemnifications, and to propose a convention for adjusting them. The Spanish Government listened to our proposition with an honorable readiness and agreed to a convention, which I now submit for your advice and consent. It does not go to the satisfaction of all our claims, but the express reservation of our right to press the validity of the residue has been made the ground of further instructions to our minister on the subject of an additional article, which it is to be hoped will not be without effect.

TH: JEFFERSON.

JANUARY 18, 1803.

Gentlemen of the Senate and of the House of Representatives:

As the continuance of the act for establishing trading houses with the Indian tribes will be under the consideration of the Legislature at its present session, I think it my duty to communicate the views which have guided me in the execution of that act, in order that you may decide on the policy of continuing it in the present or any other form, or discontinue it altogether if that shall, on the whole, seem most for the public good.

The Indian tribes residing within the limits of the United States have for a considerable time been growing more and more uneasy at the constant diminution of the territory they occupy, although effected by their own voluntary sales, and the policy has long been gaining strength with them of refusing absolutely all further sale on any conditions, insomuch that at this time it hazards their friendship and excites dangerous jealousies and perturbations in their minds to make any overture for the purchase of the smallest portions of their land. A very few tribes only are not yet obstinately in these dispositions. In order peaceably to counteract this policy of theirs and to provide an extension of territory which the rapid increase of our numbers will call for, two measures are deemed expedient. First. To encourage them to abandon hunting, to apply to the raising stock, to agriculture, and domestic manufacture, and thereby prove to themselves that less land and labor will maintain them in this better than in their former mode of living. The extensive forests necessary in the hunting life will then become useless, and they will see advantage in exchanging them for the means of improving their farms and of increasing their domestic comforts. Secondly. To multiply trading houses among them, and place within their reach those things which will contribute more to their domestic comfort than the possession of extensive but uncultivated wilds. Experience and reflection will develop to them the wisdom of exchanging what they can spare and we want for what we can spare and they want. In leading them thus to agriculture, to manufactures, and civilization; in bringing together their and our sentiments, and in preparing them ultimately to participate in the benefits of our Government, I trust and believe we are acting for their greatest good. At these trading houses we have pursued the principles of the act of Congress which directs that the commerce shall be carried on liberally, and requires only that the capital stock shall not be diminished. We consequently undersell private traders, foreign and domestic, drive them from the competition, and thus, with the good will of the Indians, rid ourselves of a description of men who are constantly endeavoring to excite in the Indian mind suspicions, fears, and irritations toward us. A letter now inclosed shows the effect of our competition on the operations of the traders, while the Indians, perceiving the advantage of purchasing from us, are soliciting generally our establishment of trading houses among them. In one quarter this is particularly interesting. The Legislature, reflecting on the late occurrences on the Mississippi, must be sensible how desirable it is to possess a respectable breadth of country on that river, from our southern limit to the Illinois, at least, so that we may present as firm a front on that as on our eastern border. We possess what is below the Yazoo, and can probably acquire a certain breadth from the Illinois and Wabash to the Ohio; but between the Ohio and Yazoo the country all belongs to the Chickasaws, the most friendly tribe within our limits, but the most decided against the alienation of lands. The portion of their country most important for us is exactly that which they do not inhabit. Their settlements are not on the Mississippi, but in the interior country. They have lately shown a desire to become agricultural, and this leads to the desire of buying implements and comforts. In the strengthening and gratifying of these wants I see the only prospect of planting on the Mississippi itself the means of its own safety. Duty has required me to submit these views to the judgment of the Legislature, but as their disclosure might embarrass and defeat their effect, they are committed to the special confidence of the two Houses.

While the extension of the public commerce among the Indian tribes may deprive of that source of profit such of our citizens as are engaged in it, it might be worthy the attention of Congress in their care of individual as well as of the general interest to point in another direction the enterprise of these citizens, as profitably for themselves and more usefully for the public. The river Missouri and the Indians inhabiting it are not as well known as is rendered desirable by their connection with the Mississippi, and consequently with us. It is, however, understood that the country on that river is inhabited by numerous tribes, who furnish great supplies of furs and peltry to the trade of another nation, carried on in a high latitude through an infinite number of portages and lakes shut up by ice through a long season. The commerce on that line could bear no competition with that of the Missouri, traversing a moderate climate, offering, according to the best accounts, a continued navigation from its source, and possibly with a single portage from the Western Ocean, and finding to the Atlantic a choice of channels through the Illinois or Wabash, the Lakes and Hudson, through the Ohio and Susquehanna, or Potomac or James rivers, and through the Tennessee and Savannah rivers. An intelligent officer, with ten or twelve chosen men, fit for the enterprise and willing to undertake it, taken from our posts where they may be spared without inconvenience, might explore the whole line, even to the Western Ocean, have conferences with the natives on the subject of commercial intercourse, get admission among them for our traders as others are admitted, agree on convenient deposits for an interchange of articles, and return with the information acquired in the course of two summers. Their arms and accouterments, some instruments of observation, and light and cheap presents for the Indians would be all the apparatus they could carry, and with an expectation of a soldier's portion of land on their return would constitute the whole expense. Their pay would be going on whether here or there. While other civilized nations have encountered great expense to enlarge the boundaries of knowledge by undertaking voyages of discovery, and for other literary purposes, in various parts and directions, our nation seems to owe to the same object, as well as to its own interests, to explore this the only line of easy communication across the continent, and so directly traversing our own part of it. The interests of commerce place the principal object within the constitutional powers and care of Congress, and that it should incidentally advance the geographical knowledge of our own continent can not but be an additional gratification. The nation claiming the territory, regarding this as a literary pursuit, which it is in the habit of permitting within its dominions, would not be disposed to view it with jealousy, even if the expiring state of its interests there did not render it a matter of indifference. The appropriation of $2,500 "for the purpose of extending the external commerce of the United States," while understood and considered by the Executive as giving the legislative sanction, would cover the undertaking from notice and prevent the obstructions which interested individuals might otherwise previously prepare in its way.

TH: JEFFERSON.

JANUARY 18, 1803.

Gentlemen of the Senate and of the House of Representatives:

I inclose a report of the Secretary of War, stating the trading houses established in the Indian territories, the progress which has been made in the course of the last year in settling and marking boundaries with the different tribes, the purchases of lands recently made from them, and the prospect of further progress in marking boundaries and in new extinguishments of title in the year to come, for which some appropriations of money will be wanting.

To this I have to add that when the Indians ceded to us the salt springs on the Wabash they expressed a hope that we would so employ them as to enable them to procure there the necessary supplies of salt. Indeed, it would be the most proper and acceptable form in which the annuity could be paid which we propose to give them for the cession. These springs might at the same time be rendered eminently serviceable to our

Western inhabitants by using them as the means of counteracting the monopolies of supplies of salt and of reducing the price in that country to a just level. For these purposes a small appropriation would be necessary to meet the first expenses, after which they should support themselves and repay those advances. These springs are said to possess the advantage of being accompanied with a bed of coal.

TH: JEFFERSON.

JANUARY 19, 1803.

Gentlemen of the Senate and of the House of Representatives:

I now lay before Congress the annual account of the fund established for defraying the contingent charges of Government. A single article of $1,440, paid for bringing home 72 seamen discharged in foreign ports from vessels sold abroad, is the only expenditure from that fund, leaving an unexpended balance of $18,560 in the Treasury.

TH: JEFFERSON.

JANUARY 24, 1803.

Gentlemen of the Senate and of the House of Representatives:

I transmit a report by the superintendent of the city of Washington on the affairs of the city committed to his care. By this you will perceive that the resales of lots prescribed by an act of the last session of Congress did not produce a sufficiency to pay the debt to Maryland to which they are appropriated, and as it was evident that the sums necessary for the interest and installments due to that State could not be produced by a sale of the other public lots without an unwarrantable sacrifice of the property, the deficiencies were of necessity drawn from the Treasury of the United States.

The office of the surveyor for the city, created during the former establishment, being of indispensable necessity, it has been continued, and to that of the superintendent, substituted instead of the board of commissioners at the last session of Congress, no salary was annexed by law. These offices being permanent, I have supposed it more agreeable to principle that their salaries should be fixed by the Legislature, and therefore have assigned them none. Their services to be compensated are from the 1st day of June last.

The marshal of the District of Columbia has, as directed by law, caused a jail to be built in the city of Washington. I inclose his statements of the expenses already incurred and of what remains to be finished. The portion actually completed has rendered the situation of the persons confined much more comfortable and secure than it has been heretofore.

TH: JEFFERSON.

FEBRUARY 3, 1803.

Gentlemen of the House of Representatives:

The inclosed letter and affidavits exhibiting matter of complaint against John Pickering, district judge of New Hampshire, which is not within Executive cognizance, I transmit them to the House of Representatives, to whom the Constitution has confided a power of instituting proceedings of redress, if they shall be of opinion that the case calls for them.

TH: JEFFERSON.

FEBRUARY 14, 1803.

Gentlemen of the Senate and of the House of Representatives:

In obedience to the ordinance for the government of the Territories of the United States requiring that the laws adopted by the governor and judges thereof shall be reported to Congress from time to time, I now transmit those which have been adopted in the Indiana Territory from January, 1801, to February, 1802, as forwarded to the office of the Secretary of State.

TH: JEFFERSON.

FEBRUARY 21, 1803.

Gentlemen of the Senate:

The Tuscarora Indians, having an interest in some lands within the State of North Carolina, asked the superintendence of the Government of the United States over a treaty to be held between them and the State of North Carolina respecting these lands. William Richardson Davie was appointed a commissioner for this purpose, and a treaty was concluded under his superintendence. This, with his letter on the subject, is now laid before the Senate for their advice and consent whether it shall be ratified.

TH: JEFFERSON.

FEBRUARY 23, 1803.

Gentlemen of the Senate and House of Representatives:

I lay before you a report of the Secretary of State on the case of the Danish brigantine *Henrick*, taken by a French privateer in 1799, retaken by an armed vessel of the United States, carried into a British island, and there adjudged to be neutral, but under allowance of such salvage and costs as absorbed nearly the whole amount of sales of the vessel and cargo. Indemnification for these losses occasioned by our officers is now claimed by the sufferers, supported by the representations of their Government. I have no doubt the Legislature will give to the subject that just attention and consideration which it is useful as well as honorable to practice in our transactions with other nations, and particularly with one which has observed toward us the most friendly treatment and regard.

TH: JEFFERSON.

PROCLAMATION.

[From the National Intelligencer, July 18, 1803.]

BY THE PRESIDENT OF THE UNITED STATES OF AMERICA.

A PROCLAMATION.

Whereas great and weighty matters claiming the consideration of the Congress of the United States form an extraordinary occasion for convening them, I do by these presents appoint Monday, the 17th day of October next, for their meeting at the city of Washington, hereby requiring their respective Senators and Representatives then and there to assemble in Congress, in order to receive such communications as may then be made to them and to consult and determine on such measures as in their wisdom may be deemed meet for the welfare of the United States.

In testimony whereof I have caused the seal of the United States to be hereunto affixed, and signed the same with my hand.

[SEAL.]   Done at the city of Washington, the 16th day of July, A. D. 1803, and in the twenty-eighth year of the Independence of the United States

TH: JEFFERSON.

By the President:

JAMES MADISON,
    Secretary.

THIRD ANNUAL MESSAGE.

OCTOBER 17, 1803.

To the Senate and House of Representatives of the United States:

In calling you together, fellow-citizens, at an earlier day than was contemplated by the act of the *last* session of Congress, I have not been insensible to the personal inconveniences necessarily resulting from an unexpected change in your arrangements. But matters of great public concernment have rendered this call necessary, and the interests you feel in these will supersede in your minds all private considerations.

Congress witnessed at their late session the extraordinary agitation produced in the public mind by the suspension of our right of deposit at the port of New Orleans, no assignment of another place having been made according to treaty. They were sensible that the continuance of that privation would be more injurious to our nation than any consequences which could flow from any mode of redress, but reposing just confidence in the good faith of the Government whose officer had committed the wrong, friendly and reasonable representations were resorted to, and the right of deposit was restored.

Previous, however, to this period we had not been unaware of the danger to which our peace would be perpetually exposed whilst so important a key to the commerce of the Western country remained under foreign power. Difficulties, too, were presenting themselves as to the navigation of other streams which, arising within our territories, pass through those adjacent. Propositions had therefore been authorized for obtaining on fair conditions the sovereignty of New Orleans and of other possessions in that quarter interesting to our quiet to such extent as was deemed practicable, and the provisional appropriation of $2,000,000 to be applied and accounted for by the President of the United States, intended as part of the price, was considered as conveying the sanction of Congress to the acquisition proposed. The enlightened Government of France saw with just discernment the importance to both nations of such liberal arrangements as might best and permanently promote the peace, friendship, and interests of both, and the property and sovereignty of all Louisiana which had been restored to them have on certain conditions been transferred to the United States by instruments bearing date the 30th of April last. When these shall have received the constitutional sanction of the Senate, they will without delay be communicated to the Representatives also for the exercise of their functions as to those conditions which are within the powers vested by the Constitution in Congress.

Whilst the property and sovereignty of the Mississippi and its waters secure an independent outlet for the produce of the Western States and an uncontrolled navigation through their whole course, free from collision with other powers and the dangers to our peace from that source, the fertility of the country, its climate and extent, promise in due season important aids to our Treasury, an ample provision for our posterity, and a wide spread for the blessings of freedom and equal laws.

With the wisdom of Congress it will rest to take those ulterior measures which may be necessary for the immediate occupation and temporary government of the country; for its incorporation into our Union; for rendering the change of government a blessing to our newly adopted brethren; for securing to them the rights of conscience and of property; for confirming to the Indian inhabitants their occupancy and self-government, establishing friendly and commercial relations with them, and for

REPLICAS OF *CLERMONT* AND *HALF MOON*

THE *OLYMPIC* ENTERING NEW YORK, JUNE, 1911

FULTON'S *CLERMONT* AND THE *OLYMPIC*

The *Clermont,* as shown in the upper panel, was about the size of an ordinary river tugboat. By comparing the tugs in the lower panel with the *Olympic* (in 1911, the largest ship afloat), some idea may be obtained of the relative power of Fulton's feeble craft and the ocean steamer of to-day.

Every patriotic American must regret that eighty per cent. of the vessels seen in our harbors are foreign-owned. The problem of restoring our merchant marine to its former high place in the commerce of the world has been frequently and fully discussed by our Presidents. Let us hope that some day we will not have to depend on foreign nations for our shipping, but that American goods will be transported in American-built and American-owned bottoms. (See "Commerce" in the encyclopedic index in volume eleven.)

ascertaining the geography of the country acquired. Such materials, for your information, relative to its affairs in general as the short space of time has permitted me to collect will be laid before you when the subject shall be in a state for your consideration.

Another important acquisition of territory has also been made since the last session of Congress. The friendly tribe of Kaskaskia Indians, with which we have never had a difference, reduced by the wars and wants of savage life to a few individuals unable to defend themselves against the neighboring tribes, has transferred its country to the United States, reserving only for its members what is sufficient to maintain them in an agricultural way. The considerations stipulated are that we shall extend to them our patronage and protection and give them certain annual aids in money, in implements of agriculture, and other articles of their choice. This country, among the most fertile within our limits, extending along the Mississippi from the mouth of the Illinois to and up the Ohio, though not so necessary as a barrier since the acquisition of the other bank, may yet be well worthy of being laid open to immediate settlement, as its inhabitants may descend with rapidity in support of the lower country should future circumstances expose that to foreign enterprise. As the stipulations in this treaty also involve matters within the competence of both Houses only, it will be laid before Congress as soon as the Senate shall have advised its ratification.

With many of the other Indian tribes improvements in agriculture and household manufacture are advancing, and with all our peace and friendship are established on grounds much firmer than heretofore. The measure adopted of establishing trading houses among them and of furnishing them necessaries in exchange for their commodities at such moderate prices as leave no gain, but cover us from loss, has the most conciliatory and useful effect on them, and is that which will best secure their peace and good will.

The small vessels authorized by Congress with a view to the Mediterranean service have been sent into that sea, and will be able more effectually to confine the Tripoline cruisers within their harbors and supersede the necessity of convoy to our commerce in that quarter. They will sensibly lessen the expenses of that service the ensuing year.

A further knowledge of the ground in the northeastern and northwestern angles of the United States has evinced that the boundaries established by the treaty of Paris between the British territories and ours in those parts were too imperfectly described to be susceptible of execution. It has therefore been thought worthy of attention for preserving and cherishing the harmony and useful intercourse subsisting between the two nations to remove by timely arrangements what unfavorable incidents might otherwise render a ground of future misunderstanding. A convention has therefore been entered into which provides for a practicable demarcation of those limits to the satisfaction of both parties.

An account of the receipts and expenditures of the year ending the 30th of September last, with the estimates for the service of the ensuing year, will be laid before you by the Secretary of the Treasury so soon as the receipts of the last quarter shall be returned from the more distant States. It is already ascertained that the amount paid into the Treasury for that year has been between $11,000,000 and $12,000,000, and that the revenue accrued during the same term exceeds the sum counted on as sufficient for our current expenses and to extinguish the public debt within the period heretofore proposed.

The amount of debt paid for the same year is about $3,100,000, exclusive of interest, and making, with the payment of the preceding year, a discharge of more than $8,500,000 of the principal of that debt, besides the accruing interest; and there remain in the Treasury nearly $6,000,000. Of these, $880,000 have been reserved for payment of the first installment due under the British convention of January 8, 1802, and two millions are what have been before mentioned as placed by Congress under the power and accountability of the President toward the price of New Orleans and other territories acquired, which, remaining untouched, are still applicable to that object and go in diminution of the sum to be funded for it.

Should the acquisition of Louisiana be constitutionally confirmed and carried into effect, a sum of nearly $13,000,000 will then be added to our public debt, most of which is payable after fifteen years, before which term the present existing debts will all be discharged by the established operation of the sinking fund. When we contemplate the ordinary annual augmentation of impost from increasing population and wealth, the augmentation of the same revenue by its extension to the new acquisition, and the economies which may still be introduced into our public expenditures, I can not but hope that Congress in reviewing their resources will find means to meet the intermediate interest of this additional debt without recurring to new taxes, and applying to this object only the ordinary progression of our revenue. Its extraordinary increase in times of foreign war will be the proper and sufficient fund for any measures of safety or precaution which that state of things may render necessary in our neutral position.

Remittances for the installments of our foreign debt having been found practicable without loss, it has not been thought expedient to use the power given by a former act of Congress of continuing them by reloans, and of redeeming instead thereof equal sums of domestic debt, although no difficulty was found in obtaining that accommodation.

The sum of $50,000 appropriated by Congress for providing gunboats remains unexpended. The favorable and peaceable turn of affairs on the Mississippi rendered an immediate execution of that law unnecessary, and time was desirable in order that the institution of that branch of our force might begin on models the most approved by experience. The same issue of events dispensed with a resort to the appropriation of $1,500,000, contemplated for purposes which were effected by happier means.

We have seen with sincere concern the flames of war lighted up again in Europe, and nations with which we have the most friendly and useful relations engaged in mutual destruction. While we regret the miseries in which we see others involved, let us bow with gratitude to that kind Providence which, inspiring with wisdom and moderation our late legislative councils while placed under the urgency of the greatest wrongs, guarded us from hastily entering into the sanguinary contest and left us only to look on and to pity its ravages. These will be heaviest on those immediately engaged. Yet the nations pursuing peace will not be exempt from all evil. In the course of this conflict let it be our endeavor, as it is our interest and desire, to cultivate the friendship of the belligerent nations by every act of justice and of innocent kindness; to receive their armed vessels with hospitality from the distresses of the sea, but to administer the means of annoyance to none; to establish in our harbors such a police as may maintain law and order; to restrain our citizens from embarking individually in a war in which their country takes no part; to punish severely those persons, citizen or alien, who shall usurp the cover of our flag for vessels not entitled to it, infecting thereby with suspicion those of real Americans and committing us into controversies for the redress of wrongs not our own; to exact from every nation the observance toward our vessels and citizens of those principles and practices which all civilized people acknowledge; to merit the character of a just nation, and maintain that of an independent one, preferring every consequence to insult and habitual wrong. Congress will consider whether the existing laws enable us efficaciously to maintain this course with our citizens in all places and with others while within the limits of our jurisdiction, and will give them the new modifications necessary for these objects. Some contraventions of right have already taken place, both within our jurisdictional limits and on the high seas. The friendly disposition of the Governments from whose agents they have proceeded, as well as their wisdom and regard for justice, leave us in reasonable expectation that they will be rectified and prevented in future, and that no act will be countenanced by them which threatens to disturb our friendly intercourse. Separated by a wide ocean from the nations of Europe and from the political interests which entangle them together, with productions and wants which render our commerce and friendship useful to them and theirs to us, it can not be the interest of any to assail us, nor ours to disturb them. We should be most unwise, indeed, were we to cast away the singular blessings of the position in which nature has placed us, the opportunity she has endowed us with of pursuing, at a distance from foreign contentions, the paths of industry, peace, and happiness, of cultivating general friendship, and of bringing collisions of interest to the umpirage of reason rather than of force. How desirable, then, must it be in a Government like ours to see its citizens adopt individually the views, the interests, and the conduct which their country should pursue, divesting themselves of those passions and partialities which tend to lessen useful friendships and to embarrass and embroil us in the calamitous scenes of Europe. Confident, fellow-citizens, that you will duly estimate the importance of neutral dispositions toward the observance of neutral conduct, that you will be sensible how much it is our duty to look on the bloody arena spread before us with commiseration indeed, but with no other wish than to see it closed, I am persuaded you will cordially cherish these dispositions in all discussions among yourselves and in all communications with your constituents; and I anticipate with satisfaction the measures of wisdom which the great interests now committed to you will give *you* an opportunity of providing, and *myself* that of approving and of carrying into execution with the fidelity I owe to my country.

TH: JEFFERSON.

SPECIAL MESSAGES.

OCTOBER 17, 1803.

Gentlemen of the Senate:

In my message of this day to both Houses of Congress I explained the circumstances which had led to the conclusion of conventions with France for the cession of the Province of Louisiana to the United States. Those conventions are now laid before you with such communications relating to them as may assist in deciding whether you will advise and consent to their ratification.

The ratification of the First Consul of France is in the hands of his chargé d'affaires here, to be exchanged for that of the United States whensoever, before the 30th instant, it shall be in readiness.

TH: JEFFERSON.

OCTOBER 21, 1803.

To the Senate and House of Representatives of the United States:

In my communication to you of the 17th instant I informed you that conventions had been entered into with the Government of France for the cession of Louisiana to the United States. These, with the advice and consent of the Senate, having now been ratified and my ratification exchanged for that of the First Consul of France in due form, they are communicated to you for consideration in your legislative capacity. You will observe that some important conditions can not be carried into execution but with the aid of the Legislature, and that time presses a decision on them without delay.

The ulterior provisions, also suggested in the same communication, for the occupation and government of the country will call for early attention. Such information relative to its government as time and distance have permitted me to obtain will be ready to be laid before you within a few days; but as permanent arrangements for this object may require time and deliberation, it is for your consideration whether you will not forthwith make such temporary provisions for the preservation in the meanwhile of order and tranquillity in the country as the case may require.

TH: JEFFERSON.

OCTOBER 24, 1803.

To the Senate of the United States:

I lay before you the convention signed on the 12th day of May last between the United States and Great Britain for settling their boundaries in the northeastern and northwestern parts of the United States, which was mentioned in my general message of the 17th instant, together with such papers relating thereto as may enable you to determine whether you will advise and consent to its ratification.

TH: JEFFERSON.

OCTOBER 31, 1803.

To the Senate of the United States of America:

I now lay before you the treaty mentioned in my general message at the opening of the session as having been concluded with the Kaskaskia Indians for the transfer of their country to us under certain reservations and conditions.

Progress having been made in the demarcation of Indian boundaries, I am now able to communicate to you a treaty with the Delawares, Shawanese, Potawatamies, Miamis, Eel-rivers, Weeas, Kickapoos, Piankeshaws, and Kaskaskias, establishing the boundaries of the territory around St. Vincennes.

Also a supplementary treaty with the Eel-rivers, Wyandots, Piankeshaws, Kaskaskias, and Kickapoos, in confirmation of the fourth article of the preceding treaty.

Also a treaty with the Choctaws, describing and establishing our demarcation of boundaries with them.

Which several treaties are accompanied by the papers relating to them, and are now submitted to the Senate for consideration whether they will advise and consent to their ratification.

TH: JEFFERSON.

NOVEMBER 4, 1803.

To the Senate and House of Representatives of the United States:

By the copy now communicated of a letter from Captain Bainbridge, of the *Philadelphia* frigate, to our consul at Gibraltar, you will learn that an act of hostility has been committed on a merchant vessel of the United States by an armed ship of the Emperor of Morocco. This conduct on the part of that power is without cause and without explanation. It is fortunate that Captain Bainbridge fell in with and took the capturing vessel and her prize, and I have the satisfaction to inform you that about the date of this transaction such a force would be arriving in the neighborhood of Gibraltar, both from the east and from the west, as leaves less to be feared for our commerce from the suddenness of the aggression.

On the 4th of September the *Constitution* frigate, Captain Preble, with Mr. Lear on board, was within two days' sail of Gibraltar, where the *Philadelphia* would then be arrived with her prize, and such explanations would probably be instituted as the state of things required, and as might perhaps arrest the progress of hostilities.

In the meanwhile it is for Congress to consider the provisional authorities which may be necessary to restrain the depredations of this power should they be continued.

TH: JEFFERSON.

NOVEMBER 14, 1803.

To the Senate and House of Representatives of the United States:

I now communicate a digest of the information I have received relative to Louisiana, which may be useful to the Legislature in providing for the government of the country. A translation of the most important laws in force in that province, now in press, shall be the subject of a supplementary communication, with such further and material information as may yet come to hand.

TH: JEFFERSON.

NOVEMBER 24, 1803.

To the House of Representatives of the United States:

In conformity with the desire expressed in the resolution of the House of Representatives of the 15th instant, I now lay before them copies of such documents as are in possession of the Executive relative to the arrest and confinement of Zachariah Cox by officers in the service of the United States in the year 1798. From the nature of the transaction some documents relative to it might have been expected from the War Office; but if any ever existed there they were probably lost when the office and its papers were consumed by fire.

TH: JEFFERSON.

NOVEMBER 25, 1803.

To the Senate and House of Representatives of the United States:

The treaty with the Kaskaskia Indians being ratified with the advice and consent of the Senate, it is now laid before both Houses in their legislative capacity. It will inform them of the obligations which the United States thereby contract, and particularly that of taking the tribe under their future protection, and that the ceded country is submitted to their immediate possession and disposal.

TH: JEFFERSON.

NOVEMBER 29, 1803.

To the Senate and House of Representatives of the United States:

I now communicate an appendix to the information heretofore given on the subject of Louisiana. You will be sensible, from the face of these papers, as well as of those to which they are a sequel, that they are not and could not be official, but are furnished by different individuals as the result of the best inquiries they had been able to make, and now given as received from them, only digested under heads to prevent repetitions.

TH: JEFFERSON.

DECEMBER 5, 1803.

To the Senate and House of Representatives of the United States:

I have the satisfaction to inform you that the act of hostility mentioned in my message of the 4th of November to have been committed by a cruiser of the Emperor of Morocco on a vessel of the United States has been disavowed by the Emperor. All differences in consequence thereof have been amicably adjusted, and the treaty of 1786 between this country and that has been recognized and confirmed by the Emperor, each party restoring to the other what had been detained or taken. I inclose the Emperor's orders given on this occasion.

The conduct of our officers generally who have had a part in these transactions has merited entire approbation.

The temperate and correct course pursued by our consul, Mr. Simpson, the promptitude and energy of Commodore Preble, the efficacious cooperation of Captains Rodgers and Campbell, of the returning squadron, the proper decision of Captain Bainbridge that a vessel which had committed an open hostility was of right to be detained for inquiry and consideration, and the general zeal of the other officers and men are honorable facts which I make known with pleasure. And to these I add what was indeed transacted in another quarter—the gallant enterprise of Captain Rodgers in destroying on the coast of Tripoli a corvette of that power of 22 guns.

I recommend to the consideration of Congress a just indemnification for the interest acquired by the captors of the *Mishouda* and *Mirboha*, yielded by them for the public accommodation.

TH: JEFFERSON.

DECEMBER 5, 1803.

To the Senate of the United States:

In compliance with the desire of the Senate expressed in their resolution of the 22d of November, on the impressment of seamen in the service of the United States by the agents of foreign nations, I now lay before the Senate a letter from the Secretary of State with a specification of the cases of which information has been received.

TH: JEFFERSON.

DECEMBER 21, 1803.

To the Senate of the United States:

On the 11th of January last I laid before the Senate, for their consideration and advice, a convention with Spain on the subject of indemnities for spoliations on our commerce committed by her subjects during the late war, which convention is still before the Senate. As this instrument did not embrace French seizures and condemnations of our vessels in the ports of Spain, for which we deemed the latter power responsible, our minister at that Court was instructed to press for an additional article, comprehending that branch of wrongs. I now communicate what has since passed on that subject. The Senate will judge whether the prospect it offers will justify a longer suspension of that portion of indemnities conceded by Spain should she now take no advantage of the lapse of the period for ratification. As the settlement of the boundaries of Louisiana will call for new negotiations on our receiving possession of that Province, the claims not obtained by the convention now before the Senate may be incorporated into those discussions.

TH: JEFFERSON.

DECEMBER 31, 1803.

To the Senate and House of Representatives of the United States:

I now lay before Congress the annual account of the fund established for defraying the contingent charges of Government. No occasion having arisen for making use of any part of it in the present year, the balance of $18,560 unexpended at the end of the last year remains now in the Treasury.

TH: JEFFERSON.

JANUARY 16, 1804.

To the Senate and House of Representatives of the United States:

In execution of the act of the present session of Congress for taking possession of Louisiana, as ceded to us by France, and for the temporary government thereof, Governor Claiborne, of the Mississippi Territory, and General Wilkinson were appointed commissioners to receive possession. They proceeded with such regular troops as had been assembled at Fort Adams from the nearest posts and with some militia of the Mississippi Territory to New Orleans. To be prepared for anything unexpected which might arise out of the transaction, a respectable body of militia was ordered to be in readiness in the States of Ohio, Kentucky, and Tennessee, and a part of those of Tennessee was moved on to the Natchez. No occasion, however, arose for their services. Our commissioners, on their arrival at New Orleans, found the Province already delivered by the commissioners of Spain to that of France, who delivered it over to them on the 20th day of December, as appears by their declaratory act accompanying this. Governor Claiborne, being duly invested with the powers heretofore exercised by the governor and intendant of Louisiana, assumed the government on the same day, and for the maintenance of law and order immediately issued the proclamation and address now communicated.

On this important acquisition, so favorable to the immediate interests of our Western citizens, so auspicious to the peace and security of the nation in general, which adds to our country territories so extensive and fertile and to our citizens new brethren to partake of the blessings of freedom and self-government, I offer to Congress and our country my sincere congratulations.

TH: JEFFERSON.

JANUARY 24, 1804.

Gentlemen of the Senate and of the House of Representatives:

I communicate for your information a letter just received from Governor Claiborne, which may throw light on the subject of the government of Louisiana, under contemplation of the Legislature. The paper being original, a return is asked.

TH: JEFFERSON.

FEBRUARY 16, 1804.

To the Senate and House of Representatives of the United States:

Information having been received some time ago that the public lands in the neighborhood of Detroit required particular attention, the agent appointed to transact business with the Indians in that quarter was instructed to inquire into and report the situation of the titles and occupation of the lands, private and public, in the neighboring settlements. His report is now communicated, that the Legislature may judge how far its interposition is necessary to quiet the legal titles, confirm the equitable, to remove the past and prevent future intrusions which have neither law nor justice for the basis.

TH: JEFFERSON.

FEBRUARY 22, 1804.

To the Senate and House of Representatives of the United States:

I communicate to Congress, for their information, a report of the surveyor of the public buildings at Washington, stating what has been done under the act of the last session concerning the city of Washington on the Capitol and other public buildings, and the highway between them.

TH: JEFFERSON.

FEBRUARY 29, 1804.

To the Senate and House of Representatives of the United States:

I communicate, for the information of Congress, a letter stating certain fraudulent practices for monopolizing lands in Louisiana, which may perhaps require legislative provisions.

TH: JEFFERSON.

MARCH 20, 1804.

To the Senate and House of Representatives of the United States:

I communicate to Congress a letter received from Captain Bainbridge, commander of the *Philadelphia* frigate, informing us of the wreck of that vessel on the coast of Tripoli, and that himself, his officers and men, had fallen into the hands of the Tripolitans. This accident renders it expedient to increase our force and enlarge our expenses in the Mediterranean beyond what the last appropriation for the naval service contemplated. I recommend, therefore, to the consideration of Congress such an addition to that appropriation as they may think the exigency requires.

TH: JEFFERSON.

MARCH 22, 1804.

To the Senate and House of Representatives of the United States:

I lay before Congress the last returns of the militia of the United States. Their incompleteness is much to be regretted, and its remedy may at some future time be a subject worthy the attention of Congress.

TH: JEFFERSON.

· PROCLAMATION.

[From Annals of Congress, Eighth Congress, second session, 1234.]

To all whom these presents shall come:

Whereas by an act of Congress authority has been given to the President of the United States, whenever he shall deem it expedient, to erect the shores, waters, and inlets of the bay and river of Mobile, and of the other rivers, creeks, inlets, and bays emptying into the Gulf of Mexico east of the said river Mobile and west thereof to the Pascagoula, inclusive, into a separate district for the collection of duties on imports and tonnage; and to establish such place within the same as he shall deem it expedient to be the port of entry and delivery for such district; and to designate such other places within the same district, not exceeding two, to be ports of delivery only:

Now know ye that I, Thomas Jefferson, President of the United States, do hereby decide that all the above-mentioned shores, waters, inlets, creeks, and rivers lying within the boundaries of the United States shall constitute and form a separate district, to be denominated "the district of Mobile;" and do also designate Fort Stoddert, within the district aforesaid, to be the port of entry and delivery for the said district.

Given under my hand this 20th day of May, 1804.

TH: JEFFERSON.

FOURTH ANNUAL MESSAGE.

NOVEMBER 8, 1804.

To the Senate and House of Representatives of the United States:

To a people, fellow-citizens, who sincerely desire the happiness and prosperity of other nations; to those who justly calculate that their own well-being is advanced by that of the nations with which they have intercourse, it will be a satisfaction to observe that the war which was lighted up in Europe a little before our last meeting has not yet extended its flames to other nations, nor been marked by the calamities which sometimes stain the footsteps of war. The irregularities, too, on the ocean, which generally harass the commerce of neutral nations, have, in distant parts, disturbed ours less than on former occasions; but in the American seas they have been greater from peculiar causes, and even within our harbors and jurisdiction infringements on the authority of the laws have been committed which have called for serious attention.

The friendly conduct of the Governments from whose officers and subjects these acts have proceeded, in other respects and in places more under their observation and control, gives us confidence that our representations on this subject will have been properly regarded.

While noticing the irregularities committed on the ocean by others, those on our own part should not be omitted nor left unprovided for. Complaints have been received that persons residing within the United States have taken on themselves to arm merchant vessels and to force a commerce into certain ports and countries in defiance of the laws of those countries. That individuals should undertake to wage private war, independently of the authority of their country, can not be permitted in a well-ordered society. Its tendency to produce aggression on the laws and rights of other nations and to endanger the peace of our own is so obvious that I doubt not you will adopt measures for restraining it effectually in future.

Soon after the passage of the act of the last session authorizing the establishment of a district and port of entry on the waters of the Mobile we learnt that its object was misunderstood on the part of Spain. Candid explanations were immediately given and assurances that, reserving our claims in that quarter as a subject of discussion and arrangement with Spain, no act was meditated in the meantime inconsistent with the peace and friendship existing between the two nations, and that conformably to these intentions would be the execution of the law. That Government had, however, thought proper to suspend the ratification of the convention of 1802; but the explanations which would reach them soon after, and still more the confirmation of them by the tenor of the instrument establishing the port and district, may reasonably be expected to replace them in the dispositions and views of the whole subject which originally dictated the convention.

I have the satisfaction to inform you that the objections which had been urged by that Government against the validity of our title to the country of Louisiana have been withdrawn, its exact limits, however, remaining still to be settled between us; and to this is to be added that, having prepared and delivered the stock created in execution of the convention of Paris of April 30, 1803, in consideration of the cession of that country, we have received from the Government of France an acknowledgment, in due form, of the fulfillment of that stipulation.

With the nations of Europe in general our friendship and intercourse are undisturbed, and from the Governments of the belligerent powers especially we continue to receive those friendly manifestations which are justly due to an honest neutrality and to such good offices consistent with that as we have opportunities of rendering.

The activity and success of the small force employed in the Mediterranean in the early part of the present year, the reenforcements sent into that sea, and the energy of the officers having command in the several vessels will, I trust, by the sufferings of war, reduce the barbarians of Tripoli to the desire of peace on proper terms. Great injury, however, ensues to ourselves, as well as to others interested, from the distance to which prizes must be brought for adjudication and from the impracticability of bringing hither such as are not seaworthy.

The Bey of Tunis having made requisitions unauthorized by our treaty, their rejection has produced from him some expressions of discontent. But to those who expect us to calculate whether a compliance with unjust demands will not cost us less than a war we must leave as a question of calculation for them also whether to retire from unjust demands will not cost them less than a war. We can do to each other very sensible injuries by war, but the mutual advantages of peace make that the best interest of both.

Peace and intercourse with the other powers on the same coast continue on the footing on which they are established by treaty.

In pursuance of the act providing for the temporary government of Louisiana, the necessary officers for the Territory of Orleans were appointed in due time to commence the exercise of their functions on the 1st day of October. The distance, however, of some of them and indispensable previous arrangements may have retarded its commencement in some of its parts. The form of government thus provided having been considered but as temporary, and open to such future improvements as further information of the circumstances of our brethren there might suggest, it will of course be subject to your consideration.

In the district of Louisiana it has been thought best to adopt the division into subordinate districts which had been established under its former government. These being five in number, a commanding officer has been appointed to each, according to the provisions of the law, and so soon as they can be at their stations that district will also be in its due state of organization. In the meantime their places are supplied by the officers before commanding there. And the functions of the governor and judges of Indiana having commenced, the government, we presume, is proceeding in its new form. The lead mines in that district offer so rich a supply of that metal as to merit attention. The report now communicated will inform you of their state and of the necessity of immediate inquiry into their occupation and titles.

With the Indian tribes established within our newly acquired limits, I have deemed it necessary to open conferences for the purpose of establishing a good understanding and neighborly relations between us. So far as we have yet learned, we have reason to believe that their dispositions are generally favorable and friendly; and with these dispositions on their part, we have in our own hands means which can not fail us for preserving their peace and friendship. By pursuing an uniform course of justice toward them, by aiding them in all the improvements which may better their condition, and especially by establishing a commerce on terms which shall be advantageous to them and only not losing to us, and so regulated as that no incendiaries of our own or any other nation may be permitted to disturb the natural effects of our just and friendly offices, we may render ourselves so necessary to their comfort and prosperity that the protection of our citizens from their disorderly members will become their interest and their voluntary care. Instead, therefore, of an augmentation of military force proportioned to our extension of frontier, I propose a moderate enlargement of the capital employed in that commerce as a more effectual, economical, and humane instrument for preserving peace and good neighborhood with them.

On this side the Mississippi an important relinquishment of native title has been received from the Delawares. That tribe, desiring to extinguish in their people the spirit of hunting and to convert superfluous lands into the means of improving what they retain, has ceded to us all the country between the Wabash and Ohio south of and including the road from the rapids toward Vincennes, for which they are to receive annuities in animals and implements for agriculture and in other necessaries. This acquisition is important, not only for its extent and fertility, but as fronting 300 miles on the Ohio, and near half that on the Wabash. The produce of the settled country descending those rivers will no longer pass in review of the Indian frontier but in a small portion, and, with the cession heretofore made by the Kaskaskias, nearly consolidates our possessions north of the Ohio, in a very respectable breadth—from Lake Erie to the Mississippi. The Piankeshaws having some claim to the country ceded by the Delawares, it has been thought best to quiet that by fair purchase also. So soon as the treaties on this subject shall have received their constitutional sanctions they shall be laid before both Houses.

The act of Congress of February 28, 1803, for building and employing a number of gunboats, is now in a course of execution to the extent there provided for. The obstacle to naval enterprise which vessels of this construction offer for our seaport towns, their utility toward supporting within our waters the authority of the laws, the promptness with which they will be manned by the seamen and militia of the place in the moment they are wanting, the facility of their assembling from different parts of the coast to any point where they are required in greater force than ordinary, the economy of their maintenance and preservation from decay when not in actual service, and the competence of our finances to this defensive provision without any new burthen are considerations which will have due weight with Congress in deciding on the expediency of adding to their number from year to year, as experience shall test their utility, until all our important harbors, by these and auxiliary means, shall be secured against insult and opposition to the laws.

No circumstance has arisen since your last session which calls for any augmentation of our regular military force. Should any improvement occur in the militia system, that will be always seasonable.

Accounts of the receipts and expenditures of the last year, with estimates for the ensuing one, will as usual be laid before you.

The state of our finances continues to fulfill our expectations. Eleven millions and a half of dollars, received in the course of the year ending the 30th of September last, have enabled us, after meeting all the ordinary expenses of the year, to pay upward of $3,600,000 of the public debt, exclusive of interest. This payment, with those of the two preceding years, has extinguished upward of twelve millions of the principal and a greater sum of interest within that period, and by a proportionate diminution of interest renders already sensible the effect of the growing sum yearly applicable to the discharge of the principal.

It is also ascertained that the revenue accrued during the last year exceeds that of the preceding, and the probable receipts of the ensuing year may safely be relied on as sufficient, with the sum already in the Treasury, to meet all the current demands of the year, to discharge upward of three millions and a half of the engagements incurred under the British and French conventions, and to advance in the further redemption of the funded debt as rapidly as had been contemplated. These, fellow-citizens, are the principal matters which I have thought it necessary at this time to communicate for your consideration and attention. Some others will be laid before you in the course of the session; but in the discharge of the great duties confided to you by our country you will take a broader view of the field of legislation. Whether the great interests of agriculture, manufactures, commerce, or navigation can within the pale of your constitutional powers be aided in any of their relations; whether laws are provided in all cases where they are wanting; whether those provided are exactly what they should be; whether any abuses take place in their administration, or in that of the public revenues; whether the organization of the public agents or of the public force is perfect in all its parts; in fine, whether anything can be done to advance the general good, are questions within the limits of your functions which will necessarily occupy your attention. In these and all other matters which you in your wisdom may propose for the good of our country you may count with assurance on my hearty cooperation and faithful execution.

TH: JEFFERSON.

SPECIAL MESSAGES.

NOVEMBER 15, 1804.

To the Senate of the United States:

I now lay before you a treaty, entered into on the 18th day of August of the present year, between the United States on one part and the Delaware Indians on the other, for the extinguishment of their title to a tract of country between the Ohio and Wabash rivers.

And another of the 27th day of the same month, between the United States and the Piankeshaws, for a confirmation of the same by the latter, together with a letter from Governor Harrison on the same subject; which treaties are submitted for your advice and consent.

TH: JEFFERSON.

NOVEMBER 15, 1804.

To the House of Representatives of the United States:

Agreeably to your resolution of the 9th instant, I now lay before you a statement of the circumstances attending the destruction of the frigate *Philadelphia*, with the names of the officers and the number of men employed on the occasion, to which I have to add that Lieutenant Decatur was thereupon advanced to be a captain in the Navy of the United States.

TH: JEFFERSON.

NOVEMBER 30, 1804.

To the Senate and House of Representatives of the United States:

I now lay before you copies of the treaties concluded with the Delaware and Piankeshaw Indians for the extinguishment of their title to the lands therein described, and I recommend to the consideration of Congress the making provision by law for carrying them into execution.

TH: JEFFERSON.

DECEMBER 13, 1804.

To the Senate of the United States:

I present for your advice a treaty entered into on behalf of the United States with the Creek Indians for the extinguishment of their right in certain lands in the forks of Oconee and Okmulgee rivers, within the State of Georgia. For the purpose of enabling you to form a satisfactory judgment on the subject, it is accompanied with the instructions of 1802, April 12, to James Wilkinson, Benjamin Hawkins, and Andrew Pickens, commissioners; those of 1803, May 5, to James Wilkinson, Benjamin Hawkins, and Robert Anderson, commissioners, and those of 1804, April 2, to Benjamin Hawkins, sole commissioner. The negotiations for obtaining the whole of the lands between the Oconee and Okmulgee have now been continued through three successive seasons under the original instructions and others supplementary to them given from time to time, as circumstances required, and the unity of the negotiation has been preserved not only by the subject, but by continuing Colonel Hawkins always one of the commissioners, and latterly the sole one. The extent of the cession to be obtained being uncertain, the limitation of price was what should be thought *reasonable according to the usual rate of compensation.* The commissioner has been induced to go beyond this limit probably by the just attentions due to the strong interest which the State of Georgia feels in making this particular acquisition, and by a despair of procuring it on more reasonable terms from a tribe which is one of those most fixed in the policy of holding fast their lands. To this may be added that if, by an alteration in the first article, instead of giving them stock which may be passed into other hands and render them the prey of speculators, an annuity shall be paid them in this case, as has hitherto been practiced in all similar cases, the price of these lands will become a pledge and guaranty for our future peace with this important tribe, and eventually an indemnity for the breach of it.

On the whole, I rest with entire satisfaction on the wisdom and counsel of those whose sanctions the Constitution has rendered necessary to the final validity of this act.

TH: JEFFERSON.

DECEMBER 31, 1804.

To the Senate and House of Representatives of the United States:

The inclosed letter, written from Malta by Richard O'Brien, our late consul at Algiers, giving some details of transactions before Tripoli, is communicated for the information of Congress.

TH: JEFFERSON.

DECEMBER 31, 1804.

To the Senate of the United States:

Most of the Indians residing within our northern boundary on this side of the Mississippi receiving from us annual aids in money and necessaries, it was a subject of complaint with the Sacs that they received nothing and were connected with us by no treaty. As they owned the country in the neighborhood of our settlements of Kaskaskia and St. Louis, it was thought expedient to engage their friendship, and Governor Harrison was accordingly instructed in June last to propose to them an annuity of $500 or $600, stipulating in return an adequate cession of territory and an exact definition of boundaries. The Sacs and Foxes acting generally as one nation, and coming forward together, he found it necessary to add an annuity for the latter tribe also, enlarging proportionably the cession of territory, which was accordingly done by the treaty now communicated, of November the 3d, with those two tribes.

This cession, giving us a perfect title to such a breadth of country on the eastern side of the Mississippi, with a command of the Ouisconsin, strengthens our means of retaining exclusive commerce with the Indians on the western side of the Mississippi—a right indispensable to the policy of governing those Indians by commerce rather than by arms.

The treaty is now submitted to the Senate for their advice and consent.

TH: JEFFERSON.

JANUARY 31, 1805.

To the House of Representatives of the United States:

In compliance with the desire of the House of Representatives, expressed in their resolution of yesterday, I have to inform them that by a letter of the 30th of May last from the Secretary of War to Samuel Hammond, a member of the House, it was proposed to him to accept a commission of colonel-commandant for the district of Louisiana when the new government there should commence. By a letter of the 30th of June he signified a willingness to accept, but still more definitively by one of October 26, a copy of which is therefore now communicated. A commission had been made out for him bearing date the 1st day of October last, and forwarded before the receipt of his letter of October 26. No later communication has been received from him, nor is anything later known of his movements.

TH: JEFFERSON.

FEBRUARY 1, 1805.

To the House of Representatives of the United States:

For some weeks past I have had reason to expect by every mail from New Orleans information which would have fully met the views of the House of Representatives, expressed in their resolution of December 31, on the subject of a post-road from the city of Washington to New Orleans; but this being not yet received, I think it my duty without further delay to communicate to the House the information I possess, however imperfect.

Isaac Briggs, one of the surveyors-general of the United States, being about to return in July last to his station at Natchez, and apprised of the anxiety existing to have a practicable road explored for forwarding the mail to New Orleans without crossing the mountains, offered his services voluntarily to return by the route contemplated, taking as he should go such observations of longitude and latitude as would enable him to delineate it exactly, and by protraction to show of what shortenings it would admit. The offer was accepted and he was furnished with an accurate sextant for his observations. The route proposed was from Washington by Fredericksburg, Cartersville, Lower Sauratown, Salisbury, Franklin Court-House in Georgia, Tuckabachee, Fort Stoddert, and the mouth of Pearl River to New Orleans. It is believed he followed this route generally, deviating at times only for special purposes, and returning again into it. His letters, herewith communicated, will shew his opinion to have been, after completing his journey, that the practicable distance between Washington and New Orleans will be a little over 1,000 miles. He expected to forward his map and special report within one week from the date of his last letter, but a letter of December 10, from another person, informs me he had been unwell, but would forward them within a week from that time. So soon as they shall be received they shall be communicated to the House of Representatives.

TH: JEFFERSON.

FEBRUARY 5, 1805.

To the Senate and House of Representatives of the United States:

The Secretary of State has lately received a note from the Danish chargé d'affaires, claiming, *in the name of his Government*, restitution in the case of the brig *Henrich*, communicated to Congress at a former session, in which note were transmitted sundry documents chiefly relating to the value and neutral character of the vessel, and to the question whether the judicial proceedings were instituted and conducted without the concurrence of the captain of the *Henrich*. As these documents appear to form a necessary appendage to those already before Congress, and throw additional light on the subject, I transmit copies of them herewith.

TH: JEFFERSON.

FEBRUARY 13, 1805.

To the Senate and House of Representatives of the United States:

In the message to Congress at the opening of the present session I informed them that treaties had been entered into with the Delaware and Piankeshaw Indians for the purchase of their right to certain lands on the Ohio. I have since received another, entered into with the Sacs and Foxes, for a portion of country on both sides of the river Mississippi. These treaties, having been advised and consented to by the Senate, have accordingly been ratified, but as they involve conditions which require legislative provision, they are now submitted to both branches for consideration.

TH: JEFFERSON.

FEBRUARY 20, 1805.

To the Senate and House of Representatives of the United States:

I communicate, for the information of Congress, a letter of September 18 from Commodore Preble, giving a detailed account of the transactions of the vessels under his command from July the 9th to the 10th of September last past.

The energy and judgment displayed by this excellent officer through the whole course of the service lately confided to him and the zeal and valor of his officers and men in the several enterprises executed by them can not fail to give high satisfaction to Congress and their country, of whom they have deserved well.

TH: JEFFERSON.

FEBRUARY 28, 1805.

To the Senate and House of Representatives of the United States:

I now lay before Congress a statement of the militia of the United States, according to the returns last received from the several States. It will be perceived that some of these are not of recent dates, and that from the States of Maryland, Delaware, and Tennessee no returns are stated. As far as appears from our records, none were ever rendered from either of these States.

TH: JEFFERSON.

FEBRUARY 28, 1805.

To the Senate and House of Representatives of the United States:

I now render to Congress the account of the fund established by the act of May 1, 1802, for defraying the contingent charges of Government. No occasion having arisen for making use of any part of the balance of $18,560 unexpended on the 31st day of December, 1803, when the last account was rendered by message, that balance has been carried to the credit of the surplus fund.

TH: JEFFERSON.

SECOND INAUGURAL ADDRESS.

Proceeding, fellow-citizens, to that qualification which the Constitution requires before my entrance on the charge again conferred on me, it is my duty to express the deep sense I entertain of this new proof of confidence from my fellow-citizens at large, and the zeal with which it inspires me so to conduct myself as may best satisfy their just expectations.

On taking this station on a former occasion I declared the principles on which I believed it my duty to administer the affairs of our Commonwealth. My conscience tells me I have on every occasion acted up to that declaration according to its obvious import and to the understanding of every candid mind.

In the transaction of your foreign affairs we have endeavored to cultivate the friendship of all nations, and especially of those with which we have the most important relations. We have done them justice on all occasions, favored where favor was lawful, and cherished mutual interests and intercourse on fair and equal terms. We are firmly convinced, and we act on that conviction, that with nations as with individuals our interests soundly calculated will ever be found inseparable from our moral duties, and history bears witness to the fact that a just nation is trusted on its word when recourse is had to armaments and wars to bridle others.

At home, fellow-citizens, you best know whether we have done well or ill. The suppression of unnecessary offices, of useless establishments and expenses, enabled us to discontinue our internal taxes. These, covering our land with officers and opening our doors to their intrusions, had already begun that process of domiciliary vexation which once entered is scarcely to be restrained from reaching successively every article of property and produce. If among these taxes some minor ones fell which had not been inconvenient, it was because their amount would not have paid the officers who collected them, and because, if they had any merit, the State authorities might adopt them instead of others less approved.

The remaining revenue on the consumption of foreign articles is paid chiefly by those who can afford to add foreign luxuries to domestic comforts, being collected on our seaboard and frontiers only, and, incorporated with the transactions of our mercantile citizens, it may be the pleasure and the pride of an American to ask, What farmer, what mechanic, what laborer ever sees a taxgatherer of the United States? These contributions enable us to support the current expenses of the Government, to fulfill contracts with foreign nations, to extinguish the native right of soil within our limits, to extend those limits, and to apply such a surplus to our public debts as places at a short day their final redemption, and that redemption once effected the revenue thereby liberated may, by a just repartition of it among the States and a corresponding amendment of the Constitution, be applied *in time of peace* to rivers, canals, roads, arts, manufactures, education, and other great objects within each State. *In time of war*, if injustice by ourselves or others must sometimes produce war, increased as the same revenue will be by increased population and consumption, and aided by other resources reserved for that crisis, it may meet within the year all the expenses of the year without encroaching on the rights of future generations by burthening them with the debts of the past. War will then be but a suspension of useful works, and a return to a state of peace a return to the progress of improvement.

I have said, fellow-citizens, that the income reserved had enabled us to extend our limits, but that extension may possibly pay for itself before we are called on, and in the meantime may keep down the accruing interest; in all events, it will replace the advances we shall have made. I know that the acquisition of Louisiana has been disapproved by some from a candid apprehension that the enlargement of our territory would endanger its union. But who can limit the extent to which the federative principle may operate effectively? The larger our association the less will it be shaken by local passions; and in any view is it not better that the opposite bank of the Mississippi should be settled by our own brethren and children than by strangers of another family? With which should we be most likely to live in harmony and friendly intercourse?

In matters of religion I have considered that its free exercise is placed by the Constitution independent of the powers of the General Government. I have therefore undertaken on no occasion to prescribe the religious exercises suited to it, but have left them, as the Constitution found them, under the direction and discipline of the church or state authorities acknowledged by the several religious societies.

The aboriginal inhabitants of these countries I have regarded with the commiseration their history inspires. Endowed with the faculties and the rights of men, breathing an ardent love of liberty and independence, and occupying a country which left them no desire but to be undisturbed, the stream of overflowing population from other regions directed itself on these shores; without power to divert or habits to contend against it, they have been overwhelmed by the current or driven before it; now reduced within limits too narrow for the hunter's state, humanity enjoins us to teach them agriculture and the domestic arts; to encourage them to that industry which alone can enable them to maintain their place in existence and to prepare them in time for that state of society which to bodily comforts adds the improvement of the mind and morals. We have therefore liberally furnished them with the implements of husbandry and household use; we have placed among them instructors in the arts of first necessity, and they are covered with the ægis of the law against aggressors from among ourselves.

But the endeavors to enlighten them on the fate which awaits their present course of life, to induce them to exercise their reason, follow its dictates, and change their pursuits with the change of circumstances have powerful obstacles to encounter; they are combated by the habits of their bodies, prejudices of their minds, ignorance, pride, and the influence of interested and crafty individuals among them who feel themselves something in the present order of things and fear to become nothing in any other. These persons inculcate a sanctimonious reverence for the customs of their ancestors; that whatsoever they did must be done through all time; that reason is a false guide, and to advance under its counsel in their physical, moral, or political condition is perilous innovation; that their duty is to remain as their Creator made them, ignorance being safety and knowledge full of danger; in short, my friends, among them also is seen the action and counteraction of good sense and of bigotry; they too have their antiphilosophists who find an interest in keeping things in their present state, who dread reformation, and exert all their faculties to maintain the ascendency of habit over the duty of improving our reason and obeying its mandates.

In giving these outlines I do not mean, fellow-citizens, to arrogate to myself the merit of the measures. That is due, in the first place, to the reflecting character of our citizens at large, who, by the weight of public opinion, influence and strengthen the public measures. It is due to the sound discretion with which they select from among themselves those to whom they confide the legislative duties. It is due to the zeal and wisdom of the characters thus selected, who lay the foundations of public happiness in wholesome laws, the execution of which alone remains for others, and it is due to the able and faithful auxiliaries, whose patriotism has associated them with me in the executive functions.

During this course of administration, and in order to disturb it, the artillery of the press has been leveled against us, charged with whatsoever its licentiousness could devise or dare. These abuses of an institution so important to freedom and science are deeply to be regretted, inasmuch as they tend to lessen its usefulness and to sap its safety. They might, indeed, have been corrected by the wholesome punishments reserved to and provided by the laws of the several States against falsehood and defamation, but public duties more urgent press on the time of public servants, and the offenders have therefore been left to find their punishment in the public indignation.

Nor was it uninteresting to the world that an experiment should be fairly and fully made, whether freedom of discussion, unaided by power, is not sufficient for the propagation and protection of truth—whether a government conducting itself in the true spirit of its constitution, with zeal and purity, and doing no act which it would be unwilling the whole world should witness, can be written down by falsehood and defamation. The experiment has been tried; you have witnessed the scene; our fellow-citizens looked on, cool and collected; they saw the latent source from which these outrages proceeded; they gathered around their public functionaries, and when the Constitution called them to the decision by suffrage, they pronounced their verdict, honorable to those who had served them and consolatory to the friend of man who believes that he may be trusted with the control of his own affairs.

No inference is here intended that the laws provided by the States against false and defamatory publications should not be enforced; he who has time renders a service to public morals and public tranquillity in reforming these abuses by the salutary coercions of the law; but the experiment is noted to prove that, since truth and reason have maintained their ground against false opinions in league with false facts, the press, confined to truth, needs no other legal restraint; the public judgment will correct false reasonings and opinions on a full hearing of all parties; and no other definite line can be drawn between the inestimable liberty of the press and its demoralizing licentiousness. If there be still improprieties which this rule would not restrain, its supplement must be sought in the censorship of public opinion.

Contemplating the union of sentiment now manifested so generally as auguring harmony and happiness to our future course, I offer to our country sincere congratulations. With those, too, not yet rallied to the same point the disposition to do so is gaining strength; facts are piercing through the veil drawn over them, and our doubting brethren will at length see that the mass of their fellow-citizens with whom they can not yet resolve to act as to principles and measures, think as they think and desire what they desire; that our wish as well as theirs is that the public

efforts may be directed honestly to the public good, that peace be cultivated, civil and religious liberty unassailed, law and order preserved,
equality of rights maintained, and that state of property, equal or unequal,
which results to every man from his own industry or that of his father's.
When satisfied of these views it is not in human nature that they should
not approve and support them. In the meantime let us cherish them
with patient affection, let us do them justice, and more than justice, in
all competitions of interest, and we need not doubt that truth, reason,
and their own interests will at length prevail, will gather them into the
fold of their country, and will complete that entire union of opinion
which gives to a nation the blessing of harmony and the benefit of all its
strength.

I shall now enter on the duties to which my fellow-citizens have again
called me, and shall proceed in the spirit of those principles which they
have approved. I fear not that any motives of interest may lead me
astray; I am sensible of no passion which could seduce me knowingly
from the path of justice, but the weaknesses of human nature and the
limits of my own understanding will produce errors of judgment sometimes injurious to your interests. I shall need, therefore, all the indulgence which I have heretofore experienced from my constituents; the
want of it will certainly not lessen with increasing years. I shall need,
too, the favor of that Being in whose hands we are, who led our fathers,
as Israel of old, from their native land and planted them in a country
flowing with all the necessaries and comforts of life; who has covered
our infancy with His providence and our riper years with His wisdom
and power, and to whose goodness I ask you to join in supplications
with me that He will so enlighten the minds of your servants, guide
their councils, and prosper their measures that whatsoever they do shall
result in your good, and shall secure to you the peace, friendship, and
approbation of all nations.

MARCH 4, 1805.

FIFTH ANNUAL MESSAGE.

DECEMBER 3, 1805.

To the Senate and House of Representatives of the United States:

At a moment when the nations of Europe are in commotion and arming
against each other, and when those with whom we have principal intercourse are engaged in the general contest, and when the countenance of
some of them toward our peaceable country threatens that even that may
not be unaffected by what is passing on the general theater, a meeting of
the representatives of the nation in both Houses of Congress has become

more than usually desirable. Coming from every section of our country, they bring with them the sentiments and the information of the whole, and will be enabled to give a direction to the public affairs which the will and the wisdom of the whole will approve and support.

In taking a view of the state of our country we in the first place notice the late affliction of two of our cities under the fatal fever which in latter times has occasionally visited our shores. Providence in His goodness gave it an early termination on this occasion and lessened the number of victims which have usually fallen before it. In the course of the several visitations by this disease it has appeared that it is strictly local, incident to cities and on the tide waters only, incommunicable in the country either by persons under the disease or by goods carried from diseased places; that its access is with the autumn and it disappears with the early frosts. These restrictions within narrow limits of time and space give security even to our maritime cities during threefourths of the year, and to the country always. Although from these facts it appears unnecessary, yet to satisfy the fears of foreign nations and cautions on their part not to be complained of in a danger whose limits are yet unknown to them I have strictly enjoined on the officers at the head of the customs to certify with exact truth for every vessel sailing for a foreign port the state of health respecting this fever which prevails at the place from which she sails. Under every motive from character and duty to certify the truth, I have no doubt they have faithfully executed this injunction. Much real injury has, however, been sustained from a propensity to identify with this endemic and to call by the same name fevers of very different kinds, which have been known at all times and in all countries, and never have been placed among those deemed contagious. As we advance in our knowledge of this disease, as facts develop the source from which individuals receive it, the State authorities charged with the care of the public health, and Congress with that of the general commerce, will become able to regulate with effect their respective functions in these departments. The burthen of quarantines is felt at home as well as abroad; their efficacy merits examination. Although the health laws of the States should be found to need no present revisal by Congress, yet commerce claims that their attention be ever awake to them.

Since our last meeting the aspect of our foreign relations has considerably changed. Our coasts have been infested and our harbors watched by private armed vessels, some of them without commissions, some with illegal commissions, others with those of legal form, but committing piratical acts beyond the authority of their commissions. They have captured in the very entrance of our harbors, as well as on the high seas, not only the vessels of our friends coming to trade with us, but our own also. They have carried them off under pretense of legal adjudication, but not daring to approach a court of justice, they have plundered and sunk them by the way or in obscure places where no evidence could arise against them, maltreated the crews, and abandoned them in boats in the open sea or on desert shores without food or covering. These enormities appearing to be unreached by any control of their sovereigns, I found it necessary to equip a force to cruise within our own seas, to arrest all vessels of these descriptions found hovering on our coasts within the limits of the Gulf Stream and to bring the offenders in for trial as pirates.

The same system of hovering on our coasts and harbors under color of seeking enemies has been also carried on by public armed ships to the great annoyance and oppression of our commerce. New principles, too, have been interpolated into the law of nations, founded neither in justice nor the usage or acknowledgment of nations. According to these a belligerent takes to itself a commerce with its own enemy which it denies to a neutral on the ground of its aiding that enemy in the war; but reason revolts at such an inconsistency, and the neutral having equal right with the belligerent to decide the question, the interests of our constituents and the duty of maintaining the authority of reason, the only umpire between just nations, impose on us the obligation of providing an effectual and determined opposition to a doctrine so injurious to the rights of peaceable nations. Indeed, the confidence we ought to have in the justice of others still countenances the hope that a sounder view of those rights will of itself induce from every belligerent a more correct observance of them.

With Spain our negotiations for a settlement of differences have not had a satisfactory issue. Spoliations during a former war, for which she had formally acknowledged herself responsible, have been refused to be compensated but on conditions affecting other claims in no wise connected with them. Yet the same practices are renewed in the present war and are already of great amount. On the Mobile, our commerce passing through that river continues to be obstructed by arbitrary duties and vexatious searches. Propositions for adjusting amicably the boundaries of Louisiana have not been acceded to. While, however, the right is unsettled, we have avoided changing the state of things by taking new posts or strengthening ourselves in the disputed territories, in the hope that the other power would not by a contrary conduct oblige us to meet their example and endanger conflicts of authority the issue of which may not be easily controlled. But in this hope we have now reason to lessen our confidence. Inroads have been recently made into the Territories of Orleans and the Mississippi, our citizens have been seized and their property plundered in the very parts of the former which had been actually delivered up by Spain, and this by the regular officers and soldiers of that Government. I have therefore found it necessary at length to give orders to our troops on that frontier to be in readiness to protect our citizens, and to repel by arms any similar aggressions in future. Other details necessary for your full information of the state of things between this country and that shall be the subject of another communication.

In reviewing these injuries from some of the belligerent powers the moderation, the firmness, and the wisdom of the Legislature will all be called into action. We ought still to hope that time and a more correct estimate of interest as well as of character will produce the justice we are bound to expect. But should any nation deceive itself by false calculations, and disappoint that expectation, we must join in the unprofitable contest of trying which party can do the other the most harm. Some of these injuries may perhaps admit a peaceable remedy. Where that is competent it is always the most desirable. But some of them are of a nature to be met by force only, and all of them may lead to it. I can not, therefore, but recommend such preparations as circumstances call for. The first object is to place our seaport towns out of the danger of insult. Measures have been already taken for furnishing them with heavy cannon for the service of such land batteries as may make a part of their defense against armed vessels approaching them. In aid of these it is desirable we should have a competent number of gunboats, and the number, to be competent, must be considerable. If immediately begun, they may be in readiness for service at the opening of the next season. Whether it will be necessary to augment our land forces will be decided by occurrences probably in the course of your session. In the meantime you will consider whether it would not be expedient for a state of peace as well as of war so to organize or class the militia as would enable us on any sudden emergency to call for the services of the younger portions, unencumbered with the old and those having families. Upward of 300,000 able-bodied men between the ages of 18 and 26 years, which the last census shews we may now count within our limits, will furnish a competent number for offense or defense in any point where they may be wanted, and will give time for raising regular forces after the necessity of them shall become certain; and the reducing to the early period of life all its active service can not but be desirable to our younger citizens of the present as well as future times, inasmuch as it engages to them in more advanced age a quiet and undisturbed repose in the bosom of their families. I can not, then, but earnestly recommend to your early consideration the expediency of so modifying our militia system as, by a separation of the more active part from that which is less so, we may draw from it when necessary an efficient corps fit for real and active service, and to be called to it in regular rotation.

Considerable provision has been made under former authorities from Congress of materials for the construction of ships of war of 74 guns. These materials are on hand subject to the further will of the Legislature.

An immediate prohibition of the exportation of arms and ammunition is also submitted to your determination.

Turning from these unpleasant views of violence and wrong, I congratulate you on the liberation of our fellow-citizens who were stranded on the coast of Tripoli and made prisoners of war. In a government bottomed on the will of all the life and liberty of every individual citizen become interesting to all. In the treaty, therefore, which has concluded our warfare with that State an article for the ransom of our citizens has been agreed to. An operation by land by a small band of our country-men and others, engaged for the occasion in conjunction with the troops of the ex-Bashaw of that country, gallantly conducted by our late consul, Eaton, and their successful enterprise on the city of Derne, contributed doubtless to the impression which produced peace, and the conclusion of this prevented opportunities of which the officers and men of our squad-ron destined for Tripoli would have availed themselves to emulate the acts of valor exhibited by their brethren in the attack of the last year. Reflecting with high satisfaction on the distinguished bravery displayed whenever occasions permitted in the late Mediterranean service, I think it would be an useful encouragement as well as a just reward to make an opening for some present promotion by enlarging our peace establishment of captains and lieutenants.

With Tunis some misunderstandings have arisen not yet sufficiently explained, but friendly discussions with their ambassador recently arrived and a mutual disposition to do whatever is just and reasonable can not fail of dissipating these, so that we may consider our peace on that coast, generally, to be on as sound a footing as it has been at any preceding time. Still, it will not be expedient to withdraw immediately the whole of our force from that sea.

The law providing for a naval peace establishment fixes the number of frigates which shall be kept in constant service in time of peace, and prescribes that they shall be manned by not more than two-thirds of their complement of seamen and ordinary seamen. Whether a frigate may be trusted to two-thirds only of her proper complement of men must depend on the nature of the service on which she is ordered; that may sometimes, for her safety as well as to insure her object, require her fullest complement. In adverting to this subject Congress will perhaps consider whether the best limitation on the Executive discretion in this case would not be by the number of seamen which may be employed in the whole service rather than by the number of the vessels. Occasions oftener arise for the employment of small than of large vessels, and it would lessen risk as well as expense to be authorized to employ them of preference. The limitation suggested by the number of seamen would admit a selection of vessels best adapted to the service.

Our Indian neighbors are advancing, many of them with spirit, and others beginning to engage in the pursuits of agriculture and household manufacture. They are becoming sensible that the earth yields subsist-ence with less labor and more certainty than the forest, and find it their interest from time to time to dispose of parts of their surplus and waste lands for the means of improving those they occupy and of subsisting their families while they are preparing their farms. Since your last session the Northern tribes have sold to us the lands between the Connecticut Reserve and the former Indian boundary and those on the Ohio from the same boundary to the rapids and for a considerable depth inland. The Chickasaws and Cherokees have sold us the country between and adjatent to the two districts of Tennessee, and the Creeks the residue of their lands in the fork of Ocmulgee up to the Ulcofauhatche. The three former purchases are important, inasmuch as they consolidate disjoined parts of our settled country and render their intercourse secure ; and the second particularly so, as, with the small point on the river which we expect is by this time ceded by the Piankeshaws, it completes our possession of the whole of both banks of the Ohio from its source to near its mouth, and the navigation of that river is thereby rendered forever safe to our citizens settled and settling on its extensive waters. The purchase from the Creeks, too, has been for some time particularly interesting to the State of Georgia.

The several treaties which have been mentioned will be submitted to both Houses of Congress for the exercise of their respective functions.

Deputations now on their way to the seat of Government from various nations of Indians inhabiting the Missouri and other parts beyond the Mississippi come charged with assurances of their satisfaction with the new relations in which they are placed with us, of their dispositions to cultivate our peace and friendship, and their desire to enter into commercial intercourse with us. A state of our progress in exploring the principal rivers of that country, and of the information respecting them hitherto obtained, will be communicated so soon as we shall receive some further relations which we have reason shortly to expect.

The receipts at the Treasury during the year ending on the 30th day of September last have exceeded the sum of $13,000,000, which, with not quite five millions in the Treasury at the beginning of the year, have enabled us after meeting other demands to pay nearly two millions of the debt contracted under the British treaty and convention, upward of four millions of principal of the public debt, and four millions of interest. These payments, with those which had been made in three years and a half preceding, have extinguished of the funded debt nearly eighteen millions of principal. Congress by their act of November 10, 1803, authorized us to borrow $1,750,000 toward meeting the claims of our citizens assumed by the convention with France. We have not, however, made use of this authority, because the sum of four millions and a half, which remained in the Treasury on the same 30th day of September last, with the receipts which we may calculate on for the ensuing year, besides paying the annual sum of $8,000,000 appropriated to the funded debt and meeting all the current demands which may be expected, will enable us to pay the whole sum of $3,750,000 assumed by the French convention and still leave us a surplus of nearly $1,000,000 at our free disposal. Should you concur in the provisions of arms and armed vessels recommended by the circumstances of the times, this surplus will furnish the means of doing so.

On this first occasion of addressing Congress since, by the choice of my constituents, I have entered on a second term of administration, I embrace the opportunity to give this public assurance that I will exert my best endeavors to administer faithfully the executive department, and will zealously cooperate with you in every measure which may tend to secure the liberty, property, and personal safety of our fellow-citizens, and to consolidate the republican forms and principles of our Government.

In the course of your session you shall receive all the aid which I can give for the dispatch of public business, and all the information necessary for your deliberations, of which the interests of our own country and the confidence reposed in us by others will admit a communication.

TH: JEFFERSON.

SPECIAL MESSAGES.

DECEMBER 6, 1805.

To the Senate and House of Representatives of the United States:

The depredations which had been committed on the commerce of the United States during a preceding war by persons under the authority of Spain are sufficiently known to all. These made it a duty to require from that Government indemnifications for our injured citizens. A convention was accordingly entered into between the minister of the United States at Madrid and the minister of that Government for foreign affairs, by which it was agreed that spoliations committed by Spanish subjects and carried into ports of Spain should be paid for by that nation, and that those committed by French subjects and carried into Spanish ports should remain for further discussion. Before this convention was returned to Spain with our ratification the transfer of Louisiana by France to the United States took place, an event as unexpected as disagreeable to Spain. From that moment she seemed to change her conduct and dispositions toward us. It was first manifested by her protest against the right of France to alienate Louisiana to us, which, however, was soon retracted and the right confirmed. Then high offense was manifested at the act of Congress establishing a collection district on the Mobile, although by an authentic declaration immediately made it was expressly confined to our acknowledged limits; and she now refused to ratify the convention signed by her own minister under the eye of his Sovereign unless we would consent to alterations of its terms which would have affected our claims against her for the spoliations by French subjects carried into Spanish ports.

To obtain justice as well as to restore friendship I thought a special mission advisable, and accordingly appointed James Monroe minister extraordinary and plenipotentiary to repair to Madrid, and in conjunction with our minister resident there to endeavor to procure a ratification of the former convention and to come to an understanding with Spain as to the boundaries of Louisiana. It appeared at once that her policy was to reserve herself for events, and in the meantime to keep our differences in an undetermined state. This will be evident from the papers now communicated to you. After nearly five months of fruitless endeavor to bring them to some definite and satisfactory result, our ministers ended the conferences without having been able to obtain indemnity for spoliations of any description or any satisfaction as to the boundaries of Louisiana, other than a declaration that we had no rights eastward of the Iberville, and that our line to the west was one which would have left us but a string of land on that bank of the river Mississippi. Our injured citizens were thus left without any prospect of retribution from the wrongdoer, and as to boundary each party was to take its own course. That which they have chosen to pursue will appear from the documents now communicated. They authorize the inference that it is their intention to advance on our possessions until they shall be repressed by an opposing force. Considering that Congress alone is constitutionally invested with the power of changing our condition from peace to war, I have thought it my duty to await their authority for using force in any degree which could be avoided. I have barely instructed the officers stationed in the neighborhood of the aggressions to protect our citizens from violence, to patrol within the borders actually delivered to us, and not to go out of them but when necessary to repel an inroad or to rescue a citizen or his property; and the Spanish officers remaining at New Orleans are required to depart without further delay. It ought to be noted here that since the late change in the state of affairs in Europe Spain has ordered her cruisers and courts to respect our treaty with her.

The conduct of France and the part she may take in the misunderstandings between the United States and Spain are too important to be unconsidered. She was prompt and decided in her declarations that our demands on Spain for French spoliations carried into Spanish ports were included in the settlement between the United States and France. She took at once the ground that she had acquired no right from Spain, and had meant to deliver us none eastward of the Iberville, her silence as to the western boundary leaving us to infer her opinion might be against Spain in that quarter. Whatever direction she might mean to give to these differences, it does not appear that she has contemplated their proceeding to actual rupture, or that at the date of our last advices from Paris her Government had any suspicion of the hostile attitude Spain had taken here; on the contrary, we have reason to believe that she was disposed to effect a settlement on a plan analogous to what our ministers had proposed, and so comprehensive as to remove as far as possible the grounds of future collision and controversy on the eastern as well as western side of the Mississippi.

The present crisis in Europe is favorable for pressing such a settlement, and not a moment should be lost in availing ourselves of it. Should it pass unimproved, our situation would become much more difficult.   Formal war is not necessary—it is not probable it will follow; but the protection of our citizens, the spirit and honor of our country require that force should be interposed to a certain degree   It will probably contribute to advance the object of peace.

But the course to be pursued will require the command of means which it belongs to Congress exclusively to yield or to deny.   To them I communicate every fact material for their information and the documents necessary to enable them to judge for themselves.   To their wisdom, then, I look for the course I am to pursue, and will pursue with sincere zeal that which they shall approve.

TH: JEFFERSON.

DECEMBER 11, 1805.

To the Senate of the United States:

I now lay before the Senate the several treaties and conventions following, which have been entered into on the part of the United States since their last session:

1. A treaty of peace and amity between the United States of America and the Bashaw, Bey, and subjects of Tripoli, in Barbary.

2. A treaty between the United States and the Wyandot, Ottawa, Chippewa, Munsee, and Delaware, Shawnee, and Potawatamie nations of Indians.

3. A treaty between the United States and the agents of the Connecticut Land Companies on one part and the Wyandot, Ottawa, Chippewa, Munsee, and Delaware, Shawnee, and Potawatamie nations of Indians.

4. A treaty between the United States and the Delawares, Potawatamies, Miamis, Eel-rivers, and Weeas.

5. A treaty between the United States and the Chickasaw Nation of Indians.

6. A treaty between the United States of America and the Cherokee Indians.

7. A convention between the United States and the Creek Nation of Indians; with the several documents necessary for their explanation.

The Senate having dissented to the ratification of the treaty with the Creeks submitted to them at their last session, which gave a sum of $200,000 for the country thereby conveyed, it is proper now to observe that instead of that sum, which was equivalent to a perpetual annuity of $12,000, the present purchase gives them an annuity of $12,000 for eight years only and of $11,000 for ten years more, the payments of which would be effected by a present sum of $130,000 placed at an annual interest of 6 per cent. If from this sum we deduct the reasonable value of the road ceded through the whole length of their country from Ocmulgee toward New Orleans, a road of indispensable necessity to us, the present convention will be found to give little more than the half of the sum which was formerly proposed to be given. This difference is thought sufficient to justify the presenting this subject a second time to the Senate.

On these several treaties I have to request that the Senate will advise whether I shall ratify them or not.

TH: JEFFERSON.

DECEMBER 23, 1805.

To the Senate and House of Representatives of the United States:

The governor and presiding judge of the Territory of Michigan have made a report to me of the state of that Territory, several matters in which being within the reach of the legislative authority only, I lay the report before Congress.

TH: JEFFERSON.

DECEMBER 31, 1805.

To the House of Representatives of the United States:

I now communicate to the House of Representatives all the information which the executive offices furnish on the subject of their resolution of the 23d instant respecting the States indebted to the United States.

TH: JEFFERSON.

JANUARY 10, 1806.

To the Senate of the United States:

In compliance with the request of the Senate expressed in their resolution of December 27, I now lay before them such documents and papers (there being no other information in my possession) as relate to complaints by the Government of France against the commerce carried on by the citizens of the United States to the French island of St. Domingo.

TH: JEFFERSON.

JANUARY 13, 1806.

To the Senate of the United States:

According to the request of the Senate of December 30, I now lay before them the correspondence of the naval commanders Barron and Rodgers and of Mr. Eaton, late consul at Tunis, respecting the progress of the war with Tripoli, antecedent to the treaty with the Bey and Regency of Tripoli, and respecting the negotiations for the same, and the commission and instructions of Mr. Eaton, with such other correspondence in possession of the offices as I suppose may be useful to the Senate in their deliberations upon the said treaty.

The instructions which were given to Mr. Lear, the consul-general at Algiers, respecting the negotiations for the said treaty accompanied the treaty and the message concerning the same, and are now with them in possession of the Senate.

So much of these papers has been extracted and communicated to the House of Representatives as relates to the principles of the cooperation between the United States and Hamet Caramalli, which is the subject of a joint message to both Houses of Congress bearing equal date with the present, and as those now communicated to the Senate comprehend the whole of that matter, I request that they may be considered as comprising the documents stated in that message as accompanying it. Being mostly originals or sole copies, a return of them is requested at the convenience of the Senate.

We have no letter from Mr. Lear respecting Tripoline affairs of later date than that of July 5, which was transmitted to the Senate with the treaty, nor, consequently, any later information what steps have been taken to carry into effect the stipulation for the delivery of the wife and children of the brother of the reigning Bashaw of Tripoli.

TH: JEFFERSON.

JANUARY 13, 1806.

To the Senate and House of Representatives of the United States:

I lay before Congress the application of Hamet Caramalli, elder brother of the reigning Bashaw of Tripoli, soliciting from the United States attention to his services and sufferings in the late war against that State; and in order to possess them of the ground on which that application stands, the facts shall be stated according to the views and information of the Executive.

During the war with Tripoli it was suggested that Hamet Caramalli, elder brother of the reigning Bashaw, and driven by him from his throne, meditated the recovery of his inheritance, and that a concert in action with us was desirable to him. We considered that concerted operations by those who have a common enemy were entirely justifiable, and might produce effects favorable to both without binding either to guarantee the objects of the other. But the distance of the scene, the difficulties of communication, and the uncertainty of our information inducing the less confidence in the measure, it was committed to our agents as one which might be resorted to if it promised to promote our success.

Mr. Eaton, however (our late consul), on his return from the Mediterranean, possessing personal knowledge of the scene and having confidence in the effect of a joint operation, we authorized Commodore Barron, then proceeding with his squadron, to enter into an understanding with Hamet if he should deem it useful; and as it was represented that he would need some aids of arms and ammunition, and even of money, he was authorized to furnish them to a moderate extent, according to the prospect of utility to be expected from it. In order to avail him of the advantages of Mr. Eaton's knowledge of circumstances, an occasional employment was provided for the latter as an agent for the Navy in that sea. Our expectation was that an intercourse should be kept up between the ex-Bashaw and the commodore; that while the former moved on by land our squadron should proceed with equal pace, so as to arrive at their destination together and to attack the common enemy by land and sea at the same time. The instructions of June 6 to Commodore Barron shew that a cooperation only was intended, and by no means an union of our object with the fortune of the ex-Bashaw, and the commodore's letters of March 22 and May 19 prove that he had the most correct idea of our intentions. His verbal instructions, indeed, to Mr. Eaton and Captain Hull, if the expressions are accurately committed to writing by those gentlemen, do not limit the extent of his cooperation as rigorously as he probably intended; but it is certain from the ex-Bashaw's letter of January 3, written when he was proceeding to join Mr. Eaton, and in which he says, "Your operations should be carried on by sea, mine by land," that he left the position in which he was with a proper idea of the nature of the cooperation. If Mr. Eaton's subsequent convention should appear to bring forward other objects, his letter of April 29 and May 1 views this convention but as provisional, the second article, as he expressly states, guarding it against any ill effect; and his letter of June 30 confirms this construction.

In the event it was found that after placing the ex-Bashaw in possession of Derne, one of the most important cities and provinces of the country, where he had resided himself as governor, he was totally unable to command any resources or to bear any part in cooperation with us. This hope was then at an end, and we certainly had never contemplated, nor were we prepared, to land an army of our own, or to raise, pay, or subsist an army of Arabs to march from Derne to Tripoli and to carry on a land war at such a distance from our resources. Our means and our authority were merely naval, and that such were the expectations of Hamet his letter of June 29 is an unequivocal acknowledgment. While, therefore, an impression from the capture of Derne might still operate at Tripoli, and an attack on that place from our squadron was daily expected, Colonel Lear thought it the best moment to listen to overtures of peace then made by the Bashaw. He did so, and while urging provisions for the United States he paid attention also to the interests of Hamet, but was able to effect nothing more than to engage the restitution of his family, and even the persevering in this demand suspended for some time the conclusion of the treaty.

In operations at such a distance it becomes necessary to leave much to the discretion of the agents employed, but events may still turn up beyond the limits of that discretion. Unable in such a case to consult his Government, a zealous citizen will act as he believes that would direct him were it apprised of the circumstances, and will take on himself the responsibility. In all these cases the purity and patriotism of the motives should shield the agent from blame, and even secure a sanction where the error is not too injurious. Should it be thought by any that the verbal instructions said to have been given by Commodore Barron to Mr. Eaton amount to a stipulation that the United States should place Hamet Caramalli on the throne of Tripoli—a stipulation so entirely unauthorized, so far beyond our views, and so onerous could not be sanctioned by our Government—or should Hamet Caramalli, contrary to the evidence of his letters of January 3 and June 29, be thought to have left the position which he now seems to regret, under a mistaken expectation that we were at all events to place him on his throne, on an appeal to the liberality of the nation something equivalent to the replacing him in his former situation might be worthy its consideration.

A nation by establishing a character of liberality and magnanimity gains in the friendship and respect of others more than the worth of mere money. This appeal is now made by Hamet Caramalli to the United States. The ground he has taken being different not only from our views but from those expressed by himself on former occasions, Mr. Eaton was desired to state whether any verbal communications passed from him to Hamet which had varied what we saw in writing. His answer of December 5 is herewith transmitted, and has rendered it still more necessary that in presenting to the Legislature the application of Hamet I should present them at the same time an exact statement of the views and proceedings of the Executive through this whole business, that they may clearly understand the ground on which we are placed. It is accompanied by all the papers which bear any relation to the principles of the cooperation, and which can inform their judgment in deciding on the application of Hamet Caramalli.

TH: JEFFERSON.

JANUARY 15, 1806.

To the Senate and House of Representatives of the United States:

I now render to Congress an account of the grant of $20,000 for the contingent charges of Government by an act making appropriations for the support of Government for the year 1805. Of that sum $1,987.50 have been necessarily applied to the support of the Territorial govern-

IMPRESSMENT OF AMERICAN SEAMAN BY BRITISH

IMPRESSMENT OF AMERICAN SEAMAN

The story of this outrage on our flag, which was of constant occurrence until the War of 1812 taught England that the "gridiron banner" meant something besides submission, is told in the article entitled "Impressment" in the index (volume eleven). Note that the seaman is being forcibly taken from an American man-of-war. The article entitled "Chesapeake, The," tells of a British captain's insolence and the American Government's tame submission to a gross outrage of this character.

ments of Michigan and Louisiana until an opportunity could occur of making a specific appropriation for that purpose. The balance of $18,012.50 remains in the Treasury.

TH: JEFFERSON.

JANUARY 17, 1806.

To the Senate and House of Representatives of the United States:

In my message to both Houses of Congress at the opening of their present session I submitted to their attention, among other subjects, the oppression of our commerce and navigation by the irregular practices of armed vessels, public and private, and by the introduction of new principles derogatory of the rights of neutrals and unacknowledged by the usage of nations.

The memorials of several bodies of merchants of the United States are now communicated, and will develop these principles and practices which are producing the most ruinous effects on our lawful commerce and navigation.

The rights of a neutral to carry on commercial intercourse with every part of the dominions of a belligerent permitted by the laws of the country (with the exception of blockaded ports and contraband of war) was believed to have been decided between Great Britain and the United States by the sentence of their commissioners mutually appointed to decide on that and other questions of difference between the two nations, and by the actual payment of the damages awarded by them against Great Britain for the infractions of that right. When, therefore, it was perceived that the same principle was revived with others more novel and extending the injury, instructions were given to the minister plenipotentiary of the United States at the Court of London, and remonstrances duly made by him on this subject, as will appear by documents transmitted herewith. These were followed by a partial and temporary suspension only, without any disavowal of the principle. He has therefore been instructed to urge this subject anew, to bring it more fully to the bar of reason, and to insist on rights too evident and too important to be surrendered. In the meantime the evil is proceeding under adjudications founded on the principle which is denied. Under these circumstances the subject presents itself for the consideration of Congress.

On the impressment of our seamen our remonstrances have never been intermitted. A hope existed at one moment of an arrangement which might have been submitted to, but it soon passed away, and the practice, though relaxed at times in the distant seas, has been constantly pursued in those in our neighborhood. The grounds on which the reclamations on this subject have been urged will appear in an extract from instructions to our minister at London now communicated.

TH: JEFFERSON.

JANUARY 17, 1806.

To the Senate and House of Representatives of the United States:

The inclosed letter from the minister plenipotentiary of the United States at the Court of London contains interesting information on the subjects of my other message of this date. It is sent separately and confidentially because its publication may discourage frank communications between our ministers generally and the Governments with which they reside, and especially between the same ministers.

TH: JEFFERSON.

JANUARY 24, 1806.

To the Senate of the United States:

A convention has been entered into between the United States and the Cherokee Nation for the extinguishment of the rights of the latter, and of some unsettled claims in the country north of the river Tennessee, therein described. This convention is now laid before the Senate for their advice and consent as to its ratification.

TH: JEFFERSON.

JANUARY 27, 1806.

To the Senate of the United States:

According to the desire of the Senate expressed in their resolution of the 10th instant, I now communicate to them a report of the Secretary of State, with its documents, stating certain new principles attempted to be introduced on the subject of neutral rights, injurious to the rights and interests of the United States. These, with my message to both Houses of the 17th instant and the documents accompanying it, fulfill the desires of the Senate as far as it can be done by any information in my possession which is authentic and not publicly known.

TH: JEFFERSON.

JANUARY 29, 1806.

To the Senate and House of Representatives of the United States:

Having received from sundry merchants at Baltimore a memorial on the same subject with those I communicated to Congress with my message of the 17th instant, I now communicate this also as a proper sequel to the former, and as making a part of the mass of evidence of the violations of our rights on the ocean.

TH: JEFFERSON.

FEBRUARY 3, 1806.

To the Senate and House of Representatives of the United States:

A letter has been received from the governor of South Carolina covering an act of the legislature of that State ceding to the United States various forts and fortifications and sites for the erection of forts in that State on the conditions therein expressed. This letter and the act it covered are now communicated to Congress.

I am not informed whether the positions ceded are the best which can be taken for securing their respective objects. No doubt is entertained that the legislature deemed them such. The river of Beaufort, particularly, said to be accessible to ships of very large size and capable of yielding them a protection which they can not find elsewhere but very far to the north, is from these circumstances so interesting to the Union in general as to merit particular attention and inquiry as to the positions on it best calculated for health as well as safety,

TH: JEFFERSON.

FEBRUARY 3, 1806.

To the Senate and House of Representatives of the United States:

In the course of the last year the following treaties and conventions for the extinguishment of Indian title to lands within our limits were entered into on behalf of the United States:

A treaty between the United States and the Wyandot, Ottawa, Chippeway, Munsee and Delaware, Shawanee and Pottawatamy nations of Indians.

A treaty between the United States and the agents of the Connecticut Land Company on one part and the Wyandot and Ottawa, Chippeway, Munsey and Delaware, Shawanee and Pottawatamy nations of Indians.

A treaty between the United States and the Delawares, Pottawatamies, Miamis, Eel-rivers, and Weas.

A treaty between the United States and the Chickasaw Nation of Indians.

Two treaties between the United States and the Cherokee Indians.

A convention between the United States and the Creek Nation of Indians.

The Senate having advised and consented to the ratification of these several treaties and conventions, I now lay them before both Houses of Congress for the exercise of their constitutional powers as to the means of fulfilling them.

TH: JEFFERSON.

FEBRUARY 6, 1806.

To the Senate and House of Representatives of the United States:

Since the date of my message of January 17 a letter of the 26th of November has been received from the minister plenipotentiary of the United States at London, covering one from the secretary for foreign affairs of that Government, which, being on the subject of that message, is now transmitted for the information of Congress. Although nothing forbids the substance of these letters from being communicated without reserve, yet so many ill effects proceed from the publications of correspondences between ministers remaining still in office that I can not but recommend that these letters be not permitted to be formally published.

TH; JEFFERSON.

FEBRUARY 19, 1806.

To the Senate and House of Representatives of the United States:

In pursuance of a measure proposed to Congress by a message of January 18, 1803, and sanctioned by their approbation for carrying it into execution, Captain Meriwether Lewis, of the First Regiment of infantry, was appointed, with a party of men, to explore the river Missouri from its mouth to its source, and, crossing the highlands by the shortest portage, to seek the best water communication thence to the Pacific Ocean; and Lieutenant Clarke was appointed second in command. They were to enter into conference with the Indian nations on their route with a view to the establishment of commerce with them. They entered the Missouri May 14, 1804, and on the 1st of November took up their winter quarters near the Mandan towns, 1,609 miles above the mouth of the river, in latitude 47° 21' 47'' north and longitude 99° 24' 45'' west from Greenwich. On the 8th of April, 1805, they proceeded up the river in pursuance of the objects prescribed to them. A letter of the preceding day, April 7th, from Captain Lewis is herewith communicated. During his stay among the Mandans he had been able to lay down the Missouri according to courses and distances taken on his passage up it, corrected by frequent observations of longitude and latitude, and to add to the actual survey of this portion of the river a general map of the country between the Mississippi and Pacific from the thirty-fourth to the fifty-fourth degree of latitude. These additions are from information collected from Indians with whom he had opportunities of communicating during his journey and residence with them. Copies of this map are now presented to both Houses of Congress. With these I communicate also a statistical view, procured and forwarded by him, of the Indian nations inhabiting the Territory of Louisiana and the countries adjacent to its northern and western borders, of their commerce, and of other interesting circumstances respecting them.

In order to render the statement as complete as may be of the Indians inhabiting the country west of the Mississippi, I add Dr. Sibley's account of those residing in and adjacent to the Territory of Orleans.

I communicate also, from the same person, an account of the Red River, according to the best information he had been able to collect.

Having been disappointed, after considerable preparation, in the purpose of sending an exploring party up that river in the summer of 1804, it was thought best to employ the autumn of that year in procuring a knowledge of an interesting branch of the river called the Washita.

This was undertaken under the direction of Mr. Dunbar, of Natchez, a citizen of distinguished science, who had aided and continues to aid us with his disinterested and valuable services in the prosecution of these enterprises. He ascended the river to the remarkable hot springs near it, in latitude 34° 31' 4.16", longitude 92° 50' 45" west from Greenwich, taking its courses and distances, and correcting them by frequent celestial observations. Extracts from his observations and copies of his map of the river from its mouth to the hot springs make part of the present communications. The examination of the Red River itself is but now commencing.

TH: JEFFERSON.

MARCH 5, 1806.

To the Senate of the United States:

According to the request of the Senate expressed in their resolution of 3d instant, I now transmit the extract of a letter from the Secretary of State to the minister plenipotentiary of the United States at Paris, the answer to that letter, and two letters from Henry Waddell, a citizen of the United States, relative to the interference of the said minister in the case of the ship *New Jersey* and to the principles alleged to have been laid down on that occasion.

There are in the office of the Department of State several printed documents in this case by the agent of those interested in the ship, which are voluminous and in French. If these be within the scope of the request of the Senate, the printed copies can be sent in immediately, but if translations be necessary some considerable time will be requisite for their execution. On this subject any further desire which the Senate shall think proper to express shall be complied with.

TH: JEFFERSON.

MARCH 7, 1806.

To the Senate of the United States:

According to the request of the Senate of yesterday, I now transmit the five printed memorials of the agent for the ship *New Jersey*, in the one of which marked B, at the ninth page, will be found the letter relative to it from the minister plenipotentiary of the United States at Paris to the French minister of the treasury, supposed to be the one designated in the resolution. We have no information of this letter but through the channel of the party interested in the ship, nor any proof of it more authentic than that now communicated.

TH: JEFFERSON.

MARCH 19, 1806.

To the Senate and House of Representatives of the United States:

It was reasonably expected that while the limits between the territories of the United States and of Spain were unsettled neither party would have innovated on the existing state of their respective positions. Some time since, however, we learnt that the Spanish authorities were advancing into the disputed country to occupy new posts and make new settlements. Unwilling to take any measures which might preclude a peaceable accommodation of differences, the officers of the United States were ordered to confine themselves within the country on this side of the Sabine River which, by delivery of its principal post, Natchitoches, was understood to have been itself delivered up by Spain, and at the same time to permit no adverse post to be taken nor armed men to remain within it. In consequence of these orders the commanding officer of Natchitoches, learning that a party of Spanish troops had crossed the Sabine River and were posting themselves on this side the Adais, sent a detachment of his force to require them to withdraw to the other side of the Sabine, which they accordingly did.

I have thought it proper to communicate to Congress the letter detailing this incident, that they may fully understand the state of things in that quarter and be enabled to make such provision for its security as, in their wisdom, they shall deem sufficient.

TH: JEFFERSON.

APRIL 11, 1806.

To the Senate and House of Representatives of the United States:

I now lay before Congress a statement of the militia of the United States according to the returns last received from the several States and Territories. It will be perceived that some of these are not of recent dates, and that from the States of Maryland and Delaware no returns are stated. As far as appears from our records, none were ever rendered from either of these States. From the Territories of Orleans, Louisiana, and Michigan complete returns have not yet been received.

TH: JEFFERSON.

APRIL 14, 1806.

To the Senate and House of Representatives of the United States:

During the blockade of Tripoli by the squadron of the United States a small cruiser, under the flag of Tunis, with two prizes, all of trifling value, attempted to enter Tripoli; was turned back, warned, and, attempting again to enter, was taken and detained as prize by the squadron. Her restitution was claimed by the Bey of Tunis with a threat of war in terms so serious that on withdrawing from the blockade of Tripoli the commanding officer of the squadron thought it his duty to repair to Tunis with his squadron and to require a categorical declaration whether peace or war was intended. The Bey preferred explaining himself by an ambassador to the United States, who on his arrival renewed the request that the vessel and her prizes should be restored. It was deemed proper to give this proof of friendship to the Bey, and the ambassador was informed the vessels would be restored. Afterwards he made a requisition of naval stores to be sent to the Bey, in order to secure a peace for the term of three years, with a threat of war if refused. It has been refused, and the ambassador is about to depart without receding from his threat or demand.

Under these circumstances, and considering that the several provisions of the act of March 25, 1804, will cease in consequence of the ratification of the treaty of peace with Tripoli, now advised and consented to by the Senate, I have thought it my duty to communicate these facts, in order that Congress may consider the expediency of continuing the same provisions for a limited time or making others equivalent.

TH: JEFFERSON.

APRIL 15, 1806.

To the Senate and House of Representatives of the United States:

The Senate having advised and consented to the ratification of a treaty concluded with the Piankeshaw Indians for extinguishing their claim to the country between the Wabash and Kaskaskia cessions, it is now laid before both Houses for the exercise of their constitutional powers as to the means of fulfilling it on our part.

TH: JEFFERSON.

APRIL 17, 1806.

To the Senate and House of Representatives of the United States:

The Senate having advised and consented to the ratification of a convention between the United States and the Cherokee Indians, concluded at Washington on the 7th day of January last, for the cession of their right to the tract of country therein described, it is now laid before both Houses of Congress for the exercise of their constitutional powers toward the fulfillment thereof.

TH: JEFFERSON.

APRIL 18, 1806.

To the Senate of the United States:

In compliance with the request of the Senate of yesterday's date, I now communicate the entire correspondence between the ambassador of Tunis and the Secretary of State, from which the Senate will see that the first application by the ambassador for restitution of the vessels taken in violation of blockade having been yielded to, the only remaining cause of difference brought forward by him is the requisition of a present of naval stores to secure a peace for three years, after which the inference is obvious that a renewal of the presents is to be expected to renew the prolongation of peace for another term. But this demand has been pressed in verbal conferences much more explicitly and pertinaciously than appears in the written correspondence. To save the delay of copying, some originals are inclosed, with a request that they be returned.

TH: JEFFERSON.

APRIL 19, 1806.

To the Senate of the United States:

I nominate James Monroe, now minister plenipotentiary of the United States at the Court of London, and William Pinkney, of Maryland, to be commissioners plenipotentiary and extraordinary for settling all matters of difference between the United States and the United Kingdoms of Great Britain and Ireland relative to wrongs committed between the parties on the high seas or other waters, and for establishing the principles of navigation and commerce between them.

James Houston, of Maryland, to be judge of the court of the United States for the district of Maryland.

Willis W. Parker, of Virginia, to be collector of the district and inspector of the revenue for the port of South Quay.

TH: JEFFERSON.

PROCLAMATIONS.

[From Annals of Congress, Ninth Congress, second session, 685.]

BY THE PRESIDENT OF THE UNITED STATES OF AMERICA.

A PROCLAMATION.

Whereas satisfactory information has been received that Henry Whitby, commanding a British armed vessel called the *Leander*, did on the 25th day of the month of April last, within the waters and jurisdiction of the United States, and near to the entrance of the harbor of New York, by a cannon shot fired from the said vessel *Leander*, commit a murder on the body of John Pierce, a citizen of the United States, then pursuing his lawful vocation within the same waters and jurisdiction of the United States and near to their shores; and that the said Henry Whitby can not at this time be brought to justice by the ordinary process of law; and

Whereas it does further appear that both before and after the said day sundry trespasses, wrongs, and unlawful interruptions and vexations on trading vessels coming to the United States, and within their waters and vicinity, were committed by the said armed vessel the *Leander*, her officers and people; by one other armed vessel called the *Cambrian*, commanded by John Nairne, her officers and people; and by one other armed vessel called the *Driver*, commanded by Slingsby Simpson, her officers and people; which vessels, being all of the same nation, were aiding and assisting each other in the trespasses, interruptions, and vexations aforesaid:

Now, therefore, to the end that the said Henry Whitby may be brought to justice and due punishment inflicted for the said murder, I do hereby especially enjoin and require all officers having authority, civil or military, and all other persons within the limits or jurisdiction of the United States, wheresoever the said Henry Whitby may be found, now or hereafter, to apprehend and secure the said Henry Whitby, and him safely and diligently to deliver to the civil authority of the place, to be proceeded against according to law.

And I do hereby further require that the said armed vessel the *Leander*, with her officers and people, and the said armed vessels the *Cambrian* and *Driver*, their officers and people, immediately and without any delay depart from the harbors and waters of the United States. And I do forever interdict the entrance of all other vessels which shall be commanded by the said Henry Whitby, John Nairne, and Slingsby Simpson, or either of them.

And if the said vessels, or any of them, shall fail to depart as aforesaid, or shall reenter the harbors or waters aforesaid, I do in that case forbid all intercourse with the said armed vessels the *Leander*, the *Cambrian*, and the *Driver*, or with any of them, and the officers and crews thereof, and do prohibit all supplies and aid from being furnished them, or any of them. And I do declare and make known that if any person from or within the jurisdictional limits of the United States shall afford any aid to either of the said armed vessels contrary to the prohibition contained in this proclamation, either in repairing such vessel or in furnishing her, her officers or crew, with supplies of any kind or in any manner whatever; or if any pilot shall assist in navigating any of the said armed vessels, unless it be for the purpose of carrying them in the first instance beyond the limits and jurisdiction of the United States, such person or persons shall on conviction suffer all the pains and penalties by the laws provided for such offenses. And I do hereby enjoin and require all persons bearing office, civil or military, within the United States, and all others citizens or inhabitants thereof, or being within the same, with vigilance and promptitude to exert their respective authorities and to be aiding and assisting to the carrying this proclamation and every part thereof into full effect.

In testimony whereof I have caused the seal of the United States to be affixed to these presents, and signed the same with my hand.

[SEAL.] Given at the city of Washington, the 3d day of May, A. D. 1806, and of the Sovereignty and Independence of the United States the thirtieth.

TH: JEFFERSON.

By the President:

JAMES MADISON,
Secretary of State.

[From Annals of Congress, Ninth Congress, second session, 686.]

BY THE PRESIDENT OF THE UNITED STATES OF AMERICA.

A PROCLAMATION.

Whereas information has been received that sundry persons, citizens of the United States or residents within the same, are conspiring and confederating together to begin and set on foot, provide, and prepare the means for a military expedition or enterprise against the dominions of Spain; that for this purpose they are fitting out and arming vessels in the western waters of the United States, collecting provisions, arms, military stores, and means; are deceiving and seducing honest and well-meaning citizens, under various pretenses, to engage in their criminal enterprises; are organizing, officering, and arming themselves for the same, contrary to the laws in such cases made and provided:

I have therefore thought proper to issue this my proclamation, warning and enjoining all faithful citizens who have been led without due knowledge or consideration to participate in the said unlawful enterprises to withdraw from the same without delay, and commanding all persons whatsoever engaged or concerned in the same to cease all further proceedings therein, as they will answer the contrary at their peril and incur prosecution with all the rigors of the law. And I hereby enjoin and require all officers, civil and military, of the United States, or of any of the States or Territories, and especially all governors and other executive authorities, all judges, justices, and other officers of the peace, all military officers of the Army or Navy of the United States, or officers of the militia, to be vigilant, each within his respective department and according to his functions, in searching out and bringing to condign punishment all persons engaged or concerned in such enterprise, in seizing and detaining, subject to the disposition of the law, all vessels, arms, military stores, or other means provided or providing for the same, and, in general, in preventing the carrying on such expedition or enterprise by all lawful means within their power; and I require all good and faithful citizens and others within the United States to be aiding and assisting herein, and especially in the discovery, apprehension, and bringing to justice of all such offenders, in preventing the execution of their unlawful designs, and in giving information against them to the proper authorities.

In testimony whereof I have caused the seal of the United States to be affixed to these presents, and have signed the same with my hand.

[SEAL.]   Given at the city of Washington on the 27th day of November, 1806, and in the year of the Sovereignty of the United States the thirty-first.

TH: JEFFERSON.

By the President:

JAMES MADISON,
     Secretary of State.

SIXTH ANNUAL MESSAGE.

DECEMBER 2, 1806.

To the Senate and House of Representatives of the United States of America in Congress assembled:

It would have given me, fellow-citizens, great satisfaction to announce in the moment of your meeting that the difficulties in our foreign relations existing at the time of your last separation had been amicably and justly terminated. I lost no time in taking those measures which were most likely to bring them to such a termination—by special missions charged with such powers and instructions as in the event of failure could leave no imputation on either our moderation or forbearance. The delays which have since taken place in our negotiations with the British Government appear to have proceeded from causes which do not forbid the expectation that during the course of the session I may be enabled to lay before you their final issue. What will be that of the negotiations for settling our differences with Spain nothing which had taken place at the date of the last dispatches enables us to pronounce. On the western side of the Mississippi she advanced in considerable force, and took post at the settlement of Bayou Pierre, on the Red River. This village was originally settled by France, was held by her as long as she held Louisiana, and was delivered to Spain only as a part of Louisiana. Being small, insulated, and distant, it was not observed at the moment of redelivery to France and the United States that she continued a guard of half a dozen men which had been stationed there. A proposition, however, having been lately made by our commander in chief to assume the Sabine River as a temporary line of separation between the troops of the two nations until the issue of our negotiations shall be known, this has been referred by the Spanish commandant to his superior, and in the meantime he has withdrawn his force to the western side of the Sabine

River. The correspondence on this subject now communicated will exhibit more particularly the present state of things in that quarter.

The nature of that country requires indispensably that an unusual proportion of the force employed there should be cavalry or mounted infantry. In order, therefore, that the commanding officer might be enabled to act with effect, I had authorized him to call on the governors of Orleans and Mississippi for a corps of 500 volunteer cavalry. The temporary arrangement he has proposed may perhaps render this unnecessary; but I inform you with great pleasure of the promptitude with which the inhabitants of those Territories have tendered their services in defense of their country. It has done honor to themselves, entitled them to the confidence of their fellow-citizens in every part of the Union, and must strengthen the general determination to protect them efficaciously under all circumstances which may occur.

Having received information that in another part of the United States a great number of private individuals were combining together, arming and organizing themselves contrary to law, to carry on a military expedition against the territories of Spain, I thought it necessary, by proclamation as well as by special orders, to take measures for preventing and suppressing this enterprise, for seizing the vessels, arms, and other means provided for it, and for arresting and bringing to justice its authors and abettors. It was due to that good faith which ought ever to be the rule of action in public as well as in private transactions, it was due to good order and regular government, that while the public force was acting strictly on the defensive and merely to protect our citizens from aggression the criminal attempts of private individuals to decide for their country the question of peace or war by commencing active and unauthorized hostilities should be promptly and efficaciously suppressed.

Whether it will be necessary to enlarge our regular force will depend on the result of our negotiations with Spain; but as it is uncertain when that result will be known, the provisional measures requisite for that, and to meet any pressure intervening in that quarter, will be a subject for your early consideration.

The possession of both banks of the Mississippi reducing to a single point the defense of that river, its waters, and the country adjacent, it becomes highly necessary to provide for that point a more adequate security. Some position above its mouth, commanding the passage of the river, should be rendered sufficiently strong to cover the armed vessels which may be stationed there for defense, and in conjunction with them to present an insuperable obstacle to any force attempting to pass. The approaches to the city of New Orleans from the eastern quarter also will require to be examined and more effectually guarded. For the internal support of the country the encouragement of a strong settlement on the western side of the Mississippi, within reach of New Orleans, will be worthy the consideration of the Legislature.

The gunboats authorized by an act of the last session are so advanced that they will be ready for service in the ensuing spring. Circumstances permitted us to allow the time necessary for their more solid construction. As a much larger number will still be wanting to place our seaport towns and waters in that state of defense to which we are competent and they entitled, a similar appropriation for a further provision for them is recommended for the ensuing year.

A further appropriation will also be necessary for repairing fortifications already established and the erection of such other works as may have real effect in obstructing the approach of an enemy to our seaport towns, or their remaining before them.

In a country whose constitution is derived from the will of the people, directly expressed by their free suffrages; where the principal executive functionaries and those of the legislature are renewed by them at short periods; where under the character of jurors they exercise in person the greatest portion of the judiciary powers; where the laws are consequently so formed and administered as to bear with equal weight and favor on all, restraining no man in the pursuits of honest industry and securing to everyone the property which that acquires, it would not be supposed that any safeguards could be needed against insurrection or enterprise on the public peace or authority. The laws, however, aware that these should not be trusted to moral restraints only, have wisely provided punishment for these crimes when committed. But would it not be salutary to give also the means of preventing their commission? Where an enterprise is meditated by private individuals against a foreign nation in amity with the United States, powers of prevention to a certain extent are given by the laws. Would they not be as reasonable and useful where the enterprise preparing is against the United States? While adverting to this branch of law it is proper to observe that in enterprises meditated against foreign nations the ordinary process of binding to the observance of the peace and good behavior, could it be extended to acts to be done out of the jurisdiction of the United States, would be effectual in some cases where the offender is able to keep out of sight every indication of his purpose which could draw on him the exercise of the powers now given by law.

The States on the coast of Barbary seem generally disposed at present to respect our peace and friendship; with Tunis alone some uncertainty remains. Persuaded that it is our interest to maintain our peace with them on equal terms or not at all, I propose to send in due time a reenforcement into the Mediterranean unless previous information shall shew it to be unnecessary.

We continue to receive proofs of the growing attachment of our Indian neighbors and of their disposition to place all their interests under the patronage of the United States. These dispositions are inspired by their confidence in our justice and in the sincere concern we feel for their welfare; and as long as we discharge these high and honorable functions with the integrity and good faith which alone can entitle us to their continuance we may expect to reap the just reward in their peace and friendship.

The expedition of Messrs. Lewis and Clarke for exploring the river Missouri and the best communication from that to the Pacific Ocean has had all the success which could have been expected. They have traced the Missouri nearly to its source, descended the Columbia to the Pacific Ocean, ascertained with accuracy the geography of that interesting communication across our continent, learnt the character of the country, of its commerce and inhabitants; and it is but justice to say that Messrs. Lewis and Clarke and their brave companions have by this arduous service deserved well of their country.

The attempt to explore the Red River, under the direction of Mr. Freeman, though conducted with a zeal and prudence meriting entire approbation, has not been equally successful. After proceeding up it about 600 miles, nearly as far as the French settlements had extended while the country was in their possession, our geographers were obliged to return without completing their work.

Very useful additions have also been made to our knowledge of the Mississippi by Lieutenant Pike, who has ascended it to its source, and whose journal and map, giving the details of his journey, will shortly be ready for communication to both Houses of Congress. Those of Messrs. Lewis, Clarke, and Freeman will require further time to be digested and prepared. These important surveys, in addition to those before possessed, furnish materials for commencing an accurate map of the Mississippi and its western waters. Some principal rivers, however, remain still to be explored, toward which the authorization of Congress by moderate appropriations will be requisite.

I congratulate you, fellow-citizens, on the approach of the period at which you may interpose your authority constitutionally to withdraw the citizens of the United States from all further participation in those violations of human rights which have been so long continued on the unoffending inhabitants of Africa, and which the morality, the reputation, and the best interests of our country have long been eager to proscribe. Although no law you may pass can take prohibitory effect till the first day of the year 1808, yet the intervening period is not too long to prevent by timely notice expeditions which can not be completed before that day.

The receipts at the Treasury during the year ending on the 30th day of September last have amounted to near $15,000,000, which have enabled us, after meeting the current demands, to pay $2,700,000 of the American claims in part of the price of Louisiana; to pay of the funded debt upward of three millions of principal and nearly four of interest, and, in addition, to reimburse in the course of the present month near two millions of 5½

EXPANSION BY PURCHASE AND DISCOVERY—THE LEWIS AND CLARK EXPEDITION AND THE LOUISIANA PURCHASE

EXPANSION BY DISCOVERY AND PURCHASE

Two events of Jefferson's time outrank in importance any other two. The first of these was the purchase from France of Louisiana Territory, for an account of which see the article entitled "Louisiana Purchase," in the index (volume eleven). The second was the exploration of the northwest from the headwaters of the Missouri to the Columbia River in Oregon by the Lewis and Clarke expedition, as a result of which we secured the States of Washington, Oregon and Idaho. See "Lewis and Clarke Expedition" in the index.

per cent stock. These payments and reimbursements of the funded debt, with those which had been made in the four years and a half preceding, will at the close of the present year have extinguished upward of twenty-three millions of principal.

The duties composing the Mediterranean fund will cease by law at the end of the present session. Considering, however, that they are levied chiefly on luxuries and that we have an impost on salt, a necessary of life, the free use of which otherwise is so important, I recommend to your consideration the suppression of the duties on salt and the continuation of the Mediterranean fund instead thereof for a short time, after which that also will become unnecessary for any purpose now within contemplation.

When both of these branches of revenue shall in this way be relinquished there will still ere long be an accumulation of moneys in the Treasury beyond the installments of public debt which we are permitted by contract to pay. They can not then, without a modification assented to by the public creditors, be applied to the extinguishment of this debt and the complete liberation of our revenues, the most desirable of all objects. Nor, if our peace continues, will they be wanting for any other existing purpose. The question therefore now comes forward, To what other objects shall these surpluses be appropriated, and the whole surplus of impost, after the entire discharge of the public debt, and during those intervals when the purposes of war shall not call for them? Shall we suppress the impost and give that advantage to foreign over domestic manufactures? On a few articles of more general and necessary use the suppression in due season will doubtless be right, but the great mass of the articles on which impost is paid are foreign luxuries, purchased by those only who are rich enough to afford themselves the use of them. Their patriotism would certainly prefer its continuance and application to the great purposes of the public education, roads, rivers, canals, and such other objects of public improvement as it may be thought proper to add to the constitutional enumeration of Federal powers. By these operations new channels of communication will be opened between the States, the lines of separation will disappear, their interests will be identified, and their union cemented by new and indissoluble ties. Education is here placed among the articles of public care, not that it would be proposed to take its ordinary branches out of the hands of private enterprise, which manages so much better all the concerns to which it is equal, but a public institution can alone supply those sciences which though rarely called for are yet necessary to complete the circle, all the parts of which contribute to the improvement of the country and some of them to its preservation. The subject is now proposed for the consideration of Congress, because if approved by the time the State legislatures shall have deliberated on this extension of the Federal trusts, and the laws shall be passed and other arrangements made for their execution, the necessary funds will be on hand and without employment. I suppose an amendment to the Constitution, by consent of the States, necessary, because the objects now recommended are not among those enumerated in the Constitution, and to which it permits the public moneys to be applied.

The present consideration of a national establishment for education particularly is rendered proper by this circumstance also, that if Congress, approving the proposition, shall yet think it more eligible to found it on a donation of lands, they have it now in their power to endow it with those which will be among the earliest to produce the necessary income. This foundation would have the advantage of being independent of war, which may suspend other improvements by requiring for its own purposes the resources destined for them.

This, fellow-citizens, is the state of the public interests at the present moment and according to the information now possessed. But such is the situation of the nations of Europe and such, too, the predicament in which we stand with some of them that we can not rely with certainty on the present aspect of our affairs, that may change from moment to moment during the course of your session or after you shall have separated. Our duty is, therefore, to act upon things as they are and to make a reasonable provision for whatever they may be. Were armies to be raised whenever a speck of war is visible in our horizon, we never should have been without them. Our resources would have been exhausted on dangers which have never happened, instead of being reserved for what is really to take place. A steady, perhaps a quickened, pace in preparations for the defense of our seaport towns and waters; an early settlement of the most exposed and vulnerable parts of our country; a militia so organized that its effective portions can be called to any point in the Union, or volunteers instead of them to serve a sufficient time, are means which may always be ready, yet never preying on our resources until actually called into use. They will maintain the public interests while a more permanent force shall be in course of preparation. But much will depend on the promptitude with which these means can be brought into activity. If war be forced upon us, in spite of our long and vain appeals to the justice of nations, rapid and vigorous movements in its outset will go far toward securing us in its course and issue, and toward throwing its burthens on those who render necessary the resort from reason to force.

The result of our negotiations, or such incidents in their course as may enable us to infer their probable issue; such further movements also on our western frontiers as may shew whether war is to be pressed there while negotiation is protracted elsewhere, shall be communicated to you from time to time as they become known to me, with whatever other information I possess or may receive, which may aid your deliberations on the great national interests committed to your charge.

TH: JEFFERSON.

SPECIAL MESSAGES.

DECEMBER 3, 1806.

To the Senate and House of Representatives of the United States:

I have the satisfaction to inform you that the negotiation depending between the United States and the Government of Great Britain is proceeding in a spirit of friendship and accommodation which promises a result of mutual advantage. Delays, indeed, have taken place, occasioned by the long illness and subsequent death of the British minister charged with that duty. But the commissioners appointed by that Government to resume the negotiation have shewn every disposition to hasten its progress. It is, however, a work of time, as many arrangements are necessary to place our future harmony on stable grounds. In the meantime we find by the communications of our plenipotentiaries that a temporary suspension of the act of the last session prohibiting certain importations would, as a mark of candid disposition on our part and of confidence in the temper and views with which they have been met, have a happy effect on its course. A step so friendly will afford further evidence that all our proceedings have flowed from views of justice and conciliation, and that we give them willingly that form which may best meet corresponding dispositions.

Add to this that the same motives which produced the postponement of the act till the 15th of November last are in favor of its further suspension, and as we have reason to hope that it may soon yield to arrangements of mutual consent and convenience, justice seems to require that the same measure may be dealt out to the few cases which may fall within its short course as to all others preceding and following it. I can not, therefore, but recommend the suspension of this act for a reasonable time, on considerations of justice, amity, and the public interests.

TH: JEFFERSON.

DECEMBER 15, 1806.

To the House of Representatives of the United States:

I lay before Congress a report of the surveyor of the public buildings, stating the progress made on them during the last season and what is proposed for the ensuing one.

I took every measure within my power for carrying into effect the request of the House of Representatives of the 17th of April last to cause the south wing of the Capitol to be prepared for their accommodation by the commencement of the present session. With great regret I found it was not to be accomplished. The quantity of freestone necessary, with the size and quality of many of the blocks, was represented as beyond what could be obtained from the quarries by any exertions which could be commanded. The other parts of the work, which might all have been completed in time, were necessarily retarded by the insufficient progress of the stonework.

TH: JEFFERSON.

JANUARY 5, 1807.

To the Senate and House of Representatives of the United States:

I transmit to each House of Congress a copy of the laws of the Territory of Michigan passed by the governor and judges of the Territory during the year 1805.

TH: JEFFERSON.

JANUARY 22, 1807.

To the Senate and House of Representatives of the United States:

Agreeably to the request of the House of Representatives communicated in their resolution of the 16th instant, I proceed to state, under the reserve therein expressed, information received touching an illegal combination of private individuals against the peace and safety of the Union, and a military expedition planned by them against the territories of a power in amity with the United States, with the measures I have pursued for suppressing the same.

I had for some time been in the constant expectation of receiving such further information as would have enabled me to lay before the Legislature the termination as well as the beginning and progress of this scene of depravity so far as it has been acted on the Ohio and its waters. From this the state of safety of the lower country might have been estimated on probable grounds, and the delay was indulged the rather because no circumstance had yet made it necessary to call in the aid of the legislative functions. Information now recently communicated has brought us nearly to the period contemplated. The mass of what I have received in the course of these transactions is voluminous, but little has been given under the sanction of an oath so as to constitute formal and legal evidence. It is chiefly in the form of letters, often containing such a mixture of rumors, conjectures, and suspicions as renders it difficult to sift out the real facts and unadvisable to hazard more than general outlines, strengthened by concurrent information or the particular credibility of the relator. In this state of the evidence, delivered sometimes, too, under the restriction of private confidence, neither safety nor justice will permit the exposing names, except that of the principal actor, whose guilt is placed beyond question.

Some time in the latter part of September I received intimations that designs were in agitation in the Western country unlawful and unfriendly to the peace of the Union, and that the prime mover in these was Aaron

Burr, heretofore distinguished by the favor of his country. The grounds of these intimations being inconclusive, the objects uncertain, and the fidelity of that country known to be firm, the only measure taken was to urge the informants to use their best endeavors to get further insight into the designs and proceedings of the suspected persons and to communicate them to me.

It was not till the latter part of October that the objects of the conspiracy began to be perceived, but still so blended and involved in mystery that nothing distinct could be singled out for pursuit. In this state of uncertainty as to the crime contemplated, the acts done, and the legal course to be pursued, I thought it best to send to the scene where these things were principally in transaction a person in whose integrity, understanding, and discretion entire confidence could be reposed, with instructions to investigate the plots going on, to enter into conference (for which he had sufficient credentials) with the governors and all other officers, civil and military, and with their aid to do on the spot whatever should be necessary to discover the designs of the conspirators, arrest their means, bring their persons to punishment, and to call out the force of the country to suppress any unlawful enterprise in which it should be found they were engaged. By this time it was known that many boats were under preparation, stores of provisions collecting, and an unusual number of suspicious characters in motion on the Ohio and its waters. Besides dispatching the confidential agent to that quarter, orders were at the same time sent to the governors of the Orleans and Mississippi Territories and to the commanders of the land and naval forces there to be on their guard against surprise and in constant readiness to resist any enterprise which might be attempted on the vessels, posts, or other objects under their care; and on the 8th of November instructions were forwarded to General Wilkinson to hasten an accommodation with the Spanish commandant on the Sabine, and as soon as that was effected to fall back with his principal force to the hither bank of the Mississippi for the defense of the interesting points on that river. By a letter received from that officer on the 25th of November, but dated October 21, we learnt that a confidential agent of Aaron Burr had been deputed to him with communications, partly written in cipher and partly oral, explaining his designs, exaggerating his resources, and making such offers of emolument and command to engage him and the army in his unlawful enterprise as he had flattered himself would be successful. The General, with the honor of a soldier and fidelity of a good citizen, immediately dispatched a trusty officer to me with information of what had passed, proceeding to establish such an understanding with the Spanish commandant on the Sabine as permitted him to withdraw his force across the Mississippi and to enter on measures for opposing the projected enterprise.

The General's letter, which came to hand on the 25th of November, as has been mentioned, and some other information received a few days earlier, when brought together developed Burr's general designs, different parts of which only had been revealed to different informants. It appeared that he contemplated two distinct objects, which might be carried on either jointly or separately, and either the one or the other first, as circumstances should direct.   One of these was the severance of the Union of these States by the Alleghany Mountains; the other an attack on Mexico.   A third object was provided, merely ostensible, to wit, the settlement of a pretended purchase of a tract of country on the Washita claimed by a Baron Bastrop.   This was to serve as the pretext for all his preparations, an allurement for such followers as really wished to acquire settlements in that country and a cover under which to retreat in the event of a final discomfiture of both branches of his real design.

He found at once that the attachment of the Western country to the present Union was not to be shaken; that its dissolution could not be effected with the consent of its inhabitants, and that his resources were inadequate as yet to effect it by force.   He took his course then at once, determined to seize on New Orleans, plunder the bank there, possess himself of the military and naval stores, and proceed on his expedition to Mexico, and to this object all his means and preparations were now directed.   He collected from all the quarters where himself or his agents possessed influence all the ardent, restless, desperate, and disaffected persons who were ready for any enterprise analogous to their characters. He seduced good and well-meaning citizens, some by assurances that he possessed the confidence of the Government and was acting under its secret patronage, a pretense which procured some credit from the state of our differences with Spain, and others by offers of land in Bastrop's claim on the Washita.

This was the state of my information of his proceedings about the last of November, at which time, therefore, it was first possible to take specific measures to meet them.   The proclamation of November 27, two days after the receipt of General Wilkinson's information, was now issued.   Orders were dispatched to every interesting point on the Ohio and Mississippi from Pittsburg to New Orleans for the employment of such force either of the regulars or of the militia and of such proceedings also of the civil authorities as might enable them to seize on all the boats and stores provided for the enterprise, to arrest the persons concerned, and to suppress effectually the further progress of the enterprise.   A little before the receipt of these orders in the State of Ohio our confidential agent, who had been diligently employed in investigating the conspiracy, had acquired sufficient information to open himself to the governor of that State and apply for the immediate exertion of the authority and power of the State to crush the combination.   Governor Tiffin and the legislature, with a promptitude, an energy, and patriotic zeal which entitle them to a distinguished place in the affection of their sister States, effected the seizure of all the boats, provisions, and other preparations within their reach, and thus gave a first blow, materially disabling the enterprise in its outset.

In Kentucky a premature attempt to bring Burr to justice without sufficient evidence for his conviction had produced a popular impression in his favor and a general disbelief of his guilt. This gave him an unfortunate opportunity of hastening his equipments. The arrival of the proclamation and orders and the application and information of our confidential agent at length awakened the authorities of that State to the truth, and then produced the same promptitude and energy of which the neighboring State had set the example. Under an act of their legislature of December 23 militia was instantly ordered to different important points, and measures taken for doing whatever could yet be done. Some boats (accounts vary from five to double or treble that number) and persons (differently estimated from 100 to 300) had in the meantime passed the Falls of Ohio to rendezvous at the mouth of Cumberland with others expected down that river.

Not apprised till very late that any boats were building on Cumberland, the effect of the proclamation had been trusted to for some time in the State of Tennessee; but on the 19th of December similar communications and instructions with those to the neighboring States were dispatched by express to the governor and a general officer of the western division of the State, and on the 23d of December our confidential agent left Frankfort for Nashville to put into activity the means of that State also. But by information received yesterday I learn that on the 22d of December Mr. Burr descended the Cumberland with two boats merely of accommodation, carrying with him from that State no quota toward his unlawful enterprise. Whether after the arrival of the proclamation, of the orders, or of our agent any exertion which could be made by that State or the orders of the governor of Kentucky for calling out the militia at the mouth of Cumberland would be in time to arrest these boats and those from the Falls of Ohio is still doubtful.

On the whole, the fugitives from the Ohio, with their associates from Cumberland or any other place in that quarter, can not threaten serious danger to the city of New Orleans.

By the same express of December 19 orders were sent to the governors of Orleans and Mississippi, supplementary to those which had been given on the 25th of November, to hold the militia of their Territories in readiness to cooperate for their defense with the regular troops and armed vessels then under command of General Wilkinson. Great alarm, indeed, was excited at New Orleans by the exaggerated accounts of Mr. Burr, disseminated through his emissaries, of the armies and navies he was to assemble there. General Wilkinson had arrived there himself on the 24th of November, and had immediately put into activity the resources of the place for the purpose of its defense, and on the 10th of December he was joined by his troops from the Sabine. Great zeal was shewn by the inhabitants generally, the merchants of the place readily agreeing to the most laudable exertions and sacrifices for manning the armed vessels with their seamen, and the other citizens manifesting unequivocal fidelity to the Union and a spirit of determined resistance to their expected assailants.

Surmises have been hazarded that this enterprise is to receive aid from certain foreign powers; but these surmises are without proof or probability. The wisdom of the measures sanctioned by Congress at its last session has placed us in the paths of peace and justice with the only powers with whom we had any differences, and nothing has happened since which makes it either their interest or ours to pursue another course. No change of measures has taken place on our part; none ought to take place at this time. With the one, friendly arrangement was then proposed, and the law deemed necessary on the failure of that was suspended to give time for a fair trial of the issue. With the same power friendly arrangement is now proceeding under good expectations, and the same law deemed necessary on failure of that is still suspended, to give time for a fair trial of the issue. With the other, negotiation was in like manner then preferred, and provisional measures only taken to meet the event of rupture. With the same power negotiation is still preferred, and provisional measures only are necessary to meet the event of rupture. While, therefore, we do not deflect in the slightest degree from the course we then assumed and are still pursuing with mutual consent to restore a good understanding, we are not to impute to them practices as irreconcilable to interest as to good faith, and changing necessarily the relations of peace and justice between us to those of war. These surmises are therefore to be imputed to the vauntings of the author of this enterprise to multiply his partisans by magnifying the belief of his prospects and support.

By letters from General Wilkinson of the 14th and 18th of December, which came to hand two days after the date of the resolution of the House of Representatives—that is to say, on the morning of the 18th instant— I received the important affidavit a copy of which I now communicate, with extracts of so much of the letters as comes within the scope of the resolution. By these it will be seen that of three of the principal emissaries of Mr. Burr whom the General had caused to be apprehended, one had been liberated by habeas corpus, and two others, being those particularly employed in the endeavor to corrupt the general and army of the United States, have been embarked by him for ports in the Atlantic States, probably on the consideration that an impartial trial could not be expected during the present agitations of New Orleans, and that that city was not as yet a safe place of confinement. As soon as these persons shall arrive they will be delivered to the custody of the law and left to such course of trial, both as to place and process, as its functionaries may direct. The presence of the highest judicial authorities, to be assembled at this place within a few days, the means of pursuing a sounder course of proceedings here than elsewhere, and the aid of the Executive means, should the judges have occasion to use them, render it equally desirable for the criminals as for the public that, being already removed from the place where they were first apprehended, the first regular arrest should take place here, and the course of proceedings receive here its proper direction.

TH: JEFFERSON.

JANUARY 26, 1807.

To the Senate and House of Representatives of the United States:

I received from General Wilkinson on the 23d instant his affidavit charging Samuel Swartwout, Peter V. Ogden, and James Alexander with the crimes described in the affidavit a copy of which is now communicated to both Houses of Congress.

It was announced to me at the same time that Swartwout and Bollman, two of the persons apprehended by him, were arrived in this city in custody each of a military officer. I immediately delivered to the attorney of the United States in this district the evidence received against them, with instructions to lay the same before the judges and apply for their process to bring the accused to justice, and put into his hands orders to the officers having them in custody to deliver them to the marshal on his application.

TH: JEFFERSON.

JANUARY 27, 1807.

To the Senate and House of Representatives of the United States:

I now render to Congress the account of the fund established for defraying the contingent expenses of Government for the year 1806. No occasion having arisen for making use of any part of the balance of $18,012.50, unexpended on the 31st day of December, 1805, that balance remains in the Treasury.

TH: JEFFERSON.

JANUARY 28, 1807.

To the Senate and House of Representatives of the United States:

By the letters of Captain Bissel, who commands at Fort Massac, and of Mr. Murrell, to General Jackson, of Tennessee, copies of which are now communicated to Congress, it will be seen that Aaron Burr passed Fort Massac on the 31st December with about ten boats, navigated by about six hands each, without any military appearance, and that three boats with ammunition were said to have been arrested by the militia at Louisville.

As the guards of militia posted on various points of the Ohio will be able to prevent any further aids passing through that channel, should any be attempted, we may now estimate with tolerable certainty the means derived from the Ohio and its waters toward the accomplishment of the purposes of Mr. Burr.

TH: JEFFERSON.

JANUARY 31, 1807.

To the Senate and House of Representatives of the United States:

In execution of the act of the last session of Congress entitled "An act to regulate the laying out and making a road from Cumberland, in the State of Maryland, to the State of Ohio," I appointed Thomas Moore, of Maryland; Joseph Kerr, of Ohio, and Eli Williams, of Maryland, commissioners to lay out the said road, and to perform the other duties assigned to them by the act. The progress which they made in the execution of the work during the last season will appear in their report now communicated to Congress. On the receipt of it I took measures to obtain consent for making the road of the States of Pennsylvania, Maryland, and Virginia, through which the commissioners proposed to lay it out. I have received acts of the legislatures of Maryland and Virginia giving the consent desired; that of Pennsylvania has the subject still under consideration, as is supposed. Until I receive full consent to a free choice of route through the whole distance I have thought it safest neither to accept nor reject finally the partial report of the commissioners. Some matters suggested in the report belong exclusively to the Legislature.

TH: JEFFERSON.

FEBRUARY 6, 1807.

To the Senate and House of Representatives of the United States:

I lay before Congress the laws for the government of Louisiana, passed by the governor and judges of the Indiana Territory at their session at Vincennes begun on the 1st of October, 1804.

TH: JEFFERSON.

FEBRUARY 6, 1807.

To the Senate and House of Representatives of the United States:

The Government of France having examined into the claim of M. de Beaumarchais against the United States, and considering it as just and legal, has instructed its minister here to make representations on the subject to the Government of the United States. I now lay his memoir thereon before the Legislature, the only authority competent to a final decision on the same.

TH: JEFFERSON.

FEBRUARY 10, 1807.

To the Senate and House of Representatives of the United States:

I communicate, for the information of Congress, a letter from Cowles Mead, secretary of the Mississippi Territory, to the Secretary of War, by which it will be seen that Mr. Burr had reached that neighborhood on the 13th of January,

TH: JEFFERSON.

FEBRUARY 10, 1807.

To the Senate and House of Representatives of the United States:

In compliance with the request of the House of Representatives expressed in their resolution of the 5th instant, I proceed to give such information as is possessed of the effect of gunboats in the protection and defense of harbors, of the numbers thought necessary, and of the proposed distribution of them among the ports and harbors of the United States.

Under present circumstances, and governed by the intentions of the Legislature as manifested by their annual appropriations of money for the purposes of defense, it has been concluded to combine, first, land batteries furnished with heavy cannon and mortars, and established on all the points around the place favorable for preventing vessels from lying before it; second, movable artillery, which may be carried, as occasion may require, to points unprovided with fixed batteries; third, floating batteries, and fourth, gunboats which may oppose an enemy at his entrance and cooperate with the batteries for his expulsion.

On this subject professional men were consulted as far as we had opportunity. General Wilkinson and the late General Gates gave their opinions in writing in favor of the system, as will be seen by their letters now communicated. The higher officers of the Navy gave the same opinions in separate conferences, as their presence at the seat of Government offered occasions of consulting them, and no difference of judgment appeared on the subject. Those of Commodore Barron and Captain Tingey, now here, are recently furnished in writing, and transmitted herewith to the Legislature.

The efficacy of gunboats for the defense of harbors and of other smooth and inclosed waters may be estimated in part from that of galleys formerly much used but less powerful, more costly in their construction and maintenance, and requiring more men. But the gunboat itself is believed to be in use with every modern maritime nation for the purposes of defense. In the Mediterranean, on which are several small powers whose system, like ours, is peace and defense, few harbors are without this article of protection. Our own experience there of the effect of gunboats for harbor service is recent. Algiers is particularly known to have owed to a great provision of these vessels the safety of its city since the epoch of their construction. Before that it had been repeatedly insulted and injured. The effect of gunboats at present in the neighborhood of Gibraltar is well known, and how much they were used both in the attack and defense of that place di ing a former war. The extensive resort to them by the two greatest naval powers in the world on an enterprise of invasion not long since in prospect shews their confidence in their efficacy for the purposes for which they are suited. By the northern powers of Europe, whose seas are particularly adapted to them, they are still more used. The remarkable action between the Russian flotilla of gunboats and galleys and a Turkish fleet of ships of the line and frigates in the Liman Sea in 1788 will be readily recollected. The latter, commanded by their most celebrated admiral, were completely defeated, and several of their ships of the line destroyed.

From the opinions given as to the number of gunboats necessary for some of the principal seaports, and from a view of all the towns and ports from Orleans to Maine, inclusive, entitled to protection in proportion to their situation and circumstances, it is concluded that to give them a due measure of protection in times of war about 200 gunboats will be requisite.

According to first ideas the following would be their general distribution, liable to be varied on more mature examination and as circumstances shall vary; that is to say:

To the Mississippi and its neighboring waters, 40 gunboats.

To Savannah and Charleston, and the harbors on each side from St. Marys to Currituck, 25.

To the Chesapeake and its waters, 20.

To Delaware Bay and River, 15.

To New York, the Sound, and waters as far as Cape Cod, 50.

To Boston and the harbors north of Cape Cod, 50.

The flotillas assigned to these several stations might each be under the care of a particular commandant, and the vessels composing them would in ordinary be distributed among the harbors within the station in proportion to their importance.

Of these boats a proper proportion would be of the larger size, such as those heretofore built, capable of navigating any seas and of reenforcing occasionally the strength of even the most distant ports when menaced with danger. The residue would be confined to their own or the neighboring harbors, would be smaller, less furnished for accommodation, and consequently less costly. Of the number supposed necessary, 73 are built or building, and the 127 still to be provided would cost from $500,000 to $600,000. Having regard to the convenience of the Treasury as well as to the resources for building, it has been thought that the one-half of these might be built in the present year and the other half the next. With the Legislature, however, it will rest to stop where we are, or at any further point, when they shall be of opinion that the number provided shall be sufficient for the object,

At times when Europe as well as the United States shall be at peace ¡t would not be proposed that more than six or eight of these vessels should be kept afloat. When Europe is in wai, treble that number might be necessary, to be distributed among those particular harbors which foreign vessels of war are in the habit of frequenting for the purpose of preserving order therein. But they would be manned in ordinary, with only their complement for navigation, relying on the seamen and militia of the port if called into action on any sudden emergency. It would be only when the United States should themselves be at war that the whole number would be brought into active service, and would be ready in the first moments of the war to cooperate with the other means for covering at once the line of our seaports. At all times those unemployed would be withdrawn into places not exposed to sudden enterprise, hauled up under sheds from the sun and weather, and kept in preservation with little expense for repairs or maintenance.

It must be superfluous to observe that this species of naval armament is proposed merely for defensive operation; that it can have but little effect toward protecting our commerce in the open seas, even on our own coast; and still less can it become an excitement to engage in offensive maritime war, toward which it would furnish no means.

TH: JEFFERSON.

FEBRUARY 11, 1807.

To the Senate and House of Representatives of the United States:

I now lay before Congress a statement of the militia of the United States according to the latest returns received by the Department of War. From two of the States no returns have ever been received.

TH: JEFFERSON.

FEBRUARY 19, 1807.

To the Senate and House of Representatives of the United States:

I transmit to Congress a letter from our ministers plenipotentiary at London, informing us that they have agreed with the British commissioners to conclude a treaty on all the points which had formed the object of their negotiation, and on terms which they trusted we would approve.

Also a letter from our minister plenipotentiary at Paris covering one to him from the minister of marine of that Government assuring him that the imperial decree lately passed was not to affect our commerce, which would still be governed by the rules of the treaty established between the two countries.

Also a letter from Cowles Mead, secretary of the Mississippi Territory, acting as governor, informing us that Aaron Burr had surrendered himself to the civil authority of that Territory.

TH: JEFFERSON.

PROCLAMATIONS.

By Thomas Jefferson, President of the United States of America.

A PROCLAMATION.

During the wars which for some time have unhappily prevailed among the powers of Europe the United States of America, firm in their principles of peace, have endeavored, by justice, by a regular discharge of all their national and social duties, and by every friendly office their situation has admitted, to maintain with all the belligerents their accustomed relations of friendship, hospitality, and commercial intercourse. Taking no part in the questions which animate these powers against each other, nor permitting themselves to entertain a wish but for the restoration of general peace, they have observed with good faith the neutrality they assumed, and they believe that no instance of a departure from its duties can be justly imputed to them by any nation. A free use of their harbors and waters, the means of refitting and of refreshment, of succor to their sick and suffering, have at all times and on equal principles been extended to all, and this, too, amidst a constant recurrence of acts of insubordination to the laws, of violence to the persons, and of trespasses on the property of our citizens committed by officers of one of the belligerent parties received among us. In truth, these abuses of the laws of hospitality have, with few exceptions, become habitual to the commanders of the British armed vessels hovering on our coasts and frequenting our harbors. They have been the subject of repeated representations to their Government. Assurances have been given that proper orders should restrain them within the limits of the rights and of the respect due to a friendly nation; but those orders and assurances have been without effect—no instance of punishment for past wrongs has taken place. At length a deed transcending all we have hitherto seen or suffered brings the public sensibility to a serious crisis and our forbearance to a necessary pause. A frigate of the United States, trusting to a state of peace, and leaving her harbor on a distant service, has been surprised and attacked by a British vessel of superior force—one of a squadron then lying in our waters and covering the transaction—and has been disabled from service, with the loss of a number of men killed and wounded. This enormity was not only without provocation or justifiable cause, but was committed with the avowed purpose of taking by force from a ship of war of the United States a part of her crew; and that no circumstance might be wanting to mark its character, it had been previously ascertained that the seamen demanded were native citizens of the United States. Having effected her purpose, she returned to anchor with her squadron within our jurisdiction. Hospitality under such circumstances ceases to be a duty, and a continuance of it with such uncontrolled abuses would tend only, by multiplying injuries and irritations, to bring on a rupture between the two nations. This extreme resort is equally opposed to the interests of both, as it is to assurances of the most friendly dispositions on the part of the British Government, in the midst of which this outrage has been committed. In this light the subject can not but present itself to that Government and strengthen the motives to an honorable reparation of the wrong which has been done, and to that effectual control of its naval commanders which alone can justify the Government of the United States in the exercise of those hospitalities it is now constrained to discontinue.

In consideration of these circumstances and of the right of every nation to regulate its own police, to provide for its peace and for the safety of its citizens, and consequently to refuse the admission of armed vessels into its harbors or waters, either in such numbers or of such descriptions as are inconsistent with these or with the maintenance of the authority of the laws, I have thought proper, in pursuance of the authorities specially given by law, to issue this my proclamation, hereby requiring all armed vessels bearing commissions under the Government of Great Britain now within the harbors or waters of the United States immediately and without any delay to depart from the same, and interdicting the entrance of all the said harbors and waters to the said armed vessels and to all others bearing commissions under the authority of the British Government.

And if the said vessels, or any of them, shall fail to depart as aforesaid, or if they or any others so interdicted shall hereafter enter the harbors or waters aforesaid, I do in that case forbid all intercourse with them, or any of them, their officers or crews, and do prohibit all supplies and aid from being furnished to them, or any of them.

And I do declare and make known that if any person from or within the jurisdictional limits of the United States shall afford any aid to any such vessel contrary to the prohibition contained in this proclamation, either in repairing any such vessel or in furnishing her, her officers or crew, with supplies of any kind or in any manner whatsoever; or if any pilot shall assist in navigating any of the said armed vessels, unless it be for the purpose of carrying them in the first instance beyond the limits and jurisdiction of the United States, or unless it be in the case of a vessel forced by distress or charged with public dispatches, as hereinafter provided for, such person or persons shall on conviction suffer all the pains and penalties by the laws provided for such offenses.

And I do hereby enjoin and require all persons bearing office, civil or military, within or under the authority of the United States, and all others citizens or inhabitants thereof, or being within the same, with vigilance and promptitude to exert their respective authorities and to be aiding and assisting to the carrying this proclamation and every part thereof into full effect.

Provided, nevertheless, that if any such vessel shall be forced into the harbors or waters of the United States by distress, by the dangers of the sea, or by the pursuit of an enemy, or shall enter them charged with dispatches or business from their Government, or shall be a public packet for the conveyance of letters and dispatches, the commanding officer, immediately reporting his vessel to the collector of the district, stating the object or causes of entering the said harbors or waters, and conforming himself to the regulations in that case prescribed under the authority of the laws, shall be allowed the benefit of such regulations respecting repairs, supplies, stay, intercourse, and departure as shall be permitted under the same authority.

In testimony whereof I have caused the seal of the United States to be affixed to these presents, and signed the same.

[SEAL.]   Given at the city of Washington, the 2d day of July, A. D. 1807, and of the Sovereignty and Independence of the United States the thirty-first.

TH: JEFFERSON.

By the President:
JAMES MADISON,
        Secretary of State.

[From Annals of Congress, Tenth Congress, first session, vol. 1, 9.]

BY THE PRESIDENT OF THE UNITED STATES OF AMERICA.

A PROCLAMATION.

Whereas great and weighty matters claiming the consideration of the Congress of the United States form an extraordinary occasion for convening them, I do by these presents appoint Monday, the 26th day of October next, for their meeting at the city of Washington, hereby requiring the respective Senators and Representatives then and there to assemble in Congress, in order to receive such communications as may then be made to them, and to consult and determine on such measures as in their wisdom may be deemed meet for the welfare of the United States.

In testimony whereof I have caused the seal of the United States to be hereunto affixed, and signed the same with my hand.

[SEAL.]   Done at the city of Washington, the 30th day of July, A. D. 1807, and in the thirty-second year of the Independence of the United States.

TH: JEFFERSON.

By the President:
JAMES MADISON,
        Secretary of State.

[From the National Intelligencer, October 19, 1807.]

By the President of the United States of America.

A PROCLAMATION.

Whereas information has been received that a number of individuals who have deserted from the Army of the United States and sought shelter without the jurisdiction thereof have become sensible of their offense and are desirous of returning to their duty, a full pardon is hereby proclaimed to each and all of such individuals as shall within four months from the date hereof surrender themselves to the commanding officer of any military post within the United States or the Territories thereof.

In testimony whereof I have caused the seal of the United States to be affixed to these presents, and signed the same with my hand.

[SEAL.]   Done at the city of Washington, the 15th day of October, A. D. 1807, and of the Independence of the United States of America the thirty-second.

TH: JEFFERSON.

By the President:
JAMES MADISON,
Secretary of State.

SEVENTH ANNUAL MESSAGE.

OCTOBER 27, 1807.

To the Senate and House of Representatives of the United States:

Circumstances, fellow-citizens, which seriously threatened the peace of our country have made it a duty to convene you at an earlier period than usual. The love of peace so much cherished in the bosoms of our citizens, which has so long guided the proceedings of their public councils and induced forbearance under so many wrongs, may not insure our continuance in the quiet pursuits of industry. The many injuries and depredations committed on our commerce and navigation upon the high seas for years past, the successive innovations on those principles of public law which have been established by the reason and usage of nations as the rule of their intercourse and the umpire and security of their rights and peace, and all the circumstances which induced the extraordinary mission to London are already known to you. The instructions given to our ministers were framed in the sincerest spirit of amity and moderation. They accordingly proceeded, in conformity therewith, to propose arrangements which might embrace and settle all the points in difference between us, which might bring us to a mutual understanding on our neutral and national rights and provide for a commercial intercourse on conditions of some equality. After long and fruitless endeavors to effect the purposes of their mission and to obtain arrangements within the limits of their instructions, they concluded to sign such as could be obtained and to send them for consideration, candidly declaring to the other negotiators at the same time that they were acting against their instructions, and that their Government, therefore, could not be pledged for ratification. Some of the articles proposed might have been admitted on a principle of compromise, but others were too highly disadvantageous, and no sufficient provision was made against the principal source of the irritations and collisions which were constantly endangering the peace of the two nations. The question, therefore, whether a treaty should be accepted in that form could have admitted but of one decision, even had no declarations of the other party impaired our confidence in it. Still anxious not to close the door against friendly adjustment, new modifications were framed and further concessions authorized than could before have been supposed necessary; and our ministers were instructed to resume their negotiations on these grounds. On this new reference to amicable discussion we were reposing in confidence, when on the 22d day of June last by a formal order from a British admiral the frigate *Chesapeake*, leaving her port for a distant service, was attacked by one of those vessels which had been lying in our harbors under the indulgences of hospitality, was disabled from proceeding, had several of her crew killed and four taken away. On this outrage no commentaries are necessary. Its character has been pronounced by the indignant voice of our citizens with an emphasis and unanimity never exceeded. I immediately, by proclamation, interdicted our harbors and waters to all British armed vessels, forbade intercourse with them, and uncertain how far hostilities were intended, and the town of Norfolk, indeed, being threatened with immediate attack, a sufficient force was ordered for the protection of that place, and such other preparations commenced and pursued as the prospect rendered proper. An armed vessel of the United States was dispatched with instructions to our ministers at London to call on that Government for the satisfaction and security required by the outrage. A very short interval ought now to bring the answer, which shall be communicated to you as soon as received; then also, or as soon after as the public interests shall be found to admit, the unratified treaty and proceedings relative to it shall be made known to you.

The aggression thus begun has been continued on the part of the British commanders by remaining within our waters in defiance of the authority of the country, by habitual violations of its jurisdiction, and at length by putting to death one of the persons whom they had forcibly taken from on board the *Chesapeake*. These aggravations necessarily lead to the policy either of never admitting an armed vessel into our harbors or of maintaining in every harbor such an armed force as may constrain obedience to the laws and protect the lives and property of our

By Thomas Jefferson President of the U. S. of America.

A Proclamation.

During the wars which, for some time, have unhappily prevailed among the powers of Europe the United States of America firm in their principles of peace have endeavored by justice, by a regular discharge of all their National & Social duties, & by every friendly office their situation has admitted to maintain with all the belligerents their accustomed relations of friendship, hospitality & commercial intercourse; taking no part in the questions which animate these powers against each other, nor permitting themselves to entertain a wish but for the restoration of general peace, they have observed with good faith the neutrality they assumed & they believe that no instance of a departure from it's duties can be justly imputed to them by any nation. A free use of their Harbours & waters, the means of refitting & of refreshment, of succour to their sick & suffering, have at all times, and on equal principles been extended to all, & this too amidst a constant recurrence of acts of insubordination to the laws, of

FIRST AND LAST PAGES OF JEFFERSON'S NEUTRALITY
PROCLAMATION.

letters & dispatches, the commanding Officer immediately reporting his Vessel to the Collector of the District, stating the
object or causes of entering the said Harbors or waters, and
conforming himself to the regulations in that case prescribed
under the Authority of the laws, shall be allowed the benefit of such regulations respecting repairs supplies stay intercourse & departure as shall be permitted under the same Authority.

In testimony whereof I have caused the Seal of the United
States to be affixed to these presents & signed the same

Given at the City of Washington the 2d day of July in the
year of our Lord 1807 & of the Sovereignty & Independance of the
United States the 31st

Th: Jefferson

By the President

Secretary of State

citizens against their armed guests; but the expense of such a standing force and its inconsistence with our principles dispense with those courtesies which would necessarily call for it, and leave us equally free to exclude the navy, as we are the army, of a foreign power from entering our limits.

To former violations of maritime rights another is now added of very extensive effect. The Government of that nation has issued an order interdicting all trade by neutrals between ports not in amity with them; and being now at war with nearly every nation on the Atlantic and Mediterranean seas, our vessels are required to sacrifice their cargoes at the first port they touch or to return home without the benefit of going to any other market. Under this new law of the ocean our trade on the Mediterranean has been swept away by seizures and condemnations, and that in other seas is threatened with the same fate.

Our differences with Spain remain still unsettled, no measure having been taken on her part since my last communications to Congress to bring them to a close. But under a state of things which may favor reconsideration they have been recently pressed, and an expectation is entertained that they may now soon be brought to an issue of some sort. With their subjects on our borders no new collisions have taken place nor seem immediately to be apprehended. To our former grounds of complaint has been added a very serious one, as you will see by the decree a copy of which is now communicated. Whether this decree, which professes to be conformable to that of the French Government of November 21, 1806, heretofore communicated to Congress, will also be conformed to that in its construction and application in relation to the United States had not been ascertained at the date of our last communications. These, however, gave reason to expect such a conformity.

With the other nations of Europe our harmony has been uninterrupted, and commerce and friendly intercourse have been maintained on their usual footing.

Our peace with the several states on the coast of Barbary appears as firm as at any former period and as likely to continue as that of any other nation.

Among our Indian neighbors in the northwestern quarter some fermentation was observed soon after the late occurrences, threatening the continuance of our peace. Messages were said to be interchanged and tokens to be passing, which usually denote a state of restlessness among them, and the character of the agitators pointed to the sources of excitement. Measures were immediately taken for providing against that danger; instructions were given to require explanations, and, with assurances of our continued friendship, to admonish the tribes to remain quiet at home, taking no part in quarrels not belonging to them. As far as we are yet informed, the tribes in our vicinity, who are most advanced in the pursuits of industry, are sincerely disposed to adhere to their friendship with us and to their peace with all others, while those more remote do not present appearances sufficiently quiet to justify the intermission of military precaution on our part.

The great tribes on our southwestern quarter, much advanced beyond the others in agriculture and household arts, appear tranquil and identifying their views with ours in proportion to their advancement. With the whole of these people, in every quarter, I shall continue to inculcate peace and friendship with all their neighbors and perseverance in those occupations and pursuits which will best promote their own well-being.

The appropriations of the last session for the defense of our seaport towns and harbors were made under expectation that a continuance of our peace would permit us to proceed in that work according to our convenience. It has been thought better to apply the sums then given toward the defense of New York, Charleston, and New Orleans chiefly, as most open and most likely first to need protection, and to leave places less immediately in danger to the provisions of the present session.

The gunboats, too, already provided have on a like principle been chiefly assigned to New York, New Orleans, and the Chesapeake. Whether our movable force on the water, so material in aid of the defensive works on the land, should be augmented in this or any other form is left to the wisdom of the Legislature. For the purpose of manning these vessels in sudden attacks on our harbors it is a matter for consideration whether the seamen of the United States may not justly be formed into a special militia, to be called on for tours of duty in defense of the harbors where they shall happen to be, the ordinary militia of the place furnishing that portion which may consist of landsmen.

The moment our peace was threatened I deemed it indispensable to secure a greater provision of those articles of military stores with which our magazines were not sufficiently furnished. To have awaited a previous and special sanction by law would have lost occasions which might not be retrieved. I did not hesitate, therefore, to authorize engagements for such supplements to our existing stock as would render it adequate to the emergencies threatening us, and I trust that the Legislature, feeling the same anxiety for the safety of our country, so materially advanced by this precaution, will approve, when done, what they would have seen so important to be done if then assembled. Expenses, also unprovided for, arose out of the necessity of calling all our gunboats into actual service for the defense of our harbors; of all which accounts will be laid before you.

Whether a regular army is to be raised, and to what extent, must depend on the information so shortly expected. In the meantime I have called on the States for quotas of militia, to be in readiness for present defense, and have, moreover, encouraged the acceptance of volunteers; and I am happy to inform you that these have offered themselves with great alacrity in every part of the Union. They are ordered to be organized and ready at a moment's warning to proceed on any service to which they may be called, and every preparation within the Executive powers has been made to insure us the benefit of early exertions.

I informed Congress at their last session of the enterprises against the public peace which were believed to be in preparation by Aaron Burr and his associates, of the measures taken to defeat them and to bring the offenders to justice. Their enterprises were happily defeated by the patriotic exertions of the militia whenever called into action, by the fidelity of the Army, and energy of the commander in chief in promptly arranging the difficulties presenting themselves on the Sabine, repairing to meet those arising on the Mississippi, and dissipating before their explosion plots engendering there. I shall think it my duty to lay before you the proceedings and the evidence publicly exhibited on the arraignment of the principal offenders before the circuit court of Virginia. You will be enabled to judge whether the defect was in the testimony, in the law, or in the administration of the law; and wherever it shall be found, the Legislature alone can apply or originate the remedy. The framers of our Constitution certainly supposed they had guarded as well their Government against destruction by treason as their citizens against oppression under pretense of it, and if these ends are not attained it is of importance to inquire by what means more effectual they may be secured.

The accounts of the receipts of revenue during the year ending on the 30th day of September last being not yet made up, a correct statement will be hereafter transmitted from the Treasury. In the meantime, it is ascertained that the receipts have amounted to near $16,000,000, which, with the five millions and a half in the Treasury at the beginning of the year, have enabled us, after meeting the current demands and interest incurred, to pay more than four millions of the principal of our funded debt. These payments, with those of the preceding five and a half years, have extinguished of the funded debt $25,500,000, being the whole which could be paid or purchased within the limits of the law and of our contracts, and have left us in the Treasury $8,500,000. A portion of this sum may be considered as a commencement of accumulation of the surpluses of revenue which, after paying the installments of debt as they shall become payable, will remain without any specific object. It may partly, indeed, be applied toward completing the defense of the exposed points of our country, on such a scale as shall be adapted to our principles and circumstances. This object is doubtless among the first entitled to attention in such a state of our finances, and it is one which, whether we have peace or war, will provide security where it is due. Whether what shall remain of this, with the future surpluses, may be usefully applied to purposes already authorized or more usefully to others requiring new authorities, or how otherwise they shall be disposed of, are questions calling for the notice of Congress, unless, indeed, they shall be superseded by a change in our public relations now awaiting the determination of others. Whatever be that determination, it is a great consolation that it will become known at a moment when the supreme council of the nation is assembled at its post, and ready to give the aids of its wisdom and authority to whatever course the good of our country shall then call us to pursue.

Matters of minor importance will be the subjects of future communications, and nothing shall be wanting on my part which may give information or dispatch to the proceedings of the Legislature in the exercise of their high duties, and at a moment so interesting to the public welfare.

TH: JEFFERSON.

SPECIAL MESSAGES.

NOVEMBER 11, 1807.

To the Senate of the United States:

Some time had elapsed after the receipt of the late treaty between the United States and Tripoli before the circumstance drew particular attention that, although by the third article the wife and children of the ex-Bashaw were to be restored to him, this did not appear either to have been done or demanded; still, it was constantly expected that explanations on the subject would be received. None, however, having arrived when Mr. Davis went as consul to Tripoli, he was instructed to demand the execution of the article. He did so, but was answered by the exhibition of a declaration, signed by our negotiator the day after the signature of the treaty, allowing four years for the restoration of the family. This declaration and the letter of Mr. Davis stating what passed on the occasion are now communicated to the Senate. On the receipt of this letter I caused the correspondence of Mr. Lear to be diligently reexamined in order to ascertain whether there might have been a communication of this paper made and overlooked or forgotten. None such, however, is found. There appears only in a journalized account of the transaction by Mr. Lear, under date of June 3, a passage intimating that he should be disposed to give time rather than suffer the business to be broken off and our countrymen left in slavery; and again, that on the return of the person who passed between himself and the Bashaw, and information that the Bashaw would require time for the delivery of the family, he consented, and went ashore to consummate the treaty. This was done the next day, and being forwarded to us as ultimately signed, and found to contain no allowance of time nor any intimation that there was any stipulation but what was in the public treaty, it was supposed that the Bashaw had, in fine, abandoned the proposition, and the instructions before mentioned were consequently given to Mr. Davis.

An extract of so much of Mr. Lear's communication as relates to this circumstance is now transmitted to the Senate, the whole of the papers having been laid before them on a former occasion. How it has happened that the declaration of June 5 has never before come to our knowledge can not with certainty be said, but whether there has been a miscarriage of it or a failure of the ordinary attention and correctness of that officer in making his communications, I have thought it due to the Senate as well as to myself to explain to them the circumstances which have withheld from their knowledge, as they did from my own, a modification which, had it been placed in the public treaty, would have been relieved from the objections which candor and good faith can not but feel in its present form.

As the restoration of the family has probably been effected, a just regard to the character of the United States will require that I make to the Bashaw a candid statement of facts, and that the sacrifices of his right to the peace and friendship of the two countries, by yielding finally to the demand of Mr. Davis, be met by proper acknowledgments and reparation on our part.

TH: JEFFERSON.

NOVEMBER 19, 1807.

To the House of Representatives of the United States:

According to the request expressed in your resolution of the 18th instant, I now transmit a copy of my proclamation interdicting our harbors and waters to British armed vessels and forbidding intercourse with them, referred to in my message of the 27th of October last.

TH: JEFFERSON.

NOVEMBER 23, 1807.

To the Senate and House of Representatives of the United States:

Agreeably to the assurance given in my message at the opening of the present session of Congress, I now lay before you a copy of the proceedings and of the evidence exhibited on the arraignment of Aaron Burr and others before the circuit court of the United States held in Virginia in the course of the present year, in as authentic form as their several parts have admitted.

TH: JEFFERSON.

NOVEMBER 23, 1807.

To the Senate of the United States:

Some circumstance, which can not now be ascertained, induced a belief that an act had passed at the last session of Congress for establishing a surveyor and inspector of revenue for the port of Stonington, in Connecticut, and commissions were signed appointing Jonathan Palmer, of Connecticut, to those offices. The error was discovered at the Treasury, and the commissions were retained; but not having been notified to me, I renewed the nomination in my message of the 9th instant to the Senate. In order to correct the error, I have canceled the temporary commissions, and now revoke the nomination which I made of the said Jonathan Palmer to the Senate.

TH: JEFFERSON.

DECEMBER 2, 1807.

To the Senate of the United States:

In compliance with the request made in the resolution of the Senate of November 30, I must inform them that when the prosecutions against Aaron Burr and his associates were instituted I delivered to the Attorney-General all the evidence on the subject, formal and informal, which I had received, to be used by those employed in the prosecutions. On the receipt of the resolution of the Senate I referred it to the Attorney-General, with a request that he would enable me to comply with it by putting into my hands such of the papers as might give information relative to the conduct of John Smith, a Senator from the State of Ohio, as an alleged associate of Aaron Burr, and having this moment received from him the affidavit of Elias Glover, with an assurance that it is the only paper in his possession which is within the term of the request of the Senate, I now transmit it for their use.

TH: JEFFERSON.

DECEMBER 7, 1807.

To the Senate and House of Representatives of the United States:

Having recently received from our late minister plenipotentiary at the Court of London a duplicate of dispatches, the original of which has been sent by the *Revenge* schooner, not yet arrived, I hasten to lay them before both Houses of Congress. They contain the whole of what has passed between the two Governments on the subject of the outrage committed by the British ship *Leopard* on the frigate *Chesapeake*. Congress will learn from these papers the present state of the discussion on that transaction, and that it is to be transferred to this place by the mission of a special minister.

While this information will have its proper effect on their deliberations and proceedings respecting the relations between the two countries, they will be sensible that, the negotiation being still depending, it is proper for me to request that the communications may be considered as confidential.

TH: JEFFERSON.

DECEMBER 18, 1807.

To the Senate and House of Representatives of the United States:

The communications now made, shewing the great and increasing dangers with which our vessels, our seamen, and merchandise are threatened on the high seas and elsewhere from the belligerent powers of Europe, and it being of the greatest importance to keep in safety these essential resources, I deem it my duty to recommend the subject to the consideration of Congress, who will doubtless perceive all the advantages which may be expected from an inhibition of the departure of our vessels from the ports of the United States.

Their wisdom will also see the necessity of making every preparation for whatever events may grow out of the present crisis.

TH: JEFFERSON.

DECEMBER 30, 1807.

To the Senate and House of Representatives of the United States:

I communicate to Congress the inclosed letters from Governor Hull, respecting the Indians in the vicinity of Detroit residing within our lines. They contain information of the state of things in that quarter which will properly enter into their view in estimating the means to be provided for the defense of our country generally.

TH: JEFFERSON.

JANUARY 8, 1808.

To the Senate and House of Representatives of the United States:

I now render to Congress the account of the fund established for defraying the contingent expenses of Government for the year 1807. Of the sum of $18,012.50, which remained unexpended at the close of the year 1806, $8,731.11 have been placed in the hands of the Attorney-General of the United States, to enable him to defray sundry expenses incident to the prosecution of Aaron Burr and his accomplices for treasons and misdemeanors alleged to have been committed by them, and the unexpended balance of $9,275.39 is now carried according to law to the credit of the surplus fund.

TH: JEFFERSON.

JANUARY 15, 1808.

To the Senate of the United States:

The posts of Detroit and Mackinac having been originally intended by the Governments which established and held them as mere depots for commerce with the Indians, very small cessions of land around them were obtained or asked from the native proprietors, and these posts depended for protection on the strength of their garrisons. The principles of our Government leading us to the employment of such moderate garrisons in time of peace as may merely take care of the post, and to a reliance on the neighboring militia for its support in the first moments of war, I have thought it would be important to obtain from the Indians such a cession in the neighborhood of these posts as might maintain a militia proportioned to this object; and I have particularly contemplated, with this view, the acquisition of the eastern moiety of the peninsula between lakes Michigan and Huron, comprehending the waters of the latter and of Detroit River, so soon as it could be effected with the perfect good will of the natives. Governor Hull was therefore appointed a commissioner to treat with them on this subject, but was instructed to confine his propositions for the present to so much of the tract before described as lay south of Saguina Bay and round to the Connecticut Reserve, so as to consolidate the new with the present settled country. The result has been an acquisition of so much only of what would have been acceptable as extends from the neighborhood of Saguina Bay to the Miami of the Lakes, with a prospect of soon obtaining a breadth of 2 miles for a communication from the Miami to the Connecticut Reserve. The treaty for this purpose entered into with the Ottoways, Chippeways, Wyandots, and Pottawattamies at Detroit on the 17th of November last is now transmitted to the Senate, and I ask their advice and consent as to its ratification.

I communicate herewith such papers as bear any material relation to the subject.

TH: JEFFERSON.

JANUARY 15, 1808.

To the Senate of the United States:

Although it is deemed very desirable that the United States should obtain from the native proprietors the whole left bank of the Mississippi to a certain breadth, yet to obliterate from the Indian mind an impression deeply made in it that we are constantly forming designs on their lands I have thought it best where urged by no peculiar necessity to leave to themselves and to the pressure of their own convenience only to come forward with offers of sale to the United States.

The Choctaws, being indebted to certain mercantile characters beyond what could be discharged by the ordinary proceeds of their huntings, and pressed for payment by those creditors, proposed at length to the United States to cede lands to the amount of their debts, and designated them in two different portions of their country. These designations not at all suiting us, their proposals were declined for that reason, and with an intimation that if their own convenience should ever dispose them to cede their lands on the Mississippi we should be willing to purchase. Still urged by their creditors, as well as by their own desire to be liberated from debt, they at length proposed to make a cession which should be to our convenience. James Robertson, of Tennessee, and Silas Dinsmore were thereupon appointed commissioners to treat with them on that subject, with instructions to purchase only on the Mississippi. On meeting their chiefs, however, it was found that such was the attachment of the nation to their lands on the Mississippi that their chiefs could not undertake to cede them; but they offered all their lands south of a line to be run from their and our boundary at the Omochita eastwardly to their boundary with the Creeks, on the ridge between the Tombigbee and Alabama, which would unite our possessions there from Natchez to Tombigbee. A treaty to this effect was accordingly signed at Pooshape-kanuk on the 16th of November, 1805; but this being against express instructions, and not according with the object then in view, I was disinclined to its ratification, and therefore did not at the last session of Congress lay it before the Senate for their advice, but have suffered it to lie unacted on.

Progressive difficulties, however, in our foreign relations have brought into view considerations other than those which then prevailed. It is now, perhaps, become as interesting to obtain footing for a strong settlement of militia along our southern frontier eastward of the Mississippi as on the west of that river, and more so than higher up the river itself. The consolidation of the Mississippi Territory and the establishing a barrier of separation between the Indians and our Southern neighbors are also important objects. The cession is supposed to contain about 5,000,000 acres, of which the greater part is said to be fit for cultivation, and no inconsiderable proportion of the first quality, on the various waters it includes; and the Choctaws and their creditors are still anxious for the sale.

I therefore now transmit the treaty for the consideration of the Senate, and I ask their advice and consent as to its ratification. I communicate at the same time such papers as bear any material relation to the subject, together with a map on which is sketched the northern limit of the cession, rather to give a general idea than with any pretension to exactness, which our present knowledge of the country would not warrant.

TH: JEFFERSON.

JANUARY 20, 1808.

To the House of Representatives of the United States:

Some days previous to your resolutions of the 13th instant a court of inquiry had been instituted at the request of General Wilkinson, charged to make the inquiry into his conduct which the first resolution desires, and had commenced their proceedings. To the judge-advocate of that court the papers and information on that subject transmitted to me by the House of Representatives have been delivered, to be used according to the rules and powers of that court.

The request of a communication of any information which may have been received at any time since the establishment of the present Government touching combinations with foreign agents for dismembering the Union or the corrupt receipt of money by any officer of the United States from the agents of foreign governments can be complied with but in a partial degree.

It is well understood that in the first or second year of the Presidency of General Washington information was given to him relating to certain combinations with the agents of a foreign government for the dismemberment of the Union, which combinations had taken place before the establishment of the present Federal Government. This information, however, is believed never to have been deposited in any public office, or left in that of the President's secretary, these having been duly examined, but to have been considered as personally confidential, and therefore retained among his private papers. A communication from the governor of Virginia to President Washington is found in the office of the President's secretary, which, although not strictly within the terms of the request of the House of Representatives, is communicated, inasmuch as it may throw some light on the subjects of the correspondence of that time between certain foreign agents and citizens of the United States.

In the first or second year of the Administration of President Adams Andrew Ellicott, then employed in designating, in conjunction with the Spanish authorities, the boundaries between the territories of the United States and Spain, under the treaty with that nation, communicated to the Executive of the United States papers and information respecting the subjects of the present inquiry, which were deposited in the Office of State. Copies of these are now transmitted to the House of Representatives, except of a single letter and a reference from the said Andrew Ellicott, which, being expressly desired to be kept secret, is therefore not communicated, but its contents can be obtained from himself in a more legal form, and directions have been given to summon him to appear as a witness before the court of inquiry.

A paper on "The Commerce of Louisiana," bearing date the 18th of April, 1798, is found in the Office of State, supposed to have been communicated by Mr. Daniel Clark, of New Orleans, then a subject of Spain, and now of the House of Representatives of the United States, stating certain commercial transactions of General Wilkinson in New Orleans. An extract from this is now communicated, because it contains facts which may have some bearing on the questions relating to him.

The destruction of the War Office by fire in the close of 1800 involved all information it contained at that date.

The papers already described therefore constitute the whole of the information on the subjects deposited in the public offices during the preceding Administrations, as far as has yet been found; but it can not be affirmed that there may be no other, because, the papers of the office being filed for the most part alphabetically, unless aided by the suggestion of any particular name which may have given such information, nothing short of a careful examination of the papers in the offices generally could authorize such an affirmation.

About a twelvemonth after I came to the administration of the Government Mr. Clark gave some verbal information to myself, as well as to the Secretary of State, relating to the same combinations for the dismemberment of the Union. He was listened to freely, and he then delivered the letter of Governor Gayoso, addressed to himself, of which a copy is now communicated. After his return to New Orleans he forwarded to the Secretary of State other papers, with a request that after perusal they should be burnt. This, however, was not done, and he was so informed by the Secretary of State, and that they would be held subject to his orders. These papers have not yet been found in the office. A letter, therefore, has been addressed to the former chief clerk, who may perhaps give information respecting them. As far as our memories enable us to say, they related only to the combinations before spoken of, and not at all to the corrupt receipt of money by any officer of the United States; consequently they respected what was considered as a dead matter, known to the preceding Administrations, and offering nothing new to call for investigations, which those nearest the dates of the transactions had not thought proper to institute.

In the course of the communications made to me on the subject of the conspiracy of Aaron Burr I sometimes received letters, some of them anonymous, some under names true or false, expressing suspicions and insinuations against General Wilkinson; but one only of them, and that anonymous, specified any particular fact, and that fact was one of those which had been already communicated to a former Administration.

No other information within the purview of the request of the House is known to have been received by any department of the Government from the establishment of the present Federal Government. That which has been recently communicated to the House of Representatives, and by them to me, is the first direct testimony ever made known to me charging General Wilkinson with the corrupt receipt of money, and the House of Representatives may be assured that the duties which this information devolves on me shall be exercised with rigorous impartiality. Should any want of power in the court to compel the rendering of testimony obstruct that full and impartial inquiry which alone can establish guilt or innocence and satisfy justice, the legislative authority only will be competent to the remedy.

TH: JEFFERSON.

JANUARY 30, 1808.

To the Senate and House of Representatives of the United States:

The Choctaws, being indebted to their merchants beyond what could be discharged by the ordinary proceeds of their huntings, and pressed for payment, proposed to the United States to cede lands to the amount of their debts, and designated them in two different portions of their country. These designations, not at all suiting us, were declined. Still urged by their creditors, as well as by their own desire to be liberated from debt, they at length proposed to make a cession which should be to our convenience. By a treaty signed at Pooshapuckanuck on the 16th of November, 1805, they accordingly ceded all their lands south of a line to be run from their and our boundary at the Omochita eastwardly to their boundary with the Creeks, on the ridge between the Tombigbee and Alabama, as is more particularly described in the treaty, containing about 5,000,000 acres, as is supposed, and uniting our possessions there from Adams to Washington County.

The location contemplated in the instructions to the commissioners was on the Mississippi. That in the treaty being entirely different, I was at that time disinclined to its ratification, and I have suffered it to lie unacted on. But progressive difficulties in our foreign relations have brought into view considerations other than those which then prevailed. It is now, perhaps, as interesting to obtain footing for a strong settlement of militia along our southern frontier eastward of the Mississippi as on the west of that river, and more so than higher up the river itself. The consolidation of the Mississippi Territory and the establishment of a barrier of separation between the Indians and our Southern neighbors are also important objects; and the Choctaws and their creditors being still anxious that the sale should be made, I submitted the treaty to the Senate, who have advised and consented to its ratification. I therefore now lay it before both Houses of Congress for the exercise of their constitutional powers as to the means of fulfilling it.

TH: JEFFERSON.

JANUARY 30, 1808.

To the House of Representatives of the United States:

The posts of Detroit and Mackinac having been originally intended by the Governments which established and held them as mere depots for commerce with the Indians, very small cessions of land around them were obtained or asked from the native proprietors, and these posts depended for protection on the strength of their garrisons. The principles of our Government leading us to the employment of such moderate garrisons in time of peace as may merely take care of the post, and to a reliance on the neighboring militia for its support in the first moments of war, I have thought it would be important to obtain from the Indians such a cession in the neighborhood of these posts as might maintain a militia proportioned to this object; and I have particularly contemplated, with this view, the acquisition of the eastern moiety of the peninsula between the lakes Michigan, Huron, and Erie, extending it to the Connecticut

Reserve so soon as it could be effected with the perfect good will of the natives.

By a treaty concluded at Detroit on the 17th of November last with the Ottoways, Chippeways, Wyandots, and Pattawatimas so much of this country has been obtained as extends from about Saguina Bay southwardly to the Miami of the Lakes, supposed to contain upward of 5,000,000 acres, with a prospect of obtaining for the present a breadth of 2 miles for a communication from the Miami to the Connecticut Reserve.

The Senate having advised and consented to the ratification of this treaty, I now lay it before both Houses of Congress for the exercise of their constitutional powers as to the means of fulfilling it.

TH: JEFFERSON.

FEBRUARY 2, 1808.

To the Senate and House of Representatives of the United States:

Having received an official communication of certain orders of the British Government against the maritime rights of neutrals, bearing date the 11th of November, 1807, I transmit them to Congress, as a further proof of the increasing dangers to our navigation and commerce, which led to the provident measure of the act of the present session laying an embargo on our own vessels.

TH: JEFFERSON.

FEBRUARY 4, 1808.

To the House of Representatives of the United States:

In my message of January 20 I stated that some papers forwarded by Mr. Daniel Clark, of New Orleans, to the Secretary of State in 1803 had not then been found in the Office of State, and that a letter had been addressed to the former chief clerk, in the hope that he might advise where they should be sought for. By indications received from him they are now found. Among them are two letters from the Baron de Carondelet to an officer serving under him at a separate post, in which his views of a dismemberment of our Union are expressed. Extracts of so much of these letters as are within the scope of the resolution of the House are now communicated. With these were found the letters written by Mr. Clark to the Secretary of State in 1803. A part of one only of these relates to this subject, and is extracted and inclosed for the information of the House. In no part of the papers communicated by Mr. Clark, which are voluminous and in different languages, nor in his letters, have we found any intimation of the corrupt receipt of money by any officer of the United States from any foreign agent. As to the combinations with foreign agents for dismembering the Union, these papers and letters offer nothing which was not probably known to my predecessors, or which could call anew for inquiries, which they had not thought necessary to institute, when the facts were recent and could be better proved. They probably believed it best to let pass into oblivion transactions which, however culpable, had commenced before this Government existed, and had been finally extinguished by the treaty of 1795.

TH: JEFFERSON.

FEBRUARY 9, 1808.

To the Senate and House of Representatives of the United States:

I communicate to Congress, for their information, a letter from the person acting in the absence of our consul at Naples, giving reason to believe, on the affidavit of a Captain Sheffield, of the American schooner *Mary Ann*, that the Dey of Algiers has commenced war against the United States. For this no just cause has been given on our part within my knowledge. We may daily expect more authentic and particular information on the subject from Mr. Lear, who was residing as our consul at Algiers.

TH: JEFFERSON.

FEBRUARY 15, 1808.

To the Senate and House of Representatives of the United States:

I communicate for the information of Congress a letter from the consul of the United States at Malaga to the Secretary of State, covering one from Mr. Lear, our consul at Algiers, which gives information that the rupture threatened on the part of the Dey of Algiers has been amicably settled, and the vessels seized by him are liberated.

TH: JEFFERSON.

FEBRUARY 19, 1808.

To the Senate and House of Representatives of the United States:

The States of Pennsylvania, Maryland, and Virginia having by their several acts consented that the road from Cumberland to the State of Ohio, authorized by the act of Congress of the 29th of March, 1806, should pass through those States, and the report of the commissioners, communicated to Congress with my message of the 31st January, 1807, having been duly considered, I have approved of the route therein proposed for the said road as far as Brownsville, with a single deviation, since located, which carries it through Uniontown.

From thence the course to the Ohio and the point within the legal limits at which it shall strike that river is still to be decided. In forming this decision I shall pay material regard to the interests and wishes of the populous parts of the State of Ohio and to a future and convenient connection with the road which is to lead from the Indian boundary near Cincinnati by Vincennes to the Mississippi at St. Louis, under authority of the act of the 21st April, 1806. In this way we may accomplish a continued and advantageous line of communication from the seat of the General Government to St. Louis, passing through several very interesting points of the Western country.

I have thought it advisable also to secure from obliteration the trace of the road so far as it has been approved, which has been executed at such considerable expense, by opening one-half of its breadth through its whole length.

The report of the commissioners, herewith transmitted, will give particular information of their proceedings under the act of the 29th March, 1806, since the date of my message of the 31st January, 1807, and will enable Congress to adopt such further measures relative thereto as they may deem proper under existing circumstances.

TH: JEFFERSON.

FEBRUARY 25, 1808.

To the Senate and House of Representatives of the United States:

The dangers to our country arising from the contests of other nations and the urgency of making preparation for whatever events might affect our relations with them have been intimated in preceding messages to Congress. To secure ourselves by due precautions an augmentation of our military force, as well regular as of volunteer militia, seems to be expedient. The precise extent of that augmentation can not as yet be satisfactorily suggested, but that no time may be lost, and especially at a season deemed favorable to the object, I submit to the wisdom of the Legislature whether they will authorize a commencement of this precautionary work by a present provision for raising and organizing some additional force, reserving to themselves to decide its ultimate extent on such views of our situation as I may be enabled to present at a future day of the session.

If an increase of force be now approved, I submit to their consideration the outlines of a plan proposed in the inclosed letter from the Secretary of War.

I recommend also to the attention of Congress the term at which the act of April 18, 1806, concerning the militia, will expire, and the effect of that expiration.

TH: JEFFERSON.

FEBRUARY 26, 1808.

To the Senate and House of Representatives of the United States:

I inclose, for the information of Congress, letters recently received from our ministers at Paris and London, communicating their representations against the late decrees and orders of France and Great Britain, heretofore transmitted to Congress. These documents will contribute to the information of Congress as to the dispositions of those powers and the probable course of their proceedings toward neutrals, and will doubtless have their due influence in adopting the measures of the Legislature to the actual crisis.

Although nothing forbids the general matter of these letters from being spoken of without reserve, yet as the publication of papers of this description would restrain injuriously the freedom of our foreign correspondence, they are communicated so far confidentially and with a request that after being read to the satisfaction of both Houses they may be returned.

TH: JEFFERSON.

MARCH 1, 1808.

To the Senate of the United States:

In compliance with the resolution of the Senate of February 26, I now lay before them such memorials and petitions for the district of Detroit, and such other information as is in my possession, in relation to the conduct of William Hull, governor of the Territory of Michigan, and Stanley Griswold, esq., while acting as secretary of that Territory.

TH: JEFFERSON.

MARCH 2, 1808.

To the Senate of the United States:

In compliance with the resolution of the Senate of November 30. 1807, I now transmit a report of the Secretary of State on the subject of impressments, as requested in that resolution. The great volume of the documents and the time necessary for the investigation will explain to the Senate the causes of the delay which has intervened.

TH: JEFFERSON.

MARCH 7, 1808.

To the Senate and House of Representatives of the United States:

In the city of New Orleans and adjacent to it are sundry parcels of ground, some of them with buildings and other improvements on them, which it is my duty to present to the attention of the Legislature. The title to these grounds appears to have been retained in the former sovereigns of the Province of Louisiana as public fiduciaries and for the purposes of the Province. Some of them were used for the residence of the governor, for public offices, hospitals, barracks, magazines, fortifications, levees, etc., others for the townhouse, schools, markets, landings, and other purposes of the city of New Orleans; some were held by religious corporations or persons, others seem to have been reserved for future disposition. To these must be added a parcel called the Batture, which

THE TRIAL FOR TREASON OF AARON BURR

THE TRIAL FOR TREASON OF AARON BURR

In 1804, after killing Hamilton in a duel, Aaron Burr set on foot a scheme of empire in the Mississippi Valley and Mexico. Those who encouraged, aided or connived in the scheme included senators, ex-senators, judges, soldiers, scholars, rich men, young men, boatmen, field hands and laborers. Andrew Jackson knew of and encouraged the plan. Anthony Merry, the British Minister, thought it would disrupt the revolted colonies and promoted it. General Wilkinson, commander of the army of the United States, was false to the Government first and to Burr later. England failing to send the desired armament and funds, Burr proposed to capture and loot the treasury and stores at Washington, and that plan having miscarried, he determined to lead his forces down to New Orleans in river boats. The United States district attorney twice tried to arrest Burr but was foiled by a corrupt judge and disappearing witnesses. Jefferson then issued his proclamation of November 27, 1806 (page 392). Ohio militiamen confiscated part of Burr's equipment lying at Marietta. Jackson betrayed his trust by letting Burr descend the Mississippi. Wilkinson, who had betrayed Burr, prepared to resist any assault the conspirators might make on New Orleans. Burr, alarmed for his safety, fled to the west bank of the Mississippi, and on January 17, 1807, surrendered himself. Although the grand jury then acquitted him, he dreaded further prosecution and fled to Alabama, where he was arrested.

The picture shows him on trial before Chief Justice Marshall in the Eagle Tavern at Richmond, Va., where he was arraigned after his capture in Alabama. The trial was a failure and Burr was acquitted. Like Benedict Arnold he fled to England, and lived and died miserably. See "Burr, Aaron," in the index in volume eleven.

requires more particular description. It is understood to have been a shoal or elevation of the bottom of the river adjacent to the bank of the suburbs of St. Mary, produced by the successive depositions of mud during the annual inundations of the river, and covered with water only during those inundations. At all other seasons it has been used by the city immemorially to furnish earth for raising their streets and court-yards, for mortar, and other necessary purposes, and as a landing or quay for unlading firewood, lumber, and other articles brought by water. This having been lately claimed by a private individual, the city opposed the claim on a supposed legal title in itself; but it has been adjudged that the legal title was not in the city. It is, however, alleged that that title, originally in the former sovereigns, was never parted with by them, but was retained in them for the uses of the city and Province, and consequently has now passed over to the United States. Until this question can be decided under legislative authority, measures have been taken according to law to prevent any change in the state of things and to keep the grounds clear of intruders. The settlement of this title, the appropriation of the grounds and improvements formerly occupied for provincial purposes to the same or such other objects as may be better suited to present circumstances, the confirmation of the uses in other parcels to such bodies, corporate or private, as may of right or on other reasonable considerations expect them, are matters now submitted to the determination of the Legislature.

The papers and plans now transmitted will give them such information on the subject as I possess, and being mostly originals, I must request that they may be communicated from the one to the other House, to answer the purposes of both,

TH: JEFFERSON.

MARCH 10, 1808.

To the Senate of the United States:

A purchase having lately been made from the Cherokee Indians of a tract of land 6 miles square at the mouth of the Chickamogga, on the Tennessee, I now lay the treaty and papers relating to it before the Senate, with an explanation of the views which have led to it.

It was represented that there was within that tract a great abundance of iron ore of excellent quality, with a stream and fall of water suitable for iron works; that the Cherokees were anxious to have works established there, in the hope of having a better supply of those implements of household and agriculture of which they have learned the use and necessity, but on the condition that they should be under the authority and control of the United States.

As such an establishment would occasion a considerable and certain demand for corn and other provisions and necessaries, it seemed probable that it would immediately draw around it a close settlement of the Cherokees, would encourage them to enter on a regular life of agriculture, familiarize them with the practice and value of the arts, attach them to property, lead them of necessity and without delay to the establishment of laws and government, and thus make a great and important advance toward assimilating their condition to ours. At the same time it offers considerable accommodation to the Government by enabling it to obtain more conveniently than it now can the necessary supplies of cast and wrought iron for all the Indians south of the Tennessee, and for those also to whom St. Louis is a convenient deposit, and will benefit such of our own citizens likewise as shall be within its reach. Under these views the purchase has been made, with the consent and desire of the great body of the nation, although not without some dissenting members, as must be the case will all collections of men. But it is represented that the dissentients are few, and under the influence of one or two interested individuals. It is by no means proposed that these works should be conducted on account of the United States. It is understood that there are private individuals ready to erect them, subject to such reasonable rent as may secure a reimbursement to the United States, and to such other conditions as shall secure to the Indians their rights and tranquillity.

The instrument is now submitted to the Senate, with a request of their advice and consent as to its ratification.

TH: JEFFERSON.

MARCH 17, 1808.

To the Senate and House of Representatives of the United States:

I have heretofore communicated to Congress the decrees of the Government of France of November 21, 1806, and of Spain of February 19, 1807, with the orders of the British Government of January and November, 1807.

I now transmit a decree of the Emperor of France of December 17, 1807, and a similar decree of the 3d of January last by His Catholic Majesty. Although the decree of France has not been received by official communication, yet the different channels of promulgation through which the public are possessed of it, with the formal testimony furnished by the Government of Spain in their decree, leave us without a doubt that such a one has been issued. These decrees and orders, taken together, want little of amounting to a declaration that every neutral vessel found on the high seas, whatsoever be her cargo and whatsoever foreign port be that of her departure or destination, shall be deemed lawful prize; and they prove more and more the expediency of retaining our vessels, our seamen, and property within our own harbors until the dangers to which they are exposed can be removed or lessened.

TH: JEFFERSON.

MARCH 18, 1808

To the Senate and House of Representatives of the United States:

The scale on which the Military Academy at West Point was originally established is become too limited to furnish the number of well-instructed subjects in the different branches of artillery and engineering which the public service calls for. The want of such characters is already sensibly felt, and will be increased with the enlargement of our plans of military preparation. The chief engineer, having been instructed to consider the subject and to propose an augmentation which might render the establishment commensurate with the present circumstances of our country, has made the report which I now transmit for the consideration of Congress.

The idea suggested by him of removing the institution to this place is also worthy of attention. Besides the advantage of placing it under the immediate eye of the Government, it may render its benefits common to the Naval Department, and will furnish opportunities of selecting on better information the characters most qualified to fulfill the duties which the public service may call for.

TH: JEFFERSON.

MARCH 22, 1808.

To the Senate and House of Representatives of the United States:

At the opening of the present session I informed the Legislature that the measures which had been taken with the Government of Great Britain for the settlement of our neutral and national rights and of the conditions of commercial intercourse with that nation had resulted in articles of a treaty which could not be acceded to on our part; that instructions had been consequently sent to our ministers there to resume the negotiations, and to endeavor to obtain certain alterations, and that this was interrupted by the transaction which took place between the frigates *Leopard* and *Chesapeake*. The call on that Government for reparation of this wrong produced, as Congress has been already informed, the mission of a special minister to this country, and the occasion is now arrived when the public interest permits and requires that the whole of these proceedings should be made known to you.

I therefore now communicate the instructions given to our minister resident at London and his communications with that Government on the subject of the *Chesapeake*, with the correspondence which has taken place here between the Secretary of State and Mr. Rose, the special minister charged with the adjustment of that difference; the instructions to our ministers for the formation of a treaty; their correspondence with the British commissioners and with their own Government on that subject; the treaty itself and written declaration of the British commissioners accompanying it, and the instructions given by us for resuming the negotiation, with the proceedings and correspondence subsequent thereto. To these I have added a letter lately addressed to the Secretary of State from one of our late ministers, which, though not strictly written in an official character, I think it my duty to communicate, in order that his views of the proposed treaty and of its several articles may be fairly presented and understood.

Although I have heretofore and from time to time made such communications to Congress as to keep them possessed of a general and just view of the proceedings and dispositions of the Government of France toward this country, yet in our present critical situation, when we find that no conduct on our part, however impartial and friendly, has been sufficient to insure from either belligerent a just respect for our rights, I am desirous that nothing shall be omitted on my part which may add to your information on this subject or contribute to the correctness of the views which should be formed. The papers which for these reasons I now lay before you embrace all the communications, official or verbal, from the French Government respecting the general relations between the two countries which have been transmitted through our minister there, or through any other accredited channel, since the last session of Congress, to which time all information of the same kind had from time to time been given them. Some of these papers have already been submitted to Congress, but it is thought better to offer them again in order that the chain of communications of which they make a part may be presented unbroken.

When, on the 26th of February, I communicated to both Houses the letter of General Armstrong to M. Champagny, I desired it might not be published because of the tendency of that practice to restrain injuriously the freedom of our foreign correspondence. But perceiving that this caution, proceeding purely from a regard to the public good, has furnished occasion for disseminating unfounded suspicions and insinuations, I am induced to believe that the good which will now result from its publication, by confirming the confidence and union of our fellow-citizens, will more than countervail the ordinary objection to such publications. It is my wish, therefore, that it may be now published.

TH: JEFFERSON.

MARCH 22, 1808.

To the Senate and House of Representatives of the United States:

In a separate message of this date I have communicated to Congress so much as may be made public of papers which give a full view of the present state of our relations with the two contending powers, France and England. Everyone must be sensible that in the details of instructions for negotiating a treaty and in the correspondence and conferences respecting it matters will occur which interest sometimes and sometimes respect or other proper motives forbid to be made public. To reconcile my duty in this particular with my desire of letting Congress know everything which can give them a full understanding of the subjects on which they are to act, I have suppressed in the documents of the other message the parts which ought not to be made public and have given them in the supplementary and confidential papers herewith inclosed, with such references as that they may be read in their original places as if still standing in them; and when these confidential papers shall have been read to the satisfaction of the House, I request their return, and that their contents may not be made public.

TH: JEFFERSON.

MARCH 25, 1808.

To the Senate and House of Representatives of the United States:

In proceeding to carry into execution the act for fortifying our forts and harbors it is found that the sites most advantageous for their defense, and sometimes the only sites competent to that defense, are in some cases the property of minors incapable of giving a valid consent to their alienation; in others belong to persons who may refuse altogether to alienate, or demand a compensation far beyond the liberal justice allowable in such cases. From these causes the defense of our seaboard, so necessary to be pressed during the present season, will in various parts be defeated unless a remedy can be applied. With a view to this I submit the case to the consideration of Congress, who, estimating its importance and reviewing the powers vested in them by the Constitution, combined with the amendment providing that private property shall not be taken for public use without just compensation, will decide on the course most proper to be pursued.

I am aware that as the consent of the legislature of the State to the purchase of the site may not in some instances have been previously obtained, exclusive legislation can not be exercised therein by Congress until that consent is given. But in the meantime it will be held under the same laws which protect the property of individuals and other property of the United States in the same State, and the legislatures at their next meetings will have opportunities of doing what will be so evidently called for by the particular interest of their own State.

TH: JEFFERSON.

MARCH 25, 1808.

To the Senate and House of Representatives of the United States:

I now lay before Congress a statement of the militia of the United States according to the latest returns received by the Department of War. From the State of Delaware alone no return has been made.

TH: JEFFERSON.

MARCH 25, 1808.

To the Senate and House of Representatives of the United States:

I transmit to both Houses of Congress a report from the surveyor of the public buildings of the progress made on them during the last session, of their present state, and of that of the funds appropriated to them. These have been much exceeded by the cost of the work done, a fact not known to me till the close of the season. The circumstances from which it arose are stated in the report of the surveyor.

TH: JEFFERSON.

MARCH 29, 1808.

To the Senate of the United States:

When the convention of the 7th of January, 1806, was entered into with the Cherokees for the purchase of certain lands, it was believed by both parties that the eastern limit, when run in the direction therein prescribed, would have included all the waters of Elk River. On proceeding to run that line, however, it was found to omit a considerable extent of those waters, on which were already settled about 200 families. The Cherokees readily consented, for a moderate compensation, that the line should be so run as to include all the waters of that river. Our commissioners accordingly entered into an explanatory convention for that purpose, which I now lay before the Senate for consideration whether they will advise and consent to its ratification. A letter from one of the commissioners, now also inclosed, will more fully explain the circumstances which led to it.

Lieutenant Pike on his journey up the Mississippi in 1805-6, being at the village of the Sioux, between the rivers St. Croix and St. Peters, conceived that the position was favorable for a military and commercial post for the United States whenever it should be thought expedient to advance in that quarter. He therefore proposed to the chiefs a cession of lands for that purpose. Their desire of entering into connection with the United States and of getting a trading house established there induced a ready consent to the proposition, and they made, by articles of agreement now inclosed, a voluntary donation to the United States of two portions of land, the one of 9 miles square at the mouth of the St. Croix, the other from below the mouth of St. Peters up the Mississippi to St. Anthonys Falls, extending 9 miles in width on each side of the Mississippi. These portions of land are designated on the map now inclosed. Lieutenant Pike on his part made presents to the Indians to some amount. This convention, though dated the 23d of September, 1805, is but lately received, and although we have no immediate view of establishing a trading post at that place, I submit it to the Senate for the sanction of their advice and consent to its ratification, in order to give to our title a full validity on the part of the United States, when ever it may be wanting, for the special purpose which constituted in the mind of the donors the sole consideration and inducement to the cession.

TH: JEFFERSON.

MARCH 30, 1808.

To the Senate and House of Representatives of the United States:

Since my message of the 22d instant letters have been received from our ministers at Paris and London, extracts from which, with a letter to General Armstrong from the French minister of foreign relations, and a letter from the British envoy residing here to the Secretary of State, I now communicate to Congress. They add to the materials for estimating the dispositions of those Governments toward this country.

The proceedings of both indicate designs of drawing us, if possible, into the vortex of their contests; but every new information confirms the prudence of guarding against these designs as it does of adhering to the precautionary system hitherto contemplated.

TH: JEFFERSON.

APRIL 2, 1808.

To the Senate and House of Representatives of the United States:

Believing that the confidence and union of our fellow-citizens at the present crisis will be still further confirmed by the publication of the letter of Mr. Champagny to General Armstrong and that of Mr. Erskine to the Secretary of State, communicated with my message of the 30th ultimo, and therefore that it may be useful to except them from the confidential character of the other documents accompanying that message, I leave to the consideration of Congress the expediency of making them public.

TH: JEFFERSON.

APRIL 8, 1808.

To the Senate of the United States:

Agreeably to the request of the Senate in their resolution of yesterday, I have examined my papers and find no letter from Matthew Nimmo of the date of November 28, 1806, nor any other from him of any date but that of January 23, 1807, now transmitted, with all the papers in my possession which accompanied it. Nor do I find any letter from John Smith, of Ohio, bearing date at any time in the month of January, 1807.

Having delivered to the Attorney-General all the papers respecting the conspiracy of Aaron Burr which came to my hands during or before his prosecution, I might suppose the letters above requested had been delivered to him; but I must add my belief that I never received such letters, and the ground of it. I am in the habit of noting daily in the list kept for that purpose the letters I receive daily by the names of the writers, and dates of time, and place, and this has been done with such exactness that I do not recollect ever to have detected a single omission. I have carefully examined that list from the 1st of November, 1806, to the last of June, 1807, and I find no note within that period of the receipt of any letter from Matthew Nimmo but that now transmitted, nor of any one of the date of January, 1807, from John Smith, of Ohio. The letters noted as received from him within that period are dated at Washington, February 2, 2, 7, and 21, which I have examined, and find relating to subjects entirely foreign to the objects of the resolution of the 7th instant; and others, dated at Cincinnati, March 27, April 6, 13, and 17, which, not being now in my possession, I presume have related to Burr's conspiracy, and have been delivered to the Attorney-General. I recollect nothing of their particular contents. I must repeat, therefore, my firm belief that the letters of Nimmo of November 28, 1806, and of John Smith of January, 1807, never came to my hands, and that if such were written (and Nimmo's letter expressly mentions his of November 28), they have been intercepted or otherwise miscarried.

TH: JEFFERSON.

APRIL 22, 1808.

To the Senate and House of Representatives of the United States:

I transmit to both Houses of Congress a letter from the envoy of His Britannic Majesty at this place to the Secretary of State on the subject of certain British claims to lands in the Territory of Mississippi, relative to which several acts have been heretofore passed by the Legislature.

TH: JEFFERSON.

PROCLAMATION.

BY THE PRESIDENT OF THE UNITED STATES OF AMERICA.

A PROCLAMATION.

Whereas information has been received that sundry persons are combined or combining and confederating together on Lake Champlain and the country thereto adjacent for the purposes of forming insurrections against the authority of the laws of the United States, for opposing the same and obstructing their execution, and that such combinations are too powerful to be suppressed by the ordinary course of judicial proceedings or by the powers vested in the marshals by the laws of the United States:

Now, therefore, to the end that the authority of the laws may be maintained, and that those concerned, directly or indirectly, in any insurrection or combination against the same may be duly warned, I have issued this my proclamation, hereby commanding such insurgents and all concerned in such combination instantly and without delay to disperse and retire peaceably to their respective abodes. And I do hereby further require and command all officers having authority, civil or military, and all other persons, civil or military, who shall be found within the vicinage of such insurrections or combinations to be aiding and assisting by all the means in their power, by force of arms or otherwise, to quell and subdue such insurrections or combinations, to seize upon all those therein concerned who shall not instantly and without delay disperse and retire to their respective abodes, and to deliver them over to the civil authority of the place, to be proceeded against according to law.

In testimony whereof I have caused the seal of the United States to be affixed to these presents, and signed the same with my hand.

[SEAL.]   Given at the city of Washington, the 19th day of April, 1808, and in the year of the Sovereignty and Independence of the United States the thirty-second.

TH: JEFFERSON.

By the President :
JAMES MADISON,
Secretary of State.

EIGHTH ANNUAL MESSAGE.

NOVEMBER 8, 1808.

To the Senate and House of Representatives of the United States:

It would have been a source, fellow-citizens, of much gratification if our last communications from Europe had enabled me to inform you that the belligerent nations, whose disregard of neutral rights has been so destructive to our commerce, had become awakened to the duty and true policy of revoking their unrighteous edicts. That no means might be omitted to produce this salutary effect, I lost no time in availing myself of the act authorizing a suspension, in whole or in part, of the several embargo laws. Our ministers at London and Paris were instructed to explain to the respective Governments there our disposition to exercise the authority in such manner as would withdraw the pretext on which the aggressions were originally founded and open the way for a renewal of that commercial intercourse which it was alleged on all sides had been reluctantly obstructed. As each of those Governments had pledged its readiness to concur in renouncing a measure which reached its adversary through the incontestable rights of neutrals only, and as the measure had been assumed by each as a retaliation for an asserted acquiescence in the aggressions of the other, it was reasonably expected that the occasion would have been seized by both for evincing the sincerity of their professions, and for restoring to the commerce of the United States its legitimate freedom. The instructions to our ministers with respect to the different belligerents were necessarily modified with a reference to their different circumstances, and to the condition annexed by law to the Executive power of suspension, requiring a decree of security to our commerce which would not result from a repeal of the decrees of France. Instead of a pledge, therefore, of a suspension of the embargo as to her in case of such a repeal, it was presumed that a sufficient inducement might be found in other considerations, and particularly in the change produced by a compliance with our just demands by one belligerent and a refusal by the other in the relations between the other and the United States. To Great Britain, whose power on the ocean is so ascendant, it was deemed not inconsistent with that condition to state explicitly that on her rescinding her orders in relation to the United States their trade would be opened with her, and remain shut to her enemy in case of his failure to rescind his decrees also. From France no answer has been received, nor any indication that the requisite change in her decrees is contemplated. The favorable reception of the proposition to Great Britain was the less to be doubted, as her orders of council had not only been referred for their vindication to an acquiescence on the part of the United States no longer to be pretended, but as the arrangement proposed, whilst it resisted the illegal decrees of France, involved, moreover, substantially the precise advantages professedly aimed at by the British orders. The arrangement has nevertheless been rejected.

This candid and liberal experiment having thus failed, and no other event having occurred on which a suspension of the embargo by the Executive was authorized, it necessarily remains in the extent originally given to it. We have the satisfaction, however, to reflect that in return for the privations imposed by the measure, and which our fellow-citizens in general have borne with patriotism, it has had the important effects of saving our mariners and our vast mercantile property, as well as of affording time for prosecuting the defensive and provisional measures called for by the occasion. It has demonstrated to foreign nations the moderation and firmness which govern our councils, and to our citizens the necessity of uniting in support of the laws and the rights of their country, and has thus long frustrated those usurpations and spoliations which, if resisted, involved war; if submitted to, sacrificed a vital principle of our national independence.

Under a continuance of the belligerent measures which, in defiance of laws which consecrate the rights of neutrals, overspread the ocean with danger, it will rest with the wisdom of Congress to decide on the course best adapted to such a state of things; and bringing with them, as they do, from every part of the Union the sentiments of our constituents, my confidence is strengthened that in forming this decision they will, with an unerring regard to the essential rights and interests of the nation, weigh and compare the painful alternatives out of which a choice is to be made. Nor should I do justice to the virtues which on other occasions have marked the character of our fellow-citizens if I did not cherish an equal confidence that the alternative chosen, whatever it may be, will be maintained with all the fortitude and patriotism which the crisis ought to inspire.

The documents containing the correspondences on the subject of the foreign edicts against our commerce, with the instructions given to our ministers at London and Paris, are now laid before you.

The communications made to Congress at their last session explained the posture in which the close of the discussions relating to the attack by a British ship of war on the frigate *Chesapeake* left a subject on which the nation had manifested so honorable a sensibility. Every view of what had passed authorized a belief that immediate steps would be taken by the British Government for redressing a wrong which the more it was investigated appeared the more clearly to require what had not been provided for in the special mission. It is found that no steps have been taken for the purpose. On the contrary, it will be seen in the documents laid before you that the inadmissible preliminary which obstructed the adjustment is still adhered to, and, moreover, that it is now brought into connection with the distinct and irrelative case of the orders in council. The instructions which had been given to our minister at London with a view to facilitate, if necessary, the reparation claimed by the United States are included in the documents communicated.

Our relations with the other powers of Europe have undergone no material changes since your last session. The important negotiations with Spain which had been alternately suspended and resumed necessarily experience a pause under the extraordinary and interesting crisis which distinguishes her internal situation.

With the Barbary Powers we continue in harmony, with the exception of an unjustifiable proceeding of the Dey of Algiers toward our consul to that Regency. Its character and circumstances are now laid before you, and will enable you to decide how far it may, either now or hereafter, call for any measures not within the limits of the Executive authority.

With our Indian neighbors the public peace has been steadily maintained. Some instances of individual wrong have, as at other times, taken place, but in no wise implicating the will of the nation. Beyond the Mississippi the Ioways, the Sacs, and the Alabamas have delivered up for trial and punishment individuals from among themselves accused of murdering citizens of the United States. On this side of the Mississippi the Creeks are exerting themselves to arrest offenders of the same kind, and the Choctaws have manifested their readiness and desire for amicable and just arrangements respecting depredations committed by disorderly persons of their tribe. And, generally, from a conviction that we consider them as a part of ourselves, and cherish with sincerity their rights and interests, the attachment of the Indian tribes is gaining strength daily—is extending from the nearer to the more remote, and will amply requite us for the justice and friendship practiced toward them. Husbandry and household manufacture are advancing among them more rapidly with the Southern than Northern tribes, from circumstances of soil and climate, and one of the two great divisions of the Cherokee Nation have now under consideration to solicit the citizenship of the United States, and to be identified with us in laws and government in such progressive manner as we shall think best.

In consequence of the appropriations of the last session of Congress for the security of our seaport towns and harbors, such works of defense have been erected as seemed to be called for by the situation of the several places, their relative importance, and the scale of expense indicated by the amount of the appropriation. These works will chiefly be finished in the course of the present season, except at New York and New Orleans, where most was to be done; and although a great proportion of the last appropriation has been expended on the former place, yet some further views will be submitted to Congress for rendering its security entirely adequate against naval enterprise. A view of what has been done at the several places, and of what is proposed to be done, shall be communicated as soon as the several reports are received.

Of the gunboats authorized by the act of December last, it has been thought necessary to build only 103 in the present year. These, with those before possessed, are sufficient for the harbors and waters most exposed, and the residue will require little time for their construction when it shall be deemed necessary.

Under the act of the last session for raising an additional military force so many officers were immediately appointed as were necessary for carrying on the business of recruiting, and in proportion as it advanced others have been added. We have reason to believe their success has been satisfactory, although such returns have not yet been received as enable me to present you a statement of the numbers engaged.

I have not thought it necessary in the course of the last season to call for any general detachments of militia or of volunteers under the laws passed for that purpose. For the ensuing season, however, they will be required to be in readiness should their service be wanted. Some small and special detachments have been necessary to maintain the laws of embargo on that portion of our northern frontier which offered peculiar facilities for evasion, but these were replaced as soon as it could be done by bodies of new recruits. By the aid of these and of the armed vessels called into service in other quarters the spirit of disobedience and abuse, which manifested itself early and with sensible effect while we were unprepared to meet it, has been considerably repressed.

Considering the extraordinary character of the times in which we live, our attention should unremittingly be fixed on the safety of our country. For a people who are free, and who mean to remain so, a well organized and armed militia is their best security. It is therefore incumbent on us at every meeting to revise the condition of the militia, and to ask ourselves if it is prepared to repel a powerful enemy at every point of our territories exposed to invasion. Some of the States have paid a laudable attention to this object, but every degree of neglect is to be found among others. Congress alone having the power to produce an uniform state of preparation in this great organ of defense, the interests which they so deeply feel in their own and their country's security will present this as among the most important objects of their deliberation.

Under the acts of March 11 and April 23 respecting arms, the difficulty of procuring them from abroad during the present situation and dispositions of Europe induced us to direct our whole efforts to the means of internal supply. The public factories have therefore been enlarged, additional machineries erected, and, in proportion as artificers can be found or formed, their effect, already more than doubled, may be increased so as to keep pace with the yearly increase of the militia. The annual sums appropriated by the latter act have been directed to the encouragement of private factories of arms, and contracts have been entered into with individual undertakers to nearly the amount of the first year's appropriation.

The suspension of our foreign commerce, produced by the injustice of the belligerent powers, and the consequent losses and sacrifices of our citizens are subjects of just concern. The situation into which we have thus been forced has impelled us to apply a portion of our industry and capital to internal manufactures and improvements. The extent of this conversion is daily increasing, and little doubt remains that the establishments formed and forming will, under the auspices of cheaper materials and subsistence, the freedom of labor from taxation with us, and of protecting duties and prohibitions, become permanent. The commerce with the Indians, too, within our own boundaries is likely to receive abundant aliment from the same internal source, and will secure to them peace and the progress of civilization, undisturbed by practices hostile to both.

The accounts of the receipts and expenditures during the year ending the 30th of September last being not yet made up, a correct statement will hereafter be transmitted from the Treasury. In the meantime it is ascertained that the receipts have amounted to near $18,000,000, which, with the eight millions and a half in the Treasury at the beginning of the year, have enabled us, after meeting the current demands and interest incurred, to pay $2,300,000 of the principal of our funded debt, and left us in the Treasury on that day near $14,000,000. Of these, $5,350,000 will be necessary to pay what will be due on the 1st day of January next, which will complete the reimbursement of the 8 per cent stock. These payments, with those made in the six years and a half preceding, will have extinguished $33,580,000 of the principal of the funded debt, being the whole which could be paid or purchased within the limits of the law and of our contracts, and the amount of principal thus discharged will have liberated the revenue from about $2,000,000 of interest and added that sum annually to the disposable surplus. The probable accumulation of the surpluses of revenue beyond what can be applied to the payment of the public debt whenever the freedom and safety of our commerce shall be restored merits the consideration of Congress. Shall it lie unproductive in the public vaults? Shall the revenue be reduced? Or shall it not rather be appropriated to the improvements of roads, canals, rivers, education, and other great foundations of prosperity and union under the powers which Congress may already possess or such amendment of the Constitution as may be approved by the States? While uncertain of the course of things, the time may be advantageously employed in obtaining the powers necessary for a system of improvement, should that be thought best.

Availing myself of this the last occasion which will occur of addressing the two Houses of the Legislature at their meeting, I can not omit the expression of my sincere gratitude for the repeated proofs of confidence manifested to me by themselves and their predecessors since my call to the administration and the many indulgences experienced at their hands. The same grateful acknowledgments are due to my fellow-citizens generally, whose support has been my great encouragement under all embarrassments. In the transaction of their business I can not have escaped error. It is incident to our imperfect nature. But I may say with truth my errors have been of the understanding, not of intention, and that the advancement of their rights and interests has been the constant motive for every measure. On these considerations I solicit their indulgence. Looking forward with anxiety to their future destinies, I trust that in their steady character, unshaken by difficulties, in their love of liberty, obedience to law, and support of the public authorities I see a sure guaranty of the permanence of our Republic ; and, retiring from the charge of their affairs, I carry with me the consolation of a firm persuasion that Heaven has in store for our beloved country long ages to come of prosperity and happiness.

TH: JEFFERSON.

SPECIAL MESSAGES.

NOVEMBER 8, 1808.

To the Senate and House of Representatives of the United States:

The documents communicated with my public message of this day contain such portions of the correspondences therein referred to, of the ministers of the United States at Paris and London, as relate to the present state of affairs between those Governments and the United States, and as may be made public. I now communicate, confidentially, such supplementary portions of the same correspondences as I deem improper for publication, yet necessary to convey to Congress full information on a subject of their deliberations so interesting to our country.

TH; JEFFERSON.

NOVEMBER 11, 1808.

To the Senate of the United States:

*　　　*　　　*　　　*　　　*　　　*　　　*

The governor of the Mississippi Territory having thought it expedient to dissolve the general assembly of that Territory, according to the authority vested in him by the ordinance of July 13, 1787, and having declared it dissolved accordingly, some doubt was suggested whether that declaration effected the dissolution of the legislative council. On mature consideration and advice I approved of the proceeding of the governor. The house of representatives of the Territory, since chosen, have consequently nominated ten persons out of whom a legislative council should be appointed. I do accordingly nominate and, by and with the advice and consent of the Senate, shall appoint John Flood McGrew, Thomas Calvit, James Lea, Alexander Montgomery, and Daniel Burnet, being five of the said ten persons, to serve as a legislative council for the said Territory, to continue in office five years, unless sooner removed according to law.

TH: JEFFERSON.

DECEMBER 13, 1808.

To the Senate and House of Representatives of the United States:

I now transmit to both Houses of Congress a report of the commissioners appointed under the act of March 29, 1806, concerning a road from Cumberland to Ohio, being a statement of the proceedings under the said act since their last report communicated to Congress, in order that Congress may be enabled to adopt such further measures as may be proper under existing circumstances.

TH: JEFFERSON.

DECEMBER 23, 1808.

To the Senate of the United States:

According to the request of the Senate in their resolution of November 14, that copies should be laid before them of all the orders and decrees of the belligerent powers of Europe, passed since 1791, affecting the commercial rights of the United States, I now transmit them a report of the Secretary of State of such of them as have been attainable in the Department of State and are supposed to have entered into the views of the Senate.

TH: JEFFERSON.

DECEMBER 27, 1808.

To the Senate of the United States:

According to the request expressed by the Senate in their resolution of November 14, I now transmit a report of the Secretary of the Treasury and statement showing, as far as returns have been received from the collectors, the number of vessels which have departed from the United States with permission, and specifying the other particulars contemplated by that resolution.

TH: JEFFERSON.

DECEMBER 30, 1808.

To the Senate and House of Representatives of the United States:

At the request of the governor, the senate, and house of representatives of the Commonwealth of Pennsylvania, I communicate certain resolutions entered into by the said senate and house of representatives, and approved by the governor, on the 23d instant. It can not but be encouraging to those whom the nation has placed in the direction of their affairs to see that their fellow-citizens will press forward in support of their country in proportion as it is threatened by the disorganizing conflicts of the other hemisphere.

TH: JEFFERSON.

DECEMBER 30, 1808.

To the Senate and House of Representatives of the United States:

I lay before the Legislature a letter from Governor Claiborne on the subject of a small tribe of Alabama Indians on the western side of the Mississippi, consisting of about a dozen families. Like other erratic tribes in that country, it is understood that they have hitherto moved from place to place according to their convenience, without appropriating to themselves exclusively any particular territory; but having now become habituated to some of the occupations of civilized life, they wish for a fixed residence. I suppose it will be the interest of the United States to encourage the wandering tribes of that country to reduce themselves to fixed habitations whenever they are so disposed. The establishment of towns and growing attachments to them will furnish in some degree pledges of their peaceable and friendly conduct. The case of this particular tribe is now submitted to the consideration of Congress.

TH: JEFFERSON.

JANUARY 6, 1809.

To the Senate and House of Representatives of the United States:

I now lay before Congress a statement of the works of defense which it has been thought necessary to provide in the first instance for the security of our seaport towns and harbors, and of the progress toward their completion. Their extent has been adapted to the scale of the appropriation and to the circumstances of the several places.

The works undertaken at New York are calculated to annoy and endanger any naval force which shall enter the harbor, and, still more, one which should attempt to lie before the city. To prevent altogether the entrance of large vessels, a line of blocks across the harbor has been contemplated, and would, as is believed, with the auxiliary means already provided, render that city safe against naval enterprise. The expense as well as the importance of the work renders it a subject proper for the special consideration of Congress.

At New Orleans two separate systems of defense are necessary—the one for the river, the other for the lake, which at present can give no aid to one another. The canal now leading from the lake, if continued into the river, would enable the armed vessels in both stations to unite, and to meet in conjunction an attack from either side. Half the aggregate force would then have the same effect as the whole, or the same force double the effect of what either can now have. It would also enable the vessels stationed in the lake when attacked by superior force to retire to a safer position in the river. The same considerations of expense and importance render this also a question for the special decision of Congress.

TH: JEFFERSON.

JANUARY 13, 1809.

To the Senate and House of Representatives of the United States:

I now render to Congress the account of the fund established for defraying the contingent expenses of Government for the year 1808. Of the $20,000 appropriated for that purpose, $2,000 were deposited in the hands of the Attorney-General of the United States to pay expenses incident to the prosecution of Aaron Burr and his accomplices for treason and misdemeanors alleged to have been committed by them; $990 were paid to the order of Governor Williams on the same account, and the balance of $17,010 remains in the Treasury unexpended.

TH: JEFFERSON.

JANUARY 17, 1809.

To the Senate and House of Representatives of the United States:

I communicate to Congress certain letters which passed between the British secretary of state, Mr. Canning, and Mr. Pinkney, our minister plenipotentiary at London. When the documents concerning the relations between the United States and Great Britain were laid before Congress at the commencement of the session, the answer of Mr. Pinkney to the letter of Mr. Canning had not been received, and a communication of the latter alone would have accorded neither with propriety nor with the wishes of Mr. Pinkney. When that answer afterwards arrived it was considered that, as what had passed by conversation had been superseded by the written and formal correspondence on the subject, the variance in the two statements of what had verbally passed was not of sufficient importance to be made the matter of a distinct and special communication. The letter of Mr. Canning, however, having lately appeared in print, unaccompanied by that of Mr. Pinkney in reply, and having a tendency to make impressions not warranted by the statements of Mr. Pinkney, it has become proper that the whole should be brought into public view.

TH: JEFFERSON.

JANUARY 24, 1809.

To the Senate of the United States:

According to the resolution of the Senate of the 17th instant, I now transmit them the information therein requested, respecting the execution of the act of Congress of February 21, 1806, appropriating $2,000,000 for defraying any extraordinary expenses attending the intercourse between the United States and foreign nations.

TH: JEFFERSON.

JANUARY 30, 1809.

To the Senate and House of Representatives of the United States:

I transmit to Congress a letter recently received from our minister at the Court of St. James, covering one to him from the British secretary of state, with his reply. These are communicated as forming a sequel to the correspondence which accompanied my message to both Houses of the 17th instant.

TH: JEFFERSON.

FEBRUARY 18, 1809.

To the Senate of the United States:

I submit a treaty, concluded at Brownstown, in the Territory of Michigan, between the United States and the Chippewas, Ottawas, Potawattamies, Wyandots, and Shawnees, on the 25th day of November last.

whereby those tribes grant to the United States two roads, therein described, for the decision of the Senate whether they will advise and consent to the ratification of it.

TH: JEFFERSON.

FEBRUARY 24, 1809.

To the Senate of the United States:

The Emperor of Russia has on several occasions indicated sentiments particularly friendly to the United States, and expressed a wish through different channels that a diplomatic intercourse should be established between the two countries. His high station and the relations of Russia to the predominant powers of Europe must give him weight with them according to the vicissitudes of the war, and his influence in negotiations for peace may be of value to the United States should arrangements of any sort affecting them be contemplated by other powers in the present extraordinary state of the world; and under the constant possibility of sudden negotiations for peace I have thought that the friendly dispositions of such a power might be advantageously cherished by a mission which should manifest our willingness to meet his good will. I accordingly commissioned in the month of August last William Short, formerly minister plenipotentiary of the United States at Madrid, to proceed as minister plenipotentiary to the Court of St. Petersburg, and he proceeded accordingly; and I now nominate him to the Senate for that appointment.

TH: JEFFERSON.

FEBRUARY 25, 1809.

To the Senate and House of Representatives of the United States:

I now lay before Congress a statement of the militia of the United States according to the latest returns received by the Department of War.

TH: JEFFERSON.

PROCLAMATION.

[From Annals of Congress, Tenth Congress, second session, 462.]

WASHINGTON, *December 30, 1808.*

The President of the United States to ——, Senator for the State of ——.

Certain matters touching the public good requiring that the Senate should be convened on Saturday, the 4th day of March next, you are desired to attend at the Senate Chamber, in the city of Washington, on that day, then and there to deliberate on such communications as shall be made to you.

TH: JEFFERSON.

James Madison

March 4, 1809, to March 4, 1817

SEE VOLUME XI.

Volume eleven is not only an index to the other volumes, not only a key that unlocks the treasures of the entire publication, but it is in itself an alphabetically arranged brief history or story of the great controlling events constituting the History of the United States.

Under its proper alphabetical classification the story is told of every great subject referred to by any of the Presidents in their official Messages, and at the end of each story the official utterances of the Presidents themselves are cited upon the subject, so that you may readily turn to the page in the body of the work itself for this original information.

Next to the possession of knowledge is the ability to turn at will to where knowledge is to be found.

JAMES MADISON

With official portrait engraved from copy of original in steel

James Madison

James Madison

JAMES MADISON was born in King George County, Va., on the 16th of March, 1751. He was the son of James Madison, the family being of English descent, and among the early settlers of Virginia. Was fitted for college by private tutors, and entered Princeton College in 1769, graduating in 1771; remained a year at college pursuing his studies. After this he returned to Virginia and began the practice of law. In 1776 was elected a member of the general assembly of Virginia, and in 1778 was appointed a member of the executive council. In the winter of 1779–80 was chosen a delegate to the Continental Congress, of which body he continued an active and prominent member till 1784. The legislature of Virginia appointed him in 1786 a delegate to a convention at Annapolis, Md., to devise a system of commercial regulations for all the States. Upon their recommendation a convention of delegates from all the States was held in Philadelphia in May, 1787. This Convention framed the Constitution of the United States, and of it Mr. Madison was a leading member. He was next a member of the convention of his State which met to consider the new Constitution for the United States. Was a member of the House of Representatives in the First Congress, taking his seat in April, 1789, and continued to be a member of the House during both of Washington's terms as President. He married Mrs. Dolly Paine Todd, of Philadelphia, in 1794, she being the widow of a Pennsylvania lawyer. Her father was a Quaker, and had removed from Virginia to Philadelphia. Declined the office of Secretary of State, vacated by Jefferson, in 1793. He retired from Congress in 1797, and in 1798 accepted a seat in the Virginia assembly. In 1801 was appointed by President Jefferson Secretary of State, which office he held during the eight years of Jefferson's Administration. In 1808 was elected President, and was reelected in 1812. On March 4, 1817, he retired from public life, and passed the remainder of his days at Montpelier, in Orange County, Va. In 1829 was chosen a member of the State convention to revise the constitution of Virginia, and was also chosen president of an agricultural society in his county. He died on the 28th day of June, 1836, and was buried at his home.

LETTER FROM THE PRESIDENT ELECT.

The President of the Senate communicated the following letter from the President elect of the United States:

CITY OF WASHINGTON, *March 2, 1809.*

HON. JOHN MILLEDGE,

President pro tempore of the Senate.

SIR: I beg leave through you to inform the honorable the Senate of the United States that I propose to take the oath which the Constitution prescribes to the President of the United States before he enters on the execution of his office on Saturday, the 4th instant, at 12 o'clock, in the Chamber of the House of Representatives.

I have the honor to be, with the greatest respect, sir, your most obedient and most humble servant,

JAMES MADISON.

FIRST INAUGURAL ADDRESS.

Unwilling to depart from examples of the most revered authority, I avail myself of the occasion now presented to express the profound impression made on me by the call of my country to the station to the duties of which I am about to pledge myself by the most solemn of sanctions. So distinguished a mark of confidence, proceeding from the deliberate and tranquil suffrage of a free and virtuous nation, would under any circumstances have commanded my gratitude and devotion, as well as filled me with an awful sense of the trust to be assumed. Under the various circumstances which give peculiar solemnity to the existing period, I feel that both the honor and the responsibility allotted to me are inexpressibly enhanced.

The present situation of the world is indeed without a parallel, and that of our own country full of difficulties. The pressure of these, too, is the more severely felt because they have fallen upon us at a moment when the national prosperity being at a height not before attained, the contrast resulting from the change has been rendered the more striking. Under the benign influence of our republican institutions, and the maintenance of peace with all nations whilst so many of them were engaged in bloody and wasteful wars, the fruits of a just policy were enjoyed in an unrivaled growth of our faculties and resources. Proofs of this were seen in the improvements of agriculture, in the successful enterprises of commerce, in the progress of manufactures and useful arts, in the increase of the public revenue and the use made of it in reducing the public debt, and in the valuable works and establishments everywhere multiplying over the face of our land.

It is a precious reflection that the transition from this prosperous condition of our country to the scene which has for some time been distressing us is not chargeable on any unwarrantable views, nor, as I trust, on any involuntary errors in the public councils. Indulging no passions which trespass on the rights or the repose of other nations, it has been the true glory of the United States to cultivate peace by observing justice, and to entitle themselves to the respect of the nations at war by fulfilling their neutral obligations with the most scrupulous impartiality. If there be candor in the world, the truth of these assertions will not be questioned; posterity at least will do justice to them.

This unexceptionable course could not avail against the injustice and violence of the belligerent powers. In their rage against each other, or impelled by more direct motives, principles of retaliation have been introduced equally contrary to universal reason and acknowledged law. How long their arbitrary edicts will be continued in spite of the demonstrations that not even a pretext for them has been given by the United States, and of the fair and liberal attempt to induce a revocation of them, can not be anticipated. Assuring myself that under every vicissitude the determined spirit and united councils of the nation will be safeguards to its honor and its essential interests, I repair to the post assigned me with no other discouragement than what springs from my own inadequacy to its high duties. If I do not sink under the weight of this deep conviction it is because I find some support in a consciousness of the purposes and a confidence in the principles which I bring with me into this arduous service.

To cherish peace and friendly intercourse with all nations having correspondent dispositions; to maintain sincere neutrality toward belligerent nations; to prefer in all cases amicable discussion and reasonable accommodation of differences to a decision of them by an appeal to arms; to exclude foreign intrigues and foreign partialities, so degrading to all countries and so baneful to free ones; to foster a spirit of independence too just to invade the rights of others, too proud to surrender our own, too liberal to indulge unworthy prejudices ourselves and too elevated not to look down upon them in others; to hold the union of the States as the basis of their peace and happiness; to support the Constitution, which is the cement of the Union, as well in its limitations as in its authorities; to respect the rights and authorities reserved to the States and to the people as equally incorporated with and essential to the success of the general system; to avoid the slightest interference with the rights of conscience or the functions of religion, so wisely exempted from civil jurisdiction; to preserve in their full energy the other salutary provisions in behalf of private and personal rights, and of the freedom of the press; to observe economy in public expenditures; to liberate the public resources by an honorable discharge of the public debts; to keep within the requisite limits a standing military force, always remembering that an armed and trained militia is the firmest bulwark of republics—that without standing armies their liberty can never be in danger, nor with large ones safe; to promote by authorized means improvements friendly to agriculture, to manufactures, and to external as well as internal commerce; to favor in like manner the advancement of science and the diffusion of information as the best aliment to true liberty; to carry on the benevolent plans which have been so meritoriously applied to the conversion of our aboriginal neighbors from the degradation and wretchedness of savage life to a participation of the improvements of which the human mind and manners are susceptible in a civilized state—as far as sentiments and intentions such as these can aid the fulfillment of my duty, they will be a resource which can not fail me.

It is my good fortune, moreover, to have the path in which I am to tread lighted by examples of illustrious services successfully rendered in the most trying difficulties by those who have marched before me. Of those of my immediate predecessor it might least become me here to speak. I may, however, be pardoned for not suppressing the sympathy with which my heart is full in the rich reward he enjoys in the benedictions of a beloved country, gratefully bestowed for exalted talents zealously devoted through a long career to the advancement of its highest interest and happiness.

But the source to which I look for the aids which alone can supply my deficiencies is in the well-tried intelligence and virtue of my fellow-citizens, and in the counsels of those representing them in the other departments associated in the care of the national interests. In these my confidence will under every difficulty be best placed, next to that which we have all been encouraged to feel in the guardianship and guidance of that Almighty Being whose power regulates the destiny of nations, whose blessings have been so conspicuously dispensed to this rising Republic, and to whom we are bound to address our devout gratitude for the past, as well as our fervent supplications and best hopes for the future.

MARCH 4, 1809.

SPECIAL SESSION MESSAGE.

Fellow-Citizens of the Senate and of the House of Representatives:

On this first occasion of meeting you it affords me much satisfaction to be able to communicate the commencement of a favorable change in our foreign relations, the critical state of which induced a session of Congress at this early period.

In consequence of the provisions of the act interdicting commercial intercourse with Great Britain and France, our ministers at London and Paris were without delay instructed to let it be understood by the French and British Governments that the authority vested in the Executive to renew commercial intercourse with their respective nations would be exercised in the case specified by that act.

Soon after these instructions were dispatched it was found that the British Government, anticipating from early proceedings of Congress at their last session the state of our laws, which has had the effect of placing the two belligerent powers on a footing of equal restrictions, and relying on the conciliatory disposition of the United States, had transmitted to their legation here provisional instructions not only to offer satisfaction for the attack on the frigate *Chesapeake*, and to make known the determination of His Britannic Majesty to send an envoy extraordinary with powers to conclude a treaty on all the points between the two countries, but, moreover, to signify his willingness in the meantime to withdraw his orders in council, in the persuasion that the intercourse with Great Britain would be renewed on the part of the United States.

These steps of the British Government led to the correspondence and the proclamation now laid before you, by virtue of which the commerce between the two countries will be renewable after the 10th day of June next.

Whilst I take pleasure in doing justice to the councils of His Britannic Majesty, which, no longer adhering to the policy which made an abandonment by France of her decrees a prerequisite to a revocation of the British orders, have substituted the amicable course which has issued thus happily, I can not do less than refer to the proposal heretofore made on the part of the United States, embracing a like restoration of the sus·pended commerce, as a proof of the spirit of accommodation which has at no time been intermitted, and to the result which now calls for our congratulations, as corroborating the principles by which the public councils have been guided during a period of the most trying embarrassments.

The discontinuance of the British orders as they respect the United States having been thus arranged, a communication of the event has been forwarded in one of our public vessels to our minister plenipotentiary at Paris, with instructions to avail himself of the important addition thereby made to the considerations which press on the justice of the French Government a revocation of its decrees or such a modification of them as that they shall cease to violate the neutral commerce of the United States.

The revision of our commercial laws proper to adapt them to the arrangement which has taken place with Great Britain will doubtless engage the early attention of Congress. It will be worthy at the same time of their just and provident care to make such further alterations in the laws as will more especially protect and foster the several branches of manufacture which have been recently instituted or extended by the laudable exertions of our citizens.

Under the existing aspect of our affairs I have thought it not inconsistent with a just precaution to have the gunboats, with the exception of those at New Orleans, placed in a situation incurring no expense beyond that requisite for their preservation and conveniency for future service, and to have the crews of those at New Orleans reduced to the number required for their navigation and safety.

I have thought also that our citizens detached in quotas of militia amounting to 100,000 under the act of March, 1808, might not improperly be relieved from the state in which they were held for immediate service. A discharge of them has been accordingly directed.

The progress made in raising and organizing the additional military force, for which provision was made by the act of April, 1808, together with the disposition of the troops, will appear by a report which the Secretary of War is preparing, and which will be laid before you.

Of the additional frigates required by an act of the last session to be fitted for actual service, two are in readiness, one nearly so, and the fourth is expected to be ready in the month of July. A report which the Secretary of the Navy is preparing on the subject, to be laid before Congress, will shew at the same time the progress made in officering and manning these ships. It will shew also the degree in which the provisions of the act relating to the other public armed ships have been carried into execution.

It will rest with the judgment of Congress to decide how far the change in our external prospects may authorize any modifications of the laws relating to the army and navy establishments.

The works of defense for our seaport towns and harbors have proceeded with as much activity as the season of the year and other circumstances would admit. It is necessary, however, to state that, the appropriations hitherto made being found to be deficient, a further provision will claim the early consideration of Congress.

The whole of the 8 per cent stock remaining due by the United States, amounting to $5,300,000, had been reimbursed on the last day of the year 1808; and on the 1st day of April last the sum in the Treasury exceeded $9,500,000. This, together with the receipts of the current year on account of former revenue bonds, will probably be nearly if not altogether sufficient to defray the expenses of the year. But the suspension of exports and the consequent decrease of importations during the last twelve months will necessarily cause a great diminution in the receipts of the year 1810. After that year, should our foreign relations be undisturbed, the revenue will again be more than commensurate to all the expenditures.

Aware of the inconveniences of a protracted session at the present season of the year, I forbear to call the attention of the Legislature to any matters not particularly urgent. It remains, therefore, only to assure you of the fidelity and alacrity with which I shall cooperate for the welfare and happiness of our country, and to pray that it may experience a continuance of the divine blessings by which it has been so signally favored.

JAMES MADISON.

MAY 23, 1809.

SPECIAL MESSAGES.

MAY 26, 1809.

To the Senate of the United States:

I now lay before Congress the report of the Secretary of War, shewing the progress made in carrying into effect the act of April, 1808, for raising an additional military force, and the disposition of the troops.

JAMES MADISON.

JUNE 4, 1809.

To the Senate of the United States:

In compliance with the request of the legislature of Pennsylvania, I transmit to Congress a copy of certain of its proceedings, communicated for the purpose by the governor of that State.

JAMES MADISON.

JUNE 15, 1809.

To the Senate of the United States:

In compliance with the resolution of the Senate of the 13th instant, I transmit extracts from letters from Mr. Pinkney to the Secretary of State, accompanied by letters and communications to him from the British secretary of state for the foreign department, all of which have been received here since the last session of Congress.

To these documents are added a communication just made by Mr. Erskine to the Secretary of State, and his answer.

JAMES MADISON.

JUNE 20, 1809.

To the Senate of the United States:

In compliance with the resolution of the Senate of the 19th instant, I transmit such information as has been received respecting exiles from Cuba arrived or expected within the United States; also a letter from General Turreau connected with that subject.

JAMES MADISON.

JUNE 26, 1809.

To the Senate of the United States:

The considerations which led to the nomination of a minister plenipotentiary to Russia being strengthened by evidence since received of the earnest desire of the Emperor to establish a diplomatic intercourse between the two countries, and of a disposition in his councils favorable to the extension of a commerce mutually advantageous, as will be seen by the extracts from letters from General Armstrong and Consul Harris herewith confidentially communicated, I nominate John Quincy Adams, of Massachusetts, to be minister plenipotentiary of the United States to the Court of St. Petersburg.

JAMES MADISON.

PROCLAMATIONS.

[From Annals of Congress, Eleventh Congress, part 2, 2060.]

BY THE PRESIDENT OF THE UNITED STATES.

A PROCLAMATION.

Whereas it is provided by the eleventh section of the act of Congress entitled "An act to interdict the commercial intercourse between the United States and Great Britain and France and their dependencies, and for other purposes," that "in case either France or Great Britain shall so revoke or modify her edicts as that they shall cease to violate the neutral commerce of the United States" the President is authorized to declare the same by proclamation, after which the trade suspended by the said act and by an act laying an embargo on all ships and vessels in the ports and harbors of the United States and the several acts supplementary thereto may be renewed with the nation so doing; and

Whereas the Honorable David Montague Erskine, His Britannic Majesty's envoy extraordinary and minister plenipotentiary, has, by the order and in the name of his Sovereign, declared to this Government that the British orders in council of January and November, 1807, will have been withdrawn as respects the United States on the 10th day of June next:

Now, therefore, I, James Madison, President of the United States, do hereby proclaim that the orders in council aforesaid will have been withdrawn on the said 10th day of June next, after which day the trade of the United States with Great Britain, as suspended by the act of Congress above mentioned and an act laying an embargo on all ships and vessels in the ports and harbors of the United States and the several acts supplementary thereto, may be renewed.

Given under my hand and the seal of the United States at Washington, [SEAL.] the 19th day of April, A.D. 1809, and of the Independence of the United States the thirty-third.

JAMES MADISON.

By the President:
R. SMITH,
Secretary of State.

[From Annals of Congress, Eleventh Congress, part 2, 2076.]

BY THE PRESIDENT OF THE UNITED STATES OF AMERICA.

A PROCLAMATION.

Whereas, in consequence of a communication from His Britannic Majesty's envoy extraordinary and minister plenipotentiary declaring that the British orders of council of January and November, 1807, would have been withdrawn on the 10th day of June last, and by virtue of authority given in such event by the eleventh section of the act of Congress entitled "An act to interdict the commercial intercourse between the United States and Great Britain and France and their dependencies, and for other purposes," I, James Madison, President of the United States, did issue my proclamation bearing date on the 19th of April last, declaring that the orders in council aforesaid would have been so withdrawn on the said 10th day of June, after which the trade suspended by certain acts of Congress might be renewed; and

Whereas it is now officially made known to me that the said orders in council have not been withdrawn agreeably to the communication and declaration aforesaid:

I do hereby proclaim the same, and, consequently, that the trade renewable on the event of the said orders, being withdrawn, is to be considered as under the operation of the several acts by which such trade was suspended.

Given under my hand and the seal of the United States at the city of Washington, the 9th day of August, A. D. 1809, and of the Independence of the said United States the thirty-fourth.

[SEAL.]

JAMES MADISON.

By the President:

    R. SMITH,
       Secretary of State.

FIRST ANNUAL MESSAGE.

NOVEMBER 29, 1809.

Fellow-Citizens of the Senate and of the House of Representatives:

At the period of our last meeting I had the satisfaction of communicating an adjustment with one of the principal belligerent nations, highly important in itself, and still more so as presaging a more extended accommodation. It is with deep concern I am now to inform you that the favorable prospect has been overclouded by a refusal of the British Government to abide by the act of its minister plenipotentiary, and by its ensuing policy toward the United States as seen through the communications of the minister sent to replace him.

Whatever pleas may be urged for a disavowal of engagements formed by diplomatic functionaries in cases where by the terms of the engagements a mutual ratification is reserved, or where notice at the time may have been given of a departure from instructions, or in extraordinary cases essentially violating the principles of equity, a disavowal could not have been apprehended in a case where no such notice or violation existed. where no such ratification was reserved, and more especially where, as is now in proof, an engagement to be executed without any such ratification was contemplated by the instructions given, and where it had with good faith been carried into immediate execution on the part of the United States.

These considerations not having restrained the British Government from disavowing the arrangement by virtue of which its orders in council were to be revoked, and the event authorizing the renewal of commercial intercourse having thus not taken place, it necessarily became a question of equal urgency and importance whether the act prohibiting that intercourse was not to be considered as remaining in legal force. This question being, after due deliberation, determined in the affirmative, a proclamation to that effect was issued. It could not but happen, however, that a return to this state of things from that which had followed an execution of the arrangement by the United States would involve difficulties. With a view to diminish these as much as possible, the instructions from the Secretary of the Treasury now laid before you were transmitted to the collectors of the several ports. If in permitting British vessels to depart without giving bonds not to proceed to their own ports it should appear that the tenor of legal authority has not been strictly pursued, it is to be ascribed to the anxious desire which was felt that no individuals should be injured by so unforeseen an occurrence; and I rely on the regard of Congress for the equitable interests of our own citizens to adopt whatever further provisions may be found requisite for a general remission of penalties involuntarily incurred.

The recall of the disavowed minister having been followed by the appointment of a successor, hopes were indulged that the new mission would contribute to alleviate the disappointment which had been produced, and to remove the causes which had so long embarrassed the good understanding of the two nations. It could not be doubted that it would at least be charged with conciliatory explanations of the step which had been taken and with proposals to be substituted for the rejected arrangement. Reasonable and universal as this expectation was, it also has not been fulfilled. From the first official disclosures of the new minister it was found that he had received no authority to enter into explanations relative to either branch of the arrangement disavowed nor any authority to substitute proposals as to that branch which concerned the British orders in council, and, finally, that his proposals with respect to the other branch, the attack on the frigate *Chesapeake*, were founded on a presumption repeatedly declared to be inadmissible by the United States, that the first step toward adjustment was due from them, the proposals at the same time omitting even a reference to the officer answerable for the murderous aggression, and asserting a claim not less contrary to the British laws and British practice than to the principles and obligations of the United States.

The correspondence between the Department of State and this minister will show how unessentially the features presented in its commencement have been varied in its progress. It will show also that, forgetting the respect due to all governments, he did not refrain from imputations on this, which required that no further communications should be received from him. The necessity of this step will be made known to His Britannic Majesty through the minister plenipotentiary of the United States in London; and it would indicate a want of the confidence due to a Government which so well understands and exacts what becomes foreign ministers near it not to infer that the misconduct of its own representative will be viewed in the same light in which it has been regarded here. The British Government will learn at the same time that a ready attention will be given to communications through any channel which may be substituted. It will be happy if the change in this respect should be accompanied by a favorable revision of the unfriendly policy which has been so long pursued toward the United States.

With France, the other belligerent, whose trespasses on our commercial rights have long been the subject of our just remonstrances, the posture of our relations does not correspond with the measures taken on the part of the United States to effect a favorable change. The result of the several communications made to her Government, in pursuance of the authorities vested by Congress in the Executive, is contained in the correspondence of our minister at Paris now laid before you.

By some of the other belligerents, although professing just and amicable dispositions, injuries materially affecting our commerce have not been duly controlled or repressed. In these cases the interpositions deemed proper on our part have not been omitted. But it well deserves the consideration of the Legislature how far both the safety and the honor of the American flag may be consulted, by adequate provisions against that collusive prostitution of it by individuals unworthy of the American name which has so much favored the real or pretended suspicions under which the honest commerce of their fellow-citizens has suffered.

In relation to the powers on the coast of Barbary, nothing has occurred which is not of a nature rather to inspire confidence than distrust as to the continuance of the existing amity. With our Indian neighbors, the just and benevolent system continued toward them has also preserved peace, and is more and more advancing habits favorable to their civilization and happiness.

From a statement which will be made by the Secretary of War it will be seen that the fortifications on our maritime frontier are in many of the ports completed, affording the defense which was contemplated, and that a further time will be required to render complete the works in the harbor of New York and in some other places. By the enlargement of the works and the employment of a greater number of hands at the public armories the supply of small arms of an improving quality appears to be annually increasing at a rate that, with those made on private contract, may be expected to go far toward providing for the public exigency.

The act of Congress providing for the equipment of our vessels of war having been fully carried into execution, I refer to the statement of the Secretary of the Navy for the information which may be proper on that subject. To that statement is added a view of the transfers of appropriations authorized by the act of the session preceding the last and of the grounds on which the transfers were made.

Whatever may be the course of your deliberations on the subject of our military establishments, I should fail in my duty in not recommending to your serious attention the importance of giving to our militia, the great bulwark of our security and resource of our power, an organization the best adapted to eventual situations for which the United States ought to be prepared.

The sums which had been previously accumulated in the Treasury, together with the receipts during the year ending on the 30th of September last (and amounting to more than $9,000,000), have enabled us to fulfill all our engagements and to defray the current expenses of Government without recurring to any loan. But the insecurity of our commerce and the consequent diminution of the public revenue will probably produce a deficiency in the receipts of the ensuing year, for which and for other details I refer to the statements which will be transmitted from the Treasury.

In the state which has been presented of our affairs with the great parties to a disastrous and protracted war, carried on in a mode equally injurious and unjust to the United States as a neutral nation, the wisdom of the National Legislature will be again summoned to the important decision on the alternatives before them. That these will be met in a spirit worthy the councils of a nation conscious both of its rectitude and of its rights, and careful as well of its honor as of its peace, I have an entire confidence; and that the result will be stamped by a unanimity becoming the occasion, and be supported by every portion of our citizens with a patriotism enlightened and invigorated by experience, ought as little to be doubted.

In the midst of the wrongs and vexations experienced from external causes there is much room for congratulation on the prosperity and happiness flowing from our situation at home. The blessing of health has never been more universal. The fruits of the seasons, though in particular articles and districts short of their usual redundancy, are more than sufficient for our wants and our comforts. The face of our country everywhere presents the evidence of laudable enterprise, of extensive capital, and of durable improvement. In a cultivation of the materials and the extension of useful manufactures, more especially in the general application to household fabrics, we behold a rapid diminution of our dependence on foreign supplies. Nor is it unworthy of reflection that this revolution in our pursuits and habits is in no slight degree a consequence of those impolitic and arbitrary edicts by which the contending nations, in endeavoring each of them to obstruct our trade with the other, have so far abridged our means of procuring the productions and manufactures of which our own are now taking the place.

Recollecting always that for every advantage which may contribute to distinguish our lot from that to which others are doomed by the unhappy spirit of the times we are indebted to that Divine Providence whose goodness has been so remarkably extended to this rising nation, it becomes us to cherish a devout gratitude, and to implore from the same omnipotent source a blessing on the consultations and measures about to be undertaken for the welfare of our beloved country.

JAMES MADISON.

SPECIAL MESSAGES.

DECEMBER 12, 1809.

To the House of Representatives of the United States:

According to the request of the House of Representatives expressed in their resolution of the 11th instant, I now lay before them a printed copy of a paper purporting to be a circular letter from Mr. Jackson to the British consuls in the United States, as received in a Gazette at the Department of State; and also a printed paper received in a letter from our minister in London, purporting to be a copy of a dispatch from Mr. Canning to Mr. Erskine of the 23d of January last.

JAMES MADISON.

DECEMBER 16, 1809.

To the Senate of the United States:

Agreeably to the request in the resolution of the 15th instant, I transmit a copy of the correspondence with the governor of Pennsylvania in the case of Gideon Olmstead.

JAMES MADISON.

DECEMBER 16, 1809.

To the House of Representatives of the United States:

Agreeably to the request expressed in the resolution of the 13th instant, I lay before the House extracts from the correspondence of the minister plenipotentiary of the United States at London.

JAMES MADISON.

DECEMBER 22, 1809.

To the Senate of the United States:

I lay before the Senate, for their consideration whether they will advise and consent to the ratification thereof, a treaty concluded on the 30th September last with the Delaware, Potawattamie, Miami, and Eel-river Miami Indian tribes northwest of the Ohio; a separate article of the same date, with the said tribes, and a convention with the Weea tribe, concluded on the 26th October last; the whole being accompanied with the explanatory documents.

JAMES MADISON.

JANUARY 3, 1810.

To the Senate and House of Representatives of the United States:

The act authorizing a detachment of 100,000 men from the militia will expire on the 30th of March next. Its early revival is recommended, in order that timely steps may be taken for arrangements such as the act contemplated.

Without interfering with the modifications rendered necessary by the defects or the inefficacy of the laws restrictive of commerce and navigation, or with the policy of disallowing to foreign armed vessels the use of our waters, it falls within my duty to recommend also that, in addition to the precautionary measure authorized by that act and to the regular troops for completing the legal establishment of which enlistments are renewed, every necessary provision may be made for a volunteer force of 20,000 men, to be enlisted for a short period and held in a state of organization and readiness for actual service at the shortest warning.

I submit to the consideration of Congress, moreover, the expediency of such a classification and organization of the militia as will best insure prompt and successive aids from that source, adequate to emergencies which may call for them.

It will rest with them also to determine how far further provision may be expedient for putting into actual service, if necessary, any part of the naval armament not now employed.

At a period presenting features in the conduct of foreign powers toward the United States which impose on them the necessity of precautionary measures involving expense, it is a happy consideration that such is the solid state of the public credit that reliance may be justly placed on any legal provision that may be made for resorting to it in a convenient form and to an adequate amount.

JAMES MADISON.

JANUARY 9, 1810.

To the Senate of the United States:

I lay before the Senate, for their consideration whether they will advise and consent to the ratification thereof, a treaty concluded on the 9th day of December last with the Kickapoo tribe of Indians, accompanied by explanations in an extract of a letter from the governor of the Indiana Territory.

JAMES MADISON.

JANUARY 15, 1810.

To the Senate of the United States:

I lay before the Senate, for their consideration whether they will advise and consent to the ratification thereof, a treaty concluded with the Great and Little Osage Indians on the 10th day of November, 1808, and the 31st day of August, 1809.

JAMES MADISON.

JANUARY 22, 1810.

To the Senate of the United States:

I transmit to the Senate a report of the Secretary of the Treasury, complying with their resolution of the 27th of December, on the subject of disbursements in the intercourse with the Barbary Powers.

JAMES MADISON.

FEBRUARY 28, 1810.

To the Senate and House of Representatives of the United States:

I now lay before you copies of the treaties concluded with the Delaware, Pottawatamie, Miami, Eel River, and Wea tribes of Indians for the extinguishment of their title to the lands therein described, and I recommend to the consideration of Congress the making provision by law for carrying them into execution.

JAMES MADISON.

MARCH 15, 1810.

To the Senate and House of Representatives of the United States:

A treaty having been entered into and duly ratified with the Kickapoo tribe of Indians for the extinguishment of their title to certain lands within the Indiana Territory, involving conditions which require legislative provision, I submit copies thereof to both branches for consideration.

JAMES MADISON.

MARCH 27, 1810.

To the House of Representatives of the United States:

In consequence of your resolution of the 26th instant, an inquiry has been made into the correspondence of our minister at the Court of London with the Department of State, from which it appears that no official communication has been received from him since his receipt of the letter of November 23 last from the Secretary of State. A letter of January 4, 1810, has been received from that minister by Mr. Smith, but being stated to be private and unofficial, and involving, moreover, personal considerations of a delicate nature, a copy is considered as not within the purview of the call of the House.

JAMES MADISON.

PROCLAMATIONS.

By the President of the United States of America.

A PROCLAMATION.

Whereas the territory south of the Mississippi Territory and eastward of the river Mississippi, and extending to the river Perdido, of which possession was not delivered to the United States in pursuance of the treaty concluded at Paris on the 30th April, 1803, has at all times, as is well known, been considered and claimed by them as being within the colony of Louisiana conveyed by the said treaty in the same extent that it had in the hands of Spain and that it had when France originally possessed it; and

Whereas the acquiescence of the United States in the temporary continuance of the said territory under the Spanish authority was not the result of any distrust of their title, as has been particularly evinced by the general tenor of their laws and by the distinction made in the application of those laws between that territory and foreign countries, but was occasioned by their conciliatory views and by a confidence in the justice of their cause and in the success of candid discussion and amicable negotiation with a just and friendly power; and

Whereas a satisfactory adjustment, too long delayed, without the fault of the United States, has for some time been entirely suspended by events over which they had no control; and

Whereas a crisis has at length arrived subversive of the order of things under the Spanish authorities, whereby a failure of the United States to take the said territory into its possession may lead to events ultimately contravening the views of both parties, whilst in the meantime the tranquillity and security of our adjoining territories are endangered and new facilities given to violations of our revenue and commercial laws and of those prohibiting the introduction of slaves ;

Considering, moreover, that under these peculiar and imperative circumstances a forbearance on the part of the United States to occupy the territory in question, and thereby guard against the confusions and contingencies which threaten it, might be construed into a dereliction of their title or an insensibility to the importance of the stake; considering that in the hands of the United States it will not cease to be a subject of fair and friendly negotiation and adjustment; considering, finally, that the acts of Congress, though contemplating a present possession by a foreign authority, have contemplated also an eventual possession of the said territory by the United States, and are accordingly so framed as in that case to extend in their operation to the same:

Now be it known that I, James Madison, President of the United States of America, in pursuance of these weighty and urgent considerations, have deemed it right and requisite that possession should be taken of the said territory in the name and behalf of the United States. William C. C. Claiborne, governor of the Orleans Territory, of which the said Territory is to be taken as part, will accordingly proceed to execute the same and to exercise over the said Territory the authorities and functions legally appertaining to his office; and the good people inhabiting the same are invited and enjoined to pay due respect to him in that character, to be obedient to the laws, to maintain order, to cherish harmony, and in every manner to conduct themselves as peaceable citizens, under full assurance that they will be protected in the enjoyment of their liberty, property, and religion.

In testimony whereof I have caused the seal of the United States to be hereunto affixed, and signed the same with my hand.

[SEAL.]   Done at the city of Washington, the 27th day of October, A. D. 1810, and in the thirty-fifth year of the Independence of the said United States.   JAMES MADISON.

By the President:

    R. SMITH,
      Secretary of State.

[From Annals of Congress, Eleventh Congress, third session, 1248.]

BY THE PRESIDENT OF THE UNITED STATES OF AMERICA.

A PROCLAMATION.

Whereas by the fourth section of the act of Congress passed on the 1st day of May, 1810, entitled "An act concerning the commercial intercourse between the United States and Great Britain and France and their dependencies, and for other purposes," it is provided "that in case either Great Britain or France shall before the 3d day of March next so revoke or modify her edicts as that they shall cease to violate the neutral commerce of the United States, which fact the President of the United States shall declare by proclamation and if the other nation shall not within three months thereafter so revoke or modify her edicts in like manner, then the third, fourth, fifth, sixth, seventh, eighth, ninth, tenth, and eighteenth sections of the act entitled 'An act to interdict the commercial intercourse between the United States and Great Britain and France and their dependencies, and for other purposes,' shall from and after the expiration of three months from the date of the proclamation aforesaid be revived and have full force and effect so far as relates to the dominions, colonies, and dependencies, and to the articles the growth, produce, or manufacture of the dominions, colonies, and dependencies, of the nation thus refusing or neglecting to revoke or modify her edicts in the manner aforesaid. And the restrictions imposed by this act shall, from the date of such proclamation cease and be discontinued in relation to the nation revoking or modifying her decrees in the manner aforesaid;" and

Whereas it has been officially made known to this Government that the edicts of France violating the neutral commerce of the United States have been so revoked as to cease to have effect on the 1st of the present month:

Now, therefore, I, James Madison, President of the United States, do hereby proclaim that the said edicts of France have been so revoked as that they ceased on the said 1st day of the present month to violate the neutral commerce of the United States, and that from the date of these presents all the restrictions imposed by the aforesaid act shall cease and be discontinued in relation to France and their dependencies.

In testimony whereof I have caused the seal of the United States to be hereunto affixed, and signed the same with my hand, at the [SEAL.] city of Washington, this 2d day of November, A. D. 1810, and of the Independence of the United States the thirty-fifth.

JAMES MADISON.

By the President:
    R. SMITH,
       Secretary of State.

SECOND ANNUAL MESSAGE.

WASHINGTON, *December 5, 1810.*

Fellow-Citizens of the Senate and of the House of Representatives:

The embarrassments which have prevailed in our foreign relations, and so much employed the deliberations of Congress, make it a primary duty in meeting you to communicate whatever may have occurred in that branch of our national affairs.

The act of the last session of Congress concerning the commercial intercourse between the United States and Great Britain and France and their dependencies having invited in a new form a termination of their edicts against our neutral commerce, copies of the act were immediately forwarded to our ministers at London and Paris, with a view that its object might be within the early attention of the French and British Governments.

By the communication received through our minister at Paris it appeared that a knowledge of the act by the French Government was followed by a declaration that the Berlin and Milan decrees were revoked, and would cease to have effect on the 1st day of November ensuing. These being the only known edicts of France within the description of the act, and the revocation of them being such that they ceased at that date to violate our neutral commerce, the fact, as prescribed by law, was announced by a proclamation bearing date the 2d day of November.

It would have well accorded with the conciliatory views indicated by this proceeding on the part of France to have extended them to all the grounds of just complaint which now remain unadjusted with the United States. It was particularly anticipated that, as a further evidence of just dispositions toward them, restoration would have been immediately made of the property of our citizens seized under a misapplication of the principle of reprisals combined with a misconstruction of a law of the United States. This expectation has not been fulfilled.

From the British Government no communication on the subject of the act has been received. To a communication from our minister at London of a revocation by the French Government of its Berlin and Milan decrees it was answered that the British system would be relinquished as soon as the repeal of the French decrees should have actually taken effect and the commerce of neutral nations have been restored to the condition in which it stood previously to the promulgation of those decrees. This pledge, although it does not necessarily import, does not exclude the intention of relinquishing, along with the orders in council, the practice of those novel blockades which have a like effect of interrupting our neutral commerce, and this further justice to the United States is the rather to be looked for, inasmuch as the blockades in question, being not more contrary to the established law of nations than inconsistent with the rules of blockade formally recognized by Great Britain herself, could have no alleged basis other than the plea of retaliation alleged as the basis of the orders in council. Under the modification of the original orders of November, 1807, into the orders of April, 1809, there is, indeed, scarcely a nominal distinction between the orders and the blockades. One of those illegitimate blockades, bearing date in May, 1806, having been expressly avowed to be still unrescinded, and to be in effect comprehended in the orders in council, was too distinctly brought within the purview of the act of Congress not to be comprehended in the explanation of the requisites to a compliance with it. The British Government was accordingly apprised by our minister near it that such was the light in which the subject was to be regarded.

On the other important subjects depending between the United States and that Government no progress has been made from which an early and satisfactory result can be relied on.

In this new posture of our relations with those powers the consideration of Congress will be properly turned to a removal of doubts which may occur in the exposition and of difficulties in the execution of the act above cited.

The commerce of the United States with the north of Europe, heretofore much vexed by licentious cruisers, particularly under the Danish flag, has latterly been visited with fresh and extensive depredations. The measures pursued in behalf of our injured citizens not having obtained justice for them, a further and more formal interposition with the Danish Government is contemplated. The principles which have been maintained by that Government in relation to neutral commerce, and the friendly professions of His Danish Majesty toward the United States, are valuable pledges in favor of a successful issue.

Among the events growing out of the state of the Spanish Monarchy, our attention was imperiously attracted to the change developing itself in that portion of West Florida which, though of right appertaining to the United States, had remained in the possession of Spain awaiting the result of negotiations for its actual delivery to them. The Spanish authority was subverted and a situation produced exposing the country to ulterior events which might essentially affect the rights and welfare of the Union. In such a conjuncture I did not delay the interposition required for the occupancy of the territory west of the river Perdido, to which the title of the United States extends, and to which the laws provided for the Territory of Orleans are applicable. With this view, the proclamation of which a copy is laid before you was confided to the governor of that Territory to be carried into effect. The legality and necessity of the course pursued assure me of the favorable light in which it will present itself to the Legislature, and of the promptitude with which they will supply whatever provisions may be due to the essential rights and equitable interests of the people thus brought into the bosom of the American family.

Our amity with the powers of Barbary, with the exception of a recent occurrence at Tunis, of which an explanation is just received, appears to have been uninterrupted and to have become more firmly established.

With the Indian tribes also the peace and friendship of the United States are found to be so eligible that the general disposition to preserve both continues to gain strength.

I feel particular satisfaction in remarking that an interior view of our country presents us with grateful proofs of its substantial and increasing prosperity. To a thriving agriculture and the improvements related to it is added a highly interesting extension of useful manufactures, the combined product of professional occupations and of household industry.

Such indeed is the experience of economy as well as of policy in these substitutes for supplies heretofore obtained by foreign commerce that in a national view the change is justly regarded as of itself more than a recompense for those privations and losses resulting from foreign injustice which furnished the general impulse required for its accomplishment. How far it may be expedient to guard the infancy of this improvement in the distribution of labor by regulations of the commercial tariff is a subject which can not fail to suggest itself to your patriotic reflections.

It will rest with the consideration of Congress also whether a provident as well as fair encouragement would not be given to our navigation by such regulations as would place it on a level of competition with foreign vessels, particularly in transporting the important and bulky productions of our own soil. The failure of equality and reciprocity in the existing regulations on this subject operates in our ports as a premium to foreign competitors, and the inconvenience must increase as these may be multiplied under more favorable circumstances by the more than countervailing encouragements now given them by the laws of their respective countries.

Whilst it is universally admitted that a well-instructed people alone can be permanently a free people, and whilst it is evident that the means of diffusing and improving useful knowledge form so small a proportion of the expenditures for national purposes, I can not presume it to be unseasonable to invite your attention to the advantages of superadding to the means of education provided by the several States a seminary of learning instituted by the National Legislature within the limits of their exclusive jurisdiction, the expense of which might be defrayed or reimbursed out of the vacant grounds which have accrued to the nation within those limits.

Such an institution, though local in its legal character, would be universal in its beneficial effects. By enlightening the opinions, by expanding the patriotism, and by assimilating the principles, the sentiments, and the manners of those who might resort to this temple of science, to be redistributed in due time through every part of the community, sources of jealousy and prejudice would be diminished, the features of national character would be multiplied, and greater extent given to social harmony. But, above all, a well-constituted seminary in the center of the nation is recommended by the consideration that the additional instruction emanating from it would contribute not less to strengthen the foundations than to adorn the structure of our free and happy system of government.

Among the commercial abuses still committed under the American flag, and leaving in force my former reference to that subject, it appears that American citizens are instrumental in carrying on a traffic in enslaved Africans, equally in violation of the laws of humanity and in defiance of those of their own country. The same just and benevolent motives which produced the interdiction in force against this criminal conduct will doubtless be felt by Congress in devising further means of suppressing the evil.

In the midst of uncertainties necessarily connected with the great interests of the United States, prudence requires a continuance of our defensive and precautionary arrangement. The Secretary of War and Secretary of the Navy will submit the statements and estimates which may aid Congress in their ensuing provisions for the land and naval forces. The statements of the latter will include a view of the transfers of appropriations in the naval expenditures and the grounds on which they were made.

The fortifications for the defense of our maritime frontier have been prosecuted according to the plan laid down in 1808. The works, with some exceptions, are completed and furnished with ordnance. Those for the security of the city of New York, though far advanced toward completion, will require a further time and appropriation. This is the case with a few others, either not completed or in need of repairs.

The improvements in quality and quantity made in the manufacture of cannon and small arms, both at the public armories and private factories, warrant additional confidence in the competency of these resources for supplying the public exigencies.

These preparations for arming the militia having thus far provided for one of the objects contemplated by the power vested in Congress with respect to that great bulwark of the public safety, it is for their consideration whether further provisions are not requisite for the other contemplated objects of organization and discipline. To give to this great mass of physical and moral force the efficiency which it merits, and is capable of receiving, it is indispensable that they should be instructed and practiced in the rules by which they are to be governed. Toward an accomplishment of this important work I recommend for the consideration of Congress the expediency of instituting a system which shall in the first instance call into the field at the public expense and for a given time certain portions of the commissioned and noncommissioned officers. The instruction and discipline thus acquired would gradually diffuse through the entire body of the militia that practical knowledge and promptitude for active service which are the great ends to be pursued. Experience has left no doubt either of the necessity or of the efficacy of competent military skill in those portions of an army in fitting it for the final duties which it may have to perform.

The Corps of Engineers, with the Military Academy, are entitled to the early attention of Congress. The buildings at the seat fixed by law for the present Academy are so far in decay as not to afford the necessary accommodation. But a revision of the law is recommended, principally with a view to a more enlarged cultivation and diffusion of the advantages of such institutions, by providing professorships for all the necessary branches of military instruction, and by the establishment of an additional academy at the seat of Government or elsewhere. The means by which war, as well for defense as for offense, are now carried on render these schools of the more scientific operations an indispensable part of every adequate system. Even among nations whose large standing armies and frequent wars afford every other opportunity of instruction these establishments are found to be indispensable for the due attainment of the branches of military science which require a regular course of study and experiment. In a government happily without the other opportunities seminaries where the elementary principles of the art of war can be taught without actual war, and without the expense of extensive and standing armies, have the precious advantage of uniting an essential preparation against external danger with a scrupulous regard to internal safety. In no other way, probably, can a provision of equal efficacy for the public defense be made at so little expense or more consistently with the public liberty.

The receipts into the Treasury during the year ending on the 30th of September last (and amounting to more than $8,500,000) have exceeded the current expenses of the Government, including the interest on the public debt. For the purpose of reimbursing at the end of the year $3,750,000 of the principal, a loan, as authorized by law, had been negotiated to that amount, but has since been reduced to $2,750,000, the reduction being permitted by the state of the Treasury, in which there will be a balance remaining at the end of the year estimated at $2,000,000. For the probable receipts of the next year and other details I refer to statements which will be transmitted from the Treasury, and which will enable you to judge what further provisions may be necessary for the ensuing years.

Reserving for future occasions in the course of the session whatever other communications may claim your attention, I close the present by expressing my reliance, under the blessing of Divine Providence, on the judgment and patriotism which will guide your measures at a period particularly calling for united councils and inflexible exertions for the welfare of our country, and by assuring you of the fidelity and alacrity with which my cooperation will be afforded.

JAMES MADISON.

SPECIAL MESSAGES.

DECEMBER 12, 1810.

To the Senate and House of Representatives of the United States:

I lay before Congress, and recommend to their early attention, a report of the Secretary of State, from which it will be seen that a very considerable demand beyond the legal appropriations has been incurred.

for the support of seamen distressed by seizures, in different parts of Europe, of the vessels to which they belonged.

JAMES MADISON.

WASHINGTON, January 3, 1811.

To the Senate and House of Representatives of the United States:

I communicate to Congress, in confidence, a letter of the 2d of December from Governor Folch, of West Florida, to the Secretary of State, and another of the same date from the same to John McKee.

I communicate in like manner a letter from the British chargé d'affaires to the Secretary of State, with the answer of the latter. Although the letter can not have been written in consequence of any instruction from the British Government founded on the late order for taking possession of the portion of West Florida well known to be claimed by the United States; although no communication has ever been made by that Government to this of any stipulation with Spain contemplating an interposition which might so materially affect the United States, and although no call can have been made by Spain in the present instance for the fulfillment of any such subsisting engagement, yet the spirit and scope of the document, with the accredited source from which it proceeds, required that it should not be withheld from the consideration of Congress.

Taking into view the tenor of these several communications, the posture of things with which they are connected, the intimate relation of the country adjoining the United States eastward of the river Perdido to their security and tranquillity, and the peculiar interest they otherwise have in its destiny, I recommend to the consideration of Congress the seasonableness of a declaration that the United States could not see without serious inquietude any part of a neighboring territory in which they have in different respects so deep and so just a concern pass from the hands of Spain into those of any other foreign power.

I recommend to their consideration also the expediency of authorizing the Executive to take temporary possession of any part or parts of the said Territory, in pursuance of arrangements which may be desired by the Spanish authorities, and for making provision for the government of the same during such possession.

The wisdom of Congress will at the same time determine how far it may be expedient to provide for the event of a subversion of the Spanish authorities within the Territory in question, and an apprehended occupancy thereof by any other foreign power.

JAMES MADISON.

JANUARY 10, 1811.

To the Senate and House of Representatives of the United States:

I communicate to Congress, in confidence, the translation of a letter from Louis de Onis to the captain-general of Caraccas.

The tendency of misrepresentations and suggestions which it may be inferred from this specimen enter into more important correspondences of the writer to promote in foreign councils at a critical period views adverse to the peace and to the best interests of our country renders the contents of the letter of sufficient moment to be made known to the Legislature.

JAMES MADISON.

JANUARY 30, 1811.

To the Senate and House of Representatives of the United States:

I transmit to Congress copies of a letter from the Secretary of the Treasury, accompanied by copies of the Laws, Treaties, and other Documents Relative to the Public Lands, as collected and arranged pursuant to the act passed April 27, 1810.

JAMES MADISON.

JANUARY 31, 1811.

To the Senate and House of Representatives of the United States:

I lay before Congress a letter from the chargé d'affaires of the United States at Paris to the Secretary of State, and another from the same to the French minister of foreign relations; also two letters from the agent of the American consul at Bordeaux to the Secretary of State.

JAMES MADISON.

FEBRUARY 16, 1811.

To the Senate and House of Representatives of the United States:

I now lay before Congress the treaty concluded on the 10th of November, 1808, on the part of the United States with the Great and Little Osage tribes of Indians, with a view to such legal provisions as may be deemed proper for fulfilling its stipulations.

JAMES MADISON.

VETO MESSAGES.

FEBRUARY 21, 1811.

To the House of Representatives of the United States:

Having examined and considered the bill entitled "An act incorporating the Protestant Episcopal Church in the town of Alexandria, in the

District of Columbia,'' I now return the bill to the House of Representatives, in which it originated, with the following objections:

Because the bill exceeds the rightful authority to which governments are limited by the essential distinction between civil and religious functions, and violates in particular the article of the Constitution of the United States which declares that ''Congress shall make no law respecting a religious establishment.'' The bill enacts into and establishes by law sundry rules and proceedings relative purely to the organization and polity of the church incorporated, and comprehending even the election and removal of the minister of the same, so that no change could be made therein by the particular society or by the general church of which it is a member, and whose authority it recognizes. This particular church, therefore, would so far be a religious establishment by law, a legal force and sanction being given to certain articles in its constitution and administration. Nor can it be considered that the articles thus established are to be taken as the descriptive criteria only of the corporate identity of the society, inasmuch as this identity must depend on other characteristics, as the regulations established are generally unessential and alterable according to the principles and canons by which churches of that denomination govern themselves, and as the injunctions and prohibitions contained in the regulations would be enforced by the penal consequences applicable to a violation of them according to the local law.

Because the bill vests in the said incorporated church an authority to provide for the support of the poor and the education of poor children of the same, an authority which, being altogether superfluous if the provision is to be the result of pious charity, would be a precedent for giving to religious societies as such a legal agency in carrying into effect a public and civil duty.

JAMES MADISON.

FEBRUARY 28, 1811.

To the House of Representatives of the United States:

Having examined and considered the bill entitled ''An act for the relief of Richard Tervin, William Coleman, Edwin Lewis, Samuel Mims, Joseph Wilson, and the Baptist Church at Salem Meeting House, in the Mississippi Territory,'' I now return the same to the House of Representatives, in which it originated, with the following objection:

Because the bill in reserving a certain parcel of land of the United States for the use of said Baptist Church comprises a principle and precedent for the appropriation of funds of the United States for the use and support of religious societies, contrary to the article of the Constitution which declares that ''Congress shall make no law respecting a religious establishment.''

JAMES MADISON.

PROCLAMATION.

[From the National Intelligencer, July 25, 1811.]

BY THE PRESIDENT OF THE UNITED STATES OF AMERICA.

A PROCLAMATION.

Whereas great and weighty matters claiming the consideration of the Congress of the United States form an extraordinary occasion for convening them, I do by these presents appoint Monday, the 4th day of November next, for their meeting at the city of Washington, hereby requiring the respective Senators and Representatives then and there to assemble in Congress, in order to receive such communications as may then be made to them, and to consult and determine on such measures as in their wisdom may be deemed meet for the welfare of the United States.

In testimony whereof I have caused the seal of the United States to be hereunto affixed, and signed the same with my hand.

[SEAL.] Done at the city of Washington, the 24th day of July, A. D. 1811, and of the Independence of the United States the thirty-sixth.

JAMES MADISON.

By the President:
JAMES MONROE,
Secretary of State.

THIRD ANNUAL MESSAGE.

WASHINGTON, *November 5, 1811.*

Fellow-Citizens of the Senate and of the House of Representatives:

In calling you together sooner than a separation from your homes would otherwise have been required I yielded to considerations drawn from the posture of our foreign affairs, and in fixing the present for the time of your meeting regard was had to the probability of further developments of the policy of the belligerent powers toward this country which might the more unite the national councils in the measures to be pursued.

At the close of the last session of Congress it was hoped that the successive confirmations of the extinction of the French decrees, so far as they violatea our neutral commerce, would have induced the Government of Great Britain to repeal its orders in council, and thereby authorize a removal of the existing obstructions to her commerce with the United States.

Instead of this reasonable step toward satisfaction and friendship between the two nations, the orders were, at a moment when least to have been expected, put into more rigorous execution; and it was communicated through the British envoy just arrived that whilst the revocation of the edicts of France, as officially made known to the British Government, was denied to have taken place, it was an indispensable condition of the repeal of the British orders that commerce should be restored to a footing that would admit the productions and manufactures of Great Britain, when owned by neutrals, into markets shut against them by her enemy, the United States being given to understand that in the meantime a continuance of their nonimportation act would lead to measures of retaliation.

At a later date it has indeed appeared that a communication to the British Government of fresh evidence of the repeal of the French decrees against our neutral trade was followed by an intimation that it had been transmitted to the British plenipotentiary here in order that it might receive full consideration in the depending discussions. This communication appears not to have been received; but the transmission of it hither, instead of founding on it an actual repeal of the orders or assurances that the repeal would ensue, will not permit us to rely on any effective change in the British cabinet. To be ready to meet with cordiality satisfactory proofs of such a change, and to proceed in the meantime in adapting our measures to the views which have been disclosed through that minister will best consult our whole duty.

In the unfriendly spirit of those disclosures indemnity and redress for other wrongs have continued to be withheld, and our coasts and the mouths of our harbors have again witnessed scenes not less derogatory to the dearest of our national rights than vexatious to the regular course of our trade.

Among the occurrences produced by the conduct of British ships of war hovering on our coasts was an encounter between one of them and the American frigate commanded by Captain Rodgers, rendered unavoidable on the part of the latter by a fire commenced without cause by the former, whose commander is therefore alone chargeable with the blood unfortunately shed in maintaining the honor of the American flag. The proceedings of a court of inquiry requested by Captain Rodgers are communicated, together with the correspondence relating to the occurrence, between the Secretary of State and His Britannic Majesty's envoy. To these are added the several correspondences which have passed on the subject of the British orders in council, and to both the correspondence relating to the Floridas, in which Congress will be made acquainted with the interposition which the Government of Great Britain has thought proper to make against the proceeding of the United States.

The justice and fairness which have been evinced on the part of the United States toward France, both before and since the revocation of her decrees, authorized an expectation that her Government would have followed up that measure by all such others as were due to our reasonable claims, as well as dictated by its amicable professions. No proof, however, is yet given of an intention to repair the other wrongs done to the United States, and particularly to restore the great amount of American property seized and condemned under edicts which, though not affecting our neutral relations, and therefore not entering into questions between the United States and other belligerents, were nevertheless founded in such unjust principles that the reparation ought to have been prompt and ample.

In addition to this and other demands of strict right on that nation, the United States have much reason to be dissatisfied with the rigorous and unexpected restrictions to which their trade with the French dominions has been subjected, and which, if not discontinued, will require at least corresponding restrictions on importations from France into the United States.

On all those subjects our minister plenipotentiary lately sent to Paris has carried with him the necessary instructions, the result of which will be communicated to you, and, by ascertaining the ulterior policy of the French Government toward the United States, will enable you to adapt to it that of the United States toward France.

Our other foreign relations remain without unfavorable changes. With Russia they are on the best footing of friendship. The ports of Sweden have afforded proofs of friendly dispositions toward our commerce in the councils of that nation also, and the information from our special minister to Denmark shews that the mission had been attended with valuable effects to our citizens, whose property had been so extensively violated and endangered by cruisers under the Danish flag.

Under the ominous indications which commanded attention it became a duty to exert the means committed to the executive department in providing for the general security. The works of defense on our maritime frontier have accordingly been prosecuted with an activity leaving little to be added for the completion of the most important ones, and, as particularly suited for cooperation in emergencies, a portion of the gunboats have in particular harbors been ordered into use. The ships of war before in commission, with the addition of a frigate, have been chiefly employed as a cruising guard to the rights of our coast, and such a disposition has been made of our land forces as was thought to promise the services most appropriate and important. In this disposition is included a force consisting of regulars and militia, embodied in the Indiana Territory and marched toward our northwestern frontier. This measure was made requisite by several murders and depredations committed by Indians, but more especially by the menacing preparations and aspect of a combination of them on the Wabash, under the influence and direction of a fanatic of the Shawanese tribe. With these exceptions the Indian tribes retain their peaceable dispositions toward us, and their usual pursuits.

I must now add that the period is arrived which claims from the legislative guardians of the national rights a system of more ample provisions for maintaining them. Notwithstanding the scrupulous justice, the protracted moderation, and the multiplied efforts on the part of the United States to substitute for the accumulating dangers to the peace of the two countries all the mutual advantages of reestablished friendship and confidence, we have seen that the British cabinet perseveres not only in withholding a remedy for other wrongs, so long and so loudly calling for it, but in the execution, brought home to the threshold of our territory, of measures which under existing circumstances have the character as well as the effect of war on our lawful commerce.

With this evidence of hostile inflexibility in trampling on rights which no independent nation can relinquish, Congress will feel the duty of putting the United States into an armor and an attitude demanded by the crisis, and corresponding with the national spirit and expectations.

I recommend, accordingly, that adequate provision be made for filling the ranks and prolonging the enlistments of the regular troops; for an auxiliary force to be engaged for a more limited term; for the acceptance of volunteer corps, whose patriotic ardor may court a participation in urgent services; for detachments as they may be wanted of other portions of the militia, and for such a preparation of the great body as will proportion its usefulness to its intrinsic capacities. Nor can the occasion fail to remind you of the importance of those military seminaries which in every event will form a valuable and frugal part of our military establishment.

The manufacture of cannon and small arms has proceeded with due success, and the stock and resources of all the necessary munitions are adequate to emergencies. It will not be inexpedient, however, for Congress to authorize an enlargement of them.

Your attention will of course be drawn to such provisions on the subject of our naval force as may be required for the services to which it may be best adapted. I submit to Congress the seasonableness also of an authority to augment the stock of such materials as are imperishable in their nature, or may not at once be attainable.

In contemplating the scenes which distinguish this momentous epoch, and estimating their claims to our attention, it is impossible to overlook those developing themselves among the great communities which occupy the southern portion of our own hemisphere and extend into our neighborhood. An enlarged philanthropy and an enlightened forecast concur in imposing on the national councils an obligation to take a deep interest in their destinies, to cherish reciprocal sentiments of good will, to regard the progress of events, and not to be unprepared for whatever order of things may be ultimately established.

Under another aspect of our situation the early attention of Congress will be due to the expediency of further guards against evasions and infractions of our commercial laws. The practice of smuggling, which is odious everywhere, and particularly criminal in free governments, where, the laws being made by all for the good of all, a fraud is committed on every individual as well as on the state, attains its utmost guilt when it blends with a pursuit of ignominious gain a treacherous subserviency, in the transgressors, to a foreign policy adverse to that of their own country. It is then that the virtuous indignation of the public should be enabled to manifest itself through the regular animadversions of the most competent laws.

To secure greater respect to our mercantile flag, and to the honest interests which it covers, it is expedient also that it be made punishable in our citizens to accept licenses from foreign governments for a trade unlawfully interdicted by them to other American citizens, or to trade under false colors or papers of any sort.

A prohibition is equally called for against the acceptance by our citizens of special licenses to be used in a trade with the United States, and against the admission into particular ports of the United States of vessels from foreign countries authorized to trade with particular ports only.

Although other subjects will press more immediately on your deliberations, a portion of them can not but be well bestowed on the just and sound policy of securing to our manufactures the success they have attained, and are still attaining, in some degree, under the impulse of causes not permanent, and to our navigation, the fair extent of which is at present abridged by the unequal regulations of foreign governments.

Besides the reasonableness of saving our manufactures from sacrifices which a change of circumstances might bring on them, the national interest requires that, with respect to such articles at least as belong to our defense and our primary wants, we should not be left in unnecessary dependence on external supplies. And whilst foreign governments adhere to the existing discriminations in their ports against our navigation, and an equality or lesser discrimination is enjoyed by their navigation in our ports, the effect can not be mistaken, because it has been seriously felt by our shipping interests; and in proportion as this takes place the advantages of an independent conveyance of our products to foreign markets and of a growing body of mariners trained by their occupations for the service of their country in times of danger must be diminished.

The receipts into the Treasury during the year ending on the 30th of September last have exceeded $13,500,000, and have enabled us to defray the current expenses, including the interest on the public debt, and to reimburse more than $5,000,000 of the principal without recurring to the loan authorized by the act of the last session. The temporary loan obtained in the latter end of the year 1810 has also been reimbursed, and is not included in that amount.

The decrease of revenue arising from the situation of our commerce, and the extraordinary expenses which have and may become necessary, must be taken into view in making commensurate provisions for the ensuing year; and I recommend to your consideration the propriety of insuring a sufficiency of annual revenue at least to defray the ordinary expenses of Government, and to pay the interest on the public debt, including that on new loans which may be authorized.

I can not close this communication without expressing my deep sense of the crisis in which you are assembled, my confidence in a wise and honorable result to your deliberations, and assurances of the faithful zeal with which my cooperating duties will be discharged, invoking at the same time the blessing of Heaven on our beloved country and on all the means that may be employed in vindicating its rights and advancing its welfare.

JAMES MADISON.

SPECIAL MESSAGES.

WASHINGTON, *November 13, 1811.*

To the Senate and House of Representatives of the United States:

I communicate to Congress copies of a correspondence between the envoy extraordinary and minister plenipotentiary of Great Britain and the Secretary of State relative to the aggression committed by a British ship of war on the United States frigate *Chesapeake*, by which it will be seen that that subject of difference between the two countries is terminated by an offer of reparation, which has been acceded to.

JAMES MADISON.

WASHINGTON, *December 18, 1811.*

To the Senate and House of Representatives of the United States:

I lay before Congress two letters received from Governor Harrison, of the Indiana Territory, reporting the particulars and the issue of the expedition under his command, of which notice was taken in my communication of November 5.

While it is deeply lamented that so many valuable lives have been lost in the action which took place on the 7th ultimo, Congress will see with satisfaction the dauntless spirit and fortitude victoriously displayed by every description of the troops engaged, as well as the collected firmness which distinguished their commander on an occasion requiring the utmost exertions of valor and discipline.

It may reasonably be expected that the good effects of this critical defeat and dispersion of a combination of savages, which appears to have been spreading to a greater extent, will be experienced not only in a ces-

THE BATTLE OF TIPPECANOE

THE BATTLE OF TIPPECANOE

November 7, 1811

Willing tools in the hands of our arch-enemy, England, the Indians were, until 1840–1850, a very real and constant source of anxiety to the Presidents. From Washington's time onward the policy had been to utilize every opportunity of thrusting the tribes westward. Tecumseh, a chieftain of remarkable intelligence and ability, sought to block the westward progress of the white man by forming a confederacy of the Indian tribes. In 1809 the United States made a purchase of 3,000,000 acres of land on the Wabash, which Tecumseh declared was fraudulent. He gathered forces on Tippecanoe Creek to prevent the occupation of the territory ceded. William Henry Harrison, then Governor of Indiana Territory, which is now Indiana, Illinois, Michigan and Wisconsin, decided to establish our title by building a fort in the disputed domain. When he came within four miles of the Indian encampment on Tippecanoe Creek he was met by a deputation of savages who requested him to abandon for the day his hostile plans, bivouac for the night on that spot, and in the morning parley with Tecumseh's brother, the Prophet. Although the spot seemed devised by nature to favor an Indian attack, Harrison complied. Two hours before daylight the Indians began picking off the troops made visible by the campfires. Unable to retaliate effectually, the troops waited doggedly for daylight. Then, at point of bayonet, they drove their foes into a swamp and wiped them and their village out of existence. The victory cost 188 men in killed and wounded, 34 of them being officers. Tecumseh's ambitious scheme of confederation was discredited and doomed from that time on.

Reference to the headings beginning with the word "Indian" in the encyclopedic index (volume eleven), will show how exhaustively the work treats Indian affairs from the very beginning of the Government to the day when the savage ceased to harass our frontiers.

sation of the murders and depredations committed on our frontier, but in the prevention of any hostile incursions otherwise to have been apprehended.

The families of those brave and patriotic citizens who have fallen in this severe conflict will doubtless engage the favorable attention of Congress.

JAMES MADISON.

WASHINGTON, *December 23, 1811.*

To the Senate and House of Representatives of the United States:

I communicate to Congress copies of an act of the legislature of New York relating to a canal from the Great Lakes to Hudson River. In making the communication I consult the respect due to that State, in whose behalf the commissioners appointed by the act have placed it in my hands for the purpose.

The utility of canal navigation is universally admitted. It is no less certain that scarcely any country offers more extensive opportunities for that branch of improvements than the United States, and none, perhaps, inducements equally persuasive to make the most of them. The particular undertaking contemplated by the State of New York, which marks an honorable spirit of enterprise and comprises objects of national as well as more limited importance, will recall the attention of Congress to the signal advantages to be derived to the United States from a general system of internal communication and conveyance, and suggest to their consideration whatever steps may be proper on their part toward its introduction and accomplishment. As some of those advantages have an intimate connection with the arrangements and exertions for the general security, it is at a period calling for those that the merits of such a system will be seen in the strongest lights.

JAMES MADISON.

WASHINGTON, *December 27, 1811.*

To the Senate and House of Representatives of the United States:

I lay before Congress copies of resolutions entered into by the legislature of Pennsylvania, which have been transmitted to me with that view by the governor of that State, in pursuance of one of the said resolutions.

JAMES MADISON.

WASHINGTON, *January 15, 1812.*

To the Senate and House of Representatives of the United States:

I transmit to Congress an account of the contingent expenses of the Government for the year 1811, incurred on the occasion of taking possession of the territory limited eastwardly by the river Perdido, and amounting to $3,396.

JAMES MADISON.

WASHINGTON, *January 16, 1812.*

To the Senate and House of Representatives of the United States:

I communicate to Congress a letter from the envoy extraordinary and minister plenipotentiary of Great Britain to the Secretary of State, with the answer of the latter.

The continued evidence afforded in this correspondence of the hostile policy of the British Government against our national rights strengthens the considerations recommending and urging the preparation of adequate means for maintaining them.

JAMES MADISON.

MARCH 3, 1812.

To the Senate and House of Representatives of the United States:

At the request of the convention assembled in the Territory of Orleans on the 22d day of November last, I transmit to Congress the proceedings of that body in pursuance of the act entitled " An act to enable the people of the Territory of Orleans to form a constitution and State government, and for the admission of the said State into the Union on an equal footing with the original States, and for other purposes."

JAMES MADISON.

MARCH 9, 1812.

To the Senate and House of Representatives of the United States:

I lay before Congress copies of certain documents which remain in the Department of State. They prove that at a recent period, whilst the United States, notwithstanding the wrongs sustained by them, ceased not to observe the laws of peace and neutrality toward Great Britain, and in the midst of amicable professions and negotiations on the part of the British Government, through its public minister here, a secret agent of that Government was employed in certain States, more especially at the seat of government in Massachusetts, in fomenting disaffection to the constituted authorities of the nation, and in intrigues with the disaffected, for the purpose of bringing about resistance to the laws, and eventually, in concert with a British force, of destroying the Union and forming the eastern part thereof into a political connection with Great Britain.

In addition to the effect which the discovery of such a procedure ought to have on the public councils, it will not fail to render more dear to the hearts of all good citizens that happy union of these States which, under Divine Providence, is the guaranty of their liberties, their safety, their tranquillity, and their prosperity.

JAMES MADISON.

APRIL 1, 1812.

To the Senate and House of Representatives of the United States:

Considering it as expedient, under existing circumstances and prospects, that a general embargo be laid on all vessels now in port, or hereafter arriving, for the period of sixty days, I recommend the immediate passage of a law to that effect.

JAMES MADISON.

APRIL 20, 1812.

To the Senate and House of Representatives of the United States:

Among the incidents to the unexampled increase and expanding interests of the American nation under the fostering influence of free constitutions and just laws has been a corresponding accumulation of duties in the several Departments of the Government, and this has been necessarily the greater in consequence of the peculiar state of our foreign relations and the connection of these with our internal administration.

The extensive and multiplied preparations into which the United States are at length driven for maintaining their violated rights have caused this augmentation of business to press on the Department of War particularly, with a weight disproportionate to the powers of any single officer, with no other aids than are authorized by existing laws. With a view to a more adequate arrangement for the essential objects of that Department, I recommend to the early consideration of Congress a provision for two subordinate appointments therein, with such compensations annexed as may be reasonably expected by citizens duly qualified for the important functions which may be properly assigned to them.

JAMES MADISON.

MAY 26, 1812.

To the Senate and House of Representatives of the United States:

I communicate to Congress, for their information, copies and extracts from the correspondence of the Secretary of State and the minister plenipotentiary of the United States at Paris. These documents will place before Congress the actual posture of our relations with France.

JAMES MADISON.

WASHINGTON, *June 1, 1812.*

To the Senate and House of Representatives of the United States:

I communicate to Congress certain documents, being a continuation of those heretofore laid before them on the subject of our affairs with Great Britain.

Without going back beyond the renewal in 1803 of the war in which Great Britain is engaged, and omitting unrepaired wrongs of inferior magnitude, the conduct of her Government presents a series of acts hostile to the United States as an independent and neutral nation.

British cruisers have been in the continued practice of violating the American flag on the great highway of nations, and of seizing and carrying off persons sailing under it, not in the exercise of a belligerent right founded on the law of nations against an enemy, but of a municipal prerogative over British subjects. British jurisdiction is thus extended to neutral vessels in a situation where no laws can operate but the law of nations and the laws of the country to which the vessels belong, and a self-redress is assumed which, if British subjects were wrongfully detained and alone concerned, is that substitution of force for a resort to the responsible sovereign which falls within the definition of war. Could the seizure of British subjects in such cases be regarded as within the exercise of a belligerent right, the acknowledged laws of war, which forbid an article of captured property to be adjudged without a regular investigation before a competent tribunal, would imperiously demand the fairest trial where the sacred rights of persons were at issue. In place of such a trial these rights are subjected to the will of every petty commander.

The practice, hence, is so far from affecting British subjects alone that, under the pretext of searching for these, thousands of American citizens, under the safeguard of public law and of their national flag, have been torn from their country and from everything dear to them; have been dragged on board ships of war of a foreign nation and exposed, under the severities of their discipline, to be exiled to the most distant and deadly climes, to risk their lives in the battles of their oppressors, and to be the melancholy instruments of taking away those of their own brethren.

Against this crying enormity, which Great Britain would be so prompt to avenge if committed against herself, the United States have in vain exhausted remonstrances and expostulations, and that no proof might be wanting of their conciliatory dispositions, and no pretext left for a continuance of the practice, the British Government was formally assured of the readiness of the United States to enter into arrangements such as could not be rejected if the recovery of British subjects were the real and the sole object. The communication passed without effect.

British cruisers have been in the practice also of violating the rights and the peace of our coasts. They hover over and harass our entering and departing commerce. To the most insulting pretensions they have added the most lawless proceedings in our very harbors, and have wantonly spilt American blood within the sanctuary of our territorial jurisdiction. The principles and rules enforced by that nation, when a neutral nation, against armed vessels of belligerents hovering near her coasts and disturbing her commerce are well known. When called on, nevertheless, by the United States to punish the greater offenses committed by her own vessels, her Government has bestowed on their commanders additional marks of honor and confidence.

Under pretended blockades, without the presence of an adequate force and sometimes without the practicability of applying one, our commerce has been plundered in every sea, the great staples of our country have been cut off from their legitimate markets, and a destructive blow aimed at our agricultural and maritime interests. In aggravation of these predatory measures they have been considered as in force from the dates of their notification, a retrospective effect being thus added, as has been done in other important cases, to the unlawfulness of the course pursued. And to render the outrage the more signal these mock blockades have been reiterated and enforced in the face of official communications from the British Government declaring as the true definition of a legal blockade "that particular ports must be actually invested and previous warning given to vessels bound to them not to enter."

Not content with these occasional expedients for laying waste our neutral trade, the cabinet of Britain resorted at length to the sweeping system of blockades, under the name of orders in council, which has been molded and managed as might best suit its political views, its commercial jealousies, or the avidity of British cruisers.

To our remonstrances against the complicated and transcendent injustice of this innovation the first reply was that the orders were reluctantly adopted by Great Britain as a necessary retaliation on decrees of her enemy proclaiming a general blockade of the British Isles at a time when the naval force of that enemy dared not issue from his own ports. She was reminded without effect that her own prior blockades, unsupported by an adequate naval force actually applied and continued, were a bar to this plea ; that executed edicts against millions of our property could not be retaliation on edicts confessedly impossible to be executed ; that retaliation, to be just, should fall on the party setting the guilty example, not on an innocent party which was not even chargeable with an acquiescence in it.

When deprived of this flimsy veil for a prohibition of our trade with her enemy by the repeal of his prohibition of our trade with Great Britain, her cabinet, instead of a corresponding repeal or a practical discontinuance of its orders, formally avowed a determination to persist in them against the United States until the markets of her enemy should be laid open to British products, thus asserting an obligation on a neutral power to require one belligerent to encourage by its internal regulations the trade of another belligerent, contradicting her own practice toward all nations, in peace as well as in war, and betraying the insincerity of those professions which inculcated a belief that, having resorted to her orders with regret, she was anxious to find an occasion for putting an end to them.

Abandoning still more all respect for the neutral rights of the United States and for its own consistency, the British Government now demands as prerequisites to a repeal of its orders as they relate to the United States that a formality should be observed in the repeal of the French decrees nowise necessary to their termination nor exemplified by British usage, and that the French repeal, besides including that portion of the decrees which operates within a territorial jurisdiction, as well as that which operates on the high seas, against the commerce of the United States should not be a single and special repeal in relation to the United States, but should be extended to whatever other neutral nations unconnected with them may be affected by those decrees. And as an additional insult, they are called on for a formal disavowal of conditions and pretensions advanced by the French Government for which the United States are so far from having made themselves responsible that, in official explanations which have been published to the world, and in a correspondence of the American minister at London with the British minister for foreign affairs such a responsibility was explicitly and emphatically disclaimed.

It has become, indeed, sufficiently certain that the commerce of the United States is to be sacrificed, not as interfering with the belligerent rights of Great Britain; not as supplying the wants of her enemies, which she herself supplies; but as interfering with the monopoly which she covets for her own commerce and navigation. She carries on a war against the lawful commerce of a friend that she may the better carry on a commerce with an enemy—a commerce polluted by the forgeries and perjuries which are for the most part the only passports by which it can succeed.

Anxious to make every experiment short of the last resort of injured nations, the United States have withheld from Great Britain, under successive modifications, the benefits of a free intercourse with their market, the loss of which could not but outweigh the profits accruing from her restrictions of our commerce with other nations. And to entitle these experiments to the more favorable consideration they were so framed as to enable her to place her adversary under the exclusive operation of them. To these appeals her Government has been equally inflexible, as if willing to make sacrifices of every sort rather than yield to the claims of justice or renounce the errors of a false pride. Nay, so far were the attempts carried to overcome the attachment of the British cabinet to its unjust edicts that it received every encouragement within the competency of the executive branch of our Government to expect that a repeal of them would be followed by a war between the United States and France, unless the French edicts should also be repealed. Even this communication, although silencing forever the plea of a disposition in the United States to acquiesce in those edicts originally the sole plea for them, received no attention.

If no other proof existed of a predetermination of the British Government against a repeal of its orders, it might be found in the correspondence of the minister plenipotentiary of the United States at London and the British secretary for foreign affairs in 1810, on the question whether the blockade of May, 1806, was considered as in force or as not in force. It had been ascertained that the French Government, which urged this blockade as the ground of its Berlin decree, was willing in the event of its removal to repeal that decree, which, being followed by alternate repeals of the other offensive edicts, might abolish the whole system on both sides. This inviting opportunity for accomplishing an object so important to the United States, and professed so often to be the desire of both the belligerents, was made known to the British Government. As that Government admits that an actual application of an adequate force is necessary to the existence of a legal blockade, and it was notorious that if such a force had ever been applied its long discontinuance had annulled the blockade in question, there could be no sufficient objection on the part of Great Britain to a formal revocation of it, and no imaginable objection to a declaration of the fact that the blockade did not exist. The declaration would have been consistent with her avowed principles of blockade, and would have enabled the United States to demand from France the pledged repeal of her decrees, either with success, in which case the way would have been opened for a general repeal of the belligerent edicts, or without success, in which case the United States would have been justified in turning their measures exclusively against France. The British Government would, however, neither rescind the blockade nor declare its nonexistence, nor permit its nonexistence to be inferred and affirmed by the American plenipotentiary. On the contrary, by representing the blockade to be comprehended in the orders in council, the United States were compelled so to regard it in their subsequent proceedings.

There was a period when a favorable change in the policy of the British cabinet was justly considered as established. The minister plenipotentiary of His Britannic Majesty here proposed an adjustment of the differences more immediately endangering the harmony of the two countries. The proposition was accepted with the promptitude and cordiality corresponding with the invariable professions of this Government. A foundation appeared to be laid for a sincere and lasting reconciliation. The prospect, however, quickly vanished. The whole proceeding was disavowed by the British Government without any explanations which could at that time repress the belief that the disavowal proceeded from a spirit of hostility to the commercial rights and prosperity of the United States; and it has since come into proof that at the very moment when the public minister was holding the language of friendship and inspiring confidence in the sincerity of the negotiation with which he was charged a secret agent of his Government was employed in intrigues having for their object a subversion of our Government and a dismemberment of our happy union.

In reviewing the conduct of Great Britain toward the United States our attention is necessarily drawn to the warfare just renewed by the savages on one of our extensive frontiers—a warfare which is known to spare neither age nor sex and to be distinguished by features peculiarly shocking to humanity. It is difficult to account for the activity and combinations which have for some time been developing themselves among tribes in constant intercourse with British traders and garrisons without connecting their hostility with that influence and without recollecting the authenticated examples of such interpositions heretofore furnished by the officers and agents of that Government.

Such is the spectacle of injuries and indignities which have been heaped on our country, and such the crisis which its unexampled forbearance and conciliatory efforts have not been able to avert. It might at least have been expected that an enlightened nation, if less urged by moral obligations or invited by friendly dispositions on the part of the United States, would have found in its true interest alone a sufficient motive to respect their rights and their tranquillity on the high seas; that an enlarged policy would have favored that free and general circulation of commerce in which the British nation is at all times interested, and which in times of war is the best alleviation of its calamities to herself as well as to other belligerents; and more especially that the British cabinet would not, for the sake of a precarious and surreptitious intercourse with hostile markets, have persevered in a course of measures which necessarily put at hazard the invaluable market of a great and growing country, disposed to cultivate the mutual advantages of an active commerce.

Other counsels have prevailed. Our moderation and conciliation have had no other effect than to encourage perseverance and to enlarge pretensions. We behold our seafaring citizens still the daily victims of lawless violence, committed on the great common and highway of nations, even within sight of the country which owes them protection. We behold our vessels, freighted with the products of our soil and industry, or returning with the honest proceeds of them, wrested from their lawful destinations, confiscated by prize courts no longer the organs of public law but the instruments of arbitrary edicts, and their unfortunate crews dispersed and lost, or forced or inveigled in British ports into British fleets, whilst arguments are employed in support of these aggressions which have no foundation but in a principle equally supporting a claim to regulate our external commerce in all cases whatsoever.

We behold, in fine, on the side of Great Britain a state of war against the United States, and on the side of the United States a state of peace toward Great Britain.

Whether the United States shall continue passive under these progressive usurpations and these accumulating wrongs, or, opposing force to force in defense of their national rights, shall commit a just cause into the hands of the Almighty Disposer of Events, avoiding all connections which might entangle it in the contest or views of other powers, and preserving a constant readiness to concur in an honorable reestablishment of peace and friendship, is a solemn question which the Constitution wisely confides to the legislative department of the Government. In recommending it to their early deliberations I am happy in the assurance that the decision will be worthy the enlightened and patriotic councils of a virtuous, a free, and a powerful nation.

Having presented this view of the relations of the United States with Great Britain and of the solemn alternative growing out of them, I proceed to remark that the communications last made to Congress on the subject of our relations with France will have shewn that since the revocation of her decrees, as they violated the neutral rights of the United States, her Government has authorized illegal captures by its privateers and public ships, and that other outrages have been practiced on our vessels and our citizens. It will have been seen also that no indemnity had been provided or satisfactorily pledged for the extensive spoliations committed under the violent and retrospective orders of the French Government against the property of our citizens seized within the jurisdiction of France. I abstain at this time from recommending to the consideration of Congress definitive measures with respect to that nation, in the expectation that the result of unclosed discussions between our minister plenipotentiary at Paris and the French Government will speedily enable Congress to decide with greater advantage on the course due to the rights, the interests, and the honor of our country.

JAMES MADISON.

JUNE 30, 1812.

To the Senate and House of Representatives of the United States:

With a view the better to adapt to the public service the volunteer force contemplated by the act passed on the 6th day of February, I recommend to the consideration of Congress the expediency of making the requisite provision for the officers thereof being commissioned by the authority of the United States.

Considering the distribution of the military forces of the United States required by the circumstances of our country, I recommend also to the consideration of Congress the expediency of providing for the appointment of an additional number of general officers, and of deputies in the Adjutant's, Quartermaster's, Inspector's, and Paymaster's departments of the Army, and for the employment in cases of emergency of additional engineers.

JAMES MADISON.

JULY 1, 1812.

To the House of Representatives of the United States:

In compliance with the resolution of the House of Representatives of the 26th of June, I transmit the information contained in the documents herewith inclosed.

JAMES MADISON.

From the Secretary of State to General George Matthews and Colonel John M'Kee.

DEPARTMENT OF STATE, *January 26, 1811.*

The President of the United States having appointed you jointly and severally commissioners for carrying into effect certain provisions of an act of Congress (a copy of which is inclosed) relative to the portion of the Floridas situated to the east of the river Perdido, you will repair to that quarter with all possible expedition, concealing from general observation the trust committed to you with that discretion which the delicacy and importance of the undertaking require.

Should you find Governor Folk or the local authority existing there inclined to surrender in an amicable manner the possession of the remaining portion or portions of West Florida now held by him in the name of the Spanish Monarchy, you are to accept in behalf of the United States the abdication of his or of the other existing authority and the jurisdiction of the country over which it extends. And should a stipulation be insisted on for the redelivery of the country at a future period, you may engage for such redelivery to the lawful sovereign.

The debts clearly due from the Spanish Government to the people of the Territory surrendered may, if insisted on, be assumed within reasonable limits and under specified descriptions to be settled hereafter as a claim against Spain in an adjustment of our affairs with her. You may also guarantee, in the name of the United States, the confirmation of all such titles to land as are clearly sanctioned by Spanish laws, and Spanish civil functionaries, where no special reasons may require changes, are to be permitted to remain in office with the assurance of a continuation of the prevailing laws, with such alterations only as may be necessarily required in the new situation of the country.

If it should be required and be found necessary, you may agree to advance, as above, a reasonable sum for the transportation of the Spanish troops.

These directions are adapted to one of the contingencies specified in the act of Congress, namely, the amicable surrender of the possession of the Territory by the local ruling authority. But should the arrangement contemplated by the statute not be made, and should there be room to entertain a suspicion of an existing design in any foreign power to occupy the country in question, you are to keep yourselves on the alert, and on the first undoubted manifestation of the approach of a force for that purpose you will exercise with promptness and vigor the powers with which you are invested by the President to preoccupy by force the Territory, to the entire exclusion of any armament that may be advancing to take the possession of it. In this event you will exercise a sound discretion in applying the powers given with respect to debts, titles to lands, civil officers, and the continuation of the Spanish laws, taking care to commit the Government on no point further than may be necessary; and should any Spanish military force remain within the country after the occupancy by the troops of the United States, you may in such case aid in their removal from the same.

The universal toleration which the laws of the United States assure to every religious persuasion will not escape you as an argument for quieting the minds of uninformed individuals who may entertain fears on that head.

The conduct you are to pursue in regard to East Florida must be regulated by the dictates of your own judgments, on a close view and accurate knowledge of the precise state of things there, and of the real disposition of the Spanish Government always recurring to the present instruction as the paramount rule of your proceedings. Should you discover an inclination in the governor of East Florida, or in the existing local authority, amicably to surrender that province into the possession of the United States, you are to accept it on the same terms that are prescribed by these instructions in relation to West Florida. And in case of the actual appearance of any attempt to take possession by a foreign power, you will pursue the same effective measures for the occupation of the Territory and for the exclusion of the foreign force as you are directed to pursue with respect to the country east of the Perdido, forming at this time the extent of Governor Folk's jurisdiction.

If you should, under these instructions, obtain possession of Mobile, you will lose no time in informing Governor Claiborne thereof, with a request that he will without delay take the necessary steps for the occupation of the same.

All ordnance and military stores that may be found in the Territory must be held as the property of the Spanish Government, to be accounted for hereafter to the proper authority, and you will not fail to transmit an inventory thereof to this Department.

If in the execution of any part of these instructions you should need the aid of a military force, the same will be afforded you upon your application to the commanding officer of the troops of the United States on that station, or to the commanding officer of the nearest post, in virtue of orders which have been issued from the War Department. And in case you should, moreover, need naval assistance, you will receive the same upon your application to the naval commander in pursuance of orders from the Navy Department.

From the Treasury Department will be issued the necessary instructions in relation to imposts and duties, and to the slave ships whose arrival is apprehended.

The President, relying upon your discretion, authorizes you to draw upon the collectors of Orleans and Savannah for such sums as may be necessary to defray unavoidable expenses that may be incurred in the execution of these instructions, not exceeding in your drafts on New Orleans $8,000 and in your drafts on Savannah $2,000, without further authority, of which expenses you will hereafter exhibit a detailed account duly supported by satisfactory vouchers.

POSTSCRIPT.—If Governor Folk should unexpectedly require and pertinaciously insist that the stipulation for the redelivery of the Territory should also include that portion of the country which is situated west of the river Perdido, you are, in yielding to such demand, only to use general words that may by implication comprehend that portion of country; but at the same time you are expressly to provide that such stipulation shall not in any way impair or affect the right or title of the United States to the same.

The Secretary of State to General Matthews.

DEPARTMENT OF STATE, *April 4, 1812.*

General MATTHEWS, etc.

SIR: I have had the honor to receive your letter of the 14th of March, and have now to communicate to you the sentiments of the President on the very interesting subject to which it relates.

I am sorry to have to state that the measures which you appear to have adopted for obtaining possession of Amelia Island and other parts of East Florida are not authorized by the law of the United States or the instructions founded on it under which you have acted.

You were authorized by the law, a copy of which was communicated to you, and by your instructions, which are strictly conformable to it, to take possession of East Florida only in case one of the following contingencies should happen: Either that the governor or other existing local authority should be disposed to place it amicably in the hands of the United States, or that an attempt should be made to take possession of it by a foreign power. Should the first contingency happen it would follow that the arrangement, being amicable, would require no force on the part of the United States to carry it into effect. It was only in case of an attempt to take it by a foreign power that force could be necessary, in which event only were you authorized to avail yourself of it.

In neither of these contingencies was it the policy of the law or purpose of the Executive to wrest the Province forcibly from Spain, but only to occupy it with a view to prevent its falling into the hands of any foreign power, and to hold that pledge under the existing peculiarity of the circumstances of the Spanish Monarchy for a just result in an amicable negotiation with Spain.

Had the United States been disposed to proceed otherwise, that intention would have been manifested by a change of the law and suitable measures to carry it into effect; and as it was in their power to take possession whenever they might think that circumstances authorized and required it, it would be the more to be regretted if possession should be effected by any means irregular in themselves and subjecting the Government of the United States to unmerited censure.

The views of the Executive respecting East Florida are further illustrated by your instructions as to West Florida. Although the United States have thought that they had a good title to the latter Province, they did not take possession until after the Spanish authority had been subverted by a revolutionary proceeding, and the contingency of the country being thrown into foreign hands had forced itself into view. Nor did they then, nor have they since, dispossessed the Spanish troops of the post which they occupied. If they did not think proper to take possession by force of a province to which they thought they were justly entitled, it could not be presumed that they should intend to act differently in respect to one to which they had not such a claim.

I may add that although due sensibility has been always felt for the injuries which were received from the Spanish Government in the last war, the present situation of Spain has been a motive for a moderate and pacific policy toward her.

In communicating to you these sentiments of the Executive on the measures you have lately adopted for taking possession of East Florida, I add with pleasure that the utmost confidence is reposed in your integrity and zeal to promote the welfare of your country. To that zeal the error into which you have fallen is imputed. But in consideration of the part which you have taken, which differs so essentially from that contemplated and authorized by the Government, and contradicts so entirely the principles on which it has uniformly and sincerely acted, you will be sensible of the necessity of discontinuing the service in which you have been employed.

You will therefore consider your powers as revoked on the receipt of this letter. The new duties to be performed will be transferred to the governor of Georgia, to whom instructions will be given on all the circumstances to which it may be proper at the present juncture to call his attention.

I have the honor to be, very respectfully, sir, your obedient servant,

JAMES MONROE.

The Secretary of State to His Excellency D. B. Mitchell, the governor of Georgia.

DEPARTMENT OF STATE, *April 10, 1812.*

SIR: The President is desirous of availing the public of your services in a concern of much delicacy and of high importance to the United States. Circumstances with which you are in some degree acquainted, but which will be fully explained by the inclosed papers, have made it necessary to revoke the powers heretofore committed to General Matthews and to commit them to you. The President is persuaded that you will not hesitate to undertake a trust so important to the nation, and peculiarly to the State of Georgia. He is the more confident in this belief from the consideration that these new duties may be discharged without interfering, as he presumes, with those of the station which you now hold.

By the act of the 15th of January, 1811, you will observe that it was not contemplated to take possession of East Florida or any part thereof, unless it should be surrendered to the United States amicably by the governor or other local authority of the Province, or against an attempt to take possession of it by a foreign power, and you will also see that General Matthews's instructions, of which a copy is likewise inclosed, correspond fully with the law.

By the documents in possession of the Government it appears that neither of these contingencies have happened; that instead of an amicable surrender by the governor or other local authority the troops of the United States have been used to dispossess the Spanish authority by force. I forbear to dwell on the details of this transaction because it is painful to recite them. By the letter to General Matthews which is inclosed, open for your perusal, you will fully comprehend the views of the Government respecting the late transaction, and by the law, the former instructions to the General, and the late letter now forwarded you will be made acquainted with the course of conduct which it is expected of you to pursue in future in discharging the duties heretofore enjoined on him.

It is the desire of the President that you should turn your attention and direct your efforts in the first instance to the restoration of that state of things in the Province which existed before the late transactions. The Executive considers it proper to restore back to the Spanish authorities Amelia Island and such other parts, if any, of East Florida as may have thus been taken from them. With this view it will be necessary for you to communicate *directly* with the governor or principal officer of Spain in that Province, and to act in harmony with him in the attainment of it. It is presumed that the arrangement will be easily and amicably made between you. I inclose you an order from the Secretary of War to the commander of the troops of the United States to evacuate the country when requested so to do by you, and to pay the same respect in future to your order in fulfilling the duties enjoined by the law that he had been instructed to do to that of General Matthews.

In restoring to the Spanish authorities Amelia Island and such other parts of East Florida as may have been taken possession of in the name of the United States there is another object to which your particular attention will be due. In the measures lately adopted by General Matthews to take possession of that Territory it is probable that much reliance has been placed by the people who acted in it on the countenance and support of the United States. It will be improper to expose these people to the resentment of the Spanish authorities. It is not to be presumed that those authorities in regaining possession of the Territory in this amicable mode from the United States will be disposed to indulge any such feeling toward them. You will, however, come to a full understanding with the Spanish governor on this subject, and not fail to obtain from him the most explicit and satisfactory assurance respecting it. Of this assurance you will duly apprise the parties interested, and of the confidence which you repose in it. It is hoped that on this delicate and very interesting point the Spanish governor will avail himself of the opportunity it presents to evince the friendly disposition of his Government toward the United States.

There is one other remaining circumstance only to which I wish to call your attention, and that relates to General Matthews himself. His gallant and meritorious services in our Revolution and patriotic conduct since have always been held in high estimation by the Government. His errors in this instance are imputed altogether to his zeal to promote the welfare of his country; but they are of a nature to impose on the Government the necessity of the measures now taken, in giving effect to which you will doubtless feel a disposition to consult, as far as may be, his personal sensibility.

I have the honor to be, etc.,

JAMES MONROE.

P. S.—Should you find it impracticable to execute the duties designated above in person, the President requests that you will be so good as to employ some very respectable character to represent you in it, to whom you are authorized to allow a similar compensation. It is hoped, however, that you may be able to attend to it in person, for reasons which I need not enter into. The expenses to which you may be exposed will be promptly paid to your draft on this Department.

The Secretary of State to D. B. Mitchell, esq., governor of Georgia.

DEPARTMENT OF STATE, *May 27, 1812.*

SIR: I have had the honor to receive your letter of the 2d instant from St. Marys, where you had arrived in discharge of the trust reposed in you by the President, in relation to East Florida.

My letter by Mr. Isaacs has, I presume, substantially answered the most important of the queries submitted in your letter, but I will give to each a more distinct answer.

By the law of which a copy was forwarded to you it is made the duty of the President to prevent the occupation of East Florida by any foreign power. It follows that you are authorized to consider the entrance, or attempt to enter, especially under existing circumstances, of British troops of any description as the case contemplated by the law, and to use the proper means to defeat it.

An instruction will be immediately forwarded to the commander of the naval force of the United States in the neighborhood of East Florida to give you any assistance, in case of emergency, which you may think necessary and require.

It is not expected, if you find it proper to withdraw the troops, that you should interfere to compel the patriots to surrender the country or any part of it to the Spanish authorities. The United States are responsible for their own conduct only; not for that of the inhabitants of East Florida. Indeed, in consequence of the compromitment of the United States to the inhabitants, you have been already instructed not to withdraw the troops, unless you find that it may be done consistently with their safety, and to report to the Government the result of your conferences with the Spanish authorities, with your opinion of their views, holding in the meantime the ground occupied.

In the present state of our affairs with Great Britain the course above pointed out is the more justifiable and proper.

I have the honor, etc.,

JAMES MONROE.

JULY 6, 1812.

To the Senate of the United States:

I transmit to the Senate copies and extracts of documents in the archives of the Department of State falling within the purview of their resolution of the 4th instant, on the subject of British impressments from American vessels. The information, though voluminous, might have been enlarged with more time for research and preparation. In some instances it might at the same time have been abridged but for the difficulty of separating the matter extraneous to the immediate object of the resolution.

JAMES MADISON.

VETO MESSAGE.

APRIL 3, 1812.

To the House of Representatives of the United States:

Having examined and considered the bill entitled "An act providing for the trial of causes pending in the respective district courts of the United States, in case of the absence or disability of the judges thereof," which bill was presented to me on the 25th of March past, I now return the same to the House of Representatives, in which it originated, with the following objections:

Because the additional services imposed by the bill on the justices of the Supreme Court of the United States are to be performed by them rather in the quality of other judges of other courts, namely, judges of the district courts, than in the quality of justices of the Supreme Court. They are to hold the said district courts, and to do and perform all acts relating to the said courts which are by law required of the district judges. The bill therefore virtually appoints, for the time, the justices of the Supreme Court to other distinct offices to which, if compatible with their original offices, they ought to be appointed by another than the legislative authority, in pursuance of legislative provisions authorizing the appointments.

Because the appeal allowed by law for the decision of the district courts to the circuit courts, whilst it corroborates the construction which regards a judge of one court as clothed with a new office, by being constituted a judge of the other, submits for correction erroneous judgments, not to superior or other judges, but to the erring individual himself, acting as sole judge in the appellate court.

Because the additional services to be required may, by distances of place and by the casualties contemplated by the bill, become disproportionate to the strength and health of the justices who are to perform them, the additional services being, moreover, entitled to no additional compensation, nor the additional expenses incurred to reimbursement. In this view the bill appears to be contrary to equity, as well as a precedent for modifications and extensions of judicial services encroaching on the constitutional tenure of judicial offices.

Because, by referring to the President of the United States questions of disability in the district judges and of the unreasonableness of delaying the suits or causes pending in the district courts, and leaving it with him in such causes to require the justices of the Supreme Court to perform additional services, the bill introduces an unsuitable relation of members of the judiciary department to a discretionary authority of the executive department.

JAMES MADISON.

PROCLAMATIONS.

[From Niles's Weekly Register, vol. 1, p. 448.]

BY THE PRESIDENT OF THE UNITED STATES.

A PROCLAMATION.

Whereas information has been received that a number of individuals who have deserted from the Army of the United States have become sensible of their offense and are desirous of returning to their duty, a full pardon is hereby granted and proclaimed to each and all such individuals as shall within four months from the date hereof surrender themselves to the commanding officer of any military post within the United States or the Territories thereof.

In testimony whereof I have caused the seal of the United States to be affixed to these presents, and signed the same with my hand.

[SEAL.] Done at the city of Washington, the 7th day of February, A. D. 1812, and of the Independence of the United States the thirty-sixth.

JAMES MADISON.

By the President:

JAMES MONROE,
Secretary of State.

[From Annals of Congress, Twelfth Congress, part 2, 2223.]

BY THE PRESIDENT OF THE UNITED STATES OF AMERICA.

A PROCLAMATION.

Whereas the Congress of the United States, by virtue of the constituted authority vested in them, have declared by their act bearing date the 18th day of the present month that war exists between the United Kingdom of Great Britain and Ireland and the dependencies thereof and the United States of America and their Territories:

Now, therefore, I, James Madison, President of the United States of America, do hereby proclaim the same to all whom it may concern; and I do specially enjoin on all persons holding offices, civil or military, under the authority of the United States that they be vigilant and zealous in discharging the duties respectively incident thereto; and I do moreover exhort all the good people of the United States, as they love their country, as they value the precious heritage derived from the virtue and valor of their fathers, as they feel the wrongs which have forced on them the last resort of injured nations, and as they consult the best means under the blessing of Divine Providence of abridging its calamities, that they exert themselves in preserving order, in promoting concord, in maintaining the authority and efficacy of the laws, and in supporting and invigorating all the measures which may be adopted by the constituted authorities for obtaining a speedy, a just, and an honorable peace.

In testimony whereof I have hereunto set my hand and caused the seal of the United States to be affixed to these presents.

[SEAL.]   Done at the city of Washington, the 19th day of June, 1812, and of the Independence of the United States the thirty-sixth.

JAMES MADISON.

By the President:

JAMES MONROE,
Secretary of State.

[From Annals of Congress, Twelfth Congress, part 2, 2224.]

BY THE PRESIDENT OF THE UNITED STATES OF AMERICA.

A PROCLAMATION.

Whereas the Congress of the United States, by a joint resolution of the two Houses, have signified a request that a day may be recommended to be observed by the people of the United States with religious solemnity as a day of public humiliation and prayer; and

Whereas such a recommendation will enable the several religious denominations and societies so disposed to offer at one and the same time their common vows and adorations to Almighty God on the solemn occasion produced by the war in which He has been pleased to permit the injustice of a foreign power to involve these United States:

I do therefore recommend the third Thursday in August next as a convenient day to be set apart for the devout purposes of rendering the Sovereign of the Universe and the Benefactor of Mankind the public homage due to His holy attributes; of acknowledging the transgressions which might justly provoke the manifestations of His divine displeasure; of seeking His merciful forgiveness and His assistance in the great duties of repentance and amendment, and especially of offering fervent supplications that in the present season of calamity and war He would take the American people under His peculiar care and protection; that He would guide their public councils, animate their patriotism, and bestow His blessing on their arms; that He would inspire all nations with a love of justice and of concord and with a reverence for the unerring precept of our holy religion to do to others as they would require that others should do to them; and, finally, that, turning the hearts of our enemies from the violence and injustice which sway their councils against us, He would hasten a restoration of the blessings of peace.

Given at Washington, the 9th day of July, A. D. 1812.

[SEAL.]   JAMES MADISON.

By the President:

JAMES MONROE,
Secretary of State.

[From Niles's Weekly Register, vol. 3, p. 101.]

BY THE PRESIDENT OF THE UNITED STATES OF AMERICA.

A PROCLAMATION.

Whereas information has been received that a number of individuals who have deserted from the Army of the United States have become sensible of their offenses and are desirous of returning to their duty, a full pardon is hereby granted and proclaimed to each and all such individuals as shall within four months from the date hereof surrender themselves to the commanding officer of any military post within the United States or the Territories thereof.

In testimony whereof I have caused the seal of the United States to be affixed to these presents, and signed the same with my hand.

[SEAL.]   Done at the city of Washington, the 8th day of October, A. D. 1812, and of the Independence of the United States the thirty-seventh.

JAMES MADISON.

By the President:

JAMES MONROE,
Secretary of State.

FOURTH ANNUAL MESSAGE.

WASHINGTON, *November 4, 1812.*

Fellow-Citizens of the Senate and of the House of Representatives:

On our present meeting it is my first duty to invite your attention to the providential favors which our country has experienced in the unusual degree of health dispensed to its inhabitants, and in the rich abundance with which the earth has rewarded the labors bestowed on it. In the successful cultivation of other branches of industry, and in the progress of general improvement favorable to the national prosperity, there is just occasion also for our mutual congratulations and thankfulness.

With these blessings are necessarily mingled the pressures and vicissitudes incident to the state of war into which the United States have been forced by the perseverance of a foreign power in its system of injustice and aggression.

Previous to its declaration it was deemed proper, as a measure of precaution and forecast, that a considerable force should be placed in the Michigan Territory with a general view to its security, and, in the event of war, to such operations in the uppermost Canada as would intercept the hostile influence of Great Britain over the savages, obtain the command of the lake on which that part of Canada borders, and maintain cooperating relations with such forces as might be most conveniently employed against other parts. Brigadier-General Hull was charged with this provisional service, having under his command a body of troops composed of regulars and of volunteers from the State of Ohio. Having reached his destination after his knowledge of the war, and possessing discretionary authority to act offensively, he passed into the neighboring territory of the enemy with a prospect of easy and victorious progress. The expedition, nevertheless, terminated unfortunately, not only in a retreat to the town and fort of Detroit, but in the surrender of both and of the gallant corps commanded by that officer. The causes of this painful reverse will be investigated by a military tribunal.

A distinguishing feature in the operations which preceded and followed this adverse event is the use made by the enemy of the merciless savages under their influence. Whilst the benevolent policy of the United States invariably recommended peace and promoted civilization among that wretched portion of the human race, and was making exertions to dissuade them from taking either side in the war, the enemy has not scrupled to call to his aid their ruthless ferocity, armed with the horrors of those instruments of carnage and torture which are known to spare neither age nor sex. In this outrage against the laws of honorable war and against the feelings sacred to humanity the British commanders can not resort to a plea of retaliation, for it is committed in the face of our example. They can not mitigate it by calling it a self-defense against men in arms, for it embraces the most shocking butcheries of defenseless families. Nor can it be pretended that they are not answerable for the atrocities perpetrated, since the savages are employed with a knowledge, and even with menaces, that their fury could not be controlled. Such is the spectacle which the deputed authorities of a nation boasting its religion and morality have not been restrained from presenting to an enlightened age.

The misfortune at Detroit was not, however, without a consoling effect. It was followed by signal proofs that the national spirit rises according to the pressure on it. The loss of an important post and of the brave men surrendered with it inspired everywhere new ardor and determination. In the States and districts least remote it was no sooner known than every citizen was ready to fly with his arms at once to protect his brethren against the bloodthirsty savages let loose by the enemy on an extensive frontier, and to convert a partial calamity into a source of invigorated efforts. This patriotic zeal, which it was necessary rather to limit than excite, has embodied an ample force from the States of Kentucky and Ohio and from parts of Pennsylvania and Virginia. It is placed, with the addition of a few regulars, under the command of Brigadier-General Harrison, who possesses the entire confidence of his fellow-soldiers, among whom are citizens, some of them volunteers in the ranks, not less distinguished by their political stations than by their personal merits.

The greater portion of this force is proceeding on its destination toward the Michigan Territory, having succeeded in relieving an important frontier post, and in several incidental operations against hostile tribes of savages, rendered indispensable by the subserviency into which they had been seduced by the enemy—a seduction the more cruel as it could not fail to impose a necessity of precautionary severities against those who yielded to it.

At a recent date an attack was made on a post of the enemy near Niagara by a detachment of the regular and other forces under the command of Major-General Van Rensselaer, of the militia of the State of New York. The attack, it appears, was ordered in compliance with the ardor of the troops, who executed it with distinguished gallantry, and were for a time victorious; but not receiving the expected support, they were compelled to yield to reenforcements of British regulars and savages. Our loss has been considerable, and is deeply to be lamented. That of the enemy, less ascertained, will be the more felt, as it includes among the killed the commanding general, who was also the governor of the Province, and was sustained by veteran troops from unexperienced soldiers, who must daily improve in the duties of the field.

Our expectation of gaining the command of the Lakes by the invasion of Canada from Detroit having been disappointed, measures were instantly taken to provide on them a naval force superior to that of the enemy. From the talents and activity of the officer charged with this object everything that can be done may be expected. Should the present season not admit of complete success, the progress made will insure for the next a naval ascendency where it is essential to our permanent peace with and control over the savages.

Among the incidents to the measures of the war I am constrained to advert to the refusal of the governors of Massachusetts and Connecticut to furnish the required detachments of militia toward the defense of the maritime frontier. The refusal was founded on a novel and unfortunate exposition of the provisions of the Constitution relating to the militia. The correspondences which will be laid before you contain the requisite information on the subject. It is obvious that if the authority of the United States to call into service and command the militia for the public defense can be thus frustrated, even in a state of declared war and of course under apprehensions of invasion preceding war, they are not one nation for the purpose most of all requiring it, and that the public safety may have no other resource than in those large and permanent military establishments which are forbidden by the principles of our free government, and against the necessity of which the militia were meant to be a constitutional bulwark.

On the coasts and on the ocean the war has been as successful as circumstances inseparable from its early stages could promise. Our public ships and private cruisers, by their activity, and, where there was occasion, by their intrepidity, have made the enemy sensible of the difference between a reciprocity of captures and the long confinement of them to their side. Our trade, with little exception, has safely reached our ports, having been much favored in it by the course pursued by a squadron of our frigates under the command of Commodore Rodgers, and in the instance in which skill and bravery were more particularly tried with those of the enemy the American flag had an auspicious triumph. The frigate *Constitution*, commanded by Captain Hull, after a close and short engagement completely disabled and captured a British frigate, gaining for that officer and all on board a praise which can not be too liberally bestowed, not merely for the victory actually achieved, but for that prompt and cool exertion of commanding talents which, giving to courage its highest character, and to the force applied its full effect, proved that more could have been done in a contest requiring more.

Anxious to abridge the evils from which a state of war can not be exempt, I lost no time after it was declared in conveying to the British Government the terms on which its progress might be arrested, without awaiting the delays of a formal and final pacification, and our chargé d'affaires at London was at the same time authorized to agree to an armistice founded upon them. These terms required that the orders in council should be repealed as they affected the United States, without a revival of blockades violating acknowledged rules, and that there should be an immediate discharge of American seamen from British ships, and a stop to impressment from American ships, with an understanding that an exclusion of the seamen of each nation from the ships of the other should be stipulated, and that the armistice should be improved into a definitive and comprehensive adjustment of depending controversies. Although a repeal of the orders susceptible of explanations meeting the views of this Government had taken place before this pacific advance was communicated to that of Great Britain, the advance was declined from an avowed repugnance to a suspension of the practice of impressments during the armistice, and without any intimation that the arrangement proposed with respect to seamen would be accepted. Whether the subsequent communications from this Government, affording an occasion for reconsidering the subject on the part of Great Britain, will be viewed in a more favorable light or received in a more accommodating spirit remains to be known. It would be unwise to relax our measures in any respect on a presumption of such a result.

The documents from the Department of State which relate to this subject will give a view also of the propositions for an armistice which have been received here, one of them from the authorities at Halifax and in Canada, the other from the British Government itself through Admiral Warren, and of the grounds on which neither of them could be accepted.

Our affairs with France retain the posture which they held at my last communications to you. Notwithstanding the authorized expectations of an early as well as favorable issue to the discussions on foot, these have been procrastinated to the latest date. The only intervening occurrence meriting attention is the promulgation of a French decree purporting to be a definitive repeal of the Berlin and Milan decrees. This proceeding, although made the ground of the repeal of the British orders in council, is rendered by the time and manner of it liable to many objections.

The final communications from our special minister to Denmark afford further proofs of the good effects of his mission, and of the amicable disposition of the Danish Government. From Russia we have the satisfaction to receive assurances of continued friendship, and that it will not be affected by the rupture between the United States and Great Britain. Sweden also professes sentiments favorable to the subsisting harmony.

With the Barbary Powers, excepting that of Algiers, our affairs remain on the ordinary footing. The consul-general residing with that Regency has suddenly and without cause been banished, together with all the American citizens found there. Whether this was the transitory effect of capricious despotism or the first act of predetermined hostility is not ascertained. Precautions were taken by the consul on the latter supposition.

The Indian tribes not under foreign instigations remain at peace, and receive the civilizing attentions which have proved so beneficial to them.

With a view to that vigorous prosecution of the war to which our national faculties are adequate, the attention of Congress will be particularly drawn to the insufficiency of existing provisions for filling up the military establishment. Such is the happy condition of our country, arising from the facility of subsistence and the high wages for every species of occupation, that notwithstanding the augmented inducements provided at the last session, a partial success only has attended the recruiting service. The deficiency has been necessarily supplied during the campaign by other than regular troops, with all the inconveniences and expense incident to them. The remedy lies in establishing more favorably for the private soldier the proportion between his recompense and the term of his enlistment, and it is a subject which can not too soon or too seriously be taken into consideration.

The same insufficiency has been experienced in the provisions for volunteers made by an act of the last session. The recompense for the service required in this case is still less attractive than in the other, and although patriotism alone has sent into the field some valuable corps of that description, those alone who can afford the sacrifice can be reasonably expected to yield to that impulse.

It will merit consideration also whether as auxiliary to the security of our frontiers corps may not be advantageously organized with a restriction of their services to particular districts convenient to them, and whether the local and occasional services of mariners and others in the seaport towns under a similar organization would not be a provident addition to the means of their defense.

I recommend a provision for an increase of the general officers of the Army, the deficiency of which has been illustrated by the number and distance of separate commands which the course of the war and the advantage of the service have required.

And I can not press too strongly on the earliest attention of the Legislature the importance of the reorganization of the staff establishment with a view to render more distinct and definite the relations and responsibilities of its several departments. That there is room for improvements which will materially promote both economy and success in what appertains to the Army and the war is equally inculcated by the examples of other countries and by the experience of our own.

A revision of the militia laws for the purpose of rendering them more systematic and better adapting them to emergencies of the war is at this time particularly desirable.

Of the additional ships authorized to be fitted for service, two will be shortly ready to sail, a third is under repair, and delay will be avoided in the repair of the residue. Of the appropriations for the purchase of materials for shipbuilding, the greater part has been applied to that object and the purchase will be continued with the balance.

The enterprising spirit which has characterized our naval force and its success, both in restraining insults and depredations on our coasts and in reprisals on the enemy, will not fail to recommend an enlargement of it.

There being reason to believe that the act prohibiting the acceptance of British licenses is not a sufficient guard against the use of them, for purposes favorable to the interests and views of the enemy, further provisions on that subject are highly important. Nor is it less so that penal enactments should be provided for cases of corrupt and perfidious intercourse with the enemy, not amounting to treason nor yet embraced by any statutory provisions.

A considerable number of American vessels which were in England when the revocation of the orders in council took place were laden with British manufactures under an erroneous impression that the nonimportation act would immediately cease to operate, and have arrived in the United States. It did not appear proper to exercise on unforeseen cases of such magnitude the ordinary powers vested in the Treasury Department to mitigate forfeitures without previously affording to Congress an opportunity of making on the subject such provision as they may think proper. In their decision they will doubtless equally consult what is due to equitable considerations and to the public interest.

The receipts into the Treasury during the year ending on the 30th of

September last have exceeded $16,500,000, which have been sufficient to defray all the demands on the Treasury to that day, including a necessary reimbursement of near three millions of the principal of the public debt. In these receipts is included a sum of near $5,850,000, received on account of the loans authorized by the acts of the last session; the whole sum actually obtained on loan amounts to $11,000,000, the residue of which, being receivable subsequent to the 30th of September last, will, together with the current revenue, enable us to defray all the expenses of this year.

The duties on the late unexpected importations of British manufactures will render the revenue of the ensuing year more productive than could have been anticipated.

The situation of our country, fellow-citizens, is not without its difficulties, though it abounds in animating considerations, of which the view here presented of our pecuniary resources is an example. With more than one nation we have serious and unsettled controversies, and with one, powerful in the means and habits of war, we are at war. The spirit and strength of the nation are nevertheless equal to the support of all its rights, and to carry it through all its trials. They can be met in that confidence. Above all, we have the inestimable consolation of knowing that the war in which we are actually engaged is a war neither of ambition nor of vainglory; that it is waged not in violation of the rights of others, but in the maintenance of our own; that it was preceded by a patience without example under wrongs accumulating without end, and that it was finally not declared until every hope of averting it was extinguished by the transfer of the British scepter into new hands clinging to former councils, and until declarations were reiterated to the last hour, through the British envoy here, that the hostile edicts against our commercial rights and our maritime independence would not be revoked; nay, that they could not be revoked without violating the obligations of Great Britain to other powers, as well as to her own interests. To have shrunk under such circumstances from manly resistance would have been a degradation blasting our best and proudest hopes; it would have struck us from the high rank where the virtuous struggles of our fathers had placed us, and have betrayed the magnificent legacy which we hold in trust for future generations. It would have acknowledged that on the element which forms three-fourths of the globe we inhabit, and where all independent nations have equal and common rights, the American people were not an independent people, but colonists and vassals. It was at this moment and with such an alternative that war was chosen. The nation felt the necessity of it, and called for it. The appeal was accordingly made, in a just cause, to the Just and All-powerful Being who holds in His hand the chain of events and the destiny of nations. It remains only that, faithful to ourselves, entangled in no connections with the views of other powers, and ever ready to accept peace from the

THE *UNITED STATES* CAPTURES THE BRITISH *MACEDONIAN*

THE UNITED STATES CAPTURES THE *MACEDONIAN*

This illustration vividly recalls Holmes's lines:

> "A crash, as when some swollen cloud,
>   Cracks o'er the tangled trees;
> With side to side, and spar to spar,
>   Whose smoking decks are these?
> I know Saint George's blood-red cross,
>   Thou mistress of the seas,
> But what is she whose streaming bars
>   Roll out before the breeze?
> Ah, well her iron ribs are knit
>   Whose thunders strive to quell
> The bellowing throats, the blazing lips
>   That pealed the Armada's knell!
> The mist has cleared, a wreath of stars
>   Rose o'er the crimson swell,
> And wavering from its mighty peak,
>   The cross of England fell."

After a ninety minute combat, on October 25, 1812, the forty-four-gun frigate *United States* forced the British *Macedonian,* also a forty-four-gun frigate, to strike her flag. The *Macedonian* had lost 104 men; the losses on the *United States* numbered, all told, 11 men.

hand of justice, we prosecute the war with united counsels and with the ample faculties of the nation until peace be so obtained and as the only means under the Divine blessing of speedily obtaining it.

JAMES MADISON.

SPECIAL MESSAGES.

NOVEMBER 12, 1812.

To the Senate and House of Representatives of the United States:

For the further information of Congress relative to the pacific advances made on the part of this Government to that of Great Britain, and the manner in which they have been met by the latter, I transmit the sequel of the communications on that subject received from the late chargé d'affaires at London.

JAMES MADISON.

NOVEMBER 17, 1812.

To the Senate and House of Representatives of the United States:

I transmit to Congress copies of a letter from the consul-general of the United States to Algiers, stating the circumstances preceding and attending his departure from that Regency.

JAMES MADISON.

WASHINGTON, *December 11, 1812.*

To the Senate and House of Representatives of the United States:

I transmit to Congress copies of a letter to the Secretary of the Navy from Captain Decatur, of the frigate *United States*, reporting his combat and capture of the British frigate *Macedonian*. Too much praise can not be bestowed on that officer and his companions on board for the consummate skill and conspicuous valor by which this trophy has been added to the naval arms of the United States.

I transmit also a letter from Captain Jones, who commanded the sloop of war *Wasp*, reporting his capture of the British sloop of war *Frolic*, after a close action, in which other brilliant titles will be seen to the public admiration and praise.

A nation feeling what it owes to itself and to its citizens could never abandon to arbitrary violence on the ocean a class of them which give such examples of capacity and courage in defending their rights on that element, examples which ought to impress on the enemy, however brave and powerful, preference of justice and peace to hostility against a country whose prosperous career may be accelerated but can not be prevented by the assaults made on it.

JAMES MADISON.

JANUARY 22, 1813.

To the Senate and House of Representatives of the United States:

I transmit, for the information of Congress, copies of a correspondence between John Mitchell, agent for American prisoners of war at Halifax, and the British admiral commanding at that station.

I transmit, for the like purpose, copies of a letter from Commodore Rodgers to the Secretary of the Navy,

JAMES MADISON.

FEBRUARY 22, 1813.

To the Senate and House of Representatives of the United States:

I lay before Congress a letter, with accompanying documents, from Captain Bainbridge, now commanding the United States frigate the *Constitution*, reporting his capture and destruction of the British frigate the *Java*. The circumstances and the issue of this combat afford another example of the professional skill and heroic spirit which prevail in our naval service. The signal display of both by Captain Bainbridge, his officers and crew, commands the highest praise.

This being a second instance in which the condition of the captured ship, by rendering it impossible to get her into port, has barred a contemplated reward of successful valor, I recommend to the consideration of Congress the equity and propriety of a general provision allowing in such cases, both past and future, a fair proportion of the value which would accrue to the captors on the safe arrival and sale of the prize.

JAMES MADISON.

FEBRUARY 24, 1813.

To the Senate and House of Representatives of the United States:

I lay before Congress copies of a proclamation of the British lieutenant-governor of the island of Bermuda, which has appeared under circumstances leaving no doubt of its authenticity. It recites a British order in council of the 26th of October last, providing for the supply of the British West Indies and other colonial possessions by a trade under special licenses, and is accompanied by a circular instruction to the colonial governors which confines licensed importations from ports of the United States to the ports of the Eastern States exclusively.

The Government of Great Britain had already introduced into her commerce during war a system which, at once violating the rights of other nations and resting on a mass of forgery and perjury unknown to other times, was making an unfortunate progress in undermining those principles of morality and religion which are the best foundation of national happiness.

The policy now proclaimed to the world introduces into her modes of warfare a system equally distinguished by the deformity of its features

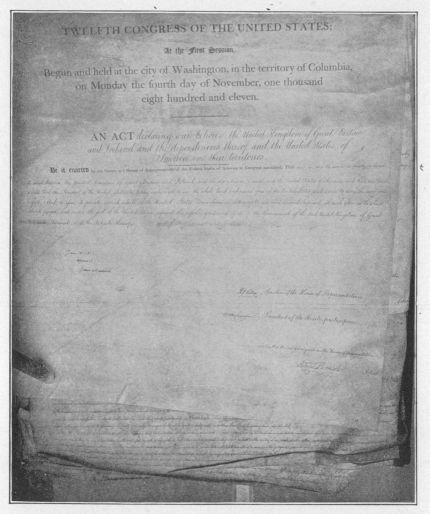

DECLARATION OF WAR AGAINST GREAT BRITAIN, WHICH
BROUGHT ON THE "WAR OF 1812."

and the depravity of its character, having for its object to dissolve the ties of allegiance and the sentiments of loyalty in the adversary nation, and to seduce and separate its component parts the one from the other.

The general tendency of these demoralizing and disorganizing contrivances will be reprobated by the civilized and Christian world, and the insulting attempt on the virtue, the honor, the patriotism, and the fidelity of our brethren of the Eastern States will not fail to call forth all their indignation and resentment, and to attach more and more all the States to that happy Union and Constitution against which such insidious and malignant artifices are directed.

The better to guard, nevertheless, against the effect of individual cupidity and treachery and to turn the corrupt projects of the enemy against himself, I recommend to the consideration of Congress the expediency of an effectual prohibition of any trade whatever by citizens or inhabitants of the United States under special licenses, whether relating to persons or ports, and in aid thereof a prohibition of all exportations from the United States in foreign bottoms, few of which are actually employed, whilst multiplying counterfeits of their flags and papers are covering and encouraging the navigation of the enemy.

JAMES MADISON.

MARCH 3, 1813.

To the House of Representatives of the United States:

Conformably to the resolution of the House of Representatives of the 27th of January last, I transmit "rolls of the persons having office or employment of a public nature under the United States."

JAMES MADISON.

VETO MESSAGE.

NOVEMBER 5, 1812.

To the Senate and House of Representatives of the United States:

The bill entitled "An act supplementary to the acts heretofore passed on the subject of an uniform rule of naturalization," which passed the two Houses at the last session of Congress, having appeared to me liable to abuse by aliens having no real purpose of effectuating a naturalization, and therefore not been signed, and having been presented at an hour too near the close of the session to be returned with objections for reconsideration, the bill failed to become a law. I also recommend that provision be now made in favor of aliens entitled to the contemplated benefit, under such regulations as will prevent advantage being taken of it for improper purposes.

JAMES MADISON.

SECOND INAUGURAL ADDRESS.

About to add the solemnity of an oath to the obligations imposed by a second call to the station in which my country heretofore placed me, I find in the presence of this respectable assembly an opportunity of publicly repeating my profound sense of so distinguished a confidence and of the responsibility united with it.   The impressions on me are strengthened by such an evidence that my faithful endeavors to discharge my arduous duties have been favorably estimated, and by a consideration of the momentous period at which the trust has been renewed.   From the weight and magnitude now belonging to it I should be compelled to shrink if I had less reliance on the support of an enlightened and generous people, and felt less deeply a conviction that the war with a powerful nation, which forms so prominent a feature in our situation, is stamped with that justice which invites the smiles of Heaven on the means of conducting it to a successful termination.

May we not cherish this sentiment without presumption when we reflect on the characters by which this war is distinguished?

It was not declared on the part of the United States until it had been long made on them, in reality though not in name; until arguments and expostulations had been exhausted; until a positive declaration had been received that the wrongs provoking it would not be discontinued; nor until this last appeal could no longer be delayed without breaking down the spirit of the nation, destroying all confidence in itself and in its political institutions, and either perpetuating a state of disgraceful suffering or regaining by more costly sacrifices and more severe struggles our lost rank and respect among independent powers.

On the issue of the war are staked our national sovereignty on the high seas and the security of an important class of citizens, whose occupations give the proper value to those of every other class.   Not to contend for such a stake is to surrender our equality with other powers on the element common to all and to violate the sacred title which every member of the society has to its protection.   I need not call into view the unlawfulness of the practice by which our mariners are forced at the will of every cruising officer from their own vessels into foreign ones, nor paint the outrages inseparable from it.   The proofs are in the records of each successive Administration of our Government, and the cruel sufferings of that portion of the American people have found their way to every bosom not dead to the sympathies of human nature.

As the war was just in its origin and necessary and noble in its objects, we can reflect with a proud satisfaction that in carrying it on no principle of justice or honor, no usage of civilized nations, no precept of courtesy or humanity, have been infringed.   The war has been waged on our part with scrupulous regard to all these obligations, and in a spirit of liberality which was never surpassed.

How little has been the effect of this example on the conduct of the enemy!

They have retained as prisoners of war citizens of the United States not liable to be so considered under the usages of war.

They have refused to consider as prisoners of war, and threatened to punish as traitors and deserters, persons emigrating without restraint to the United States, incorporated by naturalization into our political family, and fighting under the authority of their adopted country in open and honorable war for the maintenance of its rights and safety. Such is the avowed purpose of a Government which is in the practice of naturalizing by thousands citizens of other countries, and not only of permitting but compelling them to fight its battles against their native country.

They have not, it is true, taken into their own hands the hatchet and the knife, devoted to indiscriminate massacre, but they have let loose the savages armed with these cruel instruments; have allured them into their service, and carried them to battle by their sides, eager to glut their savage thirst with the blood of the vanquished and to finish the work of torture and death on maimed and defenseless captives. And, what was never before seen, British commanders have extorted victory over the unconquerable valor of our troops by presenting to the sympathy of their chief captives awaiting massacre from their savage associates. And now we find them, in further contempt of the modes of honorable warfare, supplying the place of a conquering force by attempts to disorganize our political society, to dismember our confederated Republic. Happily, like others, these will recoil on the authors; but they mark the degenerate counsels from which they emanate, and if they did not belong to a series of unexampled inconsistencies might excite the greater wonder as proceeding from a Government which founded the very war in which it has been so long engaged on a charge against the disorganizing and insurrectional policy of its adversary.

To render the justice of the war on our part the more conspicuous, the reluctance to commence it was followed by the earliest and strongest manifestations of a disposition to arrest its progress. The sword was scarcely out of the scabbard before the enemy was apprised of the reasonable terms on which it would be resheathed. Still more precise advances were repeated, and have been received in a spirit forbidding every reliance not placed on the military resources of the nation.

These resources are amply sufficient to bring the war to an honorable issue. Our nation is in number more than half that of the British Isles. It is composed of a brave, a free, a virtuous, and an intelligent people. Our country abounds in the necessaries, the arts, and the comforts of life. A general prosperity is visible in the public countenance. The means employed by the British cabinet to undermine it have recoiled on themselves;

have given to our national faculties a more rapid development, and, draining or diverting the precious metals from British circulation and British vaults, have poured them into those of the United States. It is a propitious consideration that an unavoidable war should have found this seasonable facility for the contributions required to support it. When the public voice called for war, all knew, and still know, that without them it could not be carried on through the period which it might last, and the patriotism, the good sense, and the manly spirit of our fellow-citizens are pledges for the cheerfulness with which they will bear each his share of the common burden. To render the war short and its success sure, animated and systematic exertions alone are necessary, and the success of our arms now may long preserve our country from the necessity of another resort to them. Already have the gallant exploits of our naval heroes proved to the world our inherent capacity to maintain our rights on one element. If the reputation of our arms has been thrown under clouds on the other, presaging flashes of heroic enterprise assure us that nothing is wanting to correspondent triumphs there also but the discipline and habits which are in daily progress.

MARCH 4, 1813.

SPECIAL SESSION MESSAGE.

WASHINGTON, *May 25, 1813.*

Fellow-Citizens of the Senate and of the House of Representatives:

At an early day after the close of the last session of Congress an offer was formally communicated from His Imperial Majesty the Emperor of Russia of his mediation, as the common friend of the United States and Great Britain, for the purpose of facilitating a peace between them. The high character of the Emperor Alexander being a satisfactory pledge for the sincerity and impartiality of his offer, it was immediately accepted, and as a further proof of the disposition on the part of the United States to meet their adversary in honorable experiments for terminating the war it was determined to avoid intermediate delays incident to the distance of the parties by a definitive provision for the contemplated negotiation. Three of our eminent citizens were accordingly commissioned with the requisite powers to conclude a treaty of peace with persons clothed with like powers on the part of Great Britain. They are authorized also to enter into such conventional regulations of the commerce between the two countries as may be mutually advantageous. The two envoys who where in the United States at the time of their appointment have proceeded to join their colleague already at St. Petersburg.

The envoys have received another commission authorizing them to conclude with Russia a treaty of commerce with a view to strengthen the amicable relations and improve the beneficial intercourse between the two countries.

The issue of this friendly interposition of the Russian Emperor and this pacific manifestation on the part of the United States time only can decide. That the sentiments of Great Britain toward that Sovereign will have produced an acceptance of his offered mediation must be presumed. That no adequate motives exist to prefer a continuance of war with the United States to the terms on which they are willing to close it is certain. The British cabinet also must be sensible that, with respect to the important question of impressment, on which the war so essentially turns, a search for or seizure of British persons or property on board neutral vessels on the high seas is not a belligerent right derived from the law of nations, and it is obvious that no visit or search or use of force for any purpose on board the vessels of one independent power on the high seas can in war or peace be sanctioned by the laws or authority of another power. It is equally obvious that, for the purpose of preserving to each State its seafaring members, by excluding them from the vessels of the other, the mode heretofore proposed by the United States and now enacted by them as an article of municipal policy, can not for a moment be compared with the mode practiced by Great Britain without a conviction of its title to preference, inasmuch as the latter leaves the discrimination between the mariners of the two nations to officers exposed by unavoidable bias as well as by a defect of evidence to a wrong decision, under circumstances precluding for the most part the enforcement of controlling penalties, and where a wrong decision, besides the irreparable violation of the sacred rights of persons, might frustrate the plans and profits of entire voyages; whereas the mode assumed by the United States guards with studied fairness and efficacy against errors in such cases and avoids the effect of casual errors on the safety of navigation and the success of mercantile expeditions.

If the reasonableness of expectations drawn from these considerations could guarantee their fulfillment a just peace would not be distant. But it becomes the wisdom of the National Legislature to keep in mind the true policy, or rather the indispensable obligation, of adapting its measures to the supposition that the only course to that happy event is in the vigorous employment of the resources of war. And painful as the reflection is, this duty is particularly enforced by the spirit and manner in which the war continues to be waged by the enemy, who, uninfluenced by the unvaried examples of humanity set them, are adding to the savage fury of it on one frontier a system of plunder and conflagration on the other, equally forbidden by respect for national character and by the established rules of civilized warfare.

As an encouragement to persevering and invigorated exertions to bring the contest to a happy result, I have the satisfaction of being able to appeal to the auspicious progress of our arms both by land and on the water.

In continuation of the brilliant achievements of our infant Navy, a signal triumph has been gained by Captain Lawrence and his companions in the *Hornet* sloop of war, which destroyed a British sloop of war with a celerity so unexampled and with a slaughter of the enemy so disproportionate to the loss in the *Hornet* as to claim for the conquerors the highest praise and the full recompense provided by Congress in preceding cases. Our public ships of war in general, as well as the private armed vessels, have continued also their activity and success against the commerce of the enemy, and by their vigilance and address have greatly frustrated the efforts of the hostile squadrons distributed along our coasts to intercept them in returning into port and resuming their cruises.

The augmentation of our naval force, as authorized at the last session of Congress, is in progress. On the Lakes our superiority is near at hand where it is not already established.

The events of the campaign, so far as they are known to us, furnish matter of congratulation, and show that under a wise organization and efficient direction the Army is destined to a glory not less brilliant than that which already encircles the Navy. The attack and capture of York is in that quarter a presage of future and greater victories, while on the western frontier the issue of the late siege of Fort Meigs leaves us nothing to regret but a single act of inconsiderate valor.

The provisions last made for filling the ranks and enlarging the staff of the Army have had the best effects. It will be for the consideration of Congress whether other provisions depending on their authority may not still further improve the military establishment and the means of defense.

The sudden death of the distinguished citizen who represented the United States in France, without any special arrangements by him for such a contingency, has left us without the expected sequel to his last communications, nor has the French Government taken any measures for bringing the depending negotiations to a conclusion through its representative in the United States. This failure adds to delays before so unreasonably spun out. A successor to our deceased minister has been appointed and is ready to proceed on his mission. The course which he will pursue in fulfilling it is that prescribed by a steady regard to the true interests of the United States, which equally avoids an abandonment of their just demands and a connection of their fortunes with the systems of other powers.

The receipts in the Treasury from the 1st of October to the 31st day of March last, including the sums received on account of Treasury notes and of the loans authorized by the acts of the last and the preceding sessions of Congress, have amounted to $15,412,000. The expenditures during the same period amounted to $15,920,000, and left in the Treasury on the 1st of April the sum of $1,857,000. The loan of $16,000,000, authorized by the act of the 8th of February last, has been contracted for. Of that sum more than $1,000,000 had been paid into the Treasury prior to the 1st of April, and formed a part of the receipts as above stated. The remainder of that loan, amounting to near $15,000,000, with the sum of $5,000,000 authorized to be issued in Treasury notes, and the estimated receipts from the customs and the sales of public lands, amounting to $9,300,000, and making, in the whole, $29,300,000, to be received during the last nine months of the present year, will be necessary to meet the expenditures already authorized and the engagements contracted in relation to the public debt. These engagements amount during that period to $10,500,000, which, with near one million for the civil, miscellaneous, and diplomatic expenses, both foreign and domestic, and $17,800,000 for the military and naval expenditures, including the ships of war building and to be built, will leave a sum in the Treasury at the end of the present year equal to that on the 1st of April last. A part of this sum may be considered as a resource for defraying any extraordinary expenses already authorized by law beyond the sums above estimated, and a further resource for any emergency may be found in the sum of $1,000,000, the loan of which to the United States has been authorized by the State of Pennsylvania, but which has not yet been brought into effect.

This view of our finances, whilst it shows that due provision has been made for the expenses of the current year, shows at the same time, by the limited amount of the actual revenue and the dependence on loans, the necessity of providing more adequately for the future supplies of the Treasury. This can be best done by a well-digested system of internal revenue in aid of existing sources, which will have the effect both of abridging the amount of necessary loans and, on that account, as well as by placing the public credit on a more satisfactory basis, of improving the terms on which loans may be obtained. The loan of sixteen millions was not contracted for at a less interest than about 7½ per cent, and, although other causes may have had an agency, it can not be doubted that, with the advantage of a more extended and less precarious revenue, a lower rate of interest might have sufficed. A longer postponement of this advantage could not fail to have a still greater influence on future loans.

In recommending to the National Legislature this resort to additional taxes I feel great satisfaction in the assurance that our constituents, who have already displayed so much zeal and firmness in the cause of their country, will cheerfully give any other proof of their patriotism which it calls for. Happily no people, with local and transitory exceptions never to be wholly avoided, are more able than the people of the United States to spare for the public wants a portion of their private means, whether regard be had to the ordinary profits of industry or the ordinary price of subsistence in our country compared with those in any other. And in no case could stronger reasons be felt for yielding the requisite contributions. By rendering the public resources certain and commensurate to the public exigencies, the constituted authorities will be able to prosecute the war the more rapidly to its proper issue; every hostile hope founded on a calculated failure of our resources will be cut off, and by adding to the evidence of bravery and skill in combats on the ocean and the land, and alacrity in supplying the treasure necessary to give them their fullest effect, and demonstrating to the world the public energy which our political institutions combine, with the personal liberty distinguishing them, the best security will be provided against future enterprises on the rights or the peace of the nation.

The contest in which the United States are engaged appeals for its support to every motive that can animate an uncorrupted and enlightened people—to the love of country; to the pride of liberty; to an emulation of the glorious founders of their independence by a successful vindication of its violated attributes; to the gratitude and sympathy which demand security from the most degrading wrongs of a class of citizens who have proved themselves so worthy the protection of their country by their heroic zeal in its defense; and, finally, to the sacred obligation of transmitting entire to future generations that precious patrimony of national rights and independence which is held in trust by the present from the goodness of Divine Providence.

Being aware of the inconveniences to which a protracted session at this season would be liable, I limit the present communication to objects of primary importance. In special messages which may ensue regard will be had to the same consideration.

JAMES MADISON.

SPECIAL MESSAGES.

MAY 29, 1813.

To the Senate of the United States:

The Swedish Government having repeatedly manifested a desire to interchange a public minister with the United States, and having lately appointed one with that view, and other considerations concurring to render it advisable at this period to make a correspondent appointment, I nominate Jonathan Russell, of Rhode Island, to be minister plenipotentiary of the United States to Sweden.

JAMES MADISON.

WASHINGTON, *July 6, 1813.*

To the Senate of the United States:

I have received from the committee appointed by the resolution of the Senate of the 14th day of June a copy of that resolution, which authorizes the committee to confer with the President on the subject of the nomination made by him of a minister plenipotentiary to Sweden.

Conceiving it to be my duty to decline the proposed conference with the committee, and it being uncertain when it may be convenient to explain to the committee, and through them to the Senate, the grounds of my so doing, I think it proper to address the explanation directly to the Senate. Without entering into a general review of the relations in which the Constitution has placed the several departments of the Government to each other, it will suffice to remark that the Executive and Senate, in the cases of appointments to office and of treaties, are to be considered as independent of and coordinate with each other. If they agree, the appointments or treaties are made; if the Senate disagree, they fail. If the Senate wish information previous to their final decision, the practice, keeping in view the constitutional relations of the Senate and the Executive, has been either to request the Executive to furnish it or to refer the subject to a committee of their body to communicate, either formally or informally, with the head of the proper department. The appointment of a committee of the Senate to confer immediately with the Executive himself appears to lose sight of the coordinate relation between the Executive and the Senate which the Constitution has established, and which ought therefore to be maintained.

The relation between the Senate and House of Representatives, in whom legislative power is concurrently vested, is sufficiently analogous to illustrate that between the Executive and Senate in making appointments and treaties. The two Houses are in like manner independent of and coordinate with each other, and the invariable practice of each in appointing committees of conference and consultation is to commission them to confer not with the coordinate body itself, but with a committee of that body; and although both branches of the Legislature may be too numerous to hold conveniently a conference with committees, were they to be appointed by either to confer with the entire body of the other, it may be fairly presumed that if the whole number of either branch were not too large for the purpose the objection to such a conference, being against the principle as derogating from the coordinate relations of the two Houses, would retain all its force.

I add only that I am entirely persuaded of the purity of the intentions of the Senate in the course they have pursued on this occasion, and with which my view of the subject makes it my duty not to accord, and that they will be cheerfully furnished with all the suitable information in possession of the Executive in any mode deemed consistent with the principles of the Constitution and the settled practice under it.

JAMES MADISON.

WASHINGTON, *July 20, 1813.*

To the Senate and House of Representatives of the United States:

There being sufficient ground to infer that it is the purpose of the enemy to combine with the blockade of our ports special licenses to neutral vessels or to British vessels in neutral disguises, whereby they may draw from our country the precise kind and quantity of exports essential to their wants, whilst its general commerce remains obstructed, keeping in view also the insidious discrimination between the different ports of the United States; and as such a system, if not counteracted, will have the effect of diminishing very materially the pressure of the war on the enemy, and encouraging a perseverance in it, at the same time that it will leave the general commerce of the United States under all the pressure the enemy can impose, thus subjecting the whole to British regulation in subserviency to British monopoly, I recommend to the consideration of Congress the expediency of an immediate and effectual prohibition of exports limited to a convenient day in their next session, and removable in the meantime in the event of a cessation of the blockade of our ports.

JAMES MADISON.

PROCLAMATION.

[From Niles's Weekly Register, vol. 4, p. 345.]

A PROCLAMATION.

Whereas the Congress of the United States, by a joint resolution of the two Houses, have signified a request that a day may be recommended to be observed by the people of the United States with religious solemnity as a day of public humiliation and prayer; and

Whereas in times of public calamity such as that of the war brought on the United States by the injustice of a foreign government it is especially becoming that the hearts of all should be touched with the same and the eyes of all be turned to that Almighty Power in whose hand are the welfare and the destiny of nations:

I do therefore issue this my proclamation, recommending to all who shall be piously disposed to unite their hearts and voices in addressing at one and the same time their vows and adorations to the Great Parent and Sovereign of the Universe that they assemble on the second Thursday of September next in their respective religious congregations to render Him thanks for the many blessings He has bestowed on the people of the United States; that He has blessed them with a land capable of yielding all the necessaries and requisites of human life, with ample means for convenient exchanges with foreign countries; that He has blessed the labors employed in its cultivation and improvement; that He is now blessing the exertions to extend and establish the arts and manufactures which will secure within ourselves supplies too important to remain dependent on the precarious policy or the peaceable dispositions of other nations, and particularly that He has blessed the United States with a political Constitution founded on the will and authority of the whole people and guaranteeing to each individual security, not only of his person and his property, but of those sacred rights of conscience so essential to his present happiness and so dear to his future hopes; that with those expressions of devout thankfulness be joined supplications to the same Almighty Power that He would look down with compassion on our infirmities; that He would pardon our manifold transgressions and awaken and strengthen in all the wholesome purposes of repentance and amendment; that in this season of trial and calamity He would preside in a particular manner over our public councils and inspire all citizens with a love of their country and with those fraternal affections and that mutual confidence which have so happy a tendency to make us safe at home and respected abroad; and that as He was graciously pleased heretofore to smile on our struggles against the attempts of the Government of the Empire of which these States then made a part to wrest from them the rights and privileges to which they were entitled in common with every other part and to raise them to the station of an independent and sovereign people, so He would now be pleased in like manner to bestow His blessing on our arms in resisting the hostile and persevering efforts of the same powe. to degrade us on the ocean, the common inheritance of all, from rights and immunities belonging and essential to the American people as a coequal member of the great community of independent nations; and that, inspiring our enemies with moderation, with justice, and with that spirit of reasonable accommodation which our country has continued to manifest, we may be enabled to beat our swords into plowshares and to enjoy in peace every man the fruits of his honest industry and the rewards of his lawful enterprise.

If the public homage of a people can ever be worthy the favorable regard of the Holy and Omniscient Being to whom it is addressed, it must be that in which those who join in it are guided only by their free choice, by the impulse of their hearts and the dictates of their consciences; and such a spectacle must be interesting to all Christian nations as proving that religion, that gift of Heaven for the good of man, freed from all coercive edicts, from that unhallowed connection with the powers of this world which corrupts religion into an instrument or an usurper of the policy of the state, and making no appeal but to reason, to the heart, and to the conscience, can spread its benign influence everywhere and can attract to the divine altar those freewill offerings of humble supplication, thanksgiving, and praise which alone can be acceptable to Him whom no hypocrisy can deceive and no forced sacrifices propitiate.

Upon these principles and with these views the good people of the United States are invited, in conformity with the resolution aforesaid, to dedicate the day above named to the religious solemnities therein recommended.

Given at Washington, this 23d day of July, A. D. 1813.

[SEAL.]   JAMES MADISON.

FIFTH ANNUAL MESSAGE.

WASHINGTON, *December 7, 1813.*

Fellow-Citizens of the Senate and of the House of Representatives:

In meeting you at the present interesting conjuncture it would have been highly satisfactory if I could have communicated a favorable result to the mission charged with negotiations for restoring peace. It was a just expectation, from the respect due to the distinguished Sovereign who had invited them by his offer of mediation, from the readiness with which the invitation was accepted on the part of the United States, and from the pledge to be found in an act of their Legislature for the liberality which their plenipotentiaries would carry into the negotiations, that no time would be lost by the British Government in embracing the experiment for hastening a stop to the effusion of blood. A prompt and cordial acceptance of the mediation on that side was the less to be doubted, as it was of a nature not to submit rights or pretensions on either side to the decision of an umpire, but to afford merely an opportunity, honorable and desirable to both, for discussing and, if possible, adjusting them for the interest of both.

The British cabinet, either mistaking our desire of peace for a dread of British power or misled by other fallacious calculations, has disappointed this reasonable anticipation. No communications from our envoys having reached us, no information on the subject has been received from that source; but it is known that the mediation was declined in the first instance, and there is no evidence, notwithstanding the lapse of time, that a change of disposition in the British councils has taken place or is to be expected.

Under such circumstances a nation proud of its rights and conscious of its strength has no choice but an exertion of the one in support of the other.

To this determination the best encouragement is derived from the success with which it has pleased the Almighty to bless our arms both on the land and on the water.

Whilst proofs have been continued of the enterprise and skill of our cruisers, public and private, on the ocean, and a new trophy gained in the capture of a British by an American vessel of war, after an action giving celebrity to the name of the victorious commander, the great inland waters on which the enemy were also to be encountered have presented achievements of our naval arms as brilliant in their character as they have been important in their consequences.

On Lake Erie, the squadron under command of Captain Perry having met the British squadron of superior force, a sanguinary conflict ended in the capture of the whole. The conduct of that officer, adroit as it was daring, and which was so well seconded by his comrades, justly entitles them to the admiration and gratitude of their country, and will fill an early page in its naval annals with a victory never surpassed in luster, however much it may have been in magnitude.

On Lake Ontario the caution of the British commander, favored by contingencies, frustrated the efforts of the American commander to bring on a decisive action. Captain Chauncey was able, however, to establish an ascendency on that important theater, and to prove by the manner in which he effected everything possible that opportunities only were wanted for a more shining display of his own talents and the gallantry of those under his command.

The success on Lake Erie having opened a passage to the territory of the enemy, the officer commanding the Northwestern army transferred the war thither, and rapidly pursuing the hostile troops, fleeing with their savage associates, forced a general action, which quickly terminated in the capture of the British and dispersion of the savage force.

This result is signally honorable to Major-General Harrison, by whose military talents it was prepared; to Colonel Johnson and his mounted volunteers, whose impetuous onset gave a decisive blow to the ranks of the enemy, and to the spirit of the volunteer militia, equally brave and patriotic, who bore an interesting part in the scene; more especially to the chief magistrate of Kentucky, at the head of them, whose heroism signalized in the war which established the independence of his country, sought at an advanced age a share in hardships and battles for maintaining its rights and its safety.

The effect of these successes has been to rescue the inhabitants of Michigan from their oppressions, aggravated by gross infractions of the capitulation which subjected them to a foreign power; to alienate the savages of numerous tribes from the enemy, by whom they were disappointed and abandoned, and to relieve an extensive region of country from a merciless warfare which desolated its frontiers and imposed on its citizens the most harassing services.

In consequence of our naval superiority on Lake Ontario and the opportunity afforded by it for concentrating our forces by water, operations which had been provisionally planned were set on foot against the possessions of the enemy on the St. Lawrence. Such, however, was the delay produced in the first instance by adverse weather of unusual violence and continuance and such the circumstances attending the final movements of the army, that the prospect, at one time so favorable, was not realized.

The cruelty of the enemy in enlisting the savages into a war with a nation desirous of mutual emulation in mitigating its calamities has not been confined to any one quarter. Wherever they could be turned against us no exertions to effect it have been spared. On our southwestern border the Creek tribes, who, yielding to our persevering endeavors, were gradually acquiring more civilized habits, became the unfortunate victims of seduction. A war in that quarter has been the consequence, infuriated by a bloody fanaticism recently propagated among them. It was necessary to crush such a war before it could spread among the contiguous tribes and before it could favor enterprises of the enemy into that vicinity. With this view a force was called into the service of the United States from the States of Georgia and Tennessee, which, with the nearest regular troops and other corps from the Mississippi Territory, might not only chastise the savages into present peace but make a lasting impression on their fears.

The progress of the expedition, as far as is yet known, corresponds with the martial zeal with which it was espoused, and the best hopes of a satisfactory issue are authorized by the complete success with which a well-planned enterprise was executed against a body of hostile savages by a detachment of the volunteer militia of Tennessee, under the gallant command of General Coffee, and by a still more important victory over a larger body of them, gained under the immediate command of Major-General Jackson, an officer equally distinguished for his patriotism and his military talents.

The systematic perseverance of the enemy in courting the aid of the savages in all quarters had the natural effect of kindling their ordinary propensity to war into a passion, which, even among those best disposed toward the United States, was ready, if not employed on our side, to be turned against us. A departure from our protracted forbearance to accept the services tendered by them has thus been forced upon us. But in yielding to it the retaliation has been mitigated as much as possible, both in its extent and in its character, stopping far short of the example of the enemy, who owe the advantages they have occasionally gained in battle chiefly to the number of their savage associates, and who have not controlled them either from their usual practice of indiscriminate massacre on defenseless inhabitants or from scenes of carnage without a parallel on prisoners to the British arms, guarded by all the laws of humanity and of honorable war. For these enormities the enemy are equally responsible, whether with the power to prevent them they want the will or with the knowledge of a want of power they still avail themselves of such instruments.

In other respects the enemy are pursuing a course which threatens consequences most afflicting to humanity.

A standing law of Great Britain naturalizes, as is well known, all aliens complying with conditions limited to a shorter period than those required by the United States, and naturalized subjects are in war employed by her Government in common with native subjects. In a contiguous British Province regulations promulgated since the commencement of the war compel citizens of the United States being there under certain circumstances to bear arms, whilst of the native emigrants from the United States, who compose much of the population of the Province, a number have actually borne arms against the United States within their limits, some of whom, after having done so, have become prisoners of war, and are now in our possession. The British commander in that Province, nevertheless, with the sanction, as appears, of his Government, thought proper to select from American prisoners of war and send to Great Britain for trial as criminals a number of individuals who had emigrated from the British dominions long prior to the state of war between the two nations, who had incorporated themselves into our political society in the modes recognized by the law and the practice of Great Britain, and who were made prisoners of war under the banners of their adopted country, fighting for its rights and its safety.

The protection due to these citizens requiring an effectual interposition in their behalf, a like number of British prisoners of war were put into confinement, with a notification that they would experience whatever violence might be committed on the American prisoners of war sent to Great Britain.

It was hoped that this necessary consequence of the step unadvisedly taken on the part of Great Britain would have led her Government to reflect on the inconsistencies of its conduct, and that a sympathy with the British, if not with the American, sufferers would have arrested the cruel career opened by its example.

This was unhappily not the case. In violation both of consistency and of humanity, American officers and noncommissioned officers in double the number of the British soldiers confined here were ordered into close confinement, with formal notice that in the event of a retaliation for the death which might be inflicted on the prisoners of war sent to Great Britain for trial the officers so confined would be put to death also. It was notified at the same time that the commanders of the British fleets and armies on our coasts are instructed in the same event to proceed with a destructive severity against our towns and their inhabitants.

That no doubt might be left with the enemy of our adherence to the retaliatory resort imposed on us, a correspondent number of British officers, prisoners of war in our hands, were immediately put into close confinement to abide the fate of those confined by the enemy, and the British Government has been apprised of the determination of this Government to retaliate any other proceedings against us contrary to the legitimate modes of warfare.

It is as fortunate for the United States that they have it in their power to meet the enemy in this deplorable contest as it is honorable to them that they do not join in it but under the most imperious obligations, and with the humane purpose of effectuating a return to the established usages of war.

The views of the French Government on the subjects which have been so long committed to negotiation have received no elucidation since the close of your late session. The minister plenipotentiary of the United States at Paris had not been enabled by proper opportunities to press the objects of his mission as prescribed by his instructions.

The militia being always to be regarded as the great bulwark of defense and security for free states, and the Constitution having wisely committed to the national authority a use of that force as the best provision against an unsafe military establishment, as well as a resource peculiarly adapted to a country having the extent and the exposure of the United States, I recommend to Congress a revision of the militia laws for the purpose of securing more effectually the services of all detachments called into the employment and placed under the Government of the United States.

It will deserve the consideration of Congress also whether among other improvements in the militia laws justice does not require a regulation, under due precautions, for defraying the expense incident to the first assembling as well as the subsequent movements of detachments called into the national service.

To give to our vessels of war, public and private, the requisite advantage in their cruises, it is of much importance that they should have, both for themselves and their prizes, the use of the ports and markets of friendly powers. With this view, I recommend to Congress the expediency of such legal provisions as may supply the defects or remove the doubts of the Executive authority, to allow to the cruisers of other powers at war with enemies of the United States such use of the American ports as may correspond with the privileges allowed by such powers to American cruisers.

During the year ending on the 30th of September last the receipts into the Treasury have exceeded $37,500,000, of which near twenty-four millions were the produce of loans. After meeting all demands for the public service there remained in the Treasury on that day near $7,000,000. Under the authority contained in the act of the 2d of August last for borrowing $7,500,000, that sum has been obtained on terms more favorable to the United States than those of the preceding loan made during the present year. Further sums to a considerable amount will be necessary to be obtained in the same way during the ensuing year, and from the increased capital of the country, from the fidelity with which the public engagements have been kept and the public credit maintained, it may be expected on good grounds that the necessary pecuniary supplies will not be wanting.

The expenses of the current year, from the multiplied operations falling within it, have necessarily been extensive; but on a just estimate of the campaign in which the mass of them has been incurred the cost will not be found disproportionate to the advantages which have been gained. The campaign has, indeed, in its latter stages in one quarter been less favorable than was expected, but in addition to the importance

CAPTURE OF FORT GEORGE, CANADA

THE CAPTURE OF FORT GEORGE, CANADA

May 27, 1813

A British force of 2,200 men, 1,800 of whom were regulars, held Fort George, which was directly across the Niagara River from the American Fort Niagara, where were gathered about 4,000 troops. After a twenty-minute fight, on May 27, 1813, the British fled from their stronghold, having lost 863 men besides their ammunition and supplies. Winfield Scott, who was then a colonel, is represented as leading his men through the breach into the hand-to-hand mêlée.

The engagement is more fully described in the index (volume eleven), in the article entitled "Fort George, Canada, Capture of." Also see "War of 1812."

of our naval success the progress of the campaign has been filled with incidents highly honorable to the American arms.

The attacks of the enemy on Craney Island, on Fort Meigs, on Sacketts Harbor, and on Sandusky have been vigorously and successfully repulsed; nor have they in any case succeeded on either frontier excepting when directed against the peaceable dwellings of individuals or villages unprepared or undefended.

On the other hand, the movements of the American Army have been followed by the reduction of York, and of Forts George, Erie, and Malden; by the recovery of Detroit and the extinction of the Indian war in the West, and by the occupancy or command of a large portion of Upper Canada. Battles have also been fought on the borders of the St. Lawrence, which, though not accomplishing their entire objects, reflect honor on the discipline and prowess of our soldiery, the best auguries of eventual victory. In the same scale are to be placed the late successes in the South over one of the most powerful, which had become one of the most hostile also, of the Indian tribes.

It would be improper to close this communication without expressing a thankfulness in which all ought to unite for the numerous blessings with which our beloved country continues to be favored; for the abundance which overspreads our land, and the prevailing health of its inhabitants; for the preservation of our internal tranquillity, and the stability of our free institutions, and, above all, for the light of divine truth and the protection of every man's conscience in the enjoyment of it. And although among our blessings we can not number an exemption from the evils of war, yet these will never be regarded as the greatest of evils by the friends of liberty and of the rights of nations. Our country has before preferred them to the degraded condition which was the alternative when the sword was drawn in the cause which gave birth to our national independence, and none who contemplate the magnitude and feel the value of that glorious event will shrink from a struggle to maintain the high and happy ground on which it placed the American people.

With all good citizens the justice and necessity of resisting wrongs and usurpations no longer to be borne will sufficiently outweigh the privations and sacrifices inseparable from a state of war. But it is a reflection, moreover, peculiarly consoling, that, whilst wars are generally aggravated by their baneful effects on the internal improvements and permanent prosperity of the nations engaged in them, such is the favored situation of the United States that the calamities of the contest into which they have been compelled to enter are mitigated by improvements and advantages of which the contest itself is the source.

If the war has increased the interruptions of our commerce, it has at the same time cherished and multiplied our manufactures so as to make us independent of all other countries for the more essential branches for which we ought to be dependent on none, and is even rapidly giving them an extent which will create additional staples in our future intercourse with foreign markets.

If much treasure has been expended, no inconsiderable portion of it has been applied to objects durable in their value and necessary to our permanent safety.

If the war has exposed us to increased spoliations on the ocean and to predatory incursions on the land, it has developed the national means of retaliating the former and of providing protection against the latter, demonstrating to all that every blow aimed at our maritime independence is an impulse accelerating the growth of our maritime power.

By diffusing through the mass of the nation the elements of military discipline and instruction; by augmenting and distributing warlike preparations applicable to future use; by evincing the zeal and valor with which they will be employed and the cheerfulness with which every necessary burden will be borne, a greater respect for our rights and a longer duration of our future peace are promised than could be expected without these proofs of the national character and resources.

The war has proved moreover that our free Government, like other free governments, though slow in its early movements, acquires in its progress a force proportioned to its freedom, and that the union of these States, the guardian of the freedom and safety of all and of each, is strengthened by every occasion that puts it to the test.

In fine, the war, with all its vicissitudes, is illustrating the capacity and the destiny of the United States to be a great, a flourishing, and a powerful nation, worthy of the friendship which it is disposed to cultivate with all others, and authorized by its own example to require from all an observance of the laws of justice and reciprocity. Beyond these their claims have never extended, and in contending for these we behold a subject for our congratulations in the daily testimonies of increasing harmony throughout the nation, and may humbly repose our trust in the smiles of Heaven on so righteous a cause.

JAMES MADISON.

SPECIAL MESSAGES.

DECEMBER 9, 1813.

To the Senate and House of Representatives of the United States:

The tendency of our commercial and navigation laws in their present state to favor the enemy and thereby prolong the war is more and more developed by experience. Supplies of the most essential kinds find their way not only to British ports and British armies at a distance, but the armies in our neighborhood with which our own are contending derive from our ports and outlets a subsistence attainable with difficulty, if at all, from other sources. Even the fleets and troops infesting our coasts and waters are by like supplies accommodated and encouraged in their predatory and incursive warfare.

Abuses having a like tendency take place in our import trade. British fabrics and products find their way into our ports under the name and from the ports of other countries, and often in British vessels disguised as neutrals by false colors and papers.

To these abuses it may be added that illegal importations are openly made with advantage to the violators of the law, produced by undervaluations or other circumstances involved in the course of the judicial proceedings against them.

It is found also that the practice of ransoming is a cover for collusive captures and a channel for intelligence advantageous to the enemy.

To remedy as much as possible these evils, I recommend:

That an effectual embargo on exports be immediately enacted.

That all articles known to be derived, either not at all or in any immaterial degree only, from the productions of any other country than Great Britain, and particularly the extensive articles made of wool and cotton materials, and ardent spirits made from the cane, be expressly and absolutely prohibited, from whatever port or place or in whatever vessels the same may be brought into the United States, and that all violations of the nonimportation act be subjected to adequate penalties.

That among the proofs of the neutral and national character of foreign vessels it be required that the masters and supercargoes and three-fourths at least of the crews be citizens or subjects of the country under whose flag the vessels sail.

That all persons concerned in collusive captures by the enemy or in ransoming vessels or their cargoes from the enemy be subjected to adequate penalties.

To shorten as much as possible the duration of the war it is indispensable that the enemy should feel all the pressure that can be given to it, and the restraints having that tendency will be borne with the greater cheerfulness by all good citizens, as the restraints will affect those most who are most ready to sacrifice the interest of their country in pursuit of their own.

JAMES MADISON.

JANUARY 6, 1814.

To the Senate and House of Representatives of the United States:

I transmit, for the information of Congress, copies of a letter from the British secretary of state for foreign affairs to the Secretary of State, with the answer of the latter.

In appreciating the accepted proposal of the Government of Great

Britain for instituting negotiations for peace Congress will not fail to keep in mind that vigorous preparations for carrying on the war can in no respect impede the progress to a favorable result, whilst a relaxation of such preparations, should the wishes of the United States for a speedy restoration of the blessings of peace be disappointed, would necessarily have the most injurious consequences.

JAMES MADISON.

FEBRUARY 26, 1814.

To the Senate and House of Representatives of the United States:

It has appeared that at the recovery of the Michigan Territory from the temporary possession of the enemy the inhabitants thereof were left in so destitute and distressed a condition as to require from the public stores certain supplies essential to their subsistence, which have been prolonged under the same necessity which called for them.

The deplorable situation of the savages thrown by the same event on the mercy and humanity of the American commander at Detroit drew from the same source the means of saving them from perishing by famine, and in other places the appeals made by the wants and sufferings of that unhappy description of people have been equally imperious.

The necessity imposed by the conduct of the enemy in relation to the savages of admitting their cooperation in some instances with our arms has also involved occasional expense in supplying their wants, and it is possible that a perseverance of the enemy in their cruel policy may render a further expense for the like purpose inevitable.

On these subjects an estimate from the Department of War will be laid before Congress, and I recommend a suitable provision for them.

JAMES MADISON.

MARCH 31, 1814.

To the Senate and House of Representatives of the United States:

Taking into view the mutual interests which the United States and the foreign nations in amity with them have in a liberal commercial intercourse, and the extensive changes favorable thereto which have recently taken place; taking into view also the important advantages which may otherwise result from adapting the state of our commercial laws to the circumstances now existing, I recommend to the consideration of Congress the expediency of authorizing, after a certain day, exportations, specie excepted, from the United States in vessels of the United States and in vessels owned and navigated by the subjects of powers at peace with them, and a repeal of so much of our laws as prohibits the importation of articles not the property of enemies, but produced or manufactured only within their dominions.

I recommend also, as a more effectual safeguard and encouragement to our growing manufactures, that the additional duties on imports which are to expire at the end of one year after a peace with Great Britain be prolonged to the end of two years after that event, and that, in favor of our moneyed institutions, the exportation of specie be prohibited throughout the same period.

JAMES MADISON.

PROCLAMATIONS.

[From Niles's Weekly Register, vol. 6, p. 279.]

BY THE PRESIDENT OF THE UNITED STATES OF AMERICA.

A PROCLAMATION.

Whereas information has been received that a number of individuals who have deserted from the Army of the United States have become sensible of their offenses and are desirous of returning to their duty, a full pardon is hereby granted and proclaimed to each and all such individuals as shall within three months from the date hereof surrender themselves to the commanding officer of any military post within the United States or the Territories thereof.

In testimony whereof I have caused the seal of the United States to be affixed to these presents, and signed the same with my hand.

[SEAL.]   Done at the city of Washington, the 17th day of June, A. D. 1814, and of the Independence of the United States the thirty-eighth.

JAMES MADISON.

By the President:

JAMES MONROE,
Secretary of State.

BY THE PRESIDENT OF THE UNITED STATES OF AMERICA.

A PROCLAMATION.

Whereas it is manifest that the blockade which has been proclaimed by the enemy of the whole Atlantic coast of the United States, nearly 2,000 miles in extent, and abounding in ports, harbors, and navigable inlets, can not be carried into effect by any adequate force actually stationed for the purpose, and it is rendered a matter of certainty and notoriety by the multiplied and daily arrivals and departures of the public and private armed vessels of the United States and of other vessels that no such adequate force has been so stationed; and

Whereas a blockade thus destitute of the character of a regular and legal blockade as defined and recognized by the established law of nations, whatever other purposes it may be made to answer, forms no lawful prohibition or obstacle to such neutral and friendly vessels as may choose to visit and trade with the United States; and

Whereas it accords with the interest and the amicable views of the United States to favor and promote as far as may be the free and mutually beneficial commercial intercourse of all friendly nations disposed to engage therein, and with that view to afford to their vessels destined to the United States a more positive and satisfactory security against all interruptions, molestations, or vexations whatever from the cruisers of the United States:

Now be it known that I, James Madison, President of the United States of America, do by this my proclamation strictly order and instruct all the public armed vessels of the United States and all private armed vessels commissioned as privateers or with letters of marque and reprisal not to interrupt, detain, or otherwise molest or vex any vessels whatever belonging to neutral powers or the subjects or citizens thereof, which vessels shall be actually bound and proceeding to any port or place within the jurisdiction of the United States, but, on the contrary, to render to all such vessels all the aid and kind offices which they may need or require.

Given under my hand and the seal of the United States at the city of Washington, the 29th day of June, A. D. 1814, and of the Independence of the United States the thirty-eighth.

[SEAL.]

By the President: JAMES MADISON.

JAMES MONROE,
Secretary of State.

[From Annals of Congress, Thirteenth Congress, vol. 3, 9.]

BY THE PRESIDENT OF THE UNITED STATES OF AMERICA.

A PROCLAMATION.

Whereas great and weighty matters claiming the consideration of the Congress of the United States form an extraordinary occasion for convening them, I do by these presents appoint Monday, the 19th day of September next, for their meeting at the city of Washington, hereby requiring the respective Senators and Representatives then and there to assemble in Congress, in order to receive such communications as may then be made to them and to consult and determine on such measures as in their wisdom may be deemed meet for the welfare of the United States.

In testimony whereof I have caused the seal of the United States to be hereunto affixed, and signed the same with my hand.

[SEAL.]

Done at the city of Washington, the 8th day of August, A. D. 1814, and of the Independence of the United States the thirty-ninth.

JAMES MADISON.

By the President:

JAMES MONROE,
Secretary of State.

[From Niles's Weekly Register, vol. 7, p. 2.]

BY THE PRESIDENT OF THE UNITED STATES OF AMERICA.

A PROCLAMATION.

Whereas the enemy by a sudden incursion have succeeded in invading the capital of the nation, defended at the moment by troops less numerous than their own and almost entirely of the militia, during their possession of which, though for a single day only, they wantonly destroyed the public edifices, having no relation in their structure to operations of war nor used at the time for military annoyance, some of these edifices being also costly monuments of taste and of the arts, and others depositories of the public archives, not only precious to the nation as the memorials of its origin and its early transactions, but interesting to all nations as contributions to the general stock of historical instruction and political science; and

Whereas advantage has been taken of the loss of a fort more immediately guarding the neighboring town of Alexandria to place the town within the range of a naval force too long and too much in the habit of abusing its superiority wherever it can be applied to require as the alternative of a general conflagration an undisturbed plunder of private property, which has been executed in a manner peculiarly distressing to the inhabitants, who had inconsiderately cast themselves upon the justice and generosity of the victor; and

Whereas it now appears by a direct communication from the British commander on the American station to be his avowed purpose to employ the force under his direction "in destroying and laying waste such towns and districts upon the coast as may be found assailable," adding to this declaration the insulting pretext that it is in retaliation for a wanton destruction committed by the army of the United States in Upper Canada, when it is notorious that no destruction has been committed, which, notwithstanding the multiplied outrages previously committed by the enemy was not unauthorized, and promptly shown to be so, and that the United States have been as constant in their endeavors to reclaim the enemy from such outrages by the contrast of their own example as they have been ready to terminate on reasonable conditions the war itself; and

Whereas these proceedings and declared purposes, which exhibit a deliberate disregard of the principles of humanity and the rules of civilized warfare, and which must give to the existing war a character of extended devastation and barbarism at the very moment of negotiations for peace, invited by the enemy himself, leave no prospect of safety to anything within the reach of his predatory and incendiary operations but in manful and universal determination to chastise and expel the invader:

Now, therefore, I, James Madison, President of the United States, do issue this my proclamation, exhorting all the good people thereof to unite their hearts and hands in giving effect to the ample means possessed for that purpose. I enjoin it on all officers, civil and military, to exert themselves in executing the duties with which they are respectively charged; and more especially I require the officers commanding the respective military districts to be vigilant and alert in providing for the defense thereof, for the more effectual accomplishment of which they are authorized to call to the defense of exposed and threatened places portions of the militia most convenient thereto, whether they be or be not parts of the quotas detached for the service of the United States under requisitions of the General Government.

On an occasion which appeals so forcibly to the proud feelings and patriotic devotion of the American people none will forget what they owe to themselves, what they owe to their country and the high destinies which await it, what to the glory acquired by their fathers in establishing the independence which is now to be maintained by their sons with the augmented strength and resources with which time and Heaven had blessed them.

In testimony whereof I have hereunto set my hand and caused the seal of the United States to be affixed to these presents.

[SEAL.]   Done at the city of Washington, the 1st day of September, A. D. 1814, and of the Independence of the United States the thirty-ninth.

JAMES MADISON.

By the President:
    JAMES MONROE,
        Secretary of State.

SPECIAL MESSAGE.

WASHINGTON, *September 17, 1814.*

The PRESIDENT OF THE SENATE OF THE UNITED STATES.

SIR: The destruction of the Capitol by the enemy having made it necessary that other accommodations should be provided for the meeting of Congress, chambers for the Senate and for the House of Representatives, with other requisite apartments, have been fitted up, under the direction of the superintendent of the city, in the public building heretofore allotted for the post and other public offices.

With this information, be pleased, sir, to accept assurances of my great respect and consideration.

JAMES MADISON.

THE UNFINISHED CAPITOL BURNED BY BRITISH, 1814

BURNING OF CAPITAL BY BRITISH

August 24, 1814

The British, after the ignominious flight of the American militia from the field at Bladensburg, Md., took the city of Washington, and applied the torch to the public buildings, sparing, however, the Patent Office. They withdrew hastily on the 25th.

The total loss amounted to $2,000,000.

The index (volume eleven) tells the unpleasant story, under the headings "Bladensburg, Md., Battle of," and "Washington City, D. C., Capture of."

SIXTH ANNUAL MESSAGE.

WASHINGTON, *September 20, 1814.*

Fellow-Citizens of the Senate and of the House of Representatives:

Notwithstanding the early day which had been fixed for your session of the present year, I was induced to call you together still sooner, as well that any inadequacy in the existing provisions for the wants of the Treasury might be supplied as that no delay might happen in providing for the result of the negotiations on foot with Great Britain, whether it should require arrangements adapted to a return of peace or further and more effective provisions for prosecuting the war.

That result is not yet known. If, on the one hand, the repeal of the orders in council and the general pacification in Europe, which withdrew the occasion on which impressments from American vessels were practiced, suggest expectations that peace and amity may be reestablished, we are compelled, on the other hand, by the refusal of the British Government to accept the offered mediation of the Emperor of Russia, by the delays in giving effect to its own proposal of a direct negotiation, and, above all, by the principles and manner in which the war is now avowedly carried on to infer that a spirit of hostility is indulged more violent than ever against the rights and prosperity of this country.

This increased violence is best explained by the two important circumstances that the great contest in Europe for an equilibrium guaranteeing all its States against the ambition of any has been closed without any check on the overbearing power of Great Britain on the ocean, and it has left in her hands disposable armaments, with which, forgetting the difficulties of a remote war with a free people, and yielding to the intoxication of success, with the example of a great victim to it before her eyes, she cherishes hopes of still further aggrandizing a power already formidable in its abuses to the tranquillity of the civilized and commercial world.

But whatever may have inspired the enemy with these more violent purposes, the public councils of a nation more able to maintain than it was to acquire its independence, and with a devotion to it rendered more ardent by the experience of its blessings, can never deliberate but on the means most effectual for defeating the extravagant views or unwarrantable passions with which alone the war can now be pursued against us.

In the events of the present campaign the enemy, with all his augmented means and wanton use of them, has little ground for exultation, unless he can feel it in the success of his recent enterprises against this metropolis and the neighboring town of Alexandria, from both of which his retreats were as precipitate as his attempts were bold and fortunate. In his other incursions on our Atlantic frontier his progress, often checked and chastised by the martial spirit of the neighboring citizens, has had more effect in distressing individuals and in dishonoring his arms than in promoting any object of legitimate warfare; and in the two instances mentioned, however deeply to be regretted on our part, he will find in his transient success, which interrupted for a moment only the ordinary public business at the seat of Government, no compensation for the loss of character with the world by his violations of private property and by his destruction of public edifices protected as monuments of the arts by the laws of civilized warfare.

On our side we can appeal to a series of achievements which have given new luster to the American arms. Besides the brilliant incidents in the minor operations of the campaign, the splendid victories gained on the Canadian side of the Niagara by the American forces under Major-General Brown and Brigadiers Scott and Gaines have gained for these heroes and their emulating companions the most unfading laurels, and, having triumphantly tested the progressive discipline of the American soldiery, have taught the enemy that the longer he protracts his hostile efforts the more certain and decisive will be his final discomfiture.

On our southern border victory has continued also to follow the American standard. The bold and skillful operations of Major-General Jackson, conducting troops drawn from the militia of the States least distant, particularly of Tennessee, have subdued the principal tribes of hostile savages, and, by establishing a peace with them, preceded by recent and exemplary chastisement, has best guarded against the mischief of their cooperation with the British enterprises which may be planned against that quarter of our country. Important tribes of Indians on our northwestern frontier have also acceded to stipulations which bind them to the interests of the United States and to consider our enemy as theirs also.

In the recent attempt of the enemy on the city of Baltimore, defended by militia and volunteers, aided by a small body of regulars and seamen, he was received with a spirit which produced a rapid retreat to his ships, whilst a concurrent attack by a large fleet was successfully resisted by the steady and well-directed fire of the fort and batteries opposed to it.

In another recent attack by a powerful force on our troops at Plattsburg, of which regulars made a part only, the enemy, after a perseverance for many hours, was finally compelled to seek safety in a hasty retreat, with our gallant bands pressing upon him.

On the Lakes, so much contested throughout the war, the great exertions for the command made on our part have been well repaid. On Lake Ontario our squadron is now and has been for some time in a condition to confine that of the enemy to his own port, and to favor the operations of our land forces on that frontier.

A part of the squadron on Lake Erie has been extended into Lake Huron, and has produced the advantage of displaying our command on that lake also. One object of the expedition was the reduction of Mackinaw, which failed with the loss of a few brave men, among whom was an officer justly distinguished for his gallant exploits. The expedition, ably conducted by both the land and the naval commanders, was otherwise highly valuable in its effects.

On Lake Champlain, where our superiority had for some time been undisputed, the British squadron lately came into action with the American, commanded by Captain Macdonough. It issued in the capture of the whole of the enemy's ships. The best praise for this officer and his intrepid comrades is in the likeness of his triumph to the illustrious victory which immortalized another officer and established at a critical moment our command of another lake.

On the ocean the pride of our naval arms had been amply supported. A second frigate has indeed fallen into the hands of the enemy, but the loss is hidden in the blaze of heroism with which she was defended. Captain Porter, who commanded her, and whose previous career had been distinguished by daring enterprise and by fertility of genius, maintained a sanguinary contest against two ships, one of them superior to his own, and under other severe disadvantages, till humanity tore down the colors which valor had nailed to the mast. This officer and his brave comrades have added much to the rising glory of the American flag, and have merited all the effusions of gratitude which their country is ever ready to bestow on the champions of its rights and of its safety.

Two smaller vessels of war have also become prizes to the enemy, but by a superiority of force which sufficiently vindicates the reputation of their commanders, whilst two others, one commanded by Captain Warrington, the other by Captain Blakely, have captured British ships of the same class with a gallantry and good conduct which entitle them and their companions to a just share in the praise of their country.

In spite of the naval force of the enemy accumulated on our coasts, our private cruisers also have not ceased to annoy his commerce and to bring their rich prizes into our ports, contributing thus, with other proofs, to demonstrate the incompetency and illegality of a blockade the proclamation of which is made the pretext for vexing and discouraging the commerce of neutral powers with the United States.

To meet the extended and diversified warfare adopted by the enemy, great bodies of militia have been taken into service for the public defense, and great expenses incurred. That the defense everywhere may be both more convenient and more economical, Congress will see the necessity of immediate measures for filling the ranks of the Regular Army and of enlarging the provision for special corps, mounted and unmounted, to be engaged for longer periods of service than are due from the militia. I earnestly renew, at the same time, a recommendation of such changes in the system of the militia as, by classing and disciplining for the most prompt and active service the portions most capable of it, will give to that great resource for the public safety all the requisite energy and efficiency.

The moneys received into the Treasury during the nine months ending on the 30th day of June last amounted to $32,000,000, of which near eleven millions were the proceeds of the public revenue and the remainder derived from loans. The disbursements for public expenditures during the same period exceeded $34,000,000, and left in the Treasury on the 1st day of July near $5,000,000. The demands during the remainder of the present year already authorized by Congress and the expenses incident to an extension of the operations of the war will render it necessary that large sums should be provided to meet them.

From this view of the national affairs Congress will be urged to take up without delay as well the subject of pecuniary supplies as that of military force, and on a scale commensurate with the extent and the character which the war has assumed. It is not to be disguised that the situation of our country calls for its greatest efforts. Our enemy is powerful in men and in money, on the land and on the water. Availing himself of fortuitous advantages, he is aiming with his undivided force a deadly blow at our growing prosperity, perhaps at our national existence. He has avowed his purpose of trampling on the usages of civilized warfare, and given earnests of it in the plunder and wanton destruction of private property. In his pride of maritime dominion and in his thirst of commercial monopoly he strikes with peculiar animosity at the progress of our navigation and of our manufactures. His barbarous policy has not even spared those monuments of the arts and models of taste with which our country had enriched and embellished its infant metropolis. From such an adversary hostility in its greatest force and in its worst forms may be looked for. The American people will face it with the undaunted spirit which in their revolutionary struggle defeated his unrighteous projects. His threats and his barbarities, instead of dismay, will kindle in every bosom an indignation not to be extinguished but in the disaster and expulsion of such cruel invaders. In providing the means necessary the National Legislature will not distrust the heroic and enlightened patriotism of its constituents. They will cheerfully and proudly bear every burden of every kind which the safety and honor of the nation demand. We have seen them everywhere paying their taxes, direct and indirect, with the greatest promptness and alacrity. We see them rushing with enthusiasm to the scenes where danger and duty call. In offering their blood they give the surest pledge that no other tribute will be withheld.

Having forborne to declare war until to other aggressions had been added the capture of nearly a thousand American vessels and the impressment of thousands of American seafaring citizens, and until a final declaration had been made by the Government of Great Britain that her hostile orders against our commerce would not be revoked but on conditions as impossible as unjust, whilst it was known that these orders would not otherwise cease but with a war which had lasted nearly twenty years, and which, according to appearances at that time, might last as many more; having manifested on every occasion and in every proper mode a sincere desire to arrest the effusion of blood and meet our enemy on the ground of justice and reconciliation, our beloved country, in still opposing to his persevering hostility all its energies, with an undiminished disposition toward peace and friendship on honorable terms, must carry with it the good wishes of the impartial world and the best hopes of support from an omnipotent and kind Providence.

JAMES MADISON.

SPECIAL MESSAGES.

SEPTEMBER 26, 1814.

To the Senate and House of Representatives of the United States:

I transmit to Congress, for their information, copies of a letter from Admiral Cochrane, commanding His Britannic Majesty's naval forces on the American station, to the Secretary of State, with his answer, and of a reply from Admiral Cochrane.

JAMES MADISON.

WASHINGTON, *October 10, 1814.*

To the Senate and House of Representatives of the United States:

I lay before Congress communications just received from the plenipotentiaries of the United States charged with negotiating peace with Great Britain, showing the conditions on which alone that Government is willing to put an end to the war.

The instructions to those plenipotentiaries, disclosing the grounds on which they were authorized to negotiate and conclude a treaty of peace, will be the subject of another communication.

JAMES MADISON.

WASHINGTON, *October 13, 1814.*

To the Senate and House of Representatives of the United States:

I now transmit to Congress copies of the instructions to the plenipotentiaries of the United States charged with negotiating a peace with Great Britain, as referred to in my message of the 10th instant.

JAMES MADISON.

DECEMBER 1, 1814.

To the Senate and House of Representatives of the United States:

I transmit, for the information of Congress, the communications last received from the ministers extraordinary and plenipotentiary of the United States at Ghent, explaining the course and actual state of their negotiations with the plenipotentiaries of Great Britain.

JAMES MADISON.

FEBRUARY 15, 1815.

To the Senate of the United States:

I have received from the American commissioners a treaty of peace and amity between His Britannic Majesty and the United States of America, signed by those commissioners and by the commissioners of His Britannic Majesty at Ghent on the 24th of December, 1814. The termination of hostilities depends upon the time of the ratification of the treaty by both parties. I lose no time, therefore, in submitting the treaty to the Senate for their advice and approbation.

I transmit also a letter from the American commissioners, which accompanied the treaty.

JAMES MADISON.

WASHINGTON, *February 18, 1815.*

To the Senate and House of Representatives of the United States:

I lay before Congress copies of the treaty of peace and amity between the United States and His Britannic Majesty, which was signed by the commissioners of both parties at Ghent on the 24th of December, 1814, and the ratifications of which have been duly exchanged.

While performing this act I congratulate you and our constituents upon an event which is highly honorable to the nation, and terminates with peculiar felicity a campaign signalized by the most brilliant successes.

The late war, although reluctantly declared by Congress, had become a necessary resort to assert the rights and independence of the nation. It has been waged with a success which is the natural result of the wisdom of the legislative councils, of the patriotism of the people, of the public spirit of the militia, and of the valor of the military and naval forces of the country. Peace, at all times a blessing, is peculiarly welcome, therefore, at a period when the causes for the war have ceased to operate, when the Government has demonstrated the efficiency of its powers of defense, and when the nation can review its conduct without regret and without reproach.

I recommend to your care and beneficence the gallant men whose achievements in every department of the military service, on the land and on the water, have so essentially contributed to the honor of the American name and to the restoration of peace. The feelings of conscious patriotism and worth will animate such men under every change of fortune and pursuit, but their country performs a duty to itself when it bestows those testimonials of approbation and applause which are at once the reward and the incentive to great actions.

The reduction of the public expenditures to the demands of a peace establishment will doubtless engage the immediate attention of Congress. There are, however, important considerations which forbid a sudden and general revocation of the measures that have been produced by the war. Experience has taught us that neither the pacific dispositions of the American people nor the pacific character of their political institutions can altogether exempt them from that strife which appears beyond the ordinary lot of nations to be incident to the actual period of the world, and the same faithful monitor demonstrates that a certain degree of preparation for war is not only indispensable to avert disasters in the onset, but affords also the best security for the continuance of peace. The wisdom of Congress will therefore, I am confident, provide for the maintenance of an adequate regular force; for the gradual advancement of the naval establishment; for improving all the means of harbor defense; for adding discipline to the distinguished bravery of the militia, and for cultivating the military art in its essential branches, under the liberal patronage of Government.

The resources of our country were at all times competent to the attainment of every national object, but they will now be enriched and invigorated by the activity which peace will introduce into all the scenes of domestic enterprise and labor. The provision that has been made for the public creditors during the present session of Congress must have a decisive effect in the establishment of the public credit both at home and abroad. The reviving interests of commerce will claim the legislative attention at the earliest opportunity, and such regulations will, I trust, be seasonably devised as shall secure to the United States their just proportion of the navigation of the world. The most liberal policy toward other nations, if met by corresponding dispositions, will in this respect be found the most beneficial policy toward ourselves. But there is no subject that can enter with greater force and merit into the deliberations of Congress than a consideration of the means to preserve and promote the manufactures which have sprung into existence and attained an unparalleled maturity throughout the United States during the period of the European wars. This source of national independence and wealth I anxiously recommend, therefore, to the prompt and constant guardianship of Congress.

The termination of the legislative sessions will soon separate you, fellow-citizens, from each other, and restore you to your constituents. I pray you to bear with you the expressions of my sanguine hope that the peace which has been just declared will not only be the foundation of the most friendly intercourse between the United States and Great Britain, but that it will also be productive of happiness and harmony in every section of our beloved country. The influence of your precepts and example must be everywhere powerful, and while we accord in grateful acknowledgments for the protection which Providence has bestowed upon us, let us never cease to inculcate obedience to the laws and fidelity to the Union as constituting the palladium of the national independence and prosperity.

JAMES MADISON.

WASHINGTON, *February 22, 1815.*

To the Senate and House of Representatives of the United States:

I lay before Congress copies of two ratified treaties which were entered into on the part of the United States, one on the 22d day of July, 1814, with the several tribes of Indians called the Wyandots, Delawares, Shawanees, Senakas, and Miamies; the other on the 9th day of August, 1814, with the Creek Nation of Indians.

It is referred to the consideration of Congress how far legislative provisions may be necessary for carrying any part of these stipulations into effect.

JAMES MADISON.

WASHINGTON, *February 23, 1815.*

To the Senate and House of Representatives of the United States:

Congress will have seen by the communication from the consul-general of the United States at Algiers laid before them on the 17th of November, 1812, the hostile proceedings of the Dey against that functionary. These have been followed by acts of more overt and direct warfare against the citizens of the United States trading in the Mediterranean, some of whom are still detained in captivity, notwithstanding the attempts which have been made to ransom them, and are treated with the rigor usual on the coast of Barbary.

The considerations which rendered it unnecessary and unimportant to commence hostile operations on the part of the United States being now terminated by the peace with Great Britain, which opens the prospect of an active and valuable trade of their citizens within the range of the Algerine cruisers, I recommend to Congress the expediency of an act declaring the existence of a state of war between the United States and the Dey and Regency of Algiers, and of such provisions as may be requisite for a vigorous prosecution of it to a successful issue.

JAMES MADISON.

WASHINGTON, *February 25, 1815.*

To the Senate and House of Representatives of the United States:

Peace having happily taken place between the United States and Great Britain, it is desirable to guard against incidents which during periods of war in Europe might tend to interrupt it, and it is believed in particular that the navigation of American vessels exclusively by American seamen, either natives or such as are already naturalized, would not only conduce to the attainment of that object, but also to increase the number of our seamen, and consequently to render our commerce and navigation independent of the service of foreigners who might be recalled by their governments under circumstances the most inconvenient to the United States. I recommend the subject, therefore, to the consideration of Congress, and in deciding upon it I am persuaded that they will sufficiently estimate the policy of manifesting to the world a desire on all occasions to cultivate harmony with other nations by any reasonable accommodations which do not impair the enjoyment of any of the essential rights of a free and independent people. The example on the part of the American Government will merit and may be expected to receive a reciprocal attention from all the friendly powers of Europe.

JAMES MADISON.

VETO MESSAGE.

WASHINGTON, *January 30, 1815.*

To the Senate of the United States:

Having bestowed on the bill entitled "An act to incorporate the subscribers to the Bank of the United States of America" that full consideration which is due to the great importance of the subject, and dictated by the respect which I feel for the two Houses of Congress, I am constrained by a deep and solemn conviction that the bill ought not to become a law to return it to the Senate, in which it originated, with my objections to the same.

Waiving the question of the constitutional authority of the Legislature to establish an incorporated bank as being precluded in my judgment by repeated recognitions under varied circumstances of the validity of such an institution in acts of the legislative, executive, and judicial branches of the Government, accompanied by indications, in different modes, of a concurrence of the general will of the nation, the proposed bank does not appear to be calculated to answer the purposes of reviving the public credit, of providing a national medium of circulation, and of aiding the Treasury by facilitating the indispensable anticipations of the revenue and by affording to the public more durable loans.

1. The capital of the bank is to be compounded of specie, of public

stocks, and of Treasury notes convertible into stock, with a certain proportion of each of which every subscriber is to furnish himself.

The amount of the stock to be subscribed will not, it is believed, be sufficient to produce in favor of the public credit any considerable or lasting elevation of the market price, whilst this may be occasionally depressed by the bank itself if it should carry into the market the allowed proportion of its capital consisting of public stock in order to procure specie, which it may find its account in procuring with some sacrifice on that part of its capital.

Nor will any adequate advantage arise to the public credit from the subscription of Treasury notes. The actual issue of these notes nearly equals at present, and will soon exceed, the amount to be subscribed to the bank. The direct effect of this operation is simply to convert fifteen millions of Treasury notes into fifteen millions of 6 per cent stock, with the collateral effect of promoting an additional demand for Treasury notes beyond what might otherwise be negotiable.

Public credit might indeed be expected to derive advantage from the establishment of a national bank, without regard to the formation of its capital, if the full aid and cooperation of the institution were secured to the Government during the war and during the period of its fiscal embarrassments. But the bank proposed will be free from all legal obligation to cooperate with the public measures, and whatever might be the patriotic disposition of its directors to contribute to the removal of those embarrassments, and to invigorate the prosecution of the war, fidelity to the pecuniary and general interest of the institution according to their estimate of it might oblige them to decline a connection of their operations with those of the National Treasury during the continuance of the war and the difficulties incident to it. Temporary sacrifices of interest, though overbalanced by the future and permanent profits of the charter, not being requirable of right in behalf of the public, might not be gratuitously made, and the bank would reap the full benefit of the grant, whilst the public would lose the equivalent expected from it; for it must be kept in view that the sole inducement to such a grant on the part of the public would be the prospect of substantial aids to its pecuniary means at the present crisis and during the sequel of the war. It is evident that the stock of the bank will on the return of peace, if not sooner, rise in the market to a value which, if the bank were established in a period of peace, would authorize and obtain for the public a bonus to a very large amount. In lieu of such a bonus the Government is fairly entitled to and ought not to relinquish or risk the needful services of the bank under the pressing circumstances of war.

2. The bank as proposed to be constituted can not be relied on during the war to provide a circulating medium nor to furnish loans or anticipations of the public revenue.

Without a medium the taxes can not be collected, and in the absence of specie the medium understood to be the best substitute is that of notes issued by a national bank. The proposed bank will commence and conduct its operations under an obligation to pay its notes in specie, or be subject to the loss of its charter. Without such an obligation the notes of the bank, though not exchangeable for specie, yet resting on good pledges and performing the uses of specie in the payment of taxes and in other public transactions, would, as experience has ascertained, qualify the bank to supply at once a circulating medium and pecuniary aids to the Government. Under the fetters imposed by the bill it is manifest that during the actual state of things, and probably during the war, the period particularly requiring such a medium and such a resource for loans and advances to the Government, notes for which the bank would be compellable to give specie in exchange could not be kept in circulation. The most the bank could effect, and the most it could be expected to aim at, would be to keep the institution alive by limited and local transactions which, with the interest on the public stock in the bank, might yield a dividend sufficient for the purpose until a change from war to peace should enable it, by a flow of specie into its vaults and a removal of the external demand for it, to derive its contemplated emoluments from a safe and full extension of its operations.

On the whole, when it is considered that the proposed establishment will enjoy a monopoly of the profits of a national bank for a period of twenty years; that the monopolized profits will be continually growing with the progress of the national population and wealth; that the nation will during the same period be dependent on the notes of the bank for that species of circulating medium whenever the precious metals may be wanted, and at all times for so much thereof as may be an eligible substitute for a specie medium, and that the extensive employment of the notes in the collection of the augmented taxes will, moreover, enable the bank greatly to extend its profitable issues of them without the expense of specie capital to support their circulation, it is as reasonable as it is requisite that the Government, in return for these extraordinary concessions to the bank, should have a greater security for attaining the public objects of the institution than is presented in the bill, and particularly for every practicable accommodation, both in the temporary advances necessary to anticipate the taxes and in those more durable loans which are equally necessary to diminish the resort to taxes.

In discharging this painful duty of stating objections to a measure which has undergone the deliberations and received the sanction of the two Houses of the National Legislature I console myself with the reflection that if they have not the weight which I attach to them they can be constitutionally overruled, and with a confidence that in a contrary event the wisdom of Congress will hasten to substitute a more commensurate and certain provision for the public exigencies.

JAMES MADISON.

PROCLAMATIONS.

BY THE PRESIDENT OF THE UNITED STATES

A PROCLAMATION.

The two Houses of the National Legislature having by a joint resolution expressed their desire that in the present time of public calamity and war a day may be recommended to be observed by the people of the United States as a day of public humiliation and fasting and of prayer to Almighty God for the safety and welfare of these States, His blessing on their arms, and a speedy restoration of peace, I have deemed it proper by this proclamation to recommend that Thursday, the 12th of January next, be set apart as a day on which all may have an opportunity of voluntarily offering at the same time in their respective religious assemblies their humble adoration to the Great Sovereign of the Universe, of confessing their sins and transgressions, and of strengthening their vows of repentance and amendment. They will be invited by the same solemn occasion to call to mind the distinguished favors conferred on the American people in the general health which has been enjoyed, in the abundant fruits of the season, in the progress of the arts instrumental to their comfort, their prosperity, and their security, and in the victories which have so powerfully contributed to the defense and protection of our country, a devout thankfulness for all which ought to be mingled with their supplications to the Beneficent Parent of the Human Race that He would be graciously pleased to pardon all their offenses against Him; to support and animate them in the discharge of their respective duties; to continue to them the precious advantages flowing from political institutions so auspicious to their safety against dangers from abroad, to their tranquillity at home, and to their liberties, civil and religious; and that He would in a special manner preside over the nation in its public councils and constituted authorities, giving wisdom to its measures and success to its arms in maintaining its rights and in overcoming all hostile designs and attempts against it; and, finally, that by inspiring the enemy with dispositions favorable to a just and reasonable peace its blessings may be speedily and happily restored.

Given at the city of Washington, the 16th day of November, 1814, and of the Independence of the United States the thirty-eighth.

[SEAL.]   JAMES MADISON.

BY THE PRESIDENT OF THE UNITED STATES OF AMERICA.

A PROCLAMATION.

Among the many evils produced by the wars which with little intermission have afflicted Europe and extended their ravages into other quarters of the globe for a period exceeding twenty years, the dispersion of a considerable portion of the inhabitants of different countries in sorrow and in want has not been the least injurious to human happiness nor the least severe in the trial of human virtue.

It had been long ascertained that many foreigners, flying from the dangers of their own home, and that some citizens, forgetful of their duty, had cooperated in forming an establishment on the island of Barrataria, near the mouth of the river Mississippi, for the purposes of a clandestine and lawless trade. The Government of the United States caused the establishment to be broken up and destroyed, and having obtained the means of designating the offenders of every description, it only remained to answer the demands of justice by inflicting an exemplary punishment.

But it has since been represented that the offenders have manifested a sincere penitence; that they have abandoned the prosecution of the worse cause for the support of the best, and particularly that they have exhibited in the defense of New Orleans unequivocal traits of courage and fidelity. Offenders who have refused to become the associates of the enemy in the war upon the most seducing terms of invitation and who have aided to repel his hostile invasion of the territory of the United States can no longer be considered as objects of punishment, but as objects of a generous forgiveness.

It has therefore been seen with great satisfaction that the general assembly of the State of Louisiana earnestly recommend those offenders to the benefit of a full pardon.

And in compliance with that recommendation, as well as in consideration of all the other extraordinary circumstances of the case, I, James Madison, President of the United States of America, do issue this proclamation, hereby granting, publishing, and declaring a free and full pardon of all offenses committed in violation of any act or acts of the Congress of the said United States touching the revenue, trade, and navigation thereof or touching the intercourse and commerce of the United States with foreign nations at any time before the 8th day of January, in the present year 1815, by any person or persons whomsoever being inhabitants of New Orleans and the adjacent country or being inhabitants of the said island of Barrataria and the places adjacent: *Provided*, That every person claiming the benefit of this full pardon in order to entitle himself thereto shall produce a certificate in writing from the governor of the State of Louisiana stating that such person has aided in the defense of New Orleans and the adjacent country during the invasion thereof as aforesaid.

And I do hereby further authorize and direct all suits, indictments, and prosecutions for fines, penalties, and forfeitures against any person or persons who shall be entitled to the benefit of this full pardon forthwith to be stayed, discontinued, and released; and all civil officers are hereby required, according to the duties of their respective stations, to carry this proclamation into immediate and faithful execution.

Done at the city of Washington, the 6th day of February, in the year [SEAL.] 1815, and of the Independence of the United States the thirty-ninth.

JAMES MADISON.

By the President:
   JAMES MONROE,
      Acting as Secretary of State.

[From Niles's Weekly Register, vol. 7, p. 397.]

JAMES MADISON, PRESIDENT OF THE UNITED STATES OF AMERICA.

To all and singular to whom these presents shall come, greeting:

Whereas a treaty of peace and amity between the United States of America and His Britannic Majesty was signed at Ghent on the 24th day of December, 1814, by the plenipotentiaries respectively appointed for that purpose; and the said treaty having been, by and with the advice and consent of the Senate of the United States, duly accepted, ratified, and confirmed on the 17th day of February, 1815, and ratified copies thereof having been exchanged agreeably to the tenor of the said treaty, which is in the words following, to wit:

[Here follows the treaty.]

Now, therefore, to the end that the said treaty of peace and amity may be observed with good faith on the part of the United States, I, James Madison, President as aforesaid, have caused the premises to be made public; and I do hereby enjoin all persons bearing office, civil or military, within the United States and all others citizens or inhabitants thereof or being within the same faithfully to observe and fulfill the said treaty and every clause and article thereof.

In testimony whereof I have caused the seal of the United States to be affixed to these presents, and signed the same with my hand.

[SEAL.] Done at the city of Washington, this 18th day of February, A. D. 1815, and of the Sovereignty and Independence of the United States the thirty-ninth.

JAMES MADISON.

By the President:
   JAMES MONROE,
      Acting Secretary of State.

BY THE PRESIDENT OF THE UNITED STATES OF AMERICA.

A PROCLAMATION.

The Senate and House of Representatives of the United States have by a joint resolution signified their desire that a day may be recommended to be observed by the people of the United States with religious solemnity as a day of thanksgiving and of devout acknowledgments to Almighty God for His great goodness manifested in restoring to them the blessing of peace.

No people ought to feel greater obligations to celebrate the goodness of the Great Disposer of Events and of the Destiny of Nations than the people of the United States. His kind providence originally conducted them to one of the best portions of the dwelling place allotted for the great family of the human race. He protected and cherished them under all the difficulties and trials to which they were exposed in their early days. Under His fostering care their habits, their sentiments, and their pursuits prepared them for a transition in due time to a state of independence and self-government. In the arduous struggle by which it was attained they were distinguished by multiplied tokens of His benign interposition. During the interval which succeeded He reared them into the strength and endowed them with the resources which have enabled them to assert their national rights and to enhance their national character in another arduous conflict, which is now so happily terminated by a peace and reconciliation with those who have been our enemies. And to the same Divine Author of Every Good and Perfect Gift we are indebted for all those privileges and advantages, religious as well as civil, which are so richly enjoyed in this favored land.

It is for blessings such as these, and more especially for the restoration of the blessing of peace, that I now recommend that the second Thursday in April next be set apart as a day on which the people of every religious denomination may in their solemn assemblies unite their hearts and their voices in a freewill offering to their Heavenly Benefactor of their homage of thanksgiving and of their songs of praise.

Given at the city of Washington on the 4th day of March, A. D. [SEAL.] 1815, and of the Independence of the United States the thirty-ninth.

JAMES MADISON.

BY THE PRESIDENT OF THE UNITED STATES OF AMERICA.

A PROCLAMATION.

Whereas information has been received that sundry persons citizens of the United States or residents within the same, and especially within the State of Louisiana, are conspiring together to begin and set on foot, provide, and prepare the means for a military expedition or enterprise against the dominions of Spain, with which the United States are happily at peace; that for this purpose they are collecting arms, military stores, provisions, vessels, and other means; are deceiving and seducing honest and well-meaning citizens to engage in their unlawful enterprises;

are organizing, officering, and arming themselves for the same contrary to the laws in such cases made and provided:

I have therefore thought fit to issue this my proclamation, warning and enjoining all faithful citizens who have been led without due knowledge or consideration to participate in the said unlawful enterprises to withdraw from the same without delay, and commanding all persons whatsoever engaged or concerned in the same to cease all further proceedings therein, as they will answer the contrary at their peril. And I hereby enjoin and require all officers, civil and military, of the United States or of any of the States or Territories, all judges, justices, and other officers of the peace, all military officers of the Army or Navy of the United States, and officers of the militia, to be vigilant, each within his respective department and according to his functions, in searching out and bringing to punishment all persons engaged or concerned in such enterprises, in seizing and detaining, subject to the disposition of the law, all arms, military stores, vessels, or other means provided or providing for the same, and, in general, in preventing the carrying on such expedition or enterprise by all the lawful means within their power. And I require all good and faithful citizens and others within the United States to be aiding and assisting herein, and especially in the discovery, apprehension, and bringing to justice of all such offenders, in preventing the execution of their unlawful combinations or designs, and in giving information against them to the proper authorities.

In testimony whereof I have caused the seal of the United States of America to be affixed to these presents, and signed the same with my hand.

[SEAL.]   Done at the city of Washington, the 1st day of September, A. D. 1815, and of the Independence of the said United States of America the fortieth.

JAMES MADISON.

SEVENTH ANNUAL MESSAGE.

WASHINGTON, *December 5, 1815.*

Fellow-Citizens of the Senate and of the House of Representatives:

I have the satisfaction on our present meeting of being able to communicate to you the successful termination of the war which had been commenced against the United States by the Regency of Algiers. The squadron in advance on that service, under Commodore Decatur, lost not a moment after its arrival in the Mediterranean in seeking the naval force of the enemy then cruising in that sea, and succeeded in capturing two of his ships, one of them the principal ship, commanded by the

PERRY AT LAKE ERIE

THE BATTLE OF LAKE ERIE

September 10, 1813

Here for the first time fleets flying the British and American flags met in regular line of battle.

Commodore Oliver Hazard Perry summed up the occurrence in his report as follows: "We have met the enemy and they are ours."

Perry's flagship, the *Lawrence*, led his fleet of eight vessels, manned by 400 men, against the six British vessels under Barclay, which carried more than 500 men, flying as the signal for action a flag bearing the dying words of Captain Lawrence, "Don't give up the ship!" It was a stand-up fight to the finish, with the Americans at a disadvantage, and it ended in the surrender of the British.

The picture shows Perry leaving the battered and useless *Lawrence* for the less-damaged *Niagara*.

See the article "Lake Erie, Battle of," in the index (volume eleven).

Algerine admiral. The high character of the American commander was brilliantly sustained on the occasion which brought his own ship into close action with that of his adversary, as was the accustomed gallantry of all the officers and men actually engaged. Having prepared the way by this demonstration of American skill and prowess, he hastened to the port of Algiers, where peace was promptly yielded to his victorious force. In the terms stipulated the rights and honor of the United States were particularly consulted by a perpetual relinquishment on the part of the Dey of all pretensions to tribute from them. The impressions which have thus been made, strengthened as they will have been by subsequent transactions with the Regencies of Tunis and of Tripoli by the appearance of the larger force which followed under Commodore Bainbridge, the chief in command of the expedition, and by the judicious precautionary arrangements left by him in that quarter, afford a reasonable prospect of future security for the valuable portion of our commerce which passes within reach of the Barbary cruisers.

It is another source of satisfaction that the treaty of peace with Great Britain has been succeeded by a convention on the subject of commerce concluded by the plenipotentiaries of the two countries. In this result a disposition is manifested on the part of that nation corresponding with the disposition of the United States, which it may be hoped will be improved into liberal arrangements on other subjects on which the parties have mutual interests, or which might endanger their future harmony. Congress will decide on the expediency of promoting such a sequel by giving effect to the measure of confining the American navigation to American seamen—a measure which, at the same time that it might have that conciliatory tendency, would have the further advantage of increasing the independence of our navigation and the resources for our maritime defense.

In conformity with the articles in the treaty of Ghent relating to the Indians, as well as with a view to the tranquillity of our western and northwestern frontiers, measures were taken to establish an immediate peace with the several tribes who had been engaged in hostilities against the United States. Such of them as were invited to Detroit acceded readily to a renewal of the former treaties of friendship. Of the other tribes who were invited to a station on the Mississippi the greater number have also accepted the peace offered to them. The residue, consisting of the more distant tribes or parts of tribes, remain to be brought over by further explanations, or by such other means as may be adapted to the dispositions they may finally disclose.

The Indian tribes within and bordering on the southern frontier, whom a cruel war on their part had compelled us to chastise into peace, have latterly shown a restlessness which has called for preparatory measures for repressing it, and for protecting the commissioners engaged in carrying the terms of the peace into execution.

The execution of the act for fixing the military peace establishment has been attended with difficulties which even now can only be overcome by legislative aid. The selection of officers, the payment and discharge of the troops enlisted for the war, the payment of the retained troops and their reunion from detached and distant stations, the collection and security of the public property in the Quartermaster, Commissary, and Ordnance departments, and the constant medical assistance required in hospitals and garrisons rendered a complete execution of the act impracticable on the 1st of May, the period more immediately contemplated. As soon, however, as circumstances would permit, and as far as it has been practicable consistently with the public interests, the reduction of the Army has been accomplished; but the appropriations for its pay and for other branches of the military service having proved inadequate, the earliest attention to that subject will be necessary; and the expediency of continuing upon the peace establishment the staff officers who have hitherto been provisionally retained is also recommended to the consideration of Congress.

In the performance of the Executive duty upon this occasion there has not been wanting a just sensibility to the merits of the American Army during the late war; but the obvious policy and design in fixing an efficient military peace establishment did not afford an opportunity to distinguish the aged and infirm on account of their past services nor the wounded and disabled on account of their present sufferings. The extent of the reduction, indeed, unavoidably involved the exclusion of many meritorious officers of every rank from the service of their country; and so equal as well as so numerous were the claims to attention that a decision by the standard of comparative merit could seldom be attained. Judged, however, in candor by a general standard of positive merit, the Army Register will, it is believed, do honor to the establishment, while the case of those officers whose names are not included in it devolves with the strongest interest upon the legislative authority for such provision as shall be deemed the best calculated to give support and solace to the veteran and the invalid, to display the beneficence as well as the justice of the Government, and to inspire a martial zeal for the public service upon every future emergency.

Although the embarrassments arising from the want of an uniform national currency have not been diminished since the adjournment of Congress, great satisfaction has been derived in contemplating the revival of the public credit and the efficiency of the public resources. The receipts into the Treasury from the various branches of revenue during the nine months ending on the 30th of September last have been estimated at $12,500,000; the issues of Treasury notes of every denomination during the same period amounted to the sum of $14,000,000, and there was also obtained upon loan during the same period a sum of $9,000,000, of which the sum of $6,000,000 was subscribed in cash and the sum of

$3,000,000 in Treasury notes. With these means, added to the sum of $1,500,000, being the balance of money in the Treasury on the 1st day of January, there has been paid between the 1st of January and the 1st of October on account of the appropriations of the preceding and of the present year (exclusively of the amount of the Treasury notes subscribed to the loan and of the amount redeemed in the payment of duties and taxes) the aggregate sum of $33,500,000, leaving a balance then in the Treasury estimated at the sum of $3,000,000. Independent, however, of the arrearages due for military services and supplies, it is presumed that a further sum of $5,000,000, including the interest on the public debt payable on the 1st of January next, will be demanded at the Treasury to complete the expenditures of the present year, and for which the existing ways and means will sufficiently provide.

The national debt, as it was ascertained on the 1st of October last, amounted in the whole to the sum of $120,000,000, consisting of the unredeemed balance of the debt contracted before the late war ($39,000,000), the amount of the funded debt contracted in consequence of the war ($64,000,000), and the amount of the unfunded and floating debt, including the various issues of Treasury notes, $17,000,000, which is in a gradual course of payment. There will probably be some addition to the public debt upon the liquidation of various claims which are depending, and a conciliatory disposition on the part of Congress may lead honorably and advantageously to an equitable arrangement of the militia expenses incurred by the several States without the previous sanction or authority of the Government of the United States; but when it is considered that the new as well as the old portion of the debt has been contracted in the assertion of the national rights and independence, and when it is recollected that the public expenditures, not being exclusively bestowed upon subjects of a transient nature, will long be visible in the number and equipments of the American Navy, in the military works for the defense of our harbors and our frontiers, and in the supplies of our arsenals and magazines the amount will bear a gratifying comparison with the objects which have been attained, as well as with the resources of the country.

The arrangements of the finances with a view to the receipts and expenditures of a permanent peace establishment will necessarily enter into the deliberations of Congress during the present session. It is true that the improved condition of the public revenue will not only afford the means of maintaining the faith of the Government with its creditors inviolate, and of prosecuting successfully the measures of the most liberal policy, but will also justify an immediate alleviation of the burdens imposed by the necessities of the war. It is, however, essential to every modification of the finances that the benefits of an uniform national currency should be restored to the community. The absence of the precious metals will, it is believed, be a temporary evil, but until they can again be rendered the general medium of exchange it devolves on the wisdom of Congress to provide a substitute which shall equally engage the confidence and accommodate the wants of the citizens throughout the Union. If the operation of the State banks can not produce this result, the probable operation of a national bank will merit consideration; and if neither of these expedients be deemed effectual it may become necessary to ascertain the terms upon which the notes of the Government (no longer required as an instrument of credit) shall be issued upon motives of general policy as a common medium of circulation.

Notwithstanding the security for future repose which the United States ought to find in their love of peace and their constant respect for the rights of other nations, the character of the times particularly inculcates the lesson that, whether to prevent or repel danger, we ought not to be unprepared for it. This consideration will sufficiently recommend to Congress a liberal provision for the immediate extension and gradual completion of the works of defense, both fixed and floating, on our maritime frontier, and an adequate provision for guarding our inland frontier against dangers to which certain portions of it may continue to be exposed.

As an improvement in our military establishment, it will deserve the consideration of Congress whether a corps of invalids might not be so organized and employed as at once to aid in the support of meritorious individuals excluded by age or infirmities from the existing establishment, and to procure to the public the benefit of their stationary services and of their exemplary discipline. I recommend also an enlargement of the Military Academy already established, and the establishment of others in other sections of the Union; and I can not press too much on the attention of Congress such a classification and organization of the militia as will most effectually render it the safeguard of a free state. If experience has shewn in the recent splendid achievements of militia the value of this resource for the public defense, it has shewn also the importance of that skill in the use of arms and that familiarity with the essential rules of discipline which can not be expected from the regulations now in force. With this subject is intimately connected the necessity of accommodating the laws in every respect to the great object of enabling the political authority of the Union to employ promptly and effectually the physical power of the Union in the cases designated by the Constitution.

The signal services which have been rendered by our Navy and the capacities it has developed for successful cooperation in the national defense will give to that portion of the public force its full value in the eyes of Congress, at an epoch which calls for the constant vigilance of all governments. To preserve the ships now in a sound state, to complete those already contemplated, to provide amply the imperishable materials for prompt augmentations, and to improve the existing arrangements into more advantageous establishments for the construction, the repairs, and the security of vessels of war is dictated by the soundest policy.

In adjusting the duties on imports to the object of revenue the influence of the tariff on manufactures will necessarily present itself for consideration. However wise the theory may be which leaves to the sagacity and interest of individuals the application of their industry and resources, there are in this as in other cases exceptions to the general rule. Besides the condition which the theory itself implies of a reciprocal adoption by other nations, experience teaches that so many circumstances must concur in introducing and maturing manufacturing establishments, especially of the more complicated kinds, that a country may remain long without them, although sufficiently advanced and in some respects even peculiarly fitted for carrying them on with success. Under circumstances giving a powerful impulse to manufacturing industry it has made among us a progress and exhibited an efficiency which justify the belief that with a protection not more than is due to the enterprising citizens whose interests are now at stake it will become at an early day not only safe against occasional competitions from abroad, but a source of domestic wealth and even of external commerce. In selecting the branches more especially entitled to the public patronage a preference is obviously claimed by such as will relieve the United States from a dependence on foreign supplies, ever subject to casual failures, for articles necessary for the public defense or connected with the primary wants of individuals. It will be an additional recommendation of particular manufactures where the materials for them are extensively drawn from our agriculture, and consequently impart and insure to that great fund of national prosperity and independence an encouragement which can not fail to be rewarded.

Among the means of advancing the public interest the occasion is a proper one for recalling the attention of Congress to the great importance of establishing throughout our country the roads and canals which can best be executed under the national authority. No objects within the circle of political economy so richly repay the expense bestowed on them; there are none the utility of which is more universally ascertained and acknowledged; none that do more honor to the governments whose wise and enlarged patriotism duly appreciates them. Nor is there any country which presents a field where nature invites more the art of man to complete her own work for his accommodation and benefit. These considerations are strengthened, moreover, by the political effect of these facilities for intercommunication in bringing and binding more closely together the various parts of our extended confederacy. Whilst the States individually, with a laudable enterprise and emulation, avail themselves of their local advantages by new roads, by navigable canals, and by improving the streams susceptible of navigation, the General Government is the more urged to similar undertakings, requiring a national jurisdiction and national means, by the prospect of thus systematically completing so inestimable a work; and it is a happy reflection that any defect of constitutional authority which may be encountered can be supplied in a mode which the Constitution itself has providently pointed out.

The present is a favorable season also for bringing again into view the establishment of a national seminary of learning within the District of Columbia, and with means drawn from the property therein, subject to the authority of the General Government. Such an institution claims the patronage of Congress as a monument of their solicitude for the advancement of knowledge, without which the blessings of liberty can not be fully enjoyed or long preserved; as a model instructive in the formation of other seminaries; as a nursery of enlightened preceptors, and as a central resort of youth and genius from every part of their country, diffusing on their return examples of those national feelings, those liberal sentiments, and those congenial manners which contribute cement to our Union and strength to the great political fabric of which that is the foundation.

In closing this communication I ought not to repress a sensibility, in which you will unite, to the happy lot of our country and to the goodness of a superintending Providence, to which we are indebted for it. Whilst other portions of mankind are laboring under the distresses of war or struggling with adversity in other forms, the United States are in the tranquil enjoyment of prosperous and honorable peace. In reviewing the scenes through which it has been attained we can rejoice in the proofs given that our political institutions, founded in human rights and framed for their preservation, are equal to the severest trials of war, as well as adapted to the ordinary periods of repose. As fruits of this experience and of the reputation acquired by the American arms on the land and on the water, the nation finds itself possessed of a growing respect abroad and of a just confidence in itself, which are among the best pledges for its peaceful career. Under other aspects of our country the strongest features of its flourishing condition are seen in a population rapidly increasing on a territory as productive as it is extensive; in a general industry and fertile ingenuity which find their ample rewards, and in an affluent revenue which admits a reduction of the public burdens without withdrawing the means of sustaining the public credit, of gradually discharging the public debt, of providing for the necessary defensive and precautionary establishments, and of patronizing in every authorized mode undertakings conducive to the aggregate wealth and individual comfort of our citizens.

It remains for the guardians of the public welfare to persevere in that justice and good will toward other nations which invite a return of these sentiments toward the United States; to cherish institutions which guarantee their safety and their liberties, civil and religious; and to combine with a liberal system of foreign commerce an improvement of the national advantages and a protection and extension of the independent resources of our highly favored and happy country.

In all measures having such objects my faithful cooperation ill be afforded.

JAMES MADISON.

SPECIAL MESSAGES.

WASHINGTON, *December 6, 1815.*

To the Senate of the United States:

I lay before the Senate, for their consideration and advice as to a ratification, a treaty of peace with the Dey of Algiers concluded on the 30th day of June, 1815, with a letter relating to the same from the American commissioners to the Secretary of State.

JAMES MADISON.

DECEMBER 6, 1815.

To the Senate of the United States:

I lay before the Senate, for their consideration and advice as to a ratification, a convention to regulate the commerce between the United States and Great Britain, signed by their respective plenipotentiaries on the 3d of July last, with letters relating to the same from the American plenipotentiaries to the Secretary of State, and also the declaration with which it is the intention of the British Government to accompany the exchange of the ratification of the convention.

JAMES MADISON.

WASHINGTON, *December 6, 1815.*

To the Senate of the United States:

I lay before the Senate, for their consideration and advice as to a ratification, treaties which have been concluded with the following Indian tribes, viz: Iaway tribe, Kickapoo tribe, Poutawatamie, Siouxs of the Lakes, Piankeshaw tribe, Siouxs of the River St. Peters, Great and Little Osage tribes, Yancton tribe, Mahas, Fox tribe, Teeton, Sac Nation, Kanzas tribe, Chippewa, Ottawa, Potawatamie, Shawanoe, Wyandot, Miami, Delaware, and Seneca.

I communicate also the letters from the commissioners on the part of the United States relating to their proceedings on those occasions.

JAMES MADISON.

WASHINGTON, *December 11, 1815.*

To the Senate of the United States:

I transmit the original of the convention between the United States and Great Britain, as signed by their respective plenipotentiaries, on the

3d day of July last, a copy of which was laid before the Senate on the 5th instant.

I t ansmit also a copy of the late treaty of peace with Algiers, as certified by one of the commissioners of the United States, an office copy of which was laid before the Senate on the 5th instant, the original of the treaty not having been received.

JAMES MADISON.

DECEMBER 23, 1815.

To the Senate and House of Representatives of the United States:

I lay before Congress copies of a proclamation notifying the convention concluded with Great Britain on the 3d day of July last, and that the same has been duly ratified; and I recommend to Congress such legislative provisions as the convention may call for on the part of the United States.

JAMES MADISON.

JANUARY 18, 1816.

To the Senate and House of Representatives of the United States:

The accompanying extract from the occurrences at Fort Jackson in August, 1814, during the negotiation of a treaty with the Indians shows that the friendly Creeks, wishing to give to General Jackson, Benjamin Hawkins, and others a national mark of their gratitude and regard, conveyed to them, respectively, a donation of land, with a request that the grant might be duly confirmed by the Government of the United States.

Taking into consideration the peculiar circumstances of the case, the expediency of indulging the Indians in wishes which they associated with the treaty signed by them, and that the case involves an inviting opportunity for bestowing on an officer who has rendered such illustrious services to his country a token of its sensibility to them, the inducement to which can not be diminished by the delicacy and disinterestedness of his proposal to transfer the benefit from himself, I recommend to Congress that provision be made for carrying into effect the wishes and request of the Indians as expressed by them.

JAMES MADISON.

FEBRUARY 6, 1816.

To the Senate and House of Representatives of the United States:

It is represented that the lands in the Michigan Territory designated by law toward satisfying land bounties promised the soldiers of the late army are so covered with swamps and lakes, or otherwise unfit for cultivation, that a very inconsiderable proportion can be applied to the intended grants. I recommend, therefore, that other lands be designated by Congress for the purpose of supplying the deficiency.

JAMES MADISON.

MARCH 5, 1816.

To the Senate of the United States:

In compliance with the resolution of the Senate of the 2d instant, they are informed that great losses having been sustained by citizens of the United States from unjust seizures and confiscations of their property by the late Government of Naples, it was deemed expedient that indemnification should be claimed by a special mission for that purpose. The occasion may be proper, also, for securing the use and accommodations of the Neapolitan ports, which may at any time be needed by the public ships of the United States, and for obtaining relief for the American commerce from the disadvantageous and unequal regulations now operating against it in that Kingdom.

JAMES MADISON.

MARCH 9, 1816.

To the Senate and House of Representatives of the United States:

I lay before Congress a statement of the militia of the United States according to the latest returns received by the Department of War.

JAMES MADISON.

APRIL 11, 1816.

To the Senate and House of Representatives of the United States:

With a view to the more convenient arrangement of the important and growing business connected with the grant of exclusive rights to inventors and authors, I recommend the establishment of a distinct office within the Department of State to be charged therewith, under a director with a salary adequate to his services, and with the privilege of franking communications by mail from and to the office. I recommend also that further restraints be imposed on the issue of patents to wrongful claimants, and further guards provided against fraudulent exactions of fees by persons possessed of patents.

JAMES MADISON.

APRIL 16, 1816.

To the Senate and House of Representatives of the United States:

I lay before Congress copies of a convention concluded between the United States and the Cherokee Indians on the 2d day of March last, as the same has been duly ratified and proclaimed; and I recommend that such provision be made by Congress as the stipulations therein contained may require.

JAMES MADISON.

APRIL 17, 1816.

To the Senate of the United States:

It being presumed that further information may have changed the views of the Senate relative to the importance and expediency of a mission to Naples for the purpose of negotiating indemnities to our citizens for spoliations committed by the Neapolitan Government, I nominate William Pinkney, envoy extraordinary and minister plenipotentiary to Russia, to be minister plenipotentiary to Naples, specially charged with that trust.

JAMES MADISON.

PROCLAMATIONS.

BY THE PRESIDENT OF THE UNITED STATES OF AMERICA.

A PROCLAMATION.

Whereas it has been represented that many uninformed or evil-disposed persons have taken possession of or made a settlement on the public lands of the United States which have not been previously sold, ceded, or leased by the United States, or the claim to which lands by such persons has not been previously recognized or confirmed by the United States, which possession or settlement is by the act of Congress passed on the 3d day of March, 1807, expressly prohibited; and

Whereas the due execution of the said act of Congress, as well as the general interest, requires that such illegal practices should be promptly repressed:

Now, therefore, I, James Madison, President of the United States, have thought proper to issue my proclamation commanding and strictly enjoining all persons who have unlawfully taken possession of or made any settlement on the public lands as aforesaid forthwith to remove therefrom; and I do hereby further command and enjoin the marshal, or officer acting as marshal, in any State or Territory where such possession shall have been taken or settlement made to remove, from and after the 10th day of March, 1816, all or any of the said unlawful occupants; and to effect the said service I do hereby authorize the employment of such military force as may become necessary in pursuance of the provisions of the act of Congress aforesaid, warning the offenders, moreover, that they will be prosecuted in all such other ways as the law directs.

In testimony whereof I have caused the seal of the United States of America to be affixed to these presents, and signed the same with my hand.

[SEAL.]   Done at the city of Washington, the 12th day of December, A. D. 1815, and of the Independence of the said United States of America the fortieth.   JAMES MADISON.

By the President:
    JAMES MONROE,
        Secretary of State.

[From Niles's Weekly Register, vol. 10, p. 208.]

BY THE PRESIDENT OF THE UNITED STATES.

A PROCLAMATION.

Whereas by the act entitled "An act granting bounties in land and extra pay to certain Canadian volunteers," passed the 5th March, 1816, it was enacted that the locations of the land warrants of the said volunteers should "be subject to such regulations as to priority of choice and manner of location as the President of the United States shall direct:"

Wherefore I, James Madison, President of the United States, in conformity with the provisions of the act before recited, do hereby make known that the land warrants of the said Canadian volunteers may be located agreeably to the said act at the land offices at Vincennes or Jeffersonville, in the Indiana Territory, on the first Monday in June next, with the registers of the said land offices; that the warrantees may, in person or by their attorneys or other legal representatives, in the presence of the register and receiver of the said land district, draw lots for the priority of location; and that should any of the warrants not appear for location on that day they may be located afterwards, according to their priority of presentation, the locations in the district of Vincennes to be made at Vincennes and the locations in the district of Jeffersonville to be made at Jeffersonville.

Given under my hand the 1st day of May, 1816.

                                                JAMES MADISON.
By the President:
    JOSIAH MEIGS,
        Commissioner of the General Land Office.

EIGHTH ANNUAL MESSAGE.

DECEMBER 3, 1816.

Fellow-Citizens of the Senate and of the House of Representatives:

In reviewing the present state of our country, our attention can not be withheld from the effect produced by peculiar seasons which have very generally impaired the annual gifts of the earth and threatened scarcity in particular districts. Such, however, is the variety of soils, of climates, and of products within our extensive limits that the aggregate resources for subsistence are more than sufficient for the aggregate wants. And as far as an economy of consumption, more than usual, may be necessary, our thankfulness is due to Providence for what is far more than a compensation, in the remarkable health which has distinguished the present year.

Amidst the advantages which have succeeded the peace of Europe, and that of the United States with Great Britain, in a general invigoration of industry among us and in the extension of our commerce, the value of which is more and more disclosing itself to commercial nations, it is to be regretted that a depression is experienced by particular branches of our manufactures and by a portion of our navigation. As the first proceeds in an essential degree from an excess of imported merchandise, which carries a check in its own tendency, the cause in its present extent can not be of very long duration. The evil will not, however, be viewed by Congress without a recollection that manufacturing establishments, if suffered to sink too low or languish too long, may not revive after the causes shall have ceased, and that in the vicissitudes of human affairs situations may recur in which a dependence on foreign sources for indispensable supplies may be among the most serious embarrassments.

The depressed state of our navigation is to be ascribed in a material degree to its exclusion from the colonial ports of the nation most extensively connected with us in commerce, and from the indirect operation of that exclusion.

Previous to the late convention at London between the United States and Great Britain the relative state of the navigation laws of the two countries, growing out of the treaty of 1794, had given to the British navigation a material advantage over the American in the intercourse between the American ports and British ports in Europe. The convention of London equalized the laws of the two countries relating to those ports, leaving the intercourse between our ports and the ports of the British colonies subject, as before, to the respective regulations of the parties. The British Government enforcing now regulations which prohibit a trade between its colonies and the United States in American vessels, whilst they permit a trade in British vessels, the American navigation loses accordingly, and the loss is augmented by the advantage which is given to the British competition over the American in the navigation between our ports and British ports in Europe by the circuitous voyages enjoyed by the one and not enjoyed by the other.

The reasonableness of the rule of reciprocity applied to one branch of the commercial intercourse has been pressed on our part as equally applicable to both branches; but it is ascertained that the British cabinet declines all negotiation on the subject, with a disavowal, however, of any disposition to view in an unfriendly light whatever countervailing regulations the United States may oppose to the regulations of which they complain. The wisdom of the Legislature will decide on the course which, under these circumstances, is prescribed by a joint regard to the amicable relations between the two nations and to the just interests of the United States.

I have the satisfaction to state, generally, that we remain in amity with foreign powers.

An occurrence has indeed taken place in the Gulf of Mexico which, if sanctioned by the Spanish Government, may make an exception as to that power. According to the report of our naval commander on that station, one of our public armed vessels was attacked by an overpowering force under a Spanish commander, and the American flag, with the officers and crew, insulted in a manner calling for prompt reparation. This has been demanded. In the meantime a frigate and a smaller vessel of war have been ordered into that Gulf for the protection of our commerce. It would be improper to omit that the representative of His Catholic Majesty in the United States lost no time in giving the strongest assurances that no hostile order could have emanated from his Government, and that it will be as ready to do as to expect whatever the nature of the case and the friendly relations of the two countries shall be found to require.

The posture of our affairs with Algiers at the present moment is not known. The Dey, drawing pretexts from circumstances for which the United States were not answerable, addressed a letter to this Government declaring the treaty last concluded with him to have been annulled by our violation of it, and presenting as the alternative war or a renewal of the former treaty, which stipulated, among other things, an annual tribute. The answer, with an explicit declaration that the United States preferred war to tribute, required his recognition and observance of the treaty last made, which abolishes tribute and the slavery of our captured citizens. The result of the answer has not been received. Should he renew his warfare on our commerce, we rely on the protection it will find in our naval force actually in the Mediterranean.

With the other Barbary States our affairs have undergone no change.

The Indian tribes within our limits appear also disposed to remain at peace. From several of them purchases of lands have been made particularly favorable to the wishes and security of our frontier settlements, as well as to the general interests of the nation. In some instances the titles, though not supported by due proof, and clashing those of one tribe with the claims of another, have been extinguished by double purchases, the benevolent policy of the United States preferring the augmented expense to the hazard of doing injustice or to the enforcement of justice against a feeble and untutored people by means involving or threatening an effusion of blood. I am happy to add that the tranquillity which has been restored among the tribes themselves, as well as between them and our own population, will favor the resumption of the work of civilization which had made an encouraging progress among some tribes, and that the facility is increasing for extending that divided and individual ownership, which exists now in movable property only, to the soil itself, and of thus establishing in the culture and improvement of it the true foundation for a transit from the habits of the savage to the arts and comforts of social life.

As a subject of the highest importance to the national welfare, I must again earnestly recommend to the consideration of Congress a reorganization of the militia on a plan which will form it into classes according to the periods of life more or less adapted to military services. An efficient militia is authorized and contemplated by the Constitution and required by the spirit and safety of free government. The present organization of our militia is universally regarded as less efficient than it ought to be made, and no organization can be better calculated to give to it its due force than a classification which will assign the foremost place in the defense of the country to that portion of its citizens whose activity and animation best enable them to rally to its standard. Besides the consideration that a time of peace is the time when the change can be made with most convenience and equity, it will now be aided by the experience of a recent war in which the militia bore so interesting a part.

Congress will call to mind that no adequate provision has yet been made for the uniformity of weights and measures also contemplated by the Constitution. The great utility of a standard fixed in its nature and founded on the easy rule of decimal proportions is sufficiently obvious. It led the Government at an early stage to preparatory steps for introducing it, and a completion of the work will be a just title to the public gratitude.

The importance which I have attached to the establishment of a university within this District on a scale and for objects worthy of the American nation induces me to renew my recommendation of it to the favorable consideration of Congress. And I particularly invite again their attention to the expediency of exercising their existing powers, and, where necessary, of resorting to the prescribed mode of enlarging them, in order to effectuate a comprehensive system of roads and canals, such as will have the effect of drawing more closely together every part of our country by promoting intercourse and improvements and by increasing the share of every part in the common stock of national prosperity.

Occurrences having taken place which shew that the statutory provisions for the dispensation of criminal justice are deficient in relation both to places and to persons under the exclusive cognizance of the national authority, an amendment of the law embracing such cases will merit the earliest attention of the Legislature. It will be a seasonable occasion also for inquiring how far legislative interposition may be further requisite in providing penalties for offenses designated in the Constitution or in the statutes, and to which either no penalties are annexed or none with sufficient certainty. And I submit to the wisdom of Congress whether a more enlarged revisal of the criminal code be not expedient for the purpose of mitigating in certain cases penalties which were adopted into it antecedent to experiment and examples which justify and recommend a more lenient policy.

The United States, having been the first to abolish within the extent of their authority the transportation of the natives of Africa into slavery, by prohibiting the introduction of slaves and by punishing their citizens participating in the traffic, can not but be gratified at the progress made by concurrent efforts of other nations toward a general suppression of so great an evil. They must feel at the same time the greater solicitude to give the fullest efficacy to their own regulations. With that view, the interposition of Congress appears to be required by the violations and evasions which it is suggested are chargeable on unworthy citizens who mingle in the slave trade under foreign flags and with foreign ports, and by collusive importations of slaves into the United States through adjoining ports and territories. I present the subject to Congress with a full assurance of their disposition to apply all the remedy which can be afforded by an amendment of the law. The regulations which were intended to guard against abuses of a kindred character in the trade between the several States ought also to be rendered more effectual for their humane object.

To these recommendations I add, for the consideration of Congress, the expediency of a remodification of the judiciary establishment, and of an additional department in the executive branch of the Government.

The first is called for by the accruing business which necessarily swells the duties of the Federal courts, and by the great and widening space within which justice is to be dispensed by them. The time seems to have arrived which claims for members of the Supreme Court a relief from itinerary fatigues, incompatible as well with the age which a portion of them will always have attained as with the researches and preparations which are due to their stations and to the juridical reputation of their country. And considerations equally cogent require a more convenient organization of the subordinate tribunals, which may be accomplished without an objectionable increase of the number or expense of the judges.

The extent and variety of executive business also accumulating with the progress of our country and its growing population call for an additional department, to be charged with duties now overburdening other departments and with such as have not been annexed to any department.

The course of experience recommends, as another improvement in the executive establishment, that the provision for the station of Attorney-General, whose residence at the seat of Government, official connections with it, and the management of the public business before the judiciary preclude an extensive participation in professional emoluments, be made more adequate to his services and his relinquishments, and that, with a view to his reasonable accommodation and to a proper depository of his official opinions and proceedings, there be included in the provision the usual appurtenances to a public office.

In directing the legislative attention to the state of the finances it is a subject of great gratification to find that even within the short period which has elapsed since the return of peace the revenue has far exceeded all the current demands upon the Treasury, and that under any probable diminution of its future annual products which the vicissitudes of commerce may occasion it will afford an ample fund for the effectual and early extinguishment of the public debt. It has been estimated that during the year 1816 the actual receipts of revenue at the Treasury, including the balance at the commencement of the year, and excluding the proceeds of loans and Treasury notes, will amount to about the sum of $47,000,000; that during the same year the actual payments at the Treasury, including the payment of the arrearages of the War Department as well as the payment of a considerable excess beyond the annual appropriations, will amount to about the sum of $38,000,000, and that consequently at the close of the year there will be a surplus in the Treasury of about the sum of $9,000,000.

The operations of the Treasury continued to be obstructed by difficulties arising from the condition of the national currency, but they have nevertheless been effectual to a beneficial extent in the reduction of the public debt and the establishment of the public credit. The floating debt of Treasury notes and temporary loans will soon be entirely discharged. The aggregate of the funded debt, composed of debts incurred during the wars of 1776 and 1812, has been estimated with reference to the 1st of January next at a sum not exceeding $110,000,000. The ordinary annual expenses of the Government for the maintenance of all its institutions, civil, military, and naval, have been estimated at a sum less than $20,000,000, and the permanent revenue to be derived from all the existing sources has been estimated at a sum of about $25,000,000.

Upon this general view of the subject it is obvious that there is only wanting to the fiscal prosperity of the Government the restoration of an uniform medium of exchange. The resources and the faith of the nation, displayed in the system which Congress has established, insure respect and confidence both at home and abroad. The local accumulations of the revenue have already enabled the Treasury to meet the public engagements in the local currency of most of the States, and it is expected that the same cause will produce the same effect throughout the Union; but for the interests of the community at large, as well as for the purposes of the Treasury, it is essential that the nation should possess a currency of equal value, credit, and use wherever it may circulate. The Constitu-

GENERAL HARRISON ROUTS BRITISH AND INDIANS AT THAMES RIVER, CANADA

BATTLE OF THE THAMES, CANADA

October 5, 1813

This picture illustrates a phase of the War of 1812 which is but little known. The British never hesitated to employ the tomahawk and scalping knife of the redskin. In fact, they constantly incited the Indians to repossess themselves of territory which had been ceded to us and in that way retard our settlement of the West and keep the borderers in fear of massacre.

Tecumseh, the ambitious chieftain, whose forces had been routed by Harrison at Tippecanoe, made allies of the British. His 1200 warriors retreated with 800 British regulars before the advance of 3000 Americans under Wm. Henry Harrison. Tecumseh induced the British commander to halt and give battle at a point eight miles north of the Thames. They were completely routed, Tecumseh himself being one of the killed. The picture represents him dying by a pistol shot. Six hundred of the British were captured, 18 killed and 26 wounded. The American loss in killed and wounded was about the same. The bodies of 33 Indians were found. See the index article in volume eleven, entitled "Thames, Canada, Battle of."

tion has intrusted Congress exclusively with the power of creating and regulating a currency of that description, and the measures which were taken during the last session in execution of the power give every promise of success. The Bank of the United States has been organized under auspices the most favorable, and can not fail to be an important auxiliary to those measures.

For a more enlarged view of the public finances, with a view o. the measures pursued by the Treasury Department previous to the resignation of the late Secretary, I transmit an extract from the last report of that officer. Congress will perceive in it ample proofs of the solid foundation on which the financial prosperity of the nation rests, and will do justice to the distinguished ability and successful exertions with which the duties of the Department were executed during a period remarkable for its difficulties and its peculiar perplexities.

The period of my retiring from the public service being at little distance, I shall find no occasion more proper than the present for expressing to my fellow-citizens my deep sense of the continued confidence and kind support which I have received from them. My grateful recollection of these distinguished marks of their favorable regard can never cease, and with the consciousness that, if I have not served my country with greater ability, I have served it with a sincere devotion will accompany me as a source of unfailing gratification.

Happily, I shall carry with me from the public theater other sources, which those who love their country most will best appreciate. I shall behold it blessed with tranquillity and prosperity at home and with peace and respect abroad. I can indulge the proud reflection that the American people have reached in safety and success their fortieth year as an independent nation; that for nearly an entire generation they have had experience of their present Constitution, the offspring of their undisturbed deliberations and of their free choice; that they have found it to bear the trials of adverse as well as prosperous circumstances; to contain in its combination of the federate and elective principles a reconcilement of public strength with individual liberty, of national power for the defense of national rights with a security against wars of injustice, of ambition, and of vainglory in the fundamental provision which subjects all questions of war to the will of the nation itself, which is to pay its costs and feel its calamities. Nor is it less a peculiar felicity of this Constitution, so dear to us all, that it is found to be capable, without losing its vital energies, of expanding itself over a spacious territory with the increase and expansion of the community for whose benefit it was established.

And may I not be allowed to add to this gratifying spectacle that I shall read in the character of the American people, in their devotion to true liberty and to the Constitution which is its palladium, sure presages that the destined career of my country will exhibit a Government pursuing the public good as its sole object, and regulating its means by the great principles consecrated in its charter and by those moral principles to which they are so well allied; a Government which watches over the purity of elections, the freedom of speech and of the press, the trial by jury, and the equal interdict against encroachments and compacts between religion and the state; which maintains inviolably the maxims of public faith, the security of persons and property, and encourages in every authorized mode that general diffusion of knowledge which guarantees to public liberty its permanency and to those who possess the blessing the true enjoyment of it; a Government which avoids intrusions on the internal repose of other nations, and repels them from its own; which does justice to all nations with a readiness equal to the firmness with which it requires justice from them; and which, whilst it refines its domestic code from every ingredient not congenial with the precepts of an enlightened age and the sentiments of a virtuous people, seeks by appeals to reason and by its liberal examples to infuse into the law which governs the civilized world a spirit which may diminish the frequency or circumscribe the calamities of war, and meliorate the social and beneficent relations of peace; a Government, in a word, whose conduct within and without may bespeak the most noble of all ambitions—that of promoting peace on earth and good will to man.

These contemplations, sweetening the remnant of my days, will animate my prayers for the happiness of my beloved country, and a perpetuity of the institutions under which it is enjoyed.

JAMES MADISON.

SPECIAL MESSAGES.

DECEMBER 6, 1816.

To the Senate and House of Representatives of the United States:

The ninth section of the act passed at the last session of Congress "to authorize the payment for property lost, captured, or destroyed by the enemy while in the military service of the United States, and for other purposes," having received a construction giving to it a scope of great and uncertain extent, I thought it proper that proceedings relative to claims under that part of the act should be suspended until Congress should have an opportunity of defining more precisely the cases contemplated by them. With that view I now recommend the subject to their consideration. They will have an opportunity at the same time of considering how far other provisions of the act may be rendered more clear and precise in their import.

JAMES MADISON.

DECEMBER 10, 1816.

To the Senate of the United States:

I lay before the Senate, for their consideration and advice as to a ratification, treaties concluded with the several Indian tribes according to the following statement:

A LIST OF INDIAN TRIBES WITH WHOM TREATIES HAVE BEEN MADE SINCE THE LAST SESSION OF CONGRESS.

Weas and Kickapoos tribes of Indians.—Treaty concluded at Fort Harrison between Benjamin Parke and the chiefs and headmen of those tribes the 4th June, 1816.

Ottawas, Chippewas, and Pottowotomees.—Treaty concluded at St. Louis between Governors Clarke, Edwards, and Colonel Choteau and the chiefs and headmen of those tribes on the 24th August, 1816.

Winnebago tribes.—Made by the same persons on part United States and the headmen of this tribe at St. Louis 3d June, 1816.

Sacks of Rock River.—Made by same at St. Louis 13th May, 1816.

Siouxs composing three tribes, the Siouxs of the Leaf, the Siouxs of the Broad Leaf, and the Siouxs who Shoot on the Pine-tops.—Made and concluded by the same at St. Louis 1st June, 1816.

Chickasaw tribe.—Treaty made by General Jackson, David Merrewether, esq., and Jesse Franklin, esq., and the headmen of that nation at Chickasaw council house 20th September, 1816.

Cherokee tribe.—Treaty made by General Jackson, David Merrewether, esq., and Jesse Franklin, esq., and the headmen of that nation at Turkey Town on the 4th October, 1816.

Choctaw tribe.—Treaty made by General John Coffee, John Rhea, and John McKee, esquires, and the headmen and warriors of that nation at the Choctaw trading house on the 24th of October, 1816.

JAMES MADISON.

DECEMBER 13, 1816.

To the Senate of the United States:

A treaty of commerce between the United States and the King of Sweden and Norway having been concluded and signed on the 4th day of September last by their plenipotentiaries, I lay the same before the Senate for their consideration and advice as to a ratification.

JAMES MADISON.

DECEMBER 21, 1816.

To the House of Representatives of the United States:

In compliance with the resolution of the House of Representatives of the 6th instant, I transmit to them the proceedings of the commissioner appointed under the act "to authorize the payment for property lost, captured, or destroyed by the enemy while in the military service of the United States, and for other purposes" as reported by the commissioner to the Department of War.

JAMES MADISON.

DECEMBER 26, 1816.

To the Senate and House of Representatives of the United States:

It is found that the existing laws have not the efficacy necessary to prevent violations of the obligations of the United States as a nation at peace toward belligerent parties and other unlawful acts on the high seas by armed vessels equipped within the waters of the United States.

With a view to maintain more effectually the respect due to the laws, to the character, and to the neutral and pacific relations of the United States, I recommend to the consideration of Congress the expediency of such further legislative provisions as may be requisite for detaining vessels actually equipped, or in a course of equipment, with a warlike force within the jurisdiction of the United States, or, as the case may be, for obtaining from the owners or commanders of such vessels adequate securities against the abuse of their armaments, with the exceptions in such provisions proper for the cases of merchant vessels furnished with the defensive armaments usual on distant and dangerous expeditions, and of a private commerce in military stores permitted by our laws, and which the law of nations does not require the United States to prohibit.

JAMES MADISON.

JANUARY 25, 1817.

To the Senate and House of Representatives of the United States:

I lay before Congress copies of ratified treaties between the United States and the following Indian tribes:

First. The Wea and Kickapoo.

Second. The united tribes of Ottawas, Chippawas, and Potowotomies residing on the Illinois and Melwakee rivers and their waters and on the southwestern parts of Lake Michigan.

Third. That portion of the Winnebago tribe or nation residing on the Ouisconsin River.

Fourth. The Sacs of Rock River and the adjacent country.

Fifth. Eight bands of the Siouxs, composing the three tribes called the Siouxs of the Leaf, the Siouxs of the Broad Leaf, and the Siouxs who Shoot in the Pine Tops.

Sixth. The Chickasaw tribe of Indians.

Seventh. The Cherokee tribe of Indians.

Eighth. The Chactaw tribe of Indians.

Congress will take into consideration how far legislative provisions may be necessary for carrying into effect stipulations contained in the said treaties.

JAMES MADISON.

JANUARY 31, 1817.

To the Senate and House of Representatives of the United States:

The envoy extraordinary and minister plenipotentiary of His Most Christian Majesty having renewed, under special instructions from his Government, the claim of the representative of Baron de Beaumarchais for 1,000,000 livres, which were debited to him in the settlement of his accounts with the United States, I lay before Congress copies of the memoir on that subject addressed by the said envoy to the Secretary of State.

Considering that the sum of which the million of livres in question made a part was a gratuitous grant from the French Government to the United States, and the declaration of that Government that that part of the grant was put into the hands of M. de Beaumarchais as its agent, not as the agent of the United States, and was duly accounted for by him to the French Government; considering also the concurring opinions of two Attorneys-General of the United States that the said debit was not legally sustainable in behalf of the United States, I recommend the case to the favorable attention of the Legislature, whose authority alone can finally decide on it.   JAMES MADISON.

FEBRUARY 3, 1817.

To the Senate and House of Representatives of the United States:

The Government of Great Britain, induced by the posture of the relations with the United States which succeeded the conclusion of the recent commercial convention, issued an order on the 17th day of August, 1815, discontinuing the discriminating duties payable in British ports on American vessels and their cargoes. It was not until the 22d of December following that a corresponding discontinuance of discriminating duties on British vessels and their cargoes in American ports took effect under the authority vested in the Executive by the act of March, 1816. During the period between those two dates there was consequently a failure of reciprocity or equality in the existing regulations of the two countries. I recommend to the consideration of Congress the expediency of paying to the British Government the amount of the duties remitted during the period in question to citizens of the United States, subject to a deduction of the amount of whatever discriminating duties may have commenced in British ports after the signature of that convention and been collected previous to the 17th of August, 1815.

JAMES MADISON.

FEBRUARY 6, 1817.

To the Senate and House of Representatives of the United States:

On comparing the fourth section of the act of Congress passed March 31, 1814, providing for the indemnification of certain claimants of public lands in the Mississippi Territory, with the article of agreement and cession between the United States and State of Georgia, bearing date April 30, 1802, it appears that the engagements entered into with the claimants interfere with the rights and interests secured to that State. I recommend to Congress that provision be made by law for payments to the State of Georgia equal to the amount of Mississippi stock which shall be paid into the Treasury until the stipulated sum of $1,250,000 shall be completed.

JAMES MADISON.

VETO MESSAGE.

MARCH 3, 1817.

To the House of Representatives of the United States:

Having considered the bill this day presented to me entitled "An act to set apart and pledge certain funds for internal improvements," and which sets apart and pledges funds "for constructing roads and canals, and improving the navigation of water courses, in order to facilitate, promote, and give security to internal commerce among the several States, and to render more easy and less expensive the means and provisions for the common defense," I am constrained by the insuperable difficulty I feel in reconciling the bill with the Constitution of the United States to return it with that objection to the House of Representatives, in which it originated.

The legislative powers vested in Congress are specified and enumerated in the eighth section of the first article of the Constitution, and it does not appear that the power proposed to be exercised by the bill is among the enumerated powers, or that it falls by any just interpretation within the power to make laws necessary and proper for carrying into execution those or other powers vested by the Constitution in the Government of the United States.

"The power to regulate commerce among the several States" can not include a power to construct roads and canals, and to improve the navigation of water courses in order to facilitate, promote, and secure such a commerce without a latitude of construction departing from the ordinary import of the terms strengthened by the known inconveniences which doubtless led to the grant of this remedial power to Congress.

To refer the power in question to the clause "to provide for the common defense and general welfare" would be contrary to the established and consistent rules of interpretation, as rendering the special and careful enumeration of powers which follow the clause nugatory and improper.

Such a view of the Constitution would have the effect of giving to Congress a general power of legislation instead of the defined and limited one hitherto understood to belong to them, the terms "common defense and general welfare" embracing every object and act within the purview of a legislative trust. It would have the effect of subjecting both the Constitution and laws of the several States in all cases not specifically exempted to be superseded by laws of Congress, it being expressly declared "that the Constitution of the United States and laws made in pursuance thereof shall be the supreme law of the land, and the judges of every State shall be bound thereby, anything in the constitution or laws of any State to the contrary notwithstanding." Such a view of the Constitution, finally, would have the effect of excluding the judicial authority of the United States from its participation in guarding the boundary between the legislative powers of the General and the State Governments, inasmuch as questions relating to the general welfare, being questions of policy and expediency, are unsusceptible of judicial cognizance and decision.

A restriction of the power "to provide for the common defense and general welfare" to cases which are to be provided for by the expenditure of money would still leave within the legislative power of Congress all the great and most important measures of Government, money being the ordinary and necessary means of carrying them into execution.

If a general power to construct roads and canals, and to improve the navigation of water courses, with the train of powers incident thereto, be not possessed by Congress, the assent of the States in the mode provided in the bill can not confer the power. The only cases in which the consent and cession of particular States can extend the power of Congress are those specified and provided for in the Constitution.

I am not unaware of the great importance of roads and canals and the improved navigation of water courses, and that a power in the National Legislature to provide for them might be exercised with signal advantage to the general prosperity. But seeing that such a power is not expressly given by the Constitution, and believing that it can not be deduced from any part of it without an inadmissible latitude of construction and a reliance on insufficient precedents; believing also that the permanent success of the Constitution depends on a definite partition of powers between the General and the State Governments, and that no adequate landmarks would be left by the constructive extension of the powers of Congress as proposed in the bill, I have no option but to withhold my signature from it, and to cherishing the hope that its beneficial objects may be attained by a resort for the necessary powers to the same wisdom and virtue in the nation which established the Constitution in its actual form and providently marked out in the instrument itself a safe and practicable mode of improving it as experience might suggest.

JAMES MADISON.

PROCLAMATION.

[From Annals of Congress, Fourteenth Congress, second session, 218.]

WASHINGTON, *January 1, 1817.*

To the Senators of the United States, respectively.

SIR: Objects interesting to the United States requiring that the Senate should be in session on the 4th of March next to receive such communications as may be made to it on the part of the Executive, your attendance in the Senate Chamber in this city on that day is accordingly requested.

JAMES MADISON.

ERRATA.

[These proclamations were not found in time for insertion in their proper places; see pp. 91 and 170.]

PROCLAMATION.

PHILADELPHIA, *March 1, 1791.*

The President of the United States to the President of the Senate:

Certain matters touching the public good requiring that the Senate shall be convened on Friday, the 4th instant, I have desired their attendance, as I do yours, by these presents, at the Senate Chamber in Philadelphia on that day, then and there to receive and deliberate on such communications as shall be made to you on my part.

G? WASHINGTON.

PROCLAMATION.

UNITED STATES, *March 3, 1795.*

The President of the United States to ——, Senator for the State of ——:

Certain matters touching the public good requiring that the Senate shall be convened on Monday, the 8th of June next, you are desired to attend the Senate Chamber in Philadelphia on that day, then and there to receive and deliberate on such communications as shall be made to you on my part.

G? WASHINGTON.

James Monroe

March 4, 1817, to March 4, 1825

SEE VOLUME XI.

Volume eleven is not only an index to the other volumes, not only a key that unlocks the treasures of the entire publication, but it is in itself an alphabetically arranged brief history or story of the great controlling events constituting the History of the United States.

Under its proper alphabetical classification the story is told of every great subject referred to by any of the Presidents in their official Messages, and at the end of each story the official utterances of the Presidents themselves are cited upon the subject, so that you may readily turn to the page in the body of the work itself for this original information.

Next to the possession of knowledge is the ability to turn at will to where knowledge is to be found.

HOME AT LOUDON COUNTY, VIRGINIA, OF

JAMES MONROE

With official portrait engraved from copy of original in steel

James Monroe.

James Monroe

JAMES MONROE was born April 28, 1758, in Westmoreland County, Va. He was the son of Spence Monroe and Elizabeth Jones, both natives of Virginia. When in his eighteenth year he enlisted as a private soldier in the Army to fight for independence; was in several battles, and was wounded in the engagement at Trenton; was promoted to the rank of captain of infantry. During 1777 and 1778 he acted as aid to Lord Stirling, and distinguished himself. He studied law under the direction of Thomas Jefferson, then governor of Virginia, who in 1780 appointed him to visit the army in South Carolina on an important mission. In 1782 he was elected to the Virginia assembly by the county of King George, and was by that body chosen a member of the executive council. The next year he was chosen a delegate to the Continental Congress, and remained a member until 1786; while a member he married a Miss Kortright, of New York City. Retiring from Congress, he began the practice of law at Fredericksburg, Va., but was at once elected to the legislature. In 1788 was a delegate to the State convention assembled to consider the Federal Constitution. Was a Senator from Virginia from 1790 to 1794. In May, 1794, was appointed by Washington minister to France. He was recalled in 1796, and was again elected to the legislature. In 1799 was elected governor of Virginia. In 1802 was appointed by President Jefferson envoy extraordinary to France, and in 1803 was sent to London as the successor of Rufus King. In 1805 performed a diplomatic mission to Spain in relation to the boundary of Louisiana, returning to London the following year; returned to the United States in 1808. In 1811 was again elected governor of his State, but in the same year resigned that office to become Secretary of State under President Madison. After the capture of Washington, in 1814, he was appointed to the War Department, which position he held until 1815, without relinquishing the office of Secretary of State. He remained at the head of the Department of State until the close of Mr. Madison's term. Was elected President in 1816, and reelected in 1820, retiring March 4, 1825, to his residence in Loudoun County, Va. In 1829 was elected a member of the convention called to revise the constitution of the State, and was unanimously chosen to preside over its deliberations. He was forced by ill health to retire from office, and removed to New York to reside with his son-in-law, Mr. Samuel L. Gouverneur. He died July 4, 1831, and was buried in New York City, but in 1858 his remains were removed to Richmond, Va.

LETTER FROM THE PRESIDENT ELECT.

The President of the Senate communicated the following letter from the President elect of the United States:

CITY OF WASHINGTON, *March 1, 1817.*

Hon. JOHN GAILLARD,
    President of the Senate of the United States.

SIR: I beg leave through you to inform the honorable Senate of the United States that I propose to take the oath which the Constitution prescribes to the President of the United States before he enters on the execution of his office on Tuesday, the 4th instant, at 12 o'clock, in the Chamber of the House of Representatives.

I have the honor to be, with the greatest respect, sir, your most obedient and most humble servant,

JAMES MONROE.

FIRST INAUGURAL ADDRESS.

I should be destitute of feeling if I was not deeply affected by the strong proof which my fellow-citizens have given me of their confidence in calling me to the high office whose functions I am about to assume. As the expression of their good opinion of my conduct in the public service, I derive from it a gratification which those who are conscious of having done all that they could to merit it can alone feel. My sensibility is increased by a just estimate of the importance of the trust and of the nature and extent of its duties, with the proper discharge of which the highest interests of a great and free people are intimately connected. Conscious of my own deficiency, I cannot enter on these duties without great anxiety for the result. From a just responsibility I will never shrink, calculating with confidence that in my best efforts to promote the public welfare my motives will always be duly appreciated and my conduct be viewed with that candor and indulgence which I have experienced in other stations.

In commencing the duties of the chief executive office it has been the practice of the distinguished men who have gone before me to explain the principles which would govern them in their respective Administrations. In following their venerated example my attention is naturally drawn to the great causes which have contributed in a principal degree to produce the present happy condition of the United States. They will best explain the nature of our duties and shed much light on the policy which ought to be pursued in future.

From the commencement of our Revolution to the present day almost forty years have elapsed, and from the establishment of this Constitution twenty-eight. Through this whole term the Government has been what may emphatically be called self-government. And what has been the effect? To whatever object we turn our attention, whether it relates to our foreign or domestic concerns, we find abundant cause to felicitate ourselves in the excellence of our institutions. During a period fraught with difficulties and marked by very extraordinary events the United States have flourished beyond example. Their citizens individually have been happy and the nation prosperous.

Under this Constitution our commerce has been wisely regulated with foreign nations and between the States; new States have been admitted into our Union; our territory has been enlarged by fair and honorable treaty, and with great advantage to the original States; the States, respectively protected by the National Government under a mild, parental system against foreign dangers, and enjoying within their separate spheres, by a wise partition of power, a just proportion of the sovereignty, have improved their police, extended their settlements, and attained a strength and maturity which are the best proofs of wholesome laws well administered. And if we look to the condition of individuals what a proud spectacle does it exhibit! On whom has oppression fallen in any quarter of our Union? Who has been deprived of any right of person or property? Who restrained from offering his vows in the mode which he prefers to the Divine Author of his being? It is well known that all these blessings have been enjoyed in their fullest extent; and I add with peculiar satisfaction that there has been no example of a capital punishment being inflicted on anyone for the crime of high treason.

Some who might admit the competency of our Government to these beneficent duties might doubt it in trials which put to the test its strength and efficiency as a member of the great community of nations. Here too experience has afforded us the most satisfactory proof in its favor. Just as this Constitution was put into action several of the principal States of Europe had become much agitated and some of them seriously convulsed. Destructive wars ensued, which have of late only been terminated. In the course of these conflicts the United States received great injury from several of the parties. It was their interest to stand aloof from the contest, to demand justice from the party committing the injury, and to cultivate by a fair and honorable conduct the friendship of all. War became at length inevitable, and the result has shown that our Government is equal to that, the greatest of trials, under the most unfavorable circumstances. Of the virtue of the people and of the heroic exploits of the Army, the Navy, and the militia I need not speak.

Such, then, is the happy Government under which we live—a Government adequate to every purpose for which the social compact is formed; a Government elective in all its branches, under which every citizen may by his merit obtain the highest trust recognized by the Constitution; which contains within it no cause of discord, none to put at variance one portion of the community with another; a Government which protects every citizen in the full enjoyment of his rights, and is able to protect the nation against injustice from foreign powers.

Other considerations of the highest importance admonish us to cherish our Union and to cling to the Government which supports it. Fortunate as we are in our political institutions, we have not been less so in other circumstances on which our prosperity and happiness essentially depend. Situated within the temperate zone, and extending through many degrees of latitude along the Atlantic, the United States enjoy all the varieties of climate, and every production incident to that portion of the globe. Penetrating internally to the Great Lakes and beyond the sources of the great rivers which communicate through our whole interior, no country was ever happier with respect to its domain. Blessed, too, with a fertile soil, our produce has always been very abundant, leaving, even in years the least favorable, a surplus for the wants of our fellow-men in other countries. Such is our peculiar felicity that there is not a part of our Union that is not particularly interested in preserving it. The great agricultural interest of the nation prospers under its protection. Local interests are not less fostered by it. Our fellow-citizens of the North engaged in navigation find great encouragement in being made the favored carriers of the vast productions of the other portions of the United States, while the inhabitants of these are amply recompensed, in their turn, by the nursery for seamen and naval force thus formed and reared up for the support of our common rights. Our manufactures find a generous encouragement by the policy which patronizes domestic industry, and the surplus of our produce a steady and profitable market by local wants in less-favored parts at home.

Such, then, being the highly favored condition of our country, it is the interest of every citizen to maintain it. What are the dangers which menace us? If any exist they ought to be ascertained and guarded against.

In explaining my sentiments on this subject it may be asked, What raised us to the present happy state? How did we accomplish the Revolution? How remedy the defects of the first instrument of our Union, by infusing into the National Government sufficient power for national purposes, without impairing the just rights of the States or affecting those of individuals? How sustain and pass with glory through the late war? The Government has been in the hands of the people. To the people, therefore, and to the faithful and able depositaries of their trust is the credit due. Had the people of the United States been educated in different principles, had they been less intelligent, less independent,

or **less virtuous**, can it be believed that we should have maintained the
same steady and consistent career or been blessed with the same success?
While, then, the constituent body retains its present sound and healthful
state everything will be safe. They will choose competent and faithful
representatives for every department. It is only when the people become ignorant and corrupt, when they degenerate into a populace, that
they are incapable of exercising the sovereignty. Usurpation is then an
easy attainment, and an usurper soon found. The people themselves become the willing instruments of their own debasement and ruin. Let us,
then, look to the great cause, and endeavor to preserve it in full force.
Let us by all wise and constitutional measures promote intelligence among
the people as the best means of preserving our liberties.

Dangers from abroad are not less deserving of attention. Experiencing the fortune of other nations, the United States may be again involved
in war, and it may in that event be the object of the adverse party to
overset our Government, to break our Union, and demolish us as a nation. Our distance from Europe and the just, moderate, and pacific
policy of our Government may form some security against these dangers, but they ought to be anticipated and guarded against. Many of
our citizens are engaged in commerce and navigation, and all of them
are in a certain degree dependent on their prosperous state. Many are
engaged in the fisheries. These interests are exposed to invasion in the
wars between other powers, and we should disregard the faithful admo-
nition of experience if we did not expect it. We must support our rights
or lose our character, and with it, perhaps, our liberties. A people who
fail to do it can scarcely be said to hold a place among independent nations. National honor is national property of the highest value. The
sentiment in the mind of every citizen is national strength. It ought
therefore to be cherished.

To secure us against these dangers our coast and inland frontiers
should be fortified, our Army and Navy, regulated upon just principles
as to the force of each, be kept in perfect order, and our militia be placed
on the best practicable footing. To put our extensive coast in such a
state of defense as to secure our cities and interior from invasion will be
attended with expense, but the work when finished will be permanent,
and it is fair to presume that a single campaign of invasion by a naval
force superior to our own, aided by a few thousand land troops, would
expose us to greater expense, without taking into the estimate the loss
of property and distress of our citizens, than would be sufficient for this
great work. Our land and naval forces should be moderate, but adequate
to the necessary purposes—the former to garrison and preserve our fortifications and to meet the first invasions of a foreign foe, and, while constituting the elements of a greater force, to preserve the science as well
as all the necessary implements of war in a state to be brought into activity in the event of war; the latter, retained within the limits proper in a

state of peace, might aid in maintaining the neutrality of the United States with dignity in the wars of other powers and in saving the property of their citizens from spoliation. In time of war, with the enlargement of which the great naval resources of the country render it susceptible, and which should be duly fostered in time of peace, it would contribute essentially, both as an auxiliary of defense and as a powerful engine of annoyance, to diminish the calamities of war and to bring the war to a speedy and honorable termination.

But it ought always to be held prominently in view that the safety of these States and of everything dear to a free people must depend in an eminent degree on the militia. Invasions may be made too formidable to be resisted by any land and naval force which it would comport either with the principles of our Government or the circumstances of the United States to maintain. In such cases recourse must be had to the great body of the people, and in a manner to produce the best effect. It is of the highest importance, therefore, that they be so organized and trained as to be prepared for any emergency. The arrangement should be such as to put at the command of the Government the ardent patriotism and youthful vigor of the country. If formed on equal and just principles, it can not be oppressive. It is the crisis which makes the pressure, and not the laws which provide a remedy for it. This arrangement should be formed, too, in time of peace, to be the better prepared for war. With such an organization of such a people the United States have nothing to dread from foreign invasion. At its approach an overwhelming force of gallant men might always be put in motion.

Other interests of high importance will claim attention, among which the improvement of our country by roads and canals, proceeding always with a constitutional sanction, holds a distinguished place. By thus facilitating the intercourse between the States we shall add much to the convenience and comfort of our fellow-citizens, much to the ornament of the country, and, what is of greater importance, we shall shorten distances, and, by making each part more accessible to and dependent on the other, we shall bind the Union more closely together. Nature has done so much for us by intersecting the country with so many great rivers, bays, and lakes, approaching from distant points so near to each other, that the inducement to complete the work seems to be peculiarly strong. A more interesting spectacle was perhaps never seen than is exhibited within the limits of the United States—a territory so vast and advantageously situated, containing objects so grand, so useful, so happily connected in all their parts!

Our manufactures will likewise require the systematic and fostering care of the Government. Possessing as we do all the raw materials, the fruit of our own soil and industry, we ought not to depend in the degree we have done on supplies from other countries. While we are thus dependent the sudden event of war, unsought and unexpected, can not fail to plunge us into the most serious difficulties. It is important, too, that the capital which nourishes our manufactures should be domestic, as its influence in that case instead of exhausting, as it may do in foreign hands, would be felt advantageously on agriculture and every other branch of industry. Equally important is it to provide at home a market for our raw materials, as by extending the competition it will enhance the price and protect the cultivator against the casualties incident to foreign markets.

With the Indian tribes it is our duty to cultivate friendly relations and to act with kindness and liberality in all our transactions. Equally proper is it to persevere in our efforts to extend to them the advantages of civilization.

The great amount of our revenue and the flourishing state of the Treasury are a full proof of the competency of the national resources for any emergency, as they are of the willingness of our fellow-citizens to bear the burdens which the public necessities require. The vast amount of vacant lands, the value of which daily augments, forms an additional resource of great extent and duration. These resources, besides accomplishing every other necessary purpose, put it completely in the power of the United States to discharge the national debt at an early period. Peace is the best time for improvement and preparation of every kind; it is in peace that our commerce flourishes most, that taxes are most easily paid, and that the revenue is most productive.

The Executive is charged officially in the Departments under it with the disbursement of the public money, and is responsible for the faithful application of it to the purposes for which it is raised. The Legislature is the watchful guardian over the public purse. It is its duty to see that the disbursement has been honestly made. To meet the requisite responsibility every facility should be afforded to the Executive to enable it to bring the public agents intrusted with the public money strictly and promptly to account. Nothing should be presumed against them; but if, with the requisite facilities, the public money is suffered to lie long and uselessly in their hands, they will not be the only defaulters, nor will the demoralizing effect be confined to them. It will evince a relaxation and want of tone in the Administration which will be felt by the whole community. I shall do all I can to secure economy and fidelity in this important branch of the Administration, and I doubt not that the Legislature will perform its duty with equal zeal. A thorough examination should be regularly made, and I will promote it.

It is particularly gratifying to me to enter on the discharge of these duties at a time when the United States are blessed with peace. It is a state most consistent with their prosperity and happiness. It will be my sincere desire to preserve it, so far as depends on the Executive, on just principles with all nations, claiming nothing unreasonable of any and rendering to each what is its due.

Equally gratifying is it to witness the increased harmony of opinion which pervades our Union. Discord does not belong to our system. Union is recommended as well by the free and benign principles of our Government, extending its blessings to every individual, as by the other eminent advantages attending it. The American people have encountered together great dangers and sustained severe trials with success. They constitute one great family with a common interest. Experience has enlightened us on some questions of essential importance to the country. The progress has been slow, dictated by a just reflection and a faithful regard to every interest connected with it. To promote this harmony in accord with the principles of our republican Government and in a manner to give them the most complete effect, and to advance in all other respects the best interests of our Union, will be the object of my constant and zealous exertions.

Never did a government commence under auspices so favorable, nor ever was success so complete. If we look to the history of other nations, ancient or modern, we find no example of a growth so rapid, so gigantic, of a people so prosperous and happy. In contemplating what we have still to perform, the heart of every citizen must expand with joy when he reflects how near our Government has approached to perfection; that in respect to it we have no essential improvement to make; that the great object is to preserve it in the essential principles and features which characterize it, and that that is to be done by preserving the virtue and enlightening the minds of the people; and as a security against foreign dangers to adopt such arrangements as are indispensable to the support of our independence, our rights and liberties. If we persevere in the career in which we have advanced so far and in the path already traced, we can not fail, under the favor of a gracious Providence, to attain the high destiny which seems to await us.

In the Administrations of the illustrious men who have preceded me in this high station, with some of whom I have been connected by the closest ties from early life, examples are presented which will always be found highly instructive and useful to their successors. From these I shall endeavor to derive all the advantages which they may afford. Of my immediate predecessor, under whom so important a portion of this great and successful experiment has been made, I shall be pardoned for expressing my earnest wishes that he may long enjoy in his retirement the affections of a grateful country, the best reward of exalted talents and the most faithful and meritorious services. Relying on the aid to be derived from the other departments of the Government, I enter on the trust to which I have been called by the suffrages of my fellow-citizens with my fervent prayers to the Almighty that He will be graciously pleased to continue to us that protection which He has already so conspicuously displayed in our favor.

MARCH 4, 1817.

PROCLAMATION.

[From Niles's Weekly Register, vol. 12, p. 176.]

By the President of the United States.

Whereas by an act entitled "An act providing for the sale of the tract of land at the lower rapids of Sandusky River," passed on the 27th day of April, 1816, it was enacted that all the lands in the said tract, except the reservations made in the said act, should be offered for sale to the highest bidder at Wooster, in the State of Ohio, under the direction of the register of the land office and the receiver of public moneys at Wooster, and on such day or days as shall, by a public proclamation of the President of the United States, be designated for that purpose; and

Whereas by an act entitled "An act providing for the sale of the tract of land at the British fort at the Miami of the Lake, at the foot of the rapids, and for other purposes," passed the 27th day of April, 1816, it was enacted that all the land contained in the said tract, except the reservations and exceptions made in the said act, should be offered for sale to the highest bidder at Wooster, in the State of Ohio, under the direction of the register of the land office and the receiver of public moneys at Wooster, and on such day or days as shall, by a public proclamation of the President of the United States, be designated for that purpose:

Wherefore I, James Monroe, President of the United States, in conformity with the provisions of the acts before recited, do hereby declare and make known that the lands authorized to be sold by the first-mentioned act shall be offered for sale to the highest bidder at Wooster, in the State of Ohio, on the first Monday in July next, and continue open for seven days and no longer, and that the lands authorized to be sold by the last-mentioned act shall be offered for sale to the highest bidder at the same place on the third Tuesday in July next, and continue open for seven days and no longer.

Given under my hand this 15th day of April, 1817.

By the President: JAMES MONROE.

J. MEIGS,
Commissioner of the General Land Office

FIRST ANNUAL MESSAGE.

Fellow-Citizens of the Senate and of the House of Representatives:

At no period of our political existence had we so much cause to felicitate ourselves at the prosperous and happy condition of our country. The abundant fruits of the earth have filled it with plenty. An extensive and profitable commerce has greatly augmented our revenue. The public credit has attained an extraordinary elevation. Our preparations for defense in case of future wars, from which, by the experience of all nations, we ought not to expect to be exempted, are advancing under a well-digested system with all the dispatch which so important a work will admit. Our free Government, founded on the interest and affections of the people, has gained and is daily gaining strength. Local jealousies are rapidly yielding to more generous, enlarged, and enlightened views of national policy. For advantages so numerous and highly important it is our duty to unite in grateful acknowledgments to that Omnipotent Being from whom they are derived, and in unceasing prayer that He will endow us with virtue and strength to maintain and hand them down in their utmost purity to our latest posterity.

I have the satisfaction to inform you that an arrangement which had been commenced by my predecessor with the British Government for the reduction of the naval force by Great Britain and the United States on the Lakes has been concluded, by which it is provided that neither party shall keep in service on Lake Champlain more than one vessel, on Lake Ontario more than one, and on Lake Erie and the upper lakes more than two, to be armed each with one cannon only, and that all the other armed vessels of both parties, of which an exact list is interchanged, shall be dismantled. It is also agreed that the force retained shall be restricted in its duty to the internal purposes of each party, and that the arrangement shall remain in force until six months shall have expired after notice given by one of the parties to the other of its desire that it should terminate. By this arrangement useless expense on both sides and, what is of still greater importance, the danger of collision between armed vessels in those inland waters, which was great, is prevented.

I have the satisfaction also to state that the commissioners under the fourth article of the treaty of Ghent, to whom it was referred to decide to which party the several islands in the bay of Passamaquoddy belonged under the treaty of 1783, have agreed in a report, by which all the islands in the possession of each party before the late war have been decreed to it. The commissioners acting under the other articles of the treaty of Ghent for the settlement of boundaries have also been engaged in the discharge of their respective duties, but have not yet completed them. The difference which arose between the two Governments under that treaty respecting the right of the United States to take and cure fish on the coast of the British provinces north of our limits, which had been secured by the treaty of 1783, is still in negotiation. The proposition made by this Government to extend to the colonies of Great Britain the principle of the convention of London, by which the commerce between the ports of the United States and British ports in Europe had been placed on a footing of equality, has been declined by the British Government. This subject having been thus amicably discussed between the two Governments, and it appearing that the British Government is unwilling to depart from its present regulations, it remains for Congress to decide whether they will make any other regulations in consequence thereof for the protection and improvement of our navigation.

The negotiation with Spain for spoliations on our commerce and the settlement of boundaries remains essentially in the state it held by the communications that were made to Congress by my predecessor. It has been evidently the policy of the Spanish Government to keep the nego-tiation suspended, and in this the United States have acquiesced, from an amicable disposition toward Spain and in the expectation that her Government would, from a sense of justice, finally accede to such an arrangement as would be equal between the parties. A disposition has been lately shown by the Spanish Government to move in the negotia-tion, which has been met by this Government, and should the concilia-tory and friendly policy which has invariably guided our councils be reciprocated, a just and satisfactory arrangement may be expected. It is proper, however, to remark that no proposition has yet been made from which such a result can be presumed.

It was anticipated at an early stage that the contest between Spain and the colonies would become highly interesting to the United States. It was natural that our citizens should sympathize in events which affected their neighbors. It seemed probable also that the prosecution of the con-flict along our coast and in contiguous countries would occasionally inter-rupt our commerce and otherwise affect the persons and property of our citizens. These anticipations have been realized. Such injuries have been received from persons acting under authority of both the parties, and for which redress has in most instances been withheld. Through every stage of the conflict the United States have maintained an impar-tial neutrality, giving aid to neither of the parties in men, money, ships, or munitions of war. They have regarded the contest not in the light of an ordinary insurrection or rebellion, but as a civil war between parties nearly equal, having as to neutral powers equal rights. Our ports have been open to both, and every article the fruit of our soil or of the indus-try of our citizens which either was permitted to take has been equally free to the other. Should the colonies establish their independence, it is proper now to state that this Government neither seeks nor would accept from them any advantage in commerce or otherwise which will not be equally open to all other nations. The colonies will in that event become independent states, free from any obligation to or connection with us which it may not then be their interest to form on the basis of a fair reci-procity.

In the summer of the present year an expedition was set on foot against East Florida by persons claiming to act under the authority of some of the colonies, who took possession of Amelia Island, at the mouth of the St. Marys River, near the boundary of the State of Georgia. As this Province lies eastward of the Mississippi, and is bounded by the United

States and the ocean on every side, and has been a subject of negotiation with the Government of Spain as an indemnity for losses by spoliation or in exchange for territory of equal value westward of the Mississippi, a fact well known to the world, it excited surprise that any countenance should be given to this measure by any of the colonies. As it would be difficult to reconcile it with the friendly relations existing between the United States and the colonies, a doubt was entertained whether it had been authorized by them, or any of them. This doubt has gained strength by the circumstances which have unfolded themselves in the prosecution of the enterprise, which have marked it as a mere private, unauthorized adventure. Projected and commenced with an incompetent force, reliance seems to have been placed on what might be drawn, in defiance of our laws, from within our limits; and of late, as their resources have failed, it has assumed a more marked character of unfriendliness to us, the island being made a channel for the illicit introduction of slaves from Africa into the United States, an asylum for fugitive slaves from the neighboring States, and a port for smuggling of every kind.

A similar establishment was made at an earlier period by persons of the same description in the Gulf of Mexico at a place called Galvezton, within the limits of the United States, as we contend, under the cession of Louisiana. This enterprise has been marked in a more signal manner by all the objectionable circumstances which characterized the other, and more particularly by the equipment of privateers which have annoyed our commerce, and by smuggling. These establishments, if ever sanctioned by any authority whatever, which is not believed, have abused their trust and forfeited all claim to consideration. A just regard for the rights and interests of the United States required that they should be suppressed, and orders have been accordingly issued to that effect. The imperious considerations which produced this measure will be explained to the parties whom it may in any degree concern.

To obtain correct information on every subject in which the United States are interested; to inspire just sentiments in all persons in authority, on either side, of our friendly disposition so far as it may comport with an impartial neutrality, and to secure proper respect to our commerce in every port and from every flag, it has been thought proper to send a ship of war with three distinguished citizens along the southern coast with instruction to touch at such ports as they may find most expedient for these purposes. With the existing authorities, with those in the possession of and exercising the sovereignty, must the communication be held; from them alone can redress for past injuries committed by persons acting under them be obtained; by them alone can the commission of the like in future be prevented.

Our relations with the other powers of Europe have experienced no essential change since the last session. In our intercourse with each due attention continues to be paid to the protection of our commerce, and to every other object in which the United States are interested. A strong hope is entertained that, by adhering to the maxims of a just, a candid, and friendly policy, we may long preserve amicable relations with all the powers of Europe on conditions advantageous and honorable to our country.

With the Barbary States and the Indian tribes our pacific relations have been preserved.

In calling your attention to the internal concerns of our country the view which they exhibit is peculiarly gratifying. The payments which have been made into the Treasury show the very productive state of the public revenue. After satisfying the appropriations made by law for the support of the civil Government and of the military and naval establishments, embracing suitable provision for fortifications and for the gradual increase of the Navy, paying the interest of the public debt, and extinguishing more than eighteen millions of the principal, within the present year, it is estimated that a balance of more than $6,000,000 will remain in the Treasury on the 1st day of January applicable to the current service of the ensuing year.

The payments into the Treasury during the year 1818 on account of imposts and tonnage, resulting principally from duties which have accrued in the present year, may be fairly estimated at $20,000,000; the internal revenues at $2,500,000; the public lands at $1,500,000; bank dividends and incidental receipts at $500,000; making in the whole $24,500,000.

The annual permanent expenditure for the support of the civil Government and of the Army and Navy, as now established by law, amounts to $11,800,000, and for the sinking fund to $10,000,000, making in the whole $21,800,000, leaving an annual excess of revenue beyond the expenditure of $2,700,000, exclusive of the balance estimated to be in the Treasury on the 1st day of January, 1818.

In the present state of the Treasury the whole of the Louisiana debt may be redeemed in the year 1819, after which, if the public debt continues as it now is, above par, there will be annually about five millions of the sinking fund unexpended until the year 1825, when the loan of 1812 and the stock created by funding Treasury notes will be redeemable.

It is also estimated that the Mississippi stock will be discharged during the year 1819 from the proceeds of the public lands assigned to that object, after which the receipts from those lands will annually add to the public revenue the sum of one million and a half, making the permanent annual revenue amount to $26,000,000, and leaving an annual excess of revenue after the year 1819 beyond the permanent authorized expenditure of more than $4,000,000.

By the last returns to the Department of War the militia force of the several States may be estimated at 800,000 men—infantry, artillery, and cavalry. Great part of this force is armed, and measures are taken to arm the whole. An improvement in the organization and discipline of the militia is one of the great objects which claims the unremitted attention of Congress.

The regular force amounts nearly to the number required by law, and is stationed along the Atlantic and inland frontiers.

Of the naval force it has been necessary to maintain strong squadrons in the Mediterranean and in the Gulf of Mexico.

From several of the Indian tribes inhabiting the country bordering on Lake Erie purchases have been made of lands on conditions very favorable to the United States, and, as it is presumed, not less so to the tribes themselves.

By these purchases the Indian title, with moderate reservations, has been extinguished to the whole of the land within the limits of the State of Ohio, and to a part of that in the Michigan Territory and of the State of Indiana. From the Cherokee tribe a tract has been purchased in the State of Georgia and an arrangement made by which, in exchange for lands beyond the Mississippi, a great part, if not the whole, of the land belonging to that tribe eastward of that river in the States of North Carolina, Georgia, and Tennessee, and in the Alabama Territory will soon be acquired. By these acquisitions, and others that may reasonably be expected soon to follow, we shall be enabled to extend our settlements from the inhabited parts of the State of Ohio along Lake Erie into the Michigan Territory, and to connect our settlements by degrees through the State of Indiana and the Illinois Territory to that of Missouri. A similar and equally advantageous effect will soon be produced to the south, through the whole extent of the States and territory which border on the waters emptying into the Mississippi and the Mobile. In this progress, which the rights of nature demand and nothing can prevent, marking a growth rapid and gigantic, it is our duty to make new efforts for the preservation, improvement, and civilization of the native inhabitants. The hunter state can exist only in the vast uncultivated desert. It yields to the more dense and compact form and greater force of civilized population; and of right it ought to yield, for the earth was given to mankind to support the greatest number of which it is capable, and no tribe or people have a right to withhold from the wants of others more than is necessary for their own support and comfort. It is gratifying to know that the reservations of land made by the treaties with the tribes on Lake Erie were made with a view to individual ownership among them and to the cultivation of the soil by all, and that an annual stipend has been pledged to supply their other wants. It will merit the consideration of Congress whether other provision not stipulated by treaty ought to be made for these tribes and for the advancement of the liberal and humane policy of the United States toward all the tribes within our limits, and more particularly for their improvement in the arts of civilized life.

Among the advantages incident to these purchases, and to those which have preceded, the security which may thereby be afforded to our inland

BATTLES OF PLATTSBURG AND LAKE CHAMPLAIN, 1814

THE BATTLE OF PLATTSBURG, N. Y.

September 11, 1814

This engagement is adequately described in the articles entitled "Plattsburg (N. Y.), Battle of," and "Lake Champlain, Battle of," in the index (volume eleven).

One phase of the matter, however, though not strictly military, deserves thought: The fifteen hundred inhabitants of Plattsburg, like many other Americans in New York and Vermont, throve on an illicit trade with Canada. The embargo had shut our ports to British shipping, but a constant stream of goods flowed across the border. Grains by the wagon train and meat by the herd were traded to the British army. In fact, by the natural conformation of the land the trade of northern New York and Vermont went to Canada. The St. Lawrence bore their produce instead of the Hudson; Montreal was their Capital instead of Albany. If invention had not transformed the modes of transportation that section would ultimately have connected itself politically with the Dominion.

frontiers is peculiarly important. With a strong barrier, consisting of our own people, thus planted on the Lakes, the Mississippi, and the Mobile, with the protection to be derived from the regular force, Indian hostilities, if they do not altogether cease, will henceforth lose their terror. Fortifications in those quarters to any extent will not be necessary, and the expense attending them may be saved. A people accustomed to the use of firearms only, as the Indian tribes are, will shun even moderate works which are defended by cannon. Great fortifications will therefore be requisite only in future along the coast and at some points in the interior connected with it. On these will the safety of our towns and the commerce of our great rivers, from the Bay of Fundy to the Mississippi, depend. On these, therefore, should the utmost attention, skill, and labor be bestowed.

A considerable and rapid augmentation in the value of all the public lands, proceeding from these and other obvious causes, may henceforward be expected. The difficulties attending early emigrations will be dissipated even in the most remote parts. Several new States have been admitted into our Union to the west and south, and Territorial governments, happily organized, established over every other portion in which there is vacant land for sale. In terminating Indian hostilities, as must soon be done, in a formidable shape at least, the emigration, which has heretofore been great, will probably increase, and the demand for land and the augmentation in its value be in like proportion. The great increase of our population throughout the Union will alone produce an important effect, and in no quarter will it be so sensibly felt as in those in contemplation. The public lands are a public stock, which ought to be disposed of to the best advantage for the nation. The nation should therefore derive the profit proceeding from the continual rise in their value. Every encouragement should be given to the emigrants consistent with a fair competition between them, but that competition should operate in the first sale to the advantage of the nation rather than of individuals. Great capitalists will derive all the benefit incident to their superior wealth under any mode of sale which may be adopted. But if, looking forward to the rise in the value of the public lands, they should have the opportunity of amassing at a low price vast bodies in their hands, the profit will accrue to them and not to the public. They would also have the power in that degree to control the emigration and settlement in such a manner as their opinion of their respective interests might dictate. I submit this subject to the consideration of Congress, that such further provision may be made in the sale of the public lands, with a view to the public interest, should any be deemed expedient, as in their judgment may be best adapted to the object.

When we consider the vast extent of territory within the United States, the great amount and value of its productions, the connection of its parts, and other circumstances on which their prosperity and happiness depend, we can not fail to entertain a high sense of the advantage to be derived from the facility which may be afforded in the intercourse between them by means of good roads and canals. Never did a country of such vast extent offer equal inducements to improvements of this kind, nor ever were consequences of such magnitude involved in them. As this subject was acted on by Congress at the last session, and there may be a disposition to revive it at the present, I have brought it into view for the purpose of communicating my sentiments on a very important circumstance connected with it with that freedom and candor which a regard for the public interest and a proper respect for Congress require. A difference of opinion has existed from the first formation of our Constitution to the present time among our most enlightened and virtuous citizens respecting the right of Congress to establish such a system of improvement. Taking into view the trust with which I am now honored, it would be improper after what has passed that this discussion should be revived with an uncertainty of my opinion respecting the right. Disregarding early impressions I have bestowed on the subject all the deliberation which its great importance and a just sense of my duty required, and the result is a settled conviction in my mind that Congress do not possess the right. It is not contained in any of the specified powers granted to Congress, nor can I consider it incidental to or a necessary means, viewed on the most liberal scale, for carrying into effect any of the powers which are specifically granted. In communicating this result I can not resist the obligation which I feel to suggest to Congress the propriety of recommending to the States the adoption of an amendment to the Constitution which shall give to Congress the right in question. In cases of doubtful construction, especially of such vital interest, it comports with the nature and origin of our institutions, and will contribute much to preserve them, to apply to our constituents for an explicit grant of the power. We may confidently rely that if it appears to their satisfaction that the power is necessary, it will always be granted.

In this case I am happy to observe that experience has afforded the most ample proof of its utility, and that the benign spirit of conciliation and harmony which now manifests itself throughout our Union promises to such a recommendation the most prompt and favorable result. I think proper to suggest also, in case this measure is adopted, that it be recommended to the States to include in the amendment sought a right in Congress to institute likewise seminaries of learning, for the all-important purpose of diffusing knowledge among our fellow-citizens throughout the United States.

Our manufactories will require the continued attention of Congress. The capital employed in them is considerable, and the knowledge acquired in the machinery and fabric of all the most useful manufactures is of great value. Their preservation, which depends on due encouragement is connected with the high interests of the nation.

Although the progress of the public buildings has been as favorable as circumstances have permitted, it is to be regretted that the Capitol is not yet in a state to receive you. There is good cause to presume that the two wings, the only parts as yet commenced, will be prepared for that purpose at the next session. The time seems now to have arrived when this subject may be deemed worthy the attention of Congress on a scale adequate to national purposes. The completion of the middle building will be necessary to the convenient accommodation of Congress, of the committees, and various offices belonging to it. It is evident that the other public buildings are altogether insufficient for the accommodation of the several Executive Departments, some of whom are much crowded and even subjected to the necessity of obtaining it in private buildings at some distance from the head of the Department, and with inconvenience to the management of the public business. Most nations have taken an interest and a pride in the improvement and ornament of their metropolis, and none were more conspicuous in that respect than the ancient republics. The policy which dictated the establishment of a permanent residence for the National Government and the spirit in which it was commenced and has been prosecuted show that such improvement was thought worthy the attention of this nation. Its central position, between the northern and southern extremes of our Union, and its approach to the west at the head of a great navigable river which interlocks with the Western waters, prove the wisdom of the councils which established it.

Nothing appears to be more reasonable and proper than that convenient accommodation should be provided on a well-digested plan for the heads of the several Departments and for the Attorney-General, and it is believed that the public ground in the city applied to these objects will be found amply sufficient. I submit this subject to the consideration of Congress, that such further provision may be made in it as to them may seem proper.

In contemplating the happy situation of the United States, our attention is drawn with peculiar interest to the surviving officers and soldiers of our Revolutionary army, who so eminently contributed by their services to lay its foundation. Most of those very meritorious citizens have paid the debt of nature and gone to repose. It is believed that among the survivors there are some not provided for by existing laws, who are reduced to indigence and even to real distress. These men have a claim on the gratitude of their country, and it will do honor to their country to provide for them. The lapse of a few years more and the opportunity will be forever lost; indeed, so long already has been the interval that the number to be benefited by any provision which may be made will not be great.

It appearing in a satisfactory manner that the revenue arising from imposts and tonnage and from the sale of the public lands will be fully adequate to the support of the civil Government, of the present military and naval establishments, including the annual augmentation of the latter to the extent provided for, to the payment of the interest of the public debt, and to the extinguishment of it at the times authorized, without the aid of the internal taxes, I consider it my duty to recommend to Congress their repeal. To impose taxes when the public exigencies require them is an obligation of the most sacred character, especially with a free people. The faithful fulfillment of it is among the highest proofs of their virtue and capacity for self-government. To dispense with taxes when it may be done with perfect safety is equally the duty of their representatives. In this instance we have the satisfaction to know that they were imposed when the demand was imperious, and have been sustained with exemplary fidelity. I have to add that however gratifying it may be to me regarding the prosperous and happy condition of our country to recommend the repeal of these taxes at this time, I shall nevertheless be attentive to events, and, should any future emergency occur, be not less prompt to suggest such measures and burdens as may then be requisite and proper.

JAMES MONROE.

DECEMBER 2, 1817.

SPECIAL MESSAGES.

To the Senate of the United States:

I submit to the Senate, for their consideration and advice, the following treaties entered into with several of the Indian tribes, to wit:

A treaty of peace and friendship made and concluded by William Clark, Ninian Edwards, and Auguste Choteau, commissioners on the part of the United States of America, and the chiefs and warriors of the Menomene tribe or nation of Indians, on the 30th of March, 1817, at St. Louis.

A treaty of peace and friendship made and concluded on the 4th June, 1817, at St. Louis, by William Clark, Ninian Edwards, and Auguste Choteau, commissioners on the part of the United States of America, and the chiefs and warriors of the Ottoes tribe of Indians.

A treaty of peace and friendship made and concluded on the 5th June, 1817, at St. Louis, by William Clark, Ninian Edwards, and Auguste Choteau, commissioners on the part of the United States of America, and the chiefs and warriors of the Poncarar tribe of Indians.

A treaty concluded at the Cherokee Agency on the 8th of July, 1817, between Major-General Andrew Jackson, Joseph McMinn, governor of the State of Tennessee, and General David Meriwether, commissioners of the United States of America, of the one part, and the chiefs, headmen, and warriors of the Cherokee Nation east of the Mississippi River and the chiefs, headmen, and warriors of the Cherokees on the Arkansas River, and their deputies, John D. Chisholm and James Rogers.

A treaty concluded on the 29th day of September, 1817, at the foot of the Rapids of the Miami of Lake Erie, between Lewis Cass and Duncan McArthur, commissioners of the United States, and the sachems, chiefs, and warriors of the Wyandot, Seneca, Delaware, Shawnese, Potawatamies, Ottawas, and Chippewa tribes of Indians.

The Wyandots and other tribes parties to the treaty lately concluded with them have, by a deputation to this city, requested permission to retain possession of such lands as they actually cultivate and reside on, for the ensuing year. They have also expressed a desire that the reservations made in their favor should be enlarged, representing that they had entered into the treaty in full confidence that that would be done, preferring a reliance on the justice of the United States for such extension rather than that the treaty should fail.

The Wyandots claim an extension of their reservation to 16 miles square, and the other tribes in a proportional degree. Sufficient information is not now in the possession of the Executive to enable it to decide how far it may be proper to comply with the wishes of these tribes in the extent desired. The necessary information may be obtained in the course of the next year, and if they are permitted to remain in the possession of the lands they cultivate during that time such further extension of their reservations may be made by law at the next session as justice and a liberal policy toward these people may require. It is submitted to the consideration of the Senate whether it may not be proper to annex to their advice and consent for the ratification of the treaty a declaration providing for the above objects.

JAMES MONROE.

DECEMBER 11, 1817.

WASHINGTON, *December 15, 1817.*

To the House of Representatives of the United States:

In compliance with the resolution of the House of Representatives of the 8th of this month, I transmit, for the information of the House, a report from the Secretary of State, with the documents referred to in it, containing all the information in the possession of the Executive which it is proper to disclose, relative to certain persons who lately took possession of Amelia Island and Galvezton.

JAMES MONROE.

DECEMBER 18, 1817.

To the Senate of the United States:

In compliance with the resolution of the Senate of the 11th of this month, I transmit, for the information of the Senate, a report from the

Secretary of the Treasury, relating to the progress made in surveying the several tracts of military bounty lands appropriated by Congress for the late army of the United States, and the time at which such survey will probably be completed.

JAMES MONROE.

DECEMBER 22, 1817.

To the House of Representatives:

In compliance with a resolution of the House of Representatives of the 11th of this month, requesting to be informed of the present strength of the Army of the United States, its distribution among the several military posts which it is designed to protect, and its competency to preserve and defend the fortifications amongst which it is distributed, and to aid in constructing such other military works, if any, as it may be deemed proper to erect for the more effectual security of the United States and of the Territories thereof, I now transmit a report from the Secretary of War which contains the information desired.

JAMES MONROE.

DECEMBER 29, 1817.

To the Senate of the United States:

In compliance with a resolution of the Senate of the 16th of this month, requesting information touching the execution of so much of the first article of the treaty of Ghent as relates to the restitution of slaves, which has not heretofore been communicated, I now transmit a report of the Secretary of State on that subject.

JAMES MONROE.

DECEMBER 29, 1817.

To the House of Representatives of the United States:

In compliance with a resolution of the House of Representatives of the 12th of this month, requesting to be informed whether any, and which, of the Representatives in a list thereto annexed have held offices since the 4th of March last, designating the offices, the times of appointment and acceptance, and whether they were at that time so held or when they had been resigned, I now transmit a report from the Secretary of State which contains the information desired.

JAMES MONROE.

WASHINGTON, *January 12, 1818.*

To the Senate and House of Representatives of the United States:

The claim of the representatives of the late Caron de Beaumarchais having been recommended to the favorable consideration of the Legislature by my predecessor in his message to Congress of the 31st of January last, and concurring in the sentiments therein expressed, I now transmit copies of a new representation relative to it received by the Secretary of State from the minister of France, and of a correspondence on the subject between the minister of the United States at Paris and the Duke of Richelieu, inclosed with that representation.

JAMES MONROE.

To the Senate and House of Representatives of the United States:

I have the satisfaction to inform Congress that the establishment at Amelia Island has been suppressed, and without the effusion of blood. The papers which explain this transaction I now lay before Congress.

By the suppression of this establishment and of that at Galveztown, which will soon follow, if it has not already ceased to exist, there is good cause to believe that the consummation of a project fraught with much injury to the United States has been prevented.

When we consider the persons engaged in it, being adventurers from different countries, with very few, if any, of the native inhabitants of the Spanish colonies; the territory on which the establishments were made— one on a portion of that claimed by the United States westward of the Mississippi, the other on a part of East Florida, a Province in negotiation between the United States and Spain; the claim of their leader as announced by his proclamation on taking possession of Amelia Island, comprising the whole of both the Floridas, without excepting that part of West Florida which is incorporated into the State of Louisiana; their conduct while in the possession of the island making it instrumental to every species of contraband, and, in regard to slaves, of the most odious and dangerous character, it may fairly be concluded that if the enterprise had succeeded on the scale on which it was formed much annoyance and injury would have resulted from it to the United States.

Other circumstances were thought to be no less deserving of attention. The institution of a government by foreign adventurers in the island, distinct from the colonial governments of Buenos Ayres, Venezuela, or Mexico, pretending to sovereignty and exercising its highest offices, particularly in granting commissions to privateers, were acts which could not fail to draw after them the most serious consequences. It was the duty of the Executive either to extend to this establishment all the advantages of that neutrality which the United States had proclaimed, and have observed in favor of the colonies of Spain who, by the strength of their own population and resources, had declared their independence and were affording strong proof of their ability to maintain it, or of making the discrimination which circumstances required.

Had the first course been pursued, we should not only have sanctioned all the unlawful claims and practices of this pretended Government in regard to the United States, but have countenanced a system of privateering in the Gulf of Mexico and elsewhere the ill effects of which might, and probably would, have been deeply and very extensively felt.

The path of duty was plain from the commencement, but it was painful to enter upon it while the obligation could be resisted. The law of 1811, lately published, and which it is therefore proper now to mention, was considered applicable to the case from the moment that the proclamation of the chief of the enterprise was seen, and its obligation was daily increased by other considerations of high importance already mentioned, which were deemed sufficiently strong in themselves to dictate the course which has been pursued.

Early intimation having been received of the dangerous purposes of these adventurers, timely precautions were taken by the establishment of a force near the St. Marys to prevent their effect, or it is probable that it would have been more sensibly felt.

To such establishments, made so near to our settlements in the expectation of deriving aid from them, it is particularly gratifying to find that very little encouragement was given. The example so conspicuously displayed by our fellow-citizens that their sympathies can not be perverted to improper purposes, but that a love of country, the influence of moral principles, and a respect for the laws are predominant with them, is a sure pledge that all the very flattering anticipations which have been formed of the success of our institutions will be realized. This example has proved that if our relations with foreign powers are to be changed it must be done by the constituted authorities, who alone, acting on a high responsibility, are competent to the purpose, and until such change is thus made that our fellow-citizens will respect the existing relations by a faithful adherence to the laws which secure them.

Believing that this enterprise, though undertaken by persons some of whom may have held commissions from some of the colonies, was unauthorized by and unknown to the colonial governments, full confidence is entertained that it will be disclaimed by them, and that effectual measures will be taken to prevent the abuse of their authority in all cases to the injury of the United States.

For these injuries, especially those proceeding from Amelia Island, Spain would be responsible if it was not manifest that, though committed in the latter instance through her territory, she was utterly unable to prevent them. Her territory, however, ought not to be made instrumental, through her inability to defend it, to purposes so injurious to the United States. To a country over which she fails to maintain her authority, and which she permits to be converted to the annoyance of her neighbors, her jurisdiction for the time necessarily ceases to exist. The territory of Spain will nevertheless be respected so far as it may be done consistently with the essential interests and safety of the United States. In expelling these adventurers from these posts it was not intended to make any conquest from Spain or to injure in any degree the cause of the colonies. Care will be taken that no part of the territory contemplated by the law of 1811 shall be occupied by a foreign government of any kind, or that injuries of the nature of those complained of shall be repeated; but this, it is expected, will be provided for with every other interest in a spirit of amity in the negotiation now depending with the Government of Spain.

JAMES MONROE.

JANUARY 13, 1818.

WASHINGTON, *January 23, 1818.*

To the House of Representatives of the United States:

In compliance with a resolution of the House of Representatives of the 9th of December last, requesting information of what roads have been made or are in progress under the authority of the Executive of the United States, the States and Territories through which they pass or are intended to pass, the periods when they were ordered to be made, and how far they have been executed, I now communicate a report from the Secretary of the Treasury, and likewise a report from the Secretary of War, containing the information which is desired.

JAMES MONROE.

WASHINGTON, *January 28, 1818.*

To the Senate of the United States:

In compliance with a resolution of the Senate of the 22d of this month, requesting to be informed "in what manner the troops in the service of the United States now operating against the Seminole tribe of Indians have been subsisted, whether by contract or otherwise, and whether they have been furnished regularly with rations," I now transmit a report from the Secretary of War containing the information required.

JAMES MONROE.

WASHINGTON, *January 29, 1818.*

To the House of Representatives of the United States:

In compliance with a resolution of the House of Representatives of the 23d of December last, requesting information relative to the imprisonment and detention in confinement of Richard W. Meade, a citizen of the United States, I now transmit to the House a report from the Secretary of State containing the information required.

JAMES MONROE.

To the Senate of the United States:

In compliance with a resolution of the Senate of the 8th of last month, requesting me to cause to be laid before it the proceedings which may have been had under an act entitled "An act for the gradual increase of the Navy of the United States," specifying the number of ships put on the stocks and of what class; the quantity of materials procured for ship-building, and also the sums of money which may have been paid out of the fund created by said act, and for what objects; and likewise the contracts which may have been entered into in execution of the act aforesaid on which moneys may not yet have been advanced, I now transmit a report of the Secretary of the Navy, accompanied by a report from the Board of Commissioners of the Navy, with documents which contain the information desired.

JAMES MONROE.

FEBRUARY 2, 1818

WASHINGTON, *February 6, 1818.*

To the House of Representatives of the United States:

I transmit to the House of Representatives a report of the Secretary of State, in compliance with the resolution of said House requesting information respecting the ratification of the thirteenth article of the amendments to the Constitution of the United States.

JAMES MONROE.

WASHINGTON, *February 10, 1818.*

To the Senate and House of Representatives of the United States:

As the house appropriated for the President of the United States will be finished this year, it is thought to merit the attention of the Congress in what manner it should be furnished and what measures ought to be adopted for the safe-keeping of the furniture in future. All the public furniture provided before 1814 having been destroyed with the public buildings in that year, and little afterwards procured, owing to the inadequacy of the appropriation, it has become necessary to provide almost every article requisite for such an establishment, whence the sum to be expended will be much greater than at any former period. The furniture in its kind and extent is thought to be an object not less deserving attention than the building for which it is intended. Both being national objects, each seems to have an equal claim to legislative sanction. The disbursement of the public money, too, ought, it is presumed, to be in like manner provided for by law. The person who may happen to be placed by the suffrage of his fellow-citizens in the high trust, having no personal interest in these concerns, should be exempted from undue responsibility respecting them.

For a building so extensive, intended for a purpose exclusively national, in which in the furniture provided for it a mingled regard is due to the simplicity and purity of our institutions and to the character of the people who are represented in it, the sum already appropriated has proved altogether inadequate. The present is therefore a proper time for Congress to take the subject into consideration, with a view to all the objects claiming attention, and to regulate it by law. On a knowledge of the furniture procured and the sum expended for it a just estimate may be formed regarding the extent of the building of what will still be wanting to furnish the house. Many of the articles, being of a durable nature, may be handed down through a long series of service, and being of great value, such as plate, ought not to be left altogether and at all times to the care of servants alone. It seems to be advisable that a public agent should be charged with it during the occasional absences of the President, and have authority to transfer it from one President to another, and likewise to make reports of occasional deficiencies, as the basis on which further provision should be made.

It may also merit consideration whether it may not be proper to commit the care of the public buildings, particularly the President's house and the Capitol, with the grounds belonging to them, including likewise the furniture of the latter, in a more special manner to a public agent. Hitherto the charge of this valuable property seems to have been connected with the structure of the buildings and committed to those employed in it. This guard will necessarily cease when the buildings are finished, at which time the interest in them will be proportionably augmented. It is presumed that this trust is, in a certain degree at least, incidental to the other duties of the superintendent of the public buildings, but it may merit consideration whether it will not be proper to charge him with it more explicitly, and to give him authority to employ one or more persons under him for these purposes.

JAMES MONROE.

WASHINGTON, *February 12, 1818.*

To the Senate and House of Representatives:

I lay before the House of Representatives copies of two communications received at the Department of State from the minister of Great Britain, and submit to their consideration the propriety of making such legislative provisions as may be necessary for a compliance with the representations contained in them.

By the express terms of that compact it was, when ratified by the two Governments, to be in force for the term of four years *from the day of its signature.* The revocation of all the discriminating duties became, therefore, the obligation of both Governments *from that day*, and it is conceived that every individual who has been required to pay, and who has paid, any of the extra duties revoked by the convention has a just and lawful claim upon the respective Governments for its return. From various accidents it has happened that both here and in Great Britain the cessation of the extra duties has been fixed to commence at different times. It is desirable that Congress should pass an act providing for the return of *all* the extra duties *incompatible with the terms of the convention* which have been levied upon British vessels or merchandise after the 3d of July, 1815. The British Parliament have already set the example of fixing that day for the cessation of the extra duties of export by their act of 30th of June last, and the minister of the United States in London is instructed to require the extension of the same principle to *all* the extra duties levied on vessels and merchandise of the United States in the ports of Great Britain since that day. It is not doubted that the British Government will comply with this requisition, and that the act suggested may be passed by Congress with full confidence that the reciprocal measure will receive the sanction of the British Parliament.

JAMES MONROE.

WASHINGTON, *February 23, 1818.*

To the Senate of the United States:

In compliance with a resolution of the Senate requesting me to cause to be laid before them a statement of all the arms and accouterments which have been manufactured at the different armories of the United States, with the cost of each stand, and the number delivered to each State, respectively, under the act for arming the whole body of militia, I now transmit a report from the Secretary of War, with the documents marked A, B, and C, which, together with a report to him from the Ordnance Department, contains the information required.

JAMES MONROE.

WASHINGTON, *February 23, 1818.*

To the Senate of the United States:

In compliance with a resolution of the Senate of the 19th of January, 1818, requesting information of measures which have been taken in pursuance of so much of the act to authorize the appointment of a surveyor for lands in the northern part of the Mississippi Territory, passed the 3d of March, 1817, as relates to the reservation of certain sections for the purpose of laying out and establishing towns thereon, I now transmit a report from the Secretary of the Treasury, which, with the letters and charts referred to in it, contains all the information which is desired.

JAMES MONROE.

WASHINGTON, *February 25, 1818.*

To the Senate and House of Representatives of the United States:

The commissioners of the two Governments, under the fourth article of the treaty of Ghent, having come to a decision upon the questions submitted to them, I lay before Congress copies of that decision, together with copies of the declaration signed and reported by the commissioners of this Government.

JAMES MONROE.

FEBRUARY 27, 1818.

To the House of Representatives of the United States:

I communicate herewith to the House of Representatives a copy of a letter from the governor of the State of South Carolina to the Secretary of State, together with extracts from the journals of proceedings in both branches of the legislature of that Commonwealth, relative to a proposed amendment of the Constitution, which letter and extracts are connected with the subject of my communication to the House of the 6th instant.

JAMES MONROE.

WASHINGTON, *February 28, 1818.*

To the House of Representatives of the United States:

I lay before the House a report from the Secretary of State, together with the papers relating to the claims of merchants of the United States upon the Government of Naples, in conformity with the resolution of the House of the 30th January last.

JAMES MONROE.

WASHINGTON, *March 11, 1818.*

To the Senate of the United States:

In compliance with a resolution of the Senate requesting information respecting the requisitions that were made on the contractors between the 1st of June and the 24th of December, 1817, for deposits of provisions in advance at the several posts on the frontiers of Georgia and the adjoining territory, their conduct in compliance therewith, the amount of money advanced to B. G. Orr, and the extent of his failure, with a copy of the articles of contract entered into with him, I now lay before the Senate a report from the Secretary of War, which, with the documents accompanying it, will afford the information desired.

JAMES MONROE.

WASHINGTON, *March 14, 1818.*

To the Senate and House of Representatives of the United States:

In compliance with a resolution of the Senate of the 16th of December and of the House of Representatives of the 24th of February last, I lay before Congress a report of the Secretary of State, and the papers referred to in it, respecting the negotiation with the Government of Spain. To explain fully the nature of the differences between the United States and Spain and the conduct of the parties it has been found necessary to go back to an early epoch. The recent correspondence, with the documents accompanying it, will give a full view of the whole subject, and place the conduct of the United States in every stage and under every circumstance, for justice, moderation, and a firm adherence to their rights, on the high and honorable ground which it has invariably sustained.

JAMES MONROE.

WASHINGTON, *March 16, 1818.*

To the Senate of the United States:

In compliance with a resolution of the Senate of the United States of the 31st of December last, requesting the President to cause to be laid before them a statement of the proceedings which may have been had under the act of Congress passed on the 3d March, 1817, entitled "An act to set apart and dispose of certain public lands for the encouragement and culti- vation of the vine and olive," I now transmit a report from the Secretary of the Treasury, containing all the information possessed by the Executive relating to the proceedings under the said act.

JAMES MONROE.

WASHINGTON, *March 16, 1818.*

To the Senate of the United States:

In compliance with a resolution of the Senate of the United States of the 3d of February last, requesting the President to cause to be laid before them "a statement of the progress made under the act to provide for sur- veying the coast of the United States, passed February 10, 1807, and any subsequent acts on the same subject, and the expenses incurred thereby," I transmit a report from the Secretary of the Treasury containing the information required.

JAMES MONROE.

MARCH 19, 1818.

To the Senate and House of Representatives of the United States:

In the course of the last summer a negotiation was commenced with the Government of the Netherlands with a view to the revival and modi- fication of the commercial treaty existing between the two countries, adapted to their present circumstances.

The report from the Secretary of State which I now lay before Con- gress will show the obstacles which arose in the progress of the confer- ences between the respective plenipotentiaries, and which resulted in the agreement between them then to refer the subject to the consideration of their respective Governments. As the difficulties appear to be of a na- ture which may, perhaps, for the present be more easily removed by recip- rocal legislative regulations, formed in the spirit of amity and conciliation, than by conventional stipulations, Congress may think it advisable to leave the subsisting treaty in its present state, and to meet the liberal ex- emption from discriminating tonnage duties which has been conceded in the Netherlands to the vessels of the United States by a similar exemp- tion to the vessels of the Netherlands which have arrived, or may here- after arrive, in our ports, commencing from the time when the exemption was granted to the vessels of the United States. I would further recom- mend to the consideration of Congress the expediency of extending the benefit of the same regulation, to commence from the passage of the law, to the vessels of Russia, Hamburg, and Bremen, and of making it prospectively general in favor of every nation in whose ports the vessels of the United States are admitted on the same footing as their own.

JAMES MONROE.

WASHINGTON, *March 23, 1818.*

To the Senate of the United States:

I lay before the Senate a report from the Secretary of the Navy, with the estimate of the expense which will be incurred by the establishment of two dockyards for repairing vessels of the largest size.

JAMES MONROE.

WASHINGTON, *March 25, 1818.*

To the Senate and House of Representatives of the United States:

I now lay before Congress all the information in the possession of the Executive respecting the war with the Seminoles, and the measures which it has been thought proper to adopt for the safety of our fellow-citizens on the frontier exposed to their ravages. The inclosed documents show that the hostilities of this tribe were unprovoked, the offspring of a spirit long cherished and often manifested toward the United States, and that in the present instance it was extending itself to other tribes and daily assuming a more serious aspect. As soon as the nature and object of this combination were perceived the major-general commanding the Southern division of the troops of the United States was ordered to the theater of action, charged with the management of the war and vested with the powers necessary to give it effect. The season of the year being unfavorable to active operations, and the recesses of the country affording shelter to these savages in case of retreat, may prevent a prompt termination of the war; but it may be fairly presumed that it will not be long before this tribe and its associates receive the punishment which they have provoked and justly merited.

As almost the whole of this tribe inhabits the country within the limits of Florida, Spain was bound by the treaty of 1795 to restrain them from committing hostilities against the United States. We have seen with regret that her Government has altogether failed to fulfill this obligation, nor are we aware that it made any effort to that effect. When we consider her utter inability to check, even in the slightest degree, the movements of this tribe by her very small and incompetent force in Florida, we are not disposed to ascribe the failure to any other cause. The inability, however, of Spain to maintain her authority over the territory and Indians within her limits, and in consequence to fulfill the treaty, ought not to expose the United States to other and greater injuries. When the authority of Spain ceases to exist there, the United States have a right to pursue their enemy on a principle of self-defense. In this instance the right is more complete and obvious because we shall perform only what Spain was bound to have performed herself. To the high obligations and privileges of this great and sacred right of self-defense will the movement of our troops be strictly confined. Orders have been given to the general in command not to enter Florida unless it be in pursuit of the enemy, and in that case to respect the Spanish authority wherever it is maintained; and he will be instructed to withdraw his forces from the Province as soon as he shall have reduced that tribe to order, and secure our fellow-citizens in that quarter by satisfactory arrangements against its unprovoked and savage hostilities in future.

JAMES MONROE.

WASHINGTON, *March 25, 1818.*

To the House of Representatives of the United States:

In conformity with the resolution of the House of Representatives of the 5th of December last, I now transmit a report of the Secretary of State, with a copy of the documents which it is thought proper to communicate relating to the independence and political condition of the Provinces of Spanish America.

JAMES MONROE.

WASHINGTON, *March 26, 1818.*

To the House of Representatives of the United States:

I transmit to the House of Representatives, in compliance with their resolution of March 20, such information not heretofore communicated as is in the possession of the Executive relating to the occupation of Amelia Island. If any doubt had before existed of the improper conduct of the persons who authorized and of those who were engaged in the invasion and previous occupancy of that island, of the unfriendly spirit toward the United States with which it was commenced and prosecuted, and of its injurious effect on their highest interests, particularly by its tendency to compromit them with foreign powers in all the unwarrantable acts of the adventurers, it is presumed that these documents would remove it. It appears by the letter of Mr. Pazos, agent of Commodore Aury, that the project of seizing the Floridas was formed and executed at a time when it was understood that Spain had resolved to cede them to the United States, and to prevent such cession from taking effect. The whole proceeding in every stage and circumstance was unlawful. The commission to General M'Gregor was granted at Philadelphia in direct violation of a positive law, and all the measures pursued under it by him in collecting his force and directing its movements were equally unlawful. With the conduct of these persons I have always been unwilling to connect any of the colonial governments, because I never could believe that they had

THE BATTLE OF LUNDY'S LANE

BATTLE OF LUNDY'S LANE

July 25, 1814

After this engagement both parties left the field, and so both claimed the victory. It was fought by 2500 Americans under Gen. Scott, and 4500 British under Gen. Brown. At about sunset, Scott, with a reconnoitering party of 1200, collided with the British on a road called Lundy's Lane, which led from Niagara Falls to the end of Lake Ontario. The whole American force then rushed into the conflict, which continued until midnight. Though the British abandoned their artillery, baggage and ammunition, the Americans could not move it in the night, and when they returned for it at daybreak it was too strongly defended to be taken.

The British lost 84 killed, 559 wounded, 193 missing, and 42 prisoners,— 878 all told, out of 4500. The Americans lost 171 killed, 571 wounded, and 110 missing,—a total of 852 out of 2500.

See the article entitled "Lundy's Lane, Battle of," in the index (volume eleven).

given their sanction either to the project in its origin or to the measures which were pursued in the execution of it. These documents confirm the opinion which I have invariably entertained and expressed in their favor.

JAMES MONROE.

WASHINGTON, *March 28, 1818.*

To the Senate of the United States:

In compliance with a resolution of the Senate relative to the pensioners of the United States, the sum annually paid to each, and the States or Territories in which said pensioners are respectively paid, I now transmit a report from the Secretary of War, which, with documents marked A and B, contains all the information required.

JAMES MONROE.

APRIL 6, 1818.

To the Senate of the United States:

An arrangement having been made and concluded between this Government and that of Great Britain with respect to the naval armament of the two Governments, respectively, on the Lakes, I lay before the Senate a copy of the correspondence upon that subject, including the stipulations mutually agreed upon by the two parties. I submit it to the consideration of the Senate whether this is such an arrangement as the Executive is competent to enter into by the powers vested in it by the Constitution, or is such an one as requires the advice and consent of the Senate, and, in the latter case, for their advice and consent should it be approved.

JAMES MONROE.

WASHINGTON, *April 9, 1818.*

To the Senate of the United States:

In compliance with the resolution of the Senate requesting me to cause to be laid before them a list of the names of the several agents of Indian affairs and of agents of Indian trading houses, with the pay and emolument of the agents, respectively, I now transmit a report from the Secretary of War, which contains the information required.

JAMES MONROE.

APRIL 10, 1818.

To the Senate of the United States:

In compliance with a resolution of the Senate respecting the supplies of the Northwestern army, within certain periods therein specified, by contractors, commissaries, and agents, and the expense thereby incurred, I now transmit to them a report from the Secretary of War, which, with the documents accompanying it, will afford the information required.

JAMES MONROE.

WASHINGTON, *April 15, 1818.*
To the House of Representatives of the United States:

In compliance with a resolution of the House of Representatives of the 10th instant, relative to the capture and imprisonment of certain persons, citizens of the United States, therein specifically mentioned, I now transmit a report from the Secretary of State, which, with the documents accompanying it, embraces the objects contemplated by the said resolution.

JAMES MONROE.

WASHINGTON, *April 20, 1818.*
To the Senate of the United States:

I transmit to the Senate a copy of the rules, regulations, and instructions for the naval service of the United States, prepared by the Board of Navy Commissioners in obedience to an act of Congress passed 7th of February, 1815, entitled "An act to alter and amend the several acts for establishing a Navy Department by adding thereto a Board of Commissioners."

JAMES MONROE.

PROCLAMATIONS.

BY THE PRESIDENT OF THE UNITED STATES OF AMERICA.

A PROCLAMATION.

Whereas by an act of the lieutenant-governor, council, and assembly of his Britannic Majesty's Province of Nova Scotia, passed in the year 1816, it was, among other things, enacted that from and after the 1st day of May of that year "no plaster of paris, otherwise called gypsum, which should be laden or put on board any ship or vessel at any port or place within the limits of the said Province to be transported from thence to any other port or place within or without the said limits should, directly or indirectly, be unladen or landed or put on shore at any port or place in the United States of America eastward of Boston, in the State of Massachusetts, nor unladen or put on board any American ship, vessel, boat, or shallop of any description at any port or place eastward of Boston aforesaid, under the penalty of the forfeiture of every such ship or vessel from which any such plaster of paris, or gypsum, should be unladen contrary to the provision of the said act, together with her boats, tackle, apparel, and furniture, to be seized and prosecuted in the manner thereinafter mentioned;" and

Whereas by an act of the Congress of the United States passed on the

3d day of March, 1817, it was enacted that from and after the 4th day of July then next no plaster of paris the production of any country or its dependencies from which the vessels of the United States were not permitted to bring the same article should be imported into the United States in any foreign vessel, and that all plaster of paris imported or attempted to be imported into the United States contrary to the true intent and meaning of the said act of Congress, and the vessel in which the same might be imported or attempted to be imported, together with the cargo, tackle, apparel, and furniture, should be forfeited to the United States and liable to be seized, prosecuted, and condemned in the manner therein prescribed; and

Whereas by the said act of Congress it was further enacted that the same should continue and be in force five years from January 31, 1817; provided, nevertheless, that if any foreign nation or its dependencies which at the time of the passage of the said act of Congress had in force regulations on the subject of the trade in plaster of paris prohibiting the exportation thereof to certain ports of the United States should discontinue such regulations, the President of the United States was thereby authorized to declare that fact by his proclamation, and the restrictions imposed by the said act of Congress should from the date of such proclamation cease and be discontinued in relation to the nation or its dependencies discontinuing such regulations; and

Whereas an act of the lieutenant-governor, council, and assembly of His Britannic Majesty's Province of Nova Scotia, repealing the above-mentioned act of the said Province, passed in the year 1816, has been officially communicated by his said Majesty's envoy extraordinary and minister plenipotentiary to this Government; and

Whereas by the said repealing act of the said Province of Nova Scotia, one of the dependencies of the United Kingdom of Great Britain and Ireland, the regulations at the time of the passage of the said act of Congress in force in the said Province on the subject of the trade in plaster of paris, prohibiting the exportation thereof to certain ports of the United States, have been and are discontinued:

Now, therefore, I, James Monroe, President of the United States of America, do by this my proclamation declare that fact, and that the restrictions imposed by the said act of Congress do from the date hereof cease and are discontinued in relation to His Britannic Majesty's said Province of Nova Scotia.

Given under my hand, at the city of Washington, this 23d day of April, A. D. 1818, and in the forty-second year of the Independence of the United States.

JAMES MONROE.

By the President:
JOHN QUINCY ADAMS,
Secretary of State.

BY THE PRESIDENT OF THE UNITED STATES OF AMERICA.

A PROCLAMATION.

Whereas an arrangement was entered into at the city of Washington in the month of April, A. D. 1817, between Richard Rush, esq., at that time acting as Secretary for the Department of State of the United States, for and in behalf of the Government of the United States, and the Right Honorable Charles Bagot, His Britannic Majesty's envoy extraordinary and minister plenipotentiary, for and in behalf of His Britannic Majesty, which arrangement is in the words following, to wit:

The naval force to be maintained upon the American lakes by His Majesty and the Government of the United States shall henceforth be confined to the following vessels on each side; that is—

On Lake Ontario, to one vessel not exceeding 100 tons burden and armed with one 18-pound cannon.

On the upper lakes, to two vessels not exceeding like burden each and armed with like force.

On the waters of Lake Champlain, to one vessel not exceeding like burden and armed with like force.

All other armed vessels on these lakes shall be forthwith dismantled, and no other vessels of war shall be there built or armed.

If either party should hereafter be desirous of annulling this stipulation, and should give notice to that effect to the other party, it shall cease to be binding after the expiration of six months from the date of such notice.

The naval force so to be limited shall be restricted to such services as will in no respect interfere with the proper duties of the armed vessels of the other party.

And whereas the Senate of the United States have approved of the said arrangement and recommended that it should be carried into effect, the same having also received the sanction of His Royal Highness the Prince Regent, acting in the name and on the behalf of His Britannic Majesty:

Now, therefore, I, James Monroe, President of the United States, do by this my proclamation make known and declare that the arrangement aforesaid and every stipulation thereof has been duly entered into, concluded, and confirmed, and is of full force and effect.

Given under my hand, at the city of Washington, this 28th day of April, A. D. 1818, and of the Independence of the United States the forty-second.   JAMES MONROE.

By the President:
    JOHN QUINCY ADAMS,
            Secretary of State.

BY THE PRESIDENT OF THE UNITED STATES.

A PROCLAMATION.

Whereas it appears by a proclamation of the lieutenant-governor of His Britannic Majesty's Province of New Brunswick bearing date the 10th day of April last, and officially communicated by his envoy extraordinary and minister plenipotentiary residing in the United States to this Government, that the regulations on the subject of the trade in plaster of paris, prohibiting the exportation thereof to certain ports of the United States, which were in force in the said Province at the time of the enactment of the act of the Congress of the United States entitled "An act to regulate the trade in plaster of paris," passed on the 3d day of March, 1817, have been and are discontinued:

Now, therefore, I, James Monroe, President of the United States, do hereby declare that fact, and that the restrictions imposed by the said act of Congress shall from the date hereof cease and be discontinued in relation to the said Province of New Brunswick.

Given under my hand, at the city of Washington, this 4th day of July, A. D. 1818, and in the forty-third year of the Independence of the United States.

JAMES MONROE.

By the President:
JOHN QUINCY ADAMS,
Secretary of State.

BY THE PRESIDENT OF THE UNITED STATES.

A PROCLAMATION.

Whereas by an act of the Congress of the United States of the 3d of March, 1815, so much of the several acts imposing duties on the ships and vessels and on goods, wares, and merchandise imported into the United States as imposed a discriminating duty of tonnage between foreign vessels and vessels of the United States and between goods imported into the United States in foreign vessels and vessels of the United States were repealed so far as the same respected the produce or manufacture of the nation to which such foreign ship or vessel might belong, such repeal to take effect in favor of any foreign nation whenever the President of the United States should be satisfied that the discriminating or countervailing duties of such foreign nation so far as they operate to the disadvantage of the United States have been abolished; and

Whereas satisfactory proof has been received by me from the burgomasters and senators of the free and Hanseatic city of Bremen that from and after the 12th day of May, 1815, all discriminating or countervailing duties of the said city so far as they operated to the disadvantage of the United States have been and are abolished:

Now, therefore, I, James Monroe, President of the United States of America, do hereby declare and proclaim that so much of the several acts imposing duties on the tonnage of ships and vessels and on goods, wares, and merchandise imported into the United States as imposed a discriminating duty of tonnage between vessels of the free and Hanseatic city of Bremen and vessels of the United States and between goods imported into the United States in vessels of Bremen and vessels of the United States are repealed so far as the same respect the produce or manufacture of the said free Hanseatic city of Bremen.

Given under my hand, at the city of Washington, this 24th day of July, A. D. 1818, and the forty-third year of the Independence of the United States. JAMES MONROE.

By the President:

JOHN QUINCY ADAMS,
Secretary of State.

BY THE PRESIDENT OF THE UNITED STATES.

A PROCLAMATION.

Whereas by an act of the Congress of the United States of the 3d of March, 1815, so much of the several acts imposing duties on the ships and vessels and on goods, wares, and merchandise imported into the United States as imposed a discriminating duty of tonnage between foreign vessels and vessels of the United States and between goods imported into the United States in foreign vessels and vessels of the United States were repealed so far as the same respected the produce or manufacture of the nation to which such foreign ship or vessel might belong, such repeal to take effect in favor of any foreign nation whenever the President of the United States should be satisfied that the discriminating or countervailing duties of such foreign nation so far as they operate to the disadvantage of the United States have been abolished; and

Whereas satisfactory proof has been received by me from the burgomasters and senators of the free and Hanseatic city of Hamburg that from and after the 13th day of November, 1815, all discriminating and countervailing duties of the said city so far as they operated to the disadvantage of the United States have been and are abolished:

Now, therefore, I, James Monroe, President of the United States of America, do hereby declare and proclaim that so much of the several acts imposing duties on the tonnage of ships and vessels and on goods, wares, and merchandise imported into the United States as imposed a discriminating duty of tonnage between vessels of the free and Hanseatic city of Hamburg and vessels of the United States and between goods imported into the United States in vessels of Hamburg and vessels of the United States are repealed so far as the same respect the produce or manufacture of the said free Hanseatic city of Hamburg.

Given under my hand, at the city of Washington, this 1st day of August, A. D. 1818, and the forty-third year of the Independence of the United States. JAMES MONROE.

By the President:

JOHN QUINCY ADAMS,
Secretary of State.

SECOND ANNUAL MESSAGE.

NOVEMBER 16, 1818.

Fellow-Citizens of the Senate and of the House of Representatives:

The auspicious circumstances under which you will commence the duties of the present session will lighten the burdens inseparable from the high trust committed to you. The fruits of the earth have been unusually abundant, commerce has flourished, the revenue has exceeded the most favorable anticipation, and peace and amity are preserved with foreign nations on conditions just and honorable to our country. For these inestimable blessings we can not but be grateful to that Providence which watches over the destiny of nations.

As the term limited for the operation of the commercial convention with Great Britain will expire early in the month of July next, and it was deemed important that there should be no interval during which that portion of our commerce which was provided for by that convention should not be regulated, either by arrangement between the two Governments or by the authority of Congress, the minister of the United States at London was instructed early in the last summer to invite the attention of the British Government to the subject, with a view to that object. He was instructed to propose also that the negotiation which it was wished to open might extend to the general commerce of the two countries, and to every other interest and unsettled difference between them, particularly those relating to impressment, the fisheries, and boundaries, in the hope that an arrangement might be made on principles of reciprocal advantage which might comprehend and provide in a satisfactory manner for all these high concerns. I have the satisfaction to state that the proposal was received by the British Government in the spirit which prompted it, and that a negotiation has been opened at London embracing all these objects. On full consideration of the great extent and magnitude of the trust it was thought proper to commit it to not less than two of our distinguished citizens, and in consequence the envoy extraordinary and minister plenipotentiary of the United States at Paris has been associated with our envoy extraordinary and minister plenipotentiary at London, to both of whom corresponding instructions have been given, and they are now engaged in the discharge of its duties. It is proper to add that to prevent any inconvenience resulting from the delay incident to a negotiation on so many important subjects it was agreed before entering on it that the existing convention should be continued for a term not less than eight years.

Our relations with Spain remain nearly in the state in which they were at the close of the last session. The convention of 1802, providing for the adjustment of a certain portion of the claims of our citizens for injuries sustained by spoliation, and so long suspended by the Spanish

Government, has at length been ratified by it, but no arrangement has yet been made for the payment of another portion of like claims, not less extensive or well founded, or for other classes of claims, or for the settlement of boundaries. These subjects have again been brought under consideration in both countries, but no agreement has been entered into respecting them. In the meantime events have occurred which clearly prove the ill effect of the policy which that Government has so long pursued on the friendly relations of the two countries, which it is presumed is at least of as much importance to Spain as to the United States to maintain. A state of things has existed in the Floridas the tendency of which has been obvious to all who have paid the slightest attention to the progress of affairs in that quarter. Throughout the whole of those Provinces to which the Spanish title extends the Government of Spain has scarcely been felt. Its authority has been confined almost exclusively to the walls of Pensacola and St. Augustine, within which only small garrisons have been maintained. Adventurers from every country, fugitives from justice, and absconding slaves have found an asylum there. Several tribes of Indians, strong in the number of their warriors, remarkable for their ferocity, and whose settlements extend to our limits, inhabit those Provinces. These different hordes of people, connected together, disregarding on the one side the authority of Spain, and protected on the other by an imaginary line which separates Florida from the United States, have violated our laws prohibiting the introduction of slaves, have practiced various frauds on our revenue, and committed every kind of outrage on our peaceable citizens which their proximity to us enabled them to perpetrate. The invasion of Amelia Island last year by a small band of adventurers, not exceeding 150 in number, who wrested it from the inconsiderable Spanish force stationed there, and held it several months, during which a single feeble effort only was made to recover it, which failed, clearly proves how completely extinct the Spanish authority had become, as the conduct of those adventurers while in possession of the island as distinctly shows the pernicious purposes for which their combination had been formed.

This country had, in fact, become the theater of every species of lawless adventure. With little population of its own, the Spanish authority almost extinct, and the colonial governments in a state of revolution, having no pretension to it, and sufficiently employed in their own concerns, it was in a great measure derelict, and the object of cupidity to every adventurer. A system of buccaneering was rapidly organizing over it which menaced in its consequences the lawful commerce of every nation, and particularly of the United States, while it presented a temptation to every people, on whose seduction its success principally depended. In regard to the United States, the pernicious effect of this unlawful combination was not confined to the ocean; the Indian tribes have constituted the effective force in Florida. With these tribes these adventurers had formed at an early period a connection with a view to avail themselves of that force to promote their own projects of accumulation and aggrandizement. It is to the interference of some of these adventurers, in misrepresenting the claims and titles of the Indians to land and in practicing on their savage propensities, that the Seminole war is principally to be traced. Men who thus connect themselves with savage communities and stimulate them to war, which is always attended on their part with acts of barbarity the most shocking, deserve to be viewed in a worse light than the savages. They would certainly have no claim to an immunity from the punishment which, according to the rules of warfare practiced by the savages, might justly be inflicted on the savages themselves.

If the embarrassments of Spain prevented her from making an indemnity to our citizens for so long a time from her treasury for their losses by spoliation and otherwise, it was always in her power to have provided it by the cession of this territory. Of this her Government has been repeatedly apprised, and the cession was the more to have been anticipated as Spain must have known that in ceding it she would in effect cede what had become of little value to her, and would likewise relieve herself from the important obligation secured by the treaty of 1795 and all other compromitments respecting it. If the United States, from consideration of these embarrassments, declined pressing their claims in a spirit of hostility, the motive ought at least to have been duly appreciated by the Government of Spain. It is well known to her Government that other powers have made to the United States an indemnity for like losses sustained by their citizens at the same epoch.

There is nevertheless a limit beyond which this spirit of amity and forbearance can in no instance be justified. If it was proper to rely on amicable negotiation for an indemnity for losses, it would not have been so to have permitted the inability of Spain to fulfill her engagements and to sustain her authority in the Floridas to be perverted by foreign adventurers and savages to purposes so destructive to the lives of our fellow-citizens and the highest interests of the United States. The right of self-defense never ceases. It is among the most sacred, and alike necessary to nations and to individuals, and whether the attack be made by Spain herself or by those who abuse her power, its obligation is not the less strong. The invaders of Amelia Island had assumed a popular and respected title under which they might approach and wound us. As their object was distinctly seen, and the duty imposed on the Executive by an existing law was profoundly felt, that mask was not permitted to protect them. It was thought incumbent on the United States to suppress the establishment, and it was accordingly done. The combination in Florida for the unlawful purposes stated, the acts perpetrated by that combination, and, above all, the incitement of the Indians to massacre our fellow-citizens of every age and of both sexes, merited a like treatment and received it. In pursuing these savages to an imaginary line in the woods it would have been the height of folly to have suffered that line to protect them. Had that been done the war could never cease. Even if the territory had been exclusively that of Spain and her power complete over it, we had a right by the law of nations to follow the enemy on it and to subdue him there. But the territory belonged, in a certain sense at least, to the savage enemy who inhabited it; the power of Spain had ceased to exist over it, and protection was sought under her title by those who had committed on our citizens hostilities which she was bound by treaty to have prevented, but had not the power to prevent. To have stopped at that line would have given new encouragement to these savages and new vigor to the whole combination existing there in the prosecution of all its pernicious purposes.

In suppressing the establishment at Amelia Island no unfriendliness was manifested toward Spain, because the post was taken from a force which had wrested it from her. The measure, it is true, was not adopted in concert with the Spanish Government or those in authority under it, because in transactions connected with the war in which Spain and the colonies are engaged it was thought proper in doing justice to the United States to maintain a strict impartiality toward both the belligerent parties without consulting or acting in concert with either. It gives me pleasure to state that the Governments of Buenos Ayres and Venezuela, whose names were assumed, have explicitly disclaimed all participation in those measures, and even the knowledge of them until communicated by this Government, and have also expressed their satisfaction that a course of proceedings had been suppressed which if justly imputable to them would dishonor their cause.

In authorizing Major-General Jackson to enter Florida in pursuit of the Seminoles care was taken not to encroach on the rights of Spain. I regret to have to add that in executing this order facts were disclosed respecting the conduct of the officers of Spain in authority there in encouraging the war, furnishing munitions of war and other supplies to carry it on, and in other acts not less marked which evinced their participation in the hostile purposes of that combination and justified the confidence with which it inspired the savages that by those officers they would be protected. A conduct so incompatible with the friendly relations existing between the two countries, particularly with the positive obligation of the fifth article of the treaty of 1795, by which Spain was bound to restrain, even by force, those savages from acts of hostility against the United States, could not fail to excite surprise. The commanding general was convinced that he should fail in his object, that he should in effect accomplish nothing, if he did not deprive those savages of the resource on which they had calculated and of the protection on which they had relied in making the war. As all the documents relating to this occurrence will be laid before Congress, it is not necessary to enter into further detail respecting it.

Although the reasons which induced Major-General Jackson to take these posts were duly appreciated, there was nevertheless no hesitation in deciding on the course which it became the Government to pursue. As there was reason to believe that the commanders of these posts had violated their instructions, there was no disposition to impute to their Government a conduct so unprovoked and hostile. An order was in consequence issued to the general in command there to deliver the posts— Pensacola unconditionally to any person duly authorized to receive it, and St. Marks, which is in the heart of the Indian country, on the arrival of a competent force to defend it against those savages and their associates.

In entering Florida to suppress this combination no idea was entertained of hostility to Spain, and however justifiable the commanding general was, in consequence of the misconduct of the Spanish officers, in entering St. Marks and Pensacola to terminate it by proving to the savages and their associates that they should not be protected even there, yet the amicable relations existing between the United States and Spain could not be altered by that act alone. By ordering the restitution of the posts those relations were preserved. To a change of them the power of the Executive is deemed incompetent; it is vested in Congress only.

By this measure, so promptly taken, due respect was shown to the Government of Spain. The misconduct of her officers has not been imputed to her. She was enabled to review with candor her relations with the United States and her own situation, particularly in respect to the territory in question, with the dangers inseparable from it, and regarding the losses we have sustained for which indemnity has been so long withheld, and the injuries we have suffered through that territory, and her means of redress, she was likewise enabled to take with honor the course best calculated to do justice to the United States and to promote her own welfare.

Copies of the instructions to the commanding general, of his correspondence with the Secretary of War, explaining his motives and justifying his conduct, with a copy of the proceedings of the courts-martial in the trial of Arbuthnot and Ambristie, and of the correspondence between the Secretary of State and the minister plenipotentiary of Spain near this Government, and of the minister plenipotentiary of the United States at Madrid with the Government of Spain, will be laid before Congress.

The civil war which has so long prevailed between Spain and the Provinces in South America still continues, without any prospect of its speedy termination. The information respecting the condition of those countries which has been collected by the commissioners recently returned from thence will be laid before Congress in copies of their reports, with such other information as has been received from other agents of the United States.

It appears from these communications that the Government at Buenos Ayres declared itself independent in July, 1816, having previously exercised the power of an independent government, though in the name of the

King of Spain, from the year 1810; that the Banda Oriental, Entre Rios, and Paraguay, with the city of Santa Fee, all of which are also independent, are unconnected with the present Government of Buenos Ayres; that Chili has declared itself independent and is closely connected with Buenos Ayres; that Venezuela has also declared itself independent, and now maintains the conflict with various success; and that the remaining parts of South America, except Monte Video and such other portions of the eastern bank of the La Plata as are held by Portugal, are still in the possession of Spain or in a certain degree under her influence.

By a circular note addressed by the ministers of Spain to the allied powers, with whom they are respectively accredited, it appears that the allies have undertaken to mediate between Spain and the South American Provinces, and that the manner and extent of their interposition would be settled by a congress which was to have met at Aix-la-Chapelle in September last. From the general policy and course of proceeding observed by the allied powers in regard to this contest it is inferred that they will confine their interposition to the expression of their sentiments, abstaining from the application of force. I state this impression that force will not be applied with the greater satisfaction because it is a course more consistent with justice and likewise authorizes a hope that the calamities of the war will be confined to the parties only, and will be of shorter duration.

From the view taken of this subject, founded on all the information that we have been able to obtain, there is good cause to be satisfied with the course heretofore pursued by the United States in regard to this contest, and to conclude that it is proper to adhere to it, especially in the present state of affairs.

I have great satisfaction in stating that our relations with France, Russia, and other powers continue on the most friendly basis.

In our domestic concerns we have ample cause of satisfaction. The receipts into the Treasury during the three first quarters of the year have exceeded $17,000,000.

After satisfying all the demands which have been made under existing appropriations, including the final extinction of the old 6 per cent stock and the redemption of a moiety of the Louisiana debt, it is estimated that there will remain in the Treasury on the 1st day of January next more than $2,000,000.

It is ascertained that the gross revenue which has accrued from the customs during the same period amounts to $21,000,000, and that the revenue of the whole year may be estimated at not less than $26,000,000. The sale of the public lands during the year has also greatly exceeded, both in quantity and price, that of any former year, and there is just reason to expect a progressive improvement in that source of revenue.

It is gratifying to know that although the annual expenditure has been increased by the act of the last session of Congress providing for Revolutionary pensions to an amount about equal to the proceeds of the internal duties which were then repealed, the revenue for the ensuing year will be proportionally augmented, and that whilst the public expenditure will probably remain stationary, each successive year will add to the national resources by the ordinary increase of our population and by the gradual development of our latent sources of national prosperity.

The strict execution of the revenue laws, resulting principally from the salutary provisions of the act of the 20th of April last amending the several collection laws, has, it is presumed, secured to domestic manufactures all the relief that can be derived from the duties which have been imposed upon foreign merchandise for their protection. Under the influence of this relief several branches of this important national interest have assumed greater activity, and although it is hoped that others will gradually revive and ultimately triumph over every obstacle, yet the expediency of granting further protection is submitted to your consideration.

The measures of defense authorized by existing laws have been pursued with the zeal and activity due to so important an object, and with all the dispatch practicable in so extensive and great an undertaking. The survey of our maritime and inland frontiers has been continued, and at the points where it was decided to erect fortifications the work has been commenced, and in some instances considerable progress has been made. In compliance with resolutions of the last session, the Board of Commissioners were directed to examine in a particular manner the parts of the coast therein designated and to report their opinion of the most suitable sites for two naval depots. This work is in a train of execution. The opinion of the Board on this subject, with a plan of all the works necessary to a general system of defense so far as it has been formed, will be laid before Congress in a report from the proper department as soon as it can be prepared.

In conformity with the appropriations of the last session, treaties have been formed with the Quapaw tribe of Indians, inhabiting the country on the Arkansaw, and with the Great and Little Osages north of the White River; with the tribes in the State of Indiana; with the several tribes within the State of Ohio and the Michigan Territory, and with the Chickasaws, by which very extensive cessions of territory have been made to the United States. Negotiations are now depending with the tribes in the Illinois Territory and with the Choctaws, by which it is expected that other extensive cessions will be made. I take great interest in stating that the cessions already made, which are considered so important to the United States, have been obtained on conditions very satisfactory to the Indians.

With a view to the security of our inland frontiers, it has been thought expedient to establish strong posts at the mouth of Yellow Stone River and at the Mandan village on the Missouri, and at the mouth of St. Peters on the Mississippi, at no great distance from our northern boundaries. It can hardly be presumed while such posts are maintained in the rear of the Indian tribes that they will venture to attack our peaceable inhabitants. A strong hope is entertained that this measure will likewise be productive of much good to the tribes themselves, especially in promoting the great object of their civilization. Experience has clearly demonstrated that independent savage communities can not long exist within the limits of a civilized population. The progress of the latter has almost invariably terminated in the extinction of the former, especially of the tribes belonging to our portion of this hemisphere, among whom loftiness of sentiment and gallantry in action have been conspicuous. To civilize them, and even to prevent their extinction, it seems to be indispensable that their independence as communities should cease, and that the control of the United States over them should be complete and undisputed. The hunter state will then be more easily abandoned, and recourse will be had to the acquisition and culture of land and to other pursuits tending to dissolve the ties which connect them together as a savage community and to give a new character to every individual. I present this subject to the consideration of Congress on the presumption that it may be found expedient and practicable to adopt some benevolent provisions, having these objects in view, relative to the tribes within our settlements.

It has been necessary during the present year to maintain a strong naval force in the Mediterranean and in the Gulf of Mexico, and to send some public ships along the southern coast and to the Pacific Ocean. By these means amicable relations with the Barbary Powers have been preserved, our commerce has been protected, and our rights respected. The augmentation of our Navy is advancing with a steady progress toward the limit contemplated by law.

I communicate with great satisfaction the accession of another State (Illinois) to our Union, because I perceive from the proof afforded by the additions already made the regular progress and sure consummation of a policy of which history affords no example, and of which the good effect can not be too highly estimated. By extending our Government on the principles of our Constitution over the vast territory within our limits, on the Lakes and the Mississippi and its numerous streams, new life and vigor are infused into every part of our system. By increasing the number of the States the confidence of the State governments in their own security is increased and their jealousy of the National Government proportionally diminished. The impracticability of one consolidated government for this great and growing nation will be more apparent and will be universally admitted. Incapable of exercising local authority except for general purposes, the General Government will no longer be dreaded. In those cases of a local nature and for all the great purposes for which it was instituted its authority will be cherished. Each government will acquire new force and a greater freedom of action within its proper sphere. Other inestimable advantages will follow. Our produce will be augmented to an incalculable amount in articles of the greatest value for domestic use and foreign commerce. Our navigation will in like degree be increased, and as the shipping of the Atlantic States will be employed in the transportation of the vast produce of the Western country, even those parts of the United States which are most remote from each other will be further bound together by the strongest ties which mutual interest can create.

The situation of this District, it is thought, requires the attention of Congress. By the Constitution the power of legislation is exclusively vested in the Congress of the United States. In the exercise of this power, in which the people have no participation, Congress legislate in all cases directly on the local concerns of the District. As this is a departure, for a special purpose, from the general principles of our system, it may merit consideration whether an arrangement better adapted to the principles of our Government and to the particular interests of the people may not be devised which will neither infringe the Constitution nor affect the object which the provision in question was intended to secure. The growing population, already considerable, and the increasing business of the District, which it is believed already interferes with the deliberations of Congress on great national concerns, furnish additional motives for recommending this subject to your consideration.

When we view the great blessings with which our country has been favored, those which we now enjoy, and the means which we possess of handing them down unimpaired to our latest posterity, our attention is irresistibly drawn to the source from whence they flow. Let us, then, unite in offering our most grateful acknowledgments for these blessings to the Divine Author of All Good.

JAMES MONROE.

SPECIAL MESSAGES.

NOVEMBER 30, 1818.

To the Senate of the United States:

I lay before the Senate, for their advice and consent, the several treaties which have recently been made with the Chickasaws, the Quapaws, the Wyandot, Seneca, Delaware, Shawnese, Potawatamies, Ottawas, and Chippewas, the Peoria, Kaskaskias, Mitchigamia, Cahokia, and Tamarois, the Great and Little Osages, the Weas, Potawatamies, Delaware and Miami, the Wyandot, and the four Pawnees tribes of Indians.

By reference to the journal of the commissioners it appears that George and Levi Colbert have bargained and sold to the United States the reservations made to them by the treaty of September, 1816, and that a deed of trust of the same has been made by them to James Jackson, of

Nashville.   I would therefore suggest, in case the Chickasaw treaty be approved by the Senate, the propriety of providing by law for the payment of the sum stipulated to be given to them for their reservations.

JAMES MONROE.

DECEMBER 2, 1818.

To the Senate of the United States:

I transmit to the Senate copies of such of the documents referred to in the message of the 17th of last month as have been prepared since that period.   They contain a copy of the reports of Mr. Rodney and Mr. Graham, two of the commissioners to South America, who returned first from the mission, and of the papers connected with those reports.   They also present a full view of the operations of our troops employed in the Seminole war in Florida.

It would have been gratifying to me to have communicated with the message all the documents referred to in it, but as two of our commissioners from South America made their reports a few days only before the meeting of Congress and the third on the day of its meeting, it was impossible to transmit at that time more than one copy of the two reports first made.

The residue of the documents will be communicated as soon as they are prepared.

JAMES MONROE.

WASHINGTON, *December 2, 1818.*

To the Senate of the United States:

In compliance with a resolution of the Senate of 25th of last month, requesting to be furnished with such information as may be possessed by the Executive touching the execution of so much of the first article of the late treaty of peace and amity between His Britannic Majesty and the United States as relates to the restitution of slaves, and which has not heretofore been communicated, I lay before the Senate a report made by the Secretary of State on the 1st instant in relation to that subject.

JAMES MONROE.

DECEMBER 2, 1818.

To the House of Representatives of the United States:

I transmit to the House of Representatives copies of such documents referred to in the message of the 17th ultimo as have been prepared since that period.   They present a full view of the operations of our troops employed in the Seminole war who entered Florida.

The residue of the documents, which are very voluminous, will be transmitted as soon as they can be prepared.

JAMES MONROE.

REPULSE OF BRITISH AT NEW ORLEANS, 1814

BATTLE OF NEW ORLEANS

Pakenham, with 8,000 British veterans of the Napoleonic wars, tried to wrest the city of New Orleans, with the control of the Mississippi, from Jackson's motley army of Creoles, French pirates, free negroes, San Domingans, French veterans, frontiersmen from Tennessee and Kentucky, and soldiers and sailors from the regular forces of the United States. Jackson's men fought behind a straight earthwork. The British Peninsular veterans advanced cheering. A redoubt on the far right was carried, but so terrible a fire opened on them from the line that they fled. The main attack was repulsed by riflemen from Kentucky and Tennessee. The British formed a column of sixty men front in a ditch 400 yards from the earthwork. They fell, says an eye-witness, like blades of grass before the scythe. They broke and fled; then reformed and charged. Pakenham was shot while leading them. Lambert, his successor, stopped the battle. The British had about 700 dead, of whom 85 were officers. See the index article entitled "New Orleans, Battle of," in volume eleven.

DECEMBER 12, 1818.

To the House of Representatives of the United States:

In compliance with the resolution of the House of Representatives of the 10th instant, I transmit a report of the Secretary of War, with copies of the correspondence between the governor of Georgia and Major-General Andrew Jackson on the subject of the arrest of Captain Obed Wright.

JAMES MONROE.

DECEMBER 29, 1818.

To the Senate of the United States:

I lay before the Senate, for their consideration, a convention, signed at London on the 20th of October last, between the United States and Great Britain, together with the documents showing the course and progress of the negotiation. I have to request that these documents, which are original, may be returned when the Senate shall have acted on the convention.

JAMES MONROE.

DECEMBER 31, 1818.

To the House of Representatives of the United States:

In compliance with a resolution of the House of Representatives of the 24th instant, requesting me to lay before it "copies of the correspondence, if any, between the Department of War and the governor of Georgia, in answer to the letter of the latter to the former dated on the 1st of June of the present year, communicated to the House on the 12th instant; and also the correspondence, if any, between the Department of War and General Andrew Jackson, in answer to the letter of the latter of the date 7th May, 1818, also communicated to the House on the 12th instant," I transmit a report from the Secretary of War, with a copy of an extract of a letter from Major Van De Venter, chief clerk in the Department of War, in reply to General Jackson's letter of the 7th of May, 1818.

JAMES MONROE.

DECEMBER 31, 1818.

To the House of Representatives of the United States:

In compliance with a resolution of the House of Representatives of the 7th instant, requesting me to lay before it "the proceedings which have been had under the act entitled 'An act for the gradual increase of the Navy of the United States,' specifying the number of ships which have been put on the stocks, and of what class, and the quantity and kind of materials which have been procured in compliance with the provisions of said act; and also the sums of money which have been paid out of the fund created by the said act, and for what objects; and likewise the con-tracts which have been entered into in execution of said act on which moneys may not yet have been advanced," I transmit a report from the Acting Secretary of the Navy, together with a communication from the Board of Navy Commissioners, which, with the documents accompanying it, comprehends all the information required by the House of Representatives.

JAMES MONROE.

WASHINGTON, *January 4, 1819.*

To the Senate and House of Representatives of the United States:

I transmit to Congress a proclamation, dated the 22d of last month, of the convention made and concluded at Madrid between the plenipotentiaries of the United States and His Catholic Majesty on the 11th of August, 1802, the ratifications of which were not exchanged until the 21st ultimo, together with the translation of a letter from the minister of Spain to the Secretary of State.

JAMES MONROE.

JANUARY 4, 1819.

To the Senate of the United States:

I transmit to the Senate, in pursuance of their resolution of the 30th of last month, requesting to be furnished with the instructions, including that of the 28th of July, 1818, to the plenipotentiaries of the United States who negotiated the convention with His Britannic Majesty signed on the 20th day of October in the same year, copies of all these instructions, including that particularly referred to.

JAMES MONROE.

JANUARY 11, 1819.

To the Senate of the United States:

In compliance with a resolution of the Senate of the 5th instant, requesting me "to cause to be laid before it a statement of the effective force composing the military establishment of the United States; also a statement of the different posts and garrisons at and within which troops are stationed, and the actual number of officers, noncommissioned officers, and privates at each post and garrison, respectively; also to designate in such statement the number of artillerists and the number and caliber of ordnance at each of the said posts and garrisons," I transmit a report from the Secretary of War, which, with the documents accompanying it, contains all the information required.

JAMES MONROE.

JANUARY 29, 1819.

To the House of Representatives of the United States:

I transmit to the House of Representatives, in compliance with their resolution of the 4th of this month, a report from the Secretary of State concerning the applications which have been made by any of the independent Governments of South America to have a minister or consul-general accredited by the Government of the United States, with the answers of this Government to the applications addressed to it.

JAMES MONROE.

JANUARY 30, 1819.

To the House of Representatives of the United States:

In compliance with a resolution of the House of Representatives of the 18th instant, requesting me to cause any information not already communicated to be laid before the House whether Amelia Island, St. Marks, and Pensacola yet remain in the possession of the United States, and, if so, by what laws the inhabitants are governed; whether articles imported therein from foreign countries are subject to any, and what, duties, and by what laws, and whether the said duties are collected and how; whether vessels arriving in the United States from Pensacola and Amelia Island, and in Pensacola and Amelia Island from the United States, respectively, are considered and treated as vessels arriving from foreign countries, I transmit a report from the Secretary of the Treasury, and likewise one from the Secretary of War, which will afford all the information requested by the House of Representatives.

JAMES MONROE.

FEBRUARY 2, 1819.

To the Senate of the United States:

I nominate John Overton, Newton Cannon, and Robert Weakly, of Tennessee, as commissioners to negotiate with the Chickasaw tribe of Indians for the cession of a tract of land 4 miles square, including a salt spring, reserved to the said tribe by the fourth article of a treaty concluded with the said Indians on the 19th day of October, 1818.

JAMES MONROE.

FEBRUARY 2, 1819.

To the Senate of the United States:

In compliance with a resolution of the Senate of the 13th of last month, requesting me "to cause to be laid before it a statement showing the measures that have been taken to collect the balances stated to be due from the several supervisors and collectors of the old direct tax of two millions; also a similar statement of the balances due from the officers of the old internal revenue, and to designate in such statement the persons who have been interested in the collection of the said debts and the sums by them respectively collected, and the time when the same were collected," I transmit a report of the Secretary of the Treasury, which, with the documents accompanying it, contains all the information required.

JAMES MONROE.

WASHINGTON, *February 3, 1819.*

To the Senate and House of Representatives of the United States:

I communicate to Congress copies of applications received from the minister of Great Britain in behalf of certain British subjects who have suffered in their property by proceedings to which the United States by their military and judicial officers have been parties. These injuries have been sustained under circumstances which appear to recommend strongly to the attention of Congress the claim to indemnity for the losses occasioned by them, which the legislative authority is alone competent to provide.

JAMES MONROE.

FEBRUARY 5, 1819.

To the Senate of the United States:

In compliance with a resolution of the Senate of the 25th of last month, requesting me "to cause to be laid before it a copy of the rules and regulations adopted for the government of the Military Academy at West Point; also how many cadets have been admitted into the Academy, the time of the residence of each cadet at that institution, and how many of them have been appointed officers in the Army and Navy of the United States," I transmit a report from the Secretary of War, which, with the accompanying documents, will afford all the information required by the said resolution.

JAMES MONROE.

WASHINGTON, *February 6, 1819.*

To the Senate and House of Representatives of the United States:

I transmit to Congress a copy of a letter from Governor Bibb to Major-General Jackson, connected with the late military operations in Florida. This letter has been mislaid, or it would have been communicated with the other documents at the commencement of the session.

JAMES MONROE.

FEBRUARY 6, 1819.

To the Senate and House of Representatives of the United States:

I transmit to Congress, for their consideration, applications which have been received from the minister resident of Prussia and from the senates of the free and Hanseatic cities of Hamburg and Bremen, the object of which is that the advantages secured by the act of Congress of 20th of April last to the vessels and merchandise of the Netherlands should be extended to those of Prussia, Hamburg, and Bremen. It will appear from these documents that the vessels of the United States and the merchandise laden in them are in the ports of those Governments, respectively, entitled to the same advantages in respect to imposts and duties as those of the native subjects of the countries themselves.

The principle of reciprocity appears to entitle them to the return of the same favor on the part of the United States, and I recommend it to Congress that provision to that effect may be made.

JAMES MONROE.

FEBRUARY 22, 1819.
To the Senate of the United States:

I transmit to the Senate a treaty of amity, settlement, and limits between the United States of America and His Catholic Majesty, concluded and signed this day, for the decision of the Senate as to its ratification. Copies of the correspondence between the Secretary of State and the minister from Spain connected with this subject since the renewal of the negotiation are likewise inclosed.

JAMES MONROE.

WASHINGTON, *February 26, 1819.*
To the Senate and House of Representatives of the United States:

The treaty of amity, settlement, and limits between the United States and His Catholic Majesty having been on the part of the United States ratified, by and with the advice and consent of the Senate, copies of it are now transmitted to Congress. As the ratification on the part of Spain may be expected to take place during the recess of Congress, I recommend to their consideration the adoption of such legislative measures contingent upon the event of the exchange of the ratifications as may be necessary or expedient for carrying the treaty into effect in the interval between the sessions, and until Congress at their next session may see fit to make further provision on the subject.

JAMES MONROE.

MARCH 2, 1819.
To the Senate of the United States:

A convention having been concluded between John C. Calhoun, Secretary of War, especially authorized therefor by me, and the chiefs and headmen of the Cherokee Nation of Indians, likewise duly authorized and empowered by said nation, I now lay the original instrument before the Senate for the exercise of its constitutional power respecting the ratification thereof.

JAMES MONROE.

THIRD ANNUAL MESSAGE.

WASHINGTON, *December 7, 1819.*

Fellow-Citizens of the Senate and of the House of Representatives:

The public buildings being advanced to a stage to afford accommodation for Congress, I offer you my sincere congratulations on the recommencement of your duties in the Capitol.

In bringing to view the incidents most deserving attention which have occurred since your last session, I regret to have to state that several of our principal cities have suffered by sickness, that an unusual drought has prevailed in the Middle and Western States, and that a derangement has been felt in some of our moneyed institutions which has proportionably affected their credit. I am happy, however, to have it in my power to assure you that the health of our cities is now completely restored; that the produce of the year, though less abundant than usual, will not only be amply sufficient for home consumption, but afford a large surplus for the supply of the wants of other nations, and that the derangement in the circulating paper medium, by being left to those remedies which its obvious causes suggested and the good sense and virtue of our fellow-citizens supplied, has diminished.

Having informed Congress, on the 27th of February last, that a treaty of amity, settlement, and limits had been concluded in this city between the United States and Spain, and ratified by the competent authorities of the former, full confidence was entertained that it would have been ratified by His Catholic Majesty with equal promptitude and a like earnest desire to terminate on the conditions of that treaty the differences which had so long existed between the two countries. Every view which the subject admitted of was thought to have justified this conclusion. Great losses had been sustained by citizens of the United States from Spanish cruisers more than twenty years before, which had not been redressed. These losses had been acknowledged and provided for by a treaty as far back as the year 1802, which, although concluded at Madrid, was not then ratified by the Government of Spain, nor since, until the last year, when it was suspended by the late treaty, a more satisfactory provision to both parties, as was presumed, having been made for them. Other differences had arisen in this long interval, affecting their highest interests, which were likewise provided for by this last treaty. The treaty itself was formed on great consideration and a thorough knowledge of all circumstances, the subject-matter of every article having been for years under discussion and repeated references having been made by the minister of Spain to his Government on the points respecting which the greatest difference of opinion prevailed. It was formed by a minister duly authorized for the purpose, who had represented his Government in the United States and been employed in this long-protracted negotiation several years, and who, it is not denied, kept strictly within the letter of his instructions. The faith of Spain was therefore pledged, under circumstances of peculiar force and solemnity, for its ratification. On the part of the United States this treaty was evidently acceded to in a spirit of conciliation and concession. The indemnity for injuries and losses so long before sustained, and now again acknowledged and provided for, was to be paid by them without becoming a charge on the treasury of Spain. For territory ceded by Spain other territory of great value, to which our claim was believed to be well founded, was ceded by the United States, and in a quarter more interesting to her. This cession was nevertheless received as the means of indemnifying our citizens in a considerable sum, the presumed amount of their losses. Other considerations of great weight urged the cession of this territory by Spain. It was surrounded by the Territories of the United States on every side except on that of the ocean. Spain had lost her authority over it, and, falling into the hands of adventurers connected with the savages, it was made the means of unceasing annoyance and injury to our Union in many of its most essential interests. By this cession, then, Spain ceded a territory in reality of no value to her and obtained concessions of the highest importance by the settlement of long-standing differences with the United States affecting their respective claims and limits, and likewise relieved herself from the obligation of a treaty relating to it which she had failed to fulfill, and also from the responsibility incident to the most flagrant and pernicious abuses of her rights where she could not support her authority.

It being known that the treaty was formed under these circumstances, not a doubt was entertained that His Catholic Majesty would have ratified it without delay. I regret to have to state that this reasonable expectation has been disappointed; that the treaty was not ratified within the time stipulated and has not since been ratified. As it is important that the nature and character of this unexpected occurrence should be distinctly understood, I think it my duty to communicate to you all the facts and circumstances in my possession relating to it.

Anxious to prevent all future disagreement with Spain by giving the most prompt effect to the treaty which had been thus concluded, and particularly by the establishment of a government in Florida which should preserve order there, the minister of the United States who had been recently appointed to His Catholic Majesty, and to whom the ratification by his Government had been committed to be exchanged for that of Spain, was instructed to transmit the latter to the Department of State as soon as obtained, by a public ship subjected to his order for the purpose. Unexpected delay occurring in the ratification by Spain, he requested to be informed of the cause. It was stated in reply that the great importance of the subject, and a desire to obtain explanations on certain points which were not specified, had produced the delay, and that an envoy would be dispatched to the United States to obtain such explanations of this Government. The minister of the United States offered to give full explanation on any point on which it might be desired, which proposal was declined. Having communicated this result to the Department of State in August last, he was instructed, notwithstanding the disappointment and surprise which it produced, to inform the Government of Spain that if the treaty should be ratified and transmitted here at any time before the meeting of Congress it would be received and have the same effect as if it had been ratified in due time. This order was executed, the authorized communication was made to the Government of Spain, and by its answer, which has just been received, we are officially made acquainted for the first time with the causes which have prevented the ratification of the treaty by His Catholic Majesty. It is alleged by the minister of Spain that this Government had attempted to alter one of the principal articles of the treaty by a declaration which the minister of the United States had been ordered to present when he should deliver the ratification by his Government in exchange for that of Spain, and of which he gave notice, explanatory of the sense in which that article was understood. It is further alleged that this Government had recently tolerated or protected an expedition from the United States against the Province of Texas. These two imputed acts are stated as the reasons which have induced His Catholic Majesty to withhold his ratification from the treaty, to obtain explanations respecting which it is repeated that an envoy would be forthwith dispatched to the United States. How far these allegations will justify the conduct of the Government of Spain will appear on a view of the following facts and the evidence which supports them:

It will be seen by the documents transmitted herewith that the declaration mentioned relates to a clause in the eighth article concerning certain grants of land recently made by His Catholic Majesty in Florida, which it was understood had conveyed all the lands which till then had been ungranted; it was the intention of the parties to annul these latter grants, and that clause was drawn for that express purpose and for none other. The date of these grants was unknown, but it was understood to be posterior to that inserted in the article; indeed, it must be obvious to all that if that provision in the treaty had not the effect of annulling these grants, it would be altogether nugatory. Immediately after the treaty was concluded and ratified by this Government an intimation was received that these grants were of anterior date to that fixed on by the treaty and that they would not, of course, be affected by it. The mere possibility of such a case, so inconsistent with the intention of the parties and the meaning of the article, induced this Government to demand an explanation on the subject, which was immediately granted, and which corresponds with this statement. With respect to the other act alleged, that this Government had tolerated or protected an expedition against Texas, it is utterly without foundation. Every discountenance has invariably been given to any such attempt from within the limits of the United States, as is fully evinced by the acts of the Government and the proceedings of the courts. There being cause, however, to apprehend, in the course of the last summer, that some adventurers entertained views of the kind suggested, the attention of the constituted authorities in that quarter was immediately drawn to them, and it is known that the project, whatever it might be, has utterly failed.

These facts will, it is presumed, satisfy every impartial mind that the Government of Spain had no justifiable cause for declining to ratify the treaty. A treaty concluded in conformity with instructions is obligatory, in good faith, in all its stipulations, according to the true intent and meaning of the parties. Each party is bound to ratify it. If either could set it aside without the consent of the other, there would be no longer any rules applicable to such transactions between nations. By this proceeding the Government of Spain has rendered to the United States a new and very serious injury. It has been stated that a minister would be sent to ask certain explanations of this Government; but if such were desired, why were they not asked within the time limited for the ratification? Is it contemplated to open a new negotiation respecting any of the articles or conditions of the treaty? If that were done, to what consequences might it not lead? At what time and in what manner would a new negotiation terminate? By this proceeding Spain has formed a relation between the two countries which will justify any measures on the part of the United States which a strong sense of injury and a proper regard for the rights and interests of the nation may dictate.

In the course to be pursued these objects should be constantly held in view and have their due weight. Our national honor must be maintained, and a new and a distinguished proof be afforded of that regard for justice and moderation which has invariably governed the councils of this free people. It must be obvious to all that if the United States had been desirous of making conquests, or had been even willing to aggrandize themselves in that way, they could have had no inducement to form this treaty. They would have much cause for gratulation at the course which has been pursued by Spain. An ample field for ambition is open before them, but such a career is not consistent with the principles of their Government nor the interests of the nation.

From a full view of all circumstances, it is submitted to the consideration of Congress whether it will not be proper for the United States to carry the conditions of the treaty into effect in the same manner as if it had been ratified by Spain, claiming on their part all its advantages and yielding to Spain those secured to her. By pursuing this course we shall rest on the sacred ground of right, sanctioned in the most solemn manner by Spain herself by a treaty which she was bound to ratify, for refusing to do which she must incur the censure of other nations, even those most friendly to her, while by confining ourselves within that limit we can not fail to obtain their well-merited approbation. We must have peace on a frontier where we have been so long disturbed; our citizens must be indemnified for losses so long since sustained, and for which indemnity has been so unjustly withheld from them. Accomplishing these great objects, we obtain all that is desirable.

But His Catholic Majesty has twice declared his determination to send a minister to the United States to ask explanations on certain points and to give them respecting his delay to ratify the treaty. Shall we act by taking the ceded territory and proceeding to execute the other conditions of the treaty before this minister arrives and is heard? This is a case which forms a strong appeal to the candor, the magnanimity, and the honor of this people. Much is due to courtesy between nations. By a short delay we shall lose nothing, for, resting on the ground of immutable truth and justice, we can not be diverted from our purpose. It ought to be presumed that the explanations which may be given to the minister of Spain will be satisfactory, and produce the desired result. In any event, the delay for the purpose mentioned, being a further manifestation of the sincere desire to terminate in the most friendly manner all differences with Spain, can not fail to be duly appreciated by His Catholic Majesty as well as by other powers. It is submitted, therefore, whether it will not be proper to make the law proposed for carrying the conditions of the treaty into effect, should it be adopted, contingent; to suspend its operation, upon the responsibility of the Executive, in such manner as to afford an opportunity for such friendly explanations as may be desired during the present session of Congress.

I communicate to Congress a copy of the treaty and of the instructions to the minister of the United States at Madrid respecting it; of his correspondence with the minister of Spain, and of such other documents as may be necessary to give a full view of the subject.

In the course which the Spanish Government have on this occasion thought proper to pursue it is satisfactory to know that they have not been countenanced by any other European power. On the contrary, the opinion and wishes both of France and Great Britain have not been withheld either from the United States or from Spain, and have been unequivocal in favor of the ratification. There is also reason to believe that the sentiments of the Imperial Government of Russia have been the same, and that they have also been made known to the cabinet of Madrid.

In the civil war existing between Spain and the Spanish Provinces in this hemisphere the greatest care has been taken to enforce the laws intended to preserve an impartial neutrality. Our ports have continued to be equally open to both parties and on the same conditions, and our citizens have been equally restrained from interfering in favor of either to the prejudice of the other. The progress of the war, however, has operated manifestly in favor of the colonies. Buenos Ayres still maintains unshaken the independence which it declared in 1816, and has enjoyed since 1810. Like success has also lately attended Chili and the Provinces north of the La Plata bordering on it, and likewise Venezuela.

This contest has from its commencement been very interesting to other powers, and to none more so than to the United States. A virtuous people may and will confine themselves within the limit of a strict neutrality; but it is not in their power to behold a conflict so vitally important to their neighbors without the sensibility and sympathy which naturally belong to such a case. It has been the steady purpose of this Government to prevent that feeling leading to excess, and it is very gratifying to have it in my power to state that so strong has been the sense throughout the whole community of what was due to the character and obligations of the nation that very few examples of a contrary kind have occurred.

The distance of the colonies from the parent country and the great extent of their population and resources gave them advantages which it was anticipated at a very early period would be difficult for Spain to surmount. The steadiness, consistency, and success with which they have pursued their object, as evinced more particularly by the undisturbed sovereignty which Buenos Ayres has so long enjoyed, evidently give them a strong claim to the favorable consideration of other nations. These sentiments on the part of the United States have not been withheld from other powers, with whom it is desirable to act in concert. Should it become manifest to the world that the efforts of Spain to subdue these Provinces will be fruitless, it may be presumed that the Spanish Government itself will give up the contest. In producing such a determination it can not be doubted that the opinion of friendly powers who have taken no part in the controversy will have their merited influence.

It is of the highest importance to our national character and indispensable to the morality of our citizens that all violations of our neutrality should be prevented. No door should be left open for the evasion of our laws, no opportunity afforded to any who may be disposed to take advantage of it to compromit the interest or the honor of the nation. It is submitted, therefore, to the consideration of Congress whether it may not be advisable to revise the laws with a view to this desirable result.

It is submitted also whether it may not be proper to designate by law the several ports or places along the coast at which only foreign ships of war and privateers may be admitted. The difficulty of sustaining the regulations of our commerce and of other important interests from abuse without such designation furnishes a strong motive for this measure.

At the time of the negotiation for the renewal of the commercial convention between the United States and Great Britain a hope had been entertained that an article might have been agreed upon mutually satisfactory to both countries, regulating upon principles of justice and reciprocity the commercial intercourse between the United States and the British possessions as well in the West Indies as upon the continent of

North America. The plenipotentiaries of the two Governments not having been able to come to an agreement on this important interest, those of the United States reserved for the consideration of this Government the proposals which had been presented to them as the ultimate offer on the part of the British Government, and which they were not authorized to accept. On their transmission here they were examined with due deliberation, the result of which was a new effort to meet the views of the British Government. The minister of the United States was instructed to make a further proposal, which has not been accepted. It was, however, declined in an amicable manner. I recommend to the consideration of Congress whether further prohibitory provisions in the laws relating to this intercourse may not be expedient. It is seen with interest that although it has not been practicable as yet to agree in any arrangement of this important branch of their commerce, such is the disposition of the parties that each will view any regulations which the other may make respecting it in the most friendly light.

By the fifth article of the convention concluded on the 20th of October, 1818, it was stipulated that the differences which have arisen between the two Governments with regard to the true intent and meaning of the fifth article of the treaty of Ghent, in relation to the carrying away by British officers of slaves from the United States after the exchange of the ratifications of the treaty of peace, should be referred to the decision of some friendly sovereign or state to be named for that purpose. The minister of the United States has been instructed to name to the British Government a foreign sovereign, the common friend to both parties, for the decision of this question. The answer of that Government to the proposal when received will indicate the further measures to be pursued on the part of the United States.

Although the pecuniary embarrassments which affected various parts of the Union during the latter part of the preceding year have during the present been considerably augmented, and still continue to exist, the receipts into the Treasury to the 30th of September last have amounted to $19,000,000. After defraying the current expenses of the Government, including the interest and reimbursement of the public debt payable to that period, amounting to $18,200,000, there remained in the Treasury on that day more than $2,500,000, which, with the sums receivable during the remainder of the year, will exceed the current demands upon the Treasury for the same period.

The causes which have tended to diminish the public receipts could not fail to have a corresponding effect upon the revenue which has accrued upon imposts and tonnage during the three first quarters of the present year. It is, however, ascertained that the duties which have been secured during that period exceed $18,000,000, and those of the whole year will probably amount to $23,000,000.

For the probable receipts of the next year I refer you to the statements which will be transmitted from the Treasury, which will enable you to judge whether further provision be necessary.

The great reduction in the price of the principal articles of domestic growth which has occurred during the present year, and the consequent fall in the price of labor, apparently so favorable to the success of domestic manufactures, have not shielded them against other causes adverse to their prosperity. The pecuniary embarrassments which have so deeply affected the commercial interests of the nation have been no less adverse to our manufacturing establishments in several sections of the Union.

The great reduction of the currency which the banks have been constrained to make in order to continue specie payments, and the vitiated character of it where such reductions have not been attempted, instead of placing within the reach of these establishments the pecuniary aid necessary to avail themselves of the advantages resulting from the reduction in the prices of the raw materials and of labor, have compelled the banks to withdraw from them a portion of the capital heretofore advanced to them. That aid which has been refused by the banks has not been obtained from other sources, owing to the loss of individual confidence from the frequent failures which have recently occurred in some of our principal commercial cities.

An additional cause for the depression of these establishments may probably be found in the pecuniary embarrassments which have recently affected those countries with which our commerce has been principally prosecuted. Their manufactures, for the want of a ready or profitable market at home, have been shipped by the manufacturers to the United States, and in many instances sold at a price below their current value at the place of manufacture. Although this practice may from its nature be considered temporary or contingent, it is not on that account less injurious in its effects. Uniformity in the demand and price of an article is highly desirable to the domestic manufacturer.

It is deemed of great importance to give encouragement to our domestic manufacturers. In what manner the evils which have been adverted to may be remedied, and how far it may be practicable in other respects to afford to them further encouragement, paying due regard to the other great interests of the nation, is submitted to the wisdom of Congress.

The survey of the coast for the establishment of fortifications is now nearly completed, and considerable progress has been made in the collection of materials for the construction of fortifications in the Gulf of Mexico and in the Chesapeake Bay. The works on the eastern bank of the Potomac below Alexandria and on the Pea Patch, in the Delaware, are much advanced, and it is expected that the fortifications at the Narrows, in the harbor of New York, will be completed the present year. To derive all the advantages contemplated from these fortifications it was necessary that they should be judiciously posted, and constructed with a view to permanence. The progress hitherto has therefore been slow; but as the difficulties in parts heretofore the least explored and known are surmounted, it will in future be more rapid. As soon as the survey of the coast is completed, which it is expected will be done early in the next spring, the engineers employed in it will proceed to examine for like purposes the northern and northwestern frontiers.

The troops intended to occupy a station at the mouth of the St. Peters, on the Mississippi, have established themselves there, and those who were ordered to the mouth of the Yellow Stone, on the Missouri, have ascended that river to the Council Bluff, where they will remain until the next spring, when they will proceed to the place of their destination. I have the satisfaction to state that this measure has been executed in amity with the Indian tribes, and that it promises to produce, in regard to them, all the advantages which were contemplated by it.

Much progress has likewise been made in the construction of ships of war and in the collection of timber and other materials for shipbuilding. It is not doubted that our Navy will soon be augmented to the number and placed in all respects on the footing provided for by law.

The Board, consisting of engineers and naval officers, have not yet made their final report of sites for two naval depots, as instructed according to the resolutions of March 18 and April 20, 1818, but they have examined the coast therein designated, and their report is expected in the next month.

For the protection of our commerce in the Mediterranean, along the southern Atlantic coast, in the Pacific and Indian oceans, it has been found necessary to maintain a strong naval force, which it seems proper for the present to continue. There is much reason to believe that if any portion of the squadron heretofore stationed in the Mediterranean should be withdrawn our intercourse with the powers bordering on that sea would be much interrupted, if not altogether destroyed. Such, too, has been the growth of a spirit of piracy in the other quarters mentioned, by adventurers from every country, in abuse of the friendly flags which they have assumed, that not to protect our commerce there would be to abandon it as a prey to their rapacity. Due attention has likewise been paid to the suppression of the slave trade, in compliance with a law of the last session. Orders have been given to the commanders of all our public ships to seize all vessels navigated under our flag engaged in that trade, and to bring them in to be proceeded against in the manner prescribed by that law. It is hoped that these vigorous measures, supported by like acts by other nations, will soon terminate a commerce so disgraceful to the civilized world.

In the execution of the duty imposed by these acts, and of a high trust connected with it, it is with deep regret I have to state the loss which has been sustained by the death of Commodore Perry. His gallantry in a brilliant exploit in the late war added to the renown of his country. His death is deplored as a national misfortune.

JAMES MONROE.

SPECIAL MESSAGES.

WASHINGTON, *December 7, 1819.*

To the Senate of the United States:

I transmit herewith to the Senate a collection of the commercial regulations of the different foreign countries with which the United States have commercial intercourse, which has been compiled in compliance with the resolution of the Senate of 3d March, 1817.

JAMES MONROE.

WASHINGTON, *December 14, 1819.*

To the House of Representatives of the United States:

In conformity with the resolution of the House of Representatives of the 24th of February last, I now transmit a report of the Secretary of State, with extracts and copies of several letters, touching the causes of the imprisonment of William White, an American citizen, at Buenos Ayres.

JAMES MONROE.

WASHINGTON, *December 17, 1819.*

To the Senate and House of Representatives of the United States:

Some doubt being entertained respecting the true intent and meaning of the act of the last session entitled "An act in addition to the acts prohibiting the slave trade," as to the duties of the agents to be appointed on the coast of Africa, I think it proper to state the interpretation which has been given of the act and the measures adopted to carry it into effect, that Congress may, should it be deemed advisable, amend the same before further proceeding is had under it.

The obligation to instruct the commanders of all our armed vessels to seize and bring into port all ships or vessels of the United States, wheresoever found, having on board any negro, mulatto, or person of color in violation of former acts for the suppression of the slave trade, being imperative, was executed without delay. No seizures have yet been made, but as they were contemplated by the law, and might be presumed, it seemed proper to make the necessary regulations applicable to such seizures for carrying the several provisions of the act into effect.

It is enjoined on the Executive to cause all negroes, mulattoes, or persons of color who may be taken under the act to be removed to Africa. It is the obvious import of the law that none of the persons thus taken should remain within the United States, and no place other than the coast of Africa being designated, their removal or delivery, whether carried from the United States or landed immediately from the vessels in which they were taken, was supposed to be confined to that coast. No settlement or station being specified, the whole coast was thought to be left open for the selection of a proper place at which the persons thus taken should be delivered. The Executive is authorized to appoint one or more agents residing there to receive such persons, and $100,000 are appropriated for the general purposes of the law.

On due consideration of the several sections of the act, and of its humane policy, it was supposed to be the intention of Congress that all the persons above described who might be taken under it and landed in Africa should be aided in their return to their former homes, or in their establishment at or near the place where landed. Some shelter and food would be necessary for them there as soon as landed, let their subsequent disposition be what it might. Should they be landed without such provision having been previously made, they might perish.

It was supposed, by the authority given to the Executive to appoint agents residing on that coast, that they should provide such shelter and food, and perform the other beneficent and charitable offices contemplated by the act. The coast of Africa having been little explored, and no persons residing there who possessed the requisite qualifications to entitle them to the trust being known to the Executive, to none such could it be committed. It was believed that citizens only who would go hence well instructed in the views of their Government and zealous to give them effect would be competent to these duties, and that it was not the intention of the law to preclude their appointment. It was obvious that the longer these persons should be detained in the United States in the hands of the marshals the greater would be the expense, and that for the same term would the main purpose of the law be suspended. It seemed, therefore, to be incumbent on me to make the necessary arrangements for carrying this act into effect in Africa in time to meet the delivery of any persons who might be taken by the public vessels and landed there under it.

On this view of the policy and sanctions of the law it has been decided to send a public ship to the coast of Africa with two such agents, who will take with them tools and other implements necessary for the purposes above mentioned. To each of these agents a small salary has been allowed—$1,500 to the principal and $1,200 to the other.

All our public agents on the coast of Africa receive salaries for their services, and it was understood that none of our citizens possessing the requisite qualifications would accept these trusts, by which they would be confined to parts the least frequented and civilized, without a reasonable compensation. Such allowance therefore seemed to be indispensable to the execution of the act. It is intended also to subject a portion of the sum appropriated to the order of the principal agent for the special objects above stated, amounting in the whole, including the salaries of the agents for one year, to rather less than one-third of the appropriation. Special instructions will be given to these agents, defining in precise

DEATH OF CAPTAIN LAWRENCE OF THE *CHESAPEAKE*

THE *CHESAPEAKE* CAPTURED BY THE *SHANNON*

No event in the *Chesapeake's* career contradicts the verdict of the seamen that she was hoodooed. After lying blockaded in Boston long enough to take on an entirely new crew, she sallied out to give battle to her enemy, the *Shannon*. On June 1, 1813, at 5:50 p.m. the fight began. The ships were evenly matched in size and armament, but there was no comparison between the disciplined, efficient gallantry of the British and the unskilful but courageous tactics of the Americans. After seven minutes of broadside firing, the *Chesapeake's* sails were crippled. She drifted with her bows to the *Shannon* and her decks were raked from end to end. As soon as the vessels were grappled together the British captain boarded, at the head of his men. Almost simultaneously, Lawrence fell and was borne below, crying: "Don't give up the ship! Fight her till she sinks!" But the fight was already lost. The British buried Lawrence with all the honors due to a brave but unfortunate commander and gentleman.

The previous ill-fortune of the *Chesapeake* is told in the index (volume eleven), in the article entitled "Chesapeake, The."

terms their duties in regard to the persons thus delivered to them, the disbursement of the money by the principal agent, and his accountability for the same. They will also have power to select the most suitable place on the coast of Africa at which all persons who may be taken under this act shall be delivered to them, with an express injunction to exercise no power founded on the principle of colonization or other power than that of performing the benevolent offices above recited by the permission and sanction of the existing government under which they may establish themselves. Orders will be given to the commander of the public ship in which they will sail to cruise along the coast to give the more complete effect to the principal object of the act.

JAMES MONROE.

WASHINGTON, *December 17, 1819.*

To the Senate and House of Representatives of the United States:

In compliance with a resolution of Congress of the 27th March, 1818, the journal, acts, and proceedings of the convention which formed the present Constitution of the United States have been published. The resolution directs that 1,000 copies should be printed, of which one copy should be furnished to each member of the Fifteenth Congress, and the residue to be subject to the future disposition of Congress. The number of copies sufficient to supply the members of the late Congress having been reserved for that purpose, the remainder are now deposited at the Department of State subject to the order of Congress. The documents mentioned in the resolution of the 27th March, 1818, are in the process of publication.

JAMES MONROE.

WASHINGTON, *December 24, 1819.*

To the Senate and House of Representatives of the United States:

On the 23d of February, 1803, a message from the President of the United States was transmitted to both Houses of Congress, together with the report of the then Secretary of State, Mr. Madison, upon the case of the Danish brigantine *Henrick* and her cargo, belonging to citizens of Hamburg, recommending the claim to the favorable consideration of Congress. In February, 1805, it was again presented by a message from the President to the consideration of Congress, but has not since been definitively acted upon.

The minister resident from Denmark and the consul-general from Hamburg having recently renewed applications in behalf of the respective owners of the vessel and cargo, I transmit herewith copies of their communications for the further consideration of the Legislature, upon whose files all the documents relating to the claim are still existing.

JAMES MONROE.

DECEMBER 31, 1819.

To the Senate of the United States:

I transmit to the Senate, for its advice and consent as to the ratification, three treaties which have been concluded in the course of the present year with the Kickapoos, the Chippaways, and the Kickapoos of the Vermillion by commissioners who were duly authorized for the purpose.

With the Chippaways there is a supplementary article stipulating certain advantages in their favor on condition that the same shall be ratified by the Executive, with the advice and consent of the Senate, which I likewise submit to your consideration.

JAMES MONROE.

WASHINGTON, *January 8, 1820.*

To the House of Representatives of the United States:

In compliance with a resolution of the House of Representatives of the 14th December, 1819, requesting me to cause to be laid before it any information I may possess respecting certain executions which have been inflicted in the Army of the United States since the year 1815 contrary to the laws and regulations provided for the government of the same, I transmit a report from the Secretary of War containing a detailed account in relation to the object of the said resolution.

JAMES MONROE.

WASHINGTON, *January 8, 1820.*

To the Senate of the United States:

In compliance with a resolution of the Senate of the 20th of January, 1819, requesting me " to cause a report to be laid before them at their next session of such facts as may be within the means of the Government to obtain shewing how far it may be expedient or not to provide by law for clothing the Army with articles manufactured in the United States," I transmit a report from the Secretary of War, which, with the accompanying documents, comprehends all the information required by the Senate in their resolution aforesaid.

JAMES MONROE.

WASHINGTON, *January 19, 1820.*

To the House of Representatives:

In compliance with a resolution of the House of Representatives requesting me " to lay before it at as early a day as may be convenient an account of the expenditure of the several sums appropriated for building fortifications from the year 1816 to the year 1819, inclusive, indicating the places at which works of defense have been begun, the magnitude of the works contemplated at each place, their present condition, the amount already expended, and the estimated amount requisite for the completion of each, also the mode by which the fortifications are built, by contract or otherwise,'' I now transmit to the House a report from the Secretary of War, to whom the said resolution was referred, which, with the documents accompanying it, contains all the information required.

JAMES MONROE.

WASHINGTON, *February 8, 1820.*

To the House of Representatives of the United States:

In conformity with a resolution of the House of Representatives of the 24th January, 1820, requesting me ''to inform the House what loans, if any, have been made since the peace, to private citizens, of powder, lead, and other munitions belonging to the Government by officers of any department of the Army or Navy, specifying the times, terms, objects, and extent of such loans, the names of the persons by whom and to whom made, the different times of repayment, and also the amount of the ultimate loss, if any, likely to be incurred by the Government in consequence thereof,'' I now transmit a report from the Secretary of War, which, with the accompanying documents, contains all the information that can be furnished on the subject.

JAMES MONROE.

WASHINGTON, *March 1, 1820.*

To the House of Representatives of the United States:

In compliance with a resolution of the House of Representatives of the 4th of February last, requesting to be informed what progress has been made in surveying certain parts of the coast of North Carolina and in ascertaining the latitude and longitude of the extreme points of Cape Hatteras, Cape Look Out, and Cape Fear, according to a resolution of the 19th of January, 1819, I have to state that it is intended to carry the resolution of the 19th of March into effect in the present year. The cooperation of the Board of Engineers with Naval Commissioners being necessary in executing that duty, and the Board having been engaged last year in surveying the eastern coast of our Union, it would have interfered with previous arrangements and been attended with increased expense had they been withdrawn from it. The Board will, however, be employed during the present summer in the regular execution of its duties in the survey of the coast of North Carolina, when instructions will be given it to afford the necessary aid to carry the resolution of the 19th of January of the last year into effect.

JAMES MONROE.

WASHINGTON, *March 4, 1820.*

To the Senate of the United States:

I transmit to the Senate, in pursuance of their resolution of the 4th of January last, a report from the Secretary of State, with a list of fines incurred under the act of Congress entitled "An act in addition to the act for the punishment of certain crimes against the United States," which appear from the records of the Department of State to have been remitted by the Executive authority of the United States.

JAMES MONROE.

WASHINGTON, *March 8, 1820.*

The PRESIDENT PRO TEMPORE OF THE SENATE:

I transmit to the Senate copies of sundry papers having relation to the treaty of 22d February, 1819, between the United States and Spain, which have been received at the Department of State, and have not before been communicated to the Senate.

JAMES MONROE.

WASHINGTON, *March 8, 1820.*

To the Senate and House of Representatives of the United States:

I transmit to Congress a report from the Secretary of the Treasury, which, with the accompanying documents, will shew that the act of the 20th May, 1812, respecting the northern and western boundaries of the State of Ohio, has been executed.

JAMES MONROE.

WASHINGTON, *March 17, 1820.*

To the House of Representatives of the United States:

It being stipulated by the fourth article of the articles of agreement and cession entered into on the 24th of April, 1802, with the State of Georgia that the United States should at their own expense extinguish for the use of that State, as soon as it might be done on reasonable terms, the Indian title to all the lands within its limits, and the legislature of Georgia being desirous to make a further acquisition of said lands at this time, presuming that it may be done on reasonable terms; and it being also represented that property of considerable value which had been taken by the Creek and Cherokee Indians from citizens of Georgia, the restoration of which had been provided for by different treaties, but which has never been made, it is proposed to hold a treaty with those nations, and more particularly with the Creeks, in the course of this summer. For the attainment of these objects I submit the subject to the consideration of Congress, that a sum adequate to the expenses attending such treaty may be appropriated should Congress deem it expedient.

JAMES MONROE.

WASHINGTON, *March 20, 1820.*

To the Senate of the United States:

In compliance with a resolution of the Senate of the 16th of February, 1820, requesting me to cause to be laid before it "abstracts of the bonds or other securities given under the laws of the United States by the collectors of the customs, receivers of public moneys for lands, and registers of public lands, paymasters in the Army, and pursers in the Navy, who are now in office, or who have heretofore been in office, and whose accounts remain unsettled, together with a statement of such other facts as may tend to shew the expediency or inexpediency of so far altering the laws respecting such officers that they may hereafter be appointed for limited periods, subject to removal as heretofore," I transmit to the Senate a report from the Secretary of the Treasury, which, with the documents accompanying it, will afford all the information required.

JAMES MONROE.

WASHINGTON, *March 27, 1820.*

To the Senate and House of Representatives of the United States:

I transmit to Congress an extract of a letter from the minister plenipotentiary of the United States at St. Petersburg, of the 1st of November last, on the subject of our relations with Spain, indicating the sentiments of the Emperor of Russia respecting the nonratification by His Catholic Majesty of the treaty lately concluded between the United States and Spain, and the strong interest which His Imperial Majesty takes in promoting the ratification of that treaty. Of this friendly disposition the most satisfactory assurance has been since given directly to this Government by the minister of Russia residing here.

I transmit also to Congress an extract of a letter from the minister plenipotentiary of the United States at Madrid of a later date than those heretofore communicated, by which it appears that, at the instance of the chargé d'affaires of the Emperor of Russia, a new pledge had been given by the Spanish Government that the minister who had been lately appointed to the United States should set out on his mission without delay, with full power to settle all differences in a manner satisfactory to the parties.

I have further to state that the Governments of France and Great Britain continue to manifest the sentiments heretofore communicated respecting the nonratification of the treaty by Spain, and to interpose their good offices to promote its ratification.

It is proper to add that the Governments of France and Russia have expressed an earnest desire that the United States would take no steps for the present on the principle of reprisal which might possibly tend to disturb the peace between the United States and Spain. There is good cause to presume from the delicate manner in which this sentiment has been conveyed that it is founded in a belief as well as a desire that our just objects may be accomplished without the hazard of such an extremity.

On full consideration of all these circumstances, I have thought it my duty to submit to Congress whether it will not be advisable to postpone a decision on the questions now depending with Spain until the next session. The distress of that nation at this juncture affords a motive for this forbearance which can not fail to be duly appreciated. Under such circumstances the attention of the Spanish Government may be diverted from its foreign concerns, and the arrival of a minister here be longer delayed. I am the more induced to suggest this course of proceeding from a knowledge that, while we shall thereby make a just return to the powers whose good offices have been acknowledged, and increase by a new and signal proof of moderation our claims on Spain, our attitude in regard to her will not be less favorable at the next session than it is at the present.

JAMES MONROE.

WASHINGTON, *May 9, 1820.*

To the Senate and House of Representatives of the United States:

I communicate to Congress a correspondence which has taken place between the Secretary of State and the envoy extraordinary and minister plenipotentiary of His Catholic Majesty since the message of the 27th March last, respecting the treaty which was concluded between the United States and Spain on the 22d February, 1819.

After the failure of His Catholic Majesty for so long a time to ratify the treaty, it was expected that this minister would have brought with him the ratification, or that he would have been authorized to give an order for the delivery of the territory ceded by it to the United States. It appears, however, that the treaty is still unratified and that the minister has no authority to surrender the territory. The object of his mission has been to make complaints and to demand explanations respecting an imputed system of hostility on the part of citizens of the United States against the subjects and dominions of Spain, and an unfriendly policy in their Government, and to obtain new stipulations against these alleged injuries as the condition on which the treaty should be ratified.

Unexpected as such complaints and such a demand were under existing circumstances, it was thought proper, without compromitting the Government as to the course to be pursued, to meet them promptly and to give the explanations that were desired on every subject with the utmost candor. The result has proved what was sufficiently well known before, that the charge of a systematic hostility being adopted and pursued by citizens of the United States against the dominions and subjects of Spain is utterly destitute of foundation, and that their Government in all its branches has maintained with the utmost rigor that neutrality in the civil war between Spain and the colonies which they were the first to declare. No force has been collected nor incursions made from within the United States against the dominions of Spain, nor have any naval equipments been permitted in favor of either party against the other. Their citizens have been warned of the obligations incident to the neutral condition of their country; their public officers have been instructed to see that the laws were faithfully executed, and severe examples have been made of some who violated them.

In regard to the stipulation proposed as the condition of the ratification of the treaty, that the United States shall abandon the right to recognize the revolutionary colonies in South America, or to form other relations with them when in their judgment it may be just and expedient so to do, it is manifestly so repugnant to the honor and even to the independence of the United States that it has been impossible to discuss it. In making this proposal it is perceived that His Catholic Majesty has entirely misconceived the principles on which this Government has acted in being a party to a negotiation so long protracted for claims so well founded and reasonable, as he likewise has the sacrifices which the United States have made, comparatively, with Spain in the treaty to which it is proposed to annex so extraordinary and improper a condition.

Had the minister of Spain offered an unqualified pledge that the treaty should be ratified by his Sovereign on being made acquainted with the explanations which had been given by this Government, there would have been a strong motive for accepting and submitting it to the Senate for their advice and consent, rather than to resort to other measures for redress, however justifiable and proper; but he gives no such pledge; on the contrary, he declares explicitly that the refusal of this Government to relinquish the right of judging and acting for itself hereafter, according to circumstances, in regard to the Spanish colonies, a right common to all nations, has rendered it impossible for him under his instructions to make such engagement. He thinks that his Sovereign will be induced by his communications to ratify the treaty, but still he leaves him free either to adopt that measure or to decline it. He admits that the other objections are essentially removed and will not in themselves prevent the ratification, provided the difficulty on the third point is surmounted. The result, therefore, is that the treaty is declared to have no obligation whatever; that its ratification is made to depend not on the considerations which led to its adoption and the conditions which it contains, but on a new article unconnected with it, respecting which a new negotiation must be opened, of indefinite duration and doubtful issue.

Under this view of the subject the course to be pursued would appear to be direct and obvious if the affairs of Spain had remained in the state in which they were when this minister sailed. But it is known that an important change has since taken place in the Government of that country which can not fail to be sensibly felt in its intercourse with other nations. The minister of Spain has essentially declared his inability to act in consequence of that change. With him, however, under his present powers nothing could be done. The attitude of the United States must now be assumed on full consideration of what is due to their rights, their interest and honor, without regard to the powers or incidents of the late mission. We may at pleasure occupy the territory which was intended and provided by the late treaty as an indemnity for losses so long since sustained by our citizens; but still, nothing could be settled definitively without a treaty between the two nations. Is this the time to make the pressure? If the United States were governed by views of ambition and aggrandizement, many strong reasons might be given in its favor; but they have no objects of that kind to accomplish, none which are not founded in justice and which can be injured by forbearance. Great hope is entertained that this change will promote the happiness of the Spanish nation. The good order, moderation, and humanity which have characterized the movement are the best guaranties of its success.

The United States would not be justified in their own estimation should they take any step to disturb its harmony. When the Spanish Government is completely organized on the principles of this change, as it is expected it soon will be, there is just ground to presume that our differences with Spain will be speedily and satisfactorily settled.

With these remarks I submit it to the wisdom of Congress whether it will not still be advisable to postpone any decision on this subject until the next session.

JAMES MONROE.

WASHINGTON, *May 11, 1820.*

To the Senate of the United States:

I transmit herewith to the Senate a report from the Secretary of State, together with the returns of causes depending in the courts of the United States, collected conformably to a resolution of the Senate of the 18th of January, 1819.

JAMES MONROE.

WASHINGTON, *May 12, 1820.*

The SPEAKER OF THE HOUSE OF REPRESENTATIVES:

I transmit to the House of Representatives a report from the Secretary of State, with the document prepared in pursuance of a resolution of the House of the 14th ultimo, on the subject of claims of citizens of the United States for Spanish spoliations upon their property and commerce.

JAMES MONROE.

PROCLAMATION.

By the President of the United States of America.

A PROCLAMATION.

Whereas by an act of the Congress of the United States of the 3d of March, 1815, so much of the several acts imposing duties on the ships and vessels and on goods, wares, and merchandise imported into the United States as imposed a discriminating duty of tonnage between foreign vessels and vessels of the United States and between goods imported into the United States in foreign vessels and vessels of the United States were repealed so far as the same respected the produce or manufacture of the nation to which such foreign ship or vessel might belong, such repeal to take effect in favor of any foreign nation whenever the President of the United States should be satisfied that the discriminating or countervailing duties of such foreign nation so far as they operate to the disadvantage of the United States have been abolished; and

Whereas satisfactory proof has been received by me from the burgo-masters and senate of the free and Hanseatic city of Lubeck that from and after the 30th day of October, 1819, all discriminating or countervailing duties of the said city so far as they operated to the disadvantage of the United States have been and are abolished:

Now, therefore, I, James Monroe, President of the United States of America, do hereby declare and proclaim that so much of the several acts imposing duties on the tonnage of ships and vessels and on goods, wares, and merchandise imported into the United States as imposed a discriminating duty of tonnage between vessels of the free and Hanseatic city of Lubeck and vessels of the United States and between goods imported into the United States in vessels of Lubeck and vessels of the United States are repealed so far as the same respect the produce or manufacture of the said free Hanseatic city of Lubeck.

Given under my hand, at the city of Washington, this 4th day of May, A. D. 1820, and forty-fourth year of the Independence of the United States.　　　　　　　　　　　　　　JAMES MONROE.

[SEAL.]

By the President:

John Quincy Adams, *Secretary of State*.

FOURTH ANNUAL MESSAGE.

Washington, *November 14, 1820.*

Fellow-Citizens of the Senate and of the House of Representatives:

In communicating to you a just view of public affairs at the commencement of your present labors, I do it with great satisfaction, because, taking all circumstances into consideration which claim attention, I see much cause to rejoice in the felicity of our situation. In making this remark

I do not wish to be understood to imply that an unvaried prosperity is to be seen in every interest of this great community. In the progress of a nation inhabiting a territory of such vast extent and great variety of climate, every portion of which is engaged in foreign commerce and liable to be affected in some degree by the changes which occur in the condition and regulations of foreign countries, it would be strange if the produce of our soil and the industry and enterprise of our fellow-citizens received at all times and in every quarter an uniform and equal encouragement. This would be more than we would have a right to expect under circumstances the most favorable. Pressures on certain interests, it is admitted, have been felt; but allowing to these their greatest extent, they detract but little from the force of the remarks already made. In forming a just estimate of our present situation it is proper to look at the whole in the outline as well as in the detail. A free, virtuous, and enlightened people know well the great principles and causes on which their happiness depends, and even those who suffer most occasionally in their transitory concerns find great relief under their sufferings from the blessings which they otherwise enjoy and in the consoling and animating hope which they administer. From whence do these pressures come? Not from a government which is founded by, administered for, and supported by the people. We trace them to the peculiar character of the epoch in which we live, and to the extraordinary occurrences which have signalized it. The convulsions with which several of the powers of Europe have been shaken and the long and destructive wars in which all were engaged, with their sudden transition to a state of peace, presenting in the first instance unusual encouragement to our commerce and withdrawing it in the second even within its wonted limit, could not fail to be sensibly felt here. The station, too, which we had to support through this long conflict, compelled as we were finally to become a party to it with a principal power, and to make great exertions, suffer heavy losses, and to contract considerable debts, disturbing the ordinary course of affairs by augmenting to a vast amount the circulating medium, and thereby elevating at one time the price of every article above a just standard and depressing it at another below it, had likewise its due effect.

It is manifest that the pressures of which we complain have proceeded in a great measure from these causes. When, then, we take into view the prosperous and happy condition of our country in all the great circumstances which constitute the felicity of a nation—every individual in the full enjoyment of all his rights, the Union blessed with plenty and rapidly rising to greatness under a National Government which operates with complete effect in every part without being felt in any except by the ample protection which it affords, and under State governments which perform their equal share, according to a wise distribution of power between them, in promoting the public happiness—it is impossible to behold so gratifying, so glorious a spectacle without being penetrated with the most profound and grateful acknowledgments to the Supreme Author of All Good for such manifold and inestimable blessings. Deeply impressed with these sentiments, I can not regard the pressures to which I have adverted otherwise than in the light of mild and instructive admonitions, warning us of dangers to be shunned in future, teaching us lessons of economy corresponding with the simplicity and purity of our institutions and best adapted to their support, evincing the connection and dependence which the various parts of our happy Union have on each other, thereby augmenting daily our social incorporation and adding by its strong ties new strength and vigor to the political; opening a wider range, and with new encouragement, to the industry and enterprise of our fellow-citizens at home and abroad, and more especially by the multiplied proofs which it has accumulated of the great perfection of our most excellent system of government, the powerful instrument in the hands of our All-merciful Creator in securing to us these blessings.

Happy as our situation is, it does not exempt us from solicitude and care for the future. On the contrary, as the blessings which we enjoy are great, proportionably great should be our vigilance, zeal, and activity to preserve them. Foreign wars may again expose us to new wrongs, which would impose on us new duties for which we ought to be prepared. The state of Europe is unsettled, and how long peace may be preserved is altogether uncertain; in addition to which we have interests of our own to adjust which will require particular attention. A correct view of our relations with each power will enable you to form a just idea of existing difficulties, and of the measures of precaution best adapted to them.

Respecting our relations with Spain nothing explicit can now be communicated. On the adjournment of Congress in May last the minister plenipotentiary of the United States at Madrid was instructed to inform the Government of Spain that if His Catholic Majesty should then ratify the treaty this Government would accept the ratification so far as to submit to the decision of the Senate the question whether such ratification should be received in exchange for that of the United States heretofore given. By letters from the minister of the United States to the Secretary of State it appears that a communication in conformity with his instructions had been made to the Government of Spain, and that the Cortes had the subject under consideration. The result of the deliberations of that body, which is daily expected, will be made known to Congress as soon as it is received. The friendly sentiment which was expressed on the part of the United States in the message of the 9th of May last is still entertained for Spain. Among the causes of regret, however, which are inseparable from the delay attending this transaction it is proper to state that satisfactory information has been received that measures have been recently adopted by designing persons to convert certain parts of the Province of East Florida into depots for the reception of foreign goods, from whence to smuggle them into the United States. By opening a port within the limits of Florida, immediately on our boundary where there was no settlement, the object could not be misunderstood. An early accommodation of differences will, it is hoped, prevent all such fraudulent and pernicious practices, and place the relations of the two countries on a very amicable and permanent basis.

The commercial relations between the United States and the British colonies in the West Indies and on this continent have undergone no change, the British Government still preferring to leave that commerce under the restriction heretofore imposed on it on each side. It is satisfactory to recollect that the restraints resorted to by the United States were defensive only, intended to prevent a monopoly under British regulations in favor of Great Britain, as it likewise is to know that the experiment is advancing in a spirit of amity between the parties.

The question depending between the United States and Great Britain respecting the construction of the first article of the treaty of Ghent has been referred by both Governments to the decision of the Emperor of Russia, who has accepted the umpirage.

An attempt has been made with the Government of France to regulate by treaty the commerce between the two countries on the principle of reciprocity and equality. By the last communication from the minister plenipotentiary of the United States at Paris, to whom full power had been given, we learn that the negotiation had been commenced there; but serious difficulties having occurred, the French Government had resolved to transfer it to the United States, for which purpose the minister plenipotentiary of France had been ordered to repair to this city, and whose arrival might soon be expected. It is hoped that this important interest may be arranged on just conditions and in a manner equally satisfactory to both parties. It is submitted to Congress to decide, until such arrangement is made, how far it may be proper, on the principle of the act of the last session which augmented the tonnage duty on French vessels, to adopt other measures for carrying more completely into effect the policy of that act.

The act referred to, which imposed new tonnage on French vessels, having been in force from and after the 1st day of July, it has happened that several vessels of that nation which had been dispatched from France before its existence was known have entered the ports of the United States, and been subject to its operation, without that previous notice which the general spirit of our laws gives to individuals in similar cases. The object of that law having been merely to countervail the inequalities which existed to the disadvantage of the United States in their commercial intercourse with France, it is submitted also to the consideration of Congress whether, in the spirit of amity and conciliation which it is no less the inclination than the policy of the United States to preserve in their intercourse with other powers, it may not be proper to extend relief to the individuals interested in those cases by exempting from the operation of the law all those vessels which have entered our ports without having had the means of previously knowing the existence of the additional duty.

The contest between Spain and the colonies, according to the most authentic information, is maintained by the latter with improved success. The unfortunate divisions which were known to exist some time since at Buenos Ayres it is understood still prevail. In no part of South America has Spain made any impression on the colonies, while in many parts, and particularly in Venezuela and New Grenada, the colonies have gained strength and acquired reputation, both for the management of the war in which they have been successful and for the order of the internal administration. The late change in the Government of Spain, by the reestablishment of the constitution of 1812, is an event which promises to be favorable to the revolution. Under the authority of the Cortes the Congress of Angostura was invited to open a negotiation for the settlement of differences between the parties, to which it was replied that they would willingly open the negotiation provided the acknowledgment of their independence was made its basis, but not otherwise. Of further proceedings between them we are uninformed. No facts are known to this Government to warrant the belief that any of the powers of Europe will take part in the contest, whence it may be inferred, considering all circumstances which must have weight in producing the result, that an adjustment will finally take place on the basis proposed by the colonies. To promote that result by friendly counsels with other powers, including Spain herself, has been the uniform policy of this Government.

In looking to the internal concerns of our country you will, I am persuaded, derive much satisfaction from a view of the several objects to which, in the discharge of your official duties, your attention will be drawn. Among these none holds a more important place than the public revenue, from the direct operation of the power by which it is raised on the people, and by its influence in giving effect to every other power of the Government. The revenue depends on the resources of the country, and the facility by which the amount required is raised is a strong proof of the extent of the resources and of the efficiency of the Government. A few prominent facts will place this great interest in a just light before you. On the 30th of September, 1815, the funded and floating debt of the United States was estimated at $119,635,558. If to this sum be added the amount of 5 per cent stock subscribed to the Bank of the United States, the amount of Mississippi stock and of the stock which was issued subsequently to that date, the balances ascertained to be due to certain States for military services and to individuals for supplies furnished and services rendered during the late war, the public debt may be estimated as amounting at that date, and as afterwards liquidated, to $158,713,049. On the 30th of September, 1820, it amounted to $91,993,883, having been reduced in that interval by payments $66,879,165. During this term the expenses of the Government of the United States were likewise defrayed in every branch of the civil, military, and naval establishments; the public edifices in this city have been rebuilt with considerable additions; extensive fortifications have been commenced, and are in a train of execution; permanent arsenals and magazines have been erected in various parts of the Union; our Navy has been considerably augmented, and the ordnance, munitions of war, and stores of the Army and Navy, which were much exhausted during the war, have been replenished.

By the discharge of so large a proportion of the public debt and the execution of such extensive and important operations in so short a time a just estimate may be formed of the great extent of our national resources. The demonstration is the more complete and gratifying when it is recollected that the direct tax and excise were repealed soon after the termination of the late war, and that the revenue applied to these purposes has been derived almost wholly from other sources.

The receipts into the Treasury from every source to the 30th of September last have amounted to $16,794,107.66, whilst the public expenditures to the same period amounted to $16,871,534.72, leaving in the Treasury on that day a sum estimated at $1,950,000. For the probable receipts of the following year I refer you to the statement which will be transmitted from the Treasury.

The sum of $3,000,000 authorized to be raised by loan by an act of the last session of Congress has been obtained upon terms advantageous to the Government, indicating not only an increased confidence in the faith of the nation, but the existence of a large amount of capital seeking that mode of investment at a rate of interest not exceeding 5 per cent per annum.

It is proper to add that there is now due to the Treasury for the sale of public lands $22,996,545. In bringing this subject to view I consider it my duty to submit to Congress whether it may not be advisable to extend to the purchasers of these lands, in consideration of the unfavorable change which has occurred since the sales, a reasonable indulgence. It is known that the purchases were made when the price of every article had risen to its greatest height, and that the installments are becoming due at a period of great depression. It is presumed that some plan may be devised by the wisdom of Congress, compatible with the public interest, which would afford great relief to these purchasers.

Considerable progress has been made during the present season in examining the coast and its various bays and other inlets, in the collection of materials, and in the construction of fortifications for the defense of the Union at several of the positions at which it has been decided to erect such works. At Mobile Point and Dauphin Island, and at the Rigolets, leading to Lake Pontchartrain, materials to a considerable amount have been collected, and all the necessary preparations made for the commencement of the works. At Old Point Comfort, at the mouth of James River, and at the Rip-Rap, on the opposite shore in the Chesapeake Bay, materials to a vast amount have been collected; and at the Old Point some progress has been made in the construction of the fortification, which is on a very extensive scale. The work at Fort Washington, on this river, will be completed early in the next spring, and that on the Pea Patch, in the Delaware, in the course of the next season. Fort Diamond, at the Narrows, in the harbor of New York, will be finished this year. The works at Boston, New York, Baltimore, Norfolk, Charleston, and Niagara have been in part repaired, and the coast of North Carolina, extending south to Cape Fear, has been examined, as have likewise other parts of the coast eastward of Boston. Great exertions have been made to push forward these works with the utmost dispatch possible; but when their extent is considered, with the important purposes for which they are intended—the defense of the whole coast, and, in consequence, of the whole interior—and that they are to last for ages, it will be manifest that a well-digested plan, founded on military principles, connecting the whole together, combining security with economy, could not be prepared without repeated examinations of the most exposed and difficult parts, and that it would also take considerable time to collect the materials at the several points where they would be required. From all the light that has been shed on this subject I am satisfied that every favorable anticipation which has been formed of this great undertaking will be verified, and that when completed it will afford very great if not complete protection to our Atlantic frontier in the event of another war—a protection sufficient to counterbalance in a single campaign with an enemy powerful at sea the expense of all these works, without taking into the estimate the saving of the lives of so many of our citizens, the protection of our towns and other property, or the tendency of such works to prevent war.

Our military positions have been maintained at Belle Point, on the Arkansas, at Council Bluffs, on the Missouri, at St. Peters, on the Mississippi, and at Green Bay, on the upper Lakes. Commodious barracks have already been erected at most of these posts, with such works as were necessary for their defense. Progress has also been made in opening communications between them and in raising supplies at each for the support of the troops by their own labor, particularly those most remote.

With the Indians peace has been preserved and a progress made in carrying into effect the act of Congress making an appropriation for their civilization, with the prospect of favorable results. As connected equally with both these objects, our trade with those tribes is thought to merit the attention of Congress. In their original state game is their sustenance and war their occupation, and if they find no employment from civilized powers they destroy each other. Left to themselves their extirpation is inevitable. By a judicious regulation of our trade with them we supply their wants, administer to their comforts, and gradually, as the game retires, draw them to us.   By maintaining posts far in the interior we acquire a more thorough and direct control over them, without which it is confidently believed that a complete change in their manners can never be accomplished.   By such posts, aided by a proper regulation of our trade with them and a judicious civil administration over them, to be provided for by law, we shall, it is presumed, be enabled not only to protect our own settlements from their savage incursions and preserve peace among the several tribes, but accomplish also the great purpose of their civilization.

Considerable progress has also been made in the construction of ships of war, some of which have been launched in the course of the present year.

Our peace with the powers on the coast of Barbary has been preserved, but we owe it altogether to the presence of our squadron in the Mediterranean.   It has been found equally necessary to employ some of our vessels for the protection of our commerce in the Indian Sea, the Pacific, and along the Atlantic coast.   The interests which we have depending in those quarters, which have been much improved of late, are of great extent and of high importance to the nation as well as to the parties concerned, and would undoubtedly suffer if such protection was not extended to them.   In execution of the law of the last session for the suppression of the slave trade some of our public ships have also been employed on the coast of Africa, where several captures have already been made of vessels engaged in that disgraceful traffic.

JAMES MONROE.

SPECIAL MESSAGES.

DECEMBER 12, 1820.

To the Senate of the United States:

In compliance with a resolution of the Senate of the 6th of December, requesting that the agent employed under the act entitled "An act authorizing the purchase of fire engines and building houses for the safekeeping of the same" should report in the manner stated in the said resolution his conduct in execution of the said act, I now transmit to the Senate a report from the agent, which communicates all the information which has been desired.

JAMES MONROE.

DECEMBER 14, 1820.

To the Senate of the United States:

I submit to the consideration of the Senate, for their advice and consent as to the ratification, the following treaties, concluded with the several

BATTLE OF CHIPPEWA PLAINS, CANADA, 1814

THE BATTLE OF CHIPPEWA PLAINS, CANADA

July 5, 1814

An American force of some 3500 men, under the command of Gen. Jacob Brown, crossed the Niagara River and captured Fort Erie on July 3, 1814. Following this success, Brown's army resumed its march on the morning of the 4th, its object being to meet and vanquish the British army which was gathering in force at Chippewa Plains, sixteen miles distant. Brigadier-General Winfield Scott's brigade was sent ahead and, after an arduous march over obstructed roads, came upon the British at sunset, but finding them strongly posted he fell back to await the balance of Brown's army, which arrived during the night. Next morning Brown decided to cross the Chippewa River and attack. When his troops advanced to construct the bridge they were thrown in a panic by the sight of the British army crossing the river to assail them. Scott's brigade was left to bear the brunt of the attack. He did not expect a battle and had prepared for a Fourth of July celebration. When he received word of the British advance, however, he marched his men over the bridge and charged. Almost simultaneously the British charged. The two lines drew closer together, collided, and then the British broke and fled. The British numbered 2100, and Scott's brigade 1900. See the article entitled "Chippewa Plains, Canada, Battle of," in the index (volume eleven).

Indian tribes therein mentioned since the last session of Congress, with their documents, viz: With the Weas, Kickapoos, Chippeways, Ottawas, Choctaws, and Mahas; and also a treaty with the Kickapoos amended as proposed by a resolution of the Senate at their last session.

JAMES MONROE.

WASHINGTON, *December 14, 1820.*

To the House of Representatives:

In compliance with a resolution of the House of Representatives of the 21st November last, requesting the President to lay before the House information relating to the progress and expenditures of the commissioners under the fifth, sixth, and seventh articles of the treaty of Ghent, I now transmit a report from the Secretary of State, with documents containing all the information in the possession of that Department requested by the resolution.

JAMES MONROE.

WASHINGTON, *January 1, 1821.*

To the House of Representatives of the United States:

In compliance with a resolution of the House of Representatives of the 22d of November last, requesting the President to inform that House what naval force has been stationed for the protection of the commerce of our citizens in the West India Islands and parts adjacent during the present year, and whether any depredations by pirates or others upon the property of citizens of the United States engaged in such commerce have been reported to our Government, I now submit for the information of the House a report from the Secretary of the Navy, with accompanying documents, which contains all the information in the possession of the Government required by that resolution.

JAMES MONROE.

WASHINGTON, *January 4, 1821.*

To the House of Representatives:

I communicate to the House of Representatives a report from the Secretary of State, which, with the papers accompanying it, contains all the information in the possession of the Executive requested by a resolution of the House of the 4th December last, on the subject of the African slave trade.

JAMES MONROE.

WASHINGTON, *January 4, 1821.*

To the House of Representatives:

In compliance with a resolution of the House of Representatives of the 15th of December last, requesting the President of the United States to cause to be laid before that House a statement of expenditures and receipts in the Indian Department; also the nature and extent of the contracts entered into, and with whom, from the 2d of March, 1811, to the present period, I now transmit a letter from the Secretary of War, with a report of the superintendent of Indian trade, which contains the information desired.

                    JAMES MONROE.

WASHINGTON, *January 12, 1821.*

To the House of Representatives of the United States:

I transmit to the House of Representatives a report from the Secretary of State, with the inclosed documents, relating to the negotiation for the suppression of the slave trade, which should have accompanied a message on that subject communicated to the House some time since, but which were accidentally omitted.

                    JAMES MONROE.

WASHINGTON, *January 18, 1821.*

To the Senate of the United States:

In compliance with a resolution of the Senate of the 4th instant, "requesting the President of the United States to communicate to the Senate any information he may have as to the power or authority which belonged to Don John Bonaventure Morales and to the Baron Carondelet to grant and dispose of the lands of Spain in Louisiana previously to the year 1803," I transmit a report from the Secretary of the Treasury, submitting a letter of the Commissioner of the General Land Office, with the document to which it refers.

                    JAMES MONROE.

WASHINGTON, *January 18, 1821.*

To the House of Representatives:

In compliance with a resolution of the House of Representatives requesting the President to inform the House, if in his opinion proper, whether any, and, if any, what, negotiations since the 1st of January, 1816, have been had with the Six Nations of Indians, or any portion of them, who the commissioners or agents were, the objects of the negotiation, the expenses of the same, the compensation of each commissioner, secretary, or agent, and to whom the moneys were paid, I now transmit a report from the Secretary of War communicating the information desired.

                    JAMES MONROE.

WASHINGTON, *January 31, 1821.*

To the Senate and House of Representatives:

I transmit to Congress a report from the Secretary of the Treasury submitting copies of the instructions given to the commissioners appointed under the act of the 15th of May, 1820, authorizing the location of a road from Wheeling, in the State of Virginia, to a point on the left bank of the Mississippi River between St. Louis and the mouth of the Illinois River, and copies of the report made by the said commissioners to the Treasury Department of the progress they have made in the execution of the duties prescribed by the said act, together with maps of the country through which the location is to be made.   JAMES MONROE.

FEBRUARY 5, 1821.

To the Senate of the United States:

I herewith transmit, in confidence, to the Senate reports from the Secretary of State and of the Treasury, with the papers containing the correspondence and the information in possession of the Government the communication of which was requested by the resolution of the Senate of the 23d of last month.   It is desired that the original letters may, when the Senate shall have no further use for them, be returned.

JAMES MONROE.

FEBRUARY 8, 1821.

To the Senate of the United States:

In compliance with a resolution of the Senate of the 1st instant, requesting the President of the United States "to cause to be laid before the Senate any information he may have in relation to the claims of citizens of Georgia against the Creek Nation of Indians, and why these claims, if any exist, have not been heretofore adjusted and settled under the provisions of the treaties of 1790 and 1796," I now transmit a report from the Secretary of War, with accompanying documents, which contains all the information on this subject in the possession of the Executive.

JAMES MONROE.

FEBRUARY 13, 1821.

To the Senate of the United States:

The ratification by the Spanish Government of the treaty of amity, settlement, and limits between the United States and Spain, signed on the 22d of February, 1819, and on the 24th of that month ratified on the part of the United States, has been received by the envoy extraordinary and minister plenipotentiary of that power at this place, who has given notice that he is ready to exchange the ratifications.

By the sixteenth article of that treaty it was stipulated that the ratifications should be exchanged within six months from the day of its signature, which time having elapsed before the ratification of Spain was given, a copy and translation thereof are now transmitted to the Senate for their advice and consent to receive it in exchange for the ratification of the United States heretofore executed.

The treaty was submitted to the consideration of the Cortes of that Kingdom before its ratification, which was finally given with their assent and sanction. The correspondence between the Spanish minister of foreign affairs and the minister of the United States at Madrid on that occasion is also herewith communicated to the Senate, together with a memorandum by the Secretary of State of his conference with the Spanish envoy here yesterday, when that minister gave notice of his readiness to exchange the ratifications.

The return of the original papers now transmitted, to avoid the delay necessary to the making of copies, is requested.

JAMES MONROE.

WASHINGTON, *February 22, 1821.*
To the Senate of the United States:

In compliance with a resolution of the Senate of the 16th instant, requesting "the President of the United States to cause to be laid before the Senate the original order for building the barracks at Sacketts Harbor, together with all communications between the War Department and Major-General Brown relative thereto, and the amount of public moneys expended thereon," I now transmit a report from the Secretary of War, with the papers inclosed, which contains the information desired.

JAMES MONROE.

WASHINGTON, *February 22, 1821.*
To the Senate and House of Representatives of the United States:

The treaty of amity, settlement, and limits between the United States and Spain, signed on the 22d of February, 1819, having been ratified by the contracting parties, and the ratifications having been exchanged, it is herewith communicated to Congress, that such legislative measures may be taken as they shall judge proper for carrying the same into execution.

JAMES MONROE.

WASHINGTON, *February 24, 1821.*
To the Senate and House of Representatives of the United States:

I transmit to Congress a letter from the Secretary of War, inclosing an annual return of the militia of the United States, prepared by the Adjutant and Inspector General conformably to the militia laws on that subject.

JAMES MONROE.

WASHINGTON, *February 28, 1821.*

To the Senate and House of Representatives of the United States:

I herewith transmit to Congress certain extracts and a copy of letters received by the Secretary of State from the marshal of the United States for the eastern district of Virginia, in relation to the execution of the act of the 14th of March, 1820, to provide for taking the Fourth Census, together with the answers returned to that marshal by the Secretary of State. As the time within which the assistants of the marshals can legally make their returns expired on the first Monday of the present month, it would appear by the information from the marshal at Richmond that the completion of the Fourth Census as it respects the eastern district of Virginia will have been defeated not only as it regards the period contemplated by law, but during the whole of the current year, unless Congress, to whom the case is submitted, should by an act of the present session allow further time for making the returns in question.

As connected with this subject, it is also submitted for the consideration of Congress how far the marshals ought to be liable to the payment of postage on the conveyance of the papers concerning the census and manufactures by the mail. In one instance it has been already ascertained that this item of contingent expense will amount to nearly a moiety of the compensation of the marshal for the whole of his services. If the marshals are to be relieved from this charge, provision will be necessary by law either for the admission of it in their accounts or the refunding of it by the respective postmasters.

JAMES MONROE.

WASHINGTON, *March 2, 1821.*

To the Congress of the United States:

I communicate to the two Houses of Congress copies of a treaty this day ratified on the part of the United States, concluded and signed at the Indian Springs on the 8th of January last, with the Creek Nation of Indians, in order to such legislative measures as may be necessary for giving effect to it.

JAMES MONROE.

WASHINGTON, *March 3, 1821.*

To the House of Representatives of the United States:

The treaty concluded between the United States and the Kickapoo tribe of Indians on the 30th of July, 1820, having been ratified by and with the advice and consent of the Senate, I now lay a copy of the said treaty before the House of Representatives in order to such legislative provisions being made as may be necessary to carry into effect the stipulations therein contained on the part of the United States.

JAMES MONROE.

SECOND INAUGURAL ADDRESS.

FELLOW-CITIZENS: I shall not attempt to describe the grateful emotions which the new and very distinguished proof of the confidence of my
fellow-citizens, evinced by my reelection to this high trust, has excited
in my bosom. The approbation which it announces of my conduct in the
preceding term affords me a consolation which I shall profoundly feel
through life. The general accord with which it has been expressed adds
to the great and never-ceasing obligations which it imposes. To merit
the continuance of this good opinion, and to carry it with me into my retirement as the solace of advancing years, will be the object of my most
zealous and unceasing efforts.

Having no pretensions to the high and commanding claims of my predecessors, whose names are so much more conspicuously identified with
our Revolution, and who contributed so preeminently to promote its success, I consider myself rather as the instrument than the cause of the
union which has prevailed in the late election. In surmounting, in favor
of my humble pretensions, the difficulties which so often produce division
in like occurrences, it is obvious that other powerful causes, indicating
the great strength and stability of our Union, have essentially contributed
to draw you together. That these powerful causes exist, and that they
are permanent, is my fixed opinion; that they may produce a like accord
in all questions touching, however remotely, the liberty, prosperity, and
happiness of our country will always be the object of my most fervent
prayers to the Supreme Author of All Good.

In a government which is founded by the people, who possess exclusively the sovereignty, it seems proper that the person who may be placed
by their suffrages in this high trust should declare on commencing its
duties the principles on which he intends to conduct the Administration.
If the person thus elected has served the preceding term, an opportunity
is afforded him to review its principal occurrences and to give such further explanation respecting them as in his judgment may be useful to his
constituents. The events of one year have influence on those of another,
and, in like manner, of a preceding on the succeeding Administration.
The movements of a great nation are connected in all their parts. If
errors have been committed they ought to be corrected; if the policy is
sound it ought to be supported. It is by a thorough knowledge of the
whole subject that our fellow-citizens are enabled to judge correctly of
the past and to give a proper direction to the future.

Just before the commencement of the last term the United States had
concluded a war with a very powerful nation on conditions equal and
honorable to both parties. The events of that war are too recent and
too deeply impressed on the memory of all to require a development from
me. Our commerce had been in a great measure driven from the sea,

our Atlantic and inland frontiers were invaded in almost every part; the waste of life along our coast and on some parts of our inland frontiers, to the defense of which our gallant and patriotic citizens were called, was immense, in addition to which not less than $120,000,000 were added at its end to the public debt.

As soon as the war had terminated, the nation, admonished by its events, resolved to place itself in a situation which should be better calculated to prevent the recurrence of a like evil, and, in case it should recur, to mitigate its calamities. With this view, after reducing our land force to the basis of a peace establishment, which has been further modified since, provision was made for the construction of fortifications at proper points through the whole extent of our coast and such an augmentation of our naval force as should be well adapted to both purposes. The laws making this provision were passed in 1815 and 1816, and it has been since the constant effort of the Executive to carry them into effect.

The advantage of these fortifications and of an augmented naval force in the extent contemplated, in a point of economy, has been fully illustrated by a report of the Board of Engineers and Naval Commissioners lately communicated to Congress, by which it appears that in an invasion by 20,000 men, with a correspondent naval force, in a campaign of six months only, the whole expense of the construction of the works would be defrayed by the difference in the sum necessary to maintain the force which would be adequate to our defense with the aid of those works and that which would be incurred without them. The reason of this difference is obvious. If fortifications are judiciously placed on our great inlets, as distant from our cities as circumstances will permit, they will form the only points of attack, and the enemy will be detained there by a small regular force a sufficient time to enable our militia to collect and repair to that on which the attack is made. A force adequate to the enemy, collected at that single point, with suitable preparation for such others as might be menaced, is all that would be requisite. But if there were no fortifications, then the enemy might go where he pleased, and, changing his position and sailing from place to place, our force must be called out and spread in vast numbers along the whole coast and on both sides of every bay and river as high up in each as it might be navigable for ships of war. By these fortifications, supported by our Navy, to which they would afford like support, we should present to other powers an armed front from St. Croix to the Sabine, which would protect in the event of war our whole coast and interior from invasion; and even in the wars of other powers, in which we were neutral, they would be found eminently useful, as, by keeping their public ships at a distance from our cities, peace and order in them would be preserved and the Government be protected from insult.

It need scarcely be remarked that these measures have not been resorted to in a spirit of hostility to other powers. Such a disposition does not exist toward any power.   Peace and good will have been, and will hereafter be, cultivated with all, and by the most faithful regard to justice.   They have been dictated by a love of peace, of economy, and an earnest desire to save the lives of our fellow-citizens from that destruction and our country from that devastation which are inseparable from war when it finds us unprepared for it.   It is believed, and experience has shown, that such a preparation is the best expedient that can be resorted to to prevent war.   I add with much pleasure that considerable progress has already been made in these measures of defense, and that they will be completed in a few years, considering the great extent and importance of the object, if the plan be zealously and steadily persevered in.

The conduct of the Government in what relates to foreign powers is always an object of the highest importance to the nation.   Its agriculture, commerce, manufactures, fisheries, revenue, in short, its peace, may all be affected by it.   Attention is therefore due to this subject.

At the period adverted to the powers of Europe, after having been engaged in long and destructive wars with each other, had concluded a peace, which happily still exists.   Our peace with the power with whom we had been engaged had also been concluded.   The war between Spain and the colonies in South America, which had commenced many years before, was then the only conflict that remained unsettled.   This being a contest between different parts of the same community, in which other powers had not interfered, was not affected by their accommodations.

This contest was considered at an early stage by my predecessor a civil war in which the parties were entitled to equal rights in our ports. This decision, the first made by any power, being formed on great consideration of the comparative strength and resources of the parties, the length of time, and successful opposition made by the colonies, and of all other circumstances on which it ought to depend, was in strict accord with the law of nations.   Congress has invariably acted on this principle, having made no change in our relations with either party.   Our attitude has therefore been that of neutrality between them, which has been maintained by the Government with the strictest impartiality.   No aid has been afforded to either, nor has any privilege been enjoyed by the one which has not been equally open to the other party, and every exertion has been made in its power to enforce the execution of the laws prohibiting illegal equipments with equal rigor against both.

By this equality between the parties their public vessels have been received in our ports on the same footing; they have enjoyed an equal right to purchase and export arms, munitions of war, and every other supply, the exportation of all articles whatever being permitted under laws which were passed long before the commencement of the contest; our citizens have traded equally with both, and their commerce with each has been alike protected by the Government.

Respecting the attitude which it may be proper for the United States to maintain hereafter between the parties, I have no hesitation in stating it as my opinion that the neutrality heretofore observed should still be adhered to. From the change in the Government of Spain and the negotiation now depending, invited by the Cortes and accepted by the colonies, it may be presumed that their differences will be settled on the terms proposed by the colonies. Should the war be continued, the United States, regarding its occurrences, will always have it in their power to adopt such measures respecting it as their honor and interest may require.

Shortly after the general peace a band of adventurers took advantage of this conflict and of the facility which it afforded to establish a system of buccaneering in the neighboring seas, to the great annoyance of the commerce of the United States, and, as was represented, of that of other powers. Of this spirit and of its injurious bearing on the United States strong proofs were afforded by the establishment at Amelia Island, and the purposes to which it was made instrumental by this band in 1817, and by the occurrences which took place in other parts of Florida in 1818, the details of which in both instances are too well known to require to be now recited. I am satisfied had a less decisive course been adopted that the worst consequences would have resulted from it. We have seen that these checks, decisive as they were, were not sufficient to crush that piratical spirit. Many culprits brought within our limits have been condemned to suffer death, the punishment due to that atrocious crime. The decisions of upright and enlightened tribunals fall equally on all whose crimes subject them, by a fair interpretation of the law, to its censure. It belongs to the Executive not to suffer the executions under these decisions to transcend the great purpose for which punishment is necessary. The full benefit of example being secured, policy as well as humanity equally forbids that they should be carried further. I have acted on this principle, pardoning those who appear to have been led astray by ignorance of the criminality of the acts they had committed, and suffering the law to take effect on those only in whose favor no extenuating circumstances could be urged.

Great confidence is entertained that the late treaty with Spain, which has been ratified by both the parties, and the ratifications whereof have been exchanged, has placed the relations of the two countries on a basis of permanent friendship. The provision made by it for such of our citizens as have claims on Spain of the character described will, it is presumed, be very satisfactory to them, and the boundary which is established between the territories of the parties westward of the Mississippi, heretofore in dispute, has, it is thought, been settled on conditions just and advantageous to both. But to the acquisition of Florida too much importance can not be attached. It secures to the United States a territory important in itself, and whose importance is much increased by its bearing on many of the highest interests of the Union. It opens to several of the neighboring States a free passage to the ocean, through the Province ceded, by several rivers, having their sources high up within their limits. It secures us against all future annoyance from powerful Indian tribes. It gives us several excellent harbors in the Gulf of Mexico for ships of war of the largest size. It covers by its position in the Gulf the Mississippi and other great waters within our extended limits, and thereby enables the United States to afford complete protection to the vast and very valuable productions of our whole Western country, which find a market through those streams.

By a treaty with the British Government, bearing date on the 20th of October, 1818, the convention regulating the commerce between the United States and Great Britain, concluded on the 3d of July, 1815, which was about expiring, was revived and continued for the term of ten years from the time of its expiration. By that treaty, also, the differences which had arisen under the treaty of Ghent respecting the right claimed by the United States for their citizens to take and cure fish on the coast of His Britannic Majesty's dominions in America, with other differences on important interests, were adjusted to the satisfaction of both parties. No agreement has yet been entered into respecting the commerce between the United States and the British dominions in the West Indies and on this continent. The restraints imposed on that commerce by Great Britain, and reciprocated by the United States on a principle of defense, continue still in force.

The negotiation with France for the regulation of the commercial relations between the two countries, which in the course of the last summer had been commenced at Paris, has since been transferred to this city, and will be pursued on the part of the United States in the spirit of conciliation, and with an earnest desire that it may terminate in an arrangement satisfactory to both parties.

Our relations with the Barbary Powers are preserved in the same state and by the same means that were employed when I came into this office. As early as 1801 it was found necessary to send a squadron into the Mediterranean for the protection of our commerce, and no period has intervened, a short term excepted, when it was thought advisable to withdraw it. The great interests which the United States have in the Pacific, in commerce and in the fisheries, have also made it necessary to maintain a naval force there. In disposing of this force in both instances the most effectual measures in our power have been taken, without interfering with its other duties, for the suppression of the slave trade and of piracy in the neighboring seas.

The situation of the United States in regard to their resources, the extent of their revenue, and the facility with which it is raised affords a most gratifying spectacle. The payment of nearly $67,000,000 of the public debt, with the great progress made in measures of defense and in other improvements of various kinds since the late war, are conclusive proofs of this extraordinary prosperity, especially when it is recollected that these expenditures have been defrayed without a burthen on the people, the direct tax and excise having been repealed soon after the conclusion of the late war, and the revenue applied to these great objects having been raised in a manner not to be felt. Our great resources therefore remain untouched for any purpose which may affect the vital interests of the nation. For all such purposes they are inexhaustible. They are more especially to be found in the virtue, patriotism, and intelligence of our fellow-citizens, and in the devotion with which they would yield up by any just measure of taxation all their property in support of the rights and honor of their country.

Under the present depression of prices, affecting all the productions of the country and every branch of industry, proceeding from causes explained on a former occasion, the revenue has considerably diminished, the effect of which has been to compel Congress either to abandon these great measures of defense or to resort to loans or internal taxes to supply the deficiency. On the presumption that this depression and the deficiency in the revenue arising from it would be temporary, loans were authorized for the demands of the last and present year. Anxious to relieve my fellow-citizens in 1817 from every burthen which could be dispensed with, and the state of the Treasury permitting it, I recommended the repeal of the internal taxes, knowing that such relief was then peculiarly necessary in consequence of the great exertions made in the late war. I made that recommendation under a pledge that should the public exigencies require a recurrence to them at any time while I remained in this trust, I would with equal promptitude perform the duty which would then be alike incumbent on me. By the experiment now making it will be seen by the next session of Congress whether the revenue shall have been so augmented as to be adequate to all these necessary purposes. Should the deficiency still continue, and especially should it be probable that it would be permanent, the course to be pursued appears to me to be obvious. I am satisfied that under certain circumstances loans may be resorted to with great advantage. I am equally well satisfied, as a general rule, that the demands of the current year, especially in time of peace, should be provided for by the revenue of that year.

I have never dreaded, nor have I ever shunned, in any situation in which I have been placed making appeals to the virtue and patriotism of my fellow-citizens, well knowing that they could never be made in vain, especially in times of great emergency or for purposes of high national importance. Independently of the exigency of the case, many considerations of great weight urge a policy having in view a provision of revenue to meet to a certain extent the demands of the nation, without relying altogether on the precarious resource of foreign commerce. I am satisfied that internal duties and excises, with corresponding imposts on foreign articles of the same kind, would, without imposing any serious burdens or the people, enhance the price of produce, promote our manufactures, and augment the revenue, at the same time that they made it more secure and permanent.

The care of the Indian tribes within our limits has long been an essential part of our system, but, unfortunately, it has not been executed in a manner to accomplish all the objects intended by it. We have treated them as independent nations, without their having any substantial pretensions to that rank. The distinction has flattered their pride, retarded their improvement, and in many instances paved the way to their destruction. The progress of our settlements westward, supported as they are by a dense population, has constantly driven them back, with almost the total sacrifice of the lands which they have been compelled to abandon. They have claims on the magnanimity and, I may add, on the justice of this nation which we must all feel. We should become their real benefactors; we should perform the office of their Great Father, the endearing title which they emphatically give to the Chief Magistrate of our Union. Their sovereignty over vast territories should cease, in lieu of which the right of soil should be secured to each individual and his posterity in competent portions; and for the territory thus ceded by each tribe some reasonable equivalent should be granted, to be vested in permanent funds for the support of civil government over them and for the education of their children, for their instruction in the arts of husbandry, and to provide sustenance for them until they could provide it for themselves. My earnest hope is that Congress will digest some plan, founded on these principles, with such improvements as their wisdom may suggest, and carry it into effect as soon as it may be practicable.

Europe is again unsettled and the prospect of war increasing. Should the flame light up in any quarter, how far it may extend it is impossible to foresee. It is our peculiar felicity to be altogether unconnected with the causes which produce this menacing aspect elsewhere. With every power we are in perfect amity, and it is our interest to remain so if it be practicable on just conditions. I see no reasonable cause to apprehend variance with any power, unless it proceed from a violation of our maritime rights. In these contests, should they occur, and to whatever extent they may be carried, we shall be neutral; but as a neutral power we have rights which it is our duty to maintain. For like injuries it will be incumbent on us to seek redress in a spirit of amity, in full confidence that, injuring none, none would knowingly injure us. For more imminent dangers we should be prepared, and it should always be recollected that such preparation adapted to the circumstances and sanctioned by the judgment and wishes of our constituents can not fail to have a good effect in averting dangers of every kind. We should recollect also that the season of peace is best adapted to these preparations.

If we turn our attention, fellow-citizens, more immediately to the internal concerns of our country, and more especially to those on which its future welfare depends, we have every reason to anticipate the happiest results. It is now rather more than forty-four years since we declared our independence, and thirty-seven since it was acknowledged. The talents and virtues which were displayed in that great struggle were a sure presage of all that has since followed. A people who were able to surmount in their infant state such great perils would be more competent as they rose into manhood to repel any which they might meet in their progress. Their physical strength would be more adequate to foreign danger, and the practice of self-government, aided by the light of experience, could not fail to produce an effect equally salutary on all those questions connected with the internal organization. These favorable anticipations have been realized.

In our whole system, national and State, we have shunned all the defects which unceasingly preyed on the vitals and destroyed the ancient Republics. In them there were distinct orders, a nobility and a people, or the people governed in one assembly. Thus, in the one instance there was a perpetual conflict between the orders in society for the ascendency, in which the victory of either terminated in the overthrow of the government and the ruin of the state; in the other, in which the people governed in a body, and whose dominions seldom exceeded the dimensions of a county in one of our States, a tumultuous and disorderly movement permitted only a transitory existence. In this great nation there is but one order, that of the people, whose power, by a peculiarly happy improvement of the representative principle, is transferred from them, without impairing in the slightest degree their sovereignty, to bodies of their own creation, and to persons elected by themselves, in the full extent necessary for all the purposes of free, enlightened, and efficient government. The whole system is elective, the complete sovereignty being in the people, and every officer in every department deriving his authority from and being responsible to them for his conduct.

Our career has corresponded with this great outline. Perfection in our organization could not have been expected in the outset either in the National or State Governments or in tracing the line between their respective powers. But no serious conflict has arisen, nor any contest but such as are m. naged by argument and by a fair appeal to the good sense of the people, and many of the defects which experience had clearly demonstrated in both Governments have been remedied. By steadily pursuing this course in this spirit there is every reason to believe that our system will soon attain the highest degree of perfection of which human institutions are capable, and that the movement in all its branches will exhibit such a degree of order and harmony as to command the admiration and respect of the civilized world.

Our physical attainments have not been less eminent. Twenty-five years ago the river Mississippi was shut up and our Western brethren had no outlet for their commerce. What has been the progress since that time? The river has not only become the property of the United States from its source to the ocean, with all its tributary streams (with the exception of the upper part of the Red River only), but Louisiana, with a fair and liberal boundary on the western side and the Floridas on the eastern, have been ceded to us. The United States now enjoy the complete and uninterrupted sovereignty over the whole territory from St. Croix to the Sabine. New States, settled from among ourselves in this and in other parts, have been admitted into our Union in equal participation in the national sovereignty with the original States. Our population has augmented in an astonishing degree and extended in every direction. We now, fellow-citizens, comprise within our limits the dimensions and faculties of a great power under a Government possessing all the energies of any government ever known to the Old World, with an utter incapacity to oppress the people.

Entering with these views the office which I have just solemnly sworn to execute with fidelity and to the utmost of my ability, I derive great satisfaction from a knowledge that I shall be assisted in the several Departments by the very enlightened and upright citizens from whom I have received so much aid in the preceding term. With full confidence in the continuance of that candor and generous indulgence from my fellow-citizens at large which I have heretofore experienced, and with a firm reliance on the protection of Almighty God, I shall forthwith commence the duties of the high trust to which you have called me.

MARCH 5, 1821.

PROCLAMATIONS.

By THE PRESIDENT OF THE UNITED STATES OF AMERICA.

A PROCLAMATION.

Whereas information has been received that an atrocious murder, aggravated by the additional crime of robbery, was, on the 6th or 7th day of this present month, committed in the county of Alexandria and District of Columbia on William Seaver, late of this city; and

Whereas the apprehension and punishment of the murderer or murderers and his or their accessary or accessaries will be an example due to justice and humanity and every way salutary in its operation:

I have therefore thought fit to issue this my proclamation, hereby exhorting the citizens of the United States, and particularly those of this District, and requiring all officers, according to their respective stations, to use their utmost endeavors to apprehend and bring the principal or principals, accessary or accessaries, to the said murder to justice.

And I do moreover offer a reward of $300 for each principal, if there be more than one, and $150 for each accessary before the fact, if there be more than one, who shall be apprehended after the day of the date hereof and brought to justice, to be paid upon his conviction of the crime or crimes aforesaid.

In testimony whereof I have caused the seal of the United States to be affixed to these presents, and signed the same with my hand.

[SEAL.] Done at the city of Washington, this 10th day of July, A. D. 1821, and of the Independence of the United States the forty-sixth.

JAMES MONROE.

By the President:
JOHN QUINCY ADAMS,
Secretary of State.

BY THE PRESIDENT OF THE UNITED STATES.

A PROCLAMATION.

Whereas the Congress of the United States, by a joint resolution of the 2d day of March last, entitled "Resolution providing for the admission of the State of Missouri into the Union on a certain condition," did determine and declare "that Missouri should be admitted into this Union on an equal footing with the original States in all respects whatever upon the fundamental condition that the fourth clause of the twenty-sixth section of the third article of the constitution submitted on the part of said State to Congress shall never be construed to authorize the passage of any law, and that no law shall be passed in conformity thereto, by which any citizen of either of the States of this Union shall be excluded from the enjoyment of any of the privileges and immunities to which such citizen is entitled under the Constitution of the United States: *Provided*, That the legislature of said State, by a solemn public act, shall declare the assent of the said State to the said fundamental condition, and shall transmit to the President of the United States on or before the first Monday in November next an authentic copy of said act, upon the receipt whereof the President, by proclamation, shall announce the fact, whereupon, and without any further proceeding on the part of Congress, the admission of the said State into this Union shall be considered as complete;" and

Whereas by a solemn public act of the assembly of said State of Missouri, passed on the 26th of June, in the present year, entitled "A solemn public act declaring the assent of this State to the fundamental condition contained in a resolution passed by the Congress of the United States providing for the admission of the State of Missouri into the Union on a certain condition," an authentic copy whereof has been communicated to me, it is solemnly and publicly enacted and declared that that State has assented, and does assent, that the fourth clause of the twenty-sixth section of the third article of the constitution of said State "shall never be construed to authorize the passage of any law, and that no law shall be passed in conformity thereto, by which any citizen of either of the United States shall be excluded from the enjoyment of any of the privileges and immunities to which such citizens are entitled under the Constitution of the United States:"

Now, therefore, I, James Monroe, President of the United States, in pursuance of the resolution of Congress aforesaid, have issued this my proclamation, announcing the fact that the said State of Missouri has assented to the fundamental condition required by the resolution of Congress aforesaid, whereupon the admission of the said State of Missouri into this Union is declared to be complete.

In testimony whereof I have caused the seal of the United States of America to be affixed to these presents, and signed the same with my hand.

[SEAL.]   Done at the city of Washington, the 10th day of August, A. D. 1821, and of the Independence of the said United States of America the forty-sixth.

JAMES MONROE.

By the President:

JOHN QUINCY ADAMS,
    Secretary of State.

BY THE PRESIDENT OF THE UNITED STATES OF AMERICA.

A PROCLAMATION.

Whereas by an act of the Congress of the United States of the 3d of March, 1815, so much of the several acts imposing duties on the ships and vessels and on goods, wares, and merchandise imported into the United States as imposed a discriminating duty of tonnage between foreign vessels and vessels of the United States and between goods imported into the United States in foreign vessels and vessels of the United States were repealed so far as the same respected the produce or manufacture of the nation to which such foreign ship or vessel might belong, such repeal to take effect in favor of any foreign nation whenever the President of the United States should be satisfied that the discriminating or countervailing duties of such foreign nation so far as they operate to the disadvantage of the United States have been abolished; and

Whereas satisfactory proof has been received by me, through the chargé d'affaires of the United States in Sweden, under date of the 30th day of January, 1821, that thenceforward all discriminating or countervailing duties in the Kingdom of Norway so far as they operated to the disadvantage of the United States had been and were abolished:

Now, therefore, I, James Monroe, President of the United States of

America, do hereby declare and proclaim that so much of the several acts imposing duties on the tonnage of ships and vessels and on goods, wares, and merchandise imported into the United States as imposed a discriminating duty of tonnage between vessels of the Kingdom of Norway and vessels of the United States and between goods imported into the United States in vessels of the said Kingdom of Norway and vessels of the United States are repealed so far as the same respect the produce or manufacture of the said Kingdom of Norway.

Given under my hand, at the city of Washington, this 20th day of August, A. D. 1821, and the forty-sixth year of the Independence of the United States.

JAMES MONROE.

By the President:
John Quincy Adams,
Secretary of State.

By the President of the United States of America.

A PROCLAMATION.

Whereas by an act of the Congress of the United States of the 3d of March, 1815, so much of the several acts imposing duties on the ships and vessels and on goods, wares, and merchandise imported into the United States as imposed a discriminating duty of tonnage between foreign vessels and vessels of the United States and between goods imported into the United States in foreign vessels and vessels of the United States were repealed so far as the same respected the produce or manufacture of the nation to which such foreign ship or vessel might belong, such repeal to take effect in favor of any foreign nation whenever the President of the United States should be satisfied that the discriminating or countervailing duties of such foreign nation so far as they operate to the disadvantage of the United States have been abolished; and

Whereas satisfactory proof has been received by me, under date of the 11th of May last, that thenceforward all discriminating or countervailing duties of the Dukedom of Oldenburg so far as they might operate to the disadvantage of the United States should be and were abolished upon His Highness the Duke of Oldenburg's being duly certified of a reciprocal act on the part of the United States:

Now, therefore, I, James Monroe, President of the United States of America, do hereby declare and proclaim that so much of the several acts imposing duties on the tonnage of ships and vessels and on goods, wares, and merchandise imported into the United States as imposed a discriminating duty of tonnage between vessels of the Dukedom of Oldenburg and vessels of the United States and between goods imported into the United States in vessels of the said Dukedom of Oldenburg and vessels of the United States are repealed so far as the same respect the produce or manufacture of the said Dukedom of Oldenburg.

Given under my hand, at the city of Washington, this 22d day of November, A. D. 1821, and the forty-sixth year of the Independence of the United States.

JAMES MONROE.

By the President:

JOHN QUINCY ADAMS,
Secretary of State.

FIFTH ANNUAL MESSAGE.

WASHINGTON, *December 3, 1821.*

Fellow-Citizens of the Senate and of the House of Representatives;

The progress of our affairs since the last session has been such as may justly be claimed and expected under a Government deriving all its powers from an enlightened people, and under laws formed by their representatives, on great consideration, for the sole purpose of promoting the welfare and happiness of their constituents. In the execution of those laws and of the powers vested by the Constitution in the Executive, unremitted attention has been paid to the great objects to which they extend. In the concerns which are exclusively internal there is good cause to be satisfied with the result. The laws have had their due operation and effect. In those relating to foreign powers, I am happy to state that peace and amity are preserved with all by a strict observance on both sides of the rights of each. In matters touching our commercial intercourse, where a difference of opinion has existed as to the conditions on which it should be placed, each party has pursued its own policy without giving just cause of offense to the other. In this annual communication, especially when it is addressed to a new Congress, the whole scope of our political concerns naturally comes into view, that errors, if such have been committed, may be corrected; that defects which have become manifest may be remedied; and, on the other hand, that measures which were adopted on due deliberation, and which experience has shewn are just in themselves and essential to the public welfare, should be persevered in and supported. In performing this necessary and very important duty I shall endeavor to place before you on its merits every subject that is thought to be entitled to your particular attention in as distinct and clear a light as I may be able.

By an act of the 3d of March, 1815, so much of the several acts as imposed higher duties on the tonnage of foreign vessels and on the manufactures and productions of foreign nations when imported into the United States in foreign vessels than when imported in vessels of the

United States were repealed so far as respected the manufactures and productions of the nation to which such vessels belonged, on the condition that the repeal should take effect only in favor of any foreign nation when the Executive should be satisfied that such discriminating duties to the disadvantage of the United States had likewise been repealed by such nation. By this act a proposition was made to all nations to place our commerce with each on a basis which it was presumed would be acceptable to all. Every nation was allowed to bring its manufactures and productions into our ports and to take the manufactures and productions of the United States back to their ports in their own vessels on the same conditions that they might be transported in vessels of the United States, and in return it was required that a like accommodation should be granted to the vessels of the United States in the ports of other powers. The articles to be admitted or prohibited on either side formed no part of the proposed arrangement. Each party would retain the right to admit or prohibit such articles from the other as it thought proper, and on its own conditions.

When the nature of the commerce between the United States and every other country was taken into view, it was thought that this proposition would be considered fair, and even liberal, by every power. The exports of the United States consist generally of articles of the first necessity and of rude materials in demand for foreign manufactories, of great bulk, requiring for their transportation many vessels, the return for which in the manufactures and productions of any foreign country, even when disposed of there to advantage, may be brought in a single vessel. This observation is the more especially applicable to those countries from which manufactures alone are imported, but it applies in a great extent to the European dominions of every European power and in a certain extent to all the colonies of those powers. By placing, then, the navigation precisely on the same ground in the transportation of exports and imports between the United States and other countries it was presumed that all was offered which could be desired. It seemed to be the only proposition which could be devised which would retain even the semblance of equality in our favor.

Many considerations of great weight gave us a right to expect that this commerce should be extended to the colonies as well as to the European dominions of other powers. With the latter, especially with countries exclusively manufacturing, the advantage was manifestly on their side. An indemnity for that loss was expected from a trade with the colonies, and with the greater reason as it was known that the supplies which the colonies derived from us were of the highest importance to them, their labor being bestowed with so much greater profit in the culture of other articles; and because, likewise, the articles of which those supplies consisted, forming so large a proportion of the exports of the United States, were never admitted into any of the ports of Europe except in cases of great emergency to avert a serious calamity. When no article is admitted which is not required to supply the wants of the party admitting it, and admitted then not in favor of any particular country to the disadvantage of others, but on conditions equally applicable to all, it seems just that the articles thus admitted and invited should be carried thither in the vessels of the country affording such supply and that the reciprocity should be found in a corresponding accommodation on the other side. By allowing each party to participate in the transportation of such supplies on the payment of equal tonnage a strong proof was afforded of an accommodating spirit. To abandon to it the transportation of the whole would be a sacrifice which ought not to be expected. The demand in the present instance would be the more unreasonable in consideration of the great inequality existing in the trade with the parent country.

Such was the basis of our system as established by the act of 1815 and such its true character. In the year in which this act was passed a treaty was concluded with Great Britain, in strict conformity with its principles, in regard to her European dominions. To her colonies, however, in the West Indies and on this continent it was not extended, the British Government claiming the exclusive supply of those colonies, and from our own ports, and of the productions of the colonies in return in her own vessels. To this claim the United States could not assent, and in consequence each party suspended the intercourse in the vessels of the other by a prohibition which still exists.

The same conditions were offered to France, but not accepted. Her Government has demanded other conditions more favorable to her navigation, and which should also give extraordinary encouragement to her manufactures and productions in ports of the United States. To these it was thought improper to accede, and in consequence the restrictive regulations which had been adopted on her part, being countervailed on the part of the United States, the direct commerce between the two countries in the vessels of each party has been in a great measure suspended. It is much to be regretted that, although a negotiation has been long pending, such is the diversity of views entertained on the various points which have been brought into discussion that there does not appear to be any reasonable prospect of its early conclusion.

It is my duty to state, as a cause of very great regret, that very serious differences have occurred in this negotiation respecting the construction of the eighth article of the treaty of 1803, by which Louisiana was ceded to the United States, and likewise respecting the seizure of the *Apollo*, in 1820, for a violation of our revenue laws. The claim of the Government of France has excited not less surprise than concern, because there does not appear to be a just foundation for it in either instance. By the eighth article of the treaty referred to it is stipulated that after the expiration of twelve years, during which time it was provided by the seventh or preceding article that the vessels of France and Spain should be admitted into the ports of the ceded territory without paying higher duties on merchandise or tonnage on the vessels than such as were paid by citizens of the United States, the ships of France should forever afterwards be placed on the footing of the most favored nation. By the obvious construction of this article it is presumed that it was intended that no favor should be granted to any power in those ports to which France should not be forthwith entitled, nor should any accommodation be allowed to another power on conditions to which she would not also be entitled on the same conditions. Under this construction no favor or accommodation could be granted to any power to the prejudice of France. By allowing the equivalent allowed by those powers she would always stand in those ports on the footing of the most favored nation. But if this article should be so construed as that France should enjoy, of right, and without paying the equivalent, all the advantages of such conditions as might be allowed to other powers in return for important concessions made by them, then the whole character of the stipulation would be changed. She would not be placed on the footing of the most favored nation, but on a footing held by no other nation. She would enjoy all advantages allowed to them in consideration of like advantages allowed to us, free from every and any condition whatever.

As little cause has the Government of France to complain of the seizure of the *Apollo* and the removal of other vessels from the waters of the St. Marys. It will not be denied that every nation has a right to regulate its commercial system as it thinks fit and to enforce the collection of its revenue, provided it be done without an invasion of the rights of other powers. The violation of its revenue laws is an offense which all nations punish, the punishment of which gives no just cause of complaint to the power to which the offenders belong, provided it be extended to all equally. In this case every circumstance which occurred indicated a fixed purpose to violate our revenue laws. Had the party intended to have pursued a fair trade he would have entered our ports and paid the duties; or had he intended to carry on a legitimate circuitous commerce with the United States he would have entered the port of some other power, landed his goods at the custom-house according to law, and reshipped and sent them in the vessel of such power, or of some other power which might lawfully bring them, free from such duties, to a port of the United States. But the conduct of the party in this case was altogether different. He entered the river St. Marys, the boundary line between the United States and Florida, and took his position on the Spanish side, on which in the whole extent of the river there was no town, no port or custom-house, and scarcely any settlement. His purpose, therefore, was not to sell his goods to the inhabitants of Florida, but to citizens of the United States, in exchange for their productions, which could not be done without a direct and palpable breach of our laws. It is known that a regular systematic plan had been formed by certain persons for the violation of our revenue system, which made it the more necessary to check the proceeding in its commencement.

That the unsettled bank of a river so remote from the Spanish garrisons and population could give no protection to any party in such a practice is believed to be in strict accord with the law of nations. It would not have comported with a friendly policy in Spain herself to have established a custom-house there, since it could have subserved no other purpose than to elude our revenue law. But the Government of Spain did not adopt that measure. On the contrary, it is understood that the Captain-General of Cuba, to whom an application to that effect was made by these adventurers, had not acceded to it. The condition of those Provinces for many years before they were ceded to the United States need not now be dwelt on. Inhabited by different tribes of Indians and an inroad for every kind of adventurer, the jurisdiction of Spain may be said to have been almost exclusively confined to her garrisons. It certainly could not extend to places where she had no authority. The rules, therefore, applicable to settled countries governed by laws could not be deemed so to the deserts of Florida and to the occurrences there. It merits attention also that the territory had then been ceded to the United States by a treaty the ratification of which had not been refused, and which has since been performed. Under any circumstances, therefore, Spain became less responsible for such acts committed there, and the United States more at liberty to exercise authority to prevent so great a mischief. The conduct of this Government has in every instance been conciliatory and friendly to France. The construction of our revenue law in its application to the cases which have formed the ground of such serious complaint on her part and the order to the collector of St. Marys, in accord with it, were given two years before these cases occurred, and in reference to a breach which was attempted by the subjects of another power. The application, therefore, to the cases in question was inevitable. As soon as the treaty by which these Provinces were ceded to the United States was ratified, and all danger of further breach of our revenue laws ceased, an order was given for the release of the vessel which had been seized and for the dismission of the libel which had been instituted against her.

The principles of this system of reciprocity, founded on the law of the 3d of March, 1815, have been since carried into effect with the Kingdoms of the Netherlands, Sweden, Prussia, and with Hamburg, Bremen, Lubeck, and Oldenburg, with a provision made by subsequent laws in regard to the Netherlands, Prussia, Hamburg, and Bremen that such produce and manufactures as could only be, or most usually were, first shipped from the ports of those countries, the same. being imported in vessels wholly belonging to their subjects, should be considered and admitted as their own manufactures and productions.

The Government of Norway has by an ordinance opened the ports of that part of the dominions of the King of Sweden to the vessels of the

United States upon the payment of no other or higher duties than are paid by Norwegian vessels, from whatever place arriving and with whatever articles laden. They have requested the reciprocal allowance for the vessels of Norway in the ports of the United States. As this privilege is not within the scope of the act of the 3d of March, 1815, and can only be granted by Congress, and as it may involve the commercial relations of the United States with other nations, the subject is submitted to the wisdom of Congress.

I have presented thus fully to your view our commercial relations with other powers, that, seeing them in detail with each power, and knowing the basis on which they rest, Congress may in its wisdom decide whether any change ought to be made, and, if any, in what respect. If this basis is unjust or unreasonable, surely it ought to be abandoned; but if it be just and reasonable, and any change in it will make concessions subversive of equality and tending in its consequences to sap the foundations of our prosperity, then the reasons are equally strong for adhering to the ground already taken, and supporting it by such further regulations as may appear to be proper, should any additional support be found necessary.

The question concerning the construction of the first article of the treaty of Ghent has been, by a joint act of the representatives of the United States and of Great Britain at the Court of St. Petersburg, submitted to the decision of His Imperial Majesty the Emperor of Russia. The result of that submission has not yet been received. The commissioners under the fifth article of that treaty not having been able to agree upon their decision, their reports to the two Governments, according to the provisions of the treaty, may be expected at an early day.

With Spain the treaty of February 22, 1819, has been partly carried into execution. Possession of East and West Florida has been given to the United States, but the officers charged with that service by an order from His Catholic Majesty, delivered by his minister to the Secretary of State, and transmitted by a special agent to the Captain-General of Cuba, to whom it was directed and in whom the government of those Provinces was vested, have not only omitted, in contravention of the order of their Sovereign, the performance of the express stipulation to deliver over the archives and documents relating to the property and sovereignty of those Provinces, all of which it was expected would have been delivered either before or when the troops were withdrawn, but defeated since every effort of the United States to obtain them, especially those of the greatest importance. This omission has given rise to several incidents of a painful nature, the character of which will be fully disclosed by the documents which will be hereafter communicated.

In every other circumstance the law of the 3d of March last, for carrying into effect that treaty, has been duly attended to. For the execution of that part which preserved in force, for the government of the inhabitants for the term specified, all the civil, military, and judicial powers exercised by the existing government of those Provinces an adequate number of officers, as was presumed, were appointed, and ordered to their respective stations. Both Provinces were formed into one Territory, and a governor appointed for it; but in consideration of the pre-existing division and of the distance and difficulty of communication between Pensacola, the residence of the governor of West Florida, and St. Augustine, that of the governor of East Florida, at which places the inconsiderable population of each Province was principally collected, two secretaries were appointed, the one to reside at Pensacola and the other at St. Augustine. Due attention was likewise paid to the execution of the laws of the United States relating to the revenue and the slave trade, which were extended to these Provinces. The whole Territory was divided into three collection districts, that part lying between the river St. Marys and Cape Florida forming one, that from the Cape to the Apalachicola another, and that from the Apalachicola to the Perdido the third. To these districts the usual number of revenue officers were appointed; and to secure the due operation of these laws one judge and a district attorney were appointed to reside at Pensacola, and likewise one judge and a district attorney to reside at St. Augustine, with a specified boundary between them; and one marshal for the whole, with authority to appoint a deputy. In carrying this law into effect, and especially that part relating to the powers of the existing government of those Provinces, it was thought important, in consideration of the short term for which it was to operate and the radical change which would be made at the approaching session of Congress, to avoid expense, to make no appointment which should not be absolutely necessary to give effect to those powers, to withdraw none of our citizens from their pursuits, whereby to subject the Government to claims which could not be gratified and the parties to losses which it would be painful to witness.

It has been seen with much concern that in the performance of these duties a collision arose between the governor of the Territory and the judge appointed for the western district. It was presumed that the law under which this transitory government was organized, and the commissions which were granted to the officers who were appointed to execute each branch of the system, and to which the commissions were adapted, would have been understood in the same sense by them in which they were understood by the Executive. Much allowance is due to officers employed in each branch of this system, and the more so as there is good cause to believe that each acted under the conviction that he possessed the power which he undertook to exercise. Of the officer holding the principal station, I think it proper to observe that he accepted it with reluctance, in compliance with the invitation given him, and from a high sense of duty to his country, being willing to contribute to the consummation of an event which would insure complete protection to an important part of our Union, which had suffered much from incursion and invasion, and to the defense of which his very gallant and patriotic services had been so signally and usefully devoted.

From the intrinsic difficulty of executing laws deriving their origin from different sources, and so essentially different in many important circumstances, the advantage, and indeed the necessity, of establishing as soon as may be practicable a well-organized government over that Territory on the principles of our system is apparent. This subject is therefore recommended to the early consideration of Congress.

In compliance with an injunction of the law of the 3d of March last, three commissioners have also been appointed and a board organized for carrying into effect the eleventh article of the treaty above recited, making provision for the payment of such of our citizens as have well-founded claims on Spain of the character specified by that treaty. This board has entered on its duties and made some progress therein. The commissioner and surveyor of His Catholic Majesty, provided for by the fourth article of the treaty, have not yet arrived in the United States, but are soon expected. As soon as they do arrive corresponding appointments will be made and every facility be afforded for the due execution of this service.

The Government of His Most Faithful Majesty since the termination of the last session of Congress has been removed from Rio de Janeiro to Lisbon, where a revolution similar to that which had occurred in the neighboring Kingdom of Spain had in like manner been sanctioned by the accepted and pledged faith of the reigning monarch. The diplomatic intercourse between the United States and the Portuguese dominions, interrupted by this important event, has not yet been resumed, but the change of internal administration having already materially affected the commercial intercourse of the United States with the Portuguese dominions, the renewal of the public missions between the two countries appears to be desirable at an early day.

It is understood that the colonies in South America have had great success during the present year in the struggle for their independence. The new Government of Colombia has extended its territories and considerably augmented its strength, and at Buenos Ayres, where civil dissensions had for some time before prevailed, greater harmony and better order appear to have been established. Equal success has attended their efforts in the Provinces on the Pacific. It has long been manifest that it would be impossible for Spain to reduce these colonies by force, and equally so that no conditions short of their independence would be satisfactory to them. It may therefore be presumed, and it is earnestly hoped, that the Government of Spain, guided by enlightened and liberal councils, will find it to comport with its interests and due to its magnanimity to terminate this exhausting controversy on that basis. To promote this result by friendly counsel with the Government of Spain will be the object of the Government of the United States.

In conducting the fiscal operations of the year it has been found necessary to carry into full effect the act of the last session of Congress authorizing a loan of $5,000,000. This sum has been raised at an average premium of $5.59 per centum upon stock bearing an interest at the rate of 5 per cent per annum, redeemable at the option of the Government after the 1st day of January, 1835.

There has been issued under the provisions of this act $4,735,296.30 of 5 per cent stock, and there has been or will be redeemed during the year $3,197,030.71 of Louisiana 6 per cent deferred stock and Mississippi stock. There has therefore been an actual increase of the public debt contracted during the year of $1,538,266.69.

The receipts into the Treasury from the 1st of January to the 30th of September last have amounted to $16,219,197.70, which, with the balance of $1,198,461.21 in the Treasury on the former day, make the aggregate sum of $17,417,658.91. The payments from the Treasury during the same period have amounted to $15,655,288.47, leaving in the Treasury on the last-mentioned day the sum of $1,762,370.44. It is estimated that the receipts of the fourth quarter of the year will exceed the demands which will be made on the Treasury during the same period, and that the amount in the Treasury on the 30th of September last will be increased on the 1st day of January next.

At the close of the last session it was anticipated that the progressive diminution of the public revenue in 1819 and 1820, which had been the result of the languid state of our foreign commerce in those years, had in the latter year reached its extreme point of depression. It has, however, been ascertained that that point was reached only at the termination of the first quarter of the present year. From that time until the 30th of September last the duties secured have exceeded those of the corresponding quarters of the last year $1,172,000, whilst the amount of debentures issued during the three first quarters of this year is $952,000 less than that of the same quarters of the last year.

There are just grounds to believe that the improvement which has occurred in the revenue during the last-mentioned period will not only be maintained, but that it will progressively increase through the next and several succeeding years, so as to realize the results which were presented upon that subject by the official reports of the Treasury at the commencement of the last session of Congress.

Under the influence of the most unfavorable circumstances the revenue for the next and subsequent years to the year 1825 will exceed the demands at present authorized by law.

It may fairly be presumed that under the protection given to domestic manufactures by the existing laws we shall become at no distant period a manufacturing country on an extensive scale. Possessing as we do the raw materials in such vast amount, with a capacity to augment them to an indefinite extent; raising within the country aliment of every kind to an amount far exceeding the demand for home consumption, even in the most unfavorable years, and to be obtained always at a very moderate price; skilled also, as our people are, in the mechanic arts and in every improvement calculated to lessen the demand for and the price of labor, it is manifest that their success in every branch of domestic industry may and will be carried, under the encouragement given by the present duties, to an extent to meet any demand which under a fair competition may be made upon it.

A considerable increase of domestic manufactures, by diminishing the importation of foreign, will probably tend to lessen the amount of the public revenue. As, however, a large proportion of the revenue which is derived from duties is raised from other articles than manufactures, the demand for which will increase with our population, it is believed that a fund will still be raised from that source adequate to the greater part of the public expenditures, especially as those expenditures, should we continue to be blessed with peace, will be diminished by the completion of the fortifications, dockyards, and other public works, by the augmentation of the Navy to the point to which it is proposed to carry it, and by the payment of the public debt, including pensions for military services.

It can not be doubted that the more complete our internal resources and the less dependent we are on foreign powers for every national as well as domestic purpose the greater and more stable will be the public felicity. By the increase of domestic manufactures will the demand for the rude materials at home be increased, and thus will the dependence of the several parts of our Union on each other and the strength of the Union itself be proportionably augmented. In this process, which is very desirable, and inevitable under the existing duties, the resources which obviously present themselves to supply a deficiency in the revenue, should it occur, are the interests which may derive the principal benefit from the change. If domestic manufactures are raised by duties on foreign, the deficiency in the fund necessary for public purposes should be supplied by duties on the former. At the last session it seemed doubtful whether the revenue derived from the present sources would be adequate to all the great purposes of our Union, including the construction of our fortifications, the augmentation of the Navy, and the protection of our commerce against the dangers to which it is exposed. Had the deficiency been such as to subject us to the necessity either to abandon those measures of defense or to resort to other means for adequate funds, the course presented to the adoption of a virtuous and enlightened people appeared to be a plain one. It must be gratifying to all to know that this necessity does not exist. Nothing, however, in contemplation of such important objects, which can be easily provided for, should be left to hazard. It is thought that the revenue may receive an augmentation from the existing sources, and in a manner to aid our manufactures, without hastening prematurely the result which has been suggested. It is believed that a moderate additional duty on certain articles would have that effect, without being liable to any serious objection.

The examination of the whole coast, for the construction of permanent fortifications, from St. Croix to the Sabine, with the exception of part of the territory lately acquired, will be completed in the present year, as will be the survey of the Mississippi, under the resolution of the House of Representatives, from the mouth of the Ohio to the ocean, and likewise of the Ohio from Louisville to the Mississippi. A progress corresponding with the sums appropriated has also been made in the construction of these fortifications at the points designated. As they will form a system of defense for the whole maritime frontier, and in consequence for the interior, and are to last for ages, the greatest care has been taken to fix the position of each work and to form it on such a scale as will be adequate to the purpose intended by it. All the inlets and assailable parts of our Union have been minutely examined, and positions taken with a view to the best effect, observing in every instance a just regard for economy. Doubts, however, being entertained as to the propriety of the position and extent of the work at Dauphine Island, further progress in it was suspended soon after the last session of Congress, and an order given to the Board of Engineers and Naval Commissioners to make a further and more minute examination of it in both respects, and to report the result without delay.

Due progress has been made in the construction of vessels of war according to the law providing for the gradual augmentation of the Navy, and to the extent of existing appropriations. The vessels authorized by the act of 1820 have all been completed and are now in actual service. None of the larger ships have been or will be launched for the present, the object being to protect all which may not be required for immediate service from decay by suitable buildings erected over them. A squadron has been maintained, as heretofore, in the Mediterranean, by means whereof peace has been preserved with the Barbary Powers. This squadron has been reduced the present year to as small a force as is compatible with the fulfillment of the object intended by it. From past experience and the best information respecting the views of those powers it is distinctly understood that should our squadron be withdrawn they would soon recommence their hostilities and depredations upon our commerce. Their fortifications have lately been rebuilt and their maritime force increased. It has also been found necessary to maintain a naval force on the Pacific for the protection of the very important interests of our citizens engaged in commerce and the fisheries in that sea. Vessels have likewise been employed in cruising along the Atlantic coast, in the Gulf of Mexico, on the coast of Africa, and in the neighboring seas. In the latter many piracies have been committed on our commerce, and so extensive was becoming the range of those unprincipled adventurers that there was cause to apprehend, without a timely and decisive effort to suppress them, the worst consequences would ensue. Fortunately, a considerable check has been given to that spirit by our cruisers, who have succeeded in capturing and destroying several of their vessels. Nevertheless, it is considered an object of high importance to continue these cruises until the practice is entirely suppressed. Like success has attended our efforts to suppress the slave trade. Under the flag of the United States and the sanction of their papers the trade may be considered as entirely suppressed, and if any of our citizens are engaged in it under the flags and papers of other powers, it is only from a respect to the rights of those powers that these offenders are not seized and brought home to receive the punishment which the laws inflict. If every other power should adopt the same policy and pursue the same vigorous means for carrying it into effect, the trade could no longer exist.

Deeply impressed with the blessings which we enjoy, and of which we have such manifold proofs, my mind is irresistibly drawn to that Almighty Being, the great source from whence they proceed and to whom our most grateful acknowledgments are due.

JAMES MONROE.

SPECIAL MESSAGES.

WASHINGTON, *December 16, 1821.*

To the Senate and House of Representatives of the United States:

I transmit to Congress a letter from the Secretary of the Treasury, inclosing the report of the commissioners appointed in conformity with the provisions of "An act to authorize the building of light-houses therein mentioned, and for other purposes," approved the 3d of March, 1821.

JAMES MONROE.

WASHINGTON, *December 16, 1821.*

To the House of Representatives of the United States:

By a resolution of Congress approved on the 27th of March, 1818, it was directed that the journal, acts, and proceedings of the Convention which formed the present Constitution of the United States should be published, under the direction of the President of the United States, together with the secret journals of the acts and proceedings, and the foreign correspondence (with a certain exception), of the Congress of the United States from the first meeting thereof down to the date of the ratification of the definitive treaty of peace between Great Britain and the United States, in the year 1783, and that 1,000 copies thereof should be printed, of which one copy should be furnished to each member of that (the

Fifteenth) Congress, and the residue should remain subject to the future disposition of Congress.

And by a resolution of Congress approved on the 21st April, 1820, it was provided that the secret journal, together with all the papers and documents connected with that journal, and all other papers and documents heretofore considered confidential, of the old Congress, from the date of the ratification of the definitive treaty of the year 1783 to the formation of the present Government, which were remaining in the office of the Secretary of State, should be published under the direction of the President of the United States, and that 1,000 copies thereof should be printed and deposited in the Library subject to the disposition of Congress.

In pursuance of these two resolutions, 1,000 copies of the journals and acts of the Convention which formed the Constitution have been heretofore printed and placed at the disposal of Congress, and 1,000 copies of the secret journals of the Congress of the Confederation, complete, have been printed, 250 copies of which have been reserved to comply with the direction of furnishing one copy to each member of the Fifteenth Congress; the remaining 750 copies have been deposited in the Library and are now at the disposal of Congress.

By the general appropriation act of 9th April, 1818, the sum of $10,000 was appropriated for defraying the expenses of printing done pursuant to the resolution of the 27th of March of that year. No appropriation has yet been made to defray the expenses incident to the execution of the resolution of 21st April, 1820. The whole expense hitherto incurred in carrying both resolutions into effect has exceeded by $542.56 the appropriation of April, 1818. This balance remains due to the printers, and is included in the estimates of appropriation for the year 1822. That part of the resolution of the 27th March, 1818, which directs the publication of the foreign correspondence of the Congress of the Confederation remains yet to be executed, and a further appropriation will be necessary for carrying it into effect.

JAMES MONROE.

DECEMBER 30, 1821.

To the Senate of the United States:

I transmit to the Senate a treaty of peace and amity concluded between the United States and the Dey and Regency of Algiers on the 23d of December, 1816.

This treaty is in all respects the same in its provisions with that which had been concluded on the 30th of June, 1815, and was ratified, by and with the advice and consent of the Senate, on the 26th of December of that year, with the exception of one additional and explanatory article.

The circumstances which have occasioned the delay in laying the present treaty before the Senate for their advice and consent to its ratification are, that having been received in the spring of the year 1817, during the recess of the Senate, in the interval between the time when the Department of State was vacated by its late Secretary and the entrance of his successor upon the duties of the office, and when a change also occurred of the chief clerk of the Department, it was not recollected by the officers of the Department that it remained without the constitutional sanction of the Senate until shortly before the commencement of the present session. The documents explanatory of the additional articles are likewise herewith transmitted.

JAMES MONROE.

WASHINGTON, *January 7, 1822.*

To the Congress of the United States:

I transmit a report of the Secretary of the Navy, together with a survey of the coast of North Carolina, made in pursuance of a resolution of Congress of the 19th January, 1819.

JAMES MONROE.

WASHINGTON, *January 8, 1822.*

To the Senate and House of Representatives of the United States:

In pursuance of a joint resolution of the two Houses of Congress of the 3d of March, 1821, authorizing the President to cause such number of astronomical observations to be made by methods which might, in his judgment, be best adapted to insure a correct determination of the longitude of the Capitol, in the city of Washington, from Greenwich or some other known meridian in Europe, and that he cause the data, with accurate calculations on statements founded thereon, to be laid before them at their present session, I herewith transmit to Congress the report made by William Lambert, who was selected by me on the 10th of April last to perform the service required by that resolution.

As no compensation is authorized by law for the execution of the duties assigned to Mr. Lambert, it is submitted to the discretion of Congress to make the necessary provision for an adequate allowance to him and to the assistant whom he employed to aid him in his observations.

JAMES MONROE.

JANUARY 17, 1822.

To the Senate of the United States:

I nominate the persons whose names are stated in the inclosed letter from the Secretary of War for the appointments therein respectively proposed for them.

The changes in the Army growing out of the act of the 2d of March, 1821, "to reduce and fix the military peace establishment of the United States," are exhibited in the Official Register for the year 1822, herewith submitted for the information of the Senate.

Under the late organization of the artillery arm, with the exception of the colonel of the regiment of light artillery, there were no grades higher than lieutenant-colonel recognized. Three of the four colonels of artillery provided for by the act of Congress of the 2d of March, 1821, were considered, therefore, as original vacancies, to be filled, as the good of the service might dictate, from the Army corps.

The Pay Department being considered as a part of the military establishment, and, within the meaning of the above-recited act, constituting one of the corps of the Army, the then Paymaster-General was appointed colonel of one of the regiments. A contrary construction, which would have limited the corps specified in the twelfth section of the act to the line of the Army, would equally have excluded all the other branches of the staff, as well that of the Pay Department, which was expressly comprehended among those to be reduced. Such a construction did not seem to be authorized by the act, since by its general terms it was inferred to have been intended to give a power of sufficient extent to make the reduction by which so many were to be disbanded operate with as little inconvenience as possible to the parties. Acting on these views and on the recommendation of the board of general officers, who were called in on account of their knowledge and experience to aid the Executive in so delicate a service, I thought it proper to appoint Colonel Towson to one of the new regiments of artillery, it being a corps in which he had eminently distinguished himself and acquired great knowledge and experience in the late war.

In reconciling conflicting claims provision for four officers of distinction could only be made in grades inferior to those which they formerly held. Their names are submitted, with the nomination for the brevet rank of the grades from which they were severally reduced.

It is proper also to observe that as it was found difficult in executing the act to retain each officer in the corps to which he belonged, the power of transferring officers from one corps to another was reserved in the general orders, published in the Register, till the 1st day of January last, in order that upon vacancies occurring those who had been put out of their proper corps might as far as possible be restored to it. Under this reservation, and in conformity to the power vested in the Executive by the first section of the seventy-fifth article of the general regulations of the Army, approved by Congress at the last session, on the resignation of Lieutenant-Colonel Mitchell, of the corps of artillery, Lieutenant-Colonel Lindsay, who had belonged to this corps before the late reduction, was transferred back to it in the same grade. As an additional motive to the transfer, it had the effect of preventing Lieutenant-Colonel Taylor and Major Woolley being reduced to lower grades than those which they held before the reduction, and Captain Cobb from being disbanded under the act. These circumstances were considered as constituting an extraordinary case within the meaning of the section already referred to of the Regulations of the Army. It is, however, submitted to the Senate whether this is a case requiring their confirmation; and in case that such should be their opinion, it is submitted to them for their constitutional confirmation.

JAMES MONROE.

WASHINGTON, *January 20, 1822.*

To the House of Representatives:

In compliance with a resolution of the House of Representatives "requesting the President of the United States to cause to be laid before this House an account of the expenditures made under the act to provide for the civilization of the Indian tribes, specifying the times when, the persons to whom, and the particular purpose for which such expenditures have been made," I herewith transmit a report from the Secretary of War.

JAMES MONROE.

WASHINGTON, *January 28, 1822.*

To the House of Representatives:

In compliance with the resolution of the 2d instant, I transmit a report of the Secretary of State, with all the documents relating to the misunderstanding between Andrew Jackson, while acting as governor of the Floridas, and Eligius Fromentin, judge of a court therein; and also of the correspondence between the Secretary of State and the minister plenipotentiary of His Catholic Majesty on certain proceedings in that Territory in execution of the powers vested in the governor by the Executive under the law of the last session for carrying into effect the late treaty between the United States and Spain. Being always desirous to communicate to Congress, or to either House, all the information in the possession of the Executive respecting any important interest of our Union which may be communicated without real injury to our constituents, and which can rarely happen except in negotiations pending with foreign powers, and deeming it more consistent with the principles of our Government in cases submitted to my discretion, as in the present instance, to hazard error by the freedom of the communication rather than by withholding any portion of information belonging to the subject, I have thought proper to communicate every document comprised within this call.

JAMES MONROE.

WASHINGTON, *January 30, 1822.*

To the House of Representatives of the United States:

In pursuance of a resolution of the House of Representatives of the 16th instant, requesting information with regard to outrages and abuses committed upon the persons of the officers and crews of American vessels at

The Havannah and other Spanish ports in America, and whether the
Spanish authorities have taken any measures to punish, restrain, or countenance such outrages, I herewith transmit to that House a report from
the Secretary of State, containing the information called for.

                                                 JAMES MONROE.

                                 WASHINGTON, *January 30, 1822.*

To the House of Representatives of the United States:

In pursuance of a resolution of the House of Representatives of the
8th instant, I transmit to the House of Representatives a report of the
Secretary of State, containing all the information procured by him in
relation to commissions of bankruptcy in certain districts of the United
States under the act of 4th of April, 1800, "to establish an uniform system of bankruptcy in the United States."

                                                 JAMES MONROE.

                                 WASHINGTON, *February 7, 1822.*

To the House of Representatives of the United States:

In compliance with a resolution of the House of Representatives requesting the President to "cause that House to be informed whether
the commissioners appointed to lay out the continuation of the Cumberland road from Wheeling, in the State of Virginia, through the States of
Ohio, Indiana, and Illinois to the Mississippi River, have completed the
same, and, if not completed, the reason why their duties have been suspended," I transmit a report from the Secretary of the Treasury, which
furnishes the information desired.

                                                 JAMES MONROE.

                                 WASHINGTON, *February 10, 1822.*

To the House of Representatives:

In compliance with a resolution of the House of Representatives "re-
questing the President of the United States to cause to be laid before this
House any information which he may have of the condition of the several
Indian tribes within the United States and the measures hitherto devised
and pursued for their civilization," I now transmit a report from the
Secretary of War.

                                                 JAMES MONROE.

                                 WASHINGTON, *February 23, 1822.*

To the House of Representatives:

In compliance with a resolution of the House of Representatives "requesting the President of the United States to cause to be reported to
this House whether the Indian title has been extinguished by the United

States to any lands the right of soil in which has been or is claimed by any particular State, and, if so, the conditions upon which the same has been extinguished,'' I herewith transmit a report from the Secretary of War, furnishing all the information in the possession of that Department embraced by the resolution.

JAMES MONROE.

WASHINGTON, *February 23, 1822.*
To the Senate of the United States:

In compliance with a resolution of the Senate of the 14th instant, requesting the President of the United States ''to make known to the Senate the annual disposition which has been made of the sum of $15,000 appropriated by an act of Congress of the year 1802 to promote civilization among friendly Indian tribes, showing to what tribes that evidence of the national bounty has been extended, the names of the agents who have been intrusted with the application of the money, the several amounts by them received, and the manner in which they have severally applied it to accomplish the objects of the act,'' I herewith transmit a report from the Secretary of War, furnishing all the information upon this subject in the possession of that Department.

JAMES MONROE.

WASHINGTON, *February 25, 1822.*
To the Senate and House of Representatives of the United States:

Under the appropriation made by the act of Congress of the 11th of April, 1820, for holding treaties with the Creek and Cherokee nations of Indians for the extinguishment of the Indian title to lands within the State of Georgia, pursuant to the fourth condition of the first article of the articles of agreement and cession concluded between the United States and the State of Georgia on the 24th day of April, 1802, a treaty was held with the Creek Nation, the expense of which upon the settlement of the accounts of the commissioners who were appointed to conduct the negotiation was ascertained to amount to the sum of $24,695, leaving an unexpended balance of the sum appropriated of $5,305, a sum too small to negotiate a treaty with the Cherokees, as was contemplated by the act making the appropriation. The legislature of Georgia being still desirous that a treaty should be held for further extinguishment of the Indian title to lands within that State, and to obtain an indemnity to the citizens of that State for property of considerable value, which has been taken from them by the Cherokee Indians, I submit the subject to the consideration of Congress, that a further sum, which, in addition to the balance of the former appropriation, will be adequate to the expenses attending a treaty with them, may be appropriated should Congress deem it expedient.

JAMES MONROE.

WASHINGTON, *March 4, 1822.*

To the House of Representatives of the United States:

In compliance with a resolution of the House of Representatives of the 22d ultimo, requesting the President of the United States "to cause to be laid before this House a statement showing the amount of woolens purchased for the use of the Army during the years 1820 and 1821, comprising a description of the articles, of whom the purchases were made, at what prices, and what proportion thereof was of American manufacture," I herewith transmit a report from the Secretary of War.

JAMES MONROE.

WASHINGTON, *March 8, 1822.*

To the Senate and House of Representatives of the United States:

In transmitting to the House of Representatives the documents called for by the resolution of that House of the 30th January, I consider it my duty to invite the attention of Congress to a very important subject, and to communicate the sentiments of the Executive on it, that, should Congress entertain similar sentiments, there may be such cooperation between the two departments of the Government as their respective rights and duties may require.

The revolutionary movement in the Spanish Provinces in this hemisphere attracted the attention and excited the sympathy of our fellow-citizens from its commencement. This feeling was natural and honorable to them, from causes which need not be communicated to you. It has been gratifying to all to see the general acquiescence which has been manifested in the policy which the constituted authorities have deemed it proper to pursue in regard to this contest. As soon as the movement assumed such a steady and consistent form as to make the success of the Provinces probable, the rights to which they were entitled by the law of nations as equal parties to a civil war were extended to them. Each party was permitted to enter our ports with its public and private ships, and to take from them every article which was the subject of commerce with other nations. Our citizens, also, have carried on commerce with both parties, and the Government has protected it with each in articles not contraband of war. Through the whole of this contest the United States have remained neutral, and have fulfilled with the utmost impartiality all the obligations incident to that character.

This contest has now reached such a stage and been attended with such decisive success on the part of the Provinces that it merits the most profound consideration whether their right to the rank of independent nations, with all the advantages incident to it in their intercourse with the United States, is not complete. Buenos Ayres assumed that rank by a formal declaration in 1816, and has enjoyed it since 1810 free from invasion by the parent country. The Provinces composing the Republic of Colombia, after having separately declared their independence, were united by a fundamental law of the 17th of December, 1819. A strong Spanish force occupied at that time certain parts of the territory within their limits and waged a destructive war. That force has since been repeatedly defeated, and the whole of it either made prisoners or destroyed or expelled from the country, with the exception of an inconsiderable portion only, which is blockaded in two fortresses. The Provinces on the Pacific have likewise been very successful. Chili declared independence in 1818, and has since enjoyed it undisturbed; and of late, by the assistance of Chili and Buenos Ayres, the revolution has extended to Peru. Of the movement in Mexico our information is less authentic, but it is, nevertheless, distinctly understood that the new Government has declared its independence, and that there is now no opposition to it there nor a force to make any. For the last three years the Government of Spain has not sent a single corps of troops to any part of that country, nor is there any reason to believe it will send any in future. Thus it is manifest that all those Provinces are not only in the full enjoyment of their independence, but, considering the state of the war and other circumstances, that there is not the most remote prospect of their being deprived of it.

When the result of such a contest is manifestly settled, the new governments have a claim to recognition by other powers which ought not to be resisted. Civil wars too often excite feelings which the parties can not control. The opinion entertained by other powers as to the result may assuage those feelings and promote an accommodation between them useful and honorable to both. The delay which has been observed in making a decision on this important subject will, it is presumed, have afforded an unequivocal proof to Spain, as it must have done to other powers, of the high respect entertained by the United States for her rights and of their determination not to interfere with them. The Provinces belonging to this hemisphere are our neighbors, and have successively, as each portion of the country acquired its independence, pressed their recognition by an appeal to facts not to be contested, and which they thought gave them a just title to it. To motives of interest this Government has invariably disclaimed all pretension, being resolved to take no part in the controversy or other measure in regard to it which should not merit the sanction of the civilized world. To other claims a just sensibility has been always felt and frankly acknowledged, but they in themselves could never become an adequate cause of action. It was incumbent on this Government to look to every important fact and circumstance on which a sound opinion could be formed, which has been done. When we regard, then, the great length of time which this war has been prosecuted, the complete success which has attended it in favor of the Provinces, the present condition of the parties, and the utter inability of Spain to produce any change in it, we are compelled to conclude that its fate is settled, and that the Provinces which have declared their independence and are in the enjoyment of it ought to be recognized.

Of the views of the Spanish Government on this subject no particular information has been recently received. It may be presumed that the successful progress of the revolution through such a long series of years, gaining strength and extending annually in every direction, and embracing by the late important events, with little exception, all the dominions of Spain south of the United States on this continent, placing thereby the complete sovereignty over the whole in the hands of the people, will reconcile the parent country to an accommodation with them on the basis of their unqualified independence. Nor has any authentic information been recently received of the disposition of other powers respecting it. A sincere desire has been cherished to act in concert with them in the proposed recognition, of which several were some time past duly apprised; but it was understood that they were not prepared for it. The immense space between those powers, even those which border on the Atlantic, and these Provinces makes the movement an affair of less interest and excitement to them than to us. It is probable, therefore, that they have been less attentive to its progress than we have been. It may be presumed, however, that the late events will dispel all doubt of the result.

In proposing this measure it is not contemplated to change thereby in the slightest manner our friendly relations with either of the parties, but to observe in all respects, as heretofore, should the war be continued, the most perfect neutrality between them. Of this friendly disposition an assurance will be given to the Government of Spain, to whom it is presumed it will be, as it ought to be, satisfactory. The measure is proposed under a thorough conviction that it is in strict accord with the law of nations, that it is just and right as to the parties, and that the United States owe it to their station and character in the world, as well as to their essential interests, to adopt it. Should Congress concur in the view herein presented, they will doubtless see the propriety of making the necessary appropriations for carrying it into effect.

JAMES MONROE.

WASHINGTON, *March 9, 1822.*

To the House of Representatives:

I transmit a report from the Secretary of War, together with the annual return of the militia of the United States, and an exhibit of the arms, accouterments, and ammunition of the several States and Territories of the United States, prepared in conformity with the militia laws on that subject.

JAMES MONROE.

WASHINGTON, *March 12, 1822.*

To the Senate and House of Representatives of the United States:

I lay before the Senate the copy of a supplementary report, made by William Lambert, in relation to the longitude of the Capitol from Greenwich, in pursuance of a joint resolution of the two Houses of Congress of the 3d of March, 1821, and I subjoin an extract from the letter of Mr. Lambert submitting that report.

JAMES MONROE.

WASHINGTON, *March 26, 1822.*

To the Senate and House of Representatives of the United States:

Congress having suspended the appropriation, at the last session, for the fortification at Dauphine Island, in consequence of a doubt which was entertained of the propriety of that position, the further prosecution of the work was suspended, and an order given, as intimated in the message of the 3d of December, to the Board of Engineers and Naval Commissioners to examine that part of the coast, and particularly that position, as also the position at Mobile Point, with which it is connected, and to report their opinion thereon, which has been done, and which report is herewith communicated.

By this report it appears to be still the opinion of the Board that the construction of works at both these positions is of great importance to the defense of New Orleans and of all that portion of our Union which is connected with and dependent on the Mississippi and on the other waters which empty into the Gulf of Mexico between that river and Cape Florida. That the subject may be fully before Congress, I transmit also a copy of the former report of the Board, being that on which the work was undertaken and has been in part executed. Approving as I do the opinion of the Board, I consider it my duty to state the reasons on which I adopted the first report, especially as they were in part suggested by the occurrences of the late war.

The policy which induced Congress to decide on and provide for the defense of the coast immediately after the war was founded on the marked events of that interesting epoch. The vast body of men which it was found necessary to call into the field through the whole extent of our maritime frontier, and the number who perished by exposure, with the immense expenditure of money and waste of property which followed, were to be traced in an eminent degree to the defenseless condition of the coast. It was to mitigate these evils in future wars, and even for the higher purpose of preventing war itself, that the decision was formed to make the coast, so far as it might be practicable, impregnable, and that the measures necessary to that great object have been pursued with so much zeal since.

It is known that no part of our Union is more exposed to invasion by the numerous avenues leading to it, or more defenseless by the thinness of the neighboring population, or offers a greater temptation to invasion, either as a permanent acquisition or as a prize to the cupidity of grasping invaders from the immense amount of produce deposited there, than the city of New Orleans.   It is known also that the seizure of no part of our Union could affect so deeply and vitally the immediate interests of so many States and of so many of our fellow-citizens, comprising all that extensive territory and numerous population which are connected with and dependent on the Mississippi, as the seizure of that city.   Strong works, well posted, were therefore deemed absolutely necessary for its protection.

It is not, however, by the Mississippi only, or the waters which communicate directly with or approach nearest to New Orleans, that the town is assailable.   It will be recollected that in the late war the public solicitude was excited not so much by the danger which menaced it in those directions as by the apprehension that, while a feint might be made there, the main force, landing either in the bay of Mobile or other waters between that bay and the Rigolets, would be thrown above the town in the rear of the army which had been collected there for its defense.   Full confidence was entertained that that gallant army, led by the gallant and able chief who commanded it, would repel any attack to which it might be exposed in front.   But had such a force been thrown above the town, and a position taken on the banks of the river, the disadvantage to which our troops would have been subjected, attacked in front and rear as they might have been, may easily be conceived.   As their supplies would have been cut off, they could not long have remained in the city, and, withdrawing from it, it must have fallen immediately into the hands of the force below.   In ascending the river to attack the force above, the attack must have been made to great disadvantage, since it must have been on such ground and at such time as the enemy preferred.   These considerations shew that defenses other than such as are immediately connected with the city are of great importance to its safety.

An attempt to seize New Orleans and the lower part of the Mississippi will be made only by a great power or a combination of several powers, with a strong naval and land force, the latter of which must be brought in transports which may sail in shallow water.   If the defenses around New Orleans are well posted and of sufficient strength to repel any attack which may be made on them, the city can be assailed only by a land force, which must pass in the direction above suggested, between the Rigolets and the bay of Mobile.   It becomes, therefore, an object of high importance to present such an obstacle to such an attempt as would defeat it should it be made.   Fortifications are useful for the defense of posts, to prevent the approach to cities and the passage of rivers; but as works their effect can not be felt beyond the reach of their cannon.   They are formidable in other respects by the body of men within them, which may be removed and applied to other purposes.

Between the Rigolets and the bay of Mobile there is a chain of islands, at the extremity of which is Dauphine Island, which forms, with Mobile Point, from which it is distant about 3¼ miles, the entrance into the bay of Mobile, which leads through that part of the State of Alabama to the towns of Mobile and Blakeley. The distance between Dauphine Island and the Rigolets is 90 miles. The principal islands between them are Massacre, Horn, Ship, and Cat islands, near to which there is anchorage for large ships of war. The first object is to prevent the landing of any force for the purposes above stated between the Rigolets and the bay of Mobile; the second, to defeat that force in case it should be landed. When the distance from one point to the other is considered, it is believed that it would be impossible to establish works so near to each other as to prevent the landing of such a force. Its defeat, therefore, should be effectually provided for. If the arrangement should be such as to make that result evident, it ought to be fairly concluded that the attempt would not be made, and thus we should accomplish in the best mode possible and with the least expense the complete security of this important part of our Union, the great object of our system of defense for the whole.

There are some other views of this subject which it is thought will merit particular attention in deciding the point in question. Not being able to establish a chain of posts, at least for the present, along the whole coast from the Rigolets to Dauphine Island, or on all the islands between them, at which point shall we begin? Should an attack on the city be anticipated, it can not be doubted that an adequate force would immediately be ordered there for its defense. If the enemy should despair of making an impression on the works near the town, it may be presumed that they would promptly decide to make the attempt in the manner and in the line above suggested between the Rigolets and the bay of Mobile. It will be obvious that the nearer the fortification is erected to the Rigolets with a view to this object, should it be on Cat or Ship Island, for example, the wider would the passage be left open between that work and the bay of Mobile for such an enterprise. The main army, being drawn to New Orleans, would be ready to meet such an attempt near the Rigolets or at any other point not distant from the city. It is probable, therefore, that the enemy, profiting of a fair wind, would make his attempt at the greatest distance compatible with his object from that point, and at the bay of Mobile should there not be works there of sufficient strength to prevent it. Should, however, strong works be erected there, such as were sufficient not only for their own defense against any attack which might be made on them, but to hold a force connected with that which might be drawn from the neighboring country, capable of cooperating with the force at the city, and which would doubtless be ordered to those works in the event of war, it would be dangerous for the invading force to land anywhere between the Rigolets and the bay of Mobile and to pass toward the Mississippi above the city, lest such a body might be thrown in its rear as to cut off its retreat. These considerations show the great advantage of establishing at the mouth of the bay of Mobile very strong works, such as would be adequate to all the purposes suggested.

If fortifications were necessary only to protect our country and cities against the entry of large ships of war into our bays and rivers, they would be of little use for the defense of New Orleans, since that city can not be approached so near, either by the Mississippi or in any other direction, by such vessels for them to make an attack on it. In the Gulf, within our limits west of Florida, which had been acquired since these works were decided on and commenced, there is no bay or river into which large ships of war can enter. As a defense, therefore, against an attack from such vessels extensive works would be altogether unnecessary either at Mobile Point or at Dauphine Island, since sloops of war only can navigate the deepest channel. But it is not for that purpose alone that these works are intended. It is to provide also against a formidable invasion, both by land and sea, the object of which may be to shake the foundation of our system. Should such small works be erected, and such an invasion take place, they would be sure to fall at once into the hands of the invaders and to be turned against us.

Whether the acquisition of Florida may be considered as affording an inducement to make any change in the position or strength of these works is a circumstance which also merits attention. From the view which I have taken of the subject I am of opinion that it should not. The defense of New Orleans and of the river Mississippi against a powerful invasion being one of the great objects of such extensive works, that object would be essentially abandoned if they should be established eastward of the bay of Mobile, since the force to be collected in them would be placed at too great a distance to allow the cooperation necessary for those purposes between it and that at the city; in addition to which, it may be observed that by carrying them to Pensacola or farther to the east that bay would fall immediately, in case of such invasion, into the hands of the enemy, whereby such cooperation would be rendered utterly impossible, and the State of Alabama would also be left wholly unprotected.

With a view to such formidable invasion, of which we should never lose sight, and of the great objects to which it would be directed, I think that very strong works at some point within the Gulf of Mexico will be found indispensable. I think also that those works ought to be established at the bay of Mobile—one at Mobile Point and the other on Dauphine Island—whereby the enemy would be excluded and the complete command of that bay, with all the advantages attending it, be secured to ourselves. In the case of such invasion, it will, it is presumed, be deemed necessary to collect at some point other than at New Orleans a strong force, capable of moving in any direction and affording aid to any part which may be attacked; and, in my judgment, no position presents so many advantages as a point of rendezvous for such force as the mouth of that bay. The fortification at the Rigolets will defend the entrance by one passage into Lake Pontchartrain, and also into Pearl River, which empties into the Gulf at that point. Between the Rigolets and Mobile Bay there are but two inlets which deserve the name, those of St. Louis and Pascagola, the entrance into which is too shallow even for the smallest vessels; and from the Rigolets to Mobile Bay the whole coast is equally shallow, affording the depth of a few feet of water only. Cat Island, which is nearest the Rigolets, is about 7½ miles distant from the coast and 30 from the Rigolets. Ship Island is distant about 10 miles from Cat Island and 12 from the coast. Between these islands and the coast the water is very shallow.

As to the precise depth of water in approaching those islands from the Gulf, the report of the topographical engineers not having yet been received, it is impossible to speak with precision; but admitting it to be such as for frigates and even ships of the line to enter, the anchorage at both is unsafe, being much exposed to northwest winds. Along the coast, therefore, there is no motive for such strong works on our part— no town to guard, no inlet into the country to defend—and if placed on the islands and the entrance to them is such as to admit large ships of war, distant as they are from the coast, it would be more easy for the enemy to assail them with effect.

The position, however, at Mobile Bay is essentially different. That bay takes its name from the Mobile River, which is formed by the junction of the Alabama and Tombigbee, which extend each about 300 miles into the interior, approaching at their head waters near the Tennessee River. If the enemy possessed its mouth, and fortified Mobile Point and Dauphine Island, being superior at sea it would be very difficult for us to dispossess him of either, even of Mobile Point; and holding that position, Pensacola would soon fall, as without incurring great expense in the construction of works there it would present but a feeble resistance to a strong force in its rear. If we had a work at Mobile Point only, the enemy might take Dauphine Island, which would afford him great aid in attacking the point, and enable him, even should we succeed in repelling the attack, to render us great mischief there and throughout the whole Gulf. In every view which can be taken of the subject it appears indispensable for us to command the entrance into Mobile Bay, and that decision being taken, I think the considerations which favor the occupation of Dauphine Island by a strong work are conclusive. It is proper to observe that after the repulse before New Orleans in the late war the British forces took possession of Dauphine Island and held it till the peace. Under neither of the reports of the Board of Engineers and Naval Commissioners could any but sloops of war enter the bay or the anchorage between Dauphine and Pelican islands. Both reports give to that anchorage 18 feet at low water and 20½ at high. The only difference between them consists in this, that in the first a bar leading to the anchorage, reducing the depth of water to 12 feet at low tide, was omitted. In neither case could frigates enter, though sloops of war of larger size might. The whole scope, however, of this reasoning turns on a different principle—on the works necessary to defend that bay and, by means thereof, New Orleans, the Mississippi, and all the surrounding country against a powerful invasion both by land and sea, and not on the precise depth of water in any of the approaches to the bay or to the island.

The reasoning which is applicable to the works near New Orleans and at the bay of Mobile is equally so in certain respects to those which are to be erected for the defense of all the bays and rivers along the other parts of the coast. All those works are also erected on a greater scale than would be necessary for the sole purpose of preventing the passage of our inlets by large ships of war. They are in most instances formed for defense against a more powerful invasion, both by land and sea. There are, however, some differences between the works which are deemed necessary in the Gulf and those in other parts of our Union, founded on the peculiar situation of that part of the coast. The vast extent of the Mississippi, the great outlet and channel of commerce for so many States, all of which may be affected by the seizure of that city, or of any part of the river to a great extent above it, is one of those striking peculiarities which require particular provision. The thinness of the population near the city, making it necessary that the force requisite for its defense should be called from distant parts and States, is another. The danger which the army assembled at New Orleans would be exposed to of being cut off in case the enemy should throw a force on the river above it, from the difficulty of ascending the river to attack it and of making a retreat in any other direction, is a third. For an attack on the city of New Orleans, Mobile Bay, or any part of the intermediate coast ships of war would be necessary only as a convoy to protect the transports against a naval force on their passage, and on their approach to the shore for the landing of the men, and on their return home in case they should be repulsed.

On the important subject of our defenses generally I think proper to observe that the system was adopted immediately after the late war by Congress, on great consideration and a thorough knowledge of the effects of that war—by the enormous expense attending it, by the waste of life, of property, and by the general distress of the country. The amount of debt incurred in that war and due at its conclusion, without taking into the estimate other losses, having been heretofore communicated, need not now be repeated. The interest of the debt thus incurred is four times more than the sum necessary, by annual appropriations, for the completion of our whole system of defense, land and naval, to the extent provided for and within the time specified. When that system shall be completed the expense of construction will cease, and our expenditures be proportionally diminished. Should another war occur before it is completed, the experience of the last marks in characters too strong to be mistaken its inevitable consequences; and should such war occur and find us unprepared for it, what will be our justification to the enlightened body whom we represent for not having completed these defenses? That this system should not have been adopted before the late war can not be a cause of surprise to anyone, because all might wish to avoid every expense the necessity of which might be in any degree doubtful. But with the experience of that war before us it is thought there is no cause for hesitation. Will the completion of these works and the augmentation of our Navy to the point contemplated by law require the imposition of onerous burthens on our fellow-citizens such as they can not or will not bear? Have such, or any, burthens been imposed to advance the system to its present state? It is known that no burthens whatever have been imposed; on the contrary, that all the direct or internal taxes have been long repealed, and none paid but those which are indirect and voluntary, such as are imposed on articles imported from foreign countries, most of which are luxuries, and on the vessels employed in the transportation — taxes which some of our most enlightened citizens think ought to be imposed on many of the articles for the encouragement of our manufactures, even if the revenue derived from them could be dispensed with. It is known also that in all other respects our condition as a nation is in the highest degree prosperous and flourishing, nearly half the debt incurred in the late war having already been discharged, and considerable progress having also been made in the completion of this system of defense and in the construction of other works of great extent and utility, by the revenue derived from these sources and from the sale of the public lands. I may add also that a very generous provision has been made from the same sources for the surviving officers and soldiers of our Revolutionary army. These important facts show that this system has been so far executed, and may be completed without any real inconvenience to the public. Were it, however, otherwise, I have full confidence that any burthens which might be found necessary for the completion of this system in both its branches within the term contemplated, or much sooner should any emergency require it, would be called for rather than complained of by our fellow-citizens.

From these views, applicable to the very important subject of our defenses generally as well as to the work at Dauphine Island, I think it my duty to recommend to Congress an appropriation for the latter. I considered the withholding it at the last session as the expression only of a doubt by Congress of the propriety of the position, and not as a definitive opinion. Supposing that that question would be decided at the present session, I caused the position and such parts of the coast as are particularly connected with it to be reexamined, that all the light on which the decision as to the appropriation could depend might be fully before you. In the first survey, the report of which was that on which the works intended for the defense of New Orleans, the Mississippi, the bay of Mobile, and all the country dependent on those waters were sanctioned by the Executive, the commissioners were industriously engaged about six months. I should have communicated that very able and interesting document then but from a doubt how far the interest of our country would justify its publication, a circumstance which I now mention that the attention of Congress may be drawn to it.

JAMES MONROE.

MARCH 26, 1822.

To the Senate of the United States:

Having executed the act entitled "An act to reduce and fix the military peace establishment of the United States" on great consideration and according to my best judgment, and inferring from the rejection of the nomination of Colonel Towson and Colonel Gadsden, officers of very distinguished merit, that the view which I took of that law has not been well understood, I hereby withdraw all the nominations on which the Senate has not decided until I can make a more full communication and explanation of that view and of the principles on which I have acted in the discharge of that very delicate and important duty.

JAMES MONROE.

WASHINGTON, *March 27, 1822.*

To the House of Representatives:

In compliance with a resolution of the House of Representatives of the 1st instant, requesting "the President to communicate such information as he may possess relative to any private claim against the piece of land in the Delaware River known by the name of the Peapatch, and to state if any, and what, process has been instituted in behalf of such claim," I herewith transmit a report from the Secretary of War, furnishing the information required.

JAMES MONROE.

WASHINGTON, *March 28, 1822.*

To the House of Representatives:

I transmit the original reports on the subject of the fortifications on Dauphin Island and Mobile Point, being those on which the works were undertaken and have been in part executed. The doubt expressed as to the propriety of publication is applicable to this document, which would have accompanied the message of the 26th had it been prepared in time.

JAMES MONROE.

WASHINGTON, *March 29, 1822.*

To the Senate and House of Representatives of the United States:

I transmit to Congress the translation of two letters from the minister of France to the Secretary of State, relating to the claim of the heirs of Caron de Beaumarchais upon this Government, with the documents therewith inclosed, recommending them to the favorable consideration of Congress.

JAMES MONROE.

WASHINGTON, *April 5, 1822.*

To the House of Representatives of the United States:

I communicate herewith to the House a report from the Secretary of War, containing the information requested by their resolution of the 5th ultimo.

It may be proper further to add that the secretaries of both the Territories have occasionally required and received the aid of the military force of the United States stationed within them, respectively, to carry into effect the acts of their authority.

The government of East and West Florida was under the Spanish dominion almost exclusively military. The governors of both were military officers and united in their persons the chief authority, both civil and military.

The principle upon which the act of Congress of the last session providing for the temporary government of the newly ceded Provinces was carried into execution has been communicated to Congress in my message at the opening of the session. It was to leave the authorities of the country as they were found existing at the time of the cession, to be exercised until the meeting of Congress, when it was known that the introduction of a system more congenial to our own institutions would be one of the earliest and most important subjects of their deliberations. From this, among other obvious considerations, military officers were appointed to take possession of both Provinces. But as the military command of General Jackson was to cease on the 1st of June, General Gaines, the officer next in command, then here, who was first designated to take possession of East Florida, received from me a verbal direction to give such effect to any requisition from the governor for military aid to enforce his authority as the circumstances might require. It was not foreseen that the command in both the Provinces would before further legislation by Congress on that subject devolve upon the secretaries of the Territories, but had it been foreseen the same direction would have been given as applicable to them.

No authority has been given to either of the secretaries to issue commands to that portion of the Army which is in Florida, and whenever the aid of *the military* has been required by them it has been by written requisitions to the officers commanding the troops, who have yielded compliance thereto doubtless under the directions received from General Gaines as understood by him to be authorized.

Shortly before the meeting of Congress a letter was received at the War Department from Colonel Brooke, the officer commanding at Pensacola, requesting instructions how far he was to consider these requisitions as authoritative, but the assurance that a new organization of the government was immediately to be authorized by Congress was a motive for superseding any specific decision upon the inquiry.

JAMES MONROE.

WASHINGTON, *April 6, 1822.*

To the House of Representatives of the United States:

In compliance with a resolution of the House of Representatives requesting the President of the United States to cause to be furnished to that House certain information relating to the amount of the public money paid to the Attorney-General over and above his salary fixed by law since the 1st of January, 1817, specifying the time when paid and the fund out of which such payments have been made, I transmit a paper, marked A, containing the information desired. I transmit also a paper, marked B, containing a statement of sums paid to Attorneys-General of the United States prior to the 1st of January, 1817, and in the paper marked C a like statement of sums advanced to district attorneys for services not required of them by law. These latter documents being necessary to a full view of the subject, it is thought proper to comprise them in this communication.

By the act of 24th September, 1789, instituting the office of Attorney-General, it was made his duty to prosecute and conduct all suits in the Supreme Court in which the United States should be concerned, and to give his advice and opinion upon questions of law when required by the President of the United States, or when requested by the head of any of the Departments, touching any matters that might concern their Departments. It will be seen, therefore, by the statement communicated that no money whatever has been paid to the Attorney-General for his services in that character, nor for any duty belonging to his office, beyond his salary as fixed by law.

It will also be shewn by the documents communicated that the construction given of the laws imposing duties on the Attorney-General and district attorneys have been invariably the same since the institution of the Government. On the same authority it was thought that the compensation allowed to the present Attorney-General for certain services, considering their importance and the time employed in rendering them, did not exceed, regarding precedents, what might fairly be claimed.

JAMES MONROE.

To the Senate of the United States:

Having cause to infer that the reasons which led to the construction which I gave to the act of the last session entitled "An act to reduce and fix the peace establishment of the United States" have not been well understood, I consider it my duty to explain more fully the view which I took of that act and of the principles on which I executed the very difficult and important duty enjoined on me by it.

To do justice to the subject it is thought proper to show the actual state of the Army before the passage of the late act, the force in service, the several corps of which it was composed, and the grades and number of officers commanding it. By seeing distinctly the body in all its parts on which the law operated, viewing also with a just discrimination the spirit, policy, and positive injunctions of that law with reference to precedents established in a former analogous case, we shall be enabled to ascertain with great precision whether these injunctions have or have not been strictly complied with.

By the act of the 3d of March, 1815, entitled "An act fixing the military peace establishment of the United States," the whole force in service was reduced to 10,000 men—infantry, artillery, and riflemen—exclusive of the Corps of Engineers, which was retained in its then state. The regiment of light artillery was retained as it had been organized by the act of 3d March, 1814. The infantry was formed into 9 regiments, 1 of which consisted of riflemen. The regiments of light artillery, infantry, riflemen, and Corps of Engineers were commanded each by a colonel, lieutenant-colonel, and the usual battalion and company officers; and the battalions of the corps of artillery, of which there were 8—4 for the Northern and 4 for the Southern division—were commanded by lieutenant-colonels or majors, there being 4 of each grade. There were, therefore, in the Army at the time the late law was passed 12 colonels belonging to those branches of the military establishment. Two major-generals and 4 brigadiers were likewise retained in service by this act; but the staff in several of its branches not being provided for, and being indispensable and the omission inadvertent, proceeding from the circumstances under which the act was passed, being at the close of the session, at which time intelligence of the peace was received, it was provisionally retained by the President, and provided for afterwards by the act of the 24th April, 1816. By this act the Ordnance Department was preserved as it had been organized by the act of February 8, 1815, with 1 colonel, 1 lieutenant-colonel, 2 majors, 10 captains, and 10 first, second, and third lieutenants. One Adjutant and Inspector General of the Army and 2 adjutants-general—1 for the Northern and 1 for the Southern division—were retained. This act provides also for a Paymaster-General, with a suitable number of regimental and battalion paymasters, as a part of the general staff, constituting the military peace establishment; and the Pay Department and every other branch of the staff were subjected to the Rules and Articles of War.

By the act of March 2, 1821, it was ordained that the military peace establishment should consist of 4 regiments of artillery and 7 of infantry, with such officers of engineers, ordnance, and staff as were therein specified. It is provided that each regiment of artillery should consist of 1 colonel, 1 lieutenant-colonel, 1 major, and 9 companies, with the usual company officers, 1 of which to be equipped as light artillery, and that there should be attached to each regiment of artillery 1 supernumerary captain to perform ordnance duty, thereby merging the regiment of artillery and Ordnance Department into these 4 regiments. It was provided also that each regiment of infantry should consist of 1 colonel, 1 lieutenant-colonel, 1 major, and 10 companies, with the usual company officers. The Corps of Engineers, bombardiers excepted, with the topographical engineers and their assistants, were to be retained under the existing organization. The former establishment as to the number of major-generals and brigadiers was curtailed one-half, and the office of Inspector and Adjutant General to the Army and of adjutant-general to each division annulled, and that of Adjutant-General to the Army instituted. The Quartermaster, Paymaster, and Commissary Departments were also specially provided for, as was every other branch of the staff, all of which received a new modification, and were subjected to the Rules and Articles of War.

The immediate and direct operation of this act on the military peace establishment of 1815 was that of reduction, from which no officer belonging to it was exempt, unless it might be the topographical engineers; for in retaining the Corps of Engineers, as was manifest as well by the clear import of the section relating to it as by the provisions of every other clause of the act, reference was had to the organization, and not to the officers of the Corps. The establishment of 1815 was reduced from 10,000 to about 6,000 men. The 8 battalions of artillery, constituting what was called the corps of artillery, and the regiment of light artillery as established by the act of 1815, were to be incorporated together and formed into 4 new regiments. The regiments of infantry were to be reduced from 9 to 7, the rifle regiment being broken. Three of the general officers were to be reduced, with very many of the officers belonging to the several corps of the Army, and particularly of the infantry. All the provisions of the act declare of what number of officers and men the several corps provided for by it should thenceforward consist, and not that any corps as then existing or any officer of any corps, unless the topographical engineers were excepted, should be retained. Had it been intended to reduce the officers by corps, or to exempt the officers of any corps from the operation of the law, or in the organization of the several new corps to confine the selection of the officers to be placed in them to the several corps of the like kind then existing, and not extend it to the whole military establishment, including the staff, or to confine the reduction to a proportional number of each corps and of each grade in each corps, the object in either instance might have been easily accomplished by a declaration to that effect. No such declaration was made, nor can such intention be inferred. We see, on the contrary, that every corps of the Army and staff was to be reorganized, and most of them reduced in officers and men, and that in arranging the officers from the old to the new corps full power was granted to the President to take them from any and every corps of the former establishment and place them in the latter. In this latter grant of power it is proper to observe that the most comprehensive terms that could be adopted were used, the authority being to cause the arrangement to be made from the officers of the several *corps* then in the service of the United States, comprising, of course, every corps of the staff, as well as of artillery and infantry, and not from the *corps of troops*, as in the former act, and without any limitation as to grades.

It merits particular attention that although the object of this latter act was reduction and such its effect on an extensive scale, 5 new offices were created by it—4 of the grade of colonel for the 4 regiments of artillery and that of Adjutant-General for the Army. Three of the first mentioned were altogether new, the corps having been newly created, and although 1 officer of that grade as applicable to the corps of light artillery had existed, yet as that regiment was reduced and all its parts reorganized in another form and with other duties, being incorporated into the 4 new regiments, the commander was manifestly displaced and incapable of taking the command of either of the new regiments or any station in them until he should be authorized to do so by a new appointment. The same remarks are applicable to the office of Adjutant-General to the Army. It is an office of new creation, differing from that of Adjutant and Inspector General, and likewise from that of adjutant-general to a division, which were severally annulled. It differs from the first in title, rank, and pay, and from the two latter because they had been created by law each for a division, whereas the new office, being instituted without such special designation, could have relation only to the whole Army. It was manifest, therefore, that neither of those officers had any right to this new station nor to any other station unless he should be specially appointed to it, the principle of reduction being applicable to every officer in every corps. It is proper also to observe that the duties of Adjutant-General under the existing arrangement correspond in almost every circumstance with those of the late Adjutant and Inspector General, and not with those of an adjutant-general of a division.

To give effect to this law the President was authorized by the twelfth section to cause the officers, noncommissioned officers, artificers, musicians, and privates of the several corps then in the service of the United States to be arranged in such manner as to form and complete out of the same the force thereby provided for, and to cause the supernumerary officers, noncommissioned officers, artificers, musicians, and privates to be discharged from the service.

In executing this very delicate and important trust I acted with the utmost precaution.   Sensible of what I owed to my country, I felt strongly the obligation of observing the utmost impartiality in selecting those officers who were to be retained.   In executing this law I had no personal object to accomplish or feeling to gratify—no one to retain, no one to remove.   Having on great consideration fixed the principles on which the reduction should be made, I availed myself of the example of my predecessor by appointing through the proper department a board of general officers to make the selection, and whose report I adopted.

In transferring the officers from the old to the new corps the utmost care was taken to place them in the latter in the grades and corps to which they had respectively belonged in the former, so far as it might be practicable.   This, though not enjoined by the law, appearing to be just and proper, was never departed from except in peculiar cases and under imperious circumstances.

In filling the original vacancies in the artillery and in the newly created office of Adjutant-General I considered myself at liberty to place in them any officer belonging to any part of the whole military establishment, whether of the staff or line.   In filling original vacancies—that is, offices newly created—it is my opinion, as a general principle, that Congress have no right under the Constitution to impose any restraint by law on the power granted to the President so as to prevent his making a free selection of proper persons for these offices from the whole body of his fellow-citizens.   Without, however, entering here into that question, I have no hesitation in declaring it as my opinion that the law fully authorized a selection from any branch of the whole military establishment of 1815. Justified, therefore, as I thought myself in taking that range by the very highest sanction, the sole object to which I had to direct my attention was the merit of the officers to be selected for these stations.   Three generals of great merit were either to be dismissed or otherwise provided for. The very gallant and patriotic defender of New Orleans had intimated his intention to retire, but at my suggestion expressed his willingness to accept the office of commissioner to receive the cession of the Floridas and of governor for a short time of that Territory.   As to one, therefore, there was no difficulty.   For the other two provision could only be made in the mode which was adopted.   General Macomb, who had signalized himself in the defense of Plattsburg, was placed at the head of the Corps of Engineers, to which he had originally belonged, and in which he had acquired great experience, Colonel Armistead, then at the head of that corps, having voluntarily accepted one of the new regiments of artillery, for which he possessed very suitable qualifications.   General Atkinson, likewise an officer of great merit, was appointed to the newly created office of Adjutant-General.   Brevet General Porter, an officer of great experience in the artillery, and merit, was appointed to the command of another of those regiments. Colonel Fenwick, then the oldest lieutenant-colonel of artillery, and who had suffered much in the late war by severe wounds, was appointed to a third, and Colonel Towson, who had served with great distinction in the same corps and been twice brevetted for his gallantry in the late war, was appointed to the last remaining one. General Atkinson having declined the office of Adjutant-General, Colonel Gadsden, an officer of distinguished merit and believed to possess qualifications suit-ably adapted to it, was appointed in his stead. In making the arrange ment the merits of Colonel Butler and Colonel Jones were not overlooked. The former was assigned to the place which he would have held in the line if he had retained his original lineal commission, and the latter to his commission in the line, which he had continued to hold with his staff appointment.

That the reduction of the Army and the arrangement of the officers from the old to the new establishment and the appointments referred to were in every instance strictly conformable to law will, I think, be apparent. To the arrangement generally no objection has been heard; it has been made, however, to the appointments to the original vacancies, and particularly to those of Colonel Towson and Colonel Gadsden. To those appointments, therefore, further attention is due. If they were improper it must be either that they were illegal or that the officers did not merit the offices conferred on them. The acknowledged merit of the officers and the peculiar fitness for the offices to which they were respectively appointed must preclude all objection on that head. Having already suggested my impression that in filling offices newly created, to which on no principle whatever anyone could have a claim of right, Congress could not under the Constitution restrain the free selection of the President from the whole body of his fellow-citizens, I shall only further remark that if that impression is well founded all objection to these appointments must cease. If the law imposed such restraint, it would in that case be void. But, according to my judgment, the law imposed none. An objection to the legality of those appointments must be founded either on the principle that those officers were not comprised within the corps then in the service of the United States — that is, did not belong to the peace establishment — or that the power granted by the word "arrange" imposed on the President the necessity of placing in these new offices persons of the same grade only from the old. It is believed that neither objection is well founded. Colonel Towson belonged to one of the corps then in the service of the United States, or, in other words, of the military peace establishment. By the act of 1815–16 the Pay Department, of which the Paymaster-General was the chief, was made one of the branches of the staff, and he and all those under him were subjected to the Rules and Articles of War. The appointment, therefore, of him, and especially to a new office, was strictly conformable to law.

The only difference between the fifth section of the act of 1815 for reducing the Army and the twelfth section of the act of 1821 for still further reducing it, by which the power to carry those laws into effect was granted to the President in each instance, consists in this, that by the former he was to cause the arrangement to be made of the officers, noncommissioned officers, musicians, and privates of the several *corps of troops* then in the service of the United States, whereas in the latter the term *troops* was omitted. It can not be doubted that that omission had an object, and that it was thereby intended to guard against misconstruction in so very material and important a circumstance by authorizing the application of the act unequivocally to every corps of the staff as well as of the line. With that word a much wider range was given to the act of 1815 on the reduction which then took place than under the last act. The omission of it from the last act, together with all the sanctions which were given by Congress to the construction of the law in the reduction made under the former, could not fail to dispel all doubt as to the extent of the power granted by the last law and of the pinciples which ought to guide, and on which it was thereby made the duty of the President to execute it. With respect to the other objection—that is, that officers of the same grade only ought to have been transferred to these new offices— it is equally unfounded. It is admitted that officers may be taken from the old corps and reduced and arranged in the new in inferior grades, as was done under the former reduction. This admission puts an end to the objection in this case; for if an officer may be reduced and arranged from one corps to another by an entire change of grade, requiring a new commission and a new nomination to the Senate, I see no reason why an officer may not be advanced in like manner. In both instances the grade in the old corps is alike disregarded. The transfer from it to the new turns on the merit of the party, and it is believed that the claim in this instance is felt by all with peculiar sensibility. The claim of Colonel Towson is the stronger because the arrangement of him to the office to which he is now nominated is not to one from which any officer has been removed, and to which any other officer may in any view of the case be supposed to have had a claim. As Colonel Gadsden held the office of Inspector-General, and as such was acknowledged by all to belong to the staff of the Army, it is not perceived on what ground his appointment can be objected to.

If such a construction is to be given to the act of 1821 as to confine the transfer of officers from the old to the new establishment to the *corps of troops*—that is, to the line of the Army—the whole staff of the Army in every branch would not only be excluded from any appointment in the new establishment, but altogether disbanded from the service. It would follow also that all the offices of the staff under the new arrangement must be filled by officers belonging to the new establishment after its organization and their arrangement in it. Other consequences not less serious would follow. If the right of the President to fill these original vacancies by the selection of officers from any branch of the whole military establishment was denied, he would be compelled to place in them officers of the same grade whose corps had been reduced, and they with them. The effect, therefore, of the law as to those appointments would be to legislate into office men who had been already legislated out of office, taking from the President all agency in their appointment. Such a construction would not only be subversive of the obvious principles of the Constitution, but utterly inconsistent with the spirit of the law itself, since it would provide offices for a particular grade, and fix every member of that grade in those offices, at a time when every other grade was reduced, and among them generals and other officers of the highest merit. It would also defeat every object of selection, since colonels of infantry would be placed at the head of regiments of artillery, a service in which they might have had no experience, and for which they might in consequence be unqualified.

Having omitted in the message to Congress at the commencement of the session to state the principles on which this law had been executed, and having imperfectly explained them in the message to the Senate of the 17th of January last, I deem it particularly incumbent on me, as well from a motive of respect to the Senate as to place my conduct in the duty imposed on me by that act in a clear point of view, to make this communication at this time. The examples under the law of 1815, whereby officers were reduced and arranged from the old corps to the new in inferior grades, fully justify all that has been done under the law of 1821. If the power to arrange under the former law authorized the removal of one officer from a particular station and the location of another in it, reducing the latter from a higher to an inferior grade, with the advice and consent of the Senate, it surely justifies under the latter law the arrangement of these officers, with a like sanction, to offices of new creation, from which no one had been removed and to which no one had a just claim. It is on the authority of these examples, supported by the construction which I gave to the law, that I have acted in the discharge of this high trust. I am aware that many officers of great merit, having the strongest claims on their country, have been reduced and others dismissed, but under the law that result was inevitable. It is believed that none have been retained who had not, likewise, the strongest claims to the appointments which have been conferred on them. To discriminate between men of acknowledged merit, especially in a way to affect so sensibly and materially their feelings and interests, for many of whom I have personal consideration and regard, has been a most painful duty; yet I am conscious that I have discharged it with the utmost impartiality. Had I opened the door to change in any case, even where error might have been committed, against whom could I afterwards have closed it, and into what consequences might not such a proceeding have led? The same remarks are applicable to the subject in its relation to the Senate, to whose calm and enlightened judgment, with these explanations, I again submit the nominations which have been rejected.

JAMES MONROE.

APRIL 15, 1822.

To the Senate of the United States:

In compliance with the resolution of the Senate of the 12th instant, requesting the President of the United States "to cause to be laid before the Senate the original proceedings of the board of general officers charged with the reduction of the Army under the act of the 2d of March, 1821, together with all communications to and from said board on the subject of reducing the Army, including the case submitted to the Attorney-General, and his opinion thereon," I now transmit a report from the Secretary of War, furnishing the information requested.

JAMES MONROE.

WASHINGTON, *April 15, 1822.*

To the Senate of the United States:

In compliance with a resolution of the Senate requesting the President of the United States to lay before that House any report or information which may be in his possession as to the most eligible situation on the Western waters for the erection of a national arsenal, I herewith transmit a report from the Secretary of War, containing all the information on that subject in the possession of the Executive.

JAMES MONROE.

WASHINGTON, *April 15, 1822.*

To the House of Representatives of the United States:

In compliance with a resolution of the House of Representatives of the 16th of February last, requesting the President of the United States "to communicate to that House whether any foreign government has made any claim to any part of the territory of the United States upon the coast of the Pacific Ocean north of the forty-second degree of latitude, and to what extent; whether any regulations have been made by foreign powers affecting the trade on that coast, and how it affects the interest of this Republic, and whether any communications have been made to this Government by foreign powers touching the contemplated occupation of Columbia River," I now transmit a report from the Secretary of State, containing the information embraced by that resolution.

JAMES MONROE.

WASHINGTON, *April 18, 1822.*

To the House of Representatives:

I communicate to the House of Representatives copies of sundry papers having relation to the transactions in East and West Florida, which have been received at the Department of State since my message to the two Houses of Congress of the 28th of January last, together with copies of two letters from the Secretary of State upon the same subject.

JAMES MONROE.

[The same message was sent to the Senate.]

WASHINGTON, *April 23, 1822.*

To the House of Representatives:

In compliance with a resolution of the House of Representatives of the 29th January last, requesting the President of the United States to cause to be communicated to that House certain information relative to the claim made by Jonathan Carver to certain lands within the United States near the Falls of St. Anthony, I now transmit a report of the Secretary of the Treasury, which, with the accompanying documents, contains all the information on this subject in the possession of the Executive.

JAMES MONROE.

WASHINGTON, *April 26, 1822.*

To the Senate of the United States:

I transmit to the Senate, agreeably to their resolution of yesterday, a report from the Secretary of State, with copies of the papers requested by that resolution, in relation to the recognition of the South American Provinces.

JAMES MONROE.

WASHINGTON, *April 29, 1822.*

To the House of Representatives:

I transmit to the House of Representatives a report from the Secretary of State, in pursuance of their resolution of the 29th instant,* "requesting to be furnished with a copy of the judicial proceedings in the United States court for the district of Louisiana in the case of the French slave ship *La Pensee*."

JAMES MONROE.

WASHINGTON, *April 30, 1822.*

To the Senate of the United States:

In compliance with a resolution of the Senate, requesting the President of the United States to cause to be laid before the Senate certain information respecting the practical operation of the system of subsisting the

---

*An error; so in the original message. The date of the resolution is the 18th of April.

Army under the provisions of the act passed the 14th of April, 1818, etc. I herewith transmit a report from the Secretary of War, furnishing the information required.

JAMES MONROE.

WASHINGTON, *May 1, 1822.*

To the Senate and House of Representatives of the United States:

In the message to both Houses of Congress at the commencement of their present session it was mentioned that the Government of Norway had issued an ordinance for admitting the vessels of the United States and their cargoes into the ports of that Kingdom upon the payment of no other or higher duties than are paid by Norwegian vessels, of whatever articles the said cargoes may consist and from whatever ports the vessels laden with them may come.

In communicating this ordinance to the Government of the United States that of Norway has requested the benefit of a similar and reciprocal provision for the vessels of Norway and their cargoes which may enter the ports of the United States.

This provision being within the competency only of the legislative authority of Congress, I communicate to them herewith copies of the communications received from the Norwegian Government in relation to the subject, and recommend the same to their consideration.

JAMES MONROE.

WASHINGTON, *May 1, 1822.*

To the Senate and House of Representatives of the United States:

I transmit herewith to Congress copies of letters received at the Department of State from the minister of Great Britain on the subject of the duties discriminating between imported rolled and hammered iron. I recommend them particularly to the consideration of Congress, believing that although there may be ground for controversy with regard to the application of the engagements of the treaty to the case, yet a liberal construction of those engagements would be compatible at once with a conciliatory and a judicious policy.

JAMES MONROE.

WASHINGTON, *May 4, 1822.*

To the House of Representatives of the United States:

In compliance with a resolution of the House of Representatives of the 19th of April, requesting the President "to cause to be communicated to the House, if not injurious to the public interest, any letter which may have been received from Jonathan Russell, one of the ministers who concluded the treaty of Ghent, in conformity with the indications contained in his letter of the 25th of December, 1814," I have to state that having referred the resolution to the Secretary of State, and it appearing, by a report from him, that no such document had been deposited among the archives of the Department, I examined and found among my private papers a letter of that description marked "private" by himself. I transmit a copy of the report of the Secretary of State, by which it appears that Mr. Russell, on being apprised that the document referred to by the resolution had not been deposited in the Department of State, delivered there "a paper purporting to be the duplicate of a letter written by him from Paris on the 11th of February, 1815, to the then Secretary of State, to be communicated to the House as the letter called for by the resolution."

On the perusal of the document called for I find that it communicates a difference of opinion between Mr. Russell and a majority of his colleagues in certain transactions which occurred in the negotiations at Ghent, touching interests which have been since satisfactorily adjusted by treaty between the United States and Great Britain. The view which Mr. Russell presents of his own conduct and that of his colleagues in those transactions will, it is presumed, call from the two surviving members of that mission who differed from him a reply containing their view of those transactions and of the conduct of the parties in them, and who, should his letter be communicated to the House of Representatives, will also claim that their reply should be communicated in like manner by the Executive—a claim which, on the principle of equal justice, could not be resisted. The Secretary of State, one of the ministers referred to, has already expressed a desire that Mr. Russell's letter should be communicated, and that I would transmit at the same time a communication from him respecting it.

On full consideration of the subject I have thought it would be improper for the Executive to communicate the letter called for unless the House, on a knowledge of these circumstances, should desire it, in which case the document called for shall be communicated, accompanied by a report from the Secretary of State, as above suggested. I have directed a copy to be delivered to Mr. Russell, to be disposed of as he may think proper, and have caused the original to be deposited in the Department of State, with instruction to deliver a copy to any person who may be interested.

JAMES MONROE.

WASHINGTON, *May 6, 1822.*

To the Senate and House of Representatives:

I transmit to Congress translations of two letters from Don Joaquin d'Anduaga to the Secretary of State, which have been received at the Department of State since my last message communicating copies of his correspondence with this Government.

JAMES MONROE.

Don Joaquin de Anduaga to the Secretary of State.

[Translation.]

PHILADELPHIA, *April 24, 1822.*

SIR: As soon as the news was received in Madrid of the recent occurrences in New Spain after the arrival at Vera Cruz of the Captain-General and supreme political chief appointed for those Provinces, Don Juan O. Donojú, and some papers were seen relative to those same transactions, it was feared that for forming the treaty concluded in Cordova on the 24th of August last between the said General and the traitor, Colonel Dr. Augustine Iturbide, it had been falsely supposed that the former had power from His Catholic Majesty for that act, and in a little time the correctness of those suspicions was found, as, among other things, the said O. Donojú, when on the 26th of the same August he sent this treaty to the governor of Vera Cruz, notifying him of its prompt and punctual observance, he told him that at his sailing from the Peninsula preparation for the independence of Mexico was already thought of, and that its bases were approved of by the Government and by a commission of the Cortes. His Majesty, on sight of this and of the fatal impression which so great an imposture had produced in some ultramarine Provinces, and what must without difficulty be the consequence among the rest, thought proper to order that, by means of a circular to all the chiefs and corporations beyond seas, this atrocious falsehood should be disbelieved; and now he has deigned to command me to make it known to the Government of the United States that it is false as far as General O. Donojú published beyond his instructions, by pointing out to it that he never could have been furnished with other instructions than those conformable to constitutional principles.

In compliance with this order of His Majesty, I can do no less than observe to you, sir, how unfounded one of the reasons is in your note of the 6th instant for the recognition by this Government of those of the insurgent Provinces of Spanish-America—that it was founded on the treaty made by O. Donojú with Iturbide—since not having had that power nor instruction to conclude it it is clearly null and of no value.

I repeat to you, sir, the sentiments of my distinguished consideration, and pray God that you live many years.

JOAQUIN DE ANDUAGA.

Don Joaquin de Anduaga to the Secretary of State.

[Translation.]

PHILADELPHIA, *April 26, 1822.*

JOHN QUINCY ADAMS,
    Secretary of State.

SIR: I have received your note of the 15th instant, in which you are pleased to communicate to me the reasons which induce the President not only to refuse to His Catholic Majesty the satisfaction which he demanded in his royal name for the insults offered by General Jackson to the Spanish commissaries and officers, but to approve fully of the said chief's conduct.

Before answering the contents of the said note I thought it my duty to request instructions from my Government, and therefore without delay I have laid it before them. Until they arrive, therefore, I have confined myself to two observations:

First. If in my note of the 18th of November last I said that as General Jackson had not specified the actions which had induced him to declare the Spanish officers expelled from the Floridas criminal, nor given proof of them, I thought myself authorized to declare the accusation false, I did not this through inadvertency, but upon the evident principle that every person accused has a right to declare an accusation destitute of proof false, and, much more, an accusation not pretended to be proved. This assertion of mine does not presume that I am not persuaded of the merit of the said General and of the claim which he has upon the gratitude of his country; but although it is believed the duty of his country to eulogize and reward his eminent services, yet it will be lawful for the representative of a power outraged by him to complain of his conduct. I can not persuade myself that to aggravate my said expression you could have thought that I had been wanting in due respect, it not being possible for that opinion to have entered your mind, when by his orders Mr. Forsyth had sent to the Spanish minister on the 1st of September last a note, in which, complaining of the Captain-General of the island of Cuba, he accuses him of dishonorable pecuniary motives in not having delivered the archives, without giving any proof of so injurious an assertion; and I must remark that the rank of General Mabry in Spain is at least as elevated as that of General Jackson in the United States, and that the services performed by him to his country have rendered him as worthy as he of its consideration and respect.

Second. Although you are pleased to tell me that part of the papers taken from Colonel Coppinger are ready to be delivered, which the American commissioners, *after having examined them,* have adjudged to be returned to Spain, I do not think myself authorized to admit their return in this manner, but in the mode which I demanded in my note of the 22d of November last.

As I have seen by the public papers that the President has communicated to Congress the note which you were pleased to address to me, dated the 15th instant, and that it has been ordered to be printed, I take the liberty of requesting that you will have the goodness to use your influence that this my answer may be treated in the same manner, that Congress and the public may be informed that if I have not answered the first part of it as respects the general business, it is only to wait for the instructions of my Government, but that I have answered what was personal.

I renew to you, sir, the sentiments of my distinguished consideration.

JOAQUIN DE ANDUAGA.

WASHINGTON, *May 6, 1822.*

To the Senate of the United States:

In compliance with a resolution of the Senate of the 26th of April, requesting the President of the United States "to communicate to the Senate the report of the Attorney-General relative to any persons (citizens of the United States) who have been charged with or suspected of introducing any slaves into the United States contrary to existing laws," I transmit herewith two reports from the Attorney-General.

JAMES MONROE.

WASHINGTON, *May 7, 1822.*

To the Senate of the United States:

In compliance with the resolution of the Senate of the 25th of April, requesting certain information concerning lead mines on lands of the United States, I herewith transmit a report from the Secretary of War.

JAMES MONROE.

WASHINGTON, *May 7, 1822.*

To the House of Representatives:

In compliance with the resolution of the House of Representatives of the 23d of April, requesting the President of the United States to cause to be communicated to that House certain information respecting the lead mines of the State of Missouri, I herewith transmit a report of the Secretary of War.

JAMES MONROE.

WASHINGTON, *May 7, 1822.*

To the House of Representatives:

In compliance with the resolution of the House of Representatives of the 7th of May, requesting the President to communicate to that House a letter of Jonathan Russell, esq., referred to in his message of the 4th instant, together with such communications as he may have received relative thereto from any of the other ministers of the United States who negotiated the treaty of Ghent, I herewith transmit a report from the Secretary of State, with the documents called for by that resolution.

JAMES MONROE.

VETO MESSAGE.

WASHINGTON, *May 4, 1822.*

To the House of Representatives:

Having duly considered the bill entitled ''An act for the preservation and repair of the Cumberland road,'' it is with deep regret, approving as I do the policy, that I am compelled to object to its passage and to return the bill to the House of Representatives, in which it originated, under a conviction that Congress do not possess the power under the Constitution to pass such a law.

A power to establish turnpikes with gates and tolls, and to enforce the collection of tolls by penalties, implies a power to adopt and execute a complete system of internal improvement. A right to impose duties to be paid by all persons passing a certain road, and on horses and carriages, as is done by this bill, involves the right to take the land from the proprietor on a valuation and to pass laws for the protection of the road from injuries, and if it exist as to one road it exists as to any other, and to as many roads as Congress may think proper to establish. A right to legislate for one of these purposes is a right to legislate for the others. It is a complete right of jurisdiction and sovereignty for all the purposes of internal improvement, and not merely the right of applying money under the power vested in Congress to make appropriations, under which power, with the consent of the States through which this road passes, the work was originally commenced, and has been so far executed. I am of opinion that Congress do not possess this power; that the States individually can not grant it, for although they may assent to the appropriation of money within their limits for such purposes, they can grant no power of jurisdiction or sovereignty by special compacts with the United States. This power can be granted only by an amendment to the Constitution and in the mode prescribed by it.

If the power exist, it must be either because it has been specifically granted to the United States or that it is incidental to some power which has been specifically granted. If we examine the specific grants of power we do not find it among them, nor is it incidental to any power which has been specifically granted.

It has never been contended that the power was specifically granted. It is claimed only as being incidental to some one or more of the powers which are specifically granted. The following are the powers from which it is said to be derived:

First, from the right to establish post-offices and post-roads; second, from the right to declare war; third, to regulate commerce; fourth, to pay the debts and provide for the common defense and general welfare; fifth, from the power to make all laws necessary and proper for carrying into execution all the powers vested by the Constitution in the Government of the United States or in any department or officer thereof; sixth and lastly, from the power to dispose of and make all needful rules and regulations respecting the territory and other property of the United States.

According to my judgment it can not be derived from either of those powers, nor from all of them united, and in consequence it does not exist.

Having stated my objections to the bill, I should now cheerfully communicate at large the reasons on which they are founded if I had time to reduce them to such form as to include them in this paper. The advanced stage of the session renders that impossible. Having at the commencement of my service in this high trust considered it a duty to express the opinion that the United States do not possess the power in question, and to suggest for the consideration of Congress the propriety of recommending to the States an amendment to the Constitution to vest the power in the United States, my attention has been often drawn to the subject since, in consequence whereof I have occasionally committed my sentiments to paper respecting it. The form which this exposition has assumed is not such as I should have given it had it been intended for Congress, nor is it concluded. Nevertheless, as it contains my views on this subject, being one which I deem of very high importance, and which in many of its bearings has now become peculiarly urgent, I will communicate it to Congress, if in my power, in the course of the day, or certainly on Monday next.

JAMES MONROE.

WASHINGTON, *May 4, 1822.*

To the House of Representatives:

I transmit the paper alluded to in the message of this day, on the subject of internal improvements.

JAMES MONROE.

VIEWS OF THE PRESIDENT OF THE UNITED STATES ON THE SUBJECT OF INTERNAL IMPROVEMENTS.

It may be presumed that the proposition relating to internal improvements by roads and canals, which has been several times before Congress, will be taken into consideration again either for the purpose of recommending to the States the adoption of an amendment to the Constitution to vest the necessary power in the General Government or to carry the system into effect on the principle that the power has already been granted. It seems to be the prevailing opinion that great advantage would be derived from the exercise of such a power by Congress. Respecting the right there is much diversity of sentiment. It is of the highest importance that this question should be settled. If the right exist, it ought forthwith to be exercised. If it does not exist, surely those who are friends to the power ought to unite in recommending an amendment to the Constitution to obtain it. I propose to examine this question.

The inquiry confined to its proper objects and within the most limited scale is extensive. Our Government is unlike other governments both in its origin and form. In analyzing it the differences in certain respects between it and those of other nations, ancient and modern, necessarily come into view. I propose to notice these differences so far as they are connected with the object of inquiry, and the consequences likely to result from them, varying in equal degree from those which have attended other governments. The digression, if it may be so called, will in every instance be short and the transition to the main object immediate and direct.

To do justice to the subject it will be necessary to mount to the source of power in these States and to pursue this power in its gradations and distribution among the several departments in which it is now vested. The great division is between the State governments and the General Government. If there was a perfect accord in every instance as to the precise extent of the powers granted to the General Government, we should then know with equal certainty what were the powers which remained to the State governments, since it would follow that those which were not granted to the one would remain to the other. But it is on this point, and particularly respecting the construction of these powers and their incidents, that a difference of opinion exists, and hence it is necessary to trace distinctly the origin of each government, the purposes intended by it, and the means adopted to accomplish them. By having the interior of both governments fully before us we shall have all the means which can be afforded to enable us to form a correct opinion of the endowments of each.

Before the Revolution the present States, then colonies, were separate communities, unconnected with each other except in their common relation to the Crown. Their governments were instituted by grants from the Crown, which operated, according to the conditions of each grant, in the nature of a compact between the settlers in each colony and the Crown. All power not retained in the Crown was vested exclusively in the colonies, each having a government consisting of an executive, a judiciary, and a legislative assembly, one branch of which was in every instance elected by the people. No office was hereditary, nor did any title under the Crown give rank or office in any of the colonies. In resisting the encroachments of the parent country and abrogating the power of the Crown the authority which had been held by it vested exclusively in the people of the colonies. By them was a Congress appointed, composed of delegates from each colony, who managed the war, declared independence, treated with foreign powers, and acted in all things according to the sense of their constituents. The Declaration of Independence confirmed in form what had before existed in substance. It announced to the world new States, possessing and exercising complete sovereignty, which they were resolved to maintain. They were soon after recognized by France and other powers, and finally by Great Britain herself in 1783.

Soon after the power of the Crown was annulled the people of each colony established a constitution or frame of government for themselves, in which these separate branches—legislative, executive, and judiciary—were instituted, each independent of the others. To these branches, each having its appropriate portion, the whole power of the people not delegated to Congress was communicated, to be exercised for their advantage on the representative principle by persons of their appointment, or otherwise deriving their authority immediately from them, and holding their offices for stated terms. All the powers necessary for useful purposes held by any of the strongest governments of the Old World not vested in Congress were imparted to these State governments without other checks than such as are necessary to prevent abuse, in the form of fundamental declarations or bills of right. The great difference between our governments and those of the Old World consists in this, that the former, being representative, the persons who exercise their powers do it not for themselves or in their own right, but for the people, and therefore while they are in the highest degree efficient they can never become oppressive. It is this transfer of the power of the people to representative and responsible bodies in every branch which constitutes the great improvement in the science of government and forms the boast of our system. It combines all the advantages of every known government without any of their disadvantages. It retains the sovereignty in the people, while it avoids the tumult and disorder incident to the exercise of that power by the people themselves. It possesses all the energy and efficiency of the most despotic governments, while it avoids all the oppressions and abuses inseparable from those governments.

In every stage of the conflict from its commencement until March, 1781, the powers of Congress were undefined, but of vast extent. The assemblies or conventions of the several colonies being formed by representatives from every county in each colony and the Congress by delegates from each colonial assembly, the powers of the latter for general purposes resembled those of the former for local. They rested on the same basis, the people, and were complete for all the purposes contemplated. Never was a movement so spontaneous, so patriotic, so efficient. The nation exerted its whole faculties in support of its rights, and of its independence after the contest took that direction, and it succeeded. It was, however, foreseen at a very early stage that although the patriotism of the country might be relied on in the struggle for its independence, a well-digested compact would be necessary to preserve it after obtained. A plan of confederation was in consequence proposed and taken into consideration by Congress even at the moment when the other great act which severed them from Great Britain and declared their independence was proclaimed to the world. This compact was ratified on the 21st March, 1781, by the last State, and thereupon carried into immediate effect.

The following powers were vested in the United States by the Articles of Confederation. As this, the first bond of union, was in operation nearly eight years, during which time a practical construction was given to many of its powers, all of which were adopted in the Constitution with important additions, it is thought that a correct view of those powers and of the manner in which they are executed may shed light on the subject under consideration. It may fairly be presumed that where certain powers were transferred from one instrument to the other and in the same terms, or terms descriptive only of the same powers, that it was intended that they should be construed in the same sense in the latter that they were in the former.

Article I declares that the style of the Confederacy shall be "The United States of America."

Article II. Each State retains its sovereignty, freedom, and independence, and every power and right which is not expressly delegated to the United States.

Article III. The States severally enter into a firm league of friendship with each other for their common defense, the security of their liberties, and their mutual and general welfare, binding themselves to assist each other against all force offered to or attacks made upon them on account of religion, sovereignty, trade, etc.

Article IV. The free inhabitants of each State, paupers, vagabonds, and fugitives from justice excepted, shall be entitled to all the privileges and immunities of free citizens in the several States, etc. Fugitives from justice into any of the States shall be delivered up on the demand of the executive of the State from which they fled. Full faith and credit shall be given in each State to the records and acts of every other State.

Article V. Delegates shall be annually appointed by the legislature of each State to meet in Congress on the first Monday in November, with a power to recall, etc. No State shall appoint less than two nor more than seven, nor shall any delegate hold his office for more than three in six years. Each State shall maintain its own delegates. Each State shall have one vote. Freedom of speech shall not be impeached, and the members shall be protected from arrests, except for treason, etc.

Article VI. No State shall send or receive an embassy or enter into a treaty with a foreign power. Nor shall any person holding any office of profit or trust under the United States or any State accept any present, emolument, office, or title from a foreign power. Nor shall the United States or any State grant any title of nobility. No two States shall enter into any treaty without the consent of Congress. No State shall lay any imposts or duties which may interfere with any treaties entered into by the United States. No State shall engage in war unless it be invaded or menaced with invasion by some Indian tribe, nor grant letters of marque or reprisal unless it be against pirates, nor keep up vessels of war nor any body of troops in time of peace without the consent of Congress; but every State shall keep up a well-regulated militia, etc.

Article VII. When land forces are raised by any State for the common defense, all officers of and under the rank of colonel shall be appointed by the legislature of each State.

Article VIII. All charges of war and all other expenses which shall be incurred for the common defense or general welfare shall be defrayed out of a common treasury, which shall be supplied by the several States in proportion to the value of all the land in each State granted to individuals. The taxes for paying each proportion shall be levied by the several States.

Article IX. Congress shall have the sole and exclusive right and power of determining on peace and war, except in the cases mentioned in the sixth article; of sending and receiving ambassadors; entering into alliances, except, etc.; of establishing rules for deciding what captures on land and water shall be legal; of granting letters of marque and reprisal in time of peace; appointing courts for the trial of piracies and felonies on the high seas; for deciding controversies between the States and between individuals claiming lands under two or more States whose jurisdiction has been adjusted; of regulating the alloy and value of coin struck by their authority and of foreign coin; fixing the standard of weights and measures; regulating the trade with the Indians; establishing and regulating post-offices from one State to another and throughout all the States, and exacting such postage as may be requisite to defray the expenses of the office; of appointing all officers of the land forces except the regimental; appointing all the officers of the naval forces; to ascertain the necessary sums of money to be raised for the service of the United States and appropriate the same; to borrow money and emit bills of credit; to build and equip a Navy; to agree on the number of land forces and to make requisitions on each State for its quota; that the assent of nine States shall be requisite to these great acts.

Article X regulates the powers of the committee of the States to sit in the recess of Congress.

Article XI provides for the admission of Canada into the Confederation.

Article XII pledges the faith of the United States for the payment of all bills of credit issued and money borrowed on their account.

Article XIII. Every State shall abide by the determination of the United States on all questions submitted to them by the Confederation, the Articles of the Confederation to be perpetual and not to be altered without the consent of every State.

This bond of union was soon found to be utterly incompetent to the purposes intended by it. It was defective in its powers; it was defective also in the means of executing the powers actually granted by it. Being a league of sovereign and independent States, its acts, like those of all other leagues, required the interposition of the States composing it to give them effect within their respective jurisdictions. The acts of Congress without the aid of State laws to enforce them were altogether nugatory. The refusal or omission of one State to pass such laws was urged as a reason to justify like conduct in others, and thus the Government was soon at a stand.

The experience of a few years demonstrated that the Confederation could not be relied on for the security of the blessings which had been derived from the Revolution. The interests of the nation required a more efficient Government, which the good sense and virtue of the people provided by the adoption of the present Constitution.

The Constitution of the United States was formed by a convention of delegates from the several States, who met in Philadelphia, duly authorized for the purpose, and it was ratified by a convention in each State which was especially called to consider and decide on the same. In this progress the State governments were never suspended in their functions. On the contrary, they took the lead in it. Conscious of their incompetency to secure to the Union the blessings of the Revolution, they promoted the diminution of their own powers and the enlargement of those of the General Government in the way in which they might be most adequate and efficient. It is believed that no other example can be found of a Government exerting its influence to lessen its own powers, of a policy so enlightened, of a patriotism so pure and disinterested. The credit, however, is more especially due to the people of each State, in obedience to whose will and under whose control the State governments acted.

The Constitution of the United States, being ratified by the people of the several States, became of necessity to the extent of its powers the paramount authority of the Union. On sound principles it can be viewed in no other light. The people, the highest authority known to our system, from whom all our institutions spring and on whom they depend, formed it. Had the people of the several States thought proper to incorporate themselves into one community, under one government, they might have done it. They had the power, and there was nothing then nor is there anything now, should they be so disposed, to prevent it. They wisely stopped, however, at a certain point, extending the incorporation to that point, making the National Government thus far a consolidated Government, and preserving the State governments without that limit perfectly sovereign and independent of the National Government. Had the people of the several States incorporated themselves into one community, they must have remained such, their Constitution becoming then, like the constitution of the several States, incapable of change until altered by the will of the majority. In the institution of a State government by the citizens of a State a compact is formed to which all and every citizen are equal parties. They are also the sole parties and may amend it at pleasure. In the institution of the Government of the United States by the citizens of every State a compact was formed between the whole American people which has the same force and partakes of all the qualities to the extent of its powers as a compact between the citizens of a State in the formation of their own constitution. It can not be altered except by those who formed it or in the mode prescribed by the parties to the compact itself.

This Constitution was adopted for the purpose of remedying all defects of the Confederation, and in this it has succeeded beyond any calculation that could have been formed of any human institution. By binding the States together the Constitution performs the great office of the Confederation; but it is in that sense only that it has any of the properties of that compact, and in that it is more effectual to the purpose, as it holds them together by a much stronger bond; and in all other respects in which the Confederation failed the Constitution has been blessed with complete success. The Confederation was a compact between separate and independent States, the execution of whose articles in the powers which operated internally depended on the State governments. But the great office of the Constitution, by incorporating the people of the several States to the extent of its powers into one community and enabling it to act directly on the people, was to annul the powers of the State governments to that extent, except in cases where they were concurrent, and to preclude their agency in giving effect to those of the General Government. The Government of the United States relies on its own means for the execution of its powers, as the State governments do for the execution of theirs, both governments having a common origin or sovereign, the people—the State governments the people of each State, the National Government the people of every State—and being amenable to the power which created it. It is by executing its functions as a Government thus originating and thus acting that the Constitution of the United States holds the States together and performs the office of a league. It is owing to the nature of its powers and the high source from whence they are derived—the people—that it performs that office better than the Confederation or any league which ever existed, being a compact which the State governments did not form, to which they are not parties, and which executes its own powers independently of them.

There were two separate and independent governments established over our Union, one for local purposes over each State by the people of the State, the other for national purposes over all the States by the people of the United States. The whole power of the people, on the representative principle, is divided between them. The State governments are independent of each other, and to the extent of their powers are complete sovereignties. The National Government begins where the State governments terminate, except in some instances where there is a concurrent jurisdiction between them. This Government is also, according to the extent of its powers, a complete sovereignty. I speak here, as repeatedly mentioned before, altogether of representative sovereignties, for the real sovereignty is in the people alone.

The history of the world affords no such example of two separate and independent governments established over the same people, nor can it exist except in governments founded on the sovereignty of the people. In monarchies and other governments not representative there can be no such division of power. The government is inherent in the possessor; it is his, and can not be taken from him without a revolution. In such governments alliances and leagues alone are practicable. But with us individuals count for nothing in the offices which they hold; that is, they have no right to them. They hold them as representatives, by appointment from the people, in whom the sovereignty is exclusively vested. It is impossible to speak too highly of this system taken in its twofold character and in all its great principles of two governments, completely distinct from and independent of each other, each constitutional, founded by and acting directly on the people, each competent to all its purposes, administering all the blessings for which it was instituted, without even the most remote danger of exercising any of its powers in a way to oppress the people. A system capable of expansion over a vast territory not only without weakening either government, but enjoying the peculiar advantage of adding thereby new strength and vigor to the faculties of both; possessing also this additional advantage, that while the several States enjoy all the rights reserved to them of separate and independent governments, and each is secured by the nature of the Federal Government, which acts directly on the people, against the failure of the others to bear their equal share of the public burdens, and thereby enjoys in a more perfect degree all the advantages of a league, it holds them together by a bond altogether different and much stronger than the late Confederation or any league that was ever known before—a bond beyond their control, and which can not even be amended except in the mode prescribed by it. So great an effort in favor of human happiness was never made before; but it became those who made it. Established in the new hemisphere, descended from the same ancestors, speaking the same language, having the same religion and universal toleration, born equal and educated in the same principles of free government, made independent by a common struggle and menaced by the same dangers, ties existed between them which never applied before to separate communities. They had every motive to bind them together which could operate on the interests and affections of a generous, enlightened, and virtuous people, and it affords inexpressible consolation to find that these motives had their merited influence.

In thus tracing our institutions to their origin and pursuing them in their progress and modifications down to the adoption of this Constitution two important facts have been disclosed, on which it may not be improper in this stage to make a few observations. The first is that in wresting the power, or what is called the sovereignty, from the Crown it passed directly to the people. The second, that it passed directly to the people of each colony and not to the people of all the colonies in the aggregate; to thirteen distinct communities and not to one. To these two facts, each contributing its equal proportion, I am inclined to think that we are in an eminent degree indebted for the success of our Revolution. By passing to the people it vested in a community every individual of which had equal rights and a common interest. There was no family dethroned among us, no banished pretender in a foreign country looking back to his connections and adherents here in the hope of a recall; no order of nobility whose hereditary rights in the Government had been violated; no hierarchy which had been degraded and oppressed. There was but one order, that of the people, by whom everything was gained by the change. I mention it also as a circumstance of peculiar felicity that the great body of the people had been born and educated under these equal and original institutions. Their habits, their principles, and their prejudices were therefore all on the side of the Revolution and of free republican government.

Had distinct orders existed, our fortune might and probably would have been different. It would scarcely have been possible to have united so completely the whole force of the country against a common enemy. A contest would probably have arisen in the outset between the orders for the control. Had the aristocracy prevailed, the people would have been heartless. Had the people prevailed, the nobility would probably have left the country, or, remaining behind, internal divisions would have taken place in every State and a civil war broken out more destructive even than the foreign, which might have defeated the whole movement. Ancient and modern history is replete with examples proceeding from conflicts between distinct orders, of revolutions attempted which proved abortive, of republics which have terminated in despotism. It is owing to the simplicity of the elements of which our system is composed that the attraction of all the parts has been to a common center, that every change has tended to cement the union, and, in short, that we have been blessed with such glorious and happy success.

And that the power wrested from the British Crown passed to the people of each colony the whole history of our political movement from the emigration of our ancestors to the present day clearly demonstrates. What produced the Revolution?

The violation of our rights. What rights? Our chartered rights. To whom were the charters granted, to the people of each colony or to the people of all the colonies as a single community? We know that no such community as the aggregate existed, and of course that no such rights could be violated. It may be added that the nature of the powers which were given to the delegates by each colony and the manner in which they were executed show that the sovereignty was in the people of each and not in the aggregate. They respectively presented credentials such as are usual between ministers of separate powers, which were examined and approved before they entered on the discharge of the important duties committed to them. They voted also by colonies and not individually, all the members from one colony being entitled to one vote only. This fact alone, the first of our political association and at the period of our greatest peril, fixes beyond all controversy the source from whence the power which has directed and secured success to all our measures has proceeded.

Had the sovereignty passed to the aggregate, consequences might have ensued, admitting the success of our Revolution, which might even yet seriously affect our system. By passing to the people of each colony the opposition to Great Britain, the prosecution of the war, the Declaration of Independence, the adoption of the Confederation and of this Constitution are all imputable to them. Had it passed to the aggregate, every measure would be traced to that source; even the State governments might be said to have emanated from it, and amendments of their constitutions on that principle be proposed by the same authority. In short it is not easy to perceive all the consequences into which such a doctrine might lead. It is obvious that the people in mass would have had much less agency in all the great measures of the Revolution and in those which followed than they actually had, and proportionably less credit for their patriotism and services than they are now entitled to and enjoy By passing to the people of each colony the whole body in each were kept in constant and active deliberation on subjects of the highest national importance and in the supervision of the conduct of all the public servants in the discharge of their respective duties. Thus the most effectual guards were provided against abuses and dangers of every kind which human ingenuity could devise, and the whole people rendered more competent to the self-government which by an heroic exertion they had acquired.

I will now proceed to examine the powers of the General Government, which, like the governments of the several States, is divided into three branches—a legislative, executive, and judiciary—each having its appropriate share. Of these the legislative, from the nature of its powers, all laws proceeding from it, and the manner of its appointment, its members being elected immediately by the people, is by far the most important. The whole system of the National Government may be said to rest essentially on the powers granted to this branch. They mark the limit within which, with few exceptions, all the branches must move in the discharge of their respective functions. It will be proper, therefore, to take a full and correct view of the powers granted to it.

By the eighth section of the first article of the Constitution it is declared that Congress shall have power—

First. To lay and collect taxes, duties, imposts, and excises, to pay the debts, and provide for the common defense and general welfare of the United States;

Second. To borrow money;

Third. To regulate commerce with foreign nations, and among the several States, and with the Indian tribes;

Fourth. To establish an uniform rule of naturalization and uniform laws respecting bankruptcies;

Fifth. To coin money, regulate the value thereof and of foreign coin, and fix the standard of weights and measures;

Sixth. To provide for the punishment of counterfeiting the securities and current coin of the United States;

Seventh. To establish post-offices and post-roads;

Eighth. To promote the progress of science and useful arts by securing for limited times to authors and inventors the exclusive right to their respective writings and discoveries;

Ninth. To constitute tribunals inferior to the Supreme Court, to define and punish piracies and felonies committed on the high seas, and offenses against the laws of nations;

Tenth. To declare war, grant letters of marque and reprisal, and make rules concerning captures on land and water;

Eleventh. To raise and support armies;

Twelfth. To provide and maintain a navy;

Thirteenth. To make rules for the government of the land and naval forces;

Fourteenth. To provide for calling forth the militia to execute the laws of the Union, suppress insurrections, and repel invasions;

Fifteenth. To provide for organizing, arming, and disciplining the militia, and for governing such part of them as may be in the service of the United States, reserving to the States the appointment of the officers and the authority of training the militia according to the discipline prescribed by Congress;

Sixteenth. To exercise exclusive legislation in all cases whatever over such district (not exceeding 10 miles square) as may, by the cession of particular States and the acceptance of by Congress, become the seat of Government of the United States; and to exercise like authority over all places purchased, by the consent of the legislature of the State in which the same may be, for the erection of forts, magazines, arsenals, dockyards, and other needful buildings;

Seventeenth. And to make all laws which shall be necessary and proper for carrying into execution the foregoing powers, and all other powers vested by this Constitution in the Government of the United States or in any department or officer thereof.

To the other branches of the Government the powers properly belonging to each are granted. The President, in whom the executive power is vested, is made commander in chief of the Army and Navy, and militia when called into the service of the United States. He is authorized, with the advice and consent of the Senate, two-thirds of the members present concurring, to form treaties, to nominate and, with the advice and consent of the Senate, to appoint ambassadors, other public ministers, and consuls, judges of the Supreme Court, and all other officers whose appointments are not otherwise provided for by law. He has power to grant reprieves and pardons for offenses against the United States, except in cases of impeachment. It is made his duty to give to Congress from time to time information of the state of the Union, to recommend to their consideration such measures as he may judge necessary and expedient, to convene both Houses on extraordinary occasions, to receive ambassadors, and to take care that the laws be faithfully executed.

The judicial power is vested in one Supreme Court and in such inferior courts as Congress may establish; and it is made to extend to all cases in law and equity arising under the Constitution, the laws of the United States, and treaties made under their authority. Cases affecting ambassadors and other public characters, cases of admiralty and maritime jurisdiction, causes in which the United States are a party, between two or more States, between citizens of different States, between citizens of the same State claiming grants of land under different States, between a State or the citizens thereof and foreign States, are specially assigned to these tribunals.

Other powers have been granted in other parts of the Constitution which, although they relate to specific objects, unconnected with the ordinary administration, yet, as they form important features in the Government and may shed useful light on the construction which ought to be given to the powers above enumerated, it is proper to bring into view.

By Article I, section 9, clause 1, it is provided that the migration or importation of such persons as any of the States now existing shall think proper to admit shall not be prohibited by Congress prior to the year 1808, but a tax or duty may be imposed on such importation not exceeding $10 for each person.

By Article III, section 3, clause 1, new States may be admitted by Congress into the Union, but that no new State shall be formed within the jurisdiction of another State, nor any State be formed by the junction of two or more States or parts of States without the consent of the legislature of the States concerned as well as of the United States. And by the next clause of the same article and section power is vested in Congress to dispose of and make all needful rules and regulations respecting the territory or other property belonging to the United States, with a proviso that nothing in the Constitution shall be so construed as to prejudice any claims of the United States or of any particular State.

By Article IV, section 4, the United States guarantee to every State a republican form of government and engage to protect each of them against invasion; and on application of the legislature, or of the executive when the legislature can not be convened, against domestic violence.

Of the other parts of the Constitution relating to power, some form restraints on the exercise of the powers granted to Congress and others on the exercise of the powers remaining to the States. The object in both instances is to draw more completely the line between the two governments and also to prevent abuses by either. Other parts operate like conventional stipulations between the States, abolishing between them all distinctions applicable to foreign powers and securing to the inhabitants of each State all the rights and immunities of citizens in the several States.

By the fifth article it is provided that Congress, whenever two-thirds of both Houses shall deem it necessary, shall propose amendments, or, on the application of the legislatures of two-thirds of the several States, shall call a convention for proposing amendments, which in either case shall be valid as a part of the Constitution when ratified by the legislatures of three-fourths of the several States, or by conventions in three-fourths thereof, as the one or the other mode may be proposed by Congress: *Provided*, That no State, without its consent, shall be deprived of its equal vote in the Senate, and that no amendment which may be made prior to the year 1808 shall affect the first and fourth clauses in the ninth section of the first article.

By the second section of the sixth article it is declared that the Constitution, and laws of the United States which shall be made in pursuance thereof, and all treaties made under the authority of the United States, shall be the supreme law of the land, and that the judges in every State shall be bound thereby, anything in the constitution or laws of any State to the contrary notwithstanding. This right in the National Government to execute its powers was indispensable to its existence. If the State governments had not been restrained from encroaching on the powers vested in the National Government, the Constitution, like the Confederation, would soon have been set at naught; and it was not within the limit of the human mind to devise any plan for the accomplishment of the object other than by making a national constitution which should be to the extent of its powers the supreme law of the land. This right in the National Government would have existed under the Constitution to the full extent provided for by this declaration had it not been made. To prevent the possibility of a doubt, however, on so important a subject it was proper to make the declaration.

Having presented above a full view of all the powers granted to the United States, it will be proper to look to those remaining to the States. It is by fixing the great powers which are admitted to belong to each government that we may hope to come to a right conclusion respecting those in controversy between them. In regard to the National Government, this task was easy because its powers were to be found in specific grants in the Constitution; but it is more difficult to give a detail of the powers of the State governments, as their constitutions, containing all powers granted by the people not specifically taken from them by grants to the United States, can not well be enumerated. Fortunately, a precise detail of all the powers remaining to the State governments is not necessary in the present instance. A knowledge of their great powers only will answer every purpose contemplated, and respecting these there can be no diversity in opinion. They are sufficiently recognized and established by the Constitution of the United States itself. In designating the important powers of the State governments it is proper to observe, first, that the territory contemplated by the Constitution belongs to each State in its separate character and not to the United States in their aggregate character. Each State holds territory according to its original charter, except in cases where cessions have been made to the United States by individual States. The United States had none when the Constitution was adopted which had not been thus ceded to them and which they held on the conditions on which such cession had been made. Within the individual States it is believed that they held not a single acre; but if they did it was as citizens held it, merely as private property. The territory acquired by cession lying without the individual States rests on a different principle, and is provided for by a separate and distinct part of the Constitution. It is the territory within the individual States to which the Constitution in its great principles applies, and it applies to such territory as the territory of a State and not as that of the United States. The next circumstance to be attended to is that the people composing this Union are the people of the several States, and not of the United States in the full sense of a consolidated government. The militia are the militia of the several States; lands are held under the laws of the States; descents, contracts, and all the concerns of private property, the administration of justice, and the whole criminal code, except in the cases of breaches of the laws of the United States made under and in conformity with the powers vested in Congress and of the laws of nations, are regulated by State laws. This enumeration shows the great extent of the powers of the State governments. The territory and the people form the basis on which all governments are founded. The militia constitutes their effective force. The regulation and protection of property and of personal liberty are also among the highest attributes of sovereignty. This, without other evidence, is sufficient to show that the great office of the Constitution of the United States is to unite the States together under a Government endowed with powers adequate to the purposes of its institution, relating, directly or indirectly, to foreign concerns, to the discharge of which a National Government thus formed alone could be competent.

This view of the exclusive jurisdiction of the several States over the territory within their respective limits, except in cases otherwise specially provided for, is supported by the obvious intent of the several powers granted to Congress, to which a more particular attention is now due. Of these the right to declare war is perhaps the most important, as well by the consequences attending war as by the other powers granted in aid of it. The right to lay taxes, duties, imposts, and excises, though necessary for the support of the civil government, is equally necessary to sustain the charges of war; the right to raise and support armies and a navy and to call forth and govern the militia when in the service of the United States are altogether of the latter kind. They are granted in aid of the power to make war and intended to give effect to it. These several powers are of great force and extent, and operate more directly within the limits and upon the resources of the States than any of the other powers. But still they are means only for given ends. War is declared and must be maintained, an army and a navy must be raised, fortifications must be erected for the common defense, debts must be paid. For these purposes duties, imposts, and excises are levied, taxes are laid, the lands, merchandise, and other property of the citizens are liable for them; if the money is not paid, seizures are made and the lands are sold. The transaction is terminated; the lands pass into other hands, who hold them, as the former proprietors did, under the laws of the individual States. They were means only to certain ends; the United States have nothing further to do with them. The same view is applicable to the power of the General Government over persons. The militia is called into the service of the United States; the service is performed; the corps returns to the State to which it belongs; it is the militia of such State, and not of the United States. Soldiers are required for the Army, who may be obtained by voluntary enlistment or by some other process founded in the principles of equality. In either case the citizen after the tour of duty is performed is restored to his former station in society, with his equal share in the common sovereignty of the nation. In all these cases, which are the strongest which can be given, we see that the right of the General Government is nothing more than what it is called in the Constitution, a power to perform certain acts, and that the subject on which it operates is a means only to that end; that it was both before and after that act under the protection and subject to the laws of the individual State within which it was.

To the other powers of the General Government the same remarks are applicable and with greater force. The right to regulate commerce with foreign powers was necessary as well to enable Congress to lay and collect duties and imposts as to support the rights of the nation in the intercourse with foreign powers. It is executed at the ports of the several States and operates almost altogether externally. The right to borrow and coin money and to fix its value and that of foreign coin are important to the establishment of a National Government, and particularly necessary in support of the right to declare war, as, indeed, may be considered the right to punish piracy and felonies on the high seas and offenses against the laws of nations. The right to establish an uniform rule of naturalization and uniform laws respecting bankruptcies seems to be essentially connected with the right to regulate commerce. The first branch of it relates to foreigners entering the country; the second to merchants who have failed. The right to promote the progress of useful arts and sciences may be executed without touching any of the individual States. It is accomplished by granting patents to inventors and preserving models, which may be done exclusively within the Federal district. The right to constitute courts inferior to the Supreme Court was a necessary consequence of the judiciary existing as a separate branch of the General Government. Without such inferior court in every State it would be difficult and might even be impossible to carry into effect the laws of the General Government. The right to establish post-offices and post-roads is essentially of the same character. For political, commercial, and social purposes it was important that it should be vested in the General Government. As a mere matter of regulation, and nothing more, I presume, was intended by it, it is a power easily executed and involving little authority within the States individually. The right to exercise exclusive legislation in all cases whatsoever over the Federal district and over forts, magazines, arsenals, dockyards, and other needful buildings with the consent of the State within which the same may be is a power of a peculiar character, and is sufficient in itself to confirm what has been said of all the other powers of the General Government. Of this particular grant further notice will hereafter be taken.

I shall conclude my remarks on this part of the subject by observing that the view which has been presented of the powers and character of the two Governments is supported by the marked difference which is observable in the manner of their endowment. The State governments are divided into three branches—a legislative, executive, and judiciary—and the appropriate duties of each assigned to it without any limitation of power except such as is necessary to guard against abuse, in the form of bills of right. But in instituting the National Government an entirely different principle was adopted and pursued. The Government itself is organized, like the State governments, into three branches, but its powers are enumerated and defined in the most precise form. The subject has already been too fully explained to require illustration by a general view of the whole Constitution, every part of which affords proof of what is here advanced. It will be sufficient to advert to the eighth section of the first article, being that more particularly which defines the powers and fixes the character of the Government of the United States. By this section it is declared that Congress shall have power, first, to lay and collect taxes, duties, imposts, and excises, etc.

Having shown the origin of the State governments and their endowments when first formed; having also shown the origin of the National Government and the powers vested in it, and having shown, lastly, the powers which are admitted to have remained to the State governments after those which were taken from them by the National Government, I will now proceed to examine whether the power to adopt and execute a system of internal improvement by roads and canals has been vested in the United States.

Before we can determine whether this power has been granted to the General Government it will be necessary to ascertain distinctly the nature and extent of the power requisite to make such improvements. When that is done we shall be able to decide whether such power is vested in the National Government.

If the power existed it would, it is presumed, be executed by a board of skillful engineers, on a view of the whole Union, on a plan which would secure complete effect to all the great purposes of our Constitution. It is not my intention, however, to take up the subject here on this scale. I shall state a case for the purpose of illustration only. Let it be supposed that Congress intended to run a road from the city of Washington to Baltimore and to connect the Chesapeake Bay with the Delaware and the Delaware with the Raritan by a canal, what must be done to carry the project into effect? I make here no question of the existing power. I speak only of the power necessary for the purpose. Commissioners would be appointed to trace a route in the most direct line, paying due regard to heights, water courses, and other obstacles, and to acquire the right to the ground over which the road and canal would pass, with sufficient breadth for each. This must be done by voluntary grants, or by purchases from individuals, or, in case they would not sell or should ask an exorbitant price, by condemning the property and fixing its value by a jury of the vicinage. The next object to be attended to after the road and canal are laid out and made is to keep them in repair We know that there are people in every community capable of committing voluntary injuries, of pulling down walls that are made to sustain the road, of breaking the bridges over water courses, and breaking the road itself. Some living near it might be disappointed that it did not pass through their lands and commit these acts of violence and waste from revenge or in the hope of giving it that direction, though for a short time. Injuries of this kind have been committed and are still complained of on the road from Cumberland to the Ohio. To accomplish this object Congress should have a right to pass laws to punish offenders wherever they may be found. Jurisdiction over the road would not be sufficient, though it were exclusive. It would seldom happen that the parties would be detected in the act. They would generally commit it in the night and fly far off before the sun appeared. The power to punish these culprits must therefore reach them wherever they go. They must also be amenable to competent tribunals, Federal or State. The power must likewise extend to another object not less essential or important than those already mentioned. Experience has shown that the establishment of turnpikes, with gates and tolls and persons to collect the tolls, is the best expedient that can be adopted to defray the expense of these improvements and the repairs which they necessarily require. Congress must therefore have power to make such an establishment and to support it by such regulations, with fines and penalties in the case of injuries, as may be competent to the purpose. The right must extend to all those objects, or it will be utterly incompetent. It is possessed and exercised by the States individually, and it must be possessed by the United States or the pretension must be abandoned.

Let it be further supposed that Congress, believing that they do possess the power, have passed an act for those purposes, under which commissioners have been appointed, who have begun the work. They are met at the first farm on which they enter by the owner, who forbids them to trespass on his land. They offer to buy it at a fair price or at twice or thrice its value. He persists in his refusal. Can they, on the principle recognized and acted on by all the State governments that in cases of this kind the obstinacy and perverseness of an individual must yield to the public welfare, summon a jury of upright and discreet men to condemn the land, value it, and compel the owner to receive the amount and to deliver it up to them? I believe that very few would concur in the opinion that such a power exists.

The next object is to preserve these improvements from injury. The locks of the canal are broken, the walls which sustained the road are pulled down, the bridges are broken, the road itself is plowed up, toll is refused to be paid, the gates of the canal or turnpike are forced. The offenders are pursued, caught, and brought to trial. Can they be punished? The question of right must be decided on principle. The culprits will avail themselves of every barrier that may serve to screen them from punishment. They will plead that the law under which they stand arraigned is unconstitutional, and that question must be decided by the court, whether Federal or State, on a fair investigation of the powers vested in the General Government by the Constitution. If the judges find that these powers have not been granted to Congress, the prisoners must be acquitted, and by their acquittal all claim to the right to establish such a system is at an end.

I have supposed an opposition to be made to the right in Congress by the owner of the land and other individuals charged with breaches of laws made to protect the works from injury, because it is the mildest form in which it can present itself. It is not, however, the only one. A State, also, may contest the right, and then the controversy assumes another character. Government might contend against government, for to a certain extent both the Governments are sovereign and independent of each other, and in that form it is possible, though not probable, that opposition might be made. To each limitations are prescribed, and should a contest rise between them respecting their rights and the people sustain it with anything like an equal division of numbers the worst consequences might ensue.

It may be urged that the opposition suggested by the owner of the land or by the States individually may be avoided by a satisfactory arrangement with the parties. But a suppression of opposition in that way is no proof of a right in Congress, nor could it, if confined to that limit, remove all the impediments to the exercise of the power. It is not sufficient that Congress may by the command and application of the public revenue purchase the soil, and thus silence that class of individuals, or by the accommodation afforded to individual States put down opposition on their part. Congress must be able rightfully to control all opposition or they can not carry the system into effect. Cases would inevitably occur to put the right to the test. The work must be preserved from injury, tolls must be collected, offenders must be punished. With these culprits no bargain can be made. When brought to trial they must deny the validity of the law, and that plea being sustained all claim to the right ceases.

If the United States possess this power, it must be either because it has been specifically granted or that it is incidental and necessary to carry into effect some specific grant. The advocates for the power derive it from the following sources: First, the right to establish post-offices and post-roads; second, to declare war; third, to regulate commerce among the several States; fourth, from the power to pay the debts and provide for the common defense and general welfare of the United States; fifth, from the power to make all laws necessary and proper for carrying into execution all the powers vested by the Constitution in the Government of the United States or in any department or officer thereof; sixth and lastly, from the power to dispose of and make all needful rules and regulations respecting the territory and other property of the United States. It is to be observed that there is but little accord among the advocates for this power as to the particular source from whence it is derived. They all agree, however, in ascribing it to some one or more of those above mentioned. I will examine the ground of the claim in each instance.

The first of these grants is in the following words: "Congress shall have power to establish post-offices and post-roads." What is the just import of these words and the extent of the grant? The word "establish" is the ruling term; "post-offices and post-roads" are the subjects on which it acts. The question therefore is, What power is granted by that word? The sense in which words are commonly used is that in which they are to be understood in all transactions between public bodies and individuals. The intention of the parties is to prevail, and there is no better way of ascertaining it than by giving to the terms used their ordinary import. If we were to ask any number of our most enlightened citizens, who had no connection with public affairs and whose minds were unprejudiced, what was the import of the word "establish" and the extent of the grant which it controls, we do not think there would be any difference of opinion among them. We are satisfied that all of them would answer that a power was thereby given to Congress to fix on the towns, court-houses, and other places throughout our Union at which there should be post-offices, the routes by which the mails should be carried from one post-office to another, so as to diffuse intelligence as extensively and to make the institution as useful as possible, to fix the postage to be paid on every letter and packet thus carried, to support the establishment, and to protect the post-office and mails from robbery by punishing those who should commit the offense. The idea of a right to lay off the roads of the United States on a general scale of improvement, to take the soil from the proprietor by force, to establish turnpikes and tolls, and to punish offenders in the manner stated above would never occur to any such person. The use of the existing road by the stage, mail carrier, or postboy in passing over it as others do is all that would be thought of, the jurisdiction and soil remaining to the State, with a right in the State or those authorized by its legislature to change the road at pleasure.

The intention of the parties is supported by other proof, which ought to place it beyond all doubt. In the former act of Government, the Confederation, we find a grant for the same purpose expressed in the following words: "The United States in Congress assembled shall have the sole and exclusive right and power of establishing and regulating post-offices from one State to another throughout all the United States, and exacting such postage on the papers passing through the same as may be requisite to defray the expenses of the said office." The term "establish" was likewise the ruling one in that instrument, and was evidently intended and understood to give a power simply and solely to fix where there should be post-offices. By transferring this term from the Confederation into the Constitution it was doubtless intended that it should be understood in the same sense in the latter that it was in the former instrument, and to be applied alike to post-offices and post-roads. In whatever sense it is applied to post-offices it must be applied in the same sense to post-roads. But it may be asked, If such was the intention, why were not all the other terms of the grant transferred with it? The reason is obvious. The Confederation being a bond of union between independent States, it was necessary in granting the powers which were to be exercised over them to be very explicit and minute in defining the powers granted. But the Constitution to the extent of its powers having incorporated the States into one Government like the government of the States individually, fewer words in defining the powers granted by it were not only adequate, but perhaps better adapted to the purpose. We find that brevity is a characteristic of the instrument. Had it been intended to convey a more enlarged power in the Constitution than had been granted in the Confederation, surely the same controlling term would not have been used, or other words would have been added, to show such intention and to mark the extent to which the power should be carried. It is a liberal construction of the powers granted in the Constitution by this term to include in it all the powers that were granted in the Confederation by terms which specifically defined and, as was supposed, extended their limits. It would be absurd to say that by omitting from the Constitution any portion of the phraseology which was deemed important in the Confederation the import of that term was enlarged, and with it the powers of the Constitution, in a proportional degree, beyond what they were in the Confederation. The right to exact postage and to protect the post-offices and mails from robbery by punishing the offenders may fairly be considered as incidents to the grant, since without it the object of the grant might be defeated. Whatever is absolutely necessary to the accomplishment of the object of the grant, though not specified, may fairly be considered as included in it. Beyond this the doctrine of incidental power can not be carried.

If we go back to the origin of our settlements and institutions and trace their progress down to the Revolution, we shall see that it was in this sense, and in none other, that the power was exercised by all our colonial governments. Post-offices were made for the country, and not the country for them. They are the offspring of improvement; they never go before it. Settlements are first made, after which the progress is uniform and simple, extending to objects in regular order most necessary to the comfort of man—schools, places of public worship, court-houses, and markets; post-offices follow. Roads may, indeed, be said to be coeval with settlements; they lead to all the places mentioned, and to every other which the various and complicated interests of society require.

It is believed that not one example can be given, from the first settlement of our country to the adoption of this Constitution, of a post-office being established without a view to existing roads or of a single road having been made by pavement, turnpike, etc., for the sole purpose of accommodating a post-office. Such, too, is the uniform progress of all societies. In granting, then, this power to the United States it was undoubtedly intended by the framers and ratifiers of the Constitution to convey it in the sense and extent only in which it had been understood and exercised by the previous authorities of the country.

This conclusion is confirmed by the object of the grant and the manner of its execution. The object is the transportation of the mail throughout the United States, which may be done on horseback, and was so done until lately, since the establishment of stages. Between the great towns and in other places where the population is dense stages are preferred because they afford an additional opportunity to make a profit from passengers; but where the population is sparse and on crossroads it is generally carried on horseback. Unconnected with passengers and other objects, it can not be doubted that the mail itself may be carried in every part of our Union with nearly as much economy and greater dispatch on horseback than in a stage, and in many parts with much greater. In every part of the Union in which stages can be preferred the roads are sufficiently good provided those which serve for every other purpose will accommodate them. In every other part where horses alone are used if other people pass them on horseback surely the mail carrier can. For an object so simple and so easy in its execution it would doubtless excite surprise if it should be thought proper to appoint commissioners to lay off the country on a great scheme of improvement, with the power to shorten distances, reduce heights, level mountains, and pave surfaces.

If the United States possessed the power contended for under this grant, might they not in adopting the roads of the individual States for the carriage of the mail, as has been done, assume jurisdiction over them and preclude a right to interfere with or alter them? Might they not establish turnpikes and exercise all the other acts of sovereignty above stated over such roads necessary to protect them from injury and defray the expense of repairing them? Surely if the right exists these consequences necessarily followed as soon as the road was established. The absurdity of such a pretension must be apparent to all who examine it. In this way a large portion of the territory of every State might be taken from it, for there is scarcely a road in any State which will not be used for the transportation of the mail. A new field for legislation and internal government would thus be opened.

From this view of the subject I think we may fairly conclude that the right to adopt and execute a system of internal improvement, or any part of it, has not been granted to Congress under the power to establish post-offices and post-roads; that the common roads of the country only were contemplated by that grant and are fully competent to all its purposes.

The next object of inquiry is whether the right to declare war includes the right to adopt and execute this system of improvement. The objections to it are, I presume, not less conclusive than those which are applicable to the grant which we have just examined.

Under the last-mentioned grant a claim has been set up to as much of that system as relates to roads. Under this it extends alike to roads and canals.

We must examine this grant by the same rules of construction that were applied to the preceding one. The object was to take this power from the individual States and to vest it in the General Government. This has been done in clear and explicit terms, first by granting the power to Congress, and secondly by prohibiting the exercise of it by the States. "Congress shall have a right to declare war." This is the language of the grant. If the right to adopt and execute this system of improvement is included in it, it must be by way of incident only, since there is nothing in the grant itself which bears any relation to roads and canals. The following considerations, it is presumed, prove incontestably that this power has not been granted in that or any other manner.

The United States are exposed to invasion through the whole extent of their Atlantic coast by any European power with whom we might be engaged in war—on the northern and northwestern frontier on the side of Canada by Great Britain, and on the southern by Spain or any power in alliance with her. If internal improvements are to be carried to the full extent to which they may be useful for military purposes, the power as it exists must apply to all the roads of the Union, there being no limitation to it. Wherever such improvements may facilitate the march of troops, the transportation of cannon, or otherwise aid the operations or mitigate the calamities of war along the coast or in any part of the interior they would be useful for military purposes, and might therefore be made. The power following as an incident to another power can be measured as to its extent by reference only to the obvious extent of the power to which it is incidental. So great a scope was, it is believed, never given to incidental power.

If it had been intended that the right to declare war should include all the powers necessary to maintain war, it would follow that nothing would have been done to impair the right or to restrain Congress from the exercise of any power which the exigencies of war might require. The nature and extent of this exigency would mark the extent of the power granted, which should always be construed liberally, so as to be adequate to the end. A right to raise money by taxes, duties, excises, and by loan, to raise and support armies and a navy, to provide for calling forth, arming, disciplining, and governing the militia when in the service of the United States, establishing fortifications and governing the troops stationed in them independently of the State authorities, and to perform many other acts is indispensable to the maintenance of war—no war with any great power can be prosecuted with success without the command of the resources of the Union in all these respects. These powers.

then, would of necessity and by common consent have fallen within the right to declare war had it been intended to convey by way of incident to that right the necessary powers to maintain war. But these powers have all been granted specifically with many others, in great detail, which experience had shown were necessary for the purposes of war. By specifically granting, then, these powers it is manifest that every power was thus granted which it was intended to grant for military purposes, and that it was also intended that no important power should be included in this grant by way of incident, however useful it might be for some of the purposes of the grant.

By the sixteenth of the enumerated powers, Article I, section 8, Congress are authorized to exercise exclusive legislation in all cases whatever over such district as may by cession of particular States and the acceptance of Congress, not exceeding 10 miles square, become the seat of the Government of the United State, and to exercise like authority over all places purchased by the consent of the legislature of the State in which the same shall be, for the erection of forts, magazines, arsenals, dockyards, and other useful buildings. If any doubt existed on a view of other parts of the Constitution respecting the decision which ought to be formed on the question under consideration, I should suppose that this clause would completely remove it. It has been shown after the most liberal construction of all the enumerated powers of the General Government that the territory within the limits of the respective States belonged to them; that the United States had no right under the powers granted to them, with the exception specified in this grant, to any the smallest portion of territory within a State, all those powers operating on a different principle and having their full effect without impairing in the slightest degree this right in the States; that those powers were in every instance means to ends, which being accomplished left the subject—that is, the property, in which light only land could be regarded—where it was before, under the jurisdiction and subject to the laws of the State governments.

The second number of the clause, which is applicable to military and naval purposes alone, claims particular attention here. It fully confirms the view taken of the other enumerated powers, for had it been intended to include in the right to declare war, by way of incident, any right of jurisdiction or legislation over territory within a State, it would have been done as to fortifications, magazines, arsenals, dockyards, and other needful buildings. By specifically granting the right as to such small portions of territory as might be necessary for these purposes and on certain conditions, minutely and well defined, it is manifest that it was not intended to grant it as to any other portion on any condition for any purpose or in any manner whatsoever.

It may be said that although the authority to exercise exclusive legislation in certain cases within the States with their consent may be considered as a prohibition to Congress to exercise like exclusive legislation in any other case, although their consent should be granted, it does not prohibit the exercise of such jurisdiction or power within a State as would be competent to all the purposes of internal improvement. I can conceive no ground on which the idea of such a power over any part of the territory of a State can be inferred from the power to declare war. There never can be an occasion for jurisdiction for military purposes except in fortifications, dockyards, and the like places. If the soldiers are in the field or are quartered in garrisons without the fortifications, the civil authority must prevail where they are. The government of the troops by martial law is not affected by it. In war, when the forces are increased and the movement is on a greater scale, consequences follow which are inseparable from the exigencies of the state. More freedom of action and a wider range of power in the military commanders, to be exercised on their own responsibility, may be necessary to the public safety ; but even here the civil authority of the State never ceases to operate. It is also exclusive for all civil purposes.

Whether any power short of that stated would be adequate to the purposes of internal improvement is denied. In the case of territory one government must prevail for all the purposes intended by the grant. The jurisdiction of the United States might be modified in such manner as to admit that of the State in all cases and for all purposes not necessary to the execution of the proposed power; but the right of the General Government must be complete for all the purposes above stated. It must extend to the seizure and condemnation of the property, if necessary; to the punishment of offenders for injuries to the roads and canals; to the establishment and enforcement of tolls, etc. It must be a complete right to the extent above stated or it will be of no avail. That right does not exist.

The reasons which operate in favor of the right of exclusive legislation in forts, dockyards, etc., do not apply to any other places. The safety of such works and of the cities which they are intended to defend, and even of whole communities, may sometimes depend on it. If spies are admitted within them in time of war, they might communicate intelligence to the enemy which might be fatal. All nations surround such works with high walls and keep their gates shut. Even here, however, three important conditions are indispensable to such exclusive legislation: First, the ground must be requisite for and be applied to those purposes; second, it must be purchased; third, it must be purchased by the consent of the State in which it may be. When we find that so much care has been taken to protect the sovereignty of the States over the territory within their respective limits, admitting that of the United States over such small portions and for such special and important purposes only, the conclusion is irresistible not only that the power necessary for internal improvements has not been granted, but that it has been clearly prohibited.

I come next to the right to regulate commerce, the third source from whence the right to make internal improvements is claimed. It is expressed in the following words: "Congress shall have power to regulate commerce with foreign nations and among the several States and with the Indian tribes." The reasoning applicable to the preceding claims is equally so to this. The mischief complained of was that this power could not be exercised with advantage by the individual States, and the object was to transfer it to the United States. The sense in which the power was understood and exercised by the States was doubtless that in which it was transferred to the United States. The policy was the same as to three branches of this grant, and it is scarcely possible to separate the two first from each other in any view which may be taken of the subject. The last, relating to the Indian tribes, is of a nature distinct from the others for reasons too well known to require explanation. Commerce between independent powers or communities is universally regulated by duties and imposts. It was so regulated by the States before the adoption of this Constitution equally in respect to each other and to foreign powers. The goods and vessels employed in the trade are the only subjects of regulation. It can act on none other. A power, then, to impose such duties and imposts in regard to foreign nations and to prevent any on the trade between the States was the only power granted.

If we recur to the causes which produced the adoption of this Constitution, we shall find that injuries resulting from the regulation of trade by the States respectively and the advantages anticipated from the transfer of the power to Congress were among those which had the most weight. Instead of acting as a nation in regard to foreign powers, the States individually had commenced a system of restraint on each other whereby the interests of foreign powers were promoted at their expense. If one State imposed high duties on the goods or vessels of a foreign power to countervail the regulations of such power, the next adjoining States imposed lighter duties to invite those articles into their ports, that they might be transferred thence into the other States, securing the duties to themselves. This contracted policy in some of the States was soon counteracted by others. Restraints were immediately laid on such commerce by the suffering States, and thus had grown up a state of affairs disorderly and unnatural, the tendency of which was to destroy the Union itself and with it all hope of realizing those blessings which we had anticipated from the glorious Revolution which had been so recently achieved. From this deplorable dilemma, or, rather, certain ruin, we were happily rescued by the adoption of the Constitution.

Among the first and most important effects of this great Revolution was the complete abolition of this pernicious policy. The States were brought together by the Constitution as to commerce into one community equally in regard to foreign nations and each other. The regulations that were adopted regarded us in both respects as one people. The duties and imposts that were laid on the vessels and merchandise of foreign nations were all uniform throughout the United States, and in the intercourse between the States themselves no duties of any kind were imposed other than between different ports and counties within the same State.

This view is supported by a series of measures, all of a marked character, preceding the adoption of the Constitution. As early as the year 1781 Congress recommended it to the States to vest in the United States a power to levy a duty of 5 per cent on all goods imported from foreign countries into the United States for the term of fifteen years. In 1783 this recommendation, with alterations as to the kind of duties and an extension of this term to twenty-five years, was repeated and more earnestly urged. In 1784 it was recommended to the States to authorize Congress to prohibit, under certain modifications, the importation of goods from foreign powers into the United States for fifteen years. In 1785 the consideration of the subject was resumed, and a proposition presented in a new form, with an address to the States, explaining fully the principles on which a grant of the power to regulate trade was deemed indispensable. In 1786 a meeting took place at Annapolis of delegates from several of the States on this subject, and on their report a convention was formed at Philadelphia the ensuing year from all the States, to whose deliberations we are indebted for the present Constitution.

In none of these measures was the subject of internal improvement mentioned or even glanced at. Those of 1784, 1785, 1786, and 1787, leading step by step to the adoption of the Constitution, had in view only the obtaining of a power to enable Congress to regulate trade with foreign powers. It is manifest that the regulation of trade with the several States was altogether a secondary object, suggested by and adopted in connection with the other. If the power necessary to this system of improvement is included under either branch of this grant, I should suppose that it was the first rather than the second. The pretension to it, however, under that branch has never been set up. In support of the claim under the second no reason has been assigned which appears to have the least weight.

The fourth claim is founded on the right of Congress to "pay the debts and provide for the common defense and general welfare" of the United States. This claim has less reason on its side than either of those which we have already examined. The power of which this forms a part is expressed in the following words: "Congress shall have power to lay and collect taxes, duties, imposts, and excises; to pay the debts and provide for the common defense and general welfare of the United States; but all duties, imposts, and excises shall be uniform throughout the United States."

That the second part of this grant gives a right to appropriate the public money, and nothing more, is evident from the following considerations: First. If the right of appropriation is not given by this clause, it is not given at all, there being no other grant in the Constitution which gives it directly or which has any bearing on the subject, even by implication, except the two following: First, the prohibition, which is contained in the eleventh of the enumerated powers, not to appropriate money for the support of armies for a longer term than two years; and, second, the declaration of the sixth member or clause of the ninth section of the first article that no money shall be drawn from the Treasury but in consequence of appropriations made by law. Second. This part of the grant has none of the characteristics of a distinct and original power. It is manifestly incidental to the great objects of the first part of the grant, which authorizes Congress to lay and collect taxes, duties, imposts, and excises, a power of vast extent, not granted by the Confederation, the grant of which formed one of the principal inducements to the adoption of this Constitution. If both parts of the grant are taken together (as they must be, for the one follows immediately after the other in the same sentence), it seems to be impossible to give to the latter any other construction than that contended for. Congress shall have power to lay and collect taxes, duties, imposts, and excises. For what purpose? To pay the debts and provide for the common defense and general welfare of the United States, an arrangement and phraseology which clearly show that the latter part of the clause was intended to enumerate the purposes to which the money thus raised might be appropriated. Third. If this is not the real object and fair construction of the second part of this grant, it follows either that it has no import or operation whatever or one of much greater extent than the first part. This presumption is evidently groundless in both instances. In the first because no part of the Constitution can be considered useless; no sentence or clause in it without a meaning. In the second because such a construction as made the second part of the clause an original grant, embracing the same object with the first, but with much greater power than it, would be in the highest degree absurd. The order generally observed in grants, an order founded in common sense, since it promotes a clear understanding of their import, is to grant the power intended to be conveyed in the most full and explicit manner, and then to explain or qualify it, if explanation or qualification should be necessary. This order has, it is believed, been invariably observed in all the grants contained in the Constitution. In the second because if the clause in question is not construed merely as an authority to appropriate the public money, it must be obvious that it conveys a power of indefinite and unlimited extent; that there would have been no use for the special powers to raise and support armies and a navy, to regulate commerce, to call forth the militia, or even to lay and collect taxes, duties, imposts, and excises. An unqualified power to pay the debts and provide for the common defense and general welfare, as the second part of this clause would be if considered as a distinct and separate grant, would extend to every object in which the public could be interested. A power to provide for the common defense would give to Congress the command of the whole force and of all the resources of the Union; but a right to provide for the general welfare would go much further. It would, in effect, break down all the barriers between the States and the General Government and consolidate the whole under the latter.

The powers specifically granted to Congress are what are called the enumerated powers, and are numbered in the order in which they stand, among which that contained in the first clause holds the first place in point of importance. If the power created by the latter part of the clause is considered an original grant, unconnected with and independent of the first, as in that case it must be, then the first part is entirely done away, as are all the other grants in the Constitution, being completely absorbed in the transcendent power granted in the latter part; but if the clause be construed in the sense contended for, then every part has an important meaning and effect; not a line, a word, in it is superfluous. A power to lay and collect taxes, duties, imposts, and excises subjects to the call of Congress every branch of the public revenue, internal and external, and the addition to pay the debts and provide for the common defense and general welfare gives the right of applying the money raised—that is, of appropriating it to the purposes specified according to a proper construction of the terms. Hence it follows that it is the first part of the clause only which gives a power which affects in any manner the power remaining to the States, as the power to raise money from the people, whether it be by taxes, duties, imposts, or excises, though concurrent in the States as to taxes and excises must necessarily do. But the use or application of the money after it is raised is a power altogether of a different character. It imposes no burden on the people, nor can it act on them in a sense to take power from the States or in any sense in which power can be controverted, or become a question between the two Governments. The application of money raised under a lawful power is a right or grant which may be abused. It may be applied partially among the States, or to improper purposes in our foreign and domestic concerns; but still it is a power not felt in the sense of other power, since the only complaint which any State can make of such partiality and abuse is that some other State or States have obtained greater benefit from the application than by a just rule of apportionment they were entitled to. The right of appropriation is therefore from its nature secondary and incidental to the right of raising money, and it was proper to place it in the same grant and same clause with that right. By finding them, then, in that order we see a new proof of the sense in which the grant was made, corresponding with the view herein taken of it.

The last part of this grant, which provides that all duties, imposts, and excises shall be uniform throughout the United States, furnishes another strong proof that it was not intended that the second part should constitute a distinct grant in the sense above stated, or convey any other right than that of appropriation. This provision operates exclusively on the power granted in the first part of the clause. It recites three branches of that power—duties, imposts, and excises—those only on which it could operate, the rule by which the fourth—that is, taxes—should be laid being already provided for in another part of the Constitution. The object of this provision is to secure a just equality among the States in the exercise of that power by Congress. By placing it after both the grants—that is, after that to raise and that to appropriate the public money—and making it apply to the first only it shows that it was not intended that the power granted in the second should be paramount to and destroy that granted in the first. It shows also that no such formidable power as that suggested had been granted in the second, or any power against the abuse of which it was thought necessary specially to provide. Surely if it was deemed proper to guard a specific power of limited extent and well-known import against injustice and abuse, it would have been much more so to have guarded against the abuse of a power of such vast extent and so indefinite as would have been granted by the second part of the clause if considered as a distinct and original grant.

With this construction all the other enumerated grants, and, indeed, all the grants of power contained in the Constitution, have their full operation and effect. They all stand well together, fulfilling the great purposes intended by them. Under it we behold a great scheme, consistent in all its parts, a Government instituted for national purposes, vested with adequate powers for those purposes, commencing with the most important of all, that of the revenue, and proceeding in regular order to the others with which it was deemed proper to endow it, all, too, drawn with the utmost circumspection and care. How much more consistent is this construction with the great objects of the institution and with the high character of the enlightened and patriotic citizens who framed it, as well as of those who ratified it, than one which subverts every sound principle and rule of construction and throws everything into confusion.

I have dwelt thus long on this part of the subject from an earnest desire to fix in a clear and satisfactory manner the import of the second part of this grant, well knowing from the generality of the terms used their tendency to lead into error. I indulge a strong hope that the view herein presented will not be without effect, but will tend to satisfy the unprejudiced and impartial that nothing more was granted by that part than a power to *appropriate* the public money raised under the other part. To what extent that power may be carried will be the next object of inquiry.

It is contended on the one side that as the National Government is a government of limited powers it has no right to expend money except in the performance of acts authorized by the other specific grants according to a strict construction of their powers; that this grant in neither of its branches gives to Congress discretionary power of any kind, but is a mere instrument in its hands to carry into effect the powers contained in the other grants. To this construction I was inclined in the more early stage of our Government; but on further reflection and observation my mind has undergone a change, for reasons which I will frankly unfold.

The grant consists, as heretofore observed, of a twofold power—the first to raise, the second to appropriate, the public money—and the terms used in both instances are general and unqualified. Each branch was obviously drawn with a view to the other, and the import of each tends to illustrate that of the other. The grant to raise money gives a power over every subject from which revenue may be drawn, and is made in the same manner with the grants to declare war, to raise and support armies and a navy, to regulate commerce, to establish post-offices and post-roads, and with all the other specific grants to the General Government. In the discharge of the powers contained in any of these grants there is no other check than that which is to be found in the great principles of our system, the responsibility of the representative to his constituents. If war, for example, is necessary, and Congress declare it for good cause, their constituents will support them in it. A like support will be given them for the faithful discharge of their duties under any and every other power vested in the United States. It affords to the friends of our free governments the most heartfelt consolation to know—and from the best evidence, our own experience—that in great emergencies the boldest measures, such as form the strongest appeals to the virtue and patriotism of the people, are sure to obtain the most decided approbation. But should the representative act corruptly and betray his trust, or otherwise prove that he was unworthy of the confidence of his constituents, he would be equally sure to lose it and to be removed and otherwise censured, according to his deserts. The power to raise money by taxes, duties, imposts, and excises is alike unqualified, nor do I see any check on the exercise of it other than that which applies to the other powers above recited, the responsibility of the representative to his constituents. Congress know the extent of the public engagements and the sums necessary to meet them; they know how much may be derived from each branch of revenue without pressing it too far; and, paying due regard to the interests of the people, they likewise know which branch ought to be resorted to in the first instance. From the commencement of the Government two branches of this power, duties and imposts, have been in constant operation, the revenue from which has supported the Government in its various branches and met its other ordinary engagements. In great emergencies the other two, taxes and excises, have likewise been resorted to, and neither was the right or the policy ever called in question.

If we look to the second branch of this power, that which authorizes the appropriation of the money thus raised, we find that it is not less general and unqualified than the power to raise it. More comprehensive terms than to "pay the debts and provide for the common defense and general welfare" could not have been used. So intimately connected with and dependent on each other are these two branches of power that had either been limited the limitation would have had the like effect on the other. Had the power to raise money been conditional or restricted to special purposes, the appropriation must have corresponded with it, for none but the money raised could be appropriated, nor could it be appropriated to other purposes than those which were permitted. On the other hand, if the right of appropriation had been restricted to certain purposes, it would be useless and improper to raise more than would be adequate to those purposes. It may fairly be inferred these restraints or checks have been carefully and intentionally avoided. The power in each branch is alike broad and unqualified, and each is drawn with peculiar fitness to the other, the latter requiring terms of great extent and force to accommodate the former, which have been adopted, and both placed in the same clause and sentence.

Can it be presumed that all these circumstances were so nicely adjusted by mere accident? Is it not more just to conclude that they were the result of due deliberation and design? Had it been intended that Congress should be restricted in the appropriation of the public money to such expenditures as were authorized by a rigid construction of the other specific grants, how easy would it have been to have provided for it by a declaration to that effect. The omission of such declaration is therefore an additional proof that it was not intended that the grant should be so construed.

It was evidently impossible to have subjected this grant in either branch to such restriction without exposing the Government to very serious embarrassment. How carry it into effect? If the grant had been made in any degree dependent upon the States, the Government would have experienced the fate of the Confederation. Like it, it would have withered and soon perished. Had the Supreme Court been authorized, or should any other tribunal distinct from the Government be authorized, to impose its veto, and to say that more money had been raised under either branch of this power—that is, by taxes, duties, imposts, or excises—than was necessary, that such a tax or duty was useless, that the appropriation to this or that purpose was unconstitutional, the movement might have been suspended and the whole system disorganized. It was impossible to have created a power within the Government or any other power distinct from Congress and the Executive which should control the movement of the Government in this respect and not destroy it. Had it been declared by a clause in the Constitution that the expenditures under this grant should be restricted to the construction which might be given of the other grants, such restraint, though the most innocent, could not have failed to have had an injurious effect on the vital principles of the Government and often on its most important measures. Those who might wish to defeat a measure proposed might construe the power relied on in support of it in a narrow and contracted manner, and in that way fix a precedent inconsistent with the true import of the grant. At other times those who favored a measure might give to the power relied on a forced or strained construction, and, succeeding in the object, fix a precedent in the opposite extreme. Thus it is manifest that if the right of appropriation be confined to that limit, measures may oftentimes be carried or defeated by considerations and motives altogether independent of and unconnected with their merits, and the several powers of Congress receive constructions equally inconsistent with their true import. No such declaration, however, has been made, and from the fair import of the grant, and, indeed, its positive terms, the inference that such was intended seems to be precluded.

Many considerations of great weight operate in favor of this construction, while I do not perceive any serious objections to it. If it be established, it follows that the words "to provide for the common defense and general welfare" have a definite, safe, and useful meaning. The idea of their forming an original grant, with unlimited power, superseding every other grant, is abandoned. They will be considered simply as conveying a right of appropriation, a right indispensable to that of raising a revenue and necessary to expenditures under every grant. By it, as already observed, no new power will be taken from the States, the money to be appropriated being raised under a power already granted to Congress. By it, too, the motive for giving a forced or strained construction to any of the other specific grants will in most instances be diminished and in many utterly destroyed. The importance of this consideration can not be too highly estimated, since, in addition to the examples already given, it ought particularly to be recollected that to whatever extent any specified power may be carried the right of jurisdiction goes with it, pursuing it through all its incidents. The very important agency which this grant has in carrying into effect every other grant is a wrong argument in favor of the construction contended for. All the other grants are limited by the nature of the offices which they have severally to perform, each conveying a power to do a certain thing, and that only, whereas this is coextensive with the great scheme of the Government itself. It is the lever which raises and puts the whole machinery in motion and continues the movement. Should either of the other grants fail in consequence of any condition or limitation attached to it or misconstruction of its powers, much injury might follow, but still it would be the failure of one branch of power, of one item in the system only. All the others might move on. But should the right to raise and appropriate the public money be improperly restricted, the whole system might be sensibly affected, if not disorganized. Each of the other grants is limited by the nature of the grant itself; this, by the nature of the Government only. Hence it became necessary that, like the power to declare war, this power should be commensurate with the great scheme of the Government and with all its purposes.

If, then, the right to raise and appropriate the public money is not restricted to the expenditures under the other specific grants according to a strict construction of their powers, respectively, is there no limitation to it? Have Congress a right to raise and appropriate the money to any and to every purpose according to their will and pleasure? They certainly have not. The Government of the United States is a limited Government, instituted for great national purposes, and for those only. Other interests are committed to the States, whose duty it is to provide for them. Each government should look to the great and essential purposes for which it was instituted and confine itself to those purposes. A State government will rarely if ever apply money to national purposes without making it a charge to the nation. The people of the State would not permit it. Nor will Congress be apt to apply money in aid of the State administrations for purposes strictly local in which the nation at large has no interest, although the State should desire it. The people of the other States would condemn it. They would declare that Congress had no right to tax them for such a purpose, and dismiss at the next election such of their representatives as had voted for the measure, especially if it should be severely felt. I do not think that in offices of this kind there is much danger of the two Governments mistaking their interests or their duties. I rather expect that they would soon have a clear and distinct understanding of them and move on in great harmony.

Good roads and canals will promote many very important national purposes. They will facilitate the operations of war, the movements of troops, the transportation of cannon, of provisions, and every warlike store, much to our advantage and to the disadvantage of the enemy in time of war. Good roads will facilitate the transportation of the mail, and thereby promote the purposes of commerce and political intelligence among the people. They will by being properly directed to these objects enhance the value of our vacant lands, a treasure of vast resource to the nation. To the appropriation of the public money to improvements having these objects in view and carried to a certain extent I do not see any well-founded constitutional objection.

In regard to our foreign concerns, provided they are managed with integrity and ability, great liberality is allowable in the application of the public money. In the management of these concerns no State interests can be affected, no State rights violated. The complete and exclusive control over them is vested in Congress. The power to form treaties of alliance and commerce with foreign powers, to regulate by law our commerce with them, to determine on peace or war, to raise armies and a navy, to call forth the militia and direct their operations belongs to the General Government. These great powers, embracing the whole scope of our foreign relations, being granted, on what principle can it be said that the minor are withheld? Are not the latter clearly and evidently comprised in the former? Nations are sometimes called upon to perform to each other acts of humanity and kindness, of which we see so many illustrious examples between individuals in private life. Great calamities make appeals to the benevolence of mankind which ought not to be resisted. Good offices in such emergencies exalt the character of the party rendering them. By exciting grateful feelings they soften the intercourse between nations and tend to prevent war. Surely if the United States have a right to make war they have a right to prevent it. How was it possible to grant to Congress a power for such minor purposes other than in general terms, comprising it within the scope and policy of that which conveyed it for the greater?

The right of appropriation is nothing more than a right to apply the public money to this or that purpose. It has no incidental power, nor does it draw after it any consequences of that kind. All that Congress could do under it in the case of internal improvements would be to appropriate the money necessary to make them. . For every act requiring legislative sanction or support the State authority must be relied on. The condemnation of the land, if the proprietors should refuse to sell it, the establishment of turnpikes and tolls, and the protection of the work when finished must be done by the State. To these purposes the powers of the General Government are believed to be utterly incompetent.

To the objection that the United States have no power in any instance which is not complete to all the purposes to which it may be made instrumental, and in consequence that they have no right to appropriate any portion of the public money to internal improvements because they have not the right of sovereignty and jurisdiction over them when made, a full answer has, it is presumed, been already given. It may, however, be proper to add that if this objection was well founded it would not be confined to the simple case of internal improvements, but would apply to others of high importance. Congress have a right to regulate commerce. To give effect to this power it becomes necessary to establish custom-houses in every State along the coast and in many parts of the interior. The vast amount of goods imported and the duties to be performed to accommodate the merchants and secure the revenue make it necessary that spacious buildings should be erected, especially in the great towns, for their reception. This, it is manifest, could best be performed under the direction of the General Government. Have Congress the right to seize the property of individuals if they should refuse to sell it, in quarters best adapted to the purpose, to have it valued, and to take it at the valuation? Have they a right to exercise jurisdiction within those buildings? Neither of these claims has ever been set up, nor could it, as is presumed, be sustained. They have invariably either rented houses where such as were suitable could be obtained, or, where they could not, purchased the ground of individuals, erected the buildings, and held them under the laws of the State. Under the power to establish post-offices and post-roads houses are also requisite for the reception of the mails and the transaction of the business of the several offices. These have always been rented or purchased and held under the laws of the State in the same manner as if they had been taken by a citizen. The United States have a right to establish tribunals inferior to the Supreme Court, and such have been established in every State of the Union. It is believed that the houses for these inferior courts have invariably been rented. No right of jurisdiction in them has ever been claimed, nor other right than that of privilege, and that only while the court is in session. A still stronger case may be urged. Should Congress be compelled by invasion or other cause to remove the Government to some town within one of the States, would they have a right of jurisdiction over such town, or hold even the house in which they held their session under other authority than the laws of such State? It is believed that they would not. If they have a right to appropriate money for any of these purposes, to be laid out under the protection of the laws of the State, surely they have an equal right to do it for the purposes of internal improvements.

It is believed that there is not a corporation in the Union which does not exercise great discretion in the application of the money raised by it to the purposes of its institution. It would be strange if the Government of the United States, which was instituted for such important purposes and endowed with such extensive powers, should not be allowed at least equal discretion and authority. The evil to be particularly avoided is the violation of State rights. Shunning that, it seems to be reasonable and proper that the powers of Congress should be so construed as that the General Government in its intercourse with other nations and in our internal concerns should be able to adopt all such measures lying within the fair scope and intended to facilitate the direct objects of its powers as the public welfare may require and a sound and provident policy dictate.

The measures of Congress have been in strict accord with the view taken of the right of appropriation both as to its extent and limitation, as will be shown by a reference to the laws, commencing at a very early period. Many roads have been opened, of which the following are the principal: The first from Cumberland, at the head waters of the Potomac, in the State of Maryland, through Pennsylvania and Virginia, to the State of Ohio (March 29, 1806; see vol. 4, p. 13, of the late edition of the laws). The second from the frontiers of Georgia, on the route from Athens to New Orleans, to its intersection with the thirty-first degree of north latitude (April 31, 1806, p. 58). The third from the Mississippi at a point and by a route described to the Ohio (same act). The fourth from Nashville, in Tennessee, to Natchez (same act). The fifth from the thirty-first degree of north latitude, on the route from Athens to New Orleans, under such regulations as might be agreed on between the Executive and the Spanish Government (March 3, 1807, p. 117). The sixth from the foot of the rapids of the river Miami, of Lake Erie, to the western line of the Connecticut Reserve (December 12, 1811, p. 364). The seventh from the Lower Sandusky to the boundary line established by the treaty of Greenville (same act). The eighth from a point where the United States road leading from Vincennes to the Indian boundary line, established by the treaty of Greenville, strikes the said line, to the North Bend, in the State of Ohio (January 8, 1812, p. 367). The ninth for repairing and keeping in repair the road between Columbia, on Duck River, in Tennessee, and Madisonville, in Louisiana, and also the road between Fort Hawkins, in Georgia, and Fort Stoddard (April 27, 1816, p. 104 of the acts of that year). The tenth from the Shawneetown, on the Ohio River, to the Sabine, and to Kaskaskias, in Illinois (April 27, 1816, p. 112). The eleventh from Reynoldsburg, on Tennessee River, in the State of Tennessee, through the Chickasaw Nation, to intersect the Natchez road near the Chickasaw old town (March 3, 1817, p. 252). The twelfth: By this act authority was given to the President to appoint three commissioners for the purpose of examining the country and laying out a road from the termination of the Cumberland road, at Wheeling, on the Ohio, through the States of Ohio, Indiana, and Illinois, to a point to be chosen by them, on the left bank of the Mississippi, between St. Louis and the mouth of the Illinois River, and to report an accurate plan of the said road, with an estimate of the expense of making it. It is, however, declared by the act that nothing was thereby intended to imply an obligation on the part of the United States to make or defray the expense of making the said road or any part thereof.

In the late war two other roads were made by the troops for military purposes—one from the Upper Sandusky, in the State of Ohio, through the Black Swamp, toward Detroit, and another from Plattsburg, on Lake Champlain, through the Chatauga woods toward Sacketts Harbor, which have since been repaired and improved by the troops. Of these latter there is no notice in the laws. The extra pay to the soldiers for repairing and improving those roads was advanced in the first instance from the appropriation to the Quartermaster's Department and afterwards provided for by a specific appropriation by Congress. The necessity of keeping those roads open and in good repair, being on the frontier, to facilitate a communication between our posts, is apparent.

All of these roads except the first were formed merely by cutting down the trees and throwing logs across, so as to make causeways over such parts as were otherwise impassable. The execution was of the coarsest kind. The Cumberland road is the only regular work which has been undertaken by the General Government or which could give rise to any question between the two Governments respecting its powers. It is a great work, over the highest mountains in our Union, connecting from the seat of the General Government the Eastern with the Western waters, and more intimately the Atlantic with the Western States, in the formation of which $1,800,000 have been expended. The measures pursued in this case require to be particularly noticed as fixing the opinion of the parties, and particularly of Congress, on the important question of the right. Passing through Maryland, Pennsylvania, and Virginia, it was thought necessary and proper to bring the subject before their respective legislatures to obtain their sanction, which was granted by each State by a legislative act, approving the route and providing for the purchase and condemnation of the land. This road was founded on an article of compact between the United States and the State of Ohio, under which that State came into the Union, and by which the expense attending it was to be defrayed by the application of a certain portion of the money arising from the sale of the public lands within that State. In this instance, which is by far the strongest in respect to the expense, extent, and nature of the work done, the United States have exercised no act of jurisdiction or sovereignty within either of the States by taking the land from the proprietors by force, by passing acts for the protection of the road, or to raise a revenue from it by the establishment of turnpikes and tolls, or any other act founded on the principle of jurisdiction or right. Whatever they have done has, on the contrary, been founded on the opposite principle, on the voluntary and unqualified admission that the sovereignty belonged to the State and not to the United States, and that they could perform no act which should tend to weaken the power of the State or to assume any to themselves. All that they have done has been to appropriate the public money to the construction of this road and to cause it to be constructed, for I presume that no distinction can be taken between the appropriation of money raised by the sale of the public lands and of that which arises from taxes, duties, imposts, and excises; nor can I believe that the power to appropriate derives any sanction from a provision to that effect having been made by an article of compact between the United States and the people of the then Territory of Ohio. This point may, however, be placed in a clearer light by a more particular notice of the article itself.

By an act of April 30, 1802, entitled "An act to enable the people of the eastern division of the territory northwest of the river Ohio to form a constitution and State government, and for the admission of such State into the Union on an equal footing with the original States, and for other purposes," after describing the limits of the proposed new State and authorizing the people thereof to elect a convention to form a constitution, the three following propositions were made to the convention, to be obligatory on the United States if accepted by it: First, that section No. 16 of every township, or, where such section had been sold, other lands equivalent thereto, should be granted to the inhabitants of such township for the use of free schools. Second, that the 6 miles' reservation, including the salt springs commonly called the Sciota Salt Springs, the salt springs near the Muskingum River and in the military tract, with the sections which include the same, should be granted to the said State for the use of the people thereof, under such regulations as the legislature of the State should prescribe: *Provided*, That it should never sell or lease the same for more than ten years. Third, that one-twentieth part of the proceeds of the public lands lying within the said State which might be sold by Congress from and after the 30th June ensuing should be applied to the laying out and making public roads from the navigable waters emptying into the Atlantic, to the Ohio, and through the State of Ohio, such roads to be laid out under the authority of Congress, with the consent of the several States through which they should pass.

These three propositions were made on the condition that the convention of the State should provide by an ordinance, irrevocable without the consent of the United

States, that every tract of land sold by Congress after the 30th of June ensuing should remain for the term of five years after sale exempt from every species of tax whatsoever.

It is impossible to read the ordinance of the 23d of April, 1784, or the provisions of the act of April 30, 1802, which are founded on it, without being profoundly impressed with the enlightened and magnanimous policy which dictated them. Anticipating that the new States would be settled by the inhabitants of the original States and their offspring, no narrow or contracted jealousy was entertained of their admission into the Union in equal participation in the national sovereignty with the original States. It was foreseen at the early period at which that ordinance passed that the expansion of our Union to the Lakes and to the Mississippi and all its waters would not only make us a greater power, but cement the Union itself. These three propositions were well calculated to promote these great results. A grant of land to each township for free schools, and of the salt springs to the State, which were within its limits, for the use of its citizens, with 5 per cent of the money to be raised from the sale of lands within the State for the construction of roads between the original States and the new State, and of other roads within the State, indicated a spirit not to be mistaken, nor could it fail to produce a corresponding effect in the bosoms of those to whom it was addressed. For these considerations the sole return required of the convention was that the new State should not tax the public lands which might be sold by the United States within it for the term of five years after they should be sold. As the value of these lands would be enhanced by this exemption from taxes for that term, and from which the new State would derive its proportionable benefit, and as it would also promote the rapid sale of those lands, and with it the augmentation of its own population, it can not be doubted, had this exemption been suggested unaccompanied by any propositions of particular advantage, that the convention would, in consideration of the relation which had before existed between the parties, and was about to be so much improved, most willingly have acceded to it and without regarding it as an onerous condition.

Since, then, it appears that the whole of the money to be employed in making this road was to be raised from the sale of the public lands, and which would still belong to the United States, although no mention had been made of them in the compact, it follows that the application of the money to that purpose stands upon the same ground as if such compact had not been made, and in consequence that the example in favor of the right of appropriation is in no manner affected by it.

The same rule of construction of the right of appropriation has been observed and the same liberal policy pursued toward the other new States, with certain modifications adapted to the situation of each, which were adopted with the State of Ohio. As, however, the reasoning which is applicable to the compact with Ohio in relation to the right of appropriation, in which light only I have adverted to it, is equally applicable to the several compacts with the other new States, I deem it unnecessary to take a particular notice of them.

It is proper to observe that the money which was employed in the construction of all the other roads was taken directly from the Treasury. This fact affords an additional proof that in the contemplation of Congress no difference existed in the application of money to those roads between that which was raised by the sale of lands and that which was derived from taxes, duties, imposts, and excises.

So far I have confined my remarks to the acts of Congress respecting the right of appropriation to such measures only as operate internally and affect the territory of the individual States. In adverting to those which operate externally and relate to foreign powers I find only two which appear to merit particular attention. These were gratuitous grants of money for the relief of foreigners in distress—the first in 1794 to the inhabitants of St. Domingo, who sought an asylum on our coast from the convulsions and calamities of the island; the second in 1812 to the people of

Caracas, reduced to misery by an earthquake. The considerations which were applicable to these grants have already been noticed and need not be repeated.

In this examination of the right of appropriation I thought it proper to present to view also the practice of the Government under it, and to explore the ground on which each example rested, that the precise nature and extent of the construction thereby given of the right might be clearly understood. The right to raise money would have given, as is presumed, the right to use it, although nothing had been said to that effect in the Constitution; and where the right to raise it is granted without special limitation, we must look for such limitation to other causes. Our attention is first drawn to the right to appropriate, and not finding it there we must then look to the general powers of the Government as designated by the specific grants and to the purposes contemplated by them, allowing to this (the right to raise money), the first and most important of the enumerated powers, a scope which will be competent to those purposes. The practice of the Government, as illustrated by numerous and strong examples directly applicable, ought surely to have great weight in fixing the construction of each grant. It ought, I presume, to settle it, especially where it is acquiesced in by the nation and produces a manifest and positive good. A practical construction, thus supported, shows that it has reason on its side and is called for by the interests of the Union. Hence, too, the presumption that it will be persevered in. It will surely be better to admit that the construction given by these examples has been just and proper than to deny that construction and still to practice on it—to say one thing and to do another.

Wherein consists the danger of giving a liberal construction to the right of Congress to raise and appropriate the public money? It has been shown that its obvious effect is to secure the rights of the States from encroachment and greater harmony in the political movement between the two governments, while it enlarges to a certain extent in the most harmless way the useful agency of the General Government for all the purposes of its institution. Is not the responsibility of the representative to his constituent in every branch of the General Government equally strong and as sensibly felt as in the State governments, and is not the security against abuse as effectual in the one as in the other government? The history of the General Government in all its measures fully demonstrates that Congress will never venture to impose unnecessary burdens on the people or any that can be avoided. Duties and imposts have always been light, not greater, perhaps, than would have been imposed for the encouragement of our manufactures had there been no occasion for the revenue arising from them; and taxes and excises have never been laid except in cases of necessity, and repealed as soon as the necessity ceased. Under this mild process and the sale of some hundreds of millions of acres of good land the Government will be possessed of money, which may be applied with great advantage to national purposes. Within the States only will it be applied, and, of course, for their benefit, it not being presumable that such appeals as were made to the benevolence of the country in the instances of the inhabitants of St. Domingo and Caracas will often occur. How, then, shall this revenue be applied? Should it be idle in the Treasury? That our resources will be equal to such useful purposes I have no doubt, especially if by completing our fortifications and raising and maintaining our Navy at the point provided for immediately after the war we sustain our present altitude and preserve by means thereof for any length of time the peace of the Union.

When we hear charges raised against other governments of breaches of their constitutions, or, rather, of their charters, we always anticipate the most serious consequences—communities deprived of privileges which they have long enjoyed, or individuals oppressed and punished in violation of the ordinary forms and guards of trial to which they were accustomed and entitled. How different is the situation of the United States! Nor can anything mark more strongly the great characteristics of that difference than the grounds on which like charges are raised against this Government. It is not alleged that any portion of the community or any individual has been oppressed or that money has been raised under a doubtful title. The principal charges are that a work of great utility to the Union and affecting immediately and with like advantage many of the States has been constructed; that pensions to the surviving patriots of our Revolution, to patriots who fought the battles and promoted the independence of their country, have been granted, by money, too, raised not only without oppression, but almost without being felt, and under an acknowledged constitutional power.

From this view of the right to appropriate and of the practice under it I think that I am authorized to conclude that the right to make internal improvements has not been granted by the power "to pay the debts and provide for the common defense and general welfare," included in the first of the enumerated powers; that that grant conveys nothing more than a right to appropriate the public money, and stands on the same ground with the right to lay and collect taxes, duties, imposts, and excises, conveyed by the first branch of that power; that the Government itself being limited, both branches of the power to raise and appropriate the public money are also limited, the extent of the Government as designated by the specific grants marking the extent of the power in both branches, extending, however, to every object embraced by the fair scope of those grants and not confined to a strict construction of their respective powers, it being safer to aid the purposes of those grants by the appropriation of money than to extend by a forced construction the grant itself; that although the right to appropriate the public money to such improvements affords a resource indispensably necessary to such a scheme, it is nevertheless deficient as a power in the great characteristics on which its execution depends.

The substance of what has been urged on this subject may be expressed in a few words. My idea is that Congress have an unlimited power to raise money, and that in its appropriation they have a discretionary power, restricted only by the duty to appropriate it to purposes of common defense and of general, not local, national, not State, benefit.

I will now proceed to the fifth source from which the power is said to be derived, viz, the power to make all laws which shall be necessary and proper for carrying into execution all the powers vested by the Constitution in the Government of the United States or in any department or officer thereof. This is the seventeenth and last of the enumerated powers granted to Congress.

I have always considered this power as having been granted on a principle of greater caution to secure the complete execution of all the powers which had been vested in the General Government. It contains no distinct and specific power, as every other grant does, such as to lay and collect taxes, to declare war, to regulate commerce, and the like. Looking to the whole scheme of the General Government, it gives to Congress authority to make all laws which should be deemed necessary and proper for carrying all its powers into effect. My impression has been invariably that this power would have existed substantially if this grant had not been made; for why is any power granted unless it be to be executed when required, and how can it be executed under our Government unless it be by laws necessary and proper for the purpose—that is, well adapted to the end? It is a principle universally admitted that a grant of a power conveys as a necessary consequence or incident to it the means of carrying it into effect by a fair construction of its import. In the formation, however, of the Constitution, which was to act directly upon the people and be paramount to the extent of its powers to the constitutions of the States, it was wise in its framers to leave nothing to implication which might be reduced to certainty. It is known that all power which rests solely on that ground has been systematically and zealously opposed under all governments with which we have any acquaintance; and it was reasonable to presume that under our system, where there was a division of the sovereignty between the two independent governments, the measures of the General Government would excite equal jealousy and produce an opposition not less systematic, though, perhaps, less violent. Hence the policy by the framers of our Government of securing by a fundamental declaration in the Constitution a principle which in all other governments had been left to implication only. The terms "necessary" and "proper" secure to the powers of all the grants to which the authority given in this is applicable a fair and sound construction, which is equally binding as a rule on both Governments and on all their departments.

In examining the right of the General Government to adopt and execute under this grant a system of internal improvement the sole question to be decided is whether the power has been granted under any of the other grants. If it has, this power is applicable to it to the extent stated. If it has not, it does not exist at all, for it has not been hereby granted. I have already examined all the other grants (one only excepted, which will next claim attention) and shown, as I presume, on the most liberal construction of their powers that the right has not been granted by any of them; hence it follows that in regard to them it has not been granted by this.

I come now to the last source from which this power is said to be derived, viz, the power to dispose of and make all needful rules and regulations respecting the territory or other property of the United States, which is contained in the second clause of the third section of the fourth article of the Constitution.

To form a just opinion of the nature and extent of this power it will be necessary to bring into view the provisions contained in the first clause of the section of the article referred to, which makes an essential part of the policy in question. By this it is declared that new States shall be admitted into the Union, but that no new States shall be formed or erected within the jurisdiction of any other State, nor any States be formed by the junction of two or more States or parts of States, without the consent of the legislatures of the States concerned as well as of the United States.

If we recur to the condition of our country at the commencement of the Revolution, we shall see the origin and cause of these provisions. By the charters of the several colonies limits by latitude and other descriptions were assigned to each. In commencing the Revolution the colonies, as has already been observed, claimed by those limits, although their population extended in many instances to a small portion of the territory lying within them. It was contended by some of the States after the declaration of independence that the vacant lands lying within any of the States should become the property of the Union, as by a common exertion they would be acquired. This claim was resisted by the others on the principle that all the States entered into the contest in the full extent of their chartered rights, and that they ought to have the full benefit of those rights in the event of success. Happily this controversy was settled, as all interfering claims and pretensions between the members of our Union and between the General Government and any of these members have been, in the most amicable manner and to the satisfaction of all parties. On the recommendation of Congress the individual States having such territory within their chartered limits ceded large portions thereof to the United States on condition that it should be laid off into districts of proper dimensions, the lands to be sold for the benefit of the United States, and that the districts be admitted into the Union when they should obtain such a population as it might be thought proper and reasonable to prescribe. This is the territory and this the property referred to in the second clause of the fourth article of the Constitution.

All the States which had made cessions of vacant territory except Georgia had made them before the adoption of the Constitution, and that State had made a proposition to Congress to that effect which was under consideration at the time the Constitution was adopted. The cession was completed after the adoption of the Constitution. It was made on the same principle and on similar conditions with those which had been already made by the other States. As differences might arise respecting the right or the policy in Congress to admit new States into the Union under the new Government, or to make regulations for the government of the territory ceded in the intermediate state, or for the improvement and sale of the public lands, or to accept other cessions, it was thought proper to make special provisions for these objects, which was accordingly done by the above-recited clause in the Constitution.

Thus the power of Congress over the ceded territory was not only limited to these special objects, but was also temporary. As soon as the territory became a State the jurisdiction over it as it had before existed ceased. It extended afterwards only to the unsold lands, and as soon as the whole were sold it ceased in that sense also altogether. From that moment the United States have no jurisdiction or power in the new States other than in the old, nor can it be obtained except by an amendment of the Constitution.

Since, then, it is manifest that the power granted to Congress to dispose of and make all needful regulations respecting the territory and other property of the United States relates solely to the territory and property which had been ceded by individual States, and which after such cession lay without their respective limits, and for which special provision was deemed necessary, the main power of the Constitution operating internally, not being applicable or adequate thereto, it follows that this power gives no authority, and has even no bearing on the question of internal improvement. The authority to admit new States and to dispose of the property and regulate the territory is not among the enumerated powers granted to Congress, because the duties to be performed under it are not among the ordinary duties of that body, like the imposition of taxes, the regulation of commerce, and the like. They are objects in their nature special, and for which special provision was more suitable and proper.

Having now examined all the powers of Congress under which the right to adopt and execute a system of internal improvement is claimed and the reasons in support of it in each instance, I think that it may fairly be concluded that such a right has not been granted. It appears and is admitted that much may be done in aid of such a system by the right which is derived from several of the existing grants, and more especially from that to appropriate the public money. But still it is manifest that as a system for the United States it can never be carried into effect under that grant nor under all of them united, the great and essential power being deficient, consisting of a right to take up the subject on principle; to cause our Union to be examined by men of science, with a view to such improvements; to authorize commissioners to lay off the roads and canals in all proper directions; to take the land at a valuation if necessary, and to construct the works; to pass laws with suitable penalties for their protection; and to raise a revenue from them, to keep them in repair, and make further improvement by the establishment of turnpikes and tolls, with gates to be placed at the proper distances.

It need scarcely be remarked that this power will operate, like many others now existing, without affecting the sovereignty of the States except in the particular offices to be performed. The jurisdiction of the several States may still exist over the roads and canals within their respective limits, extending alike to persons and property, as if the right to make and protect such improvements had not been vested in Congress. The right, being made commensurate simply with the purposes indispensable to the system, may be strictly confined to them. The right of Congress to protect the works by laws imposing penalties would operate on the same principles as the right to protect the mail. The act being punishable only, a jurisdiction over the place would be altogether unnecessary and even absurd.

In the preceding inquiry little has been said of the advantages which would attend the exercise of such a power by the General Government. I have made the inquiry under a deep conviction that they are almost incalculable, and that there was a general concurrence of opinion among our fellow-citizens to that effect. Still, it may not be improper for me to state the grounds upon which my own impression is founded. If it sheds no additional light on this interesting part of the subject, it will at least show that I have had more than one powerful motive for making the inquiry. A general idea is all that I shall attempt.

The advantages of such a system must depend upon the interests to be affected by it and the extent to which they may be affected, and those must depend on the capacity of our country for improvement and the means at its command applicable to that object.

I think that I may venture to affirm that there is no part of our globe comprehending so many degrees of latitude on the main ocean and so many degrees of longitude into the interior that admits of such great improvement and at so little expense. The Atlantic on the one side, and the Lakes, forming almost inland seas, on the other, separated by high mountains, which rise in the valley of the St. Lawrence and determine in that of the Mississippi, traversing from north to south almost the whole interior, with innumerable rivers on every side of those mountains, some of vast extent, many of which take their sources near to each other, give the great outline. The details are to be seen on the valuable maps of our country.

It appears by the light already before the public that it is practicable and easy to connect by canals the whole coast from its southern to its northern extremity in one continued inland navigation, and to connect in like manner in many parts the Western lakes and rivers with each other. It is equally practicable and easy to facilitate the intercourse between the Atlantic and the Western country by improving the navigation of many of the rivers which have their sources near to each other in the mountains on each side, and by good roads across the mountains between the highest navigable points of those rivers. In addition to the example of the Cumberland road, already noticed, another of this kind is now in train from the head waters of the river James to those of the Kanawha; and in like manner may the Savannah be connected with the Tennessee. In some instances it is understood that the Eastern and Western waters may be connected together directly by canals. One great work of this kind is now in its progress and far advanced in the State of New York, and there is good reason to believe that two others may be formed, one at each extremity of the high mountains above mentioned, connecting in the one instance the waters of the St. Lawrence with Lake Champlain, and in the other some of the most important of the Western rivers with those emptying into the Gulf of Mexico, the advantage of which will be seen at the first glance by an enlightened observer.

Great improvements may also be made by good roads in proper directions through the interior of the country. As these roads would be laid out on principle on a full view of the country, its mountains, rivers, etc., it would be useless, if I had the knowledge, to go into detail respecting them. Much has been done by some of the States, but yet much remains to be done with a view to the Union.

Under the colonial governments improvements of this kind were not thought of. There was, it is believed, not one canal and little communication from colony to colony. It was their policy to encourage the intercourse between each colony and the parent country only. The roads which were attended to were those which led from the interior of each colony to its principal towns on the navigable waters. By those routes the produce of the country was carried to the coast, and shipped thence to the mercantile houses in London, Liverpool, Glasgow, or other towns to which the trade was carried on. It is believed that there was but one connected route from North to South at the commencement of the Revolution, and that a very imperfect one. The existence and principle of our Union point out the necessity of a very different policy.

The advantages which would be derived from such improvements are incalculable. The facility which would thereby be afforded to the transportation of the whole of the rich productions of our country to market would alone more than amply compensate for all the labor and expense attending them. Great, however, as is that advantage, it is one only of many and by no means the most important. Every power of the General Government and of the State governments connected with the strength and resources of the country would be made more efficient for the purposes intended by them. In war they would facilitate the transportation of men, ordnance, and provisions, and munitions of war of every kind to every part of our extensive coast and interior on which an attack might be made or threatened. Those who have any knowledge of the occurrences of the late war must know the good effect which would result in the event of another war from the command of an interior navigation alone along the coast for all the purposes of war as well as of commerce between the different parts of our Union. The impediments to all military operations which proceeded from the want of such a navigation and the reliance which was placed, notwithstanding those impediments, on such a commerce can not be forgotten. In every other line their good effect would be most sensibly felt. Intelligence by means of the Post-Office Department would be more easily, extensively, and rapidly diffused. Parts the most remote from each other would be brought more closely together. Distant lands would be made more valuable, and the industry of our fellow-citizens on every portion of our soil be better rewarded.

It is natural in so great a variety of climate that there should be a corresponding difference in the produce of the soil; that one part should raise what the other might want. It is equally natural that the pursuits of industry should vary in like manner; that labor should be cheaper and manufactures succeed better in one part than in another; that were the climate the most severe and the soil less productive, navigation, the fisheries, and commerce should be most relied on. Hence the motive for an exchange for mutual accommodation and active intercourse between them. Each part would thus find for the surplus of its labor, in whatever article it consisted, an extensive market at home, which would be the most profitable because free from duty.

There is another view in which these improvements are of still more vital importance. The effect which they would have on the bond of union itself affords an inducement for them more powerful than any which have been urged or than all of them united. The only danger to which our system is exposed arises from its expansion over a vast territory. Our union is not held together by standing armies or by any ties other than the positive interests and powerful attractions of its parts toward each other. Ambitious men may hereafter grow up among us who may promise to themselves advancement from a change, and by practicing upon the sectional interests, feelings, and prejudices endeavor under various pretexts to promote it. The history of the world is replete with examples of this kind—of military commanders and demagogues becoming usurpers and tyrants, and of their fellow-citizens becoming their instruments and slaves. I have little fear of this danger, knowing well how strong the bond which holds us together is and who the people are who are thus held together; but still, it is proper to look at and to provide against it, and it is not within the compass of human wisdom to make a more effectual provision than would be made by the proposed improvements. With their aid and the intercourse which would grow out of them the parts would soon become so compacted and bound together that nothing could break it.

The expansion of our Union over a vast territory can not operate unfavorably to the States individually. On the contrary, it is believed that the greater the expansion within practicable limits—and it is not easy to say what are not so—the greater the advantage which the States individually will derive from it. With governments separate, vigorous, and efficient for all local purposes, their distance from each other can have no injurious effect upon their respective interests. It has already been shown that in some important circumstances, especially with the aid of these improvements, they must derive great advantage from that cause alone—that is, from their distance from each other. In every other way the expansion of our system must operate favorably for every State in proportion as it operates favorably for the

Union. It is in that sense only that it can become a question with the States, or, rather, with the people who compose them. As States they can be affected by it only by their relation to each other through the General Government and by its effect on the operations of that Government. Manifest it is that to any extent to which the General Government can sustain and execute its functions with complete effect will the States—that is, the people who compose them—be benefited. It is only when the expansion shall be carried beyond the faculties of the General Government so as to enfeeble its operations to the injury of the whole that any of the parts can be injured. The tendency in that stage will be to dismemberment and not to consolidation. This danger should, therefore, be looked at with profound attention as one of a very serious character. I will remark here that as the operations of the National Government are of a general nature, the States having complete power for internal and local purposes, the expansion may be carried to very great extent and with perfect safety. It must be obvious to all that the further the expansion is carried, provided it be not beyond the just limit, the greater will be the freedom of action to both Governments and the more perfect their security, and in all other respects the better the effect will be to the whole American people. Extent of territory, whether it be great or small, gives to a nation many of its characteristics. It marks the extent of its resources, of its population, of its physical force. It marks, in short, the difference between a great and a small power.

To what extent it may be proper to expand our system of government is a question which does not press for a decision at this time. At the end of the Revolutionary war, in 1783, we had, as we contended and believed, a right to the free navigation of the Mississippi, but it was not until after the expiration of twelve years, in 1795, that that right was acknowledged and enjoyed. Further difficulties occurred in the bustling of a contentious world when, at the expiration of eight years more, the United States, sustaining the strength and energy of their character, acquired the Province of Louisiana, with the free navigation of the river from its source to the ocean and a liberal boundary on the western side. To this Florida has since been added, so that we now possess all the territory in which the original States had any interest, or in which the existing States can be said, either in a national or local point of view, to be in any way interested. A range of States on the western side of the Mississippi, which already is provided for, puts us essentially at ease. Whether it will be wise to go further will turn on other considerations than those which have dictated the course heretofore pursued. At whatever point we may stop, whether it be at a single range of States beyond the Mississippi or by taking a greater scope, the advantage of such improvements is deemed of the highest importance. It is so on the present scale. The further we go the greater will be the necessity for them.

It can not be doubted that improvements for great national purposes would be better made by the National Government than by the governments of the several States. Our experience prior to the adoption of the Constitution demonstrated that in the exercise by the individual States of most of the powers granted to the United States a contracted rivalry of interest and misapplied jealousy of each other had an important influence on all their measures to the great injury of the whole. This was particularly exemplified by the regulations which they severally made of their commerce with foreign nations and with each other. It was this utter incapacity in the State governments, proceeding from these and other causes, to act as a nation and to perform all the duties which the nation owed to itself under any system which left the General Government dependent on the States, which produced the transfer of these powers to the United States by the establishment of the present Constitution. The reasoning which was applicable to the grant of any of the powers now vested in Congress is likewise so, at least to a certain extent, to that in question. It is natural that the States individually in making improvements should look to their particular and local interests. The members composing their respective legislatures represent the people of each State only, and might not feel themselves at liberty to look to objects in these respects beyond that limit. If the resources of the Union were to be brought into operation under the direction of the State assemblies, or in concert with them, it may be apprehended that every measure would become the object of negotiation, of bargain and barter, much to the disadvantage of the system, as well as discredit to both governments. But Congress would look to the whole and make improvements to promote the welfare of the whole. It is the peculiar felicity of the proposed amendment that while it will enable the United States to accomplish every national object, the improvements made with that view will eminently promote the welfare of the individual States, who may also add such others as their own particular interests may require.

The situation of the Cumberland road requires the particular and early attention of Congress. Being formed over very lofty mountains and in many instances over deep and wide streams, across which valuable bridges have been erected, which are sustained by stone walls, as are many other parts of the road, all these works are subject to decay, have decayed, and will decay rapidly unless timely and effectual measures are adopted to prevent it.

The declivities from the mountains and all the heights must suffer from the frequent and heavy falls of water and its descent to the valleys, as also from the deep congelations during our severe winters. Other injuries have also been experienced on this road, such as the displacing the capping of the walls and other works, committed by worthless people either from a desire to render the road impassable or to have the transportation in another direction, or from a spirit of wantonness to create employment for idlers. These considerations show that an active and strict police ought to be established over the whole road, with power to make repairs when necessary, to establish turnpikes and tolls as the means of raising money to make them, and to prosecute and punish those who commit waste and other injuries.

Should the United States be willing to abandon this road to the States through which it passes, would they take charge of it, each of that portion within its limits, and keep it in repair? It is not to be presumed that they would, since the advantages attending it are exclusively national, by connecting, as it does, the Atlantic with the Western States, and in a line with the seat of the National Government. The most expensive parts of this road lie within Pennsylvania and Virginia, very near the confines of each State and in a route not essentially connected with the commerce of either.

If it is thought proper to vest this power in the United States, the only mode in which it can be done is by an amendment of the Constitution. The States individually can not transfer the power to the United States, nor can the United States receive it. The Constitution forms an equal and the sole relation between the General Government and the several States, and it recognizes no change in it which shall not in like manner apply to all. If it is once admitted that the General Government may form compacts with individual States not common to the others, and which the others might even disapprove, into what pernicious consequences might it not lead? Such compacts are utterly repugnant to the principles of the Constitution and of the most dangerous tendency. The States through which this road passes have given their sanction only to the route and to the acquisition of the soil by the United States, a right very different from that of jurisdiction, which can not be granted without an amendment to the Constitution, and which need not be granted for the purposes of this system except in the limited manner heretofore stated. On full consideration, therefore, of the whole subject I am of opinion that such an amendment ought to be recommended to the several States for their adoption.

I have now essentially executed that part of the task which I imposed on myself of examining the right of Congress to adopt and execute a system of internal improvement, and, I presume, have shown that it does not exist. It is, I think, equally manifest that such a power vested in Congress and wisely executed would have the happiest effect on all the great interests of our Union. It is, however, my opinion that the power should be confined to great national works only, since if it were unlimited it would be liable to abuse and might be productive of evil. For all minor improvements the resources of the States individually would be fully adequate, and by the States such improvements might be made with greater advantage than by the Union, as they would understand better such as their more immediate and local interests required.

In the view above presented I have thought it proper to trace the origin of our institutions, and particularly of the State and National Governments, for although they have a common origin in the people, yet, as the point at issue turned on what were the powers granted to the one government and what were those which remained to the other, I was persuaded that an analysis which should mark distinctly the source of power in both governments, with its progress in each, would afford the best means for obtaining a sound result. In our political career there are, obviously, three great epochs. The colonial state forms the first; the Revolutionary movement from its commencement to the adoption of the Articles of Confederation the second, and the intervening space from that event to the present day the third. The first may be considered the infant state. It was the school of morality, of political science and just principles. The equality of rights enjoyed by the people of every colony under their original charters forms the basis of every existing institution, and it was owing to the creation by those charters of distinct communities that the power, when wrested from the Crown, passed directly and exclusively to the people of each colony. The Revolutionary struggle gave activity to those principles, and its success secured to them a permanent existence in the governments of our Union, State and National. The third epoch comprises the administration under the Articles of Confederation, with the adoption of the Constitution and administration under it. On the first and last of these epochs it is not necessary to enlarge for any purpose connected with the object of this inquiry. To the second, in which we were transferred by a heroic exertion from the first to the third stage, and whose events give the true character to every institution, some further attention is due. In tracing in greater detail the prominent acts of a movement to which we owe so much I shall perform an office which, if not useful, will be gratifying to my own feelings, and I hope not unacceptable to my readers.

Of the Revolutionary movement itself sentiments too respectful, too exalted, can not be entertained. It is impossible for any citizen having a just idea of the dangers which we had to encounter to read the record of our early proceedings and to see the firmness with which they were met and the wisdom and patriotism which were displayed in every stage without being deeply affected by it. An attack on Massachusetts was considered an attack on every colony, and the people of each moved in her defense as in their own cause. The meeting of the General Congress in Philadelphia on the 6th of September, 1774, appears to have been the result of a spontaneous impulse in every quarter at the same time. The first public act proposing it, according to the Journals of the First Congress, was passed by the house of representatives of Connecticut on the 3d of June of that year; but it is presumed that the first suggestion came from Massachusetts, the colony most oppressed, and in whose favor the general sympathy was much excited. The exposition which that Congress made of grievances, in the petition to the King, in the address to the people of Great Britain, and in that to the people of the several colonies, evinced a knowledge so profound of the English constitution and of the general principles of free government and of liberty, of our rights founded on that constitution and on the charters of the several colonies, and of the numerous and egregious violations which had been committed of them, as must have convinced all impartial minds that the talent on this side of the Atlantic was at least equal to that on the other. The spirit in which those papers were drawn, which was known to be in strict accord with the public sentiment, proved that, although the whole people cherished a connection with the parent country and were desirous of preserving it on just principles, they nevertheless stood embodied at the parting line, ready to separate forever if a redress of grievances, the alternative offered, was not promptly rendered. That alternative was rejected, and in consequence war and dismemberment followed.

The powers granted to the delegates of each colony who composed the First Congress looked primarily to the support of rights and to a redress of grievances, and, in consequence, to the restoration of harmony, which was ardently desired. They justified, however, any extremity in case of necessity. They were ample for such purposes, and were executed in every circumstance with the utmost fidelity. It was not until after the meeting of the Second Congress, which took place on the 10th May, 1775, when full proof was laid before it of the commencement of hostilities in the preceding month by a deliberate attack of the British troops on the militia and inhabitants of Lexington and Concord, in Massachusetts, that war might be said to be decided on, and measures were taken to support it. The progress even then was slow and reluctant, as will be seen by their second petition to the King and their second address to the people of Great Britain, which were prepared and forwarded after that event. The arrival, however, of large bodies of troops and the pressure of war in every direction soon dispelled all hope of accommodation.

On the 15th of June, 1775, a commander in chief of the forces raised and to be raised for the defense of American liberty was appointed by the unanimous vote of Congress, and his conduct in the discharge of the duties of that high trust, which he held through the whole of the war, has given an example to the world for talents as a military commander; for integrity, fortitude, and firmness under the severest trials; for respect to the civil authority and devotion to the rights and liberties of his country, of which neither Rome nor Greece have exhibited the equal. I saw him in my earliest youth, in the retreat through Jersey, at the head of a small band, or rather in its rear, for he was always next the enemy, and his countenance and manner made an impression on me which time can never efface. A lieutenant then in the Third Virginia Regiment, I happened to be on the rear guard at Newark, and I counted the force under his immediate command by platoons as it passed me, which amounted to less than 3,000 men. A deportment so firm, so dignified, so exalted, but yet so modest and composed, I have never seen in any other person.

On the 6th July, 1775, Congress published a declaration of the causes which compelled them to take up arms, and immediately afterwards took measures for augmenting the Army and raising a navy; for organizing the militia and providing cannon and small arms and military stores of every kind; for raising a revenue and pushing the war offensively with all the means in their power. Nothing escaped the attention of that enlightened body. The people of Canada were invited to join the Union, and a force sent into the province to favor the Revolutionary party, which, however, was not capable of affording any essential aid. The people of Ireland were addressed in terms manifesting due respect for the sufferings, the talents, and patriotism of that portion of the British Empire, and a suitable acknowledgment was made to the assembly of Jamaica for the approbation it had expressed of our cause and the part it had taken in support of it with the British Government.

On the 2d of June, 1775, the convention of Massachusetts, by a letter signed by their president, of May the 10th, stated to Congress that they labored under difficulties for the want of a regular form of government, and requested to be favored with explicit advice respecting the taking up and exercising the powers of civil government, and declaring their readiness to submit to such a general plan as the Congress might direct for the colonies, or that they would make it their great study to establish such a form of government there as should not only promote their own advantage, but the union and interest of all America. To this application an answer was given on the

9th, by which it was recommended to the convention "to write letters to the inhabitants of the several places entitled to representation in assembly, requesting them to choose such representatives, and that the assembly, when chosen, should elect councilors, and that said assembly or council should exercise the powers of government until a governor of His Majesty's appointment will consent to govern the colony according to its charter."

On the 18th October of the same year the delegates from New Hampshire laid before Congress an instruction from their convention "to use their utmost endeavors to obtain the advice and direction of Congress with respect to a method for administering justice and regulating their civil police." To this a reply was given on the 3d November, by which it was recommended to the convention "to call a full and free representation of the people, and that the representatives, if they thought it necessary, should establish such a form of government as in their judgment would best promote the happiness of the people and most effectually secure peace and good order in the Province during the continuance of the present dispute between Great Britain and the colonies."

On the 4th November it was resolved by Congress "that if the convention of South Carolina shall find it necessary to establish a form of government in that colony it be recommended to that convention to call a full and free representation of the people; and the said representatives, if they think it necessary, shall establish such a form of government as in their judgment will best promote the happiness of the people and most effectually secure peace and good order in the colony during the continuance of the present dispute between Great Britain and the colonies."

On the 4th December following a resolution passed recommending the same measure, and precisely in the same words, to the convention of Virginia.

On the 10th May, 1776, it was recommended to the respective assemblies and conventions of the united colonies, where no government sufficient to the exigencies of their affairs had been established, "to adopt such government as should, in the opinion of the representatives of the people, best conduce to the happiness and safety of their constituents in particular and America in general."

On the 7th June resolutions respecting independence were moved and seconded, which were referred to a committee of the whole on the 8th and 10th, on which latter day it was resolved to postpone a decision on the first resolution or main question until the 1st July, but that no time might be lost in case the Congress agree thereto that a committee be appointed to prepare a declaration to the effect of that resolution.

On the 11th June, 1776, Congress appointed a committee to prepare and digest a plan of confederation for the colonies. On the 12th July the committee reported a draft of articles, which were severally afterwards debated and amended until the 15th November, 1777, when they were adopted. These articles were then proposed to the legislatures of the several States, with a request that if approved by them they would authorize their delegates to ratify the same in Congress, and, which being done, to become conclusive. It was not until the 21st of March, 1781, as already observed, that they were ratified by the last State and carried into effect.

On the 4th July, 1776, independence was declared by an act which arrested the attention of the civilized world and will bear the test of time. For force and condensation of matter, strength of reason, sublimity of sentiment and expression, it is believed that no document of equal merit exists. It looked to everything, and with a reach, perspicuity, and energy of mind which seemed to be master of everything.

Thus it appears, in addition to the very important charge of managing the war, that Congress had under consideration at the same time the Declaration of Independence, the adoption of a confederation for the States, and the propriety of instituting State governments, with the nature of those governments, respecting which it had been consulted by the conventions of several of the colonies. So great a trust was never reposed before in a body thus constituted, and I am authorized to add, looking to the great result, that never were duties more ably or faithfully performed.

The distinguishing characteristic of this movement is that although the connection which had existed between the people of the several colonies before their dismemberment from the parent country was not only not dissolved but increased by that event, even before the adoption of the Articles of Confederation, yet the preservation and augmentation of that tie were the result of a new creation, and proceeded altogether from the people of each colony, into whose hands the whole power passed exclusively when wrested from the Crown. To the same cause the greater change which has since occurred by the adoption of the Constitution is to be traced.

The establishment of our institutions forms the most important epoch that history hath recorded. They extend unexampled felicity to the whole body of our fellow-citizens, and are the admiration of other nations. To preserve and hand them down in their utmost purity to the remotest ages will require the existence and practice of virtues and talents equal to those which were displayed in acquiring them. It is ardently hoped and confidently believed that these will not be wanting.

PROCLAMATIONS.

By the President of the United States.

A PROCLAMATION.

Whereas by the second section of an act of Congress of the 6th of May last, entitled "An act in addition to the act concerning navigation, and also to authorize the appointment of deputy collectors," it is provided that in the event of the signature of any treaty or convention concerning the navigation or commerce between the United States and France the President of the United States, if he should deem the same expedient, may suspend by proclamation until the end of the next session of Congress the operation of the act entitled "An act to impose a new tonnage duty on French ships and vessels, and for other purposes," and also to suspend, as aforesaid, all other duties on French vessels or the goods imported in the same which may exceed the duties on American vessels and on similar goods imported in the same; and

Whereas a convention of navigation and commerce between the United States of America and His Majesty the King of France and Navarre has this day been duly signed by John Quincy Adams, Secretary of State, on the part of the United States, and by the Baron Hyde de Neuville, envoy extraordinary and minister plenipotentiary from France, on the part of His Most Christian Majesty, which convention is in the words following:

[Here follows the treaty.]

Now, therefore, be it known that I, James Monroe, President of the United States, in pursuance of the authority aforesaid, do hereby suspend from and after the 1st day of October next until the end of the next session of Congress, the operation of the act aforesaid, entitled "An act to impose a new tonnage duty on French ships and vessels, and for other purposes," and also all other duties on French vessels and the goods being the growth, produce, and manufacture of France imported in the same which may exceed the duties on American vessels and on similar goods imported in the same, saving only the discriminating duties payable on French vessels and on articles the growth, produce, and manufacture of France imported in the same stipulated by the said convention to be paid.

In testimony whereof I have caused the seal of the United States to be affixed to these presents, and signed the same with my hand.

[SEAL.] Done at Washington, the 24th day of June, A. D. 1822, and of the Independence of the United States the forty-sixth.

JAMES MONROE.

By the President:

JOHN QUINCY ADAMS,
Secretary of State.

BY THE PRESIDENT OF THE UNITED STATES OF AMERICA.

A PROCLAMATION.

Whereas by an act of the Congress of the United States passed on the 6th day of May last it was provided that on satisfactory evidence being given to the President of the United States that the ports in the islands or colonies in the West Indies under the dominion of Great Britain have been opened to the vessels of the United States the President should be, and thereby was, authorized to issue his proclamation declaring that the ports of the United States should thereafter be open to the vessels of Great Britain employed in the trade and intercourse between the United States and such islands or colonies, subject to such reciprocal rules and restrictions as the President of the United States might by such proclamation make and publish, anything in the laws entitled "An act concerning navigation" or an act entitled "An act supplementary to an act concerning navigation" to the contrary notwithstanding; and

Whereas satisfactory evidence has been given to the President of the United States that the ports hereinafter named in the islands or colonies in the West Indies under the dominion of Great Britain have been opened to the vessels of the United States; that is to say, the ports of Kingston, Savannah le Mar, Montego Bay, Santa Lucia, Antonio, St. Ann, Falmouth, Maria, Morant Bay, in Jamaica; St. George, Grenada; Roseau, Dominica; St. Johns, Antigua; San Josef, Trinidad; Scarborough, Tobago; Road Harbour, Tortola; Nassau, New Providence; Pittstown, Crooked Island; Kingston, St. Vincent; Port St. George a l Port Hamilton, Bermuda; any port where there is a custom-house, Bahamas; Bridgetown, Barbadoes; St. Johns, St. Andrews, New Brunswick; Halifax, Nova Scotia; Quebec, Canada; St. Johns, Newfoundland; Georgetown, Demerara; New

Amsterdam, Berbice; Castries, St. Lucia; Besseterre, St. Kitts; Charlestown, Nevis; and Plymouth, Montserrat:

Now, therefore, I, James Monroe, President of the United States of America, do hereby declare and proclaim that the ports of the United States shall hereafter, and until the end of the next session of the Congress of the United States, be open to the vessels of Great Britain employed in the trade and intercourse between the United States and the islands and colonies hereinbefore named, anything in the laws entitled "An act concerning navigation" or an act entitled "An act supplementary to an act concerning navigation" to the contrary notwithstanding, under the following reciprocal rules and restrictions, namely:

To vessels of Great Britain, bona fide British built, owned and the master and three-fourths of the mariners of which at least shall belong to Great Britain, or any United States built ship or vessel which has been sold to and become the property of British subjects, such ship or vessel being also navigated with a master and three-fourths of the mariners at least belonging to Great Britain: *And provided always*, That no articles shall be imported into the United States in any such British ship or vessel other than articles of the growth, produce, or manufacture of the British islands and colonies in the West Indies when imported in British vessels coming from any such island or colony, and articles of the growth, produce, or manufacture of the British colonies in North America or of the island of Newfoundland in vessels coming from the port of St. Johns, in that island, or from any of the aforesaid ports of the British colonies in North America.

Given under my hand, at the city of Washington, this 24th day of August, A. D. 1822, and in the forty-seventh year of the Independence of the United States. JAMES MONROE.

By the President:

JOHN QUINCY ADAMS, *Secretary of State.*

SIXTH ANNUAL MESSAGE.

WASHINGTON, *December 3, 1822.*

Fellow-Citizens of the Senate and House of Representatives:

Many causes unite to make your present meeting peculiarly interesting to our constituents. The operation of our laws on the various subjects to which they apply, with the amendments which they occasionally require, imposes annually an important duty on the representatives of a free people. Our system has happily advanced to such maturity that I am not aware that your cares in that respect will be augmented. Other causes exist which are highly interesting to the whole civilized world, and to no portion of it more so, in certain views, than to the United

States. Of these causes and of their bearing on the interests of our Union I shall communicate the sentiments which I have formed with that freedom which a sense of duty dictates. It is proper, however, to invite your attention in the first instance to those concerns respecting which legislative provision is thought to be particularly urgent.

On the 24th of June last a convention of navigation and commerce was concluded in this city between the United States and France by ministers duly authorized for the purpose. The sanction of the Executive having been given to this convention under a conviction that, taking all its stipulations into view, it rested essentially on a basis of reciprocal and equal advantage, I deemed it my duty, in compliance with the authority vested in the Executive by the second section of the act of the last session of the 6th of May, concerning navigation, to suspend by proclamation until the end of the next session of Congress the operation of the act entitled "An act to impose a new tonnage duty on French ships and vessels, and for other purposes," and to suspend likewise all other duties on French vessels or the goods imported in them which exceeded the duties on American vessels and on similar goods imported in them. I shall submit this convention forthwith to the Senate for its advice and consent as to the ratification.

Since your last session the prohibition which had been imposed on the commerce between the United States and the British colonies in the West Indies and on this continent has likewise been removed. Satisfactory evidence having been adduced that the ports of those colonies had been opened to the vessels of the United States by an act of the British Parliament bearing date on the 24th of June last, on the conditions specified therein, I deemed it proper, in compliance with the provision of the first section of the act of the last session above recited, to declare, by proclamation bearing date on the 24th of August last, that the ports of the United States should thenceforward and until the end of the next session of Congress be opened to the vessels of Great Britain employed in that trade, under the limitation specified in that proclamation.

A doubt was entertained whether the act of Congress applied to the British colonies on this continent as well as to those in the West Indies, but as the act of Parliament opened the intercourse equally with both, and it was the manifest intention of Congress, as well as the obvious policy of the United States, that the provisions of the act of Parliament should be met in equal extent on the part of the United States, and as also the act of Congress was supposed to vest in the President some discretion in the execution of it, I thought it advisable to give it a corresponding construction.

Should the constitutional sanction of the Senate be given to the ratification of the convention with France, legislative provisions will be necessary to carry it fully into effect, as it likewise will be to continue in force, on such conditions as may be deemed just and proper, the intercourse which has been opened between the United States and the British colonies. Every light in the possession of the Executive will in due time be communicated on both subjects.

Resting essentially on a basis of reciprocal and equal advantage, it has been the object of the Executive in transactions with other powers to meet the propositions of each with a liberal spirit, believing that thereby the interest of our country would be most effectually promoted. This course has been systematically pursued in the late occurrences with France and Great Britain, and in strict accord with the views of the Legislature. A confident hope is entertained that by the arrangement thus commenced with each all differences respecting navigation and commerce with the dominions in question will be adjusted, and a solid foundation be laid for an active and permanent intercourse which will prove equally advantageous to both parties.

The decision of His Imperial Majesty the Emperor of Russia on the question submitted to him by the United States and Great Britain, concerning the construction of the first article of the treaty of Ghent, has been received. A convention has since been concluded between the parties, under the mediation of His Imperial Majesty, to prescribe the mode by which that article shall be carried into effect in conformity with that decision. I shall submit this convention to the Senate for its advice and consent as to the ratification, and, if obtained, shall immediately bring the subject before Congress for such provisions as may require the interposition of the Legislature.

In compliance with an act of the last session a Territorial government has been established in Florida on the principles of our system. By this act the inhabitants are secured in the full enjoyment of their rights and liberties, and to admission into the Union, with equal participation in the Government with the original States on the conditions heretofore prescribed to other Territories. By a clause in the ninth article of the treaty with Spain, by which that Territory was ceded to the United States, it is stipulated that satisfaction shall be made for the injuries, if any, which by process of law shall be established to have been suffered by the Spanish officers and individual Spanish inhabitants by the late operations of our troops in Florida. No provision having yet been made to carry that stipulation into effect, it is submitted to the consideration of Congress whether it will not be proper to vest the competent power in the district court at Pensacola, or in some tribunal to be specially organized for the purpose.

The fiscal operations of the year have been more successful than had been anticipated at the commencement of the last session of Congress.

The receipts into the Treasury during the three first quarters of the year have exceeded the sum of $14,745,000. The payments made at the Treasury during the same period have exceeded $12,279,000, leaving in the Treasury on the 30th day of September last, including $1,168,592.24

which were in the Treasury on the 1st day of January last, a sum exceeding $4,128,000.

Besides discharging all demands for the current service of the year, including the interest and reimbursement of the public debt, the 6 per cent stock of 1796, amounting to $80,000, has been redeemed. It is estimated that, after defraying the current expenses of the present quarter and redeeming the two millions of 6 per cent stock of 1820, there will remain in the Treasury on the 1st of January next nearly $3,000,000. It is estimated that the gross amount of duties which have been secured from the 1st of January to the 30th of September last has exceeded $19,500,000, and the amount for the whole year will probably not fall short of $23,000,000.

Of the actual force in service under the present military establishment, the posts at which it is stationed, and the condition of each post, a report from the Secretary of War which is now communicated will give a distinct idea. By like reports the state of the Academy at West Point will be seen, as will be the progress which has been made on the fortifications along the coast and at the national armories and arsenals.

The position on the Red River and that at the Sault of St. Marie are the only new posts that have been taken. These posts, with those already occupied in the interior, are thought to be well adapted to the protection of our frontiers. All the force not placed in the garrisons along the coast and in the ordnance depots, and indispensably necessary there, is placed on the frontiers.

The organization of the several corps composing the Army is such as to admit its expansion to a great extent in case of emergency, the officers carrying with them all the light which they possess to the new corps to which they might be appointed.

With the organization of the staff there is equal cause to be satisfied. By the concentration of every branch with its chief in this city, in the presence of the Department, and with a grade in the chief military station to keep alive and cherish a military spirit, the greatest promptitude in the execution of orders, with the greatest economy and efficiency, are secured. The same view is taken of the Military Academy. Good order is preserved in it, and the youth are well instructed in every science connected with the great objects of the institution. They are also well trained and disciplined in the practical parts of the profession. It has been always found difficult to control the ardor inseparable from that early age in such manner as to give it a proper direction. The rights of manhood are too often claimed prematurely, in pressing which too far the respect which is due to age and the obedience necessary to a course of study and instruction in every such institution are sometimes lost sight of. The great object to be accomplished is the restraint of that ardor by such wise regulations and government as, by directing all the energies of the youthful mind to the attainment of useful knowledge, will keep it within a just subordination and at the same time elevate it to the highest purposes. This object seems to be essentially obtained in this institution, and with great advantage to the Union.

The Military Academy forms the basis, in regard to science, on which the military establishment rests. It furnishes annually, after due examination and on the report of the academic staff, many well-informed youths to fill the vacancies which occur in the several corps of the Army, while others who retire to private life carry with them such attainments as, under the right reserved to the several States to appoint the officers and to train the militia, will enable them, by affording a wider field for selection, to promote the great object of the power vested in Congress of providing for the organizing, arming, and disciplining the militia. Thus by the mutual and harmonious cooperation of the two governments in the execution of a power divided between them, an object always to be cherished, the attainment of a great result, on which our liberties may depend, can not fail to be secured. I have to add that in proportion as our regular force is small should the instruction and discipline of the militia, the great resource on which we rely, be pushed to the utmost extent that circumstances will admit.

A report from the Secretary of the Navy will communicate the progress which has been made in the construction of vessels of war, with other interesting details respecting the actual state of the affairs of that Department. It has been found necessary for the protection of our commerce to maintain the usual squadrons on the Mediterranean, the Pacific, and along the Atlantic coast, extending the cruises of the latter into the West Indies, where piracy, organized into a system, has preyed on the commerce of every country trading thither. A cruise has also been maintained on the coast of Africa, when the season would permit, for the suppression of the slave trade, and orders have been given to the commanders of all our public ships to seize our own vessels, should they find any engaged in that trade, and to bring them in for adjudication.

In the West Indies piracy is of recent date, which may explain the cause why other powers have not combined against it. By the documents communicated it will be seen that the efforts of the United States to suppress it have had a very salutary effect. The benevolent provision of the act under which the protection has been extended alike to the commerce of other nations can not fail to be duly appreciated by them.

In compliance with the act of the last session entitled "An act to abolish the United States trading establishments," agents were immediately appointed and instructed, under the direction of the Secretary of the Treasury, to close the business of the trading houses among the Indian tribes and to settle the accounts of the factors and subfactors engaged in that trade, and to execute in all other respects the injunctions of that act in the mode prescribed therein. A final report of their proceedings shall be communicated to Congress as soon as it is received.

It is with great regret I have to state that a serious malady has deprived us of many valuable citizens at Pensacola and checked the progress of some of those arrangements which are important to the Territory. This effect has been sensibly felt in respect to the Indians who inhabit that Territory, consisting of the remnants of several tribes who occupy the middle ground between St. Augustine and Pensacola, with extensive claims but undefined boundaries. Although peace is preserved with those Indians, yet their position and claims tend essentially to interrupt the intercourse between the eastern and western parts of the Territory, on which our inhabitants are principally settled. It is essential to the growth and prosperity of the Territory, as well as to the interests of the Union, that these Indians should be removed, by special compact with them, to some other position or concentrated within narrower limits where they are. With the limited means in the power of the Executive, instructions were given to the governor to accomplish this object so far as it might be practicable, which was prevented by the distressing malady referred to. To carry it fully into effect in either mode additional funds will be necessary, to the provision of which the powers of Congress alone are competent. With a view to such provision as may be deemed proper, the subject is submitted to your consideration, and in the interim further proceedings are suspended.

It appearing that so much of the act entitled "An act regulating the staff of the Army," which passed on the 14th April, 1818, as relates to the commissariat will expire in April next, and the practical operation of that department having evinced its great utility, the propriety of its renewal is submitted to your consideration.

The view which has been taken of the probable productiveness of the lead mines, connected with the importance of the material to the public defense, makes it expedient that they should be managed with peculiar care. It is therefore suggested whether it will not comport with the public interest to provide by law for the appointment of an agent skilled in mineralogy to superintend them, under the direction of the proper department.

It is understood that the Cumberland road, which was constructed at a great expense, has already suffered from the want of that regular superintendence and of those repairs which are indispensable to the preservation of such a work. This road is of incalculable advantage in facilitating the intercourse between the Western and the Atlantic States. Through it the whole country from the northern extremity of Lake Erie to the Mississippi, and from all the waters which empty into each, finds an easy and direct communication to the seat of Government, and thence to the Atlantic. The facility which it affords to all military and commercial operations, and also to those of the Post-Office Department, can not be estimated too highly. This great work is likewise an ornament and an honor to the nation. Believing that a competent power to adopt and execute a system of internal improvement has not been granted to Congress, but that such a power, confined to great national purposes and with proper limitations, would be productive of eminent advantage to our Union, I have thought it advisable that an amendment of the Constitution to that effect should be recommended to the several States. A bill which assumed the right to adopt and execute such a system having been presented for my signature at the last session, I was compelled, from the view which I had taken of the powers of the General Government, to negative it, on which occasion I thought it proper to communicate the sentiments which I had formed, on mature consideration, on the whole subject. To that communication, in all the views in which the great interest to which it relates may be supposed to merit your attention, I have now to refer. Should Congress, however, deem it improper to recommend such an amendment, they have, according to my judgment, the right to keep the road in repair by providing for the superintendence of it and appropriating the money necessary for repairs. Surely if they had the right to appropriate money to make the road they have a right to appropriate it to preserve the road from ruin. From the exercise of this power no danger is to be apprehended. Under our happy system the people are the sole and exclusive fountain of power. Each government originates from them, and to them alone, each to its proper constituents, are they respectively and solely responsible for the faithful discharge of their duties within their constitutional limits; and that the people will confine their public agents of every station to the strict line of their constitutional duties there is no cause to doubt. Having, however, communicated my sentiments to Congress at the last session fully in the document to which I have referred, respecting the right of appropriation as distinct from the right of jurisdiction and sovereignty over the territory in question, I deem it improper to enlarge on the subject here.

From the best information that I have been able to obtain it appears that our manufactures, though depressed immediately after the peace, have considerably increased, and are still increasing, under the encouragement given them by the tariff of 1816 and by subsequent laws. Satisfied I am, whatever may be the abstract doctrine in favor of unrestricted commerce, provided all nations would concur in it and it was not liable to be interrupted by war, which has never occurred and can not be expected, that there are other strong reasons applicable to our situation and relations with other countries which impose on us the obligation to cherish and sustain our manufactures. Satisfied, however, I likewise am that the interest of every part of our Union, even of those most benefited by manufactures, requires that this subject should be touched with the greatest caution, and a critical knowledge of the effect to be produced by the slightest change. On full consideration of the subject in all its relations I am persuaded that a further augmentation may now be made of the duties on certain foreign articles in favor of our own and without affecting injuriously any other interest.   For more precise details I refer you to the communications which were made to Congress during the last session.

So great was the amount of accounts for moneys advanced during the late war, in addition to others of a previous date which in the regular operations of the Government necessarily remained unsettled, that it required a considerable length of time for their adjustment.   By a report from the First Comptroller of the Treasury it appears that on the 4th of March, 1817, the accounts then unsettled amounted to $103,068,876.41, of which, on the 30th of September of the present year, $93,175,396.56 had been settled, leaving on that day a balance unsettled of $9,893,479.85. That there have been drawn from the Treasury, in paying the public debt and sustaining the Government in all its operations and disbursements, since the 4th of March, 1817, $157,199,380.96, the accounts for which have been settled to the amount of $137,501,451.12, leaving a balance unsettled of $19,697,929.84.   For precise details respecting each of these balances I refer to the report of the Comptroller and the documents which accompany it.

From this view it appears that our commercial differences with France and Great Britain have been placed in a train of amicable arrangement on conditions fair and honorable in both instances to each party; that our finances are in a very productive state, our revenue being at present fully competent to all the demands upon it; that our military force is well organized in all its branches and capable of rendering the most important service in case of emergency that its number will admit of; that due progress has been made, under existing appropriations, in the construction of fortifications and in the operations of the Ordnance Department; that due progress has in like manner been made in the construction of ships of war; that our Navy is in the best condition, felt and respected in every sea in which it is employed for the protection of our commerce; that our manufactures have augmented in amount and improved in quality; that great progress has been made in the settlement of accounts and in the recovery of the balances due by individuals, and that the utmost economy is secured and observed in every Department of the Administration.

Other objects will likewise claim your attention, because from the station which the United States hold as a member of the great community of nations they have rights to maintain, duties to perform, and dangers to encounter.

A strong hope was entertained that peace would ere this have been concluded between Spain and the independent governments south of the United States in this hemisphere.   Long experience having evinced the competency of those governments to maintain the independence which they had declared, it was presumed that the considerations which induced their recognition by the United States would have had equal weight with

Oak hill October 17.th 1823

Dear Sir

I transmit to you two dispatches, which were reciev'd from Mr Rush, while I was lately in Washington, which involve interests of the highest importance. They contain two letters from Mr Canning, suggesting designs of the holy alliance, against the Independence of So. America, & proposing a cooperation, between G. Britain & the U States, in support of it, against the members of that alliance. The project, aims in the first instance, at a mere expression of opinion, some what in the abstract, but which it is expected by Mr Canning, will have a great political effect, by defeating the combination. By Mr Rush's answers, which are also inclosed, you will see the light in which he views the subject, & the extent to which he may have gone. Many important considerations are involved in this proposition. 1st shall we entangle ourselves, at all, in European politicks, & wars, on the side of any power, against others, presuming that a concert by agreement, of the kind proposed, may lead to that result? 2d. If a case can exist in which a sound maxim, may, & ought to be departed from, is not the present instance, precisely that case? 3d. Has not the epoch arrived when G. Britain must take her stand,

either

on the side of the monarchies of Europe, or of the U. States,
& in consequence, either in favor of Despotism or of liberty
& may it not be presumed, that no one of that majesty,
no government, but sufd on the present occurrence, as
that, which it deems the most suitable, to announce &
mark the commencement of that career.

My own impression is that we ought to meet the propo=
sal of the British govt. & to make it known, that we
would view an interference on the part of the European
powers, and specially an attack on the Colonies, by
them, as an attack on ourselves, presuming that if
they succeed with these, they would extend it to us. I
am sensible however of the extent & difficulty of the
question, & shall be happy to have your, & Mr. Madi=
sons opinions on it. I do not wish to trouble
either of you with my ill affairs, but the project on
which is, involves the high interest, for which we
have so long & so faithfully, & harmoniously
contended together. I beg you now & so therefore to
peruse the dispatches, with an interpretation of the
motives —

With great respect & regard I am dear
Your friend   James Monroe

other powers, and that Spain herself, yielding to those magnanimous feelings of which her history furnishes so many examples, would have terminated on that basis a controversy so unavailing and at the same time so destructive. We still cherish the hope that this result will not long be postponed.

Sustaining our neutral position and allowing to each party while the war continues equal rights, it is incumbent on the United States to claim of each with equal rigor the faithful observance of our rights according to the well-known law of nations. From each, therefore, a like cooperation is expected in the suppression of the piratical practice which has grown out of this war and of blockades of extensive coasts on both seas, which, considering the small force employed to sustain them, have not the slightest foundation to rest on.

Europe is still unsettled, and although the war long menaced between Russia and Turkey has not broken out, there is no certainty that the differences between those powers will be amicably adjusted. It is impossible to look to the oppressions of the country respecting which those differences arose without being deeply affected. The mention of Greece fills the mind with the most exalted sentiments and arouses in our bosoms the best feelings of which our nature is susceptible. Superior skill and refinement in the arts, heroic gallantry in action, disinterested patriotism, enthusiastic zeal and devotion in favor of public and personal liberty are associated with our recollections of ancient Greece. That such a country should have been overwhelmed and so long hidden, as it were, from the world under a gloomy despotism has been a cause of unceasing and deep regret to generous minds for ages past. It was natural, therefore, that the reappearance of those people in their original character, contending in favor of their liberties, should produce that great excitement and sympathy in their favor which have been so signally displayed throughout the United States. A strong hope is entertained that these people will recover their independence and resume their equal station among the nations of the earth.

A great effort has been made in Spain and Portugal to improve the condition of the people, and it must be very consoling to all benevolent minds to see the extraordinary moderation with which it has been conducted. That it may promote the happiness of both nations is the ardent wish of this whole people, to the expression of which we confine ourselves; for whatever may be the feelings or sentiments which every individual under our Government has a right to indulge and express, it is nevertheless a sacred maxim, equally with the Government and people, that the destiny of every independent nation in what relates to such improvements of right belongs and ought to be left exclusively to themselves.

Whether we reason from the late wars or from those menacing symptoms which now appear in Europe, it is manifest that if a convulsion should take place in any of those countries it will proceed from causes which have no existence and are utterly unknown in these States, in which there is but one order, that of the people, to whom the sovereignty exclusively belongs. Should war break out in any of those countries, who can foretell the extent to which it may be carried or the desolation which it may spread? Exempt as we are from these causes, our internal tranquillity is secure; and distant as we are from the troubled scene, and faithful to first principles in regard to other powers, we might reasonably presume that we should not be molested by them. This, however, ought not to be calculated on as certain. Unprovoked injuries are often inflicted, and even the peculiar felicity of our situation might with some be a cause for excitement and aggression. The history of the late wars in Europe furnishes a complete demonstration that no system of conduct, however correct in principle, can protect neutral powers from injury from any party; that a defenseless position and distinguished love of peace are the surest invitations to war, and that there is no way to avoid it other than by being always prepared and willing for just cause to meet it. If there be a people on earth whose more especial duty it is to be at all times prepared to defend the rights with which they are blessed, and to surpass all others in sustaining the necessary burthens, and in submitting to sacrifices to make such preparations, it is undoubtedly the people of these States.

When we see that a civil war of the most frightful character rages from the Adriatic to the Black Sea; that strong symptoms of war appear in other parts, proceeding from causes which, should it break out, may become general and be of long duration; that the war still continues between Spain and the independent governments, her late Provinces, in this hemisphere; that it is likewise menaced between Portugal and Brazil, in consequence of the attempt of the latter to dismember itself from the former, and that a system of piracy of great extent is maintained in the neighboring seas, which will require equal vigilance and decision to suppress it, the reasons for sustaining the attitude which we now hold and for pushing forward all our measures of defense with the utmost vigor appear to me to acquire new force.

The United States owe to the world a great example, and, by means thereof, to the cause of liberty and humanity a generous support. They have so far succeeded to the satisfaction of the virtuous and enlightened of every country. There is no reason to doubt that their whole movement will be regulated by a sacred regard to principle, all our institutions being founded on that basis. The ability to support our own cause under any trial to which it may be exposed is the great point on which the public solicitude rests. It has been often charged against free governments that they have neither the foresight nor the virtue to provide at the proper season for great emergencies; that their course is improvident and expensive; that war will always find them unprepared, and, whatever may be its calamities, that its terrible warnings will be disregarded and forgotten as soon as peace returns. I have full confidence that this chargé so far as relates to the United States will be shewn to be utterly destitute of truth.

JAMES MONROE.

SPECIAL MESSAGES.

To the Senate of the United States: DECEMBER 4, 1822.

The convention between the United States and France, concluded at Washington on the 24th day of June last, is now transmitted to the Senate for their advice and consent with regard to its ratification, together with the documents relating to the negotiation, which may serve to elucidate the deliberations of the Senate concerning its objects and the purposes to which it was adapted.

JAMES MONROE.

To the Senate of the United States: DECEMBER 4, 1822.

I transmit herewith to the Senate, for their constitutional consideration and decision thereon, a convention between the United States and Great Britain, concluded at St. Petersburg on the 12th day of July last, under the mediation of His Imperial Majesty of all the Russias, together with the documents appertaining thereto, and which may elucidate the motives for its negotiation and the objects for the accomplishment of which it is intended.

JAMES MONROE.

WASHINGTON, *December 6, 1822.*

To the House of Representatives of the United States:

In compliance with the resolution of the House of Representatives of the 7th of May last, requiring that a plan for the peace establishment of the Navy of the United States and also of the Marine Corps should be communicated to that House at the present session, I transmit a report of the Secretary of the Navy, containing a plan which has been prepared for the proposed establishment.

JAMES MONROE.

WASHINGTON, *December 7, 1822.*

To the Senate of the United States:

In compliance with the resolution of the Senate of the 8th of May last, requesting "information relative to the copper mines on the southern shore of Lake Superior, their number, value, and position, the names of the Indian tribes who claim them, the practicability of extinguishing their titles, and the probable advantages which may result to the Republic from the acquisition and working these mines," I herewith transmit a report from the Secretary of War, which comprises the information desired in the resolution referred to.

JAMES MONROE.

WASHINGTON, *December 9, 1822.*

To the Senate of the United States:

Recent information of the multiplied outrages and depredations which have been committed on our seamen and commerce by the pirates in the West Indies and Gulf of Mexico, exemplified by the death of a very meritorious officer, seems to call for some prompt and decisive measures on the part of the Government. All the public vessels adapted to that service which can be spared from other indispensable duties are a ready employed in it; but from the knowledge which has been acquired of the places from whence these outlaws issue and to which they escape from danger it appears that it will require a particular kind of force, capable of pursuing them into the shallow waters to which they retire, effectually to suppress them. I submit to the consideration of the Senate the propriety of organizing such force for that important object.

JAMES MONROE.

[The same message, dated December 6, 1822, was sent to the House of Representatives.]

WASHINGTON, *December 9, 1822.*

To the Senate of the United States:

In compliance with a resolution of the Senate of the 22d of February last, "requesting the President of the United States to cause to be collected and communicated to the Senate at the commencement of the next session of Congress the best information which he may be able to obtain relative to certain Christian Indians and the lands intended for their benefit on the Muskingum, in the State of Ohio, granted under an act of Congress of June 1, 1796, to the Society of the United Brethren for Propagating the Gospel among the Heathen, showing as correctly as possible the advance or decline of said Indians in numbers, morals, and intellectual endowments; whether the lands have inured to their sole benefit, and, if not, to whom, in whole or in part, have such benefits accrued," I transmit a report from the Secretary of War with the accompanying documents.

JAMES MONROE.

WASHINGTON, *January 3, 1823.*

To the Senate of the United States:

In compliance with the three resolutions of the Senate of the 5th April 1822, requesting the President of the United States to communicate detail the expenses of building each vessel of war authorized by the act of the 2d of January, 1813, and its supplements, and also the names, number, grade, etc., of the officers and men employed at each navy-yard and naval station during the two years immediately preceding the 1st of January, 1822, I herewith transmit a report from the Secretary of the Navy, with the accompanying documents, which contains the desired information.

JAMES MONROE.

WASHINGTON, *January 3, 1823.*

To the House of Representatives of the United States:

In compliance with the resolutions of the House of Representatives of the 8th of January, 7th May, and 17th December, 1822, requesting the President of the United States to cause to be laid before that House a detailed statement of the current expenses of the Ordnance Department for the years 1817, 1818, 1819, 1820, and 1821, and as much as can be shewn for the year 1822, and also the number and local position of each of the armories, arsenals, and magazines of the United States, the total expense of constructing and repairing the same up to the year 1821; the number of cannon and other arms annually made at each, and the expenses of each armory and arsenal for each year from 1816 to 1821, inclusive, I herewith transmit a report from the Secretary of War, accompanied by such documents as will be found to contain the desired information.

JAMES MONROE.

WASHINGTON, *January 3, 1823.*

To the House of Representatives of the United States:

In compliance with the resolution of the House of Representatives of the United States of the 19th of December, 1822, requesting the President of the United States to cause to be laid before that House the several laws which have been made by the governor and legislative council of Florida, together with such information as may be in the possession of the Executive, I herewith transmit a report from the Secretary of State, with the accompanying documents, which contains the information desired.

JAMES MONROE.

WASHINGTON, *January 6, 1823.*

To the House of Representatives of the United States:

In compliance with the resolution of the House of Representatives of the 19th of December last, requesting the President of the United States to communicate to the House the progress which has been made in the execution of the act of the last session entitled "An act to abolish the Indian trading establishments," with a report from the factories, respectively, as the same were made to him, I transmit a report from the Secretary of the Treasury, with the documents referred to by that resolution. In further execution of the act of the last session treaties have since been made with the Osage and Sac Indians by which those tribes have severally relinquished to the United States their right under preceding treaties to the maintenance of a factory within each, respectively.

JAMES MONROE.

JANUARY 6, 1823.

To the Senate:

I transmit to the Senate, for their advice and consent as to the ratification, treaties which have been made with the Osage and Sac tribes of Indians in execution of the provision contained in the act of the last session entitled "An act to abolish the Indian trading establishments."

JAMES MONROE.

WASHINGTON, *January 10, 1823.*

To the Senate of the United States:

In compliance with a resolution of the Senate requesting the President of the United States "to cause to be laid before the Senate the number of arms required annually to supply the militia of the West according to acts of Congress; the probable number necessary to be placed in military deposits located or to be located on the Western waters; the cost of transportation of arms to the Western States and deposits; the probable cost of manufacturing arms in the West; the probable cost of erecting at this time on the Western waters such an armory as that at Harpers Ferry or at Springfield, and such other information as he may deem important to establish the expediency of erecting on the Western waters a national armory," I herewith transmit a report from the Secretary of War containing the desired information.

JAMES MONROE.

WASHINGTON, *January 16, 1823.*

The VICE-PRESIDENT OF THE UNITED STATES AND PRESIDENT OF THE SENATE:

The convention concluded and signed at St. Petersburg on the 21st of July last under the mediation of His Imperial Majesty the Emperor of all the Russias having been ratified by the three powers parties thereto, and the ratifications of the same having been duly exchanged, copies of it are now communicated to Congress, to the end that the measures for carrying it on the part of the United States into execution may obtain the cooperation of the Legislature necessary to the accomplishment of some of its provisions. A translation is subjoined of three explanatory documents, in the French language, referred to in the fourth article of the convention and annexed to it. The agreement executed at the exchange of the ratifications is likewise communicated.

JAMES MONROE.

[The same message was addressed to the Speaker of the House of Representatives.]

JANUARY 22, 1823.

To the Senate of the United States:

In compliance with a resolution of December 12, 1822, requesting that the President would cause to be laid before the Senate a statement exhibiting the amount in aggregate of the goods, wares, and merchandise exported from the United States to France, and imported from thence, in each year from and after the year 1814 to the year 1820, discriminating in the reports between the articles of the growth, produce, or manufacture of the United States and those of foreign countries, and also stating the national character of the vessels in which such exports and imports have been made, I transmit a report from the Secretary of the Treasury, which contains the information desired.

JAMES MONROE.

JANUARY 22, 1823.

To the Senate and House of Representatives:

In carrying fully into effect the intention of Congress in making an appropriation of $5,000 by the act of the 14th April, 1820, for the survey of the Ohio and the Mississippi rivers from the Rapids of the Ohio at Louisville to the Balize, for the purpose of facilitating and ascertaining the most practicable route of improving the navigation of these rivers, orders were given through the proper department to the Board of Engineers to examine and survey the said rivers with reference to those objects, and to report their opinion thereon, which they have done, and which report I now communicate for the information of Congress.

JAMES MONROE.

WASHINGTON, *January 25, 1823.*

To the House of Representatives:

I transmit herewith to the House of Representatives a report from the Secretary of State, together with the documents which contain the information requested by the resolution of the House of the 19th of December last, relating to the establishment at the mouth of Columbia River.

JAMES MONROE.

To the Senate and House of Representatives of the United States:

I transmit herewith a letter from the Secretary of the Navy, containing one from Captain John Rodgers, president of the Naval Board, accompanied by a description of the inclined plane, dock, and fixtures for hauling up ships, and an estimate of the cost and materials and workmanship necessary for the completion of a dock and wharves, proposed to be connected with the inclined plane constructed at the navy-yard, Washington, and recommend the same to the attentive consideration of Congress.

It is confidently believed that this invention combines advantages so highly useful as to justify the appropriation required.

JANUARY 28, 1823.   JAMES MONROE.

FEBRUARY 3, 1823.

To the Senate of the United States:

Having lately received a memorial from the legislative council of the Territory of Florida on subjects very interesting to the inhabitants of the Territory and also to the United States, which require legislative provision, I transmit the same to Congress and recommend it to their consideration.

JAMES MONROE.

[The same message was addressed to the Speaker of the House of Representatives.]

WASHINGTON, *February 3, 1823.*

To the Senate and House of Representatives of the United States:

I transmit herewith a resolution of the legislature, with an extract of a letter from the governor, of Georgia, and a memorial of the legislature of Missouri, relative to the extinguishment of the Indian title to lands within the limits of these States, respectively. Believing the present time to be propitious for holding treaties for the attainment of cessions of land from the Indians within those States, I submit the subject to the consideration of Congress, that adequate appropriations for such treatie may be made should Congress deem it expedient.

JAMES MONROE.

FEBRUARY 4, 1823.

To the House of Representatives of the United States:

In compliance with the resolution of the House of Representatives of the 12th of December last, requesting the President "to communicate to the House such information as he might possess with regard to any expedition prepared in the United States and having sailed from thence within the year 1822 against the territory or dependency of any power in amity with the United States, and to inform the House whether any measures have been taken to bring to condign punishment persons who have been concerned in such expedition contrary to the laws," I transmit to the House reports from the Secretaries of State and of the Treasury, with the documents mentioned in each. Those documents contain all the information in possession of the Executive relating to the subject of the resolution.

That a force of a very limited extent has been equipped in the ports of the United States and sailed from thence for the purpose described in the resolution is manifest from the documents now communicated. The reports from the collectors of Philadelphia and New York will shew in what manner this equipment escaped their notice.

The first information of this equipment was received from St. Bartholomews, the place of its rendezvous. This was confirmed afterwards from Curracoa with an account of its failure. Should any of those persons return within the jurisdiction of the United States care will be taken that the laws applicable to such offenses are duly enforced against them. Whether any aid was afforded by others to the parties engaged in this unlawful and contemptible adventure in the ports in which it was planned, inconsistent with ordinary commercial transactions and contrary to the laws of the United States, will be referred to the Attorney-General, on whose advice any measures in regard to them will depend.

JAMES MONROE.

FEBRUARY 6, 1823.

To the House of Representatives:

In compliance with a resolution of the House of Representatives of the 28th of January last, requesting information "whether the treaty concluded with the Choctaw Nation of Indians on the 18th of October, 1820, has been executed so far as respects the cession of certain lands to said nation west of the river Mississippi, and if possession has been given of the lands ceded to them; if not, that he assign the reasons which prevented the immediate execution of the stipulations of said treaty, and whether the difficulties have diminished or increased by the delay in its execution," I communicate a report from the Secretary of War, with the documents referred to in it.

JAMES MONROE.

FEBRUARY 10, 1823.

To the Senate of the United States:

In compliance with a resolution of the Senate of February 3, requesting a statement of the number and size of cannon, mortars, and howitzers necessary for the armament of the fortifications already built and intended to be built, with an estimate of the sum necessary for their construction, I transmit a report from the Secretary of War, prepared in execution of instructions given him to that effect.

JAMES MONROE.

WASHINGTON, *February 13, 1823.*

To the House of Representatives of the United States:

In compliance with a resolution of the House of Representatives of 22d January last, requesting the communication to the House of all the correspondence between the Governments of the United States and Great Britain relating to the negotiation of the convention of the 20th October, 1818, which may not be inconsistent with the public interest, I transmit herewith to the House a report from the Secretary of State, together with the papers requested by the resolution of the House.

JAMES MONROE.

FEBRUARY 14, 1823.

To the Senate of the United States:

In compliance with a resolution of the Senate of the 11th of this month, requesting the President to cause to be communicated to the Senate an estimate of the amount of land in the State of Georgia to which the Indian title has been extinguished by the United States since the cession of a portion of the territory of Georgia to the United States, with a statement of the cost of such extinguishment, and also an estimate of the amount of land within the said State to which the Indian title still remains to be extinguished, and by what tribes claimed, I transmit a report from the Secretary of War, which contains the information desired.

JAMES MONROE.

FEBRUARY 17, 1823.

To the House of Representatives of the United States:

In compliance with a resolution of the House of Representatives of the 17th of December, requesting the President to communicate to the House a statement of the amount expended for the current expenses of the Ordnance Department during the years 1817, 1818, 1819, 1820, and 1821, and as much as can be shewn for the year 1822, with the items for which the money was expended, the place where and the persons to whom paid, what quantity of timber has been procured for gun carriages and caissons, its cost annually, and where deposited; the quantity of ordnance of every kind that has been procured during those years or paid for, and the whole amount of arms of every description now belonging to the

United States; the sum expended in the purchase of sites for arsenals since the peace, the cost of the buildings erected thereon, and whether all those arsenals are necessary for the service of the United States, I transmit a report from the Secretary of War, with the documents mentioned therein, which contains the information desired.

JAMES MONROE.

WASHINGTON, *February 18, 1823.*

The VICE-PRESIDENT OF THE UNITED STATES AND PRESIDENT OF THE SENATE:

The convention of navigation and commerce between the United States of America and His Majesty the King of France and Navarre, concluded and signed at Washington on the 24th of June, 1822, with the first separate article thereto annexed, having been ratified by the two parties, and the ratifications of the same having been duly exchanged, copies of it and of the separate article referred to are now communicated to the two Houses of Congress, to the end that the necessary measures for carrying it into execution on the part of the United States may be adopted by the Legislature.

JAMES MONROE.

[The same message was sent to the House of Representatives.]

FEBRUARY 19, 1823.

To the House of Representatives of the United States:

In compliance with a resolution of the House of Representatives of the 11th of December last, I transmit to the House a report from the Secretary of the Treasury, containing the information requested, of the amount of moneys advanced to agents, subagents, contractors, subcontractors, or individuals since the 1st of January, 1817, which have not been accounted for on settlement, and of the loss sustained in each case, the sureties taken, and the names of the sureties.

JAMES MONROE.

WASHINGTON, *February 19, 1823.*

To the House of Representatives of the United States:

I transmit to the House of Representatives, in pursuance of a resolution of that House of the 31st of last month, a report from the Secretary of State, relative to the commissioners appointed for the purpose of ascertaining the titles and claims to land in Florida.

JAMES MONROE.

FEBRUARY 19, 1823.

To the House of Representatives of the United States:

I transmit to the House of Representatives an additional report from the Secretary of the Treasury, with the documents referred to therein, containing further information of the proceedings in execution of the law of the last session respecting the trade with the Indian tribes, called for by the resolution of the 19th of December last.

JAMES MONROE.

FEBRUARY 22, 1823.

To the House of Representatives of the United States:

In compliance with a resolution of the House of Representatives of the 11th of this month, requesting information whether any prize agents have neglected to render an account of their agency and to pay over the money in their hands, the names of those who have failed, the sums unaccounted for, and whether any of those thus failing are in the employ of the Government, and their compensation has been in consequence suspended, I transmit a report from the Secretary of the Navy, with the documents referred to by him.

JAMES MONROE.

FEBRUARY 25, 1823.

To the Congress of the United States:

I transmit to Congress the general returns of the militia of the several States and Territories for the year 1822, with an account of the arms, accouterments, ammunition, ordnance, etc., belonging to each as far as the returns have been received, in compliance with the provision of the act of 1803.

JAMES MONROE.

FEBRUARY 25, 1823.

To the Senate of the United States:

By a resolution of the 27th of December last the President of the United States was requested to communicate to the Senate such information as he might possess respecting the political state of the island of St. Domingo; whether the Government thereof was claimed by any European nation, what our commercial relations with the Government of the island were, and whether any further commercial relations with that Government would be consistent with the interest and safety of the United States.

From the import of the resolution it is inferred that the Senate were fully aware of the delicate and interesting nature of the subject embraced by it in all its branches. The call supposes something peculiar in the nature of the Government of that island and in the character of its population, to which attention is due. Impressed always with an anxious desire to meet every call of either House for information, I most willingly comply in this instance and with a view to the particular circumstances alluded to.

In adverting to the political state of St. Domingo I have to observe that the whole island is now united under one Government, under a constitution which retains the sovereignty in the hands of the people of color, and with provisions which prohibit the employment in the Government of all white persons who have emigrated there since 1816, or who may hereafter emigrate there, and which prohibit also the acquisition by such persons of the right of citizenship or to real estate in the island. In the exercise of this sovereignty the Government has not been molested by any European power. No invasion of the island has been made or attempted by any power. It is, however, understood that the relations between the Government of France and the island have not been adjusted, that its independence has not been recognized by France, nor has peace been formally established between the parties.

The establishment of a Government of people of color in the island on the principles above stated evinces distinctly the idea of a separate interest and a distrust of other nations. Had that jealousy been confined to the inhabitants of the parent country it would have been less an object of attention; but by extending it to the inhabitants of other countries with whom no difference ever existed the policy assumes a character which does not admit of a like explanation. To what extent that spirit may be indulged or to what purposes applied our experience has yet been too limited to enable us to form a just estimate. These are inquiries more peculiarly interesting to the neighboring islands. They nevertheless deserve the attention of the United States.

Between the United States and the island a commercial intercourse exists, and it will continue to be the object of this Government to promote it. Our commerce there has been subjected to higher duties than have been imposed on like articles from some other nations. It has nevertheless been extensive, proceeding from the wants of the respective parties and the enterprise of our citizens. Of this discrimination to our injury we had a right to complain and have complained. It is expected that our commercial intercourse with the island will be placed on the footing of the most favored nation. No preference is sought in our favor, nor ought any to be given to others. Regarding the high interest of our happy Union and looking to every circumstance which may by any possibility affect the tranquillity of any part, however remotely, and guarding against such injury by suitable precautions, it is the duty of this Government to promote by all the means in its power and by a fair and honorable policy the best interest of every other part, and thereby of the whole. Feeling profoundly the force of this obligation, I shall continue to exert with unwearied zeal my best faculties to give it effect.

JAMES MONROE.

WASHINGTON, *February 26, 1823.*

To the House of Representatives of the United States:

I transmit to the House of Representatives, in pursuance of a resolution of that House of the 30th January last, a report from the Secretary of State, containing the information required in relation to the transactions of the commissioners under the sixth and seventh articles of the treaty of Ghent, and also as to the measures which have been taken under the fourth article of the treaty with Spain of the 22d of February, 1819, for fixing the boundary line described in the third article of the last-mentioned treaty.   JAMES MONROE.

WASHINGTON, *February 27, 1823.*

To the House of Representatives:

I transmit to the House of Representatives a report from the Secretary of State, made in pursuance of their resolution of the 21st of January last, requesting the President of the United States to cause to be arranged and laid before that House a digest shewing such changes in the commercial regulations of the different foreign countries with which the United States have intercourse as shall have been adopted and come to the knowledge of the Executive subsequently to the formation of the digest communicated to the Senate on the 7th December, 1819.

JAMES MONROE.

WASHINGTON, *February 28, 1823.*

To the House of Representatives of the United States:

I transmit to the House of Representatives a report from the Secretary of State, with copies of sundry papers which should have been included among those which accompanied my message of the 13th instant, being part of the correspondence with Great Britain relating to the negotiation of the convention of 20th of October, 1818, but which were accidentally omitted from the papers communicated to the House with that message.

JAMES MONROE.

WASHINGTON, *February 28, 1823.*

To the House of Representatives:

In compliance with a resolution of the House of Representatives of the 24th of January, requesting the President to communicate to the House the number of persons and the amount due from each whose compensation has been withheld or suspended, in pursuance of the law prohibiting payments to persons in arrears to the United States; whether the amount withheld has been applied in all cases to the extinguishment of their debts to the Government; whether the said laws have been enforced in all cases against securities who are liable for the payment of any arrears due; whether any disbursing officer, within the knowledge of the President, has given conclusive evidence of his insolvency, and, if so, whether he is still retained in the service of the United States, I transmit to the House a report from the Secretary of the Treasury, with the documents mentioned therein.

The report has been confined to the operations of the law. Respecting the circumstances of individuals in their transactions without the sphere of their public duties I have no means of information other than those which are common to all. JAMES MONROE.

WASHINGTON, *March 1, 1823.*

To the House of Representatives of the United States:

In compliance with a resolution of the House of Representatives of this day, requesting information of the measures taken with regard to the illegal blockade of the ports of the Spanish Main, and to depredations of privateers fitted out from Porto Rico and other Spanish islands on the commerce of the United States, I transmit to the House a report from the Secretary of State containing the information required by the resolution. JAMES MONROE.

SEVENTH ANNUAL MESSAGE.

WASHINGTON, *December 2, 1823.*

Fellow-Citizens of the Senate and House of Representatives:

Many important subjects will claim your attention during the present session, of which I shall endeavor to give, in aid of your deliberations, a just idea in this communication. I undertake this duty with diffidence, from the vast extent of the interests on which I have to treat and of their great importance to every portion of our Union. I enter on it with zeal from a thorough conviction that there never was a period since the establishment of our Revolution when, regarding the condition of the civilized world and its bearing on us, there was greater necessity for devotion in the public servants to their respective duties, or for virtue, patriotism, and union in our constituents.

Meeting in you a new Congress, I deem it proper to present this view of public affairs in greater detail than might otherwise be necessary. I do it, however, with peculiar satisfaction, from a knowledge that in this respect I shall comply more fully with the sound principles of our

Government. The people being with us exclusively the sovereign, it is indispensable that full information be laid before them on all important subjects, to enable them to exercise that high power with complete effect. If kept in the dark, they must be incompetent to it. We are all liable to error, and those who are engaged in the management of public affairs are more subject to excitement and to be led astray by their particular interests and passions than the great body of our constituents, who, living at home in the pursuit of their ordinary avocations, are calm but deeply interested spectators of events and of the conduct of those who are parties to them. To the people every department of the Government and every individual in each are responsible, and the more full their information the better they can judge of the wisdom of the policy pursued and of the conduct of each in regard to it. From their dispassionate judgment much aid may always be obtained, while their approbation will form the greatest incentive and most gratifying reward for virtuous actions, and the dread of their censure the best security against the abuse of their confidence. Their interests in all vital questions are the same, and the bond, by sentiment as well as by interest, will be proportionably strengthened as they are better informed of the real state of public affairs, especially in difficult conjunctures. It is by such knowledge that local prejudices and jealousies are surmounted, and that a national policy, extending its fostering care and protection to all the great interests of our Union, is formed and steadily adhered to.

A precise knowledge of our relations with foreign powers as respects our negotiations and transactions with each is thought to be particularly necessary. Equally necessary is it that we should form a just estimate of our resources, revenue, and progress in every kind of improvement connected with the national prosperity and public defense. It is by rendering justice to other nations that we may expect it from them. It is by our ability to resent injuries and redress wrongs that we may avoid them.

The commissioners under the fifth article of the treaty of Ghent, having disagreed in their opinions respecting that portion of the boundary between the Territories of the United States and of Great Britain the establishment of which had been submitted to them, have made their respective reports in compliance with that article, that the same might be referred to the decision of a friendly power. It being manifest, however, that it would be difficult, if not impossible, for any power to perform that office without great delay and much inconvenience to itself, a proposal has been made by this Government, and acceded to by that of Great Britain, to endeavor to establish that boundary by amicable negotiation. It appearing from long experience that no satisfactory arrangement could be formed of the commercial intercourse between the United States and the British colonies in this hemisphere by legislative acts while each party pursued its own course without agreement or concert with the other, a proposal has been made to the British Government to regulate this com-